The Official CompTIA® A+® Core 1 and Core 2 Instructor Guide (Exams 220-1001 and 220-1002)

Volume 1

The Official CompTIA® A+® Core 1 and Core 2 Instructor Guide (Exams 220-1001 and 220-1002)

COURSE EDITION: 1.01

Acknowledgements

James Pengelly, Author
Pamela J. Taylor, Author
Brian Sullivan, Media Designer
Peter Bauer, Content Editor

Thomas Reilly, Vice President Learning
Katie Hoenicke, Director of Product Management
James Chesterfield, Manager, Learning Content and Design
Becky Mann, Senior Manager, Product Development

Notices

DISCLAIMER

While CompTIA, Inc. takes care to ensure the accuracy and quality of these materials, we cannot guarantee their accuracy, and all materials are provided without any warranty whatsoever, including, but not limited to, the implied warranties of merchantability or fitness for a particular purpose. The use of screenshots, photographs of another entity's products, or another entity's product name or service in this book is for editorial purposes only. No such use should be construed to imply sponsorship or endorsement of the book by nor any affiliation of such entity with CompTIA. This courseware may contain links to sites on the Internet that are owned and operated by third parties (the "External Sites"). CompTIA is not responsible for the availability of, or the content located on or through, any External Site. Please contact CompTIA if you have any concerns regarding such links or External Sites.

TRADEMARK NOTICES

CompTIA®, A+®, and the CompTIA logo are registered trademarks of CompTIA, Inc., in the U.S. and other countries. All other product and service names used may be common law or registered trademarks of their respective proprietors.

COPYRIGHT NOTICE

Table of Contents

Using the Official CompTIA® A+® Core 1 and Core 2 Instructor Guide (Exams 220-1001 and 220-1002)

Welcome to the Instructor

Welcome to the only materials on the market today developed by CompTIA to prepare learners for CompTIA certification exams. You can utilize *The Official CompTIA® A+® Core 1 and Core 2 (Exams 220-1001 and 220-1002)* curriculum to present world-class instructional experiences whether:

- Your students are participating with you in the classroom or virtually.
- You are presenting in a continuous event or in an extended teaching plan, such as an academic semester.
- Your presentation takes place synchronously with the students or asynchronously.
- Your students have physical courseware or are using digital materials.
- You have any combination of these instructional dimensions.

To make the best use of *The Official CompTIA® A+® Core 1 and Core 2 (Exams 220-1001 and 220-1002)* materials in any or all of these dimensions, be sure to review all of the components of the CompTIA CHOICE platform. The CompTIA CHOICE platform is developed and hosted by Logical Operations and has been customized specifically for Official CompTIA Content.

Preparing to Teach

Effectively presenting the information and skills in this course requires adequate preparation in any presentation modality. As such, as an instructor, you should familiarize yourself with the content of the entire course, including its organization and instructional approaches. You should review each of the activities and exercises so you can facilitate them during the learning event. Also, make sure you review the tips for presenting in the different dimensions; these instructor tips are available as notes in the margins of your Instructor Guide.

In addition to the curriculum itself, Microsoft® PowerPoint® slides, data files, and other course-specific support material may be available by downloading the files from the CHOICE Course screen. Be sure to obtain the course files prior to your learning event and make sure you distribute them to your students.

Course Facilitator Icons

Throughout the Instructor Guide, you may see various instructor-focused icons that provide suggestions, answers to problems, and supplemental information for you, the instructor.

Instructor Icon	Instructor Icon Descriptive Text
Show Slide(s)	The **Show Slide** icon provides a prompt to the instructor to display a specific slide from the provided PowerPoint files.
Teaching Tip	The **Teaching Tip** icons provide additional guidance and background that you may want to utilize during specific parts of the course, including lecture, whiteboard sketching, or demonstrations.
Interaction Opportunity	The **Interaction Opportunity** provides suggestions on different ways to engage with students, either through discussions or activities.

Digital Software Updates

Software vendors mentioned in this course may at any time deploy software updates digitally, resulting in changes that may not be reflected dynamically in this course. Stay up to date with product updates and be ready to adapt the material to any changes in the user interface.

Presentation Tips for the *The Official CompTIA® A+® Core 1 and Core 2 (Exams 220-1001 and 220-1002)* Course

Here are some useful tips for presenting the *The Official CompTIA® A+® Core 1 and Core 2 (Exams 220-1001 and 220-1002)* course.

- With the latest revision of the certification exams and corresponding exam objectives, a significant amount of new content has been added to this edition of the course. You might need to employ time-saving techniques, such as asking participants to read some of the content as "homework" and then spending very little classroom time on that content, to ensure that you can cover all of the content included in the course manual.
- If you will have remote participants for your class, it is strongly recommended that you position a camera directly above a work area so that remote students can watch as you or other participants work with the various hardware components throughout the course.
- Throughout the course, when software or applications are being installed or updated that might take considerable time, consider having students start the install or update, then present the related content. You might also consider having the install or update begin before a scheduled classroom break.
- In the troubleshooting topics, you might have to send students out of the physical classroom in order to introduce errors and issues into their devices. For remote participants, you might want to also introduce issues into your devices so that you can demonstrate how to troubleshoot and correct the errors.
- The **Video** icon provides access to different videos that can be incorporated into the course. These videos, developed exclusively for CompTIA by ITPro.TV, provide demonstrations of key activities in the course. These are a good alternative to show if you do not have access to all equipment mentioned in the course.

Course-Specific Technical Requirements

Hardware

For this course, you will need one HOST and one WORKBENCH computer for each student and the instructor, along with some additional components and equipment.

Each HOST computer will run Windows® 10, Hyper-V®, and multiple virtual machines and will need the following minimum hardware configurations:

- 2 GHz multicore x64 CPU with virtualization support
- 8 to 16 GB RAM (More RAM provides better VM performance.)
- 200 GB free disk space (An SSD will provide much better performance than an HDD.)
- DVD-ROM drive
- Ethernet network cards supported by the Windows® host OS (Windows® 10)
- Internet access (Contact your local network administrator.)

 Note: Some activities require web access for the HOST. VMs should not be connected to the Internet or to the physical classroom network.

- Keyboard and mouse (or other pointing device)
- 1,024 x 768 resolution monitor recommended

Each WORKBENCH computer should be capable of running Windows® 10 (1803 build).

Software

For each HOST computer, you will need product ISOs and (where applicable) product keys/ licenses for the following software:

- Windows® 10 x64 Pro/Enterprise Branch 1803 or later with Hyper-V® installed
- Windows® 8.1 Pro/Enterprise x64 Edition
- Windows® 7 Professional/Enterprise x64 Edition SP1 (Build 7601)
- Windows® Server 2016 Standard Edition
- CentOS 7 x64 (A prebuilt VM is provided. You will only need to provide an ISO if you want to demonstrate or run an attended installation of Linux.)

 Note: If you do not have the specific builds available, future versions of Windows® 10 or Server 2016 should not substantially affect the activity steps. However, security and virus definition updates could cause some of the tools used in the activities to fail; if this is the case, disable Windows® Defender. Windows® 7 must have SP1 installed.

For each WORKBENCH computer, you will need:

- Product ISOs and (where applicable) product keys/licenses for Windows® 10 x64 Pro/Enterprise Branch 1803
- CPU-Z (**www.cpuid.com/softwares/cpu-z.html**)

You will also need:

- A variety of peripherals such as keyboards and mice, different kinds of displays and cabling, microphones and speakers, and webcams.
- A variety of upgrade components such as storage drives, graphics adapters, power supplies, and RAM.
- A variety of laptops and mobile devices.
- Cleaning kits, toolkits, and testing equipment such as multimeters and power supply testers.
- Printing and networking equipment.
- IoT/home automation equipment.

Setting Up the Course

A detailed Setup Guide is provided on the **Instructor Resources** tile of the CHOICE Course screen. It includes complete instructions for setting up instructor and student computers to complete all of the hands-on activities in this course.

Presentation Planners

The lesson durations given in the course content are estimates based on a typical class experience. Your presentation timing and flow may vary based on factors such as the size of the class, whether students are in specialized job roles, whether you plan to incorporate videos or other assets from the CHOICE Course screen into the course, and so on.

Because the content can be presented in a continuous flow or separately across a multi-session series, several sample presentation planners are provided on the **Instructor Resources** tile of the CHOICE Course screen. You can use these sample planners to determine how you will conduct the class to meet the needs of your own situation.

About This Course

CompTIA A+ certified professionals are proven problem solvers. They support today's core technologies from security to cloud to data management and more. CompTIA A+ is the industry standard for launching IT careers into today's digital world. It is the only industry recognized credential with performance-based items to prove pros can think on their feet to perform critical IT support tasks in the moment. It is trusted by employers around the world to identify the go-to person in end point management and technical support roles. CompTIA A+ is regularly re-invented by IT experts to ensure that it validates core skills and abilities demanded in the workplace.

The Official CompTIA® A+® Core 1 and Core 2 (Exams 220-1001 and 220-1002) course provides the background knowledge and skills you will require to be a successful A+ technician. It will help you prepare to take the CompTIA A+ Core Series certification examinations (exam numbers 220-1001 and 220-1002), in order to become a CompTIA A+ Certified Professional.

Course Description

Target Student

This course is designed for individuals who have basic computer user skills and who are interested in obtaining a job as an entry-level IT technician. This course is also designed for students who are seeking the CompTIA A+ certification and who want to prepare for the CompTIA A+ Core 1 220-1001 Certification Exam and the CompTIA A+ Core 2 220-1002 Certification Exam.

Prerequisites

To ensure your success in this course, you should have experience with basic computer user skills, be able to complete tasks in a Microsoft® Windows® environment, be able to search for, browse, and access information on the Internet, and have basic knowledge of computing concepts. You can obtain this level of skills and knowledge by taking the following official CompTIA courses:

* *The Official CompTIA® IT Fundamentals+ (Exam FC0-U61)*

Note: The prerequisites for this course might differ significantly from the prerequisites for the CompTIA certification exams. For the most up-to-date information about the exam prerequisites, complete the form on this page: **https://certification.comptia.org/training/exam-objectives**

Course Objectives

In this course, you will install, configure, optimize, troubleshoot, repair, upgrade, and perform preventive maintenance on personal computers, digital devices, and operating systems.

You will:

* Support operating systems.
* Install and configure PC system unit components and peripheral devices.
* Install, configure, and troubleshoot display and multimedia devices.
* Install, configure, and troubleshoot storage devices.
* Install, configure, and troubleshoot internal system components.
* Install, configure, and maintain operating systems.
* Maintain and troubleshoot Microsoft Windows.
* Explain network infrastructure concepts.
* Configure and troubleshoot network connections.
* Manage users, workstations, and shared resources.
* Implement client virtualization and cloud computing.
* Implement physical security.
* Secure workstations and data.

- Troubleshoot workstation security issues.
- Support and troubleshoot laptops.
- Support and troubleshoot mobile devices.
- Install, configure, and troubleshoot print devices.
- Implement operational procedures.

The CompTIA CHOICE Home Screen

Logon and access information for your CHOICE environment will be provided with your class experience. The platform is your entry point to the learning experience, of which this course manual is only one part.

On the Home screen, you can access the Course screens for your specific courses. Visit the Course screen both during and after class to make use of the world of support and instructional resources that make up the learning experience.

Each Course screen will give you access to the following resources:

- **Classroom**: A link to your training provider's classroom environment.
- **eBook**: An interactive electronic version of the printed book for your course.
- **Files**: Any course files available to download.
- **Checklists**: Step-by-step procedures and general guidelines you can use as a reference during and after class.
- **Videos**: Brief videos, developed exclusively for CompTIA by ITPro.TV, provide demonstrations of key activities in the course. These are a good alternative to view if you do not have access to all equipment mentioned in the course.
- **Assessment**: A series of different assessments for each lesson as well as an overall course self-assessment.

Depending on the nature of your course and the components chosen by your learning provider, the CHOICE Course screen may also include access to elements such as:

- LogicalLABs, a virtual technical environment for your course.
- CertMaster Practice, an adaptive knowledge assessment and practice test platform.
- Various partner resources related to the courseware.
- Related certifications or credentials.
- A link to your training provider's website.
- Notices from the CHOICE administrator.
- Newsletters and other communications from your learning provider.
- Mentoring services.

Visit your CHOICE Home screen often to connect, communicate, and extend your learning experience!

How to Use This Book

As You Learn

This book is divided into lessons and topics, covering a subject or a set of related subjects. In most cases, lessons are arranged in order of increasing proficiency.

The results-oriented topics include relevant and supporting information you need to master the content. Each topic has various types of activities designed to enable you to solidify your understanding of the informational material presented in the course. Information is provided for reference and reflection to facilitate understanding and practice.

Data files for various activities as well as other supporting files for the course are available by download from the CHOICE Course screen. In addition to sample data for the course exercises, the course files may contain media components to enhance your learning and additional reference materials for use both during and after the course.

Checklists of procedures and guidelines can be used during class and as after-class references when you're back on the job and need to refresh your understanding.

At the back of the book, you will find a glossary of the definitions of the terms and concepts used throughout the course. You will also find an index to assist in locating information within the instructional components of the book. In many electronic versions of the book, you can click links on key words in the content to move to the associated glossary definition, and on page references in the index to move to that term in the content. To return to the previous location in the document after clicking a link, use the appropriate functionality in your PDF viewing software.

As You Review

Any method of instruction is only as effective as the time and effort you, the student, are willing to invest in it. In addition, some of the information that you learn in class may not be important to you immediately, but it may become important later. For this reason, we encourage you to spend some time reviewing the content of the course after your time in the classroom.

As a Reference

The organization and layout of this book make it an easy-to-use resource for future reference. Taking advantage of the glossary, index, and table of contents, you can use this book as a first source of definitions, background information, and summaries.

Course Icons

Watch throughout the material for the following visual cues.

Student Icon	Student Icon Descriptive Text
	A **Note** provides additional information, guidance, or hints about a topic or task.
	A **Caution** note makes you aware of places where you need to be particularly careful with your actions, settings, or decisions, so that you can be sure to get the desired results of an activity or task.
	Video notes show you where an associated video is particularly relevant to the content. These videos can be accessed through the Video tile in CHOICE.
	Checklists provide job aids you can use after class as a reference to perform skills back on the job. Access checklists from your CHOICE Course screen.
	Additional **Practice Questions** are available in the Assessment tile in your CHOICE Course screen.

Lesson 1

Supporting Operating Systems

LESSON INTRODUCTION

As a professional IT support representative or PC service technician, your job will include installing, configuring, maintaining, and troubleshooting personal computer operating systems, applications, hardware, and networks. Before you can perform any of these tasks, you need to understand the basics of what an operating system is, including the various versions, features, components, and technical capabilities. With this knowledge, you can provide effective support for all types of system environments.

The operating system is the software that provides a user interface to the computer hardware and provides an environment in which to run software applications and create computer networks. In this lesson, you will identify the basic types, functions, features, and tools of operating systems, with a particular focus on Microsoft® Windows®.

LESSON OBJECTIVES

In this lesson, you will:

- Compare common OSs and their purposes and features.

- Identify procedures and techniques to employ when troubleshooting.

- Use administrative tools and system utilities in different versions of Windows.

- Perform file management using Explorer and command prompt tools.

- Use the command-line tools and the Disk Management console to configure disks, volumes, arrays, and mount points.

- Use Device Manager and Control Panel/Settings to configure power management, display and sound devices, and to remove devices.

Topic A

Identify Common Operating Systems

EXAM OBJECTIVES COVERED
1002-1.1 Compare and contrast common operating system types and their purposes.
1002-1.2 Compare and contrast features of Microsoft Windows versions.

In this topic, you will identify the types and functions of personal computer (PC) and mobile device operating systems. The first step is to learn about the various operating systems available today, and to identify those that are commonly used on PCs and those that are used on tablets and smartphones.

Without a user-friendly operating system, most people would not be capable of using their computers or mobile devices to successfully perform the tasks required of them. As an IT professional, being familiar with the different types of operating systems can help you to support a variety of computer and mobile device environments.

WHAT IS AN OPERATING SYSTEM?

Show Slide(s)
What is an Operating System?

Teaching Tip
Point out that the OS is like glue, holding the bits of the computing platform together.

A computer requires an **operating system (OS)** in order to function. The operating system provides the interface between the hardware, application programs, and the user. The operating system handles many of the basic system functions, such as interaction with the system hardware and input/output.

An operating system is generally made up of a number of core files—called the **kernel** —with additional **device drivers** and **programs** to provide extended functionality. The earliest operating systems for PCs, such as Microsoft's Disk Operating System (DOS), used a command-line user interface or simple menu systems. Windows and software applications for Windows were marked by the use of a **Graphical User Interface (GUI)**. This helped to make computers easier to use by non-technical staff and home users.

 Note: Actually, some DOS applications presented a GUI, of a kind. Windows is sometimes described as a WIMP (Window, Icon, Menu, Pointing device) interface.

The **desktop style** favored by a particular OS or OS version is a powerful factor in determining customer preferences for one OS over another.

OS TYPES

Show Slide(s)
OS Types

The market for operating systems is divided into four main sections:

- Business client—an OS designed to work as a client in business networks.
- Network Operating System (NOS)—an OS designed to run on servers in business networks.
- Home client—an OS designed to work on standalone or workgroup PCs in a home or small office.
- Cell phone (smartphone)/Tablet—an OS designed to work with a handheld portable device. This type of OS must have a touch-operated interface.

COMPATIBILITY ISSUES

A software application is coded to run on a particular OS. You cannot install an app written for iOS® on an Android™ smartphone. The developer must create a different version of the app. This can be relatively easy for the developer or quite difficult, depending on the way the app is coded and the target platforms. The application or app "ecosystem," or the range of software available for a particular OS, is another big driver of customer acceptance for a particular OS product.

Compatibility also affects version updates to operating system software. There is always a chance that some change in the new OS version will cause software (or hardware device drivers) written for an older version not to work properly. In the business client market, this makes companies very reluctant to update to new OS versions without extensive testing. As extensive testing is very expensive, they are generally reluctant to adopt new versions without a compelling need to do so.

 Note: These compatibility concerns are being mitigated somewhat by the use of web applications and cloud services. A web application only needs the browser to be compatible, not the whole OS. The main compatibility issue for a web application is supporting a touch interface and a very wide range of display resolutions on the different devices that might connect to it.

Finally, compatibility also affects the way that computers running different operating systems can communicate on data networks. The computers cannot "talk" to one another directly. The operating systems must support common network protocols that allow data to be exchanged in a standard format.

MICROSOFT WINDOWS

Microsoft Windows is the dominant commercial PC OS, estimated to be installed on 90% of the world's desktop and laptop computers. The **Windows Server** OS is also widely used on private network servers and Internet servers running web, email, and social networking apps.

Like most software, Windows and Windows Server® have been released in a number of versions over the years. Historically, a new version would have to be purchased, though upgrade discounts were usually available. A new version may introduce significant changes in desktop styles and user interface of Windows and add new features and support for new types of hardware. On the downside, a new version may not be compatible with hardware and software applications designed for earlier versions.

One of the main functions of an OS is to provide an interface (or **shell**) between the user and the computer hardware and software. Windows has a number of interface components designed both for general use and for more technical configuration and troubleshooting.

The top level of the user interface is the **desktop**. This is displayed when Windows starts and the user logs on. The desktop contains icons to launch applications and possibly user data files. The desktop also contains the Start Menu or **Start Screen** and taskbar, which are used to launch and control applications.

MICROSOFT WINDOWS VERSIONS

Let's start by taking a look at the most popular versions of Windows currently in use. Other operating systems will be examined more closely later in the course.

 Show Slide(s)
Compatibility Issues

 Show Slide(s)
Microsoft Windows

 Teaching Tip

Give an overview of Windows versions so that learners are familiar with the timeline and can identify which versions remain in widespread use.

Note that learners don't need to learn release dates or market share for the exam.

Windows Server isn't mentioned explicitly on the syllabus but Active Directory is. Just make learners aware that it is a "parallel" version to the desktop OS.

 Show Slide(s)
Microsoft Windows Versions (3 slides)

 Teaching Tip

This course assumes that learners have basic familiarity with user-level features of Windows, such as the desktop, taskbar, icons, and windows.

WINDOWS 10

Windows 10, first released in 2015, is the current version. Windows 10 aims to provide a consistent user experience across different types of devices, including desktop PCs, laptops, tablets, and smartphones.

When installed to a PC or laptop, Windows 10 retains the user desktop and taskbar familiar from legacy versions but uses a touch-optimized **Start Screen** interface to access apps and programs. This replaces the old Start Menu. As well as shortcuts, the **Start Screen** can display app tiles, which can contain live or actively updated content. These app tiles are fully customizable.

Windows 10 (1803) desktop and Start Screen. (Screenshot used with permission from Microsoft.)

Interaction Opportunity

Ask learners to start Windows 10 on the HOST PC and locate desktop features such as icons, the taskbar, notification area, **Start** button, and **Start Screen**. Show them how to access customization options for the desktop, **Start Screen** and taskbar.

The **Start Screen** is activated by selecting the **Start** button ▣ or by pressing the **Windows** key, which might also be labeled the **Start** key.

 *Note: On a smartphone or tablet, the **Start Screen** replaces the desktop entirely.*

WINDOWS 10 FEATURE UPDATES

With Windows 10, Microsoft indicated that they would no longer release new versions of Windows, but would instead maintain the OS with **feature updates** on a periodic basis. Thus, the current version of Windows, at the time of writing, is still Windows 10. This approach is known as "Windows as a service." Feature updates for Windows 10 are identified with a name and number. For example, in July 2016, Microsoft released a Windows 10 feature update called Windows 10 Anniversary Update. This release was identified with the number 1607, which corresponds to the year (2016) and month (07/ July) of release. The full name of the current version of Windows 10 at the time of writing is Windows 10 Spring Creators Update (1803), replacing the Fall Creators Update (1709).

In addition to feature updates, Windows is updated periodically with **quality updates**. Quality updates do not usually make radical changes to Windows, though some do include new features. Quality updates might sometimes cause compatibility problems with some hardware devices and software applications, but this is less likely than with feature updates.

Windows 10 Mobile

Microsoft has developed versions of Windows for mobile devices, including Windows CE, Windows Phone® 7, and Windows Phone 8. None of these have enjoyed the same sort of success as Windows has in the PC market.

With Windows 10 Mobile, Microsoft has adopted a consistent user interface and code base across all types of devices. Windows 10 Mobile has a very small smartphone market share compared to Android and iOS. Microsoft develops and sells Windows 10 Mobile smartphones and Surface® tablets.

WINDOWS 8 AND WINDOWS 8.1

Compared to earlier versions, Windows 8 (released in 2012) and Windows 8.1 (2013) imposed significant user interface changes to provide better support for touchscreens. One of these changes was the first use of the **Start Screen**. Not all of the changes were popular with users familiar with Windows 7, however. Windows 10 addressed this feedback and was also made available as a free upgrade to Windows 8. Consequently, Windows 10 very quickly replaced Windows 8 and Windows 8 is not that widely used, having about 7% market share at the time of writing.

As well as introducing the **Start Screen** for the first time, in Windows 8, some of the search and configuration settings are accessed as **charms**. The Charms bar is opened by swiping from the right of the screen.

 Teaching Tip

The **Start Screen** caused Microsoft a great deal of grief with users in the first iteration of Windows 8, and trying to operate it with a mouse is indeed a difficult experience. On a PC, it's best to use the keyboard— just press the **Windows** key and type the name of what you want to run.

Another issue was the lack of any obvious way to shut down the PC. Power options were accessed via the Charms bar.

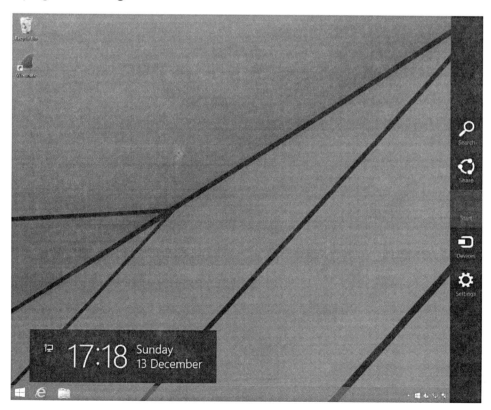

Windows 8.1 showing the Charms bar. (Screenshot used with permission from Microsoft.)

On a desktop PC, you can move the mouse pointer down from the top-right or (more simply) press **Windows**+**C**. The Charms bar was discontinued in Windows 10.

 *Note: Windows 8 was swiftly updated to Windows 8.1 to address some issues with the interface, principally the lack of a **Start** button and forcing use of the **Start Screen** at boot rather than the desktop. In other respects, references to Windows 8 in this course can be taken to apply to Windows 8.1, too. There was never a Windows 9.*

WINDOWS 7

Prior to Windows 8, there was Windows 7 (2009), Windows Vista (2007), and Windows XP (2001). Of these, Windows 7 is still widely used, with an estimated installation base of around 45% of all PCs. Despite no longer being officially supported by Microsoft, Windows XP is still installed on about 5% of devices. Windows Vista never achieved a significant market share.

Windows 7 uses the "classic" Start Menu user interface. The Start Menu contains icon shortcuts to recently used programs and some of the main folders and utilities. The All Programs submenu contains the shortcuts to all the other desktop applications installed on the computer.

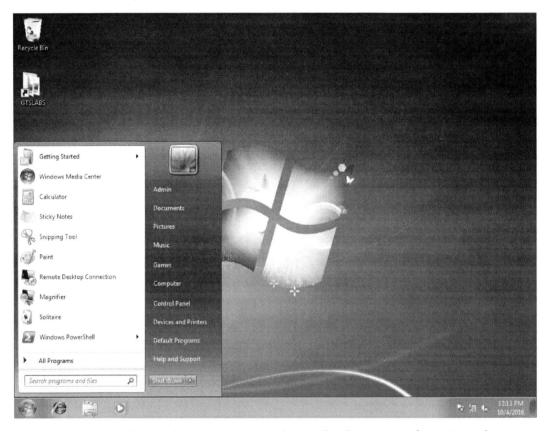

Windows 7 desktop and Start Menu. (Screenshot used with permission from Microsoft.)

 Note: According to the CompTIA exam objectives, you will not be expected to support Windows Vista or Windows XP.

WINDOWS EDITIONS

Each version of Windows is available in different editions. Editions are used by Microsoft to create different markets for Windows. Windows 7 editions included

---

 Interaction Opportunity

If learners ask about the feature differences among the various version of Windows, consider having them perform a web search for *feature comparison microsoft windows* and review the search results with the class, The **Comparison of Microsoft Windows versions** article in Wikipedia contains over a dozen tables describing the features of each version of Windows that has been released over the years. Point out the release timeline graph at the end of the article to show the many versions of Windows that have been released.

 Show Slide(s)

Windows Editions

 Teaching Tip

Make sure you differentiate between the concepts of editions and versions.

Note that "Windows 10 Education" is the Education Enterprise edition, while "Pro Education" is more like the Pro edition.

Windows 10 Mobile counts as another edition, and there is also a Windows 10 Mobile Enterprise.

Starter, Home Basic, Home Premium, Professional, Enterprise, and Ultimate. Windows 10 is available in the following editions:

- Windows 10 Home—designed for domestic consumers and Small Office Home Office (SOHO) business use. The Home edition cannot be used to join a Windows domain network.
- Windows 10 Pro—designed for small and medium-sized businesses. The "Professional" edition comes with networking and management features designed to allow network administrators more control over each client device.
- Windows 10 Enterprise/Windows 10 Enterprise (Long Term Servicing Channel)— similar to the Pro edition but designed for volume licensing by medium and large enterprises.
- Windows 10 Education/Pro Education—variants of the Enterprise and Pro editions designed for licensing by schools and colleges.

 Note: The Windows 7 Ultimate edition was a "superset" with all the features from other editions. Ultimate editions were discontinued with Windows 8. The distinction between basic and premium home editions was also abandoned. Windows 8 has an unnamed edition—sometimes referred to as "Windows 8 Core"—rather than a "Home" edition.

WINDOWS IN THE CORPORATE WORLD

The principal distinguishing feature of the Professional/Pro, Enterprise, Ultimate, and Education editions (regardless of version) is the ability to join a **domain network**. A personal user or small business owner can just administer each machine they own individually. On a corporate network, it is necessary to manage user accounts and system policies centrally, because there are more machines to manage and security requirements are higher. This centralized management is provided by joining each computer to a domain, where the accounts are configured on Domain Controller (DC) servers. Some other notable corporate features are as follows:

- **BitLocker**—enables the user to encrypt all the information on a disk drive. Encryption means that data on the device is protected even if someone steals it (as long as they cannot crack the user password). BitLocker is included with Windows 7 Enterprise and Ultimate, Windows 8 Pro and Enterprise, and Windows 10 Pro, Enterprise, and Education editions.
- **Encrypting File System (EFS)**—where BitLocker encrypts an entire drive, EFS can be used to apply file- or folder-level encryption. EFS is included with Windows 7 Professional, Enterprise, and Ultimate, Windows 8 Pro and Enterprise, and Windows 10 Pro, Enterprise, and Education editions.
- **BranchCache**—an enterprise might have computers installed at different geographic locations needing to view and update data at a central office. As the Wide Area Network (WAN) links from each location to the office might be quite slow, it can be useful for the remote computers to share access to a single cache of data from shared folders and files or document portals such as SharePoint sites. This reduces the amount of WAN traffic because each client does not have to download its own copy individually. BranchCache is supported on Windows 7 Enterprise and Ultimate, Windows 8 Enterprise, and Windows 10 Pro, Enterprise, and Education editions.

 Note: The Pro/Professional editions support a limited type of BranchCache for Background Intelligent Transfer Service (BITS) communications only. Most document and file sharing uses HyperText Transfer Protocol (HTTP) or Server Message Block (SMB), and these types of transfers are only supported by the Enterprise/Ultimate editions. BITS might be used for tasks such as patch deployment or image-based installs.

 Interaction Opportunity

Ask learners to run **About your PC** to view the edition installed on their HOST PCs. Point out the option to perform an edition upgrade.

 Show Slide(s)

Windows in the Corporate World

 Teaching Tip

For purposes of the exam, note that BitLocker is NOT included with Windows 7 Professional.

Note that encryption technologies will be covered later in the course.

Show Slide(s)
Windows for Personal Use

Teaching Tip
Another difference between Home and Home Premium was support for Aero desktop-compositing effects, but hopefully learners won't need to know that for the exam. Home Basic also couldn't be used to create homegroups, only join them.

Show Slide(s)
32-bit and 64-bit Windows

Show Slide(s)
Windows System Limits (3 slides)

Teaching Tip
You might want to note the existence of the "Pro for Workstations" edition, which supports 6 TB memory.

WINDOWS FOR PERSONAL USE

Windows Media Center is a Microsoft app allowing the computer to be used as a sort of home entertainment appliance, such as playing DVDs (several other functions of the product are no longer supported). Media Center was included in the Windows 7 Home Premium, Professional, Enterprise, and Ultimate editions. It is the principal distinction between the Windows 7 Home Basic and Windows 7 Home Premium editions. It became a paid-for add-on in Windows 8 and was discontinued in Windows 10.

If Media Center is not available, a DVD player is available from Microsoft. Third-party software is required to playback commercial Blu-ray™ discs.

32-BIT AND 64-BIT WINDOWS

Each version and edition of Windows is available as 32-bit or 64-bit (x64) software. 64-bit editions of Windows can run most 32-bit applications software, though there may be some exceptions (you should check with the software vendor). The reverse is not true, however; a 32-bit version of Windows cannot run 64-bit applications software.

64-bit editions of Windows also require 64-bit hardware device drivers authorized ("signed") by Microsoft. If the vendor has not produced a 64-bit driver, the hardware device will not be usable.

WINDOWS SYSTEM LIMITS

The versions and editions of Windows have different restrictions in terms of CPU types and features and memory supported. Windows 10 has the following system limits:

Feature	Home	Pro	Education	Enterprise
SMP (Multiple CPUs)	No	2-way	2-way	2-way
Multicore	Yes	Yes	Yes	Yes
RAM limitations (32-bit)	4 GB	4 GB	4 GB	4 GB
RAM limitations (64-bit)	128 GB	2 TB	2 TB	6 TB

Windows 8 has the following system limits:

Feature	Core	Pro/Enterprise
SMP	No	2-way
Multicore	Yes	Yes
RAM limitations (32-bit)	4 GB	4 GB
RAM limitations (64-bit)	128 GB	512 GB

Windows 7 has the following system limits:

Feature	Home Basic	Home Premium	Professional	Enterprise	Ultimate
64-bit Edition	Yes	Yes	Yes	Yes	Yes
SMP	No	No	2-way	2-way	2-way
Multicore	Yes	Yes	Yes	Yes	Yes
RAM limitations (32-bit)	4 GB	4 GB	4 GB	4 GB	4 GB

Feature	Home Basic	Home Premium	Professional	Enterprise	Ultimate
RAM limitations (64-bit)	8 GB	16 GB	192 GB	192 GB	192 GB

The Windows 7 Starter edition was only available to system builders (OEMs) for installation on netbooks and sub-notebooks. It supports up to 2 GB RAM. There is no 64-bit version of the Starter edition.

OS LIFECYCLES

An **end of life system** is one that is no longer supported by its developer or vendor. End of life systems no longer receive security updates and so represent a critical vulnerability for a company's security systems if any remain in active use.

Microsoft products are subject to a support lifecycle policy. Windows versions are given five years of mainstream support and five years of extended support (during which only security updates are shipped). Support is contingent on the latest Service Pack being applied (non-updated versions of Windows are supported for 24 months following the release of the SP). Windows 10 retirement schedules for feature updates —referred to as "end of service"—are 18 months, except for September updates for Education/Enterprise editions only, which are supported for 30 months.

To find out when Microsoft products will be retired or how long specific products will be supported, visit the Microsoft Product Lifecycle Search tool at **support.microsoft.com/lifecycle/search**.

When you plan to install a new version of an operating system as an upgrade, you must check that your computer meets the hardware requirements for the new version. As operating system software such as Windows 10 moves towards more of a service model, with quite frequent feature updates, it could be the case that an update has its own system requirements that were different from the original. Plus, Microsoft points out that the core hardware requirements for Windows 10 are the same as those for Windows 7. Other factors might impact your ability to apply a feature update, including support for third-party driver or applications software.

APPLE OPERATING SYSTEMS

In 1984, when the IBM PC was the dominant desktop standard, Steve Jobs and Steve Wozniak created a new type of personal computer—the Apple® Macintosh® (or Mac®). It was revolutionary because it came with a graphical user interface at a time when IBM's PC used the command-line/text menu DOS operating system. The Mac has never matched Windows' huge user base, although its current incarnation does have a truly devoted following.

APPLE MAC OS/OS X/macOS

The main difference between Mac OS and other operating systems is that the OS is only supplied with Apple-built computers. You cannot purchase Mac OS and install it on an ordinary PC. This helps to make Mac OS stable but does mean that there is far less choice in terms of buying extra hardware.

Show Slide(s)
OS Lifecycles

Teaching Tip
Learners shouldn't need to know end of life dates for the exam, but you might want to briefly discuss the support status for different Windows versions. Windows 7 is in extended support until 2020. Windows 8.0 is no longer supported. Windows 8.1 continues in extended support through 2023.

Show Slide(s)
Apple Operating Systems (2 slides)

Teaching Tip
Mac OS has about 9% market share at the time of writing.

Interaction Opportunity
Poll learners to see who uses Macs at home or at work, and who uses Windows.

macOS desktop. (Screenshot courtesy of Apple.)

The current lines—OS X® and more recently macOS®—were re-developed from the kernel of another type of operating system called UNIX. This kernel is supplemented with additional code to implement the Mac's graphical interface and system utilities and to maintain compatibility with older Mac OS applications. macOS gets periodic "dot" version updates. At the time of writing, the current version is 10.14 or "Mojave," and updates are being released to existing customers free-of-charge.

As there is a tight link between the models of Mac computers and the OS, Apple makes specific update limitations about whether a new version of macOS can be installed to a Mac computer. Check **support.apple.com** for the technical specification for any particular macOS release. Apple does not publish end of life policies.

APPLE iOS

iOS is the operating system for Apple's iPhone® smartphone and iPad® tablet. While also derived from UNIX, iOS is a closed source operating system. This means that the code used to design the software is kept confidential and can only be modified by Apple. macOS and iOS have some similarities but they are not compatible; an app developed for iOS will not run on macOS.

On an iOS device, apart from volume and power, the only external button is the Home key, which returns the user to the home screen "desktop."

The interface is then entirely controlled via touch. Point to icons to open apps, swipe or flick from left-to-right to access the keyboard and search, or flick right-to-left to view more icons. Re-arrange icons by tapping and holding for a few seconds. The icons will then "wobble" and can be dragged to a different page or into the dock taskbar at the bottom. Press the Home key to save.

To view and manage open apps, double-click the Home key to open the Multitasking bar.

Teaching Tip

iOS has about 12% smartphone market share, compared to Android's 87%. Note that the Home key is being dropped with iPhone X.

Support for native iOS apps is being built into the latest release of macOS (Mojave). Translating a native iOS app to run on the desktop is still not a straightforward task, however.

Interaction Opportunity

Poll learners to see who uses iPhones and iPads.

iOS 11 running on an iPhone 7. (Screenshot courtesy of Apple.)

Touch can be operated either with your fingers or with a special soft-touch stylus. There are many more gestures in addition to those listed above. For example, shaking the device is often used to activate undo. There are also external keyboards available and most Apple devices support Siri®, a voice recognition system and personal assistant.

New versions are released approximately every year with various .x updates. Version 12 is current at time of writing. Apple makes new versions freely available, though older hardware devices may not support all the features of a new version, or may not be supported at all. As with macOS, update limitations are published at **support.apple.com** but there are no end of life policies.

UNIX-BASED OPERATING SYSTEMS

Windows and macOS dominate the desktop/workstation/laptop market, but a third "family" of operating systems is very widely used on a larger range of devices.

UNIX

UNIX is a trademark for a family of operating systems originally developed at Bell Laboratories beginning in the late 1960s. All UNIX® systems share a kernel/shell architecture, with the kernel providing the core functionality and the interchangeable shells providing the user interface. Unlike Windows and macOS, UNIX is portable to different hardware platforms; versions of UNIX can run on everything from personal computers to mainframes and on many types of computer processors.

LINUX

Originally developed by Linus Torvalds, **Linux** is based on UNIX. UNIX was developed over decades by various commercial, academic, and not-for-profit organizations. This resulted in several versions, not all of which are compatible, and many of which are

 Show Slide(s)

UNIX-Based Operating Systems (2 slides)

 Teaching Tip

Although UNIX is not on the exam objectives, it is included here because of its relationship to Linux and macOS.

 Teaching Tip

Note that Linux is not that widely used as a desktop system (though the derived Chrome OS is very popular within the education sector) but is very widely used as a server OS (one estimate is that Linux powers 70% of the top 10 million domains).

 Interaction Opportunity

Ask learners if they have any experience in using Linux as a desktop or a server OS.

proprietary or contain copyrighted or patented code or features. Linux® was developed as a fully open source alternative to UNIX (and for that matter, to Windows and macOS and iOS).

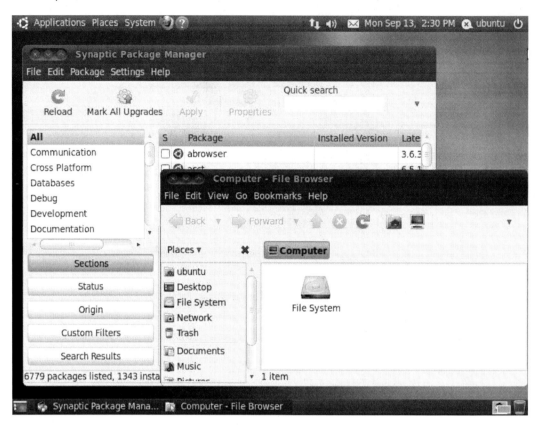

Ubuntu Linux.

Linux can be used as a desktop or server OS. There are many distributions or distros, notably SUSE®, Red Hat®, CentOS, Fedora®, Debian®, Ubuntu®, and Mint®. Each distro adds specific packages and interfaces to the generic Linux kernel and provides different support options. Linux does not require a graphical interface, though many distributions provide one.

IBM®, Sun/Oracle®, and Novell® are among the vendors producing end-user applications for Linux. As a desktop OS it tends to be used in schools and universities more than in business or in the home. As a server OS, it dominates the market for web servers. It is also used very widely as the OS for "smart" appliances and Internet of Things (IoT) devices.

CHROME OS

Chrome OS is derived from Linux, via an open source OS called Chromium™. Chrome OS™ itself is proprietary. Chrome OS is developed by Google to run on specific laptop (Chromebook) and PC (Chromebox) hardware. This hardware is designed for the budget and education markets.

Chrome OS was primarily developed to use web applications. In a web application, the software is hosted on a server on the Internet and the client connects to it using a browser. The client computer does not need to be particularly powerful as the server does most of the processing. Chrome OS provides a minimal environment compared to Windows. This means that there is less chance of some other software application or hardware device driver interfering with the function of the browser.

There are also "packaged" apps available for use offline and Chrome OS can run apps developed for Android.

Teaching Tip

The exam objectives classify Chrome as a cell phone/tablet OS but it's better known as a workstation OS. There is now a Chrometab (produced by Acer), and some Chromebooks are hybrid laptop/tablets. There are some rumors that Google plans to replace both Chrome OS and Android with a new OS (code named Fuchsia).

ANDROID

Android is a smartphone/tablet OS developed by the Open Handset Alliance, primarily driven by Google. Unlike iOS, it is an open-source OS, based on Linux. The software code is made publicly available (**source.android.com**). This means that there is more scope for hardware vendors, such as Acer®, Asus®, HTC®, Huawei®, LG, Motorola®, OnePlus, Oppo™, Samsung®, Sony®, and Xiamoi to produce vendor-specific versions.

Teaching Tip

As noted above, Android dominates the market by volume (around 87% of smartphones).

Interaction Opportunity

Ask Android users to raise their hands, and point out the iPhone/Android split.

Android lollipop home screen.

Like iOS, Android is updated with new major (1.x) and minor (x.1) versions, each of which is named after some kind of sweet stuff. At the time of writing, current versions include 7.1 (Nougat) and 8.1 (Oreo). Because handset vendors produce their own editions of Android, device compatibility for new versions is more mixed compared with iOS.

End of life policies and update restrictions for particular handsets are determined by the handset vendor rather than any kind of overall Android authority. Companies ordering handsets in bulk as employee devices may be able to obtain their own guarantees.

Interaction Opportunity

Ask learners to check the OS version on their own phones (tap **Settings→System→About** for Android and **Settings→General→About** for iOS). Optionally, if you have Internet access, ask them to locate the support policy for their smartphones.

Activity 1-1
Discussing OS Types

 Show Slide(s)

Activity: Discussing OS Types

SCENARIO

Answer the following questions to check your understanding of the topic.

---

1. You receive a call from a customer who is confused after upgrading his Windows 7 Home Premium edition computer to Windows 10. The user cannot find the **All Programs** menu.

    What should you advise?

    Users often need assistance when an OS version changes the desktop style or user interface. In Windows 10, the **Start** Menu and the **All Programs** submenu have been replaced by the **Start Screen**. The user can scroll in the **Start Screen** or use **Instant Search** to find any app. To use **Instant Search**, press the **Windows** key and type the app name.

2. **In terms of system hardware, what is the main advantage of a 64-bit version of Windows?**

    Support for more than 4 GB RAM.

3. You are advising a customer whose business is expanding. The business owner needs to provision an additional 30 desktop computers, some of which will be installed at a second office location. The business is currently run with a workgroup network of five Windows 7 Home Premium desktop computers and one file server.

    Why might you suggest licenses for an edition of Windows 10 that supports corporate needs for the new computer and has upgrades for the old computers? Which specific edition(s) could you recommend?

    Without a domain, accounts must be configured on each computer individually. With over 30 computers to manage at two locations, this would be a substantial task so switching to a domain network, where the accounts can be configured on the server, is likely to save costs in the long term. The **BranchCache** feature would also allow computers at the second office to minimize bandwidth usage when downloading documents (Enterprise edition only) and updates from the main office. You can suggest either Windows 10 Pro or Windows 10 Enterprise for use on a domain. As Windows moves towards a service model, subscription-based licensing of the Enterprise edition is becoming the mainstream choice.

4. A customer asks whether an iOS app that your company developed will also work on her Apple macOS computer.

    What issue does this raise and what answer might you give?

    The issue here is compatibility between different operating systems. Even though both are produced by Apple, iOS and macOS use different environments so the iOS app cannot be installed directly. Your company might make a macOS version. Also (and do not worry if you did not include this in your answer), with the latest version of macOS (Mojave), support for native iOS apps is being provisioned so this might be something you can offer in the future.

5. **Apart from Windows and macOS, what operating system options are there for client PCs?**

    The other main choice is one of the distributions of Linux. A company might also use some sort of UNIX. Finally, Chrome OS is installed on Chromebox PCs. These are often used by educational institutions and businesses who rely primarily on web applications, rather than locally installed desktop software.

6. You are advising a customer with an older model Android smartphone. The customer wants to update to the latest version of Android, but using the update option results in a **No updates available** message.

    What type of issue is this, and what advice can you provide?

    This is an issue with update limitations. Android is quite a fragmented market, and customers must depend on the handset vendor to implement OS updates for a particular model. The customer can only check the handset vendor's website or helpline to find out if a version update will ever be supported for that model.

Topic B
Troubleshooting Methodology

EXAM OBJECTIVES COVERED
1001-5.1 Given a scenario, use the best practice methodology to resolve problems.

Teaching Tip

The basic troubleshooting procedure is covered early (before the details of supporting particular OS, hardware, or network technologies) because the troubleshooting model is critical to many of the other topics in the course.

Often, computer technicians spend a large percentage of their time troubleshooting the various software and hardware components used in computers, networks, and printers. Before you can even begin to troubleshoot a physical problem with a piece of hardware or diagnose an error thrown up by a software program, you need to understand the basics of troubleshooting and some best practices used.

The most elaborate toolkit and expensive diagnostic software can be useless if you do not have a consistent plan for solving problems. Even experienced technicians can sometimes overlook obvious problems or solutions. Troubleshooting can be extremely challenging, but if you follow common best practices and basic troubleshooting procedures, you will often be able to determine the specific cause of a problem, as well as possible solutions to the problem.

TROUBLESHOOTING BASICS

Show Slide(s)

Troubleshooting Basics

Teaching Tip

Ideally, give an example or two of troubleshooting scenarios you have had to deal with (and perhaps, how you could have approached them better if you'd followed the process of identify, analyze, test, evaluate, and document).

To some extent, being an effective troubleshooter simply involves having a detailed knowledge of how something is supposed to work and of the sort of things that typically go wrong. However, the more complex a system is, the less likely it is that this sort of information will be at hand, so it is important to develop general troubleshooting skills to approach new and unexpected situations confidently.

Troubleshooting is a process of problem solving. It is important to realize that problems have causes, symptoms, and consequences. For example:

- A computer system has a fault in the hard disk drive (cause).
- Because the disk drive is faulty, the computer is displaying a "blue screen" (symptom).
- Because of the fault, the user cannot do any work (consequence).

From a business point-of-view, resolving the consequences of the problem is more important than solving the original cause. For example, the most effective solution might be to provide the user with another workstation, then get the drive replaced.

It is also important to realize that the cause of a specific problem might be the symptom of a larger problem. This is particularly true if the same problem recurs. For example, you might ask why the disk drive is faulty—is it a one-off error or are there problems in the environment, supply chain, and so on?

PROBLEM MANAGEMENT

Show Slide(s)

Problem Management

Any organization that has to deal with more than a few problems every week will have a system in place for **problem management**. The basis of problem management is the identification, prioritization, and ownership of **incidents**. The process of problem management is as follows:

1. A user contacts the help desk, perhaps by phone or email. An operator or technician is assigned to the incident and a job ticket is generated.

2. The user describes the problem to the operator, who may ask clarifying questions. The operator categorizes the problem, assesses how urgent it is, and how long it will take to fix.
3. The operator may take the user through initial troubleshooting steps. If these do not work, the job may be escalated to deskside support or a senior technician.
4. Troubleshooting continues until the problem is resolved. At that point, the user is contacted to confirm that the problem has been fixed. The job ticket is updated with details of the problem and how it was resolved. The ticket is then considered closed.

At each stage, the problem management system can track the ownership of the problem (who is dealing with it) and its status (what has been done). At each stage of problem management, you need to consider and be guided by corporate policies, procedures, and impacts before making changes. An enterprise network is, by definition, highly interconnected. Even small changes can have major, unintended impacts, so it is imperative that you follow established change management procedures and know when to seek authority to make a change.

THE COMPTIA A+ TROUBLESHOOTING MODEL

Here are the steps in CompTIA's A+ troubleshooting model:

1. Identify the problem.
   - Question user and identify user changes to computer.
   - Perform backups before making changes.
   - Inquire regarding environmental or infrastructure changes.
   - Review system and application logs.
2. Establish a theory of probable cause (question the obvious and if necessary conduct internal or external research based on symptoms).
3. Test the theory to determine cause:
   - Once theory is confirmed, determine next steps to resolve problem.
   - If theory is not confirmed, re-establish new theory or escalate.
4. Establish a plan of action to resolve the problem and implement the solution.
5. Verify full system functionality, and if applicable, implement preventative measures.
6. Document findings, actions, and outcomes.

Show Slide(s)
The CompTIA A+ Troubleshooting Model (2 slides)

Teaching Tip
Encourage learners to memorize these steps in their proper order.

These steps and the approach and attitude you should apply when troubleshooting are explained in a bit more detail in the next section.

 Note: A methodical process is the ideal, but troubleshooting in help desk and IT support departments is often a time-critical process. In the real world, you often have to balance being methodical with being efficient.

CUSTOMER SERVICE AND COMMUNICATIONS SKILLS

Employers value "soft skills," such as being able to communicate and use questioning, as highly as technical skills. Troubleshooting is one area where soft skills are vital:

- A user may be upset or angry—perhaps they have lost work or cannot get an expensive, new computer to work.
- A user may not be technically knowledgeable.

It is your job to calm the user and to help him or her give you the information you need to diagnose and solve the problem. You need to be able to ask questions that the user can answer simply, without having to know anything about the computer or its software, and guide him or her through basic troubleshooting steps. When speaking

Show Slide(s)
Customer Service and Communications Skills

Teaching Tip
Emphasize the reasoning behind the use of open/closed questioning techniques.

with a user, try to be calm and polite. Do not interrupt when the user is speaking. Do not use technical language (jargon) or abbreviations that are likely to confuse.

OPEN AND CLOSED QUESTIONING

The basis of getting troubleshooting information from users is asking good questions. Questions are commonly divided into two types:

- Open questions invite someone to explain in their own words. Examples are, "What is the problem?", "What happens when you try to switch the computer on?", "Were you able to complete this task before, and if so, when did you notice there was an issue?", and "What types of changes have you noticed since the last time you completed this task?"
- Closed questions invite a Yes/No answer or a fixed response. Examples include, "Can you see any text on the screen?" or "What does the error message say?"

Open questions are good to start with as they help to avoid making your own assumptions about what is wrong and encourage the user to give you all the information that he or she is able to. However, you should not trust the user's judgment completely. The user may be inexperienced or have formed a false impression of what is going wrong. Try to establish factual information rather than asking for the user's opinion.

Closed questions can be used to "drill down" into the nature of the problem and guide a user towards giving you information that is useful.

DEVELOPING A TROUBLESHOOTING MINDSET

Troubleshooting is not just the application of technical knowledge and expertise; the approach you choose to take is equally important.

- Be calm—if you are calm, it instills confidence in the customer and will also prevent you from making rash decisions.
- Take breaks—troubleshooting requires a great deal of concentration. After a long period of working on the same task, the mind can become fatigued and concentration is reduced. Consider taking breaks or leaving the problem for a while to refresh your mind.
- Challenge assumptions—a problem may be reported that is similar to one that you have experienced before, but you should not assume that the problem is identical. Although the symptoms may be similar, the problem and its solution could be completely different. Always treat each problem as a new challenge. Be prepared to try something different. If you have decided what the problem is, but cannot seem to solve it, it may be that you are incorrect. Be prepared to start again from the beginning with an open mind.
- Assess costs and impacts—remember, you must account for corporate policies and evaluate the impact of a problem. A particular problem might be a stimulating challenge, but if resolving it is not the highest priority in terms of business needs, you need to give up on finding "The Answer" and use a shortcut to get to a solution. When assessing whether to repair a part, consider the cost of the part and the cost of your time to perform the repair. In many circumstances, replacement is the most effective option.
- Know when to give up!—you will not always be able to fix the problem yourself. Be prepared to pass the problem on rather than wasting the customer's time!

PROBLEM IDENTIFICATION

When troubleshooting, unless the problem is very simple, it is best to work methodically to ensure that you diagnose the correct problem and choose the best way to resolve it.

Show Slide(s)

Problem Identification
(2 slides)

The traditional method for problem solving is to find the cause of the problem and then to seek to remove or resolve that cause. If you switch your television on and the screen remains dark, you would seek out the cause and then remove it. Finding the actual cause may involve identifying several possible causes and then checking them out one by one to determine a probable cause. If your television stops working, you could ask yourself, "Is the problem in the television?", "Has the fuse blown?", "Is there a problem at the broadcasting station rather than with my television?". With all problems we run through a list of possibilities before making a decision. The trick is to do this methodically (so that possible causes are not overlooked) and efficiently (so that the problem can be solved quickly).

Troubleshooting is not just a problem-solving process, though. It requires effective decision-making. Sometimes there is no simple solution to a problem. There may be several solutions and which is best might not be obvious. An apparent solution might solve the symptoms of the problem but not the cause. A solution might be impractical or too costly. Finally, a solution might be the cause of further problems, which could be even worse than the original problem.

BE PREPARED

Before you visit a user or customer to fix a problem, ensure that you have all the necessary hardware and software tools, documentation, and any other information you may need to avoid repeated and unnecessary trips between your office and the customer's location.

If you are instructing a user over the phone or by email, make sure you offer clear, concise, and accurate instructions.

If troubleshooting requires that the system be taken offline, make sure that this is scheduled appropriately and sensitively. Remember that troubleshooting may involve more than fixing a particular problem; it is about maintaining the resources that users need to do their work.

PERFORM BACKUPS

Consider the importance of data stored on the local computer when performing troubleshooting or maintenance. Check when a backup was last made. If a backup has not been made, perform one before changing the system configuration, if at all possible. The simplest way of making a backup before troubleshooting is to use drive imaging software.

QUESTION THE USER

The first report of a problem will typically come from a user or another technician, and they will be one of the best sources of information, if you can ask the right questions. Before you begin examining settings in Windows or taking the PC apart, spend some time gathering as much information as you can about the problem. Ensure you ask the user to describe *all* of the circumstances. Some good questions to ask include:

- What are the exact error messages appearing on the screen or coming from the speaker? Remember that the error could reveal a symptom, not a cause.
- Has anyone else experienced the same problem?
- How long has the problem been occurring?
- What changes have been made recently to the system? Were these changes initiated by you, or via another support request?

  The latest change to a system is very often the cause of the problem. If something worked previously, then excepting mechanical failures, it is likely that the problem has arisen because of some user-initiated change or some environmental or infrastructure change. If something has never worked, a different approach is required.
- Has anything been tried to solve the problem?

Sources of Information

SOURCES OF INFORMATION

Of course, you cannot always rely on the user to let you know everything that has happened. To diagnose a problem, you may also need to use the following techniques:

- Make a physical inspection—look and listen. You may be able to see or hear a fault (scorched motherboard, "sick"-sounding disk drive, no fan noise, and so on).
- If the symptoms of the problem are no longer apparent, a basic technique is to reproduce the problem—that is, repeat the exact circumstances that produced the failure or error. Some problems are intermittent, though, which means that they cannot be repeated reliably. Issues that are transitory or difficult to reproduce are often the hardest to troubleshoot.
- Check system and application logs or diagnostic software for information.
- Check the system documentation, such as installation or maintenance logs, for useful information.
- Consult any other technicians that might have worked on the system recently or might be working at the moment on some related issue. Consider that environmental or infrastructure changes might have been instigated by a different group within the company. Perhaps you are responsible for application support and the network infrastructure group has made some changes without issuing proper notice.

Determination of Probable Causes

DETERMINATION OF PROBABLE CAUSES

If you obtain accurate answers to your initial questions, you will have determined the severity of the problem (how many are affected), a rough idea of where to look (hardware or OS for instance), and whether to look for a recent change or an oversight in configuration.

You diagnose a problem by identifying the symptoms. From knowing what causes such symptoms, you can consider possible cause to determine the most probable cause and then devise tests to show whether it is the cause or not. Sometimes symptoms derive from more than one cause; while this type of problem is rarer, it is much harder to troubleshoot. A computer system comprises a number of components. Fault finding needs to identify which component is faulty.

QUESTIONING THE OBVIOUS

There are two good ways to consider a computer problem systematically:

- Step through what should happen, either yourself or by observing the user, and identify the point at which there is a failure or error.
- Work up or down layers—for example, power, hardware components, drivers/firmware, software, network, user actions.

With either approach, do not overlook the obvious—sometimes seemingly intractable problems are caused by the simplest things.

Note: A basic technique when troubleshooting a cable, connector, or device is to have a "known good" duplicate on hand. This is another copy of the same cable or device that you know works that you can use to test by substitution. This approach very quickly identifies "non-causes."

Unless a problem is trivial, break the troubleshooting process into compartments or categories. If you can isolate your investigation to a particular subsystem by eliminating "non-causes," you can troubleshoot the problem more quickly. For example, when troubleshooting a PC, you might work as follows:

1. Decide whether the problem is hardware or software related (Hardware).
2. Decide which hardware subsystem is affected (Disk).

3. Decide whether the problem is in the disk unit or connectors and cabling (Connector).
4. Test your theory.

When you have drilled down like this, the problem should become obvious. Of course, you could have made the wrong choice at any point, so you must be prepared to go back and follow a different path.

> **Note:** *If you are really unlucky, two (or more) components may be faulty. Another difficulty lies in assessing whether a component itself is faulty or whether it is not working because of a related component.*

RESEARCHING THE PROBLEM

One of the most useful troubleshooting skills is being able to do research; to find information quickly. Learn to use web and database search tools so that you can locate information that is relevant and useful. Identify different knowledge sources available to you. Consider both internally available documentation and problem logs and external support resources, such as vendor support or forums.

RE-ESTABLISHING A NEW THEORY

If your theory is not proven by the tests you make or the research you undertake, you must establish a new theory. If one does not suggest itself from what you have discovered so far, there may be more lengthy procedures you can use to diagnose a cause—remember to assess business needs before embarking on very lengthy and possibly disruptive tests. Is there a simpler workaround that you are overlooking?

If a problem is particularly intractable, you can do the reverse of the above process and take the system down to its base configuration (the minimum needed to run). When (if) this is working, you can then add peripherals and devices or software subsystems one-by-one, testing after each, until eventually the problem is located. This is time-consuming, but may be necessary if nothing else is providing a solution.

PROBLEM ESCALATION

Be aware that you may not have all the answers all the time. Consider consulting your colleagues, Internet discussion groups, or manufacturers' help lines. This will not only help you to solve the problem more quickly or identify a better solution than you had considered yourself, but will also increase your knowledge and experience.

Show Slide(s)
Problem Escalation

If you cannot solve a problem yourself, it is better to escalate it than to waste a lot of time trying to come up with an answer. Formal escalation routes depend on the type of support service you are operating and the terms of any warranties or service contracts that apply. Some obvious escalation routes include:

*   Senior staff/Knowledge Experts/Subject Matter Experts/technical staff/developers/ programmers/administrators within your company.
*   Suppliers and manufacturers—warranty and support contracts and helplines or web contact portals.
*   Other support contractors/consultants, websites, and social media.

Choosing whether to escalate a problem is complex as you have to balance the need to resolve a problem in a timely fashion with what might be additional costs and the burdens/priorities that senior staff are already coping with. You should be guided by policies and practices in the company you work for. When you escalate a problem, make sure that what you have found out or attempted so far is documented. Failing that, describe the problem clearly to whoever is taking over or providing you with assistance.

If you are completing troubleshooting steps under instruction from another technician —the vendor's support service, for instance—make sure you properly understand the steps you are being asked to take, especially if it requires disassembly of a component or reconfiguration of software that you are not familiar with.

SOLUTION IMPLEMENTATION AND TESTING

Show
Slide(s)
Solution
Implementation and
Testing

If you have established and tested a theory of cause, it should be apparent what steps are required to resolve the issue. There are typically three solutions to an IT problem:

- Repair—you need to determine whether the cost of repair makes this the best option.
- Replace—often more expensive and may be time-consuming if a part is not available. There may also be an opportunity to upgrade the part or software.
- Workaround—as any software developer will tell you, not all problems are critical. If neither repair nor replacement is cost-effective, it may be best either to find a workaround or just to document the issue and move on.

> **Note:** *If a part or system is under warranty, you can return the broken part for a replacement. To do this, you normally need to obtain a Returned Materials Authorization (RMA) ticket from the vendor.*

When you consider solutions, you have to assess the cost and time required. Another consideration is potential effects on the rest of the system that your plan of action may have and whether you have authorization to proceed. A typical example is applying a software patch, which might fix a given problem but cause other programs not to work. This is where an effective change and configuration management system comes into play, as it should help you to understand how different systems are interconnected and cause you to seek the proper authorization for your plan.

IMPLEMENT THE SOLUTION

If you do not have authorization to implement a solution, you will need to escalate the problem to more senior personnel. If applying the solution is disruptive to the wider network or business, you also need to consider the most appropriate time to schedule the reconfiguration work and plan how to notify other network users. When you make a change to the system as part of implementing a solution, test after each change. If the change does not fix the problem, reverse it and then try something else. If you make a series of changes without recording what you have done, you could find yourself in a tricky position.

VERIFICATION AND DOCUMENTATION

Show
Slide(s)
Verification and
Documentation

Teaching
Tip
Testing/verifying
solutions is heavily
stressed in the exam
objectives.

When you apply a solution, test that it fixes the reported problem and that the system as a whole continues to function normally. Tests could involve any of the following:

- Trying to use a component.
- Substituting the component for a "known good" one.
- Inspecting a component to see whether it is properly connected or damaged or whether any status or indicator lights show a problem.
- Disabling or uninstalling the component (if it might be the cause of a wider problem).
- Consulting documentation and software tools such as Device Manager to confirm a component is configured properly.
- Updating software or a device driver.

Before you can consider a problem closed, you should both be satisfied in your own mind that you have resolved it and get the customer's acceptance that it has been fixed. Restate what the problem was and how it was resolved then confirm with the customer that the incident log can be closed.

PREVENTIVE MEASURES

To fully solve a problem, you should try to eliminate any factors that could cause the problem to reoccur. For example, if the power cable on a PC blows a fuse, you should not only replace the fuse, but also check to see if there are any power problems in the building that may have caused the fuse to blow in the first place. If a computer is infected with a virus, ensure that the antivirus software is updating itself regularly and users are trained to avoid malware risks.

DOCUMENT FINDINGS, ACTIONS, AND OUTCOMES

Most troubleshooting takes place within the context of a ticket system. This shows who is responsible for any particular problem and what its status is. This gives you the opportunity to add a complete description of the problem and its solution (findings, actions, and outcomes).

This is very useful for future troubleshooting, as problems fitting into the same category can be reviewed to see if the same solution applies. Troubleshooting steps can be gathered into a "Knowledge Base" or Frequently Asked Questions (FAQ) of support articles. It also helps to analyze IT infrastructure by gathering statistics on what types of problems occur and how frequently.

The other value of a log is that it demonstrates what the support department is doing to help the business. This is particularly important for third-party support companies, who need to prove the value achieved in service contracts. When you complete a problem log, remember that people other than you may come to rely on it. Also, logs may be presented to customers as proof of troubleshooting activity. Write clearly and concisely, checking for spelling and grammar errors.

Teaching Tip

The importance of documentation is very heavily stressed in the exam objectives.

Interaction Opportunity

If you have time and Internet access, ask learners to look at some help desk/ticket management systems, such as Zoho, Zendesk, or Spiceworks, to identify key features. They could also look at some Knowledge Bases and support forums, such as Tom's Hardware, Bleeping Computer, or MajorGeeks.

Activity 1-2
Discussing Troubleshooting Methodology

 Show Slide(s)

Activity: Discussing Troubleshooting Methodology

SCENARIO

Answer the following questions to check your understanding of the topic.

---

1. You are dealing with a support request and think that you have identified the probable cause of the reported problem.

    What should be your next troubleshooting step?

    Test the theory to determine the cause.

2. **If you have to open the system case to troubleshoot a computer, what should you check before proceeding?**

    That data on the PC has been backed up. You should always verify that you have a backup before beginning any troubleshooting activities.

3. You receive a support call from a user.

    What should be your first troubleshooting step?

    Question the user to establish all the circumstances surrounding the problem.

4. **Why does it help to categorize a problem when troubleshooting?**

    A step-by-step analysis of the problem helps by making sure you approach it methodically and troubleshooting within a more limited area is simpler.

5. **If another technician says to you, "We'll have to strip this back to base?", what do they mean, and at which specific step of troubleshooting are you likely to be?**

    Bringing a system "back to base" means re-building a troublesome system from its core components. You can then add extra devices one by one until the source of the fault is revealed. This can be time-consuming so is likely to be something you would try if you are testing a theory of probable cause unsuccessfully, and you need to establish a new theory.

6. **What should you do if you cannot determine the cause of a problem?**

    You could consult a colleague, refer to product documentation, or search the web. It might also be appropriate to escalate the problem to more senior support staff.

7. You think you have discovered the solution to a problem in a product Knowledge Base, and the solution involves installing a software patch.

   What should be your next troubleshooting step?

   Identify any negative consequences in applying the software patch, then devise an implementation plan to install the file. You need to schedule the work so as to minimize disruption. You should also make a plan to rollback the installation, should that prove necessary.

8. **After applying a troubleshooting repair, replacement, or upgrade, what should you do next?**

   Test that the fix works and that the system as a whole is functional. You might also implement preventative measures to reduce the risk of the problem occurring again.

9. **What is the last step in the best practice methodology for troubleshooting and how might it be implemented?**

   Document findings, actions, and outcomes. You can use spreadsheet or database tools, but using ticket-based management system software to create incident logs is best.

Topic C

Use Windows Features and Tools

EXAM OBJECTIVES COVERED
1002-1.4 Given a scenario, use appropriate Microsoft command line tools.
1002-1.5 Given a scenario, use Microsoft operating system features and tools.
1002-1.6 Given a scenario, use Microsoft Windows Control Panel utilities.
1002-2.6 Compare and contrast the differences of basic Microsoft Windows OS security settings.

Teaching Tip

As mentioned earlier, this course assumes that learners have basic familiarity with how Windows works in terms of operating the taskbar, windows, shortcut keys, basic Control Panel/Settings configuration, and so on. This topic provides an overview of the administrative tools—consoles, command prompt, registry, etc.

Emphasize that exam candidates must know how to run each tool and must be able to match each tool to an appropriate task.

Show Slide(s)

Windows Settings and Control Panel (2 slides)

As an administrator, you will manage the computer through a graphic user interface (GUI) for some tasks and through a command line interface for others. In this topic, you will examine some of the administrative tools and utilities for Windows computers.

When you configure or troubleshoot a computer, you need to do so with an account that has sufficient privileges to make major changes to OS settings and files. If misused, these privileges could be a significant threat to the security of the computer system and network. In this topic, you will also learn how to exercise administrative privileges safely.

WINDOWS SETTINGS AND CONTROL PANEL

Many tools are used to configure Windows settings and hardware devices. Some of the tools are accessible to ordinary users; others need administrative privileges to run.

CONTROL PANEL

In Windows 7, the **Control Panel** is the best place to start configuring your system. The icons in the Control Panel represent applets used to configure a part of the system.

Windows 7 Control Panel showing 1) Task groups; 2) Configuration applets; 3) Navigation breadcrumb; 4) Search box. (Screenshot used with permission from Microsoft.)

Most applets are added by Windows but some software applications, such as antivirus software, add their own applets. Configuration information entered via Control Panel is ultimately stored in the Windows registry database.

You can access Control Panel through the Start Menu. In addition, certain applets are accessible by viewing object properties straight from the desktop or from Explorer.

Control Panel applets are arranged by category by default, although you can display "All items" via the breadcrumb or the "View by" menu. Note that options with the 🛡 icon on or next to them will require you to authorize use of the command through User Account Control (UAC).

Interaction Opportunity

This topic does have a hands-on activity, but encourage learners to open each tool on their HOST computer as you discuss it.

WINDOWS SETTINGS

Windows Settings is a touchscreen-enabled "app" interface for managing a Windows 10 computer.

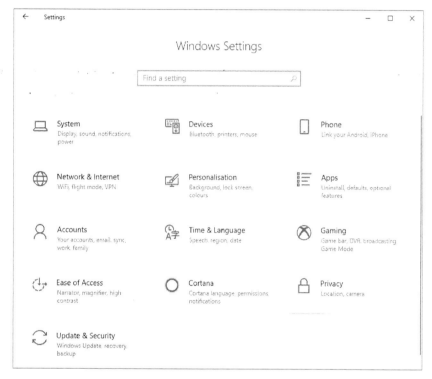

Windows Settings app. (Screenshot used with permission from Microsoft.)

Most of the standard Windows 10 configuration settings can be located within Windows Settings, but not all of them. Some options are still configured via Control Panel. Each Windows 10 feature update tends to move more configuration options from Control Panel to Windows Settings, though.

> **Note:** *In Windows 8, this app is referred to as "PC Settings" and is accessed via the Charms bar.*

Show Slide(s)

User Accounts (3 slides)

Teaching Tip

This course covers more advanced user/ group management (Local Users and Groups console) in the networking/sharing topics.

USER ACCOUNTS

A **user account** is the principal means of controlling access to computer and network resources and rights or privileges. Resources include access to files, folders, or printers; rights or privileges refers to the ability to make configuration changes or read/modify a data file. Each resource is configured with an access list, which is a list of users and their permissions for that resource.

A user account is protected by authenticating the account owner—making them provide some data that is known or held only by them.

Each user account is also associated with a profile, stored in a subfolder of the **Users** folder. The profile contains per-user registry settings (ntuser.dat) and the default document folders. Software applications might also write configuration information to the profile.

ADMINISTRATOR AND STANDARD USER ACCOUNTS

When the OS is first installed, the account created or used during setup is a powerful local administrator account. The account is assigned membership of the local Administrators group. Generally speaking, you should only use this account to manage the computer—install applications and devices, perform troubleshooting, and so on.

You should create ordinary user accounts for day-to-day access to the computer. This is done by putting additional users of the computer in the **Standard users** group. Standard users cannot change the system configuration and are restricted to saving data files within their own user profile folder or the Public profile. For example, a user named David with standard privileges could save files only within C:\Users\David or C:\Users\Public. Administrators can access any folder on the computer.

 Note: *Windows protects system folders from non-root administrative users. These folders are owned by a system account (such as **TrustedInstaller**). This provides more protection against malware and misconfiguration. It is possible for any administrator account to take ownership of a system folder and override these protections, though.*

USER ACCOUNT MANAGEMENT

The **User Accounts** applet in Control Panel allows users to manage their accounts. Users can manage local and network passwords and choose a picture to represent them on the log on screen.

User Accounts applet in Windows 7. (Screenshot used with permission from Microsoft.)

Administrators can create and delete accounts or change the type of account (between administrator and user).

LOCAL AND MICROSOFT ACCOUNTS

In Windows 8 and Windows 10, the **User Accounts** applet is still present and can still be used to change an account name or type, but it cannot be used to create new accounts. That function, plus most other account functions, is performed in the **Accounts** section of Windows Settings. Windows 8/10 accounts can either be local accounts (like Windows 7 user accounts) or linked to a **Microsoft account**, which gives access to Microsoft's cloud services and syncs desktop settings across multiple devices.

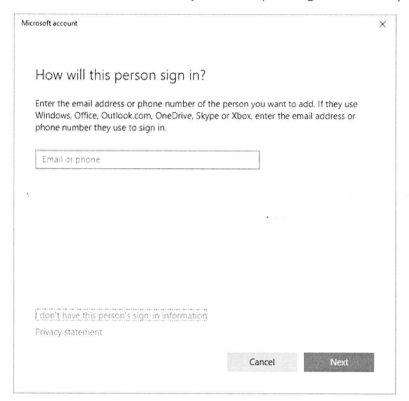

Creating a new account. (Screenshot used with permission from Microsoft.)

*Note: To learn more, check the **Video** tile on the CHOICE Course screen for any videos that supplement the content for this lesson.*

Access the Checklist tile on your CHOICE Course screen for reference information and job aids on How to Create a User Account in Windows 10.

UAC

User Account Control (UAC) is a solution to the problem of elevated privileges. In order to change important settings on the computer, such as installing drivers or software, administrative privileges are required. Previous versions of Windows make dealing with typical administrative tasks as an ordinary user very difficult, meaning that most users were given administrative privileges as a matter of course. This makes the OS more usable but it also makes it much more vulnerable, as any malicious software infecting the computer would run with the same administrative privileges.

Teaching Tip

Microsoft accounts used to be called **Live accounts**. The services are still hosted by live.com (onedrive.live.com, outlook.live.com, and so on), but the **Live** brand is no longer used.

Local accounts now require security challenge responses to be configured. Discuss how to approach this when configuring "generic" or "shared" administrator accounts. You can skip the questions by configuring the account with no password initially and then setting the password later.

Show Slide(s)

UAC (2 slides)

UAC SECURE DESKTOP

Accounts with administrative privileges are mediated by UAC. UAC counters the problem of escalated privileges by first extending some system privileges to ordinary users but then running accounts in a sandbox mode. Tasks that require UAC are shown with a Security Shield icon.

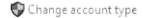 Change account type

Security Shield icon showing that changing this setting will require UAC authorization. (Screenshot used with permission from Microsoft.)

When a user needs to exercise administrative rights, she or he must explicitly confirm use of those rights:

- If the logged in account has standard privileges, an administrator's credentials must be entered via the authorization dialog box.
- If the logged in account is already an administrator, the user must still click through the authorization dialog box.

The desktop darkens into a special secure desktop mode to prevent third-party software from imitating the authorization dialog box.

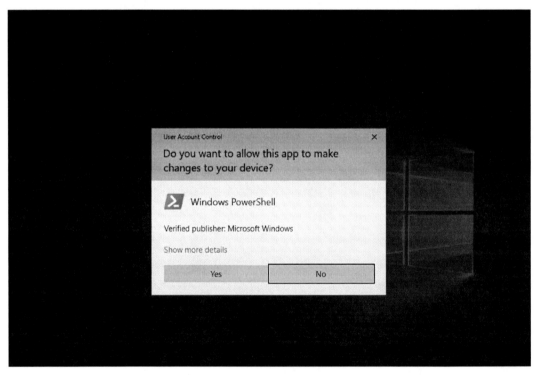

UAC requiring confirmation of the use of administrator privileges. This account is an administrator so only a confirmation is required—no credentials have to be supplied. (Screenshot used with permission from Microsoft.)

CONFIGURING UAC

UAC protects the system from malware running with elevated administrator privileges. This is a good thing, but if you need to perform numerous system administration tasks at the same time, UAC can prove frustrating. You can configure UAC notifications to appear more or less frequently by using the configuration option in the User Accounts applet.

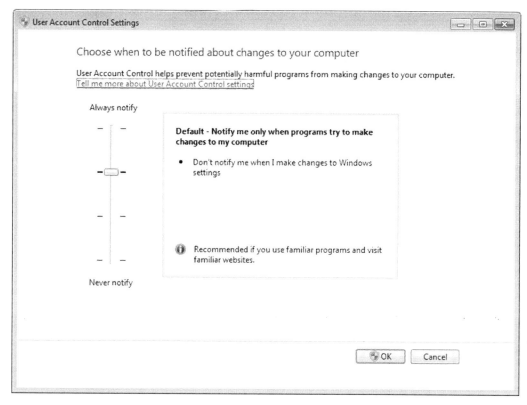

Configuring UAC notifications. (Screenshot used with permission from Microsoft.)

ADMINISTRATIVE TOOLS

One of the options in Control Panel is the **Administrative Tools** shortcut.

Show Slide(s)

Administrative Tools (3 slides)

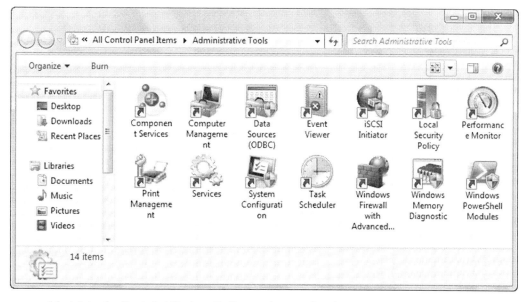

Administrative Tools in Windows 7. (Screenshot used with permission from Microsoft.)

Administrative Tools contains several shortcuts, giving you the ability to define and configure various advanced system settings and processes. There are also tools to assist with troubleshooting the system.

DEFAULT MICROSOFT MANAGEMENT CONSOLES

Administrative Tools is a collection of pre-defined Microsoft Management Consoles (MMCs). Each console contains one or more snap-ins that are used to modify various settings. The principal consoles are:

- **Component Services**—enables you to register new server applications or reconfigure security permissions for existing services.
- **Computer Management**—the default management console with multiple snap-ins to configure local users and groups, disks, services, devices, and so on.

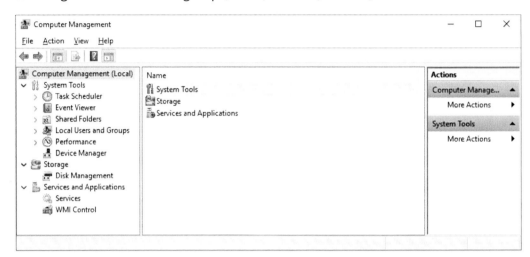

The default Computer Management console in Windows 10 with the configuration snap-ins shown on the left. (Screenshot used with permission from Microsoft.)

- **Data Sources**—control connections to databases set up on the local computer.
- **Event Viewer**—allows monitoring of Windows logs. System, security, and application events are recorded in these logs. There are also application- and service-specific logs.
- **Local Security Policy**—allows you to view and edit the current security policy. A computer that is a member of a domain will have the security settings defined in the domain security policy.
- **Print Management**—set properties and monitor local printers and manage printer sharing on the network.
- **Reliability and Performance Monitoring**—view the performance of the local computer.
- **Services**—start, stop, and pause services.

 Note: *Windows 10 adds quite a few more shortcuts under Administrative Tools, including* **Disk Cleanup**, **System Configuration**, **System Information**, *and* **Task Scheduler**.

MMC CUSTOMIZATION

As well as using the default consoles, you may find it useful to create your own. Consoles can be configured for each administrator and the details saved as a file with an MSC extension in their Start Menu folders.

 Note: *Most MMC snap-ins can be used to manage either the local computer or a remote computer (a computer elsewhere on the network).*

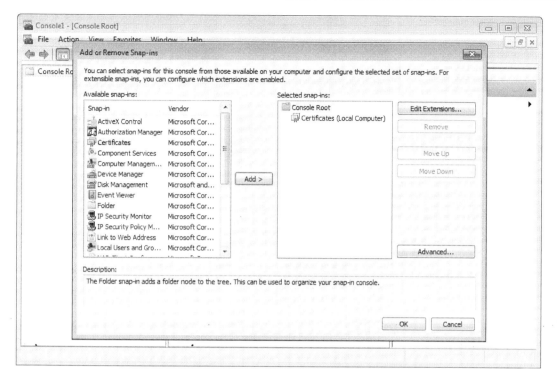

Adding a Snap-in in Windows 7. (Screenshot used with permission from Microsoft.)

*Note: To learn more, check the **Video** tile on the CHOICE Course screen for any videos that supplement the content for this lesson.*

Access the Checklist tile on your CHOICE Course screen for reference information and job aids on How to Create Custom MMCs in Windows.

ACCESS OPTIONS FOR SYSTEM TOOLS

Control Panel and Administrative Tools contain most of the shortcuts for the system features, but there are other ways of accessing key tools.

Show Slide(s)

Access Options for System Tools (2 slides)

COMPUTER/THIS PC

The **Computer** object (renamed **This PC** in Windows 8/10) provides access to your local drives, printers, and any network drives that have been mapped. To browse resources, open **Computer/This PC** then the icon that represents the resource you want to view.

By right-clicking the icon itself and selecting the **Properties** option from the menu, you can access System properties. You can also right-click and select **Manage** to open the default Computer Management console.

WinX/POWER USERS MENU

Pressing **Windows**+**X** or right-clicking the **Start** button shows a shortcut menu including Control Panel, Windows Settings, and File Explorer, but also management utilities such as Device Manager, Computer Management, Command Prompt, and Windows PowerShell®.

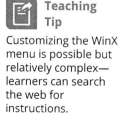

Teaching Tip

Customizing the WinX menu is possible but relatively complex— learners can search the web for instructions.

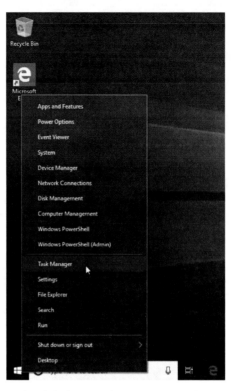

Windows 10 WinX menu (right-click the Start button). (Screenshot used with permission from Microsoft.)

 Note: *Contents of the WinX menu do change frequently. For example, the Control Panel link is no longer included in Windows 10 (1803).*

INSTANT SEARCH BOX AND RUN COMMAND

The **Instant Search** box on the Start Menu/**Start Screen** will execute programs and configuration options using simple names. You can open any file or program by pressing the **Windows** key then typing the path to the file. In the case of registered programs and utilities, you simply need to type the program file name or utility name.

Alternatively, you can access the **Run** dialog box using **Windows**+**R** or entering `run` into the search box.

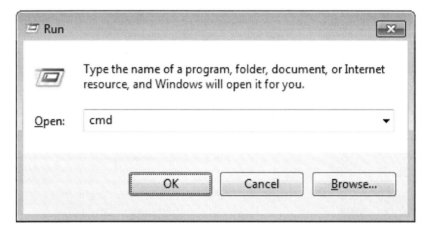

Run dialog box. (Screenshot used with permission from Microsoft.)

Note: *The* `run` *command is useful if you want to execute a program with switches that modify the operation of the software. For example, Microsoft Office programs can be executed using safe mode switches for troubleshooting.*

.MSC EXTENSIONS AND THE RUN LINE

There are several management consoles that you can access via the Run line by using the .MSC extension. For example:

- `devmgmt.msc` opens the Device Manager console.
- `diskmgmt.msc` opens the Disk Management console.
- `compmgmt.msc` opens the Computer Management console.

COMMAND LINE TOOLS

Most configuration of Windows can be done via convenient GUI tools, such as the management consoles and Control Panel. In some circumstances, though, it is necessary to use a command prompt to configure or troubleshoot a system. As you learn the commands, you may also find it quicker to use the command shell for actions such as file management. Learning commands is also valuable if you have to write scripts to automate Windows.

 **Show Slide(s)**

Command Line Tools (4 slides)

COMMAND PROMPT

You can run any command from the **Run** dialog box. However, to input a series of commands or to view output from commands, you need to use the command shell (`cmd.exe`). To open the prompt, type `cmd` in the **Run** dialog box or **Instant Search** box.

 Note: *Alternatively, you can type* `command` *to achieve the same thing. This used to be specifically a DOS command interpreter, but now just links to cmd.exe.*

You may need to run the command prompt with elevated privileges in order to execute a command. If a command cannot be run, the error message "The requested operation requires elevation" is displayed.

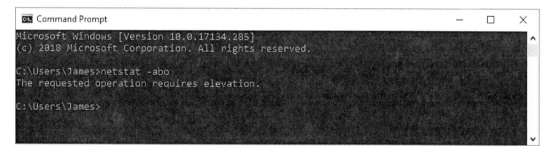

Trying to run a command that requires elevation. You must open a new command prompt window as administrator. (Screenshot used with permission from Microsoft.)

You cannot continue within the same window. You need to open a new command prompt as administrator. Right-click the command prompt shortcut and select **Run as administrator** then confirm the UAC prompt. Alternatively, type `cmd` in the Instant Search box then press **Ctrl+Shift+Enter**.

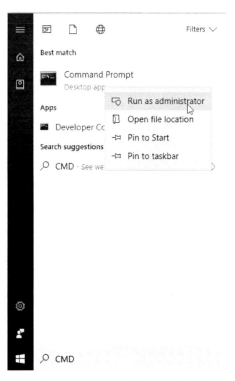

Opening an elevated command prompt. (Screenshot used with permission from Microsoft.)

When run as administrator, the title bar shows "Administrator: Command Prompt" and the default folder is C:\Windows\System32 rather than C:\Users*Username*.

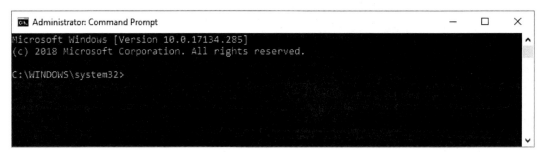

Elevated command prompt. (Screenshot used with permission from Microsoft.)

Teaching Tip

Also note use of **Tab** + Arrow keys to cycle through previously entered commands.

You may also want to note the file/folder name completion feature when working at the command line. Press **Tab** and the interpreter will fill in the first folder/file in the directory. Alternatively, type a few letters and press **Tab** and the interpreter will fill in the name.

Note: *You can use this technique to open other utilities, such as Explorer or Notepad, with administrative privileges.*

COMMAND SYNTAX

To run a command, type it at the prompt (>) using the command name and any switches and arguments using the proper syntax. When you have typed the command, press **Enter** to execute it.

The syntax of a command lists which arguments you must use (plus ones that are optional) and the effect of the different switches. Switches are usually preceded by the forward slash escape character.

Note: *If an argument includes a space, it may need to be entered within quotes (."..").*

As you enter commands, the prompt fills up with text. If this is distracting, you can use the `cls` command to clear the screen.

Some commands, such as `nslookup` or `telnet`, can operate in interactive mode. This means that using the command starts that program and from that point, the prompt will only accept input relevant to the program. To exit the program you use the `exit` or `quit` command (or press **Ctrl+C**). The `exit` command will close the cmd window if not used within an interactive command.

GETTING HELP

The command prompt includes a rudimentary help system. If you type `help` at the command prompt then press **Enter**, a list of available commands is displayed. If you enter `help` *CommandName*, help on that command is displayed, listing the syntax and switches used for the command. You can also display help on a particular command by using the `/?` switch (for example, `netstat /?` displays help on the `netstat` command).

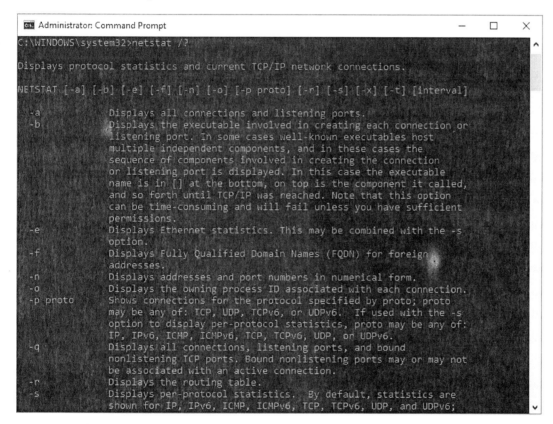

Help on the netstat command. (Screenshot used with permission from Microsoft.)

TEXT EDITORS

Many files used by the operating system and applications are in a binary file format that can only be interpreted by the application. A plain text file can be modified in any text editor, but if it is saved through an application other than a basic text editor, it could be converted to a binary format and so become unusable. Windows supplies the basic text editor Notepad to modify text files. There are many third-party alternatives with better features, however.

RUN COMMAND

You can also execute commands from **Instant Search** or from the **Run** dialog box. If a command is interactive, it will open a command prompt window for input. If a command is non-interactive, the command prompt window will open briefly and close again as the command executes. If you want to force a command into interactive mode, use the `cmd /k` keyword before the command (for example, `cmd /k ipconfig`).

WINDOWS SHUTDOWN OPTIONS

Show Slide(s)

Windows Shutdown Options

Teaching Tip

The original release of Windows 8 buried the **Shut Down** command within the **Settings** Charm, which frustrated a lot of users.

When the user wants to finish using Windows, simply disconnecting the power runs a risk of losing data or corrupting system files. There are various choices for closing or suspending a session:

- Shut down (`/s`)—close all open programs and services before powering off the computer. The user should save changes in any open files first but will be prompted to save any open files during shut down.
- Standby/Sleep—save the current session to memory and put the computer into a minimal power state.
- Hibernate (`/h`)—save the current session to disk before powering off the computer.
- Log off (`/l`)—close all open programs and services started under the user account but leave the computer running.
- Switch user—log on to another user account, leaving programs and files under the current account open.
- Lock—secure the desktop with a password while leaving programs running.
- Restart (`/r`)—close all open programs and services before rebooting without powering down. This is also called a soft reset.

These options can be selected from the Start Menu/**Start Screen** or by pressing **Ctrl +Alt+Del**.

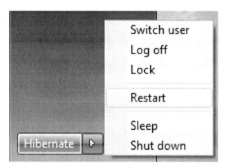

Options on the Windows 7 power button. (Screenshot used with permission from Microsoft.)

 Note: One of the "quirks" of Windows 8.0 was the lack of an obvious way to select the Shut Down command. Microsoft expected users to just use the physical power button, which on a modern computer invokes a shut down command (soft power) rather than a hard reset (unless you keep the power button pressed down). Users were reluctant to adopt this method, no doubt following years of IT departments telling them not to turn off a computer that way. The power options in Windows 8.0 are accessed via the Charms bar. The Start button and a power button on the Start Screen was returned in 8.1. In Windows 10, it appears right above the Start button, where no one can miss it.

The computer can also be shut down at a command prompt by using the `shutdown` command plus the relevant switch (shown in the previous figure). If a shutdown is in progress, `shutdown /a` aborts it (if used quickly enough). The `/t nn` switch can be used to specify delay in seconds before shutdown starts; the default is 30 seconds.

THE WINDOWS REGISTRY

The Windows registry provides a remotely accessible database for storing operating system, device, and software application configuration information. When you boot a Windows machine, the registry is populated with information about hardware detected in your system. During boot, Windows extracts information from the registry, such as which device drivers to load and in what order. Device drivers also send and receive data from the registry. The drivers receive load parameters and configuration data. Finally, whenever you run a setup program or configure the system via Control Panel/Settings or Administrative Tools, it will add or change data in the registry.

The registry does have a dedicated tool called `regedit` for direct editing, but it is not the tool you would use on an everyday basis to modify configuration data. Control Panel/Settings and Administrative Tools are better options for most tasks.

REGISTRY STRUCTURE

The registry is structured as a set of five root keys that contain computer and user databases. The computer database includes information about hardware and software installed on the computer. The user database includes the information in user profiles, such as desktop settings, individual preferences for certain software, and personal printer and network settings.

Root Key Name	Description
HKEY_LOCAL_ MACHINE	Hardware information such as bus type, system memory, device drivers, and startup control data. HKLM also contains the Security Accounts Manager (SAM) password file (not viewable) and system-wide software settings.
HKEY_CLASSES_ROOT	Object Linking And Embedding (OLE) and file association data.
HKEY_CURRENT_USER	Contains the profile for the user who is currently logged on, including environment variables, desktop settings, network connections, printers, and application preferences.
HKEY_USERS	Contains all actively loaded user profiles, including HKEY_CURRENT_ USER, which always refers to a child of HKEY_USERS, and the default profile.
HKEY_CURRENT_CONFIG	Contains system and software configuration information specific to this session.

SUBKEYS AND VALUES

Each root key can contain subkeys and data items called value entries. Subkeys are analogous to folders and the value entries are analogous to files. A value entry has three parts: the name of the value, the data type of the value, and the value itself. The following table lists the different data types.

Data Type	Description
REG_BINARY	Raw binary data. Most hardware component information is stored as binary data and displayed in hex format.
REG_DWORD	Data represented by a 4-byte number. Many parameters for device drivers and services are this type and can be displayed in binary, hex, or decimal format.
REG_SZ	A string or sequence of characters representing human-readable text.

Show Slide(s)

The Windows Registry (2 slides)

Teaching Tip

The exam objectives specify using `regedit`, so this section may go a bit beyond what is required. However, support technicians will need to navigate the registry and be aware of the types of data that can be added as values as part of their working knowledge.

The "H" in "HKEY" stands for "Handle to".

Data Type	Description
REG_MULTI_SZ	A multiple string. Values that contain lists or multiple text values are usually this type. Entries are separated by NULL characters.
REG_EXPAND_SZ	An expandable data string, which is text that contains a variable to be replaced when called by an application. For example, the string %SystemRoot% would be replaced by the actual location of the folder containing the Windows system files.

REGISTRY DATABASE FILES

The registry database is stored in binary files called **hives**. A hive comprises a single file (with no extension), a .LOG file (containing a transaction log), and a .SAV file (a copy of the key as it was at the end of setup). The system hive also has an .ALT backup file. Most of these files are stored in the %SystemRoot%\System32\Config folder, but hive files for user profiles are stored in the folder holding the user's profile. The following table shows the standard hives.

Hive	Files
HKEY_CURRENT_CONFIG	system, system.alt, system.log, system.sav
HKEY_CURRENT_USER	ntuser.dat, ntuser.dat.log
HKEY_LOCAL_MACHINE \SAM	ssam, sam.log, sam.savv
HKEY_LOCAL_MACHINE\ SECURITY	security, security.log, security.sav
HKEY_LOCAL_MACHINE\ SOFTWARE	software, software.log, software.sav
HKEY_LOCAL_MACHINE\ SYSTEM	system, system.alt, system.log, system.sav
HKEY_USERS\.DEFAULT	default, default.log, default.sav
HKEY_CLASSES_ROOT	Not stored in a hive but built from the \SOFTWARE \CLASSES keys in CURRENT_USER and LOCAL_MACHINE

EDITING THE REGISTRY

You can start the Registry Editor by running `regedit` via **Instant Search**, the **Run** dialog box, or the command prompt. You can use it to view or edit the registry and to back up and restore portions of the registry.

Use the **Find** tool (**Ctrl**+**F**) to search for a key or value. If you want to copy portions of the registry database and use them on other computers, select **File→Export Registry File**. The file will be exported in a registry-compatible format and can be merged into another computer's registry by double-clicking the file (or calling it from a script).

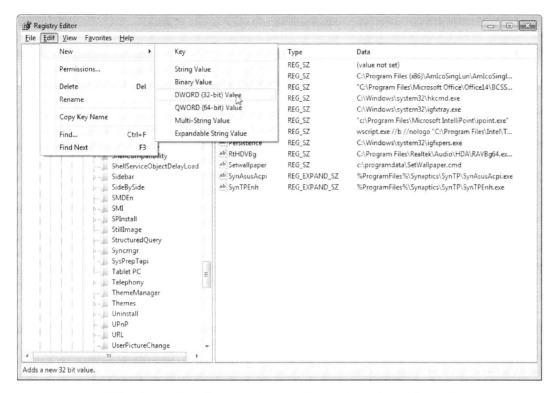

Editing the registry. (Screenshot used with permission from Microsoft.)

A registration file is a plain text file. If you merge changes from a .reg file back to the registry, additions that you have made to the registry will not be overwritten.

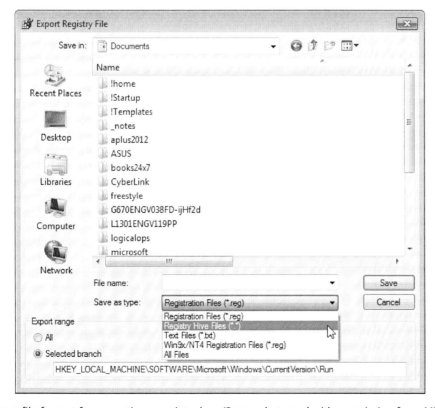

Selecting a file format for exporting a registry key. (Screenshot used with permission from Microsoft.)

Use the **Registry Hive Files** format to create a binary copy of that portion of the registry. Restoring from the binary file will remove any additions you made, as well as reversing the changes.

 *Note: To learn more, check the **Video** tile on the CHOICE Course screen for any videos that supplement the content for this lesson.*

 Access the Checklist tile on your CHOICE Course screen for reference information and job aids on How to Edit the Windows Registry.

Activity 1-3

Discussing Windows Features and Tools

Show Slide(s)

Activity: Discussing Windows Features and Tools

SCENARIO

Answer the following questions to check your understanding of the topic.

1. A user asks you how they can change **Ease of Access** settings.

   In which management interface(s) are these settings located in the different versions of Windows?

   User-level features like this are configured via the Control Panel in Windows 7. In Windows 8 and Windows 10, there are **Ease of Access** settings in both the Control Panel and in the **PC Settings**/Windows **Settings** app but don't worry if you just answered "**Settings** app." It is also worth remembering that you can use **Instant Search** to return a list of user configuration options quickly.

2. You receive a call from a Windows 7 user who wants to "speed his computer up." After questioning him, you find that he is actually getting frustrated at having to click through UAC authorizations. He asks how to turn them off.

   Explain how this is done. Should you offer any other advice?

   There are several ways to disable User Account Control (UAC) but the simplest is via the **User Accounts** applet in Control Panel. You can also just search for "UAC" to open the dialog box. You should advise the customer that UAC is an important security feature and that by disabling it, his computer will be more vulnerable to malware.

3. **True or false? Each version of Windows has an Administrative Tools shortcut folder in Control Panel.**

   True—the contents do vary from version to version though.

4. **When would you use the** `mmc` **command?**

   A Microsoft Management Console (MMC) is used for Windows administration. Running `mmc` opens an empty console. You would do this to create a custom toolkit of the snap-ins used to configure advanced features of Windows. You can save the custom console for future use.

5. You are attempting to run a command but receive the message **The requested operation requires elevation.**

   What must you do to run the command?

   Open a new command prompt window with sufficient privileges. You can right-click the **Command Prompt** icon and select **Run as administrator** or press **Ctrl+Shift+Enter** with the icon selected.

6. **Why might you run the** `shutdown` **command with the** `/t` **switch?**

   To specify a delay between running the command and shutdown starting. You might do this to give users a chance to save work or to ensure that a computer is restarted overnight.

7. **What tasks would you perform using the** `regedit` **tool?**

   This tool allows you to make manual changes to the Window Registry database. You can also use it to export and back up portions of the registry. You might also import registry files to apply a suggested fix.

Activity 1-4

Using Windows Features and Tools

Show Slide(s)

Activity: Using Windows Features and Tools

BEFORE YOU BEGIN

The hands-on activities in this course use Virtual Machines (VMs) within the Hyper-V hypervisor. The VMs have been pre-installed on your HOST computer. Your instructor will explain how to sign-on to the HOST computer.

If you are confident, try to complete the numbered steps independently. If you need guidance in completing a task, refer to the lettered sub-steps.

SCENARIO

In the first part of this activity, you will compare the desktop styles of Windows 10, Windows 7, and Windows 8.1. Think about which version you would recommend to a corporate client, based on ease of use. Later in the activity, you will identify the admin tools best suited to particular tasks and how to access them.

Note: Activities may vary slightly if the software vendor has issued digital updates. Your instructor will notify you of any changes.

Teaching Tip

If learners aren't confident using Windows, get them to practice basic tasks on the HOST before using the VMs. Learners should be able to use the **Start Screen**, use the taskbar (manipulate application windows and switch between them confidently), navigate the file system by using Explorer (change view settings and use search).

1. Use **Hyper-V Manager** to start the **PC1 VM** and sign on using the account **Admin** and password **Pa$$w0rd**.

    a) Click in the **Instant Search** box and type *hyperv*.

    b) Select the icon for **Hyper-V Manager** in the search results.

    c) In the **Virtual Machines** panel, right-click **PC1** and select **Start**.

    d) Double-click the VM to open the connection window.

Teaching Tip

Notify students of any changes to activities based on digital software updates issued by the software vendor.

You can start, stop, or configure each VM through its own connection window in Hyper-V Manager. (Screenshot used with permission from Microsoft.)

    e) With the user name **Admin** shown, click in the box and type **Pa$$w0rd** and then press **Enter** to sign on.

Windows 10 boots to the desktop. This is the default behavior for a PC (or VM). Tablet mode boots to the **Start Screen**. This mode is selected automatically on tablet hardware, or you can apply it using **Notification icon→Tablet mode**.

f) On the taskbar, select the **Notification** icon to view the options.

g) Select the **Start** button and explore the layout of the **Start Screen**.

The first column contains shortcuts to frequently used settings and folder locations. The middle pane lists all apps installed on the computer. The last pane can be configured with app tile shortcuts and live files.

Teaching Tip

Point out the differences in desktop styles and the Start/taskbar layout.

2. Start the **PC2 VM** and sign on using the account ***Admin*** and ***Pa$$w0rd*** for the password. Compare the Windows 7 desktop to Windows 10.

a) Select the **Hyper-V Manager** window. In the **Virtual Machines** panel, right-click **PC2** and select **Start**. Double-click the **VM** to open the connection window.

b) Press **Ctrl+Alt+End** to show the sign-on screen.

> **Note:** *When the mouse is within the VM window, keyboard commands work on the VM, not on the HOST. The only exception is that pressing **Ctrl+Alt+Del** while in the VM does send the command to the host, so in the VM, you need to press **Ctrl+Alt+End** in instances where you would normally press **Ctrl+Alt +Del**.*

c) Select **Switch User**, then select **Other User** to use a different account to the one shown initially.

d) In the **User name** box, type **.\Admin**. Type **Pa$$w0rd** in the **Password** box and then press **Enter**.

This VM is joined to a domain but the domain server is not started. Using .\ tells Windows to use a local account for authentication, rather than the domain server.

e) Compare the Windows 7 desktop and taskbar to the Windows 10 desktop.

f) On **PC2**, select the **Start** button and explore the layout of the Start Menu. Observe the links to the configuration applets and the shortcuts in the **All Programs** submenu.

Interaction Opportunity

Poll learners to discover which version is preferred—does anyone put Windows 8.1 at the top?

If there is time, discuss how interface changes promote or hinder version upgrades by corporate customers. You might want to discuss how the idea of Windows as a Service might be viewed by corporate customers. Is it better to keep the interface "fresh" or "familiar"?

3. Start the **Windows 8.1 VM** and sign on with the same account details as you used previously. Compare the Windows 8.1 desktop to Windows 7 and Windows 10.

a) Start the **PC3 VM** and open a connection window.

b) Sign on to the **Admin** account using the **Pa$$w0rd** credential.

This Windows 8.1 build boots to the **Start Screen**. Also, you might see a tip showing how to access the Charms bar.

c) See if you can follow the tip instructions to show the Charms bar—move the cursor to the top-right corner of the connection window and then pull down. If you struggle with this, press **Windows+C** instead.

d) From the **Charms** bar, select **Settings**. Note the **Power** icon.

Later patches for Windows 8.1 include the **Power** icon at the top of the **Start Screen**.

e) Press the **Windows** key to toggle between the **Start Screen** and desktop.

f) With the desktop showing, right-click the taskbar and select **Properties**. Select the **Navigation** tab. Note the option to boot to the desktop rather than the **Start Screen**. Select **Cancel**.

g) Show the **Start Screen** again. Move the mouse to the bottom of the window and select the arrow that appears.

This shows all the apps installed on the computer.

h)   Examine some of the differences to Windows 10.

In Windows 10, the account options and access to the power button and settings are more conveniently placed on the left of the **Start Screen**. It is also easier to browse the **All Apps** list.

You won't use Windows 8.0 in these activities, but you should be aware that this version of Windows shipped without a **Start** button.

This is the Windows 8.0 desktop—note the lack of a Start button. (Screenshot used with permission from Microsoft.)

4.   Use the **Windows 10 VM** to create a new standard user account. Sign on with the new account and try to escalate the account privileges to trigger a UAC prompt.

a)   Switch to the **PC1** connection window. In the VM, select **Start** then select the **Settings** icon.

b)   Select **Accounts→Other people→Add someone else to this PC**.

> **Note:** *In some builds of Windows 10, instead of **Add someone else to this PC**, you might see **Family & other people**. Selecting either of these options opens the same dialog box.*

c)   Type the name **Sam** and the password **Pa$$w0rd** as requested.

> **Caution:** *You are using the same weak password for every account in these activities. You must NEVER do this outside of a training environment.*

d)   Input some text in response to the security questions.

A real user would use these to recover a forgotten password, but it does not matter what you enter for this activity.

e)   Select **Next** to create the account.

f)   Select **Start**, then select the **account icon** and select **Sign out**.

g)   In the VM connection window, select **View→Enhanced session**.

This setting needs to be turned off because of the security settings on the VM.

h)   Click to dismiss the privacy shade, and then select **Other user**.

 **Teaching Tip**

If **Other user** is not listed, have students select **Sam** from the list in the lower left of the screen.

i) In the **User name** box, type **.\Sam**. Type *Pa$$w0rd* in the **Password** box and then press **Enter**. Wait while Windows configures the account profile.

j) Press the **Windows** key, and then type *control panel*. Select **Control Panel** from the search results.

k) In the **Control Panel** window, from the **View by** list box, select **Small icons**. Observe the full list of configurable applets.

Windows 10 retains quite a few configuration settings in the Control Panel interface.

l) Select **User Accounts** and then select **Manage User Accounts**.

This triggers the UAC authorization dialog box and secure desktop. You must enter the credentials of an administrator account to continue.

m) Select **No**.

Teaching Tip

In some Windows 10 builds, instead of **Manage User Accounts**, learners might see **Manage another account**.

Teaching Tip

Microsoft is trying to deprecate use of Control Panel but it is still quite important. Learners can browse the web for tips on "fixing" the WinX menu contents.

5. Open the default management console on the Windows 10 and Windows 7 VMs and compare them. Create a custom management console with the **Certificates** snap-in on the Windows 7 (PC2) VM.

a) On the **PC1 VM**, right-click the **Start** button to show the WinX menu. This contains shortcuts to a selection of administrative tools.

In this Windows 10 build (1803), shortcuts to the legacy command prompt and Control Panel are no longer present.

b) Select **Computer Management**.

This is the default management console. Amongst other things, you can use it to view logs, configure accounts, and manage devices, disks, and services.

c) Switch to the **PC2 VM** and right-click the **Start** button. Notice that there is no WinX menu. Select **Start** instead, then right-click **Computer** and select **Manage**.

Computer Management is almost identical between Windows 7 and Windows 10.

d) Select **Start**, then type *mmc* and press **Enter**. Select **Yes** to accept the UAC authorization.

Because you are signed in with an administrator account, you do not need to enter credentials.

e) In the **Console1** window, select **File→Add/Remove Snap-in**.

f) Select **Certificates** and select the **Add** button. With **My user account** selected, select **Finish**. Select **OK**.

g) Select **File→Add/Remove Snap-in→Certificates→Add**. This time, select **Computer account** and select **Next**. With **Local computer** selected, select **Finish**. Select **OK**.

You have configured a console to use to manage digital certificates installed on the computer and under a user account.

h) Select **File→Save**. Type *Certificates* and select **Save**.

i) Close the console.

j) Select **Start→Control Panel**. Compare the applets to those present in Windows 10.

6. In Windows 7, open a command prompt and use the `help`, `notepad`, `chkdsk`, and `shutdown` commands.

a) In the **PC2 VM**, select **Start** and then type *cmd* and press **Enter**.

b) Type `help` and press **Enter**. Browse the list of supported commands.

c) Right-click the title bar and select **Edit→Select All**. Press **Enter**.

This copies the contents of the command window.

d) Type `notepad` and press **Enter**.

This opens the text editor utility in a new window.

e) Press **Ctrl+V** to paste the command output into the Notepad window.

f) Close the file, saving it as *commands*.

g) Close the Notepad window.

h) Back in the command prompt window, type `cmd /?` and press **Enter**.

The syntax of the command interpreter is shown.

i)   Read a couple of pages, then press **Ctrl+C** to cancel and return to the prompt.

j)   Type `chkdsk` and press **Enter**. Note the error message.

k)   Select **Start** then type `cmd` and press **Ctrl+Shift+Enter**. Select **Yes** to confirm the UAC prompt.

l)   Type `chkdsk` and press **Enter**.

      This time, the command executes.

m)   Run the following command to restart the computer after a short delay:
      `shutdown /r /t 30`

7. The registry is a database of computer and user configuration settings. Usually changes are made by program installers and uninstallers and the Windows administrative tools, but in some circumstances you may need to make edits directly. Open the Registry Editor on the Windows 7 VM.

    a)   Switch to the **PC2 VM**. If necessary, log in as **Admin**. Select **Start**, type *regedit*, then select the shortcut found in the results. Select **Yes** at the UAC prompt.

          You can now see the registry hives in the left-hand pane (there are five).

    b)   Select the arrow next to **HKEY_LOCAL_MACHINE** to see its subkeys. Expand **SYSTEM** by selecting its arrow. You can see more than one control set. These are discrete configuration sets. Expand **CurrentControlSet**.

          This is the working configuration set.

8. Back up a subkey, then modify a value and revert the change by using your backup file.

    a)   In the **Registry Editor**, navigate to **HKEY_CURRENT_USER→ Control Panel→Desktop**. This section of the registry contains per-user settings, stored in the account profile as NTUSER.dat.

    b)   In the right panel, scroll down and locate the **Wallpaper** value. You can see that a wallpaper is currently set.

    c)   From the **Registry Editor** menu, select **File→Export**. Verify that the **Export range** option is set to **Selected branch** and **Save as type** is set to **Registration Files** (the binary format). In the **File Name** text box, type *backup* and then select **Save**.

          You have saved the user's desktop settings to a REG file, including their wallpaper setting.

    d)   Right-click the desktop and select **Personalize**. Select **DesktopBackground.** From the **Picture location** list, select **Solid color**. Choose any color and then select **Save changes**.

    e)   Switch to the **Registry Editor** and press **F5** to refresh the data. The wallpaper value should now be blank.

    f)   From the **Registry Editor** menu, select **File→Import**. Double-click the backup file.

    g)   Select **OK** at the confirmation dialog box.

    h)   Sign out and sign back in to verify that the original background has been restored.

Interaction Opportunity

Point out the different data types used by value entries. Note that **REG_SZ** is a string (text).

Optionally, ask learners to look at HKEY_USERS too. Note the SID that identifies the account. The "short" SIDs are system accounts.

9. If you have time, explore the **Settings** app on Windows 10 and Windows 8.1. You do not need to look at every option—just try to form an understanding of the major headings and configuration pages. In Windows 10, focus on important sections, such as System, Devices, Network, and Update & Security.

Teaching Tip

Learners don't need to learn the layout of **Settings** for the exam (the objectives don't mention it explicitly). If there is time, ask them to identify the main categories and some of the subcategories in important sections.

10. At the end of each activity, you need to close the VMs. You will always discard any changes you made.

    a)   From the connection window, select **Action→Revert**. If prompted, select the **Revert** button to confirm.

    b)   Repeat to revert the other VMs.

Note: *You can also revert each VM by using the **Hyper-V Manager** console. Right-click the VM and select **Revert**. At the end of the activity, the state of each VM should be listed as **Off**.*

Topic D
Manage Files in Windows

EXAM OBJECTIVES COVERED
1002-1.4 Given a scenario, use appropriate Microsoft command line tools.
1002-1.5 Given a scenario, use Microsoft operating system features and tools.
1002-1.6 Given a scenario, use Microsoft Windows Control Panel utilities.
1002-2.6 Compare and contrast the differences of basic Microsoft Windows OS security settings.

File management is a critical part of using a computer. As a computer support professional, you will often have to assist users with locating files. You should also be familiar with the Windows system folders and know how to perform file management at the command prompt as well as the GUI.

WINDOWS FILE AND FOLDER MANAGEMENT TOOLS

File Explorer provides hierarchical access to the system objects, drives, folders, and files stored on the computer. Explorer enables you to open, copy, move, rename, view, and delete files and folders.

Note: File Explorer was previously called "Windows Explorer." It is often just referred to as "Explorer," as the process is run from the file `explorer.exe`*.*

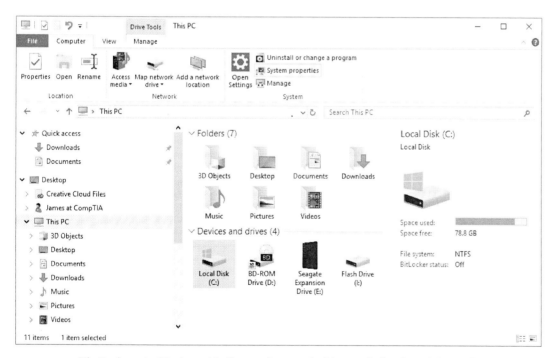

File Explorer in Windows 10. (Screenshot used with permission from Microsoft.)

Explorer appears as a two-paned window showing the hierarchical structure of your system. The left pane shows folders and the right pane shows the contents of the

Teaching Tip
While "Explorer" is a content example for objective 1002-1.5, this topic assumes learners are familiar with basic file move/copy/rename/delete operations and know how to use the Recycle Bin.

Show Slide(s)
Windows File and Folder Management Tools

Teaching Tip
Point out the desktop hierarchy and how user profiles are stored under the different versions of Windows.

You might also want to discuss roaming profiles. Home folders and folder redirection are covered later in the course.

currently selected folder. Arrow symbols are used to indicate parts of the hierarchy that can be expanded or collapsed.

 *Note: You can navigate the whole thing using the keyboard. Use **Tab** and **Shift+Tab** to switch between panes. Use the **Up** and **Down** arrows to move between folders and **Left** and **Right** arrows to expand and collapse trees.*

The basic principle is that ordinary users can write (save data files) only to their profile folders and a special public profile. All other areas of the file system are protected; accessible only to accounts with administrative privileges.

SYSTEM HIERARCHIES IN WINDOWS VERSIONS

Show Slide(s)

System Hierarchies in Windows Versions (3 slides)

In Windows, system objects are organized in a hierarchy. While the system objects themselves remain much the same, their exact name and place in the hierarchy changes from Windows version to Windows version. The basic purpose of the system objects is to mediate user access to personal files stored within their own folder plus local drives and network shares.

WINDOWS 7 SYSTEM HIERARCHY

In Windows 7, each profile folder contains subfolders for different types of files (documents, pictures, music, video, and so on). User access to the profile folder is largely mediated through the Libraries feature. Libraries are virtual folders that can represent content saved in different locations in the file system and on different file systems. For example, a documents library could show the contents of the user's documents folder and a USB drive.

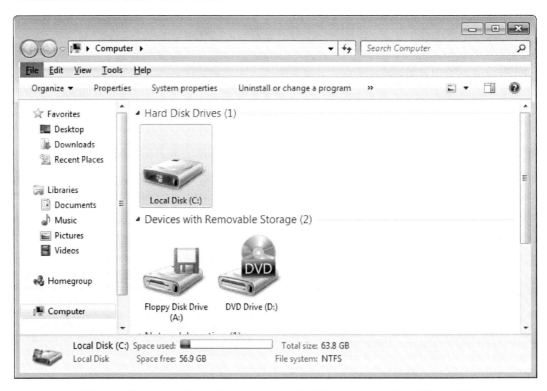

Windows 7 system objects. (Screenshot used with permission from Microsoft.)

The Computer system object allows the user to explore the contents of any local drives attached to the PC. The Network and Homegroup objects show servers and their shared files and printers on the local network. Favorites is a place for users to add shortcuts to other folders or locations in the file system.

WINDOWS 8 SYSTEM HIERARCHY

In Windows 8, the computer object is named This PC and contains the user's desktop, the main document folders (including a downloads folder for files saved via the browser), and any local drives. The Libraries feature is hidden by default. Network, Homegroup, and Favorites work in the same way as Windows 7. The top level may also contain the OneDrive® object, which allows access to a cloud-based storage folder linked to the user's Microsoft account.

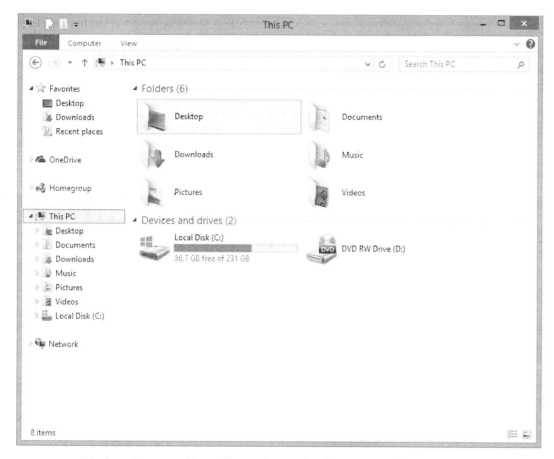

Windows 8 system objects. (Screenshot used with permission from Microsoft.)

WINDOWS 10 SYSTEM HIERARCHY

When browsing the computer using File Explorer in Windows 10, two top-level categories are shown in the navigation pane. Quick access contains shortcuts to folders that are most useful (replacing Favorites). These can be modified by dragging and dropping. By default, it contains shortcuts to your personal Desktop, Downloads, Documents, and Pictures folders.

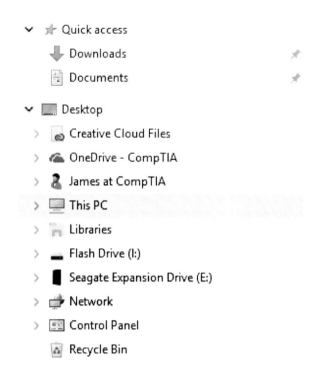

File Explorer navigation pane showing top-level categories in Windows 10. (Screenshot used with permission from Microsoft.)

The second top-level category is the Desktop. Under the "Desktop" object, you can find the following categories:

- **OneDrive**—if you sign into the computer with a Microsoft account, this shows the files and folders saved to your cloud storage service on the Internet. As you can see from the screenshot, other cloud service providers may add links here, too.
- **User account**—the folders belonging to your account profile. For example, in the previous screenshot, the user account is listed as "James at CompTIA."
- **This PC**—access to user-generated files in the user's profile plus the hard drives and removable storage drives available to the PC.
- **Libraries**—these can be used to create views of folders and files stored in different locations and on different disks. As with Windows 8, Libraries may be hidden by default, unless the computer was upgraded from Windows 7.
- **Network**—contains computers, shared folders, and shared printers available over the network.
- **Control Panel**—options for configuring legacy Windows features. Most configuration is now performed via the Settings app rather than Control Panel.
- **Recycle Bin**—provides an option for recovering files and folders that have been recently deleted.

Show Slide(s)

Drives, Folders, and Files

Teaching Tip

Even though it is acceptable to use the A: or B: drive letters now that floppy drives are defunct, not many people do.

DRIVES, FOLDERS, AND FILES

The top-level categories in the navigation pane show "logical" system objects. Actual data storage is configured on one or more drives. Each drive can have folders and files stored on it.

LOCAL DRIVES

Within the Computer/This PC object, drives are referred to by letters and optional labels. A "drive" can be a single physical disk or a partition on a disk. A drive can also point to a shared network folder "mapped" to a drive letter. By convention, the A: drive is the floppy disk (very rarely seen these days) and the C: drive is the partition on the primary fixed disk holding the Windows installation.

Every drive contains a directory called the **root directory**. The root directory is represented by the backslash (\ ). For example, the root directory of the C: drive is C:\. Below the root directory is a hierarchical structure of directories called subdirectories. A sample directory structure is shown in the diagram.

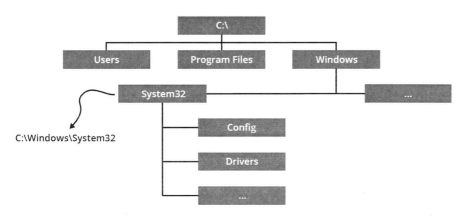

Typical Windows directory structure.

Files may be placed at each level but the root, and certain other folders are designated as system and protected from use by standard users. While it is possible to create subfolders off the root folder, it is much better to keep user data within the profile subfolder within "Users."

FOLDER CREATION

You can use the shortcut or File menus to create a new folder within another object. Windows has various folder naming rules that must be followed when modifying the folder structure:

Teaching Tip

Note that Windows 10 supports longer path names if configured in the Registry.

- No two subfolders within the same folder may have the same name. Subfolders of different folders may have the same name, though.
- Folder names may not contain the following reserved characters: \ / : * ? " < > |
- The full path to an object (including any file name and extension) may not usually exceed 260 characters.

A warning message is displayed if these rules are not followed and the user is prompted to enter a new folder name.

Note: Folder and file names are case aware, which means that the system preserves case in the name as entered but does not regard the case as significant for operations such as detecting duplicate names or indexing.

FILE CREATION

Files are the containers for the data that is used and modified through the operating system and applications. Files store either text or binary data. Text data is human-readable, while binary data can only be interpreted by a software application compatible with that file type. Most user-generated files are created via the Save command of an application.

Files follow a similar naming convention to folders, except that the last part of the file name represents a **file extension**, which describes what type of file it is. The extension is used by Windows to associate the file with an application. The extension is divided from the rest of the file name by a period. By convention, extensions were three characters, but there are many applications (such as Microsoft Office) that now use four or more characters for the file extension. By default, the extension is not shown to the user.

 Note: You can use a period as part of the main part of the file name, too. It is the last period that delimits the file extension.

SYSTEM FILES

System files are the files that are required for the operating system to function. These files are typically hidden because their deletion can prevent the computer from working properly. For system files, both the file extension and the location of the file in the system hierarchy are important, as they help the computer recognize it as a system file.

The root directory of a typical Windows installation normally contains the following files and subdirectories:

- **Windows**—the system root, containing drivers, logs, add-in applications, system and registry files (notably the System32 subdirectory), fonts, and so on.

 Note: System32 contains most of the applications and utilities used to manage and configure Windows. This is true even of 64-bit versions of Windows. 32-bit Dynamic Link Libraries (DLL) running under 64-bit Windows are stored in the SYSWOW64 folder.

- **Program Files/Program Files (x86)**—subdirectories for installed applications software. In 64-bit versions of Windows, a Program Files (x86) folder is created to store 32-bit applications.
- **Users**—storage for users' profile settings and data. Each user has a folder named after their user account. This subfolder contains NTUSER.DAT (registry data) plus subfolders for "Documents," "Music," "Pictures," "Downloads," "Saved Games," "Searches," and so on. The profile folder also contains hidden subfolders used to store application settings and customizations, favorite links, shortcuts, temporary files, and so on. There is also a "Public" profile, which is used for sharing documents between users on the same computer. The Users folder also contains a subfolder called "Default," which is the template for new user profiles.
- **bootmgr**—this file can present boot options when the computer starts. It reads information from the Boot Configuration Data (BCD) store, which is usually stored in a hidden System Reserved partition.
- **pagefile.sys**—Virtual Memory pagefile. Virtual memory is used to store data used by running applications when there is not enough system memory (RAM).

 Note: In Windows 8 and Windows 10, you will also see a swapfile.sys file. This is used by Windows Store apps.

- **hiberfil.sys**—image of memory contents saved when the computer is put into hibernation.

FILE ATTRIBUTES

A file's name is just one of its **attributes**. Other attributes include the date the file was created, accessed, or modified; its size; its description; and the following markers, which can be enabled or disabled.

Attribute	Usage
Read-only (R)	Prevents changes being saved back to the file. The user will be prompted to create another file containing the modified data.

Attribute	Usage
Hidden (H)	Specifies whether the file is visible in the default view (it is possible to adjust Windows to display hidden files and folders, though).
System (S)	Specifies that the file should not be accessible to ordinary users.
Archive (A)	Shows whether a file has changed since the last backup.

Files stored on a drive formatted using the NTFS file system have extended attributes, including permissions, compression, and encryption.

PERMISSIONS

To view, create, modify, or delete a file in a folder, you need the correct permissions on that folder. Permissions can also be applied to individual files. Administrators can obtain full permissions over any file, but standard users can generally only view and modify files stored either in their profile or in the public profile. If a user attempts to view or save a file with insufficient permissions to do so, Windows displays an Access Denied error message.

Custom permissions can be configured for a file or folder using the **Security** tab in its properties dialog box.

 Show Slide(s)
Permissions

 Teaching Tip

The goal is to give a quick overview of permissions concepts here. The complexities of NTFS versus share permissions plus inheritance and moving/copying between NTFS and non-NTFS drives is covered later in the course.

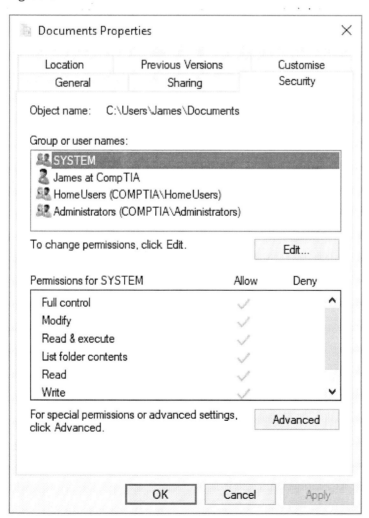

Viewing permissions for a folder object. (Screenshot used with permission from Microsoft.)

To configure permissions, you first select the account to which the permissions apply. You can then set the appropriate permission level. In simple terms, the permissions available are as follows:

Permission	Allows the user to:
Full control	Do anything with the object, including change its permissions and its owner.
Modify	Do most things with an object but not to change its permissions or owner.
Read/list/execute	View the contents of a file or folder or start a program.
Write	Read a file and change it, or create a file within a folder, but not to delete it.

FOLDER OPTIONS

Show Slide(s)

Folder Options (3 slides)

The **Folder Options** applet in Control Panel (or the **Tools** menu in Explorer or **Options** button in File Explorer) governs how Explorer shows folders and files. On the **General** tab, you can set options for the layout of Explorer windows.

Folder Options dialog box—General tab in Windows 7. (Screenshot used with permission from Microsoft.)

On the **View** tab, you can configure a number of settings for how folders and files are shown.

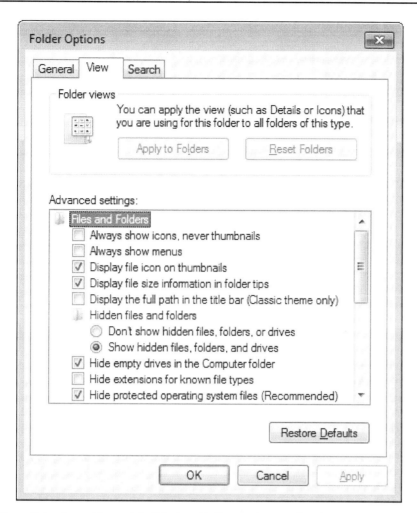

Folder Options dialog box—View tab in Windows 7. (Screenshot used with permission from Microsoft.)

You should pay particular attention to the following settings:

- Hide extensions for known file types—Windows files are identified by a three- or four-character extension following the final period in the file name. The file extension determines which software application is used to open, edit, or print the file by default. Overtyping the file extension (when renaming a file) can make it difficult to open, so extensions are normally hidden from view.
- Hidden files and folders—a file or folder can be marked as "Hidden" through its file attributes. Files marked as hidden are not shown by default but can be revealed by setting the **Show hidden files, folders, and drives** option. Note that this will not show "system" files, unless the following option is also disabled.
- Hide protected operating system files—this configures "system" files as hidden. It is worth noting that in Windows, File/Resource Protection prevents users (even administrative users) from deleting these files anyway.

You can configure file search behavior on the **Search** tab. Search is also governed by how the Indexing Options applet is configured. This allows you to define indexed locations and rebuild the index. A corrupted index is a common cause of search problems.

In Windows 10, you can use the **View** menu ribbon to toggle hidden items and file extensions without going through the **Folder Options** dialog box.

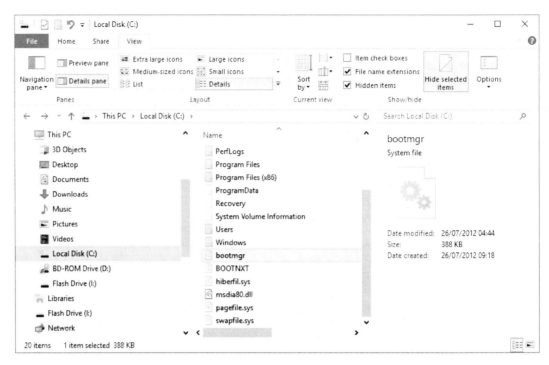

Setting view options in the Windows 10 version of File Explorer. (Screenshot used with permission from Microsoft.)

DIRECTORY NAVIGATION AT THE COMMAND PROMPT

Show Slide(s)

Directory Navigation at the Command Prompt (3 slides)

Teaching Tip

Exam candidates need to know the usage and switches for these command-line tools.

Even under a GUI-operated OS such as Windows, it is important for a PC technician to be able to complete file management and configuration operations using the command prompt. Some actions can be completed more quickly using commands; some commands can only be issued from a command-line; and sometimes the GUI may not be available.

DIRECTORIES AND THE COMMAND PROMPT

If the root directory of the C: drive is selected, the command prompt will display C:\> The greater than sign (>) at the end of the prompt separates the prompt information from your input. If you change from the current directory (in this example, the root directory) to a first-level directory called "Windows," the prompt would become C: \Windows>.

Changing to a second-level directory called "System32" would change the prompt to C: \Windows\System32\>.

A backslash (\ ) is used to separate each directory level.

> **Note:** *While Windows uses the backslash to delimit directories, if you type a path using forward slashes in Explorer or at the command prompt, it will still be interpreted correctly. The Linux file system uses forward slashes.*

THE DEFAULT DRIVE

Each drive is assigned its own drive letter. When using the command prompt from Windows, the default path will usually be *%HomePath%* (for example, C:\Users\David). If the command prompt is open using **Run as administrator**, the default path will be C: \Windows\System32.

To change the working drive, just enter the drive letter followed by a colon and press **Enter**. For example, E: changes to the "E" drive. The prompt will change to E:\> indicating that the default drive is now drive E.

Note: *If you try to switch to a removable drive when the disk is not in the drive, it will generate an error.*

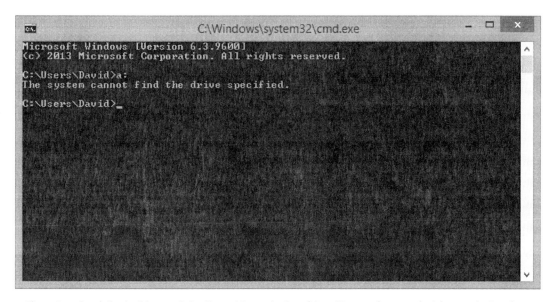

Changing the default drive and dealing with a missing drive. (Screenshot used with permission from Microsoft.)

CHANGING THE CURRENT DIRECTORY (CD)

To find a particular file, it is often necessary to move around the directory structure. The `cd` (chdir) command is used to change the current directory. You can change to any directory by entering the full path, such as: `cd c:\users\david`

There are a number of shortcuts, however. If the current directory is "C:\Users\David" and you want to change to "C:\Users\David\Documents," enter: `cd documents`

If the current directory is "C:\Users\David\Documents" and you want to move up to the parent directory, enter: `cd ..`

If the current directory is "C:\Users\David" and you want to change to the root directory of the drive, enter: `cd\`

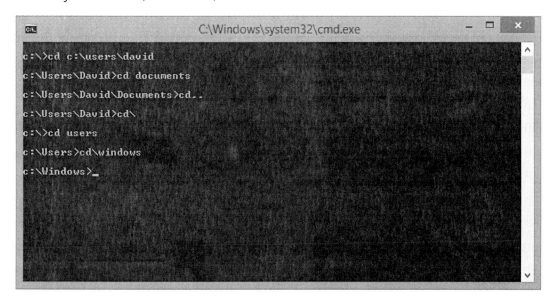

Navigating directories with the cd command. (Screenshot used with permission from Microsoft.)

If the current directory is "C:\Users" and you want to change to "C:\Windows," enter: `cd\windows`

It is not possible to move across from one directory to another at the same level. To reach "C:\Windows" from "C:\Users," the command has to return to the root directory and then select the chosen branch.

Commands such as `cd\` or `cd..` do not require a space. A common error is to use `cd\Directory` when `cd Directory` is required. To move further down the directory structure, use a space. The command `cd\Directory` sends the prompt back to the root directory from where it would then attempt to move into "Directory."

LISTING FILES AND DIRECTORIES (DIR)

Use the `dir` command to list the files and subdirectories from either the current drive and directory or from a specified drive and directory.

dir command. (Screenshot used with permission from Microsoft.)

A subdirectory will be listed with <DIR> next to it in normal view or with square brackets [Windows] around the name if dir/w is used to list in wide view. To view all files and directories within the current directory, enter: `dir`

To view the files and directories in the root directory of the "A:" drive when your current drive is "C:" enter: `dir A:\`

The \ following the A: is important. Typing just `dir A:` or `dir C:` would list the files present in the current directory for that drive (the last one used). To view files in a specific directory on drive A, you must type the full path; for example, `dir A: \backups`

If the current directory has more than one screen of files and directories, type:

- `dir/w` (lists files using wide format with no file details).
- `dir/p` (lists files one screen at a time).
- `dir/w/p` (both of the above).

You can present files in a particular order using the `/o:x` switch, where x could be `n` to list by name, `s` to list by size, `e` to list by extension, or `d` to list by date. The date field can be set by the `/t:x` switch, where x is `c` for created on, `a` for last access, or `w` for last modified.

Another useful switch is /a:x, which displays files with the attribute indicated by x (r for Read-only, h for hidden, s for system, and a for archive).

WILDCARDS (QUESTION MARK [?] AND ASTERISK [*])

A **wildcard** character allows you to use unspecified characters with the command. A question mark (?) means a single unspecified character. For example, the command dir ????????.log will display all .log files with 8 characters in the file name.

The asterisk can be used to indicate a string of unspecified characters. The following examples show possible ways to use the asterisk with the dir command:

- dir *.*—displays all files and directories in the current directory.
- dir *.doc—displays all files with the DOC extension in the current directory.
- dir let*.doc—same as the previous example, but only shows files with LET as the first characters of the name.
- dir let*.doc /s—same as the previous example, but also searches subdirectories.
- dir *.—displays all files without an extension. This is often used to view directories.

FILE MANAGEMENT AT THE COMMAND PROMPT

Show Slide(s)
File Management at the Command Prompt

The move and copy commands provide the ability to transfer files from one disk or directory to another from a command prompt. Both commands use a three-part syntax: COMMAND *Source Destination* where *Source* is the drive name, path, and name of the files to be moved/copied and *Destination* is the drive name and path of the new location. When using copy, you can enter a different filename to create a duplicate in the same directory. For example, you want to copy all the files from the "C:\Documents" directory to the "C:\Backup" directory. You also want to move any files with a "txt" extension from the "C:\Backup" directory to the "C:\Backup\Archive" directory.

Teaching Tip
You are not presenting any of the switches for these commands, as there are a lot. Focus instead on choosing an appropriate command for a given purpose. For example, you might just use

COPYING DIRECTORY STRUCTURES

xcopy is a utility that allows you to copy the contents of more than one directory at a time and retain the directory structure. The syntax for xcopy is as follows: xcopy *Source [Destination] [Switches]*.

You can use switches to include or exclude files and folders by their attributes. Check the command help for additional switches and syntax.

robocopy

robocopy (or "robust copy") is another file copy utility. It was previously available in the Windows Resource Kit but is now included as a native command in Windows. Microsoft now recommends using robocopy rather than xcopy.

robocopy is designed to work better with long file names and NTFS attributes. Check the command help for additional switches and syntax.

copy to copy a single file, but if you want to copy a complex folder as part of a script or backup operation, then xcopy or robocopy would be a better choice.

 Note: Despite the name, you can also use robocopy to move files (/mov switch).

RENAMING A FILE

To change a file name, use the `ren` command. The syntax of this command is: `ren OldName NewName`. For example, to rename the ReadMe.txt file to ReadNow.doc, use the following command: `ren readme.txt readnow.doc`

To rename multiple files, wildcard characters may be used. For example, ren *.txt *.doc will rename all files with an extension of TXT to DOC.

 Note: Changing a file extension is not usually a good idea, as the file will no longer be associated with the application used to open it.

DELETING A FILE

To remove a file from a directory or a disk, use the `del` command. The `erase` command has identical usage. The following switches are available with the `del` command:

Switch	Use
/p	Prompt to delete for each file.
/f	Suppress prompt for read-only files.
/q	Suppress prompt on wildcard delete.
/s	Delete files from subdirectories.
/a:	Delete files with particular attributes (for example, /a:r) or without particular attributes (for example, /a:-r).

CREATING A DIRECTORY

To create a directory, use the `md` or `mkdir` command. For example, to create a directory called "Data" in the current directory, type `md Data`. To create a directory called "Docs" in a directory called "Data" on the A drive, when the current path is "C:\," type `md A:\Data\Docs`

REMOVING A DIRECTORY

To delete an empty directory, type `rd Directory`. If the directory is not empty, you can remove files and subdirectories from it using the `rd /s` command. You can also use the `/q` switch to suppress confirmation messages (quiet mode).

 Note: To learn more, check the Video tile on the CHOICE Course screen for any videos that supplement the content for this lesson.

 Access the Checklist tile on your CHOICE Course screen for reference information and job aids on How to Copy Files and Folders at the Command Prompt.

Activity 1-5

Discussing File Management in Windows

Show
Slide(s)

Activity: Discussing File
Management in
Windows

SCENARIO

Answer the following questions to check your understanding of the topic.

1. **Which is or are the main location(s) for system files in Windows?**

   The **Windows** folder (or system root) contains the files used to run Windows itself. **Program Files** contains the executable and settings files installed by desktop applications. You might also mention that the **Users** folder contains user settings files, user-specific application data, and user-generated data files. There are also some additional hidden folders (notably **ProgramData**) but do not worry if you have not included these.

2. **True or false? In Windows 7, libraries cannot contain network folders.**

   False—this is one of the main reasons for using libraries. They can consolidate a "view" of files stored in different locations on different file systems. This includes shared folders on network servers and removable drives.

3. You receive a call from a user trying to save a file and receiving an "Access Denied" error.

   Assuming a normal configuration with no underlying file corruption, encryption, or malware issue, what is the cause and what do you suggest?

   The user does not have "Write" or "Modify" permission to that folder. If there is no configuration issue, you should advise the user about the storage locations permitted for user-generated files. If there were a configuration issue, you would investigate why the user had not been granted the correct permissions for the target folder.

4. You need to assist a user in changing the extension of a file.

   Assuming default Explorer view settings, what steps must the user take?

   The user must first show file extensions, using the **View** tab in the **Folder Options** applet. In Windows 8/10, extensions can be shown through a check box on the **View** menu ribbon. The user can then right-click the file and select **Rename** or press **F2** and overtype the extension part.

5. **What is the effect of running the `cd..` command?**

   Change the directory focus to the parent directory (equivalent of Up One Folder).

6. Which Windows command is probably best suited for scripting file backup operations?

The `robocopy` command offers more options than `xcopy` so will usually be the better choice. The `copy` command is quite basic and probably not suitable.

Topic E

Manage Disks in Windows

EXAM OBJECTIVES COVERED
1002-1.3 Summarize general OS installation considerations and upgrade methods.
1002-1.4 Given a scenario, use appropriate Microsoft command line tools.
1002-1.5 Given a scenario, use Microsoft operating system features and tools.

Much of the time the default options for Windows Setup will take care of preparing the computer's fixed disk storage for use. Equally, there will be plenty of occasions in your career when you need to configure custom partitions, use different file systems, or configure software RAID. This topic will teach you how to perform such disk management tasks using the console and command-line tools.

DISK PARTITIONS

A mass storage device or fixed disk, such as Hard Disk Drive (HDD) or Solid State Drive (SSD), requires partitioning and formatting before it can be used. The Disk Management snap-in is used to configure partitions, or you can use `diskpart` from a command line. For a new installation, you can configure and format partitions using the Setup program.

PARTITIONING

Partitioning the physical disk is the act of dividing it into logically separate storage areas, often referred to as "drives." You must create at least one partition on a fixed disk before performing a high-level format to create a file system. Typically, this is done through Windows Setup when building a new PC or through Disk Management when adding an extra disk.

Information about partitions is stored in a Master Boot Record (MBR), which is located in the first 512 byte sector on the disk. The GUI (Globally Unique Identifier) Partition Table (GPT) provides a more up-to-date scheme to address some of the limitations of MBR.

Under Windows, disks can be configured as either basic or dynamic. Configuring dynamic disks enables the use of multiple disks for single "volumes" and is discussed later.

Note: Volume (or drive) is a term used at the OS level to refer to a contiguous storage area formatted with a single file system. This could mean a partition on a hard disk, a CD-ROM, a floppy disk, or a RAID virtual disk spanning multiple hard disks. The term partition is more specific than volume—it refers to an area on a hard disk or SSD.

MBR-STYLE PARTITIONING

With basic storage and MBR-style partitions, a given physical disk can contain up to four primary partitions, any one of which can be marked as active, and therefore made bootable. This allows for four different "drives" on the same physical disk and for multiple operating systems (a **multiboot system**). You might also use partitions to create discrete areas for user data file storage, storing log files, or hosting databases. Each drive can be formatted with a different file system.

Teaching Tip

Stress the importance of knowing how to create partitions and the differences between NTFS and FAT.

Show Slide(s)

Disk Partitions

Teaching Tip

Learners need to know the partition/volume lingo.

Teaching Tip

Note that there is very little reason to choose MBR over GPT. You would only choose MBR if GPT were not supported by the PC BIOS.

Each primary partition contains a boot sector, or Partition Boot Record (PBR)/Volume Boot Record (VBR), at the start of the partition. When a partition is marked as active, its boot sector is populated with a record that points to the Windows boot loader (typically C:\Windows\System32\winload.exe). This active partition is also referred to as the **system partition** or system reserved partition.

The drive containing the operating system files (the system root) is referred to as the **boot partition**. This can be on a logical drive in an extended partition and does not have to be the same as the system drive. The typical installation options for Windows create a "hidden" system reserved partition (with no drive letter) and label the boot partition as drive C:.

If for some reason four drives are insufficient, then three primary partitions can be created and the remaining disk space allocated to an extended partition, which itself can be divided into as many logical drives as needed. Extended partitions do not have boot sectors and cannot be made active.

GPT-STYLE PARTITIONING

A disk with no existing partitions on it can be converted to use the GPT-style partition format. All currently supported versions of Windows have read/write support for GPT disks. GPT is required on the boot device for 64-bit versions of Windows when installed to a computer with Unified Extensible Firmware Interface (UEFI) firmware. A computer with older Basic Input/Output System (BIOS) firmware will normally have to use MBR.

One of the features of GPT is support for more than four primary partitions. Windows allows up to 128 partitions with GPT. GPT also supports larger partitions (2 TB+) and a backup copy of the partition entries. A GPT-style disk includes a Protective MBR for compatibility with systems that do not recognize GPT.

 Note: For Windows 10 on a UEFI PC, Microsoft's recommendation is to create a number of additional hidden utility partitions, including one for the Recovery Environment (RE). You can read more about Microsoft's recommended partition scheme at **docs.microsoft.com/en-us/windows-hardware/manufacture/desktop/configure-uefigpt-based-hard-drive-partitions**.

FILE SYSTEMS

Show Slide(s)
File Systems (2 slides)

Teaching Tip
Windows must be installed on an NTFS boot partition.

High-level formatting prepares a partition for use with an operating system. The format process creates a file system on the disk partition. Each partition can be formatted using a different file system. Drives for use with Windows should generally be formatted using NTFS, which is more efficient and supports advanced features such as permissions, encryption, and quota management. The older FAT/FAT32 system can be used for compatibility with legacy versions of Windows or other operating systems in a dual-boot environment.

CLUSTERS

The smallest unit of storage on a fixed disk has traditionally been the 512 byte **sector**. A file system is not restricted to using a single sector as the basic unit of storage, however. The file system can group sectors into **clusters** (or Allocation Units) of 2, 4, or 8 sectors. Smaller clusters make more efficient use of the disk capacity, but using larger clusters can improve file Input/Output (I/O) performance, especially when working with large files.

As fixed disk sizes have increased, some disk models now use Advanced Format, with 4 kilobyte (4K) sector sizes. If supported by the OS and PC firmware, these can be used in native mode; if not, the drive controller will usually present the disk in 512 emulated (512e) mode.

NEW TECHNOLOGY FILE SYSTEM (NTFS)

The **New Technology File System (NTFS)** is a proprietary file system developed exclusively for use with Windows. It provides a 64-bit addressing scheme, allowing for very large volumes and file sizes. In theory, the maximum volume size is 16 Exabytes, but actual implementations of NTFS are limited to between 137 GB and 256 Terabytes, depending on the version of Windows and the allocation unit size. The key NTFS features are:

- **Recovery**—NTFS utilizes sector sparing and transaction tracking to provide reliable data transfer. When data is written to an NTFS volume, it is re-read and verified. In the event of a problem, the sector concerned is marked as bad and the data relocated. Transaction tracking logs all disk and file system activity, making recovery after power outage a faster and more reliable process.
- **Security**—NTFS has many security features. These include file permissions and ownership, file access audit trails, quota management, and Encrypting File System (EFS).
- **POSIX Compliance**—in efforts to support the UNIX/Linux community, Microsoft engineered the NTFS file system to support case sensitive naming, hard links, and other key features required by UNIX/Linux applications. Although the file system is case-sensitive capable and preserves case, Windows does not insist upon case sensitive naming.
- **Compression**—NTFS allows file- or folder-level compression.
- **Indexing**—the Indexing Service creates a catalog of file and folder locations and properties, speeding up searches.
- **Dynamic Disks**—this is a disk management feature allowing space on multiple physical disks to be combined into volumes.

 Note: Windows Home/Core editions do not support dynamic disks or encryption. There is a cipher.exe tool to allow the user to decrypt files but no option to perform encryption of files or folders.

The only significant drawback of NTFS is that it is not fully supported by operating systems other than Windows. macOS can read NTFS drives but cannot write to them. Linux distributions and utilities may be able to support NTFS to some degree.

FAT

The **FAT** file system is named for its method of organization—the File Allocation Table. This 16-bit table of values provides links from one allocation unit to another.

 Note: FAT was originally designed as a 12-bit file system for floppy disks (FAT12). The 16-bit version (FAT16) was developed for the first PCs to ship with hard drives.

FAT16

A **FAT16** system does not support the recovery or security features of NTFS. The maximum volume size is either 2 GB or 4 GB, depending on the version in use, and the maximum file size is the volume size minus 1 byte. Its only significant feature is that it is compatible with all Microsoft operating systems plus macOS and Linux, and therefore ideal in a multiboot environment or for removable media that must be shared between different operating systems.

FAT32

FAT32 does not differ greatly from FAT16. Because it has a 32-bit allocation table, it supports larger volumes than FAT16—nominally up to 2 TB, though the Windows Setup program will only format partitions up to 32 GB in size. It suffers from the same reliability and security issues as FAT16. The maximum file size is 4 GB minus 1 byte.

Teaching Tip

Encourage exam candidates to study all the features of NTFS and FAT.

Teaching Tip

You can use some third-party macOS software to enable NTFS write operations.

Again, it is ideal in a multiboot or removable storage environment with Windows 9x, macOS, or Linux, but it is not supported by DOS.

EXFAT

Another option is a 64-bit version of FAT called **exFAT**. exFAT is designed for use with removable hard drives and flash media. Like NTFS, exFAT supports large volumes (128 petabytes) and file sizes (16 exabytes). Its real use is not for massive drives, however, but for better performance on moderate size volumes (up to 1 TB) than NTFS. There is also support for access permissions but not compression or encryption.

CDFS

The CD File System (CDFS or ISO 9660) is a legacy file system used for CD optical disc media (CD-ROM and CD-R). CDFS supports two main data writing modes: mode 1 has better error correction, whereas mode 2 allows more data to be written to the disc. Joliet is an extension to CDFS that enables long file name support and Unicode characters in file names.

UDF (ISO 13346)

The Universal Disk Format (UDF or ISO 13346) is an updated file system for optical media with support for multisession writing. It is the standard used by Windows, where it is referred to as Live File System, for CD and DVD recordable and rewritable discs. There are several different versions of UDF, with 2.01 being the default in Windows. Blu-ray reading and writing requires version 2.5 and third-party software.

THE WINDOWS DISK MANAGEMENT CONSOLE

Show
Slide(s)

The Windows Disk
Management Console
(6 slides)

Windows provides the **Disk Management** console to format disks and manage partitions. The utility displays a summary of any fixed and removable drives attached to the system. The top pane lists drives; the bottom pane lists disks, with information about the partitions created on each disk and any unpartitioned space.

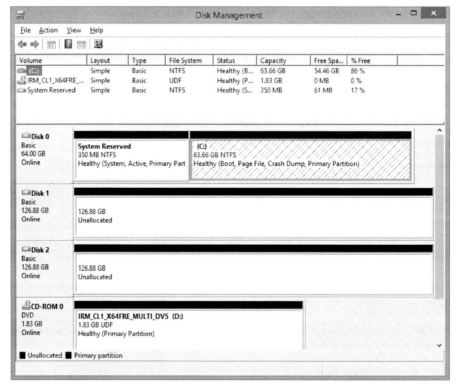

Disk Management utility in Windows 8.1. (Screenshot used with permission from Microsoft.)

To open the tool, right-click **Computer/This PC** and select **Manage** then select the **Disk Management** icon under **Storage**. You can also use the WinX menu (right-click **Start**).

INITIALIZING DISKS

If you add a hard disk to the system, you will be prompted to initialize it when you start Disk Management. You can choose whether to use the MBR or GPT partition style for the new disk.

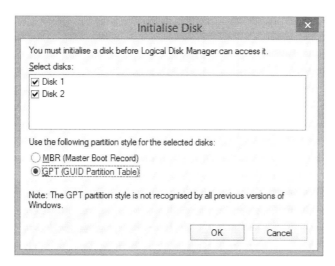

Initializing newly detected disks—note the option to choose between MBR and GPT. (Screenshot used with permission from Microsoft.)

When a disk has been initialized, you can create partitions on it. You can also create a new partition on an existing disk if there is unpartitioned space on the disk.

ADDING DRIVES AND ASSIGNING DRIVE LETTERS

To create a new partition, right-click an area of unallocated space and select **New Simple Volume**. Complete the wizard to select:

- Amount of disk space to use (in megabytes—recall that 1024 MB is 1 GB).

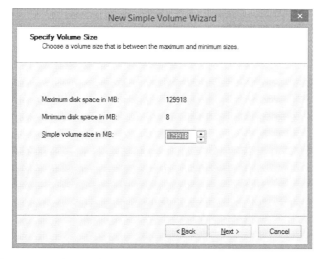

New Simple Volume Wizard—configuring volume size. (Screenshot used with permission from Microsoft.)

- Assign a drive letter or a mount point. You can also choose not to assign a drive or mount point, in which case the volume will be inaccessible via Explorer.

 Teaching Tip

Remind learners that Windows reports disk and file sizes by using binary units in decimal notation (the interface should really use GiB and MiB, for instance). Disk vendors use decimal units, where 1 GB equals 1,000 MB. For example, a disk described by the vendor as being 500 GB will be reported by Disk Management as having 465.7 "GB" of available space.

New Simple Volume Wizard—configuring access path. (Screenshot used with permission from Microsoft.)

FORMATTING THE DRIVE

To complete the wizard, you must select a file system to use to format the new partition. You can make the following choices:

- NTFS or FAT for the file system.
- Allocation unit size—default settings are usually best (selects a size based on the volume size). As a rule of thumb, a small allocation unit size is efficient if the disk stores mainly small files or vice versa, but a typical desktop machine will make equal use of small and large files.
- Volume label—shown in Explorer along with the drive letter.
- Quick format—a full format checks the disk for bad sectors; selecting the quick format option skips this check.

New Simple Volume Wizard—formatting the volume. (Screenshot used with permission from Microsoft.)

Note: Both types of format remove references to existing files in the volume boot record but the actual sectors are not "scrubbed" or zeroed. Existing files will be overwritten as new files are added to the volume, but in principle data can be recovered from a formatted disk (using third-party tools). A secure format utility prevents this by overwriting each sector with a zero value, sometimes using multiple passes.

Having set up the disk structure, if you want to change it in the future, then partitions can be managed using the shortcut menu, which contains options to mark a partition as active, re-format or delete it, or change its drive letter. You can also access the volume properties sheet, which contains options for the disk performance tools and access permissions and quota management (on NTFS volumes).

 Note: *You cannot format or delete system or boot partitions.*

SPLITTING AND EXTENDING PARTITIONS

You can shrink or extend simple volumes formatted with NTFS and unformatted volumes. Shrinking a volume then creating a new volume on the same disk allows you to "split" the original volume. Shrinking a volume is contingent on the files stored in the volume. If there is an unmovable file, the volume cannot be shrunk past it. Extending a volume is contingent on the amount of space left on the physical disk.

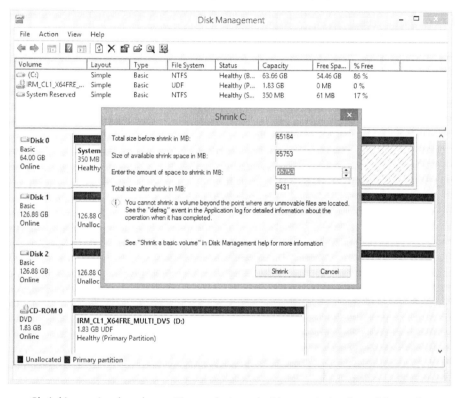

Shrinking a simple volume. (Screenshot used with permission from Microsoft.)

 Note: *Before trying to shrink a volume, disable the hibernation file and pagefile, then clean up and defragment the disk. It may be worth trying a third-party defragmentation utility to try to move files that Windows' built-in Defragmenter cannot.*

DISK ARRAYS

Dynamic storage allows the creation of volumes spanning multiple disks (an **array**). Dynamic disks can only be read by the Professional/Enterprise (and Ultimate) editions of Windows.

 Show Slide(s)

Disk Arrays (2 slides)

 Teaching Tip

Simple, spanned, and striped volumes are incredibly risky. If any of the underlying disks fail, the whole volume is lost.

The only conceivable use is to temporarily "rescue" an installation that has run out of disk space, then back it up and reinstall to a larger drive.

Mirrored drives were finally enabled in Windows 7 (they were previously a server-only feature). Note that this only means the Professional/Enterprise/Ultimate editions; Windows 7 Home editions still don't support dynamic disks.

Windows 8 adds the ability to create RAID5 volumes.

Note: Windows Home/Core editions do not support dynamic disks at all, so if you were to configure dynamic disks under Windows 7 Professional, then move the disks to a computer running Windows 7 Home Premium, the volumes would not be readable. Also, the option to convert from basic to dynamic disks is disabled on laptops.

Only fixed disks can be used. A fixed disk is one installed within the computer and connected by the SATA or NVMe (PCI Express) bus. Disks connected via USB, Thunderbolt, or eSATA cannot be converted to dynamic.

DYNAMIC VOLUME TYPES

Dynamic volumes can be in the following configurations:

- **Simple**—occupies space on a single disk. There is little difference in practice between this and a basic volume.
- **Spanned**—a volume using space on two or more disks. This arrangement is also referred to as JBOD (Just a Bunch Of Disks).
- **Striped**—a volume using space on two or more disks configured using RAID 0 to improve performance. Basically data is written across all disks, whereas spanned just uses up space on the volume using the standard file access pattern.

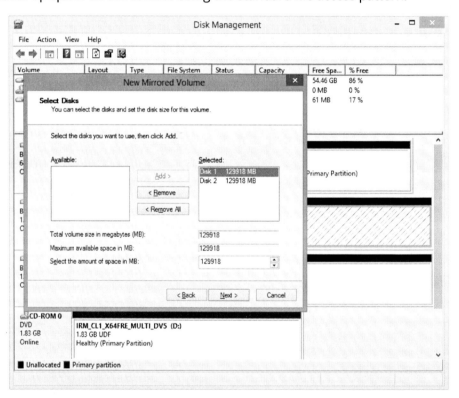

Creating a mirrored volume dynamic disk array. (Screenshot used with permission from Microsoft.)

- **Mirrored**—a volume where one disk stores a copy (mirror) of the other disk. This provides redundancy (RAID 1). Redundancy means that one of the disks can fail, but the volume will still be accessible.
- **RAID 5**—a volume where data is spread across three or more disks. The system writes parity information alongside the data. If one of the disks is damaged, the remaining data can be combined with the remaining parity information to keep the volume functioning. RAID 5 is only supported under Windows 8/10.

MANAGING VOLUMES

When a mirrored volume has been set up, you have two options for converting the mirror set back to a simple volume:

- Breaking the mirror leaves the data in the volumes on both disks intact. You would also use this option to replace one of the disks in the mirror set (install the physical disk then use the **Add Mirror** command on the existing volume).

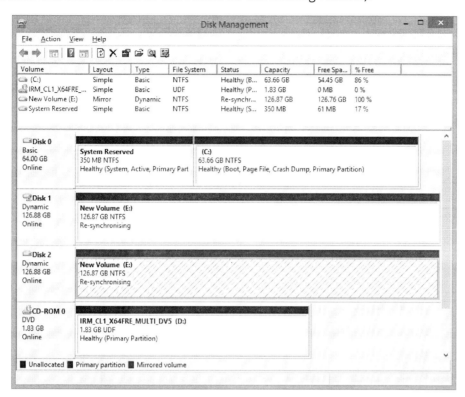

When a physical disk underlying a mirrored volume fails, you can install another disk and add it to the mirror—a resynching process will start to copy data from the first disk to the second. (Screenshot used with permission from Microsoft.)

- Removing a mirror deletes the volume (and any files it contains) from that disk, leaving the volume on the other disk as a simple volume.

 Note: Spanned and striped volumes offer flexibility, but if any of the disks in the array fail, all data on the volume will be lost. Only mirroring and RAID 5 provide redundancy.

A dynamic disk can be converted back to basic, but the volumes (and any data on them) must be deleted first. As with basic partitions, volumes must be formatted (NTFS or FAT/FAT32) before they can be available to the OS.

DRIVE STATUS INDICATORS

Each disk and drive displays status indicators in the Disk Management program. Disks can have the following status indicators:

- **Online**—The disk is OK.
- **Not Initialized**—When you add a new unpartitioned disk, a wizard runs, prompting you to initialize, partition, and format the disk. If you cancel the wizard, the disk will appear as Not Initialized. Right-click to start the wizard again.
- **Unreadable**—The disk is damaged. This message can be transitory so try right-clicking the **Disk Management** tool and selecting **Rescan Disks**. If the disk is still shown as unreadable, you would have to use third-party tools to try to recover data from it.

 Show
Slide(s)

Drive Status Indicators

 Teaching
Tip

Exam candidates need to be able to interpret and act upon these status indicators.

- **Foreign**—if you configure a disk as dynamic on one computer, then install the disk in another computer, it will be marked as foreign. Right-click the disk and select **Import Foreign Disk** to make it accessible to the system.
- **Offline/Missing**—a disk configured as dynamic cannot be read. This could be a transitory error but is more likely to indicate that the drive or I/O to the drive is damaged, a cable is unplugged, the disk has been switched off, and so on. There are two options:
  - If the disk can be restored, use the **Reactivate Disk** option to add it back to the array.
  - If the disk cannot be restored, use the **Remove Disk** option.

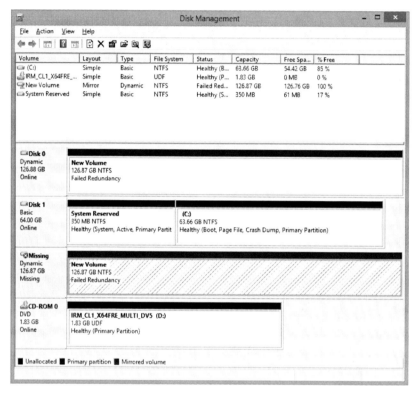

One of the disks underlying the mirrored volume is missing and consequently the volume is marked as failed. (Screenshot used with permission from Microsoft.)

Volumes (or partitions) can have the following status indicators:

- **Healthy**—The volume is formatted and ready to read and write data. Healthy (System) indicates that the volume contains the boot loader, whereas Healthy (Active) represents the system volume used to boot. Healthy (Boot) represents a volume containing an OS, whereas Healthy (Page File) shows one storing a pagefile. A drive may also display as Healthy (At Risk), which means that a number of I/O errors are occurring—a good sign that the disk or controller is failing.
- **Failed/Unknown**—This either indicates a damaged disk (basic) or a dynamic volume where the supporting disk drives are not available. You need to check the status of the devices (if cabling and power are OK, the disk[s] or controller may have been damaged). A volume listed as "Unknown" has an unreadable boot sector.
- **Failed Redundancy**—A RAID volume that is still working but that is no longer fault tolerant. You should identify the failed disk and replace it.
- **Regenerating**—When a disk is brought back into a damaged RAID 5 volume, the controller begins regenerating parity information for the volume. It should be accessible during this period, but performance will be worse.
- **Resynching**—Occurs when a disk is restored to a mirrored volume.

- **Formatting**—A user-initiated format is in progress. Wait for the format to complete before trying to access the volume.

STORAGE SPACES

As mentioned previously, dynamic disks can only be configured on local fixed disks. Windows 8/10 comes with a **Storage Spaces** feature, allowing arrays to be configured across all kinds of storage devices, including USB-connected disks. Also, Storage Spaces is available in the "core" and home editions, unlike dynamic disks.

To configure a storage space, first select the drives that you want to add to the pool. You can then configure what type of redundancy to configure (mirrored or parity), format the volume, and assign a drive letter.

Show Slide(s)

Storage Spaces (2 slides)

Adding drives to a storage space pool. (Screenshot used with permission from Microsoft.)

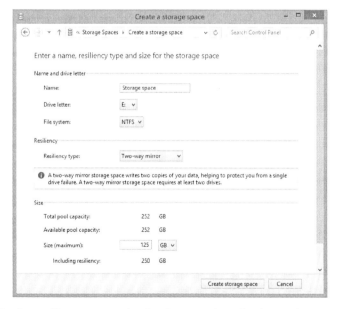

Configuring drive letter, file system, and redundancy options for the pool. (Screenshot used with permission from Microsoft.)

Show Slide(s)

Mount Points and Disk Images

Teaching Tip

Mount points enable everything to be "contained" within a user's profile and saves them having to shift from drive-to-drive.

Note that this is the way Linux makes file systems on different disk devices available.

MOUNT POINTS AND DISK IMAGES

A **mount point** means that rather than allocating a drive letter to a volume, it is accessed from a designated folder in the file system. The host file system must be

NTFS but the volume mounted can be formatted with any type of file system. For example, you might partition and format a removable hard disk then mount it as a DATA volume within a user's Documents folder. To assign a volume to a mount point, first create a folder at the point in the file system you want to mount the drive. This folder must be empty. Next, either run the **New Partition/Volume Wizard** or unassign the drive letter from an existing partition and mount it (use the **Change Drive Letter and Paths** shortcut menu to do this).

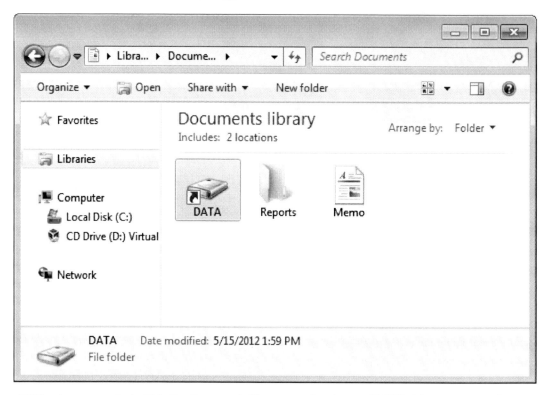

DATA volume mounted within the Documents library—notice that no "DATA" drive appears under any of the drive letters. (Screenshot used with permission from Microsoft.)

Disk images are used with virtualization software to store data written to a virtual machine's hard drive. Windows supports mounting Windows Hyper-V disk image files (VHD and VHDX) within the local file system (right-click **Disk Management** and select **Attach VHD**). An ISO image is a file copy of a CD or DVD. Windows 7 cannot mount ISO images natively, though there is third-party software available to do this, but Windows 8/10 can. You can also burn an image to a physical disc through Explorer.

DISK AND VOLUME MANAGEMENT AT THE COMMAND PROMPT

Show Slide(s)

Disk and Volume Management at the Command Prompt (2 slides)

The Disk Management snap-in is easy to use but there are some circumstances where you may need to manage volumes at a command prompt.

THE diskpart COMMAND

The `diskpart` command is the command interface underlying the **Disk Management** tool. It can be run at an elevated Windows command prompt or Windows Recovery Environment/Pre-installation Environment.

 *Note: The **Disk Management** tool prevents you from completing certain destructive actions, such as deleting the system or boot volume. diskpart is not restricted in this way, so use it with care.*

There are too many options in `diskpart` to cover here, but the basic process of inspecting disks and partitions is as follows:

1. Run the `diskpart` utility then enter `select disk 0` at the prompt (or the number of the disk you want to check).
2. Type `detail disk` and then press **Enter** to display configuration information for the disk. The utility should report that the partitions (or volumes) are healthy.

   If `diskpart` reports that the hard disk has no partitions, the partition table may have become corrupted by a virus. You may be able to resolve this by partitioning and formatting the drive.
3. Enter either `select partition 0` or `select volume 0` at the prompt (or the number of the partition or volume you want to check).
4. Enter either `detail partition` or `detail volume` to view information about the object. You can now use commands such as `assign` (change the drive letter), `delete` (destroy the volume), or `extend`.
5. Enter `exit` to quit diskpart.

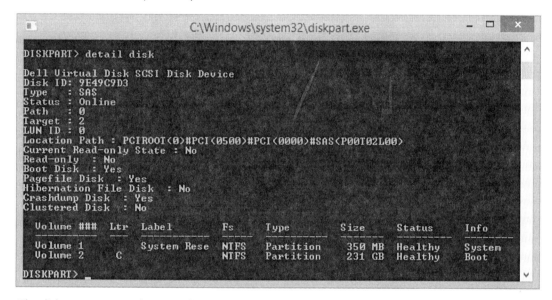

The diskpart program showing a hard disk partition structure. (Screenshot used with permission from Microsoft.)

THE format COMMAND

The `format` command formats (or re-formats) the drive using the specified file system. This process deletes any data existing on the drive.

 Note: You can convert a FAT drive to NTFS without losing data using the command `convert volume /fs:ntfs`. It is not possible to convert back from NTFS. A full backup of the disk should always be taken before converting.

The basic command is `format volume`, where volume is a drive letter or volume name. The main switches are as follows.

Switch	Use
`/fs:`	Specify the file system (such as NTFS, exFAT, FAT32, or FAT).
`/v:`	Enter a label for the volume. If you do not include this switch, you are prompted for a label when format is complete.
`/q`	Perform a quick format (does not scan for bad sectors).

Switch	Use
/a:	Specify the size of allocation units (512, 1024, 2048, 4096, 8192, 16K, 32K, 64K). If omitted, the default size depends on the size of the volume.
/x	Force the volume to dismount. This will cause file errors for users with files open on the volume.
/c	Enable file compression if using NTFS. It's not usually a good idea to enable compression on the drive root, especially if the drive contains system files. Use folder properties to enable compression on a case-by-case basis.

Activity 1-6
Discussing Windows Disk Management

SCENARIO
Answer the following questions to check your understanding of the topic.

1. **If a single physical disk is divided into three partitions, how many different file systems can be supported?**

   Three—each partition can use a different file system.

2. **What is the difference between the boot partition and the system partition?**

   The system partition contains the boot files; the boot partition contains the system root (OS files).

3. **What type of partitioning scheme must a disk use if Windows is installed to a 64-bit UEFI-based computer?**

   GPT-style partitioning.

4. **True or false? A volume or partition MUST be assigned a drive letter to access it via Explorer.**

   False—assigning a drive letter is common practice, but a partition can be mounted to any point in the file system.

5. You are troubleshooting a problem and find a disk marked as "foreign" listed under **Drive Management**.

   What does this mean?

   The disk was configured as dynamic under a different computer then installed in this one. You need to import the disk to make it usable.

6. A customer with a Windows 10 Home computer contacts you. She stores family photos on the computer's hard disk, but says she has read about disk failure and worries that they might be at risk.

   Is she right to be concerned and what solutions can you suggest?

   The customer is right to consider the risk and take steps to mitigate it. One option is to make a backup of the files so that they are always stored on at least two devices. You could also suggest configuring the RAID-like functionality available with the **Storage Spaces** feature of Windows 10. Note that you cannot recommend **Dynamic Disks** as that is not available with the Home edition. Using both **Storage Spaces** and an offsite backup method, such as copying to a cloud drive, will give the best protection.

7. **Is the command** `format d: /fs:exfat /q` **valid? If so, what is its effect, and what precaution might you need to take before running it?**

    Yes, it is valid. It formats drive D with the exFAT file system by using a quick format (does not scan for bad sectors). This will delete the file table on the drive so existing data files can be overwritten—the formatted drive will appear to be empty in Explorer. If there are existing files that need to be preserved, they should be backed up before running the `format` command.

8. Diagnose the configuration and error status shown in this exhibit.

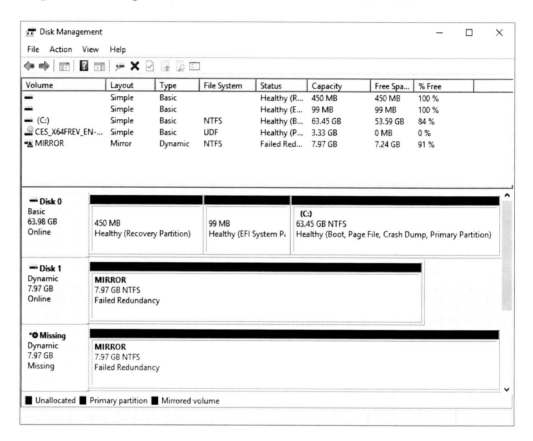

(Screenshot used with permission from Microsoft.)

Examine the screenshot. Can you explain the current configuration, the status of the configuration, and next steps to remedy the error?

You should be able to identify that a mirrored volume has been configured using the **Dynamic Disks** feature. One of the disks is missing—you cannot tell why from the screenshot, but it could have been physically removed or is damaged. You might also be able to identify from the **Failed redundancy** message that the volume has been reactivated, so data files are still accessible. The volume is at risk though, as failure of the remaining disk would result in complete data loss. You need to back up files on the volume as a matter of urgency. You should then either repair the mirror with the old drive or a new drive. If it is not possible to repair the mirror, you should recreate it with a new disk and restore files from backup.

Activity 1-7

Managing Files, Folders, and Disks in Windows

Show Slide(s)

Activity: Managing Files, Folders, and Disks in Windows

BEFORE YOU BEGIN

Complete this activity using Hyper-V Manager and the PC1 (Windows 10) and PC2 (Windows 7) VMs.

SCENARIO

In this activity, you will add and configure storage devices for the VMs and use the file management tools.

---

1. Start the **PC2** VM, and sign on as **Admin** and use **Pa$$w0rd** for the password. Browse system objects and folders to understand the file system hierarchy in Windows 7.

    a) Open the **Hyper-V Manager** window. In the **Virtual Machines** panel, right-click **PC2** and select **Start**. Double-click the VM to open the connection window.

    b) Press **Ctrl+Alt+End** to show the sign-on screen. Select **Switch User** and then select **Other User** to use a different account to the one shown initially. In the **User name** box, type **.\Admin**. Type **Pa$$w0rd** in the **Password** box, and then press **Enter**.

    c) On the taskbar, select the **Windows Explorer** icon.

    d) In the left pane, select the **Computer** icon. The **Computer** object contains the drives mapped to drive letters. In this case, you can see the boot disk (**Local disk C:**) and removable drives such as the DVD drive (**D:**).

    e) In the left pane, select the arrow to expand **Computer** and then select **Local disk (C:)** to show the folders off the root of the C: drive in the main pane.

    Most of the folders shown here are created during the installation of Windows.

    • **Program Files/Program Files (x86)**—contains the files installed by software applications.

    • **Users**—contains subfolders for each user account, which store user profile configuration files and user-generated files.

    • **Windows**—the files used by Windows itself.

    f) In the left pane, select the **Libraries** icon.

    User content is designed to be accessed via libraries. A library is a virtual storage location that can be configured to show the contents of designated folders. The default libraries show the contents of the user's personal profile and the public profile for **Documents**, **Music**, **Pictures**, and **Videos**.

    > **Note:** *Note that the **Libraries** feature is still available in Windows 8/10 but is hidden by default. Microsoft now emphasizes the use of OneDrive to store documents, rather than the local file system.*

    g) From the **Start Menu**, select the **Admin** user name.

    This opens another **Explorer** window showing the full contents of the profile. As you can see, there is the folder for the **Desktop**, as well as ones for **Favorites**, **Saved Searches**, **Downloads**, and so on. Each user can create new folders and files within their own folders. Creating folders and files outside this area may require administrator privileges.

h) In **Explorer**, press **Alt** to show the menu bar and select **Tools→Folder options→View**. Under **Advanced settings**, select **Show hidden files, folders, and drives**, and uncheck **Hide extensions for known file types** and **Hide protected operating system files**.

i) Select **Yes** to confirm, and then select **OK** to apply the changes.

j) In the user folder, look at some of the system files and folders that have been revealed:

- **NTUSER** contains registry settings related to the user account.
- **AppData** contains settings and temporary files related to software applications.

k) In the navigation pane, select **Local Disk (C:)**. Observe the files and folders that have been revealed since you last looked at the object.

Teaching Tip

Note that on a real PC, you would also find hiberfil.sys in the root of the boot drive.

- **Recycle Bin**—this is the "literal" location of the temporary holding area for deleted files.
- **ProgramData**—applications can write information to this folder without requiring administrator privileges. It is used for configuration settings that apply to all users.
- **System Volume Information**—this holds information used by NTFS recovery and indexing features, such as system restore points.
- **Pagefile.sys**—this is the virtual memory file.

l) Open the **C:\Windows** folder.

This contains the Windows system files. Note particularly the following folders:

- **System32**—this contains many drivers and shared libraries (DLLs). As this is a 64-bit edition of Windows, there is also a SysWOW64 folder for 32-bit DLLs.
- **winsxs**—if you right-click this folder and select **Properties** you will find it is very large (about 6 GB). Unfortunately, you can't do anything to reduce that! This folder underpins the system protection features of Windows and allows multiple versions of DLLs to co-exist.

Teaching Tip

See if learners can anticipate why they are using the same size for each disk.

2. Use Hyper-V to create two virtual hard disks and add them to the **PC1** VM.

a) On the **HOST PC**, in the **Hyper-V Manager** console, right-click **PC1** and select **Settings**.

b) In **Settings for PC1**, in the navigation pane, select **SCSI Controller**. In the details pane, select **Hard Drive** and then select the **Add** button.

c) In the details pane, select the **New** button.

The **New Virtual Hard Disk Wizard** is displayed. Complete the wizard by working through the following steps.

d) If a **Before You Begin** page appears, check **Do not show this page again** and select **Next**.

e) On the **Choose Disk Type** page, select **Dynamically expanding** and then click **Next**.

f) On the **Specify Name and Location** page, in the **Name** box, type *RAIDA*. In the **Location** box, amend the path to *C:\COMPTIA-LABS\TEMP* and then select **Next**.

g) In the **Size** box, type *8*. Select **Finish**.

h) Select the **Apply** button.

i) In **Settings for PC1**, select **SCSI Controller** again. In the details pane, select **Hard Drive** and then select the **Add** button. Complete the wizard to configure another **8 GB** disk named ***RAIDB***.

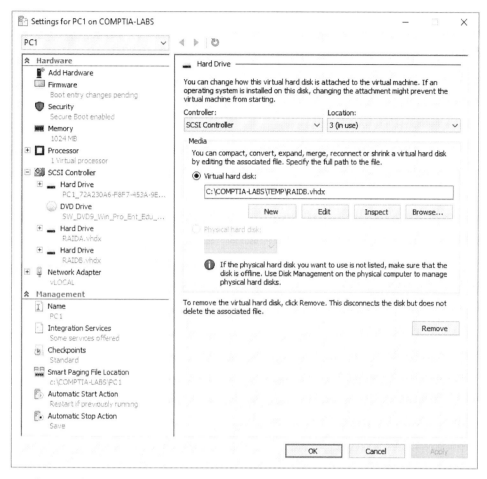

Configuring the VM with two additional hard disks. (Screenshot used with permission from Microsoft.)

j) In the **Settings for PC1** dialog box, select **OK**.

3. Configure a simple partition on one of the new disks. Use **NTFS** formatting, the label **LABFILES**, and assign drive letter **L**.

a) Start **PC1** and sign on to the ***Admin*** account with the ***Pa$$w0rd*** credential.

b) Right-click **Start** and select **Disk Management**.

A dialog box appears because new disks have been detected. If you look behind the dialog box, you should see that the new disks are marked **Unknown**.

c) Select **OK** to initialize the disks using GPT partitioning.

The new disks are now marked **Online**.

d) Right-click the unallocated space on **Disk 1** and select **New Simple Volume**. Complete the **New Simple Volume** wizard by selecting the following options. Select **Next**.

e) On the **Specify Volume Size** page, select **Next** to accept the default value and use all available space on the disk.

f) Select **Assign the following drive letter** and then select **L**. Select **Next**.

g) From the **File system** box, leave **NTFS** selected and verify that **Perform a quick format** is checked. In the **Volume label** box, type ***LABFILES***

h) Select **Next** then **Finish**.

When formatting is complete, the partition is marked as **Healthy**.

i) Leave the Disk Management console open.

4. Browse the system objects and folders in Windows 10 to compare them to Windows 7. Observe folder permissions to distinguish the permissions set on a user folder to those set on a system folder.

   a) On the taskbar, select the **File Explorer** icon.

   b) Observe that the layout of objects in the navigation pane is different to Windows 7.

   The computer object (**This PC**) contains the profile folders as well as local drives. The **Libraries** object is "replaced" by **OneDrive** (though you can show Libraries too).

   c) Browse the **Local Disk (C:)** drive. Verify that the system folders are the same as Windows 7.

   d) Right-click **Documents** and select **Properties**. Select the **Security** tab. Observe that the **Admin** user plus **SYSTEM** and **Administrators** group accounts are listed. Each account has Full Control. Select **Cancel**.

   e) Right-click the **Windows** folder and select **Properties**. Select the **Security** tab. Observe that there are no individual user accounts listed. Most of the group account permissions are not shown (they are allocated special permissions). The **Users** group account can view the folder but cannot make changes. Select **Cancel**.

5. Practice performing directory navigation at the command line.

   a) Open a command prompt, then type `cd..` and press **Enter**.

   This changes the prompt focus to the parent directory.

   b) Type `cd\` and press **Enter** to go to the root directory of drive C:.

   c) Enter `dir` to get a file and directory listing. Is everything displayed?

   Hidden files are not shown.

   d) Enter `dir/?` to view help for the command. Which switches are required to display everything displayed?

   ```
   dir /a:hs
   ```

   e) Enter `dir` with the switches required to list hidden files.

Teaching Tip

Point out that commands issued at the Windows command prompt are not case sensitive.

6. In this step, you will identify some of the differences between copy, xcopy, and robocopy. You need to copy the contents of the **C:\LABFILES** folder to a **DATA** folder on the L drive. The **DATA** folder does not currently exist.

   a) Run the following command and note the errors:

   ```
   copy C:\LABFILES\* L:\DATA\
   ```

   b) Try the following command:

   ```
   copy C:\LABFILES\* L:\DATA
   ```

   c) Look at the last message in the output—does it seem odd? Browse the **L** drive in **Explorer**. You will see a **DATA** file with no extension. Open the **Data** file in **Notepad**, and verify that the contents of the copied files is shown in this file. Close Notepad and delete the DATA file.

   d) Now try the first command again but use `xcopy` rather than `copy`:

   ```
   xcopy C:\LABFILES\* L:\DATA\
   ```

   Does it work?

   It copies the files but not the subdirectories.

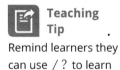

Teaching Tip

Remind learners they can use / ? to learn the switches.

   e) Work out the `xcopy` command to duplicate completely the contents of C:\LABFILES to the L:\DATA folder. What is the command you need to use?

   ```
   xcopy C:\LABFILES\* L:\DATA\ /s /e /y
   ```

   f) Run the command to verify it works as you expect it to work.

   g) Use the **tree L:\DATA** command to obtain a directory listing of the folder **DATA** to check you have used **XCOPY** correctly.

   You should see several subfolders, including some "empty" ones—if you have made a mistake, use the `rd` command to remove the **DATA** folder.

Both `copy` and `xcopy` are now deprecated in favor of `robocopy` (robust copy).

7. **Work out the `robocopy` command to move files smaller than 10 KB from the DATA folder to a SmallData folder on the L: drive.**

    ```
    robocopy C:\LABFILES L:\SmallData\ /s /e /mov /max:
    10241
    ```

8. **Work out the `robocopy` command to recreate the directory structure of c: \LABFILES: within a DataLayout folder on the L: drive.**

    One way to do it is `robocopy C:\LABFILES L:\DataLayout\ / create /s /e`. But this creates 0 KB placeholder file names as well as the directories. To recreate only the directories, use : `robocopy C: \LABFILES L:\DataLayout\ /create /e /xf *`

9. In this step, you will explore options for configuring software RAID (Redundant Array of Independent Disks). Mirroring means that each file write is duplicated to two disks. If one disk fails, the volume will continue to work. The drawback is that only 50% of the disk space is available. As the next task, reconfigure the LABFILES partition as a mirrored volume and mount it as LABFILES to the **Public** user folder.

    a) Switch to the **Disk Management** console. Right-click **Disk 1** and select **Convert to Dynamic Disk**. In the dialog box, check **Disk 2** also and select **OK**. In the **Disks to Convert** dialog box, select **Convert**. Confirm by selecting **Yes**.

    b) Right-click the **LABFILES** volume and select **Add Mirror**. In the dialog box, select **Disk 2** then select the **Add Mirror** button.

    c) Observe that when synching is complete, the volume is marked as **Healthy**.

        The color-coding of the volume is different to that of the partitions on Disk 0 (the disk hosting the system and boot partitions). This color indicates that the volume is mirrored.

    d) Right-click the volume and select **Change Drive Letter and Paths**. Select the **Add** button. Select the **Browse** button.

    e) Expand **C:→Users→Public** then select the **New Folder** button. Type *LABFILES* and press **Enter**. Select **OK** to choose the folder. Select **OK**.

    f) Use File Explorer to browse the **C:\Users\Public** folder. Note the icon for the mounted volume. Open it to check that the files you copied survived the conversion.

Teaching Tip

Remind learners that in a "real" environment, you should never perform a configuration task like this without making a backup first.

10. Observe the effect on the array of a disk "failure." You can simulate this by disabling the disk device.

    a) Right-click **Start** and select **Device Manager**.

    b) Expand **Disk drives**. Right-click the last **Microsoft Virtual Disk** item in the list and select **Disable device**. Confirm the prompt by selecting **Yes**. Select **Yes** to restart.

    c) Sign back on and open the **Disk Management** console again. Note the status messages.

        The volume continues to function using the single device. If the other disk were to fail the volume would be lost. When a volume is in this state, make sure it is backed up and then try to restore the second disk and rebuild the mirror.

11. Disk Management is the easiest way to perform disk configuration. However, you can also use command line tools. These tools should be used with care! In this step, explore the use of `diskpart` commands.

    a) Open a command prompt, then type **`diskpart`** and press **Enter** to start the disk utility. Select **Yes** at the UAC prompt.

        A new elevated command prompt window is opened.

b) Type `help` and press **Enter** to view a list of commands.

c) Enter the command `list disk`

d) Enter the command `select disk 0` followed by `detail disk` to display the configuration of the boot disk.

This contains three volumes. There is a system reserved volume with no drive letter formatted with FAT32 and a boot volume (holding the Windows files) with the drive letter C: assigned and formatted with NTFS. There is also a recovery tools partition. All volumes are of the partition type.

e) Enter the command `list partition` followed by `list volume`.

Partitions are configured on hard disks. A volume is often mapped to a single partition but as you can see, there are other types of volume, including the optical drive and the mirrored volume you created earlier.

```
▒ C:\Windows\system32\diskpart.exe                              —    □    ✕
Type    : SAS
Status  : Online
Path    : 0
Target  : 0
LUN ID  : 0
Location Path : UNAVAILABLE
Current Read-only State : No
Read-only  : No
Boot Disk  : Yes
Pagefile Disk  : Yes
Hibernation File Disk  : No
Crashdump Disk  : Yes
Clustered Disk  : No

  Volume ###  Ltr  Label        Fs     Type        Size     Status     Info
  ----------  ---  -----------  -----  ----------  -------  ---------  --------
  Volume 2         Recovery     NTFS   Partition   499 MB   Healthy    ·
  Volume 3    C                 NTFS   Partition    39 GB   Healthy    Boot
  Volume 4                      FAT32  Partition    99 MB   Healthy    System

DISKPART> list partition

  Partition ###  Type              Size      Offset
  -------------  ----------------  -------   -------
  Partition 1    Recovery          499 MB    1024 KB
  Partition 2    System             99 MB    500 MB
  Partition 3    Reserved           16 MB    599 MB
  Partition 4    Primary            39 GB    615 MB

DISKPART> list volume

  Volume ###  Ltr  Label        Fs     Type        Size     Status     Info
  ----------  ---  -----------  -----  ----------  -------  ---------  --------
  Volume 0    L    LABFILES     NTFS   Mirror      8174 MB  Failed Rd
              C:\Users\Public\LABFILES\
  Volume 1    D    CPBA_X64FRE  UDF    DVD-ROM     4800 MB  Healthy
  Volume 2         Recovery     NTFS   Partition   499 MB   Healthy
  Volume 3    C                 NTFS   Partition    39 GB   Healthy    Boot
  Volume 4                      FAT32  Partition    99 MB   Healthy    System
```

Viewing information about volumes and partitions via diskpart. (Screenshot used with permission from Microsoft.)

f) Enter the command `select partition 2` followed by `detail partition`. Verify that the partition is marked system .

g) Enter the command `select volume 3` followed by `detail volume` to show information about the volume's properties.

h) Enter the command `select disk 1` followed by `detail disk` to display the configuration of the remaining disk underpinning the LABFILES volume.

i) Enter the command `select volume 0` followed by `detail volume` to show information about the volume's properties.

This is the mirrored volume you configured.

j) Enter `assign letter=T` to change the drive letter used for the mirrored volume. Run `list volume` to verify the changes.

k) Type `remove mount=C:\Users\Public\LABFILES` and press **Enter**.

l) Type `exit` then press **Enter** to quit the utility. Leave the other command prompt open.

m) Observe the changes in Explorer.

   C:\Users\Public\LABFILES is now an ordinary (empty) folder again but the data files are still present on drive **T**. You haven't deleted any information; just changed the way it is accessed.

12. The `format` utility can be used to format any disk to use the FAT, FAT32, or NTFS file system, but the process deletes any existing data or directory structure on the drive. Re-format the mirrored volume with the FAT32 file system.

   a) In the original command prompt, type `format t: /fs:fat32` and press **Enter**. Observe the error.

   b) Close the command prompt, then select **Start** and type `cmd`, then press **Ctrl+Shift+Enter**. Confirm the UAC prompt by selecting **Yes**.

   c) Type `format t: /fs:fat32` and press **Enter**.

   d) When prompted, confirm the volume label as **LABFILES** and then confirm the format by pressing **y** and then **Enter**.

   e) When formatting is complete, enter the volume label as *TOOLS* and close the command prompt window.

   f) Use Windows Explorer to verify that the files and folders you copied to the drive are no longer present.

13. At the end of each activity, you need to close the VMs. You will always discard any changes you made.

   a) From the connection window, select **Action→Revert**. If prompted, select the **Revert** button to confirm.

   b) Repeat to revert the PC2 VM.

   c) On the **HOST**, open **File Explorer** and browse to **C:\COMPTIA-LABS\TEMP**. Press **Ctrl+A** to select all the files and then press **Delete**. Confirm by selecting the **Yes** button.

    Note: When a VM is reverted, both changes to the disks and changes to settings are discarded.

Topic F

Manage Devices in Windows

EXAM OBJECTIVES COVERED
1002-1.5 Given a scenario, use Microsoft operating system features and tools.
1002-1.6 Given a scenario, use Microsoft Windows Control Panel utilities.

Teaching Tip

This topic concludes the initial look at Windows and operating systems with an overview of device configuration tools, in preparation for switching the focus to hardware in the next few lessons.

Show Slide(s)

Power Options

Teaching Tip

Discuss ACPI and the different power states.

In this topic, you will use the Control Panel and Device Manager to install and configure PC peripheral devices and hardware settings under Windows.

POWER OPTIONS

Power management allows Windows to selectively reduce or turn off the power supplied to hardware components. This is important to avoid wasting energy when the computer is on but not being used and to maximize run-time when on battery power. Power management requires three compatible components:

*   Hardware—devices that support power management are often labeled Energy Star, after the US Environmental Protection Agency scheme. It is important for the CPU, motherboard, hard disks, and display screen to support power management.
*   Firmware—almost all chipsets support the power management standard Advanced Configuration and Power Interface (ACPI) but you may need to check that it has been enabled.
*   Operating System—current versions of Windows provide full ACPI compatibility.

 Note: Power management is more important on mobile devices but can be configured on desktops in much the same way.

One basic feature of ACPI is to support different power-saving modes. The computer can be configured to enter a power saving mode automatically; for example, if there is no use of an input device for a set period. The user can also put the computer into a power-saving state rather than shutting down.

There are several levels of ACPI power mode, starting with S0 (powered on) and ending with S5 (soft power off) and G3 (mechanically powered off). In-between these are different kinds of power-saving modes:

*   **Standby/Suspend to RAM**—cuts power to most devices (for example, the CPU, monitor, disk drives, and peripherals) but maintains power to the memory. This is also referred to as ACPI modes S1-S3.
*   **Hibernate/Suspend to Disk**—saves any data in memory (open files) to disk (as hiberfil.sys in the root of the boot volume) then turns the computer off. This is also referred to as ACPI mode S4.

In Windows, power management is implemented as the sleep and hybrid sleep modes:

*   A laptop goes into the standby state as normal; if running on battery power, it will switch from standby to hibernate before the battery runs down.
*   A desktop creates a hibernation file then goes into the standby state. This is referred to as hybrid sleep mode. It can also be configured to switch to the full hibernation state after a defined period.
*   Windows 8 supports an alternative mode called Connected Standby or InstantGo, updated to Modern Standby in Windows 10. These utilize a device's ability to

function in an S0 low-power idle mode to maintain network connectivity without consuming too much energy. This option is only available with compatible hardware.

 Note: *You can also set a specific device (such as the display or hard drive) to enter a power-saving state if it goes unused for a defined period (sleep timers). Note that some monitors still consume quite a lot of power in standby mode.*

CONFIGURING POWER OPTIONS

The **Power Options** Control Panel applet lets you configure power management settings via a system of power plans. These enable the user to switch between different sets of preconfigured options easily. Each power plan can be customized, or new plans can be defined and saved.

As well as configuring events for the power button or closing the lid of a laptop, the "shut down" option in Start Menu can be customized; so clicking the button could make the computer sleep while closing the lid could activate the hibernate routine. These settings can be defined for all plans (use the **Choose what the power button does** link in the bar on the left shown in the dialog box in the following figure) or on a per-plan basis (select the plan then configure advanced settings).

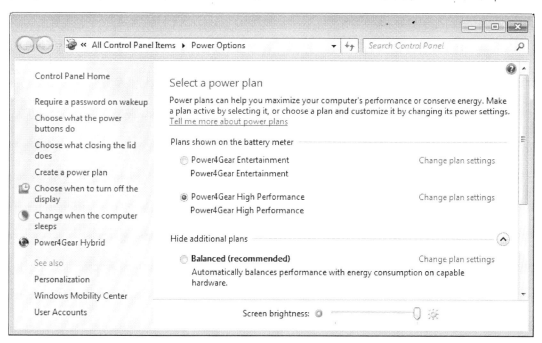

Configuring power management in Windows 7. (Screenshot used with permission from Microsoft.)

Advanced settings allow you to configure a very wide range of options, including CPU states, search and indexing behavior, display brightness, and so on.

There is no GUI option to disable hibernation (and consequently delete hiberfil.sys). This can be done via the command line (`powercfg -h off | on`).

In Windows 10, you can still configure power plans via the Power Options applet but you can also set basic options quickly via the **Power & sleep** page in Windows Settings.

DISPLAY AND SOUND DEVICES

You can configure the way Windows appears through Personalization settings in Control Panel/Settings. This allows you to select and customize themes, which set the appearance of the desktop environment, such as the wallpaper, screen saver, color scheme, and font size used.

 Show Slide(s)
Display and Sound Devices

 Teaching Tip

These settings are of limited importance to modern display equipment, but learners should know how to access them.

Note that they might be useful when configuring older projector equipment as an external display.

CONFIGURING THE DISPLAY RESOLUTION

Most computers are now used with TFT display screens. These screens are really designed to be used only at their native resolution. Windows should detect this and configure itself appropriately. If you do need to adjust the resolution, right-click the desktop and select **Screen resolution** (Windows 7) or **Display settings** (Windows 8/10). Alternatively, you can open the applets via Control Panel/Settings.

COLOR DEPTH AND REFRESH RATE

You might want to change the number of bits used to represent colors at some point; perhaps to make a legacy application work better. From the Screen resolution/Display settings applet, select **Advanced display settings**, and then on the **Adapter** tab for the monitor, select **List All Modes**. Choose an appropriate resolution and color depth mode. Windows 8/10 only supports 32-bit color.

TFTs work at a pre-set refresh rate. If you have a CRT and need to tweak the rate, you can do this on the **Monitor** tab via **Advanced display settings**.

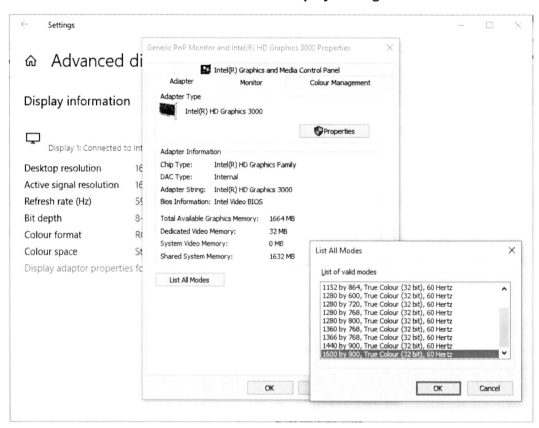

Checking the modes supported by a TFT monitor—various resolutions are available but all at 32-bit color and 60 Hertz refresh rate. (Screenshot used with permission from Microsoft.)

SOUND SETTINGS

Use the **Sound** applet in Control Panel/Settings to test microphone, headset, or speaker hardware and configure settings.

If you have multiple devices, you can choose the defaults on the **Playback** and **Recording** tabs and test levels for audio input and output.

The **Communications** tab lets you set an option to reduce other sounds if the device receives or places a telephone call. The **Sounds** tab lets you configure which noises Windows makes in response to actions and events, such as a calendar reminder or warning dialog box.

Use the icon in the Notification Area to control the volume.

HARDWARE DEVICE CONFIGURATION AND MANAGEMENT

Most hardware devices use **Plug-and-Play**. This means that Windows automatically detects when a new device is connected, locates drivers for it, and installs and configures it, with minimal user input. In some cases, you may need to install the hardware vendor's driver before connecting the device. The vendor usually provides a setup program to accomplish this.

Show Slide(s)

Hardware Device Configuration and Management (4 slides)

 Note: When using a 64-bit edition of Windows, you must obtain 64-bit device drivers. 32-bit drivers will not work.

There may also be circumstances where you need to install a device manually, disable or remove a device, or update a device's driver.

ADD HARDWARE WIZARD

The Add Hardware/Add a Device wizard (in Control Panel) supports the manual addition of devices while Device Manager (in Administrative Tools, the Computer Management snap-in, or Control Panel) is used to configure them.

The precise stages in the **Add Hardware** or **Add a Device** wizards are different between the various versions of Windows, but in all of them—by selecting the appropriate options—you can get to the point where you choose which hardware you want to install manually.

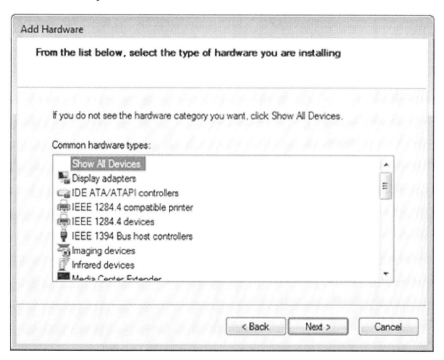

Installing a device manually. (Screenshot used with permission from Microsoft.)

Choose the type of hardware from the list then select from the list of manufacturers and models, and Windows will attempt to allocate it resources.

DEVICES AND PRINTERS

In Windows 7 and Windows 8, **Devices and Printers** is the location for the basic user-configurable settings for peripheral devices attached to the computer. Double-clicking an icon brings up the device's status page and available configuration options (referred to as the Device Stage). The shortcut menu for each device also allows you to set configurable properties, start a troubleshooter (devices with an ⚠ icon are not working properly), or remove the device from the computer.

Devices and Printers in Windows 7. (Screenshot used with permission from Microsoft.)

THE DEVICES PAGE

In Windows 10, the **Devices** page in Windows Settings provides options for adding and configuring peripherals.

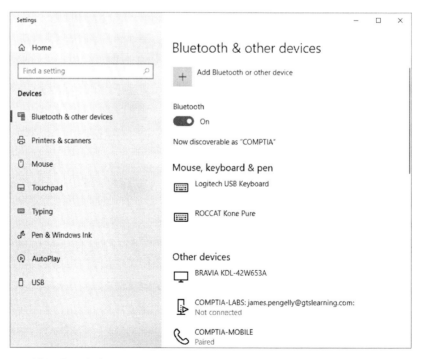

Devices page within the Windows 10 Settings app. (Screenshot used with permission from Microsoft.)

DEVICE MANAGER

When you have installed a device, check that it works. It is a good sign if the device is recognized by Windows, but you should still perform a functional test. For example, print a test page when installing a printer, test file copy when installing removable media, or test audio and video playback when installing multimedia devices.

Device Manager (`devmgmt.msc`) allows you to view and edit the properties of installed hardware. You can change device settings, update drivers, and resolve any known conflicts.

VERIFYING DEVICE INSTALLATION

Beyond installation of its driver, a device's configuration will include an interrupt address (IRQ) and various other properties, including memory addresses and I/O ranges. All hardware devices need a unique configuration so that they can communicate with the processor and other system components. Hopefully, if all your devices are fairly recent, Windows will be able to detect them and install them properly. There may be circumstances where you need to check the system resources assigned to a device, however. You can use the **View** menu in Device Manager to see which resources are assigned to which device.

Show Slide(s)
Device Manager (3 slides)

Teaching Tip
Learners need to pay attention to the status indicators in Device Manager.

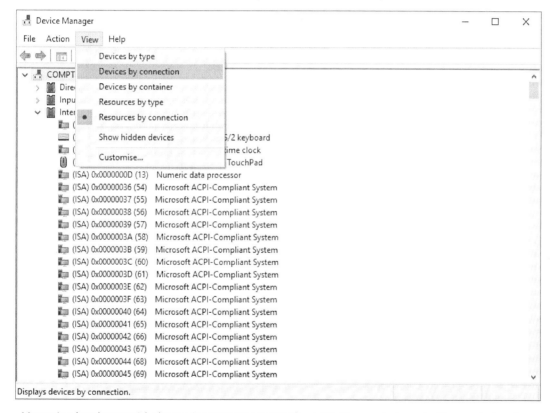

Managing hardware with the Device Manager in Windows 10. (Screenshot used with permission from Microsoft.)

UPDATING AND TROUBLESHOOTING A DEVICE

Sometimes Windows can determine a device's type and function, but cannot locate a driver for the device (perhaps there is no driver included on the Windows setup media or in Windows Update). In this case, you may find an "Unknown Device" or device of a "generic" type listed in the Device Manager with a yellow exclamation mark indicating a problem.

If the device has never worked, check that it (or the driver installed) is compatible with the OS. Manufacturers often release updated drivers to fix known problems. The update can normally be obtained as a download from the support area of the manufacturer's website. Once downloaded, the driver may come with a setup program to install it or may need to be installed manually.

 Note: *If a device is not working properly, a warning message is usually displayed in the notification area.*

To update or troubleshoot a device manually, in the Device Manager hardware tree, locate the device, right-click it, and select **Properties** to display the device settings. The **General** tab displays status information for the device. Use the **Update Driver** button on the **Drivers** tab to install a new driver.

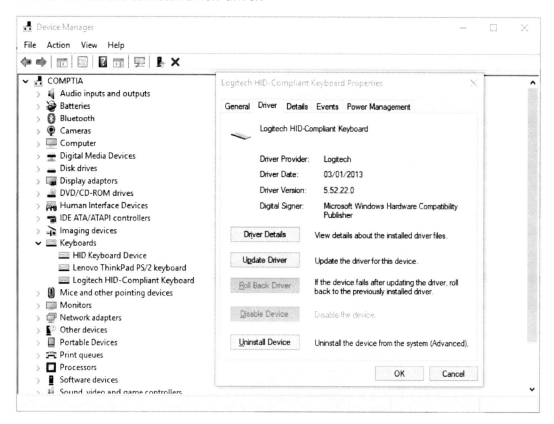

Using device properties to investigate driver version. (Screenshot used with permission from Microsoft.)

 Note: *When installing drivers, always check the laptop (or PC) vendor's site for an OEM version of the driver first. Devices used by system builders can be slightly different from retail versions and may need a different driver to work properly with the chipset and firmware. This is more often the case with laptops than desktop PCs.*

If a device supports Plug-and-Play and is hot swappable, you can remove it from the computer without having to uninstall it. Before removing a storage device, close any

applications that might be using it, then select the **Safely Remove Hardware** icon in the notification area on the taskbar and choose the option to stop or eject the device. Otherwise, you can uninstall a device prior to physically removing it by right-clicking in Device Manager and selecting **Uninstall**.

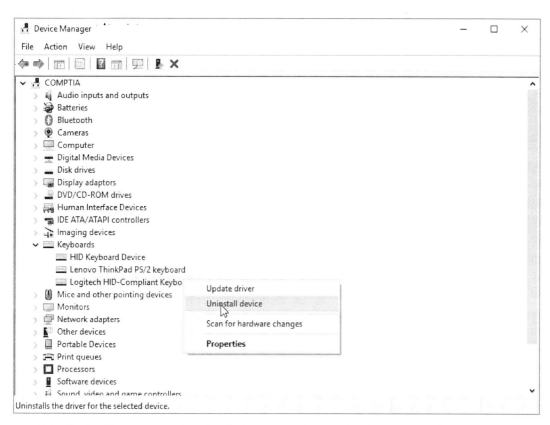

Using Device Manager to uninstall a device. (Screenshot used with permission from Microsoft.)

Teaching Tip

Point out that you can show hidden devices by using the **View** menu. Uninstalling such "ghost devices" can sometimes solve hardware or system stability issues.

There is also an option in Device Manager to Disable a device, which you might use if it is not working with the current driver and want to make it inaccessible to users while you find a replacement or to improve system security by disabling unused devices (such as modems). Disabled devices are shown with a down arrow.

HARDWARE DIAGNOSTICS

If you cannot diagnose a hardware driver or configuration problem via Device Manager, there are other tools you can use to get more information.

Show Slide(s)

Hardware Diagnostics (3 slides)

TROUBLESHOOTING APP

Windows is bundled with a number of automated troubleshooting utilities. These guide you through the process of installing and configuring a device correctly. The troubleshooters are available from Control Panel in Windows 7 or the Settings app in Windows 10.

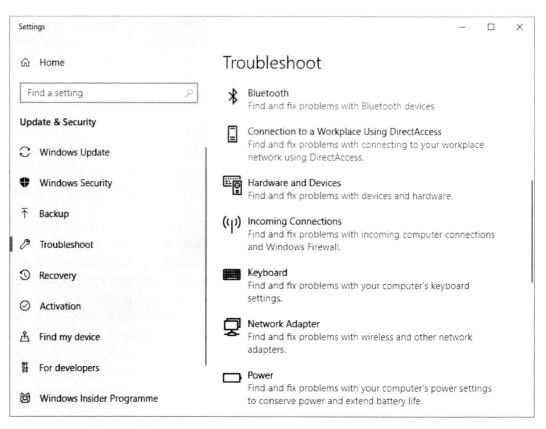

Selection of the troubleshooting tools in Windows 10. (Screenshot used with permission from Microsoft.)

SYSTEM INFORMATION

The System Information (`msinfo32`) application provides a Windows interface to some of the configuration information contained in the registry.

Category	Description
System Summary	Information about operating system and firmware versions and registration details.
Hardware Resources	The I/O, IRQ, and memory address settings used by the CPU to communicate with a component.
Components	A detailed list of all running devices. including configuration information such as IRQ.
Software Environment	Various information including drivers, environment settings, and network connections.

Note: *It's* `msinfo32` *even if you're using a 64-bit version of Windows—there is no such thing as "msinfo64."*

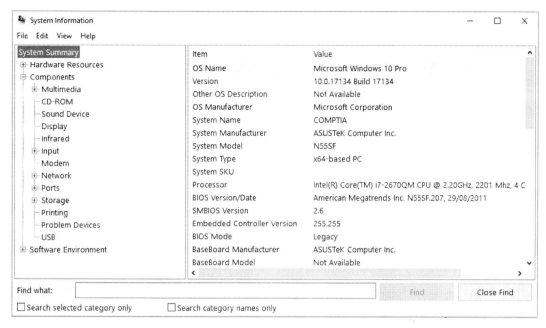

System Information. (Screenshot used with permission from Microsoft.)

DirectX DIAGNOSTIC TOOL

The DirectX Diagnostic Tool (`dxdiag`) displays a report on the system's DirectX configuration, which determines its ability to support 3D graphics and sound.

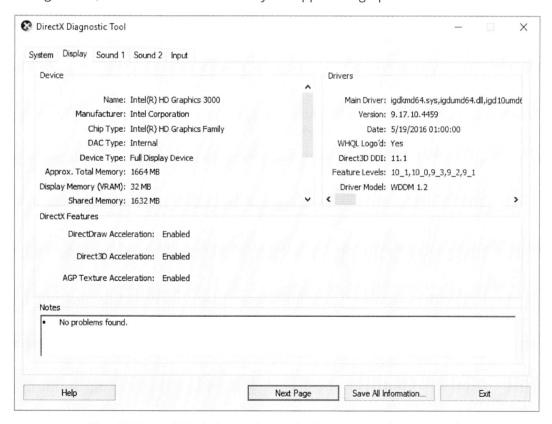

DirectX Diagnostic Tool. (Screenshot used with permission from Microsoft.)

Activity 1-8
Discussing Windows Device Management

 Show Slide(s)

Activity: Discussing Windows Device Management

SCENARIO

Answer the following questions to check your understanding of the topic.

1. You are supporting a user with a Windows 10 Home PC. The user has installed a computer game, but the game will not run. The computer is fitted with a dedicated graphics adapter. You determine that the adapter driver should be updated, but there is no newer driver available via Windows Update.

   How should you proceed?

   Browse the graphics adapter vendor's website and use the card's model number in the driver search tool to look for the latest version. Compare the version information for the driver on the website to the installed version (use **Device Manager** to check the installed version number). If the website driver is newer, download and run the setup file to install and configure it. You should ensure that the setup file is digitally signed by the vendor. If the driver is only provided as a compressed archive, extract the driver files then use the **Update Driver** button in **Device Manager** to select it for use with the adapter.

2. You are supporting a user who has installed a vendor keyboard driver. The keyboard no longer functions correctly.

   Under Windows 10, what are the steps to revert to the previous driver?

   Open **Device Manager** from the WinX menu, **Instant Search**, or the **Computer Management** console. Expand **Keyboards** then right-click the device and select **Properties**. On the **Driver** tab, select **Rollback Driver**.

3. A Windows 7 Professional user is trying to join a video conference and cannot hear any sound from her headset or the computer's built-in speakers.

   Which tool can you suggest using to try to remedy the fault?

   There is an automated Windows Troubleshooting tool for diagnosing and correcting problems with audio playback. You should advise the customer to open the **Troubleshooting** applet in **Control Panel** and select the troubleshooter for audio playback.

4. You are troubleshooting an issue with a wireless adapter. When you open **Device Manager**, you find the device's icon is shown with a down arrow superimposed.

What does this mean and why might this configuration have been imposed?

The icon indicates that the device has been disabled. It could be that there was a fault or there may be a network configuration or security reason for disabling the adapter. In this sort of situation, use incident logs and device documentation to establish the reason behind the configuration change.

5. Identify how to open the tool shown in this exhibit. (Screenshot used with permission from Microsoft.)

What single word command can you use to open the tool shown in the exhibit? For what sort of troubleshooting task might you need to use the information shown?

Run the **System Information** tool using the `msinfo32` command. Each hardware device uses hardware resources such as an Interrupt Request (IRQ) line to communicate with the processor. You might need to investigate these if using devices that are not Plug-and-Play compatible.

6. You are assisting a laptop user. While she was away from her desk, the laptop has powered off. The user was in the middle of working on a file and had forgotten to save changes.

Can you reassure her and advise on the best course of action?

When a computer goes into a power saving mode, it will either maintain a small amount of power to the memory modules or write the contents of memory to a hibernation file on disk. Consequently, the user should be able to start the laptop again and the desktop will resume with the open file still there. You should advise the customer to save changes to files regularly however.

Summary

In this lesson, you supported operating systems. By increasing your familiarity with the types of operating systems in use, as well as the tools and capabilities of each, you are well on the way to gaining the knowledge and expertise expected of an A+ technician.

Which versions of Windows do you expect to support?

A: Answers will vary, but might include a mixture of Windows 7 and Windows 10.

Which part of the CompTIA A+ Troubleshooting Model do you expect to find most challenging, and why?

A: Answers will vary, but might include identifying the problem, because some symptoms can be caused by unusual issues.

 *Practice Question: Additional practice questions are available on the CompTIA CHOICE platform within the **Assessments** tile.*

Lesson 2

Installing and Configuring PC Components

LESSON INTRODUCTION

You have been looking at how the operating system runs the computer and how you can use OS tools to configure the settings and hardware. A very large percentage of the work that most IT technicians do entails working with hardware, including installing, upgrading, repairing, configuring, maintaining, optimizing, and troubleshooting computer components.

In this lesson, you will turn your attention to the computer's system components and peripheral devices. You will see how they are connected and configured to create a customizable PC platform.

LESSON OBJECTIVES

In this lesson, you will:

- Use appropriate safety procedures for avoiding hazards associated with PC support and minimize the risk of damage from ESD.
- Identify PC components.
- Identify common connection interfaces and the cables and connectors used with them.
- Install peripheral devices.

Topic A

Use Appropriate Safety Procedures

 EXAM OBJECTIVES COVERED
1002-4.4 Explain common safety procedures.

To complete PC support tasks without damaging the equipment that you are servicing or causing physical injury to yourself or others, there are several tools to use and operational procedures to follow in order to get the job done quickly, safely, and correctly. In this topic, you will identify the best practices for PC technicians to follow to promote electrical and environmental safety.

LOCAL GOVERNMENT REGULATIONS

When performing PC maintenance work, you may need to take account of compliance with government regulations. Regulations that typically affect PC maintenance or the installation of new equipment are:

- Health and safety laws: Keeping the workplace free from hazards.
- Building codes: Ensuring that fire prevention and electrical systems are intact and safe.
- Environmental regulations: Disposing of waste correctly.

For example, in the United States, the most common safety regulations are those issued by the federal government, such as the Occupational Safety and Health Administration (OSHA), and state standards regarding employee safety. OSHA-compliant employers must provide:

- A workplace that is free from recognized hazards that could cause serious physical harm.
- Personal protective equipment designed to protect employees from certain hazards.
- Communication—in the form of labeling, Material Safety Data Sheets (MSDSs), and training about hazardous materials.

While specific regulations may vary from country to country and state to state, in general employers are responsible for providing a safe and healthy working environment for their employees. Employees have a responsibility to use equipment in the workplace in accordance with the guidelines given to them and to report any hazards. Employees should also not interfere with any safety systems, including signs or warnings or devices such as firefighting equipment. Employees should not introduce or install devices, equipment, or materials to the workplace without authorization or without making an assessment of the installation.

HEALTH AND SAFETY PROCEDURES

A company's health and safety procedures should be set out in a handbook, possibly as part of an employee's induction handbook. Health and safety procedures should:

- Identify what to do in the event of a fire or other emergency.
- Identify responsible persons (for example, for overall health and safety, nominated first aiders, fire marshals, and so on).

 Teaching Tip

This topic focuses on electrical safety and ESD precautions. Depending on student interest and skill levels, you might also want to elaborate on other types of safety issues and countermeasures.

Show Slide(s)

Local Government Regulations

 Teaching Tip

Discuss the health and safety procedures that are in place in your training environment.

Show Slide(s)

Health and Safety Procedures

- Identify hazardous areas in the workspace and precautions to take when entering them.
- Describe best practice for use and care of the workspace and equipment within it.
- Establish an incident reporting procedure for detecting and eliminating workplace hazards and accidents.

GENERAL EMERGENCY PROCEDURES

Here is a general procedure for emergency situations:

1. Raise the alarm and contact the emergency services, giving them a description of the emergency and your location.
2. If possible, make the scene safe. For example, if you are faced with a fire, establish that you have an escape route, or if faced with electrical shock, disconnect the power (if it is safe for you to do so).
3. If you have training and it is safe to do so, do what you can to tackle the emergency (for example, give first aid or use firefighting equipment).

Of course, circumstances might dictate that you do something differently. It is vital that you keep calm and do not act rashly.

ELECTRICAL HAZARDS

The most prevalent physical hazards that computer technicians face are electrical hazards. Electricity is necessary to run a computer, but it can also damage sensitive computer equipment, and in some cases, pose a danger to humans. Following established best practices for promoting electrical safety will protect not only the computer equipment that you work on, but also your personal safety and the safety of others.

Electrical equipment can give an electric shock if it is broken, faulty, or installed incorrectly. An electric shock can cause muscle spasms, severe burns, or even kill (electrocution).

Electrical currents can pass through metal and most liquids, so neither should be allowed to come into contact with any electrical device installations. Damaged components or cables are also a risk and should be replaced or isolated immediately. It is important to test electrical devices regularly. The frequency will depend on the environment in which the device is used. In some countries, **portable appliance testing (PAT)** carried out by a qualified electrician or technician ensures that a device is safe to use.

The human body is an electrical conductor and a resistor, so a current will pass through it and make it heat up, manifesting as a burn if the current is strong enough. A current can interfere with the body's nervous system, which also uses electrical signals. This might manifest as spasm or paralysis or in a severe case cause a heart attack. Collateral injuries occur when involuntary muscle contractions caused by the shock cause the body to fall or come in contact with sharp edges or electrically live parts.

Electricity can hurt you even if you are careful and avoid becoming part of an electrical ground circuit. The heat generated by an electric arc or electrical equipment can burn your skin or set your clothes on fire.

 Note: High voltages (over about 30V) are more dangerous because they have the power to push more current through you (skin's resistance drops at higher voltages), but it is the current that causes the actual damage. This is why static electricity is not dangerous to you, despite the high voltages. More current will flow if a larger area of your body is exposed.

 Show Slide(s)

General Emergency Procedures

 Teaching Tip

Stress that this is a general procedure: There is no list of responses that are appropriate for different situations. A degree of common sense is required.

The most important thing is to keep calm.

 Show Slide(s)

Electrical Hazards

 Teaching Tip

Remind learners that current is a flow of electrons, and voltage is the "pressure" that pushes the electrons through a conductor.

Show
Slide(s)

Fuses

FUSES

An electrical device must be fitted with a **fuse** appropriate to its power output. A fuse blows if there is a problem with the electrical supply, breaking the circuit to the power source. Fuses come in different ratings, such as 3A, 5A, and 13A. A device's instructions will indicate what rating of fuse to use, but most computer equipment is rated at 3A or 5A. If the fuse fitted is rated too low, it will blow too easily; if the rating is too high, it may not blow when it should (it will allow too much current to pass through the device).

If multiple devices need to be attached to a single power point, a power strip of sockets should be used. If too many devices are attached to a single point, there is a risk that they will overheat and cause a fire. "Daisy-chaining" one power strip to another is dangerous. The total amperage of devices connected to the strip must not exceed the strip's maximum load (typically 12 amps).

Show
Slide(s)

Equipment Grounding
(2 slides)

Teaching
Tip

If possible, point out features of electrical safety systems within the training environment.

EQUIPMENT GROUNDING

Electrical equipment must also be **grounded** (or earthed). If there is a fault that causes metal parts in the equipment to become live, a ground provides a path of least resistance for the electrical current to flow away harmlessly. Most computer products (PCs, printers, and so on) are connected to the building ground via the power plug. However, the large metal equipment racks often used to house servers and network equipment must also be grounded. Do not disconnect the ground wire. If it has to be removed, make sure it is replaced by a competent electrician.

Grounding terminals and wires. (Image by phadventure © 123RF.com.)

HIGH VOLTAGE DEVICE SAFETY

Show
Slide(s)

High Voltage Device
Safety

Most of the internal circuitry in a computer is low voltage (12 V or less) and low current, so there is not much of a threat to your personal safety. However, there are exceptions to this, and these exceptions can be very dangerous. Power supplies, CRT monitors, the inverter card in an LCD display's fluorescent backlight, and laser printers can carry dangerously high levels of voltage. Charges held in capacitors can persist for hours after the power supply is turned off. You should not open these units unless you have been specifically trained to do so. Adhere to all printed warnings, and never remove or break open any safety devices that carry such a warning.

 Caution: *Never insert anything into the power supply fan to get it to rotate. This approach does not work, and it is dangerous.*

ELECTRICAL FIRE SAFETY

Faulty electrical equipment can pose a fire risk. If the equipment allows more current to flow through a cable than the cable is rated for, the cable will heat up. This could ignite flammable material close to the cable. If an electrical wire does start a fire, it is important to use the correct type of extinguisher to put it out. Many extinguishers use water or foam, which can be dangerous if used near live electrical equipment. The best type to use is a Carbon Dioxide (CO_2) gas extinguisher. CO_2 extinguishers have a black label. Dry powder extinguishers can also be used, though these can damage electronic equipment.

Show Slide(s)
Electrical Fire Safety

 Caution: *Care must be taken in confined spaces as the CO_2 plus smoke from the fire will quickly replace the available oxygen, making it hard to breathe.*

You should also ensure that the electricity supply is turned off. This should happen automatically (the fuses for the circuit should trip), but make sure you know the location of the power master switches for a building.

GUIDELINES FOR WORKING SAFELY WITH ELECTRICAL SYSTEMS

 Note: *All of the Guidelines for this lesson are available as checklists from the **Checklist** tile on the CHOICE Course screen.*

Show Slide(s)
Guidelines for Working Safely with Electrical Systems

Consider these guidelines as you prepare to work with electrical equipment.

ELECTRICAL SAFETY

Follow these guidelines to work safely with electrical systems:

- Do not work on electrical systems unless you have a good understanding of the risks and appropriate safety procedures.
- Do not attempt repair work when you are tired; you may make careless mistakes, and your primary diagnostic tool, deductive reasoning, will not be operating at full capacity.
- Do not assume anything without checking it out for yourself. A ground wire might have been disconnected or never properly installed, for example.
- Disconnect the power to a circuit if you must handle it.
- Hold down the power button on the device to ensure the circuits are drained of residual power.
- Test live parts with a multimeter to ensure that no voltage is present.
- Always use properly insulated tools and never grip a tool by its metal parts.

 Note: *It is especially important not to touch the live parts of multimeter probes, as these may be connected to an energized circuit. Handle the probes by the insulated sheaths only.*

- Take care not to touch any part of a circuit with both hands to reduce the risk of a serious shock. This is called the "hand in pocket" rule. It reduces the chance that the current will pass through your chest and cause a heart attack.
- Make sure your hands and the surrounding area are dry. Sweat can make your hands more conductive.
- Do not leave any spill hazards in the vicinity and ensure you are not standing on a wet floor.
- Do not wear jewelry, a wrist watch, or other items such as name badges that may dangle from your neck or wrist, as they can cause a short circuit or become trapped by moving parts.

ENVIRONMENTAL SAFETY

Show Slide(s)
Environmental Safety

In addition to electrical hazards, there are other environmental issues that computer technicians must deal with on a regular basis. The health and safety of you and those around you should always be your highest priority. Recognizing potential environmental hazards and properly dealing with them in a safe manner is a critical responsibility for a CompTIA® A+® technician.

Category	Description
Trip hazards	A **trip hazard** is caused by putting any object in pathways where people walk.
Lifting and carrying risks	Lifting a heavy object in the wrong way can damage your back or cause muscle strains and ligament damage. You may also drop the object and injure yourself or damage the object. Lifting and manual handling risks are not limited to particularly heavy objects. An object that is large or awkward to carry could cause you to trip over or walk into something else. An object that has sharp or rough edges or contains a hot or corrosive liquid could cause you to cut or hurt yourself.

TOXIC WASTE HANDLING

Show Slide(s)
Toxic Waste Handling

Teaching Tip

There is some overlap between the safety procedures used for handling and disposal and environmental impact concepts, such as MSDS. The latter will be covered later in the course.

The conditions surrounding computer equipment can be an issue when there is a large number of airborne particles flowing in and around various devices. Contaminants can be either gaseous, such as ozone; particles, such as dust; or organic, which comes from industrial processing of fossil fuels or plastics. There is also a risk of poisonous or corrosive chemicals leaking from faulty equipment. Special care must be taken in respect of the following device types:

- **CRT monitors:** A cathode ray tube (CRT) is an older type of computer monitor. These are very heavy and bulky and can contain substantial amounts of hazardous materials, notably lead. They also contain a glass vacuum tube and high-voltage capacitors. While the tube is designed to be shatter resistant, it is still potentially very hazardous if dropped. The capacitors represent a high risk of electric shock.
- **Batteries:** Swollen or leaking batteries from laptop computers or within cell phones and tablets must be handled very carefully and stored within appropriate containers. Use gloves and safety goggles to minimize any risk of burns from corrosive material.
- **Electronic devices (PCs, cell phones, and tablets):** Many components in electronic devices contain toxins and heavy metals, such as lead, mercury, and arsenic. These toxins may be present in batteries, in circuit boards, and in plastics used in the case. These toxins are harmful to human health if ingested and

damaging to the environment. This means that you must not dispose of electronic devices as general waste in landfill or incinerators. If an electronic device cannot be donated for reuse, it must be disposed of through an approved waste management and recycling facility.

- **Toner kits and cartridges**: Photocopier and laser printer toner is an extremely fine powder. The products in toner powder are not classed as hazardous to health but any dust in substantial concentration is a nuisance as it may cause respiratory tract irritation.

GUIDELINES FOR WORKING SAFELY AMONG ENVIRONMENTAL HAZARDS

Here are some guidelines to help you work safely when environmental hazards are present.

 Show Slide(s)

Guidelines for Working Safely Among Environmental Hazards (2 slides)

ENVIRONMENTAL SAFETY

Follow these guidelines to work safely among environmental hazards:

- When installing equipment, ensure that cabling is secured, using cable ties or cable management products if necessary. Check that cables running under a desk cannot be kicked out by a user's feet. Do not run cabling across walkways or, if there is no option but to do so, use a cord protector to cover the cabling.
- When servicing equipment, do not leave devices (PC cases for instance) in walkways or near the edge of a desk (where it could be knocked off). Be careful about putting down heavy or bulky equipment (ensure that it cannot topple).
- When you need to lift or carry items, be aware of what your weight limitations are, as well as any restrictions and guidance set forth in your job description or site safety handbook. Weight limitations will vary depending on context. For example, a 50 pound limitation for lifting and carrying an object while holding it close to your body is not the same as lifting an object from a shelf above your head.
- If necessary, you should obtain protective clothing (gloves and possibly goggles) for handling equipment and materials that can be hazardous.
- Lift heavy objects safely. To do so:
  1. Plant your feet around the object with one foot slightly toward the direction in which you are going to move.
  2. Bend your knees to reach the object while keeping your back as straight as is possible and comfortable and your chin up.
  3. Find a firm grip on the object then lift smoothly by straightening your legs—do not jerk the object up.
  4. Carry the object while keeping your back straight.
- Lower heavy objects safely, by reversing the lifting process; keep your chin up and bend at the knees. Take care not to trap your fingers or to lower the object onto your feet.
- If you cannot lift an object because it is too awkward or heavy, then get help from a coworker, or use a cart to relocate the equipment. If you use a cart, make sure the equipment is tightly secured during transport. Do not stack loose items on a cart. If you need to carry an object for some distance, make sure that the route is unobstructed and that the pathway (including stairs or doorways) is wide and tall enough.
- Follow these guidelines when working with toxic materials.
  - Never disassemble a CRT and never try to stack old units on top of one another.
  - Use gloves and safety goggles to minimize any risk of burns from corrosive materials from batteries, cell phones, and tablets.

- Use an air filter mask that fits over your mouth and nose when servicing toner kits and cartridges to avoid breathing in the particles. People who suffer from asthma or bronchitis should avoid changing toner cartridges where possible. Loose toner must be collected carefully using an approved toner vacuum and sealed within a strong plastic waste container. Get the manufacturer's advice about disposing of loose toner safely. It must not be sent directly to a landfill.

ESD

Show Slide(s)

ESD

Teaching Tip

Point out that static electricity is high "pressure" (voltage) but low flow (current), which is why it is less harmful to humans.

Static electricity is a high voltage (potential difference) stored in an insulated body. **Electrostatic discharge (ESD)** occurs when a path is created that allows electrons to rush from a statically charged body to another with an unequal charge. The electricity is released with a spark. The charge follows the path of least resistance, so it can occur between an electrical ground, such as a doorknob or a computer chassis, and a charged body, such as a human hand.

Although the voltage is high, the amount of ESD current sustained is very low, so static electricity is not that harmful. It can, however, be slightly painful. You might have felt a small shock when reaching for a metal door handle for instance. You can feel a discharge of over about 2500V. A discharge of 20,000V or more could produce a visible spark. Walking over an untreated carpet in dry conditions could create a charge of around 35,000V.

The human body is mostly water and so does not generate or store static electricity very well. Unfortunately, our clothes are often made of synthetic materials, such as nylon and polyester, which act as good generators of static electricity and provide insulating layers that allow charges to accumulate. Humidity and climate also affect the likelihood of ESD. The risk increases during dry, cool conditions when humidity is low. In humid conditions, such as before or during a storm, the residual charge can bleed into the environment before it can increase sufficiently to be harmful to electrical components.

An electronic component, such as a memory or logic chip, is composed of fine, conductive metal oxides deposited on a small piece of silicon. Its dimensions are measured in fractions of a micron (one millionth of a meter). Any static electricity discharged into this structure will flash-over (spark) between the conductive tracks, damaging or even vaporizing them. A transistor designed to work with 1-3V can be damaged by a charge of under 100V, though most have ESD protection circuits that improve this tolerance.

A static discharge may make a chip completely unusable. If not, it is likely to fail at some later time. Damage occurring in this way can be hidden for many months and might only manifest itself in occasional failures.

COMPONENT HANDLING

Show Slide(s)

Component Handling (3 slides)

Teaching Tip

Stress that while anti-static measures reduce the risk of ESD damage to computers, they raise the risk of electric shock. It is vital to check any equipment used regularly and to follow proper procedures.

By eliminating unnecessary activities that create static charges and by removing unnecessary materials that are known charge generators, you can protect against ESD-related damage and injuries. There are several other prevention techniques that you can use to protect yourself and equipment when you are working with computer components.

- **Self-grounding**, or manual dissipation of static buildup by touching a grounded object prior to touching any electronic equipment. You can accomplish this by touching an unpainted part of a metal computer chassis or other component.
- Using an anti-ESD wrist strap or leg strap can dissipate static charges more effectively than self-grounding. The band should fit snugly around your wrist or ankle to maximize contact with the skin. Do not wear it over clothing. The strap ground is made either using a grounding plug that plugs into a wall socket or a

crocodile clip that attaches to a grounded point or an unpainted part of the computer's metal chassis.

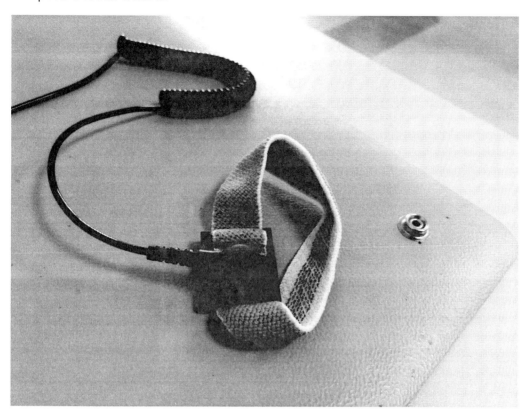

Electrostatic Discharge ESD wrist strap on ESD mat. (Image by Audrius Merfeldas © 123RF.com.)

• An anti-ESD service mat is also useful. Sensitive components can be placed on the mat safely. The mats contain a snap that you connect to the wrist or leg strap. If the technician's clothing has the potential to produce static charges, an ESD smock, which covers from the waist up, can be helpful.

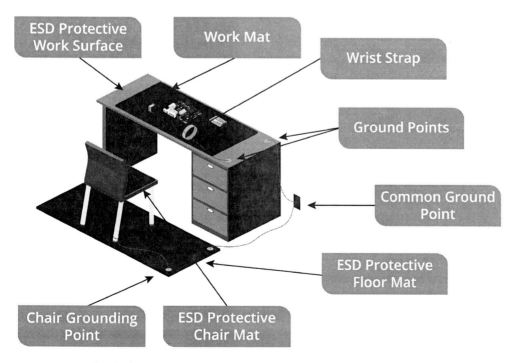

An example of a basic electrostatic discharge (ESD) workstation. (Image © 123RF.com.)

- Electronic components, assemblies, and spare parts, known as **field replaceable units (FRUs)** are often shipped in **antistatic bags** to protect them from ESD damage.

ANTISTATIC BAG TYPES

Antistatic packaging includes either anti-ESD shielding or dissipative material.

- Anti-ESD Shielding—this packaging reduces the risk of ESD because it is coated with a conductive material (such as a nickel compound). This material prevents static electricity from discharging through the inside of the bag. These bags are usually a shiny grey metallic color. To protect the contents of the bag fully, you should seal it, or at least fold the top over and seal that down.
- Dissipative Packaging—this light pink or blue packaging reduces the build-up of static in the general vicinity of the contents by being slightly more conductive than normal. A plastic bag or foam packaging may be sprayed with an anti-static coating or have anti-static materials added to the plastic compound. This is used to package non-static-sensitive components packed in proximity to static-sensitive components.

GUIDELINES FOR PROTECTING COMPONENTS FROM ESD DAMAGE

Show Slide(s)

Guidelines for Protecting Components from ESD Damage

Here are some guidelines to help you protect your electronic components from ESD damage.

ESD PROTECTION

Follow these guidelines to protect electronic components from damage due to ESD:

- Use proper component handling and storage procedures whenever you are performing PC maintenance work.
- To protect components and equipment from ESD damage:
  - Make sure that your body and clothing are drained of static electricity before starting work.
  - If possible, work in an uncarpeted area.
  - The simplest (but least effective) means of self-grounding is to touch an unpainted metal part of the PC, such as the power supply unit, before you handle a sensitive component. This is only a temporary solution and a static charge could build up again.

 Caution: Do not leave the PC plugged in if you open the case for servicing. Your safety is more important than the risk of damaging some PC components.

  - Where possible, handle vulnerable components by holding the edges of the plastic mounting card, and avoid touching the surfaces of the chips themselves.
- Use ESD wrist or ankle straps and dissipative floor mats.

 Note: Ensure that the strap has a working current-limiting resistor for safety (straps should be tested daily). Do not use a grounding plug if there is any suspicion of a fault in the socket or in the building's electrical wiring, or if the wiring is not regularly inspected and tested.

 *Note: To learn more, check the **Video** tile on the CHOICE Course screen for any videos that supplement the content for this lesson.*

Activity 2-1

Implementing an Anti-ESD Service Kit

BEFORE YOU BEGIN

Your instructor will provide you with an anti-static kit.

You will be performing this activity at your WORKBENCH PC.

SCENARIO

You are assisting with introducing recently hired employees to the safety culture. You will need to demonstrate safe use of an anti-static kit and answer questions about safety procedures and hazards.

1. **Describe the equipment you should use to prevent static electricity on your body from damaging the equipment on which you are working.**

   An anti-ESD service kit comprising an anti-ESD wrist strap, grounding cord and plug, and a conductive mat. The grounding plug should be connected to an earthed point.

2. Your instructor will provide you with an anti-static service kit. Prepare it for use and allow your instructor to check that you have connected everything correctly.

   You can refer to the figure in the **Component Handling** section for assistance.

3. **True or False? If you are using an anti-static floor mat, you do not need any other anti-ESD service equipment.**

   False. A mat should be used with a wrist strap. You may also need ESD-safe packaging for storing components.

4. **In which atmospheric conditions is the risk of ESD highest?**

   During cool, dry conditions when humidity is low. When humidity is high, the static electricity can dissipate through the moisture present in the air.

5. **Electrical injuries include electrocution, shock, and collateral injury. Would you be injured if you are not part of the electrical ground current?**

   Yes, you could receive a thermal burn from the head of an electric arc or electric equipment. Your clothes can catch on fire, or your skin can be burned.

Show Slide(s)

Activity: Implementing an Anti-ESD Service Kit

Teaching Tip

Hand out one anti-static service kit per learner. They will need these for the remainder of the activities, but remember to collect the kits again after class unless you are letting learners take their toolkits away with them.

Make sure that you check each learner's anti-static service kit setup to ensure that they have correctly connected their wrist-strap, grounding cord etc.

Also ask learners to check the installation of standard classroom PCs - note measures to prevent trip hazards, etc.

6. **Which computer component presents the most danger from electrical shock?**

   ○ System boards

   ○ Hard drives

   ● Power supplies

   ○ System unit

7. **What component helps to protect users of electrical equipment against a short circuit?**

   ○ Resistor

   ● Fuse

   ○ Power supply

   ○ ESD wrist strap

8. **What care should you take when lifting a heavy object?**

   The main concern is damaging your back. Lift slowly using your legs for power not your back muscles.

9. **What should you do before transporting a bulky object?**

   Check that there is a clear path to the destination point. If you cannot carry the object safely, get help or use a cart.

Topic B
PC Components

EXAM OBJECTIVES COVERED
1001-3.5 Given a scenario, install and configure motherboards, CPUs, and add-on cards.

If you are not familiar with the various components that a computer is made up of, it can seem like a jigsaw puzzle. Like most puzzles, each part of a computer connects to other parts in a specific place, but generally, you will find that the pieces fit together almost exactly the same way from one system to another. To help you put the puzzle together, you need to understand what these pieces look like and what they do.

SYSTEM CASE TYPES

A **desktop computer** refers to a PC that is not designed to be used on the move. The components of a desktop computer system are divided between those that are designed to be handled by the user (peripheral devices) and those that would be damaged or dangerous if exposed.

The **system case** (or **chassis**) is a plastic and metal box that houses this second class of components, such as the motherboard, Central Processing Unit (CPU), memory, adapter cards, disk drives, and power supply unit. System units are also often referred to as boxes, main units, or base units.

There are two basic types of system unit: Tower and Small Form Factor (SFF). These types are available in different sizes. Be aware that while a small case may be desirable because it takes up less space, it has less room inside for installing extra devices and is less effective at cooling.

A **tower case** is designed to sit vertically on a surface, so that it is taller than it is wide. Tower cases come in four basic sizes: full, mid, mini, and slim line.

- Full tower cases are usually used for PC servers. These require the extra internal space for additional hard disks, adapter cards, and redundant power supply units.
- Mid tower cases are used for high-end user PCs. These PCs do require extra devices and adapter cards, but not as many as a server.
- Mini tower cases are usually used for office or home PCs where the requirement for additional internal devices and adapter cards is limited.
- Slimline cases require low-profile adapter cards but can be oriented horizontally or vertically.

Teaching Tip

If learners have completed the CompTIA IT Fundamentals+ course, they should have a basic understanding of computer processing (input, output, processing, and storage), and the functions of the CPU, system memory, disk drives, and video adapters. If learners have not completed the prerequisite course, you might need to provide some extra explanation as you discuss these technologies.

Show Slide(s)

System Case Types (3 slides)

Teaching Tip

Explain that for the first part of the course, you will focus on desktop hardware, and later, you will cover laptops and other mobile hardware components.

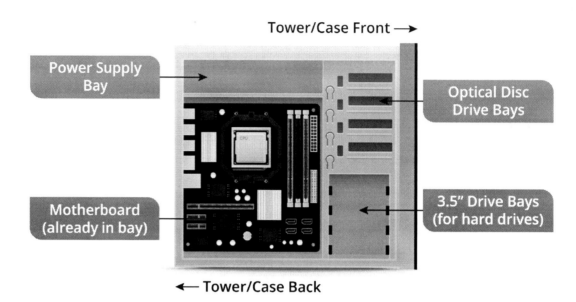

Computer tower with main panel removed showing an attached motherboard and areas for optical disc drives, 3.5" drive bays, and a power supply bay. (Image © 123RF.com.)

Small Form Factor (SFF) case designs are semi-portable, space-saving designs typically used for domestic entertainment or Media Center systems that will not look out of place in a living room. They are usually cube-like or super slimline. SFF cases can hold only a limited number of components.

Desktop computers can also be purchased as **all-in-one units**. All-in-one means that all the computer components, except the keyboard and mouse, are contained within the monitor case.

All-in-one PC. (Image © 123RF.com.)

PARTS OF THE SYSTEM CASE

To perform PC maintenance and component upgrades, you must understand how to open a desktop computer's case.

Show
Slide(s)

Parts of the System
Case (4 slides)

- Each case has a **cover**, which is removed by either undoing the screws at the back or pressing together clips that release it. Cases based on the slimline design have a hinged cover that releases to allow access to the motherboard.
- The **front panel** provides access to the removable media drives, a power on/off switch, a reset switch, and LEDs (Light Emitting Diodes) to indicate drive operation. The front cover can be removed but may require the side panel to be removed first in order to access the screws or clips that secure it.

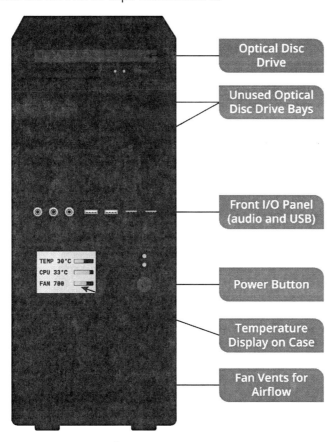

Front of case. (Image © 123RF.com.)

Note: Some cases feature tool-free access (that is, they are secured by clips). Some cases use proprietary screw fittings to prevent unauthorized access to the internal components.

- The **rear panel** has cut-out slots aligned with the position of **adapter card** slots. These slots should either be covered by an adapter card or a metal strip known as a **blanking plate**. Uncovered slots can disrupt the proper flow of air around components in the PC and cause overheating and also increase the amount of dust in the system.

  There is also a cut-out aligned with the motherboard's Input/Output (I/O) ports. These allow for the connection of peripheral devices.

  The rear panel provides access to the Power Supply Unit (PSU) sockets. The PSU has an integral fan exhaust. Care should be taken that it is not obstructed, as this will adversely affect cooling. There may be an additional case fan.

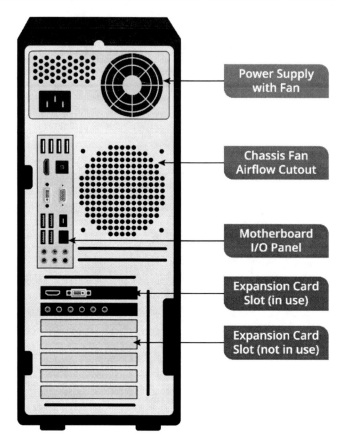

Rear panel of a PC. (Image © 123RF.com.)

Show Slide(s)

Repair or Replace?

REPAIR OR REPLACE?

PC components that are easily user-replaceable (or upgradeable) are referred to as **field replaceable units (FRUs)**. Due to economic factors, most components of a PC are not worth repairing; instead they are simply replaced with a new unit ("swapped out").

Show Slide(s)

Guidelines for PC Disassembly

GUIDELINES FOR PC DISASSEMBLY

Here are some guidelines for disassembling PCs.

PC DISASSEMBLY

Before you start to disassemble a PC, consider the following guidelines:

- Back up all data stored on the internal drive(s) to protect important data.
- Create a clean work environment with plenty of working space where you can set the PC at a comfortable height.
- Gather all necessary tools and equipment. A notepad and pen may be useful for making diagrams and notes. A digital camera is also useful for recording the layout of components.
- Make sure that all devices are powered off and unplugged from the building power before disconnecting them.
- Take anti-static precautions to minimize the chance of damaging sensitive components. Place static-sensitive components, such as processors and memory, in anti-static bags.

Note: *To learn more, check the* **Video** *tile on the CHOICE Course screen for any videos that supplement the content for this lesson.*

Access the Checklist tile on your CHOICE Course screen for reference information and job aids on How to Disassemble a Personal Computer.

MOTHERBOARDS

A printed circuit board, variously called the **motherboard**, **mobo**, **system board**, or **main board**, houses the processor, chipset, memory, and expansion slots. The type of motherboard influences system speed and upgrade capabilities. There are many motherboard manufacturers, including AOpen (Acer), ASRock, ASUSTek, Biostar, EVGA Corporation, Gigabyte, Intel, MSI, Shuttle, Tyan, and Via.

The motherboard is attached to the case by using **standoffs**. These hold the motherboard firmly and ensure no other part of it touches the case. The standoffs are positioned in holes that line up in the same position in the case and the motherboard (as long as they use compatible form factors). Standoffs are either brass ones secured by screws or plastic ones that snap into place.

MOTHERBOARD FORM FACTORS

The form factor of the motherboard describes its shape, layout, and the type of case and power supply that can be used. Two motherboards may have exactly the same functionality but different form factors; the difference is the layout of the components on the motherboard.

The following table describes common motherboard form factors.

Form Factor	Description
ATX	• The Advanced Technology Extended (ATX) specification was developed by Intel in 1995 to provide a new design for PC motherboards, updating the previous AT form factor. • Full size ATX boards are 12 inches wide by 9.6 inches deep (or 305 x 244 mm). • ATX boards can contain up to seven expansion slots.
Micro-ATX	• The Micro-ATX (mATX) standard specifies a 9.6-inch (244 x 244 mm) square board. • mATX boards have fewer expansion slots than ATX boards (up to 4 compared to a maximum of 7 for full-sized ATX boards). **Note:** *Most mATX boards can be mounted in ATX cases.*

Show Slide(s)

Motherboards

Teaching Tip

Exam candidates might need to be able to identify the parts of a motherboard from a diagram. If you have samples of different motherboards, you could pass them around now. Emphasize that these form factors can be matched to different case types.

Show Slide(s)

Motherboard Form Factors

Teaching Tip

The "I" in ITX could stand for information. Via originally planned to use the form factor in an "Information PC" product.

Form Factor	Description
Mini-ITX	• Small Form Factor (SFF) PCs are becoming popular as home machines (and in image-conscious offices). SFF PCs often use Via's Mini-ITX form factor. • Mini-ITX is 6.7 inches (170 x 170 mm) square with one expansion slot. *Note: Most mini-ITX boards can be mounted in ATX cases.*
Other ITX-based form factors	There are also smaller nano-, pico-, and mobile-ITX form factors, but these are used for embedded systems and portables, rather than PCs. *Note: No commercial motherboards were ever produced from the original plain ITX specification.*

MOTHERBOARD CONNECTOR TYPES

Show Slide(s)

Motherboard Connector Types

All motherboards have connectors for the same sort of components: CPU, memory, disk drives, peripherals, and so on. However, the type and number of these connectors depends upon the motherboard model.

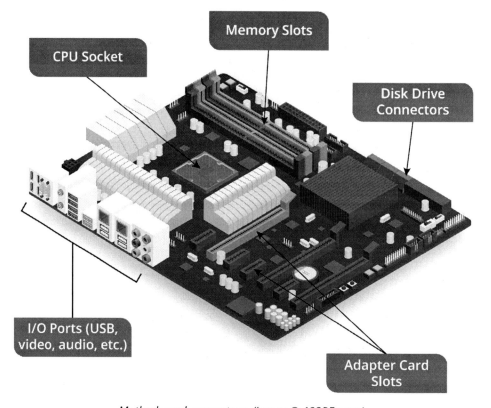

Motherboard connectors. (Image © 123RF.com.)

CPU SOCKETS

Show Slide(s)

CPU Sockets

New motherboards are generally released to support new CPU designs. Most PC CPUs are manufactured by Intel and AMD, and these vendors use different socket designs.

Also, because technology changes rapidly, a given motherboard will only support a limited number of CPU models. CPU models are closely tied to the chipset and memory subsystem. This means that there is less scope for upgrading the CPU than used to be the case. You could not, for instance, take a motherboard designed for the Core 2 CPU and plug an AMD Phenom CPU into it. Both the physical interface (socket) and system architecture have diverged along proprietary lines since the old socket 7 interface.

The CPU is typically inserted into a squarish socket, located close to the memory sockets, and then covered by a heatsink and fan.

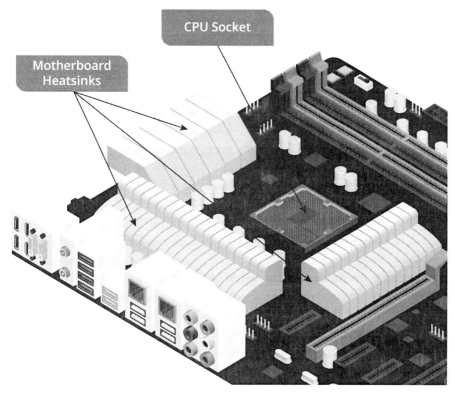

Motherboard CPU socket and heatsinks. (Image © 123RF.com.)

MEMORY SLOTS

All the software and data processed by a computer is ultimately stored as binary code; strings of ones and zeroes. This program code is stored in system memory.

System memory uses a type of memory technology called **Random Access Memory (RAM)**. Program code is loaded into RAM so that it can be accessed and executed by the processor. RAM also holds data, such as the contents of a spreadsheet or document, while it is being modified. System RAM is volatile; it loses its contents when power is removed.

System RAM is normally packaged as Dual Inline Memory Modules (DIMMs) fitted to motherboard slots. DIMM slots have catches at either end, are located close to the CPU socket, and are often color-coded. Note that there are various RAM technologies (DDR3 versus DDR4, for instance) and the DIMMs are specific to a particular DDR version. A label next to the slots should identify the type of DIMMs supported.

The capabilities of the memory controller and number of physical slots determine how much memory can be fitted.

Show Slide(s)

Memory Slots

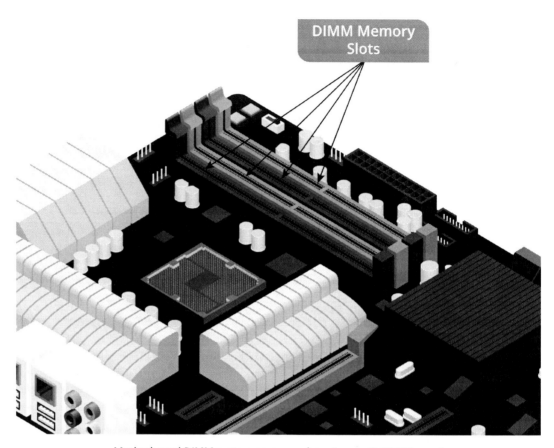

Motherboard DIMM system memory slots. (Image © 123RF.com.)

CHIPSET AND MEMORY ARCHITECTURE

Show Slide(s)

Chipset and Memory Architecture

The **chipset** consists of several controllers that handle the transfer of data between the CPU and various devices. Examples of controllers include the following:

- System memory controller.
- Input/Output (I/O) controller to handle disk drives and expansion buses.
- Controllers for any integrated video, sound, and network (cabled and wireless) interfaces.

 Note: *Intel and AMD manufacture all the CPUs used in PCs, but there are various chipset vendors. Some of the major names include ATI (now owned by AMD), NVIDIA, SiS, ULi, and VIA.*

The chipset is soldered onto the motherboard and cannot be upgraded. The type of chipset on the motherboard can affect the choice of processor and multiprocessing support, type and amount of system memory supported, and type(s) of system bus supported.

The link between the CPU and system memory is a key factor in determining system performance. Historically, PCs used a chipset split into two sections: the northbridge and the southbridge. The main function of the northbridge is as the system memory controller, connecting the processor to RAM. The southbridge is designed to control all of the I/O functions not handled by the northbridge. These are older, slower technologies, such as USB.

As memory, video, and fixed disk technologies improved, the northbridge/southbridge architecture became a bottleneck to performance. Newer CPUs and chipsets use different designs, with Intel and AMD both introducing different architectures. The general trend is for subsystems that require a lot of bandwidth—notably the system memory controller and graphics controller—to be incorporated on the same chip as the CPU itself (referred to as "on die").

CMOS AND RTC BATTERIES

On older computers, **CMOS** RAM stored the PC's basic configuration and any settings made via the CMOS/system firmware setup program. CMOS stands for Complementary Metal-Oxide Semiconductor, which describes the manufacturing process used to make the RAM chip.

CMOS devices require very little power to operate and use a small battery to maintain their settings. The **CMOS battery** is a coin cell lithium battery. These batteries typically last for 5-10 years.

On current motherboards, configuration data is stored in a Non-Volatile RAM (NVRAM) chip such as flash memory, rather than in CMOS RAM. Flash memory does not require battery-backup. A CMOS battery is still used to power the **Real Time Clock (RTC)**, however, and may be referred to as the **RTC battery** or **clock battery**. The RTC keeps track of the actual date and time.

Show Slide(s)

CMOS and RTC Batteries (2 slides)

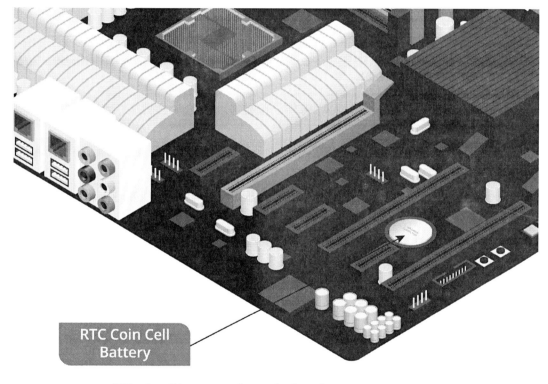

RTC Coin Cell Battery

RTC coin cell battery on the motherboard. (Image © 123RF.com.)

BUS ARCHITECTURE

Computers transmit data using electrical signals and process and store it using components called transistors and capacitors. An electrical pathway on the motherboard or through cabling that carries the signals is referred to as a **bus**. Physically, a bus is implemented on the motherboard as tiny wires (called **traces**) running between components. The bus carries information being processed by the computer (data) and information about where the data is located in memory (address). The bus also carries power to a component and the timing signals that synchronize data transfers between components.

Show Slide(s)

Bus Architecture

Teaching Tip

Point out the key functions of the bus: addressing and data transfer, plus timing signals and power.

The term "bus architecture" usually means an expansion bus, used to connect peripheral devices. However, a variety of buses exist within a PC. Also, the way that bus designs are implemented has changed considerably as PC technology has developed and improved.

INTERNAL AND EXTERNAL BUSES

Show Slide(s)

Internal and External Buses

One way of categorizing types of buses is to divide them into internal and external. An internal bus, or **local** bus, connects core components, such as the CPU, memory, and the system controllers.

An external bus, or **expansion bus**, allows additional components to be connected to the computer. These components could be peripheral devices (located outside the case) or adapter cards (located inside the case).

External bus technologies do not necessarily extend outside the computer case. For example, PCI, the most popular expansion bus standard, provides connections to internal adapter cards only. A genuinely external bus (like SCSI, USB, or Firewire) extends the bus wires outside the computer case using cabling. The distinction between internal and external bus types has also become a lot less clear as one bus technology will be used to perform both types of role (for example, PCI Express).

EXPANSION SLOTS

Show Slide(s)

Expansion Slots (2 slides)

Teaching Tip

If you have examples of motherboards with different expansion slot types, you can pass them around at this point.

Expansion slots enable you to install plug-in adapter cards in a computer to extend the range of functions it can perform. There are several expansion bus types and many different types of adapter card.

Computers can support more than one expansion bus. PCs use a multi-bus design, to support older technologies and allow for upgrades. For example, a PC might support PCI and PCI Express for adding internal adapter cards plus USB to allow the connection of peripherals.

RISER CARDS

Some PC case designs are slimline, meaning that there is not enough space for full height expansion cards. This problem is addressed by providing a **riser card** at right angles to the main board, enabling you to connect additional adapters to the system in an orientation that is parallel to the motherboard and thus save space within the system case.

> *Note: Another option is to use low profile adapter cards. A low profile card is about half the height of a standard card and so fits within a slimline case.*

Historically, the LPX and NLX form factors were designed as riser architectures. Most manufacturers just use the ATX riser card specification. This specifies a 2x11 connector plus a PCI connector for the riser card.

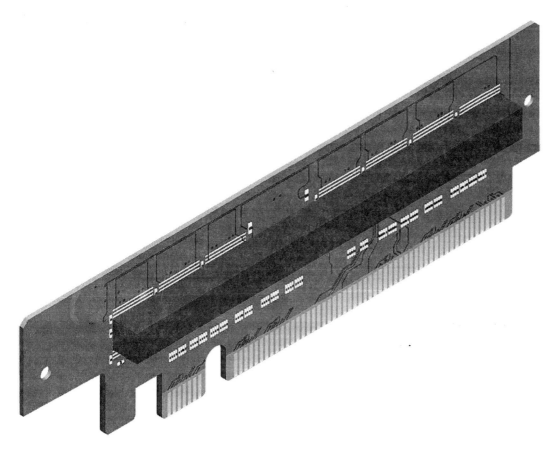

A riser card. (Image © 123RF.com.)

Note: **Daughter board** *is a general computing and electronics term for any circuit board that plugs into another circuit board. In personal computing, a daughter board can be used as a more general term for adapter cards. Sometimes, in casual usage, the term is used interchangeably with the term riser card, but technically they are not the same.*

SYSTEM CLOCK AND BUS SPEED

The **system clock** synchronizes the operation of all parts of the PC and provides the basic timing signal for the CPU. Clock speeds are measured in Megahertz (MHz) or Gigahertz (GHz). The clock consists of a clock generator that sets up a timing signal and clock multipliers that take the timing signal produced by the generator and apply a multiplication factor to produce different timing signals for different types of buses. This means that one type of bus can work at a different speed (or frequency) to another type of bus.

PCI BUS

The **Peripheral Component Interconnect (PCI) bus** was introduced in 1994 with the Pentium processor. It is still an important technology in terms of adapter card provision, though it is being superseded by PCI Express. Several versions of PCI have been released subsequently to the first commercial version (2.0). Information about PCI standards is published at pcisig.org. The different capabilities are summarized here.

Show Slide(s)
System Clock and Bus Speed

Teaching Tip
Emphasize the differences between the system clock and the RTC clock. System clocks control timing signals between system components, whereas RTC clocks keep track of the current date and time.

Show Slide(s)
PCI Bus (3 slides)

BUS WIDTH AND CLOCK SPEED

- PCI supports up to 5 devices (though each device can have up to 8 different functions) and allocates system resources by using Plug-and-Play. Bandwidth on the PCI bus is shared between all devices. PCI supports **bus mastering**, meaning that the device can control the bus to transfer data to and from memory, without requiring the CPU. The PCI architecture is a 32-bit-wide parallel bus working at 33.3 MHz, achieving a transfer rate of up to 133 MBps (that is, 32 bits divided by 8 to get 4 bytes, then multiplied by the clock rate of 33.3).
- Later versions allowed for 66 MHz operation (giving a 32-bit bus 266 MBps bandwidth) and a 64-bit wide bus (266 MBps at 33.3 MHz or 533 MBps at 66 MHz). 64-bit and 66 MHz cards and buses are not commonly found on desktop PCs, however.

ADAPTER CARD AND SLOT FORM FACTORS

Originally, PCI cards were designed for 5V signaling, but the PCI 2.1 specification also allows for 3.3V and dual voltage cards. In order to prevent the wrong type of PCI card from being inserted (for example, a 3.3V card in a 5V PCI slot), the keying for the three types of cards is different.

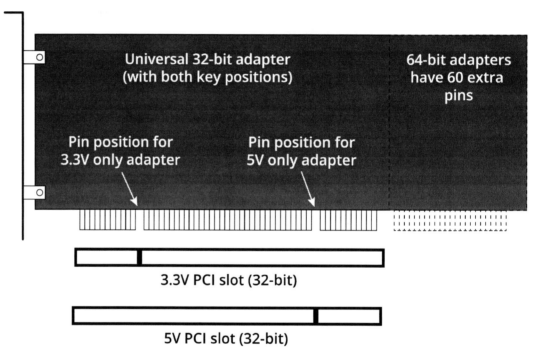

PCI card and slot form factors. The exact number of pins is not shown in this image. (Image © 123RF.com.)

On a 5V card and slot, the key is at pins 50-51; on a 3.3V adapter, the key is at pins 12-13.

64-bit compatible slots and adapters have an extra 60 pins, making the slots distinctively longer. A 32-bit card can be inserted into a 64-bit slot (as long as it is not a 5V card).

 Note: *PCI 2.3 deprecates the use of 5V cards and most cards are universal. The vast majority of cards and slots for desktop systems are 32-bit. 64-bit PCI is more a feature of server-level systems.*

Regardless of the voltage used for signaling, PCI slots can deliver up to 25W of power to an adapter.

A dual voltage (universal) adapter has both keys.

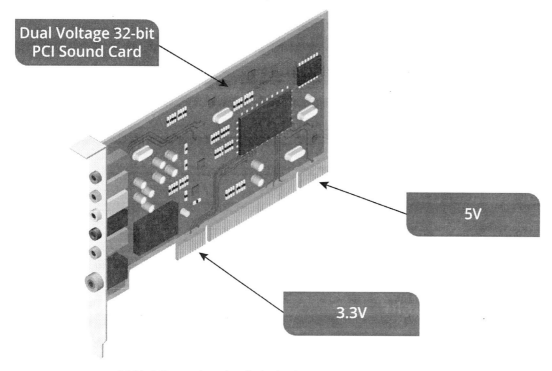

32-bit PCI sound card with dual voltage. (Image © 123RF.com.)

PCI EXPRESS BUS

As CPU and memory bus speeds increased over the years, PCI represented a substantial bottleneck to computer performance. PCI is a parallel interface. Parallel interface speeds are limited by the problem of timing each signal (data skew). They are also more complex and costly to implement. Another performance barrier is the fact that the bandwidth of the PCI bus is shared between all the components connected to it, and only one component can make use of the bus at any one time. This is a particular problem for video, disk access, and networking.

Various fixes were implemented to remove critical bottlenecks. These fixes added to the complexity of chip design, and over time the PCI bus simply became inadequate. **PCI Express (PCIe)** was released by Intel in 2004 as the replacement for the PCI architecture. PCIe uses point-to-point serial communications, meaning that each component can have a dedicated link to any other component. Connections are made via a switch, which routes data between components and can provide Quality of Service (QoS) to any component that needs it (for example, to prioritize real-time video over non-time critical data).

Show Slide(s)

PCI Express Bus (3 slides)

Teaching Tip

PCIe has superseded PCI/AGP, but most motherboards still have PCI slots.

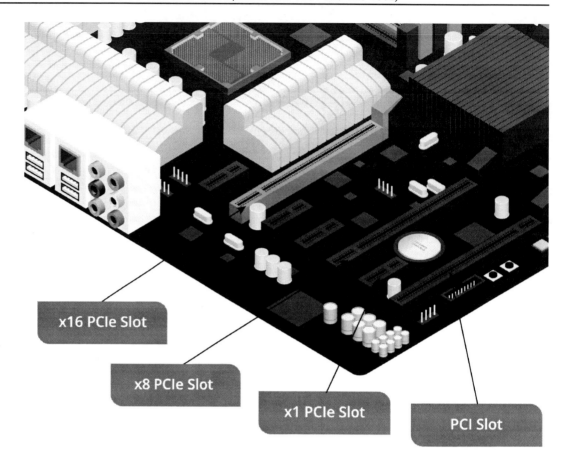

x16 PCIe Slot

x8 PCIe Slot

x1 PCIe Slot

PCI Slot

Motherboard PCI and PCI Express expansion slots. (Image © 123RF.com.)

Teaching Tip

The total number of lanes supported by the chipset might not be what you expect from looking at the slots. For example, a chipset might support a maximum of 24 lanes despite having 2x16 slots and a couple of x1 slots. Using two graphics adapters in both x16 slots would mean that they could only use x8 lanes. The specification allows for x32 lanes, but this type of slot is almost never used, and x4 slots are not common, either.

Each point-to-point connection is referred to as a **link**. The link sends both data and control/timing instructions. A link can make use of one or more **lanes**. Each lane consists of two wire pairs (four wires in total) using low voltage differential signaling. One pair is used to transmit and the other to receive (bi-directional).

- A given component can support a specific number of lanes (usually x1, x4, x8, or x16), and the switch negotiates the maximum possible number of lanes to use (for example, x8 and x16 devices would use 8 lanes). Each lane supports a transfer rate of 250 MBps in each direction. Most graphics cards use x16 links (4 GBps in each direction).
- A card will fit in any port with an equal or greater number of lanes. For example, a x8 card will fit in a x8 or x16 socket (up-plugging) and work at x8, but it will not fit in a x1 or x4 slot (down-plugging). x4, x8, and x16 slots are physically the same length but parts of the slot will be blanked out for x4 and x8.

PCIe is software compatible with PCI, meaning that PCI ports can be included on a motherboard (to support legacy adapter cards) but PCI cards cannot be fitted into PCIe sockets.

PCIe can supply up to 75W to a device via the motherboard slot. An extra 75W power can be supplied via a PCIe power connector. PCIe also features power management functions and support for hot swappable and hot pluggable adapters.

PCIe VERSIONS

The original PCIe standard has been subject to several version updates. PCI Express 2 compatible motherboards and adapters support transfer rates of 500 MBps per lane. Version 2.0 motherboards and adapters are interchangeable with earlier version 1.1

devices, though the added performance benefits are realized only if both components support version 2.

PCIe 2.1 specifies a power draw from the slot of up to 150W and an 8-pin auxiliary power connector delivering another 150W. This change introduced potential compatibility problems with v1.0 devices but these can often be fixed via a firmware update.

PCIe 3 further increases transfer rates to around 1 GBps per lane while maintaining backward-compatibility. The PCIe 4 standard doubles transfer rates again, to roughly 2 GBps per lane, whereas PCIe 5, while still being finalized at the time of writing, will almost double it again (to nearly 4 GBps per lane).

 Note: You will also see the term GigaTransfers per second (GT/s) used to describe PCIe speeds. These values do not exclude the bits transmitted as signaling and encoding overhead.

 Teaching Tip

PCIe 5 is expected to be implemented on commercial motherboards in 2019.

STORAGE BUS (SATA AND IDE)

A **storage bus** is a special type of expansion bus dedicated to communicating with storage devices, such as hard disks, solid state drives, and optical drives (CD/DVD/Blu-ray). Host Bus Adapters (HBAs) provide a connection point for internal mass storage devices, such as hard drives, optical drives, and tape drives. There used to be two main bus standards for attaching internal storage devices to a PC: Parallel ATA (PATA), which is also known as Integrated Drive Electronics (IDE) or Enhanced IDE (EIDE), and Small Computer System Interface (SCSI).

Both IDE and SCSI used parallel transfers of data per clock signal to improve bandwidth. As circuitry and encoding methods have improved, these parallel transmission technologies have been superseded by faster serial bus types. Consequently, IDE and SCSI have now largely been replaced by SATA (Serial ATA).

 Show Slide(s)

Storage Bus (SATA and IDE) (2 slides)

 Teaching Tip

Limit your presentation to introducing IDE and SATA connectors in this section. Details of the interfaces are covered later in the course.

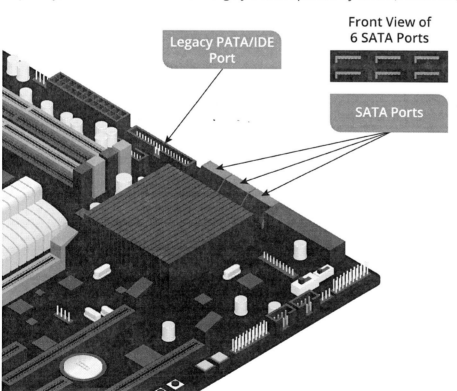

Motherboard SATA and legacy PATA/IDE ports. (Image © 123RF.com.)

A SATA port accepts a compact 7-pin connector and can be used to attach a single device. Most full size motherboards have 4 built-in SATA ports.

 Note: *What is called IDE today is technically Enhanced IDE (EIDE). Original IDE specifications were published even further in the past.*

OTHER MOTHERBOARD CONNECTORS

Show Slide(s)
Other Motherboard Connectors (2 slides)

In addition to slots and sockets for the major components, motherboards also include connectors for things like case buttons and fans.

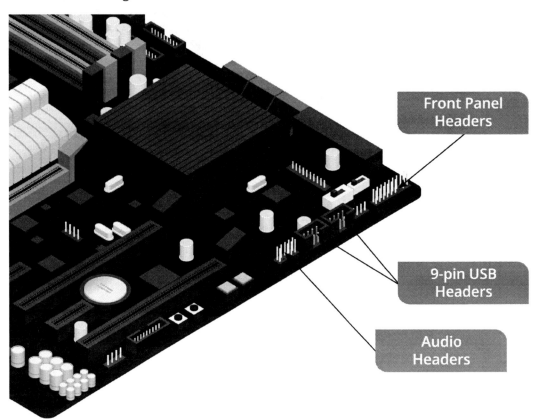

Motherboard front panel, USB, and audio headers. (Image © 123RF.com.)

These connector types are described in the following table.

Connector Type	Description
Internal USB connectors	A computer will normally feature one or two front USB ports to connect peripherals, as well as more on the back. Internal USB connections are made via 9-pin headers, which accept up to two 4-pin port connections (the 9th pin is to orient the cable correctly).

Connector Type	Description
Front panel connectors	Components on the front panel of the case connect to headers on the motherboard. Typically, front panel connectors can include:
	• Power button (soft power): On modern computers, the power button sends a signal to the PC that can be interpreted by the OS (as a command to shut down for instance) rather than actually switching the PC off. Holding down the power button for a few seconds will cut the power, however.
	• Drive (HDD) activity lights: These show when an internal hard disk is being accessed.
	• Audio ports: These allow headphones and a microphone to be connected to the computer.
	When disassembling the system, you should make a diagram of how these connectors are plugged in (position and orientation). If you do not have a diagram, you will have to refer to the motherboard documentation or go by any labels printed on the wires and headers. These are not always very easy to follow, however, which is why you should always make a diagram (or take a digital photo) to refer to.
Power and fan connectors	The motherboard also contains various connection points for the power supply and fans.
	• The power connector is usually a 24-pin white or black block.
	• Fan connectors are smaller. There will be one for the CPU and one or more for the case fans.
	There is no current standard that dictates the size and form factor of fan connectors. Common connectors include:
	• A 3-pin Molex KK connector, commonly used to connect a fan directly to the motherboard.
	• A 4-pin Molex KK connector that is similar in function to the 3-pin KK connector, except that it has an extra pin to provide the ability to control the speed of the fan.
	• A 4-pin Molex connector that connects directly to the system's power supply.

Note: In some systems, the system firmware monitors the fan speed. In order for this to happen, the power supply requires an external fan connector that is attached to the motherboard. The fan does not draw power from the connector; it only is used to provide information to the system firmware. Based on the information received, the system can increase the fan speed for improved cooling or decrease the fan speed when less cooling is needed so that the system operates more quietly.

JUMPER SETTINGS

When upgrading components such as the CPU, you may have to change the position of **jumpers** on the motherboard. A jumper is a small plastic clip containing a metal conductor that fits over two contacts on the motherboard. The position of the clip completes a circuit that configures the motherboard in one way or another.

Note: *There may be a motherboard reset jumper. Setting this may allow you to restore the system from a failed firmware update, forgotten system supervisor password, and so on.*

Activity 2-2

Discussing PC Components

SCENARIO

Answer the following questions to check your understanding of the topic.

Show
Slide(s)

Activity: Discussing PC
Components

1. **Describe how you would open a PC case to access the motherboard.**

   Power down the PC and remove the power cable. With the power cable removed, hold the power button down for a few seconds to ensure PC is completely de-energized. Then, remove any screws holding the case cover in place, and slide the cover out from the retaining clips. This should expose the motherboard. You would usually need to remove other panels only to access storage devices.

2. **At the rear of a system case are slots for adapter card ports. Why should these be covered with blanking plates if not in use?**

   The fan system is designed to draw cool air across the motherboard and blow out warm air. Large holes in the chassis disrupt this air flow. Also dust will be able to settle on the system components more easily.

3. You have been servicing a computer but when you have finished you find that it will not turn on. There was no power problem before and you have verified that the computer is connected to a working electrical outlet.

   What is the most likely explanation?

   The cable connecting the power button to the motherboard could have been disconnected and either not reconnected or not properly reconnected.

4. **What is the main function of the chipset?**

   Provides controllers for the CPU to interface with other components (memory and expansion bus for instance) and adapters to provide functions such as video and audio, and Ethernet and wireless networking on the motherboard.

5. **True or false? The Real Time Clock controls the timing of signals between the CPU and other components.**

   False. The system clock controls timing; the Real Time Clock keeps track of the calendar date and time.

6. **What type of socket is used to install system memory?**

   Dual Inline Memory Module (DIMM).

7. **You have a x8 PCIe storage adapter card—can you fit this in a x16 slot?**

   Yes—this is referred to as up-plugging. On some motherboards it may only function as a x1 device though.

8. **What is the bandwidth of a PCIe v2.0 x16 graphics adapter?**

   8 GBps in each direction (full duplex). PCIe v2 supports 500 MBps per lane.

9. You also need to help new hires identify the different types of motherboards used in computers deployed throughout the company.

   What type of motherboard is displayed here, and what characteristics did you use to help you identify the board type?

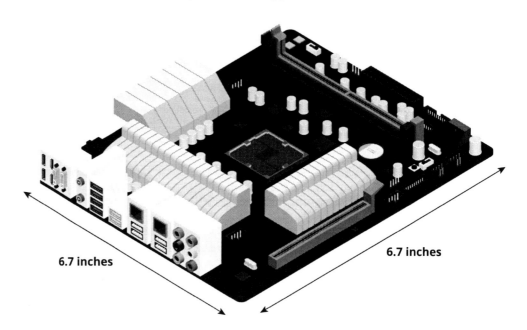

6.7 inches

6.7 inches

Based on its small size dimensions and compact component design, this motherboard is a mini-ITX.

10. **What type of motherboard is displayed here, and what characteristics did you use to help you identify the board type?**

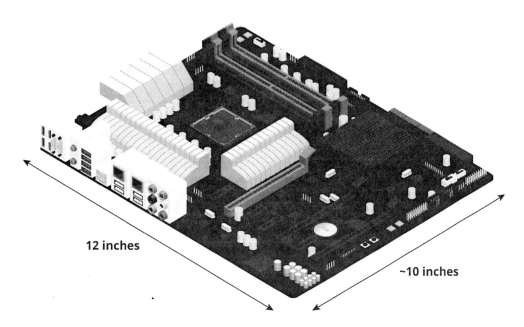

12 inches

~10 inches

You can tell by the large size and large number of available components and slots that this motherboard is an ATX.

Topic C
Common Connection Interfaces

EXAM OBJECTIVES COVERED
1001-3.1 Explain basic cable types, features, and their purposes.
1001-3.2 Identify common connector types.
1001-3.5 Given a scenario, install and configure motherboards, CPUs, and add-on cards.

You need to be able to identify how components are connected together to form a complete computer system. In this topic, you will compare PC and device connection interfaces and their characteristics.

A PC is made up of many different components. All of these components need to be able to communicate with each other so that the computer can function properly. As PC designs have evolved over the years, several connection technologies have been implemented to provide communication among computer components. As a computer technician, identifying the methods used to connect devices to a computer will enable you to install, upgrade, and replace PC components quickly and effectively.

INTERFACES, PORTS, AND CONNECTIONS

Show Slide(s)

Interfaces, Ports, and Connections (2 slides)

Teaching Tip

Logical ports are discussed later in the course, when networking topics are introduced.

Teaching Tip

Emphasize that a connection is the combination of ports, connectors, and cables that establish the link between components.

Some people might use the terms interface, port, and connection interchangeably, but there are some differences among the three.

INTERFACE

An **interface** is the point at which two devices connect and communicate with each other.

PORT

A physical **Port** is a hardware interface that you can use to connect devices to a computer. The port can also be referred to as an endpoint.

- The port transfers electronic signals between the device and the system unit.
- A port is either an electrically wired socket or plug, or it can be a wireless transmission device.
- Ports can vary by shape, by color, by the number and layout of the pins or connectors contained within the port, by the signals the port carries, and by the port's location.
- Ports exist for both internal and external devices. External ports often have a graphical representation of the type of device that should be connected to it, such as a small picture of a monitor adjacent to the video port.

CONNECTIONS

Computer **connections** are the physical access points that enable a computer to communicate with internal or external devices. They include the ports on both the computer and the connected devices, plus a transmission medium, which is either a cable with connectors at each end or a wireless technology. Personal computer connections can be categorized by the technology or standard that was used to develop the device.

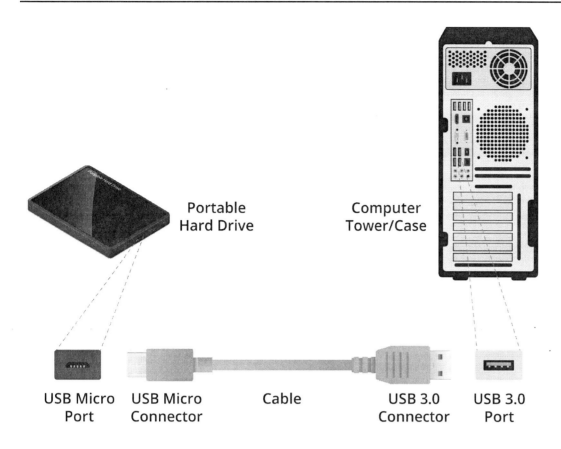

A computer connection between an external USB hard drive and a desktop computer. (Image © 123RF.com.)

Ports are often described as being **male**, meaning they have pin connectors, or **female**, meaning they have hole connectors. This gender orientation means that it is virtually impossible to connect them incorrectly. Many connectors and ports are also **keyed** to prevent them from being inserted the wrong way around.

I/O PORTS AND CABLES

Input and output **(I/O) ports** allow additional devices to be connected to the PC. Some ports are designed for a particular type of device (such as a graphics port). Other ports (such as USB) support different device types.

External ports are positioned at the rear or front of the PC through cut-outs in the case. They can be provided on the motherboard or with an expansion card.

 Teaching Tip

While not as widely used as they once were, learners should memorize these color codes.

 Show Slide(s)

I/O Ports and Cables

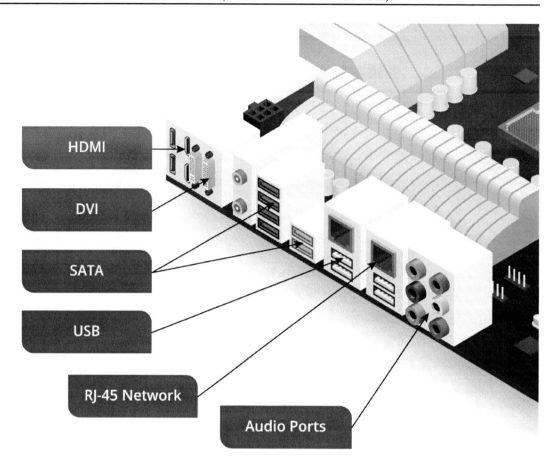

I/O ports on a motherboard. (Image © 123RF.com.)

USB CONNECTORS

Show Slide(s)

USB Connectors (4 slides)

Teaching Tip

Exam candidates need to remember information such as the differing data rates and connector types for each version of USB.

The **Universal Serial Bus (USB)** has become the standard means of connecting peripheral devices to a computer. It is an example of a multipurpose cable that can be used to attach a wide range of peripherals and storage devices.

 Note: USB has not historically been used as a display interface (to attach a monitor). That is changing as the USB-C connector (discussed later) is becoming more widely adopted.

A USB bus consists of a **host controller** and up to 127 devices.

 Note: To overcome the limitations of sharing bandwidth, most PC chipsets feature multiple USB controllers, each of which has only three or four ports.

A device can be a **hub** (providing ports for additional devices) or function. Functions are divided into classes, such as human interface (keyboards and mice), mass storage (disk drives), printer, audio device, and so on.

USB STANDARDS

There have been several iterations of the USB standard. Each new version introduces better data rates. A version update may also define new connector form factors and other improvements. The **USB 2.0 (HighSpeed) standard** specifies a data rate of 480 Mbps. Note that this bandwidth is shared between all devices attached to the same host.

The USB 3.0 standard introduces a **SuperSpeed mode**. SuperSpeed improves the bus bandwidth tenfold (to 5 Gbps or 5000 Mbps) and makes the link full duplex, so a device can send and receive at up to 5 Gbps simultaneously. USB 3.1 defines a **SuperSpeed+ mode** with a data rate of 10 Gbps. USB 3.2 promises 20 Gbps, but only over USB-C ports and cabling (discussed later).

Note: USB 3 controllers actually feature two sub-controllers. One controller handles SuperSpeed-capable devices while the other supports legacy HighSpeed, FullSpeed, and LowSpeed USB v1.1 and v2.0 devices. Consequently legacy devices will not slow down SuperSpeed-capable devices. There are changes to the way the bus works to try to improve "real-world" bandwidth too.

USB 3.x receptacles and connectors often have a blue connector tab or housing to distinguish them.

USB POWER

Power is supplied by the host at 5V and a single device may draw up to 500 mA (milli-amps) or 2.5 W (increased to 4.5 W with the USB 3.0 specification). Devices that require more power than this, such as printers, must be connected to an external power supply.

Note: Devices supporting fast charging can supply 7.5 W if the port is in charging mode (no data transfer is possible in charging mode). Devices conforming to the USB Power Delivery version 2.0 specification are able to deliver up to 100 W of power.

USB ON THE GO (OTG)

USB On the Go (OTG) allows a port to function either as a host or as a device. For example, a port on a smartphone might operate as a device when connected to a PC but as a host when connected to a keyboard.

USB CONNECTORS AND PORTS

USB connectors are *always* inserted with the USB symbol facing up. There have been several versions of the USB standard and these versions have often introduced new connector form factors.

The main connectors for USB 2.0 are:

- Type A (4-pin)—for connection to the host. The connector and port are shaped like flat rectangles.
- Type B (4-pin)—for connection to a device. The connector and port are square, with a beveled top. There are also small form factor versions of the type B connector and port:
  - Type B Mini (5-pin)—a smaller connector for connection to a device. This type of connector was seen on early digital cameras but is no longer widely used. The additional pin supports USB OTG.

    Note: There were also a number of non-standard mini B connectors used on various digital camera models.

  - Type B Micro (5-pin)—an updated connector for smaller devices, such as smartphones and tablets. The micro connector is distinctively flatter than the older mini type connector.

USB 2.0

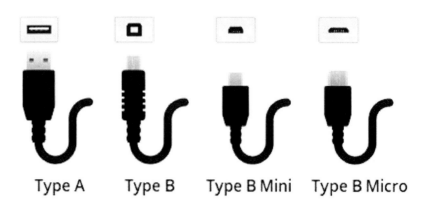

USB 2.0 ports and connectors. (Image © 123RF.com.)

A USB cable can feature Type A to Type A connectors but most convert from one type to another (Type A to Type B or Type A to Micro Type B for instance).

In USB 3.0, there are 9-pin versions of the Type A, Type B, and Type B Micro connectors. USB 3.0 Type A connections are physically compatible with USB 1.1 and 2.0 connections, but the Type B/Type B Micro connections are not. So, for example, you could plug a USB 2.0 Type A cable into a USB 3.0 port, but you could not plug a USB 3.0 Type B cable into a USB 2.0 Type B port.

USB 3.0 and 3.1

USB 3.0 and 3.1 connectors and ports (from left to right): Type A, Type B, Micro Type B, Type C. (Image © 123RF.com.)

As you can see, USB has historically featured a bewildering range of connector types. USB 3.1 defines a new USB-C 24-pin connector type. This should provide a single consistent hardware interface for the standard. The connector is reversible, meaning it can be inserted either way up. The connector design is also more secure and robust. USB-C can use the same type of connector at both ends or you can obtain USB-C to USB Type A or Type B converter cables.

CABLE LENGTH

The maximum cable length for LowSpeed devices is 3m while for FullSpeed and HighSpeed the limit is 5m. Vendors may provide longer cables however. SuperSpeed-capable cables do not have an official maximum length but up to about 3m is recommended.

OTHER PERIPHERAL CONNECTOR TYPES

USB is the dominant interface for PC peripherals, but you may also come across cabled devices requiring different connections.

Show Slide(s)
Other Peripheral Connector Types

THUNDERBOLT (TB)

The **Thunderbolt (TB)** interface was developed by Intel® and is primarily used on Apple® workstations and laptops. Thunderbolt® can be used as a display interface (like DisplayPort or HDMI) and as a general peripheral interface (like USB). In its first two versions, Thunderbolt uses the same physical interface as MiniDP and is compatible with DisplayPort, so that displays with a MiniDP port can be connected to a host via Thunderbolt. Thunderbolt ports are distinguished from MiniDP by a lightning bolt icon.

The USB-C form factor adopted for Thunderbolt 3. (Image © 123RF.com.)

Version 2 of the standard supports links of up to 20 Gbps. Up to six devices can be connected to a single port by daisy-chaining the devices. You can also use a dock or hub device to channel a variety of ports (TB, USB, HDMI, and Ethernet, for instance) via a single Thunderbolt port on the host PC or laptop.

Thunderbolt version 3 changes the physical interface to use the same port, connector, and cabling as USB-C. Converter cables are available to connect Thunderbolt 1 or 2 devices to Thunderbolt 3 ports. A USB device plugged into a Thunderbolt 3 port will function normally but Thunderbolt devices will not work if connected to a USB port that is not Thunderbolt-enabled. Thunderbolt 3 supports up to 40 Gbps over a short, high-quality cable (up to 0.5m/1.6ft).

LIGHTNING

Apple's iPhone® and iPad® mobile devices use a proprietary 8-pin **Lightning** port and connector. The Lightning connector is reversible (can be inserted either way up).

Apple Lightning connector and port. (Image © 123RF.com.)

The Lightning port is found only on Apple's mobile devices. To connect such a device to a PC, you need a suitable adapter cable, such as Lightning-to-USB A or Lightning-to-USB C.

SERIAL PORTS (RS-232 AND DB-9)

The **serial port** (or **RS-232**) is so-called because data is transmitted over one wire one bit at a time. Start, stop, and parity bits are used to format and verify data transmission. While modern interfaces like USB are also serial, an RS-232 interface uses much less sophisticated signaling methods. Consequently, an RS-232 serial port supports data rates up to about 115 Kbps only.

9-pin serial connector and port. (Image © 123RF.com.)

Serial ports are generally associated with connecting external modems, used to establish dial-up Internet connections, though even this function has largely been superseded by USB. You may also come across serial ports on network equipment, where a serial connection can be used to manage the device.

RS-232 (Recommended Standard #232) specifies a 25-pin hardware interface, but in practice, PC manufacturers used the cheaper 9-pin D-shell (**DB-9**) male port shown above.

In Windows®, the serial port is referred to as a **Communications (COM) port**.

Note: You might also come across the term PS/2. This was a serial interface used to attach mice and keyboards. PS/2 ports use a 6-pin mini-DIN format.

STORAGE CONNECTOR TYPES

USB and Thunderbolt are examples of multipurpose cables used to attach different kinds of external peripheral device (though it is also possible to use USB cabling within the system case). Internal storage devices use different types of interface, though.

- **SATA and eSATA connectors.**

    Serial Advanced Technology Attachment (SATA) is the standard means of attaching internal storage drives to a desktop PC. Each SATA host adapter port supports a single device.

    Internal SATA cables can be up to 1 m (39"). The cables are terminated with compact 7-pin connectors.

Show Slide(s)
Storage Connector Types (2 slides)

Teaching Tip
Use this section to provide a quick overview. Storage device capabilities and configuration is covered later in the course.

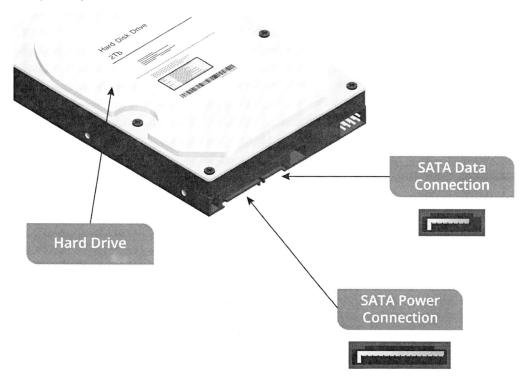

SATA data and power ports on a hard drive. (Image © 123RF.com.)

There is also an **eSATA standard** for the attachment of external drives, with a 2 m (78") cable. You must use an eSATA cable to connect to an external eSATA port; you cannot use an internal SATA cable. **eSATAp** is a non-standard powered port used by some vendors that is compatible with both USB and SATA (with an eSATAp cable). The USB interface dominates the external drive market, however.

Note: The main drawback of eSATA compared to USB or Thunderbolt external drives is that power is not supplied over the cable. This is not so much of an issue for 3.5" drives, which require a separate power supply anyways, but it limits the usefulness of eSATA for 2.5" portable drives.

- **SCSI.**

    Modern connection interfaces use serial communications. These serial links can achieve Mbps and Gbps speeds because of improved signaling and encoding methods. Back when serial interfaces were much slower, PC vendors used parallel data transmission to support better transfer rates. While a serial interface essentially transfers 1 bit at a time, a parallel interface transfers 8 bits (1 byte) or more. This requires more wires in the cable and more pins in the connectors, meaning parallel interfaces are very bulky.

Internal PC storage devices often used Parallel ATA (PATA)/Enhanced Integrated Drive Electronics (EIDE) connections. This supported transfer rates up to about 133 MBps. Workstations and servers requiring more speed would use the **Small Computer Systems Interface (SCSI)** bus instead. SCSI could support up to 320 MBps data rates. While you will not come across any new systems shipping with SCSI connections, you might need to support legacy systems that use SCSI.

SCSI could be used for both internal devices and external peripherals (such as scanners and printers) but you are very, very unlikely to find it used anywhere except for the connection of internal disk drives. While early SCSI types used 50-pin connectors, you are only likely to come across High Density (HD) 68-pin connectors or Single Connector Attachment (SCA) 80-pin connectors. SCA incorporates both a power connector and configuration wires, allowing for hot swappable drives.

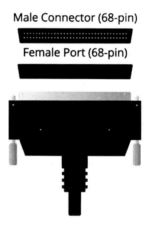

Internal and external male HD connectors. (Image © 123RF.com.)

Also, you should note that while parallel SCSI as a physical interface has almost completely disappeared, the software interface and command set are used in many other storage technologies, including Serial Attached SCSI (SAS), Firewire, and Storage Area Networks (SAN).

- **Molex connectors.**

As well as a data connection, an internal hard drive needs to be connected to the computer power supply. A computer power supply will come with a number of peripheral power connectors. For older devices, this power connection is made using **Molex connectors** and ports. A Molex connector is usually white and has 4 pins plus red, yellow, and black wires.

A Molex connector. (Image © 123RF.com.)

 Note: *SATA drives are more likely to use the SATA power connector. Some devices might have both types of power connectors.*

NETWORK CONNECTOR TYPES

Network connections also use dedicated cable types, rather than multipurpose cabling such as USB and Thunderbolt.

 **Show Slide(s)**

Network Connector Types

- **RJ-45.**

    Most computers have a network adapter already installed as part of the motherboard chipset. The network adapter will have an RJ-45 port to connect the computer to the network, via another RJ-45 port in the network equipment. This port will be marked "LAN" (Local Area Network).

    An **RJ-45 (Registered Jack) connector** is used with twisted pair cable for Ethernet local area networking products. Twisted pair is a type of copper cabling where pairs of insulated conductors are twisted around one another, to minimize electrical interference.

RJ-45 port and connector. (Image © 123RF.com.)

RJ-45 connectors are used with 4-pair (8-wire) cables. The connectors are also referred to as 8P8C, standing for 8-position/8-contact. This means that all eight "potential" wire positions are supplied with contacts, so that they can all carry signals if needed.

- **RJ-11.**

Smaller **RJ-11 connectors** are used with 2- or 3-pair UTP or with flat ribbon "silver satin" phone cables. Typically only one pair carries the dial tone and voice circuit (also called the Tip and Ring wires after the way older phono plugs were wired). The other pair is usually unused but can be deployed for a secondary circuit. RJ-11 connectors are used for telephone systems (for example, to connect a modem to a phone jack).

RJ-11 port and connector. (Image © 123RF.com.)

 Note: An RJ-11 connector only has two contacts (6P2C); to use more pairs, an RJ-14 (6P4C) connector is required. This is physically the same size as RJ-11 but has more wired contacts.

EXPANSION CARDS

 Show Slide(s)

Expansion Cards

 Teaching Tip

This course mentions only the expansion cards listed in the A+ Core 1 (220-1001) exam objectives. Remind learners that there are many other sorts of expansion cards available in today's marketplace. Also point out that video and sound cards are discussed in the next lesson.

Expansion cards (or add-on cards) can be installed on the motherboard to add functions or ports not provided as part of the chipset. An expansion card can be fitted to an appropriate slot (PCI or PCIe) on the motherboard.

- **I/O Adapters and Storage Cards.**

  Most Input/Output (I/O) bus functions are provided on the motherboard, which will typically have USB ports for external peripherals and SATA ports for internal storage drives. An adapter card can be installed to provide additional ports or a bus type that is not supported on the motherboard. Typical examples include an eSATA host adapter to make external storage ports available, a flash memory card reader, a card with extra USB ports, or a card supporting wireless peripherals, such as Bluetooth®.

- **Network Interface Cards (NICs).**

  Most computers have a network adapter already installed as part of the motherboard chipset. However, there may be occasions when you need to install an add-on Network Interface Card (NIC) or need to upgrade an adapter to use a different type of network, bandwidth, or cabling.

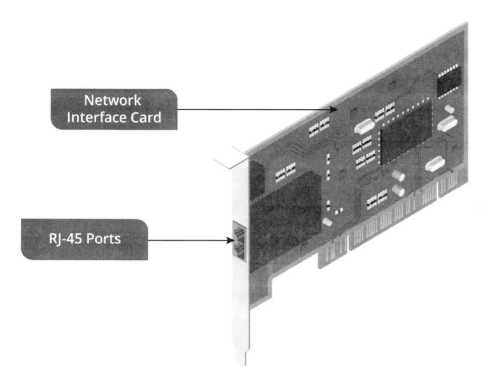

RJ-45 ports on a Network Interface Card (NIC). (Image © 123RF.com.)

A Wi-Fi adapter can be added to connect to a wireless network. Wi-Fi adapters are developed to different 802.11 standards (802.11a/b/g/n/ac).

*Note: To learn more, check the **Video** tile on the CHOICE Course screen for any videos that supplement the content for this lesson.*

Access the Checklist tile on your CHOICE Course screen for reference information and job aids on How to Install and Remove Expansion Cards.

Activity 2-3
Identifying Connection Interfaces

SCENARIO
Answer the following questions to check your understanding of the topic.

1. **In this graphic, identify the (A) audio ports, (B) video ports, and (C) USB ports.**

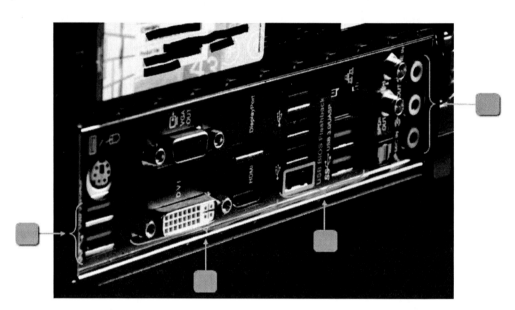

Moving from left to right, the components should be labeled: C, B, C, A.

2. **You are speaking with a junior technician. He is not sure what is meant by a "keyed" connector. Can you tell him?**

A keyed connector has a catch or slot to ensure that it cannot be inserted the wrong way round or used with an incompatible port.

3. **What is the nominal data rate of a USB port supporting SuperSpeed+?**

Normally 10 Gbps, but devices supporting USB 3.2 can use up to 20 Gbps over USB-C cabling.

4. **True or false? USB-C ports and cables are compatible with Apple Lightning ports and cables.**

False.

5.   **What type of device would you connect a Molex cable to?**

A Molex cable is a power cable. Normally, devices such as disk drives and optical drives require more power than can be delivered over the data bus. Note that most drives actually use SATA power connectors these days.

6.   **Why would you install an I/O adapter card?**

To make more or different kinds of ports available (SCSI, USB, or SATA typically).

Activity 2-4
Demonstrating PC Disassembly and Reassembly

Show Slide(s)

Activity: Demonstrating PC Disassembly and Reassembly

Teaching Tip

You might want to provide different PCs for the workbench-type activities than for the Hyper-V activities.

If you have a variety of PCs in the room, encourage learners to move to another desk and perform the same exercise on another PC. You might need to provide login credentials.

Also ask learners to check the installation of standard classroom PCs - note measures to prevent trip hazards, etc.

BEFORE YOU BEGIN

Your instructor will provide you with a WORKBENCH PC system to use to complete this activity. Make sure you find out the account credentials used to sign in. If a PC is not available for use in this activity, use the reference images provided instead.

You will perform this activity at your WORKBENCH PC.

SCENARIO

You are responsible for familiarizing new technical support staff on the hardware used by the company. You are going to show how to remove the PC case to compile information about the components installed to add to system inventory documentation.

---

1. Open a PC case and identify components on the motherboard.

   a) The PC should be powered off and cables to devices should all be disconnected. If not, shut down the PC then remove all the cables, starting with the power connector.

   b) Carefully lift the system unit onto your workbench and remove the system case cover.

   Use this image if you don't have a computer to open.

c)   Without touching anything inside the system unit, identify the following components. You can move cables if they obstruct your view, but be careful not to dislodge them from their connectors. If you do not have access to a PC, identify the location of components in the image above instead. You will not be able to see as much as with a physical inspection, so do not worry if you cannot identify exact numbers and types.

- CPU
- Memory slots (number and type—DDR3 or DDR4 for instance)
- Expansion slots (number of each type)
- Drive ports (number of each type)
- Power connectors (P1 and fans)
- RTC battery
- Front panel connectors

2.   **Draw a diagram showing the layout of the components you identified above.**

In the reference image, there are four DIMMs (DDR4 but the label is not legible), two of which are used. From top to bottom, the PCIe slots are x1, x16 (occupied by graphics adapter card), x4 (hard to see), and x16. There are two SATA ports on the right edge, connecting two HDDs. The card below them is an SSD connected to an M.2 port. There are actually two more SATA ports in the middle of the board, but these are obscured by the CPU heat sink—you can follow the cable back to the optical drive bay though. The RTC battery is just visible below the CPU, and learners should be able to make out the fan connections. The P1 connector is beneath the jumble of cables. Some of the front panel connectors on the bottom edge are easy to pick out from the cables. It isn't easy to identify their type, though (from left to right: audio in, USB, speaker). The connectors for another set of USB ports plus LED and power are beneath the cable ties.

3.   **Write down any problems you might suspect with the way the system is built (for example, cables not connected to devices, scorch marks, excessive dust or dirt, and so on).**

Responses will vary depending on the systems being examined.

4.   When you have finished, replace the system case cover.

5.   Identify the external ports.

Your system likely has a different number of ports, different ports, and different locations for some items. Use this image if you don't have a physical PC to examine.

6.   **What ports can you identify?**

USB 3 ports and plugs have blue tabs and usually an "SS" label for SuperSpeed. USB 2 ports and plugs are supposed to have white tabs but this is not so commonly observed. In the reference image, starting on the left there are two PS/2 ports (mouse and keyboard). Note that it is quite common for vendors to continue to include these on servers and workstations for use with KVM. Next to them is an RJ-45 port above two USB 2.0 ports. In the next block, there are two DP++ (DisplayPort) video ports and one DVI port. You haven't covered video ports yet, so don't worry if you can't identify the exact type. Next in the image are four USB 3 ports and finally the audio ports. The dedicated graphics adapter has a DVI and DP++ port.

7.   Demonstrate how to identify external ports on your WORKBENCH PC.

a)   Inspect the PC and complete the table below to show the number of available ports (remember that there could be connectors on the back and the front of the PC).

Port Type	Number/Notes
USB 2	
USB 3	
Thunderbolt (MiniDP or USB type)	
Network (RJ-45)	
Other (display connectors, for instance)	

b)   Check the ports carefully to ensure that none are damaged (for example, pins that are broken, bent, or missing or mounting bolts that are loose or missing).

8.   Check the case labeling for the following information (this would be used to obtain support):

Information	Details
Vendor (OEM)	
Model Number	
Serial Number/ Service Tag	

9.   Finally, demonstrate how to set up the PC for use again.

a)   If the cabling is fine, connect the devices in the following order, taking care not to damage the connectors and to secure them properly (note that some devices might not be available to you—check with your instructor if you are unsure):

•   Mouse
•   Keyboard
•   Display screen
•   Microphone and speakers
•   Display power plug
•   PC power plug

b)   Check the routing of cables so that there are no trip hazards. Optionally, adjust the monitor so that it is the correct height for use (the top edge should be at eye level).

c)   When your instructor has checked the system, press the power button to turn it on.

d)   As the PC powers up, listen and look for the following signs that the computer is operating normally.

•   Power LED comes on.
•   Fans start spinning.

- Hard disk activity—LED flickers and there may be some soft noise but grinding or clicking indicates a problem.
- System firmware messages on the screen—if you do not see anything, check the display is connected and switched on.
- Windows logo on the screen.

e) Verify that the keyboard and mouse work. Sign in to the PC using the credentials provided.

10. Your instructor might provide you with examples of device connections and interfaces and ask you or other participants to identify them.

 **Interaction Opportunity**

Consider displaying various examples of device connectors and interfaces, and ask participants to identify them. This can be an opportunity to generate discussion on the differences between the various types of connections and where they might be used.

Topic D

Install Peripheral Devices

EXAM OBJECTIVES COVERED
1001-3.6 Explain the purposes and uses of various peripheral types.

Much of the work that you will perform as a PC technician will involve installing and configuring various hardware and software components. As an IT professional, you will often find yourself setting up end-user workstations or helping those end users with the hardware they need to make their daily lives easier. Installing and configuring peripheral components—like keyboards and mice, or even more specialized devices—are some of the more common tasks that you will perform.

INPUT DEVICES

Show Slide(s)

Input Devices

Input devices—or **Human Interface Devices (HIDs)**—are peripherals that enable the user to enter data and select commands. Computers need user input such as directions or commands and user interaction with the programs that are included in order to produce something of use.

Keyboards and pointing devices are the standard input devices for personal computers these days, but there is an ever-growing number of input devices available for the user to interact with in a variety of ways. As well as command input, security systems often require different ways for users to input credentials to access an account or authorize a payment.

KEYBOARDS

Show Slide(s)

Keyboards (2 slides)

Interaction Opportunity

Poll learners to find out what types of keyboards they use.

The **keyboard** is the longest serving type of input device. Historically, keyboards were connected via the 6-pin mini-DIN PS/2 port. This is colored purple to differentiate it from the identical form factor mouse connector. All keyboards are now USB or wireless (typically Bluetooth), though.

Extended PC keyboards feature a number of special command keys (Alt and Ctrl plus keys such as Print Screen, NumLock, Scroll Lock, Start, Shortcut, and Function). A numeric keypad can be used to allow faster entry of numeric data or as an additional set of arrow keys (the function is toggled by NumLock). Multimedia keyboards may also feature programmable keys and buttons that can be used for web browsing, playing CDs/DVDs, and so on.

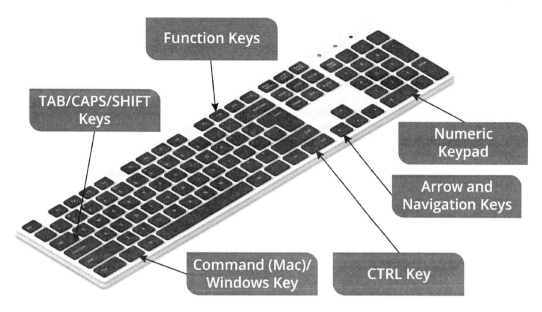

An extended keyboard. (Image © 123RF.com.)

When selecting a keyboard for a user, in addition to considering its ergonomics, you should also consider whether the keyboard offers additional features (such as customizable hot keys and scrolling) as well as wireless connectivity.

An ergonomic keyboard. (Image by Dmitriy Melnikov © 123RF.com.)

Most keyboards designed for use with Latin scripts use the QWERTY key layout. There are different layouts though, such as the small differences between US and UK layouts, the Dvorak alternative layout for Latin script, and keyboards for different scripts, such as Cyrillic. It is important that the keyboard type is set correctly in the OS.

In Windows, the type of keyboard layout is configured through the **Language** applet in Control Panel/Settings so that the computer knows which symbol to use when a particular key or key combination is pressed.

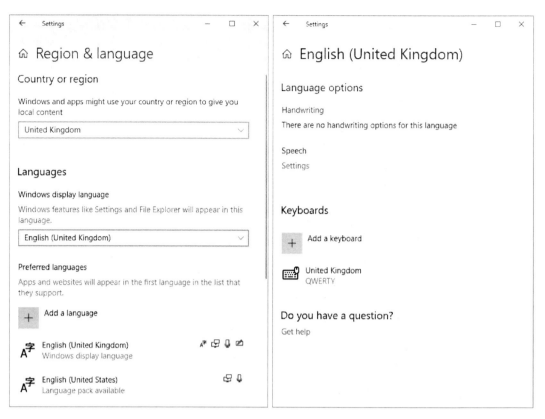

Language and input options in Windows 10.

POINTING DEVICES

Show Slide(s)

Pointing Devices (2 slides)

Interaction Opportunity

Again, poll learners to ask about the types of pointing devices they use.

While a keyboard can be used to navigate a window (using **Tab** and arrow keys, for instance), most operating systems are designed to be used with some sort of **pointing device**. A pointing device is usually used to move a cursor to select and manipulate objects on the screen.

MOUSE

The **mouse** is the main type of pointing device for graphical software. Mice use the same interfaces as keyboards (the PS/2 port for a mouse is color-coded green, though). There are three main types:

- Mechanical mouse—this contains rollers to detect the movement of a ball housed within the mouse case. As the user moves the mouse on a mat or other firm surface, the ball is moved and the rollers and circuitry translate that motion to move a cursor on the screen. Mechanical mice are no longer in production.
- Optical mouse—this uses LEDs to detect movement over a surface.
- Laser mouse—this uses an infrared laser, which gives greater precision than an optical mouse.

A basic mouse, with a scroll wheel and four buttons (two main buttons on top and two side buttons). (Image © 123RF.com.)

Another distinguishing feature of different mouse models is the number of buttons (between two and four), which can be customized to different functions, and the presence of a scroll wheel, used (obviously) for scrolling and as a clickable extra button. Mice are also distinguished by their size and shape. Smaller mice are useful with portable systems; some mice are marketed on the basis of their ergonomic shape.

TOUCHPAD

A **touchpad** is a small, touch-sensitive pad where you run your finger across the surface to send electronic signals to the computer to control the pointer on the screen. Touchpads can have buttons like a mouse or trackball, or the touch pad can be configured to detect finger taps on its surface and process those signals like button clicks.

Laptop Touchpad

Touchpad on a laptop. (Image © 123RF.com.)

Touchpads are most closely associated with laptop computers but it is possible to use them as peripheral devices with PCs, too. An external touchpad is connected using USB or Bluetooth.

GAME CONTROLLERS

PC games are mostly designed for use with the mouse and keyboard but some games (flight simulators, for instance) benefit from the use of a game controller, such as a **joystick** or **game pad**. There are also controllers for specific game types, such as steering wheels for driving games and light guns for shooting games. As with most other peripherals, wired game controllers are connected using USB, whereas wireless models use Bluetooth. Joysticks can also be used as input devices by people who have difficulty using a mouse or keyboard.

A game controller. (Image © 123RF.com.)

KVM SWITCHES

Show Slide(s)

KVM Switches

Interaction Opportunity

Ask why this is considered an input/output device, and point out that many KVM switches, particularly for servers using KVM over IP, still include PS/2 ports.

A **Keyboard, Video, Mouse (KVM) switch** allows multiple computers (typically servers) to be controlled via a single keyboard, mouse, and monitor. Some switches designed for home use also support speaker and microphone ports. Each computer's ports are cabled to the switch, then a single cable runs from the switch to the input and output devices.

A KVM switch with front and back views. (Image © 123RF.com.)

Simple desktop KVM switches support two devices; control is usually switched using a key sequence such as **Scroll Lock** + **Scroll Lock** + an arrow key (such as **Right Arrow**).

Server-level KVM switches may support 10 or more ports and have more sophisticated controls.

SECURITY INPUT DEVICES

Security input devices provide protection against unauthorized access to computing devices and resources. Commonly implemented security input devices include biometric devices and card readers.

Show Slide(s)

Security Input Devices (3 slides)

BIOMETRIC AUTHENTICATION DEVICES

Biometric devices are used to perform authentication. **Authentication** means identifying someone as a valid user of the computer or network.

Biometrics is an automated method of recognizing a person based on a physiological or behavioral characteristic unique to the individual, such as a retina pattern, fingerprint, or voice pattern. Biometric technologies are becoming the foundation of an extensive array of highly secure identification and personal verification solutions. Biometric input devices can add an additional layer of physical security or information security by verifying the identity of the person attempting to gain access to a location or device.

Biometric devices will need to be installed and configured, and then initialized for the specific end user who will be using the device. The initial biometric authentication "object" for the user (be it a fingerprint, retina scan, pass phrase, etc.) must first be captured and stored. Then the user will have to test the device to make sure that it accurately verifies his or her identity against the authentication object, permitting them access to the location or device.

Touching a fingerprint scanner. (Image © 123RF.com.)

Whether or not a biometric device is being deployed will likely be a decision made based on an organizational security policy or standard. If biometric devices will be deployed at individual workstations, you will need to determine the specific biometric device's connector requirements; as most use a USB connection, you will need to make sure that the user's computer has an available USB port to connect the device.

SMART CARD READERS

A **smart card reader** provides a slot or NFC (contactless) interface to interact with a **smart card**. The reader is typically a peripheral device attached via a USB port but may be built into some laptop models. The microprocessor embedded in the smart card is used to store a digital certificate to prove the identity of the holder. The use of the certificate token is combined with a PIN or password to protect against loss or theft.

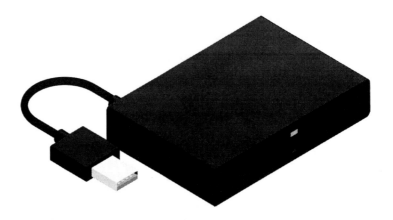

A smart card reader. (Image © 123RF.com.)

MAGNETIC STRIP/CHIP READERS

In the days before microprocessors could be made small enough to embed in a plastic wafer, the account number and other details of a credit or bank card were encoded in a magnetic strip. All bank-issued cards retain these magnetic strips for compatibility with legacy systems. When the card is swiped through a magnetic reader, the reader obtains the account details from the card. As with smart card readers, these would be attached as a USB peripheral.

A chip reader works in the same way as a smartcard reader but is designed to work specifically with bank cards to support Point of Sale (POS) systems.

NFC AND TAP PAY DEVICES

As mentioned above, a smart card can be contact-based or contactless. Many contactless readers use the **Near Field Communications (NFC) protocol**. NFC is a very short range radio link based on **Radio Frequency ID (RFID)**. NFC normally works at up to 2 inches (6cm) at data rates of 106, 212, and 424 Kbps.

As well as cards, NFC sensors are now often integrated with smartphones, allowing their use as a kind of "electronic wallet." As with a chip reader, an NFC/tap pay terminal would be attached to the computer via a USB cable as part of a POS system.

NFC mobile payment between a smartphone and a payment processor. (Image © 123RF.com.)

SIGNATURE PADS

Signature recognition uses a signature pad and a database of approved signatures. A user signs the signature pad, and the recognition system analyzes the individual behavior of the person signing, such as the strokes used and the pressure applied while signing, to verify the identity of the user.

If not hard-wired into a system (such as a security system), a signature capture pad used with a smaller device like a personal computer typically connects via a USB connection.

A signature pad and pen. (Image © 123RF.com.)

INSTALLATION AND CONFIGURATION CONSIDERATIONS

Peripheral devices for Windows computers are **Plug-and-Play**. This means that they can be added to the computer and the operating system will detect the device automatically and prompt you to configure it using a hardware or device setup wizard. Most devices also come with setup programs which will do the same job. They are required if the OS does not ship with the drivers required by the device.

 Show Slide(s)

Installation and Configuration Considerations (2 slides)

 Teaching Tip

Emphasize that it is a best practice to use the latest driver for a peripheral.

SYSTEM RESOURCES

When you install a new device, such as a network card, sound card, or internal modem into a PC, it must be allocated a set of **system resources** that enable it to communicate with the CPU and memory without conflicting with other devices. This process is handled by Plug-and-Play.

Resource	Description
Memory Range/I/O Address	Every device in the PC has its own set of unique memory addresses in an area called the **I/O address** map. The I/O address is a means for the CPU to communicate with a device. The address map is a block of system memory 65,536 bytes (64 KB) in size. The I/O port is referred to using its hexadecimal (or port) address in the range of 0000-FFFF.
Interrupts (IRQ)	An I/O address tells the CPU where to look in memory to communicate with a device, but it must also know when to communicate with it! This is accomplished by the device raising an **Interrupt Request (IRQ)**. Under the early PC architecture, each device was allocated an IRQ "line" from 0 to 15. Allocating the same IRQ to two devices was the cause of many problems on these early computers. Modern PCs use more advanced interrupt controllers to facilitate interrupts from multiple devices on a bus such as PCI or PCIe. Some core system components are still allocated IRQs from the 0 to 15 range, though.

HOT SWAP

Most devices connected over USB are hot swappable. This means that the device can be added to or removed from the computer while it is switched on. Devices attached via legacy interfaces may need the PC to be restarted.

 Note: *You may also see the term hot pluggable used. Technically, a hot pluggable device can be installed while the system is running but cannot necessarily be removed safely without shutting down the computer. A fully hot swappable device can be added or removed without an OS restart.*

DRIVERS

Before connecting a device, you may need to install its **driver** using the vendor-supplied software. A driver is software that creates an interface between the device and the operating system. It may also include tools for configuring and optimizing the device. Many devices have drivers that are shipped along with Windows or made available over Windows Update, but even in that case the vendor may be able to supply a more up-to-date driver. Output devices such as monitors and speakers do not generally require drivers, but input devices such as mice, keyboards, and touchscreens do.

CONNECTIONS

Assuming the correct driver is available to the OS, adding and removing external peripherals is then just a case of plugging or unplugging the connector into the correct type of socket. USB has simple push/pull connectors that are keyed to prevent incorrect insertion. Connectors for legacy ports often have screws to hold them in place. RJ-11 and RJ-45 connectors have a plastic clip that must be pressed down to remove.

CONFIGURATION

The OS will detect and install the device automatically. You can then use Device Manager, Control Panel, Windows Settings, or the vendor-supplied software to configure user settings.

GUIDELINES FOR INSTALLING PERIPHERAL DEVICES

Follow these guidelines for working with peripheral devices.

 Show Slide(s)

Guidelines for Installing Peripheral Devices

INSTALLING PERIPHERAL DEVICES

Here are some guidelines for you to consider when you are adding or removing peripheral devices:

- Always read the manufacturer's instructions and check that the device is compatible with the PC and operating system.
- Hold the connector, not the cable, when removing a lead.
- Inspect the connector and port for damage (notably broken or bent pins) before attaching a lead.
- Take care to align the connector carefully and do not use excessive force, to avoid damaging the pins.
- Check whether the device requires an external power source.

 *Note: To learn more, check the **Video** tile on the CHOICE Course screen for any videos that supplement the content for this lesson.*

 Access the Checklist tile on your CHOICE Course screen for reference information and job aids on How to Install and Remove Peripheral Devices.

Activity 2-5

Discussing Peripheral Device Installation

Show Slide(s)

Activity: Discussing Peripheral Device Installation

SCENARIO

Answer the following questions to check your understanding of the topic.

1. A remote user has requested a Dvorak keyboard for use with her Windows 10 computer. The device has arrived and the user connected it to a USB port. She contacts support saying that the keyboard "isn't typing properly."

    What is the likely cause of this issue?

    The appropriate keyboard layout has not been selected in **Settings**.

2. You are contacted by another remote user. The user has a laptop and desktop computer. The user wants to know if there is a device that would allow them to use the same peripheral devices with both systems without having to switch cables over all the time.

    What is your answer?

    Yes, you can use a Keyboard Video Mouse (KVM) switch for this purpose.

3. You are supporting a client setting up a Point of Sale system.

    Which peripheral device types or functions should she consider?

    A POS system reads the information stored on the customer's payment card or digital wallet. Historically, this information was stored in the card's magnetic strip. Most POS devices retain a magnetic reader as a backup mechanism. The majority of bank cards now also store the account information in an embedded chip, which can be read by inserting the card into the reader. This chip may also support contactless use or NearField Communications (NFC). A customer can also store the card details in a smartphone and use the smartphone's NFC chip to make payments. Not all POS readers support contactless and it would carry a slight price premium, so your client should decide whether it is important to offer this payment method to her customers.

4. You have finished copying some files to a USB memory stick.

    What should you do before unplugging the stick?

    Use the **Safely Remove Hardware** icon to stop the device.

Summary

In this lesson, you identified common safety procedures, core hardware components, and various connection interfaces, and you installed peripheral components.

Have you encountered situations where appropriate safety procedures were not followed? Which safety precautions do you think will be most important to follow?

A: Answers will vary depending on learners' experience and environment. In work areas with a lot of high voltage equipment, electrical safety issues should be paramount, while in work areas that contain a lot of computer equipment, ESD precautions might be deemed most important .

Will there be any specialty input devices that you will need to install or configure at your workplace? How might this affect your day-to-day activities as an IT professional?

A: Answers will vary according to the type of business where the individual works or expects to work. If the company has a great need for security, biometric devices may be incorporated at many key levels of entry, including computers. Specialty input devices might include touch screens, barcode readers, gamepads, or interactive whiteboards. Having knowledge of various types of devices, how they work, and how they are installed and configured will be necessary. Keeping up with evolving technology will likely be necessary as well.

 *Practice Question: Additional practice questions are available on the CompTIA CHOICE platform within the **Assessments** tile.*

Lesson 3

Installing, Configuring, and Troubleshooting Display and Multimedia Devices

LESSON INTRODUCTION

This lesson focuses on installing, configuring, and troubleshooting display and multimedia devices. The video and audio subsystems provide the main ways that information is output from the computer and presented to the user. Multimedia devices can also be used as inputs—to record sound from a microphone, import pictures from a scanner or camera, or capture video from a webcam.

LESSON OBJECTIVES

In this lesson, you will:

- Install and configure display devices.

- Troubleshoot display device issues.

- Install and configure multimedia devices.

Topic A

Install and Configure Display Devices

EXAM OBJECTIVES COVERED
1001-3.1 Explain basic cable types, features, and their purposes.
1001-3.5 Given a scenario, install and configure motherboards, CPUs, and add-on cards.
1001-3.6 Explain the purposes and uses of various peripheral types.

Output devices are those that transmit information from the computer system to the user, whether as video/graphics (display), audio (speakers), or hard copy (printer). The video subsystem is the main type of output provided with a PC. Graphics output is provided by some sort of display unit or monitor plus a video card, which generates the signals to drive the monitor.

DISPLAY DEVICE TYPES

Show Slide(s)

Display Device Types

Display devices include monitors, projectors, and VR headsets. You will work most often with monitors, as they are required by practically every desktop and portable computer.

Some notable manufacturers of display devices include ViewSonic®, Iiyama, Sony, Panasonic, Toshiba, LG, Acer®, Sanyo, and Mitsubishi.

MONITORS

Show Slide(s)

Monitors

Historically, computer monitors used the same sort of cathode ray tube (CRT) technology as consumer television sets. A CRT requires an analog signal from the display adapter to form the picture. CRTs are also very bulky. In the last decade or so, flat panel displays have replaced CRTs. Flat panels use digital signaling, are much thinner and lighter, and use less power than CRTs.

Teaching Tip

CRTs are no longer called out as a type of display device that learners need to know about for the exam, but some troubleshooting content examples refer to CRT-specific issues, so you might want to explain the term.

LCDs

Flat panel **Liquid Crystal Displays (LCDs)** are the standard display type for PC systems and laptops. Liquid crystals are chemicals whose properties change with the application of voltage. In modern types of LCD, voltages "twist" the molecules in the liquid crystal to block the passage of light to some degree to set the pixel to the required color.

Each picture element (pixel) in a color LCD comprises cells (or subpixels) with filters to generate the three primary colors (red, green, and blue). Each pixel is addressed by a transistor to vary the intensity of each cell, therefore creating the gamut (range of colors) that the display can generate. In the types of flat panel used for computer displays, the liquid crystal elements and transistors are placed on a **Thin Film Transistor (TFT)** and such LCD panels are often just referred to as "TFTs." TFTs designed for use with PCs are usually of two types:

- **Twisted Nematic (TN)**—produces acceptable results and good response times. Low response times make the display prone to motion blur and "trails."
- **In-Plane Switching (IPS)**—the different arrangement of the cells in IPS panels delivers better color reproduction at a wider range of viewing angles (especially vertical viewing angles) than TN-type displays. The trade-off is slightly worse response times.

TFTs are driven by a digital signal, but many older models come with analog-digital converters so they can accept an analog signal from an interface such as Video Graphics Array (VGA).

A desktop computer with a TFT display. (Image © 123RF.com.)

LCD BACKLIGHTS

A TFT panel must be illuminated to produce a clear image. In cheaper displays, the **backlight** is a **Cold Cathode Fluorescent (CCFL)** bulb. In most modern TFTs, the backlight is provided by an array of Light Emitting Diodes (LED) rather than a fluorescent bulb. There are a number of different types of LED lighting:

- Edge lit—the LEDs are arranged around the screen rather than behind it. A diffuser is used to try to make the light evenly bright across the whole of the screen.
- Backlit—the LEDs are positioned in an array behind the TFT. This should illuminate the panel more evenly. The disadvantage is that the panel will be slightly thicker. A full array LED backlight can also allow for local dimming, where the LEDs can be selectively dimmed in zones, improving contrast ratio (and power efficiency).
- Color temperature—the backlight can either generate a uniform white light (WLED) or be composed of some combination of RGB or GB LEDs, to allow for different color "temperatures."

OLED DISPLAYS

An **OLED (Organic LED)** display is a newer type of device, often used for small screens (in smartphones, for instance), though more full-scale OLED monitors are starting to appear. One advantage of OLED is that it does not require a separate backlight, making the representation of "True Black" much better and allowing the display to be thinner, lighter, and consume less power. Also, OLEDs can be made from plastic with no requirement for a layer of glass. This means that the display can be curved to different shapes. Manufacturers are even experimenting with flexible, roll-up displays.

DIGITAL PROJECTORS

A **video projector** is a large format display, suitable for use in a presentation or at a meeting. The image is projected onto a screen or wall using a lens system. Some types of projectors are portable; others are fixed in place.

Show Slide(s)
Digital Projectors

Teaching Tip
Point out that DLP relates to digital projectors.

A DLP projector. (Image © 123RF.com.)

Like display monitors, projectors can use different imaging technologies:

- Cathode Ray Tube (CRT)—you may come across legacy projectors using this analog format, but they are not widely marketed anymore.
- Liquid Crystal Display (LCD)—this is a similar technology to that used in display screens except that the lamp used to project the image is much more powerful than a backlight.
- **Digital Light Processing (DLP)**—developed by Texas Instruments. Each pixel in a DLP device is represented by a mirror, which can be tilted towards or away from the lamp, and color filters to create the required shade.
- Laser projector—a lampless projector still uses LCD or DLP imaging but replaces the bulb light source with laser light. Some systems use three lasers (red, green, and blue) while others use a single laser with splitters and phosphors to generate different shades.

Note: Take care when handling projectors. During use, the bulb becomes very hot and while it is hot will be very fragile. Allow a projector to cool completely before attempting to move it.

VR HEADSETS

A **Virtual Reality (VR) headset** is a device that fits over your eyes and ears. It aims to replace sights and sounds from the real world with images and noises generated by a computer application. The headset also comes with handheld controllers to allow you to move the avatar representing you in the virtual space and interact with the virtual environment.

VR is mostly used for games but has other obvious applications for meetings and social networking that is likely to see it more widely adopted in business networks in the next few years. There are two main types of headsets: **tethered VR headsets** are self-contained devices, whereas **mobile VR headsets** are designed to use a specific smartphone model (or range of models) to provide the display.

Tethered headsets, such as the HTC Vive® and Oculus Rift, require an HDMI port plus a number of USB ports on the host PC. While not current at the time of writing, it is likely that most systems will adopt a single USB-C cable in the near future. Tethered VR headsets have substantial system requirements for the CPU, graphics adapter, and system memory.

Note: Make sure the surrounding area is free from obstructions and trip hazards so that the wearer is less likely to hurt themselves or damage anything in the nearby environment.

DISPLAY DEVICE SETTINGS AND FEATURES

Display devices are evaluated on the following characteristics:

- **Resolution and analog versus digital output. Resolution** is the number of **pixels** (picture elements) used to create the image. Resolution is quoted as the number of horizontal and vertical pixels (for example, if the resolution is 640x480, the image is 640 pixels wide by 480 pixels high). Each pixel can be a different color. The total number of colors supported in the image is referred to as the **color depth** (or bit depth). Early (very early) computer monitors had limited color support, such as 8-bit (256 colors). Modern TFTs will support either 18-bit or 24-bit (or higher) color.

  A video card (the component that generates the screen image) can support a number of resolutions (limited by the card's bandwidth; higher resolutions require more data). If the resolution set is greater than the monitor's maximum resolution, then the display will be unstable or will not show anything.

  While **analog display** devices (such as legacy Cathode Ray Tube [CRT] monitors) can support a range of resolutions, **digital display** devices such as TFTs have a **native resolution**, based on the number of pixels in the display. An analog device such as CRT can support a number of output resolutions without losing quality (the "crispness" of an image). TFTs only support lower resolutions by interpolating the image, which makes it look "fuzzy."

- **Screen size and aspect ratio.** For flat panels, the quoted screen size is always the viewable area, measured diagonally. Most screens are around 20" but premium models are available up to 30." **Aspect ratio** is the width of the screen divided by the height. Flat panels are either 4:3 or widescreen (16:9 or 16:10), with widescreen models now dominating the market. One feature of some flat panels is the ability to pivot the display through 90 degrees (making it 3:4 or 9:16).

   Note: Consumer widescreen (for DVD movies) is 16:9, but many PC widescreen display formats are 16:10 to leave room for on-screen controls above or below the movie.

- **Refresh rate.** In an analog device, **refresh rate** is the speed at which the CRT redraws the image, measured in hertz (Hz). If the refresh rate is not high enough (below about 70 Hz), there will be a noticeable flicker as the image is redrawn. This can cause eyestrain and headache. TFTs are not refreshed in the same way and do not suffer from flicker, but the refresh rate in a TFT still has an impact on the quality of the image (in particular, how smoothly objects in motion are displayed).

  Whereas refresh rate is the number of times the display device updates the display (regardless of whether the image is changed or not), the **frame rate** is the number of times the image in a video stream changes per second. This can be expressed in Hertz or Frames per Second (fps). The refresh rate needs to be synched to the frame rate. For example, a display device with a 120 Hz refresh rate displays a 30 fps video stream at a ratio of 4:1. Standard TFTs have a refresh rate of 60 Hz with more expensive models featuring 120 or 240 Hz.

  Response rate is the time taken for a pixel to change color, measured in milliseconds (ms). The best quality TFTs have a response rate of 8 ms or lower. High response rates (over 20 ms) can lead to "ghosting" or "trails" when the image changes quickly.

- **Brightness, contrast ratio, and illuminance. Luminance** is the perceived brightness of a display screen, measured in candelas per square meter (cd/m²). Typically, TFTs are between 200 and 300 cd/m² though panels designed for home entertainment or gaming may be 500 cd/m² or better. **Contrast ratio** is a measure of luminance of white compared to black. Higher ratios (above 600:1) indicate that displays can display "true blacks" and better saturated (more intense) colors.

 Show
Slide(s)
Display Device Settings and Features

 Teaching
Tip
Exam candidates need to know the most common display types and the resolutions and color depths at which they can run.

When evaluating projectors, the critical performance factor is **illuminance** or light projecting power rather than luminance/brightness. With a flat panel, you want to evaluate how bright it appears when you look at it. With a projector, you want to evaluate the brightness of the image it projects onto another surface. Projectors are normally rated in lumens (or more specifically ANSI lumens, which represents a particular set of test conditions). A projector rated at around 3000 lumens will be able to display clear images with a small amount of ambient light (a room with the curtains closed and overhead lighting dimmed, for instance). A projector rated at 6000 lumens would be able to display a clear image in a sunlit room. Do note that the larger the image, the greater the projecting power needs to be to maintain the same image clarity.

- **Viewing angle and privacy filters.** The image on a flat panel darkens and distorts to some degree if not viewed straight on. Although this is not an issue for desktop use, it can affect use of the screen for viewing movies or as a presentation device. Manufacturers may quote acceptable viewing angles in marketing literature, but these values are not usually comparable to one another. As mentioned above, IPS-type flat panels perform better at wide angles than TN-type panels.

  A **privacy filter** prevents anyone but the user from reading the screen. IPS-type TFTs are designed to be viewed from wide angles. This is fine for home entertainment use but raises the risk that someone would be able to observe confidential information shown on a user's monitor. A privacy filter restricts the viewing angle to the person directly in front of the screen.

- **Coatings.** A display can come with either a matte or a gloss coating. A **gloss coating** helps the display to appear "richer" but also reflects more light, which can cause problems with screen glare and reflections of background objects. A **matte coating** may be superficially less impressive but is generally better suited to office work. **Antiglare covers** are available if the ambient lighting causes problems with the display.

VGA STANDARDS

Show Slide(s)
VGA Standards

IBM® created **Video Graphics Array (VGA)** as a standard for the resolution and color depth of computer displays. VGA specifies a resolution of 640x480 with 16 colors (4-bit color) at 60 Hz. VGA also specifies other lower resolution modes with more colors, but 640x480 is what is commonly referred to as "VGA."

Increasing any one of resolution, color depth, or refresh rate increases the amount of bandwidth required for the video signal and the amount of processing that the CPU or Graphics Processing Unit (GPU) must do and the amount of system or graphics memory required.

The VGA standard is long obsolete but was further developed by the Video Electronics Standards Association (VESA) as **Super VGA (SVGA)**. SVGA was originally 800x600 @ 4-bit or 8-bit color. This was very quickly extended as the capabilities of graphics cards and monitors increased with the de facto XGA standard providing 1024x768 resolution, better color depths, and higher refresh rates. Resolutions for modern display systems use some variant of the XGA "standard" (in fact, these are labels rather than standards) or a High Definition (HD) resolution, similar to that found on consumer electronics and media. Some of the more popular XGA and HD resolutions in use are as follows.

Standard	Resolution	Aspect Ratio
WXGA (Widescreen XGA)	1280x800	Widescreen (16:10)
SXGA (Super XGA)	1280x1024	5:4
HD	1366x768	Widescreen (16:9)
WSXGA	1440x900	Widescreen (16:10)
HD+	1600x900	Widescreen (16:9)

Standard	Resolution	Aspect Ratio
Full HD	1920x1080	Widescreen (16:9)
QHD (Quad HD)	2560x1440	Widescreen (16:9)
4K UHD (Ultra HD)	3840x2160	Widescreen (16:9)

DISPLAY DEVICE CONNECTIONS AND CABLES

There are many different types of video connectors and cabling. An individual model of any one video card, monitor, or projector will often support more than one cable type. When computers were primarily used with CRT monitors, the graphics adapter would generate an analog video signal to drive the monitor. Now that most screens use TFT technology, the video signal is usually digital. Many digital monitors can take an incoming analog video signal but need to convert it back to digital (so the signal is being converted from digital to analog and then from analog back to digital).

VGA PORTS AND CONNECTORS

The distinctive blue, 15-pin **Video Graphics Array (VGA) port** (HD15F/DE-15) was the standard analog video interface for PC devices for a very long time. Up until a few years ago, even new video cards and monitors usually included it, though it is starting to be phased out completely now.

The connector is a D-shell type (HD15M) with screws to secure it to the port. The screws very frequently become stuck or the housing bolt comes undone when you try to unscrew the connector.

Show Slide(s)
Display Device Connections and Cables

Teaching Tip
Point out that most interfaces now use digital, rather than analog, signaling.

Show Slide(s)
VGA Ports and Connectors

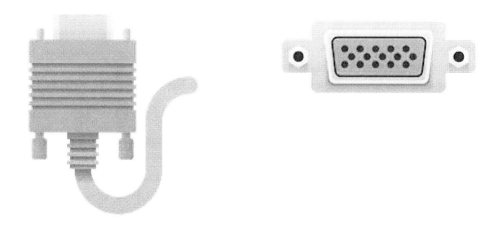

A VGA connector and port. (Image © 123RF.com.)

The interface is analog, meaning that it carries a continuous, variable signal for Red, Green, and Blue (RGB) component video.

Better quality cables (generally speaking, the thicker the better) use shielded coaxial wiring and support longer lengths at better resolutions. Low quality cable may only be able to support 800x600. The cable may be marketed with the highest resolution it can support—UXGA (1600x1200), for instance. Most VGA cable does not exceed 5 m but a good quality cable might be able to support sub-HD resolutions at lengths of up to 30 m.

**Show
Slide(s)**

DVI Ports and
Connectors (2 slides)

DVI PORTS AND CONNECTORS

Digital Visual Interface (DVI) is a video cable type designed for flat panel display equipment. While popular for a short period after its introduction in 1999, DVI is now being phased out in favor of better-established technologies, such as HDMI®, DisplayPort™, and Thunderbolt™. You are unlikely to see DVI used on new display devices or computers.

There are five types of DVI, supporting different configurations for bandwidth and analog/digital signaling. The pin configuration of the connectors identifies what type of DVI is supported by a particular port.

- DVI-A
- DVI-D (single link)
- DVI-I (single link)
- DVI-D (dual link)
- DVI-I (dual link)

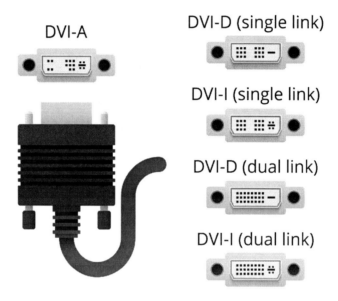

DVI port and connector types. (Image © 123RF.com.)

DVI-I supports both analog equipment (such as CRTs) and digital. DVI-A supports only analog equipment and DVI-D supports only digital.

DVI bandwidth in single-link mode is 3.7 Gbps, enough for full HD resolution (1920x1200) at a frame rate of 60 fps. More bandwidth can be obtained through connectors that support dual-link mode. Dual-link supports over 7.4 Gbps, enough for HDTV @ 85 fps. A single-link connector can be plugged into a dual-link port, but not vice versa.

There are economy and premium brands of DVI cable. Cables have to support an HD signal at a length of at least 5 m (16.5 ft). Better quality cable will support longer lengths. The quality cable uses thicker wiring and better shielding.

HDMI PORTS AND CONNECTORS

**Show
Slide(s)**

HDMI Ports and
Connectors (2 slides)

The **High Definition Multimedia Interface (HDMI)** is the most widely used graphic device interface. It is ubiquitous on consumer electronics, such as televisions and Blu-ray players, as well as computer equipment. HDMI supports both video and audio digital streams, plus remote control (CEC) and digital content protection (HDCP).

Note: *HMDI carries only a digital signal. It does not support analog monitors.*

HDMI cabling is specified to different HDMI versions with different bandwidth capabilities. Notably, version 1.4 adds support for 4K (4096x2160@24Hz). 4K is the format used in digital cinemas and consequently represents something of a Holy Grail for home cinema enthusiasts. The Ultra HD (3840x2160) format is often also branded "4K."

Version 1.4 also allows the controller (typically a computer) and display device (an IP-capable TV, for instance) to establish a Fast Ethernet (100 Mbps) network link over an HDMI With Ethernet cable.

At the time of writing, HDMI is on version 2.1. This supports 48 Gbps bandwidth, or up to 10K at 120 Hz.

HDMI uses a proprietary 19-pin (Type A) connector. There is a Type B connector (29-pin) to support dual-link connections but it is not widely used.

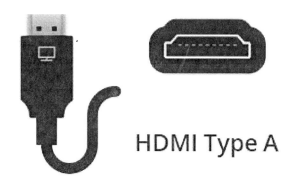

HDMI Type A port and connector. (Image © 123RF.com.)

HDMI v1.3 introduced the Mini HDMI connector (Type C) for use on portable devices, such as camcorders. This is more compact but has the same number of pins. HDMI v1.4 also introduced the even smaller Micro HDMI connector (Type D), still with 19 pins.

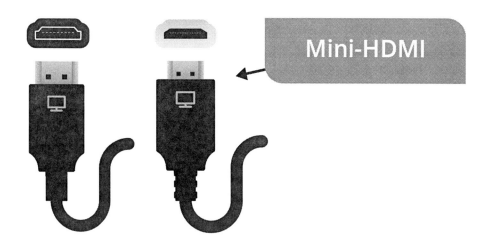

From left to right: HDMI connector and port, Mini-HDMI connector and port. (Image © 123RF.com.)

HDMI cable is rated as either Standard (Category 1) or High Speed (Category 2). High Speed cable supports greater lengths and is required for v1.4 features, such as 4K and

3D. HDMI version 2.0 and 2.1 specify Premium High Speed (up to 18 Gbps) and Ultra High Speed (up to 48 Gbps) cable ratings.

HDMI is backward-compatible with DVI-D using a suitable adapter cable. This means that (for example) a DVI-D graphics adapter could be connected to an HDMI port on the display device.

DISPLAYPORT PORTS AND CONNECTORS

Show Slide(s)

DisplayPort Ports and Connectors (2 slides)

Teaching Tip

DisplayPort is being replaced by Thunderbolt and USB-C.

HDMI was principally developed by consumer electronics companies (Hitachi, Panasonic, Sony, and so on) and requires a royalty to use. **DisplayPort** was developed by the Video Electronics Standards Association (VESA), the organization largely representing PC graphics adapter and display technology companies. It is a royalty-free standard intended to complement HDMI.

Unlike other video and audio standards, it transmits packetized data, in the same sort of way as PCI Express. Like PCI Express, bandwidth can be allocated in bonded lanes (up to 4). Each lane can be given a different data rate. In v1.2 of the standard, each lane can be allocated a 1.62, 2.7, or 5.4 Gbps data rate. The maximum data rate for a 4-lane link is 17.28 Gbps. Like HDMI v1.4, there is support for 48-bit color, 3D, 4K/UHD, and HDCP. There is also an auxiliary channel that allows (for example) a microphone-enabled display to feed the audio signal back to the PC without additional cabling.

DisplayPort supports both copper and fiber-optic cabling. DisplayPort-certified copper cable must be capable of supporting 2560x1600 (WQXGA resolution) over 2 m. It also supports multiple monitors "daisy-chained" on the same cable.

A DP++ DisplayPort port and connector. (Image © 123RF.com.)

DisplayPort uses a 20-pin connector. A DP++ port allows a connection with DVI-D and HDMI devices (using a suitable adapter cable). There is also a mini DisplayPort format (MiniDP or mDP), developed by Apple and licensed to other vendors.

THUNDERBOLT AND USB-C PORTS AND CONNECTORS

Show Slide(s)

Thunderbolt and USB-C Ports and Connectors

Historically, computer video used dedicated cable types such as HDMI or DisplayPort. Modern computer display equipment is quickly adopting the USB-C connector interface. USB-C can carry HDMI or DisplayPort signaling (with an adapter cable) but would usually be used with Thunderbolt 3 signaling for video support.

A USB-C connector with Thunderbolt 3 support. (Image © 123RF.com.)

 Note: Not all USB-C ports support Thunderbolt 3. Look for the flash icon on the port or confirm using the system documentation.

VIDEO ADAPTERS AND CONVERTERS

Many video cards provide support for older display standards. It might be that the video card itself is quite old but it can be useful for newer video cards to support interfaces that might only be found on older monitors and projectors. If there is no port common to both the computer and the monitor, you may be able to use a converter or adapter cable to connect them.

It will often be the case where the graphics adapter comes with a physical interface that is not supported by the display device. In this scenario, you can use a converter cable or adapter plug to connect the devices:

DVI TO HDMI

DVI is not supported on many consumer devices so you may use this type of adapter to connect a laptop to a TV set. There is no signal conversion involved so this can be performed by a passive cable.

 Show Slide(s)

Video Adapters and Converters (2 slides)

 Teaching Tip

Emphasize the difference between an adapter and a converter. Adapters solve the problem of incompatible cables, whereas converters solve the problem of incompatible signals.

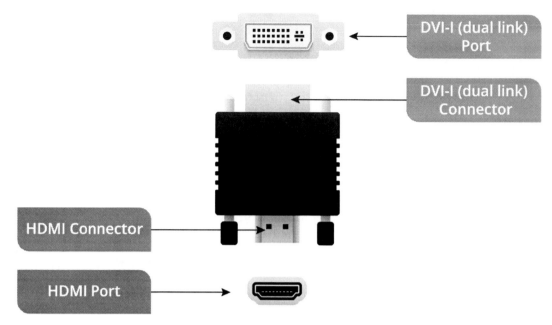

HDMI to DVI-I adapter. (Image © 123RF.com.)

DVI OR HDMI TO VGA

Older flat panels may only come with VGA ports so this type of converter can be used to connect them up to newer computing devices. Unless going from DVI-I (analog) to VGA, this type of converter requires an active Digital to Analog Converter (DAC) chip. Note that the converter will not be accepted by HDCP-protected content.

For instance, a VGA to DVI-I adapter would carry an analog signal only, while an HDMI to VGA converter cable converts between digital and analog inputs or outputs.

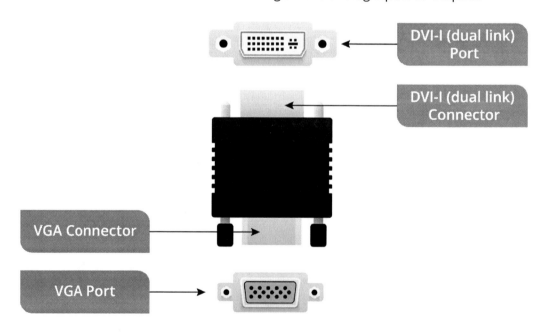

VGA to DVI-I adapter. (Image © 123RF.com.)

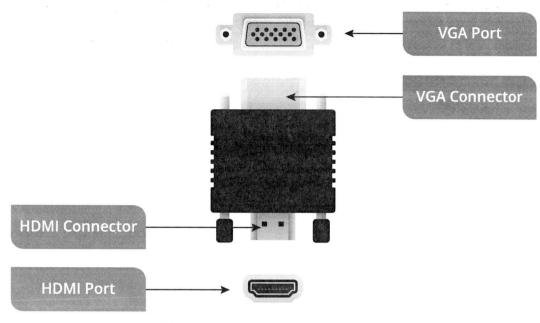

HDMI to VGA adapter. (Image © 123RF.com.)

DISPLAYPORT/THUNDERBOLT TO DVI

This type of adapter would allow you to connect a computing device of a "certain age" to newer display devices (or vice versa). No signal conversion is involved so only a simple passive cable with appropriate connectors on each end is required.

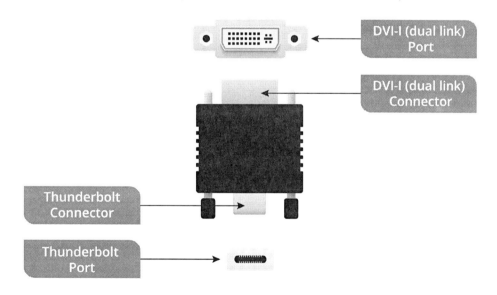

A Thunderbolt to DVI-I adapter. (Image © 123RF.com.)

VIDEO CARDS

The **video card** (or **graphics adapter**) generates the signal to send to the monitor or projector. The video card may make use of the system CPU and memory, but most add-in cards are highly sophisticated pieces of equipment, essentially computers in their own right.

 Note: *Be aware that the terms video, graphics, and display are used interchangeably to refer to these adapters (or cards).*

 Show Slide(s)
Video Cards

 Teaching Tip
Point out that top-end graphics adapters can be almost as expensive as CPUs.

Low-end graphics adapters are likely to be included with the motherboard chipset or as part of the CPU itself. This is also referred to as an **onboard adapter**. If a computer is to be used for 3D gaming, Computer Aided Design (CAD), or digital artwork, a better quality adapter is required. This can be installed as an **add-on card** via a PCIe slot. Most graphics adapters are based on chipsets by ATI/AMD (Radeon chipset), NVIDIA (GeForce and nForce chipsets), SiS, VIA, and Intel.

ADAPTER COMPONENTS

Show Slide(s)

Adapter Components

Teaching Tip

A high-end card is really only required for games, though even some office applications now have quite demanding graphics requirements. A low spec (integrated) adapter is the hallmark of all the cheap systems out there.

The core of a video adapter is the **Graphics Processing Unit (GPU)**. This is a microprocessor like the CPU, but designed and optimized for processing instructions that render 2D and 3D images on-screen. High-end cards are differentiated based on the following features:

- **Clock speed**—as with the CPU, the clock speed is the basic measure of performance, but the internal architecture (pipeline) of the GPU is another important factor.
- **Shader units**—support the special effects built into games and other software. These units perform calculations that allow for 3D shading, realistic shadows and lighting, surface textures, translucency, and so on.
- **Frame rate**—the basic test for a GPU is the frame rate it can produce for a particular game or application. 25 fps is about the minimum to make a game playable.

3D cards need a substantial amount of memory for processing and texture effects. A dedicated card may be fitted with up to 12 GB GDDR RAM at the high-end; around 2 GB would be more typical of current mid-range performance cards. The width and speed of the memory bus between the graphics RAM and GPU are also important. Low end cards use shared memory (that is, the adapter uses the system RAM). Some cards may use a mix of dedicated and shared memory.

Note:

Graphics Double Data Rate (GDDR) memory technology is similar to the DDR modules used for system RAM.

Most modern cards use a PCIe x16 interface. Dual cards, using two (or more) slots, are also available. With NVIDIA cards, this is accomplished using Scalable Link Interface (SLI); AMD/ATI dual cards are branded CrossFire.

SUPPORT FOR DISPLAY INTERFACES

Modern cards will support at least one digital interface (DVI, HDMI, DisplayPort, or Thunderbolt). Some cards may support other interfaces, such as VGA, but such support for analog display interfaces is increasingly unlikely. Having multiple connectors on the card also allows for the attachment of multiple display devices, even if the connectors are different types.

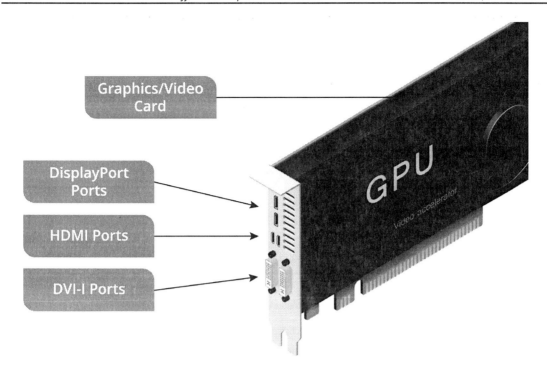

A video/graphics card with DisplayPort, HDMI, and DVI-I ports. (Image © 123RF.com.)

GRAPHICS APIs

To work with 3D games and design applications, graphics cards need to be compliant with the specified version of one of the major graphics application programming interfaces (APIs):

- DirectX®—Microsoft's specification. DirectX also specifies sound and multimedia APIs.
- OpenGL®—developed by Silicon Graphics.

CONFIGURATION TOOLS FOR DISPLAY DEVICES

Once the adapter card has been installed and the monitor connected via a suitable cable, Windows should detect the devices and make them available for use via Plug and Play.

If the computer has an onboard adapter, you may need to disable it via the system setup (BIOS) program after installing an add-on card. In some cases though, the utility supplied with the adapter will support selecting the default input and specifying use of a particular adapter for a particular task or process.

Basic display settings, such as the resolution, can be configured via a built-in operating system tool, such as Windows Settings or Windows Control Panel. Alternatively, an adapter card might ship with a dedicated management utility. You would normally access this via an icon in the notification area.

Show Slide(s)

Configuration Tools for Display Devices

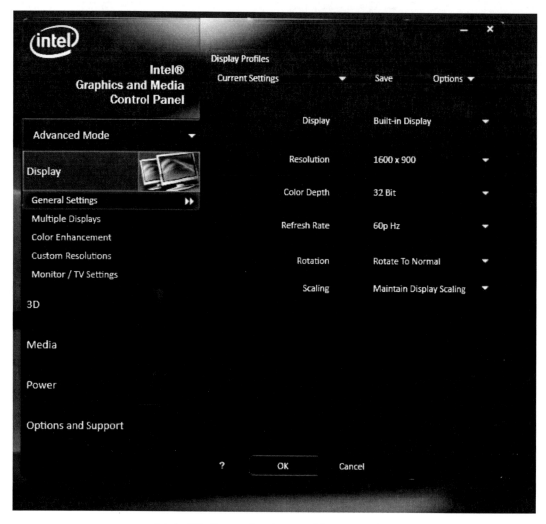

Intel utility for configuring graphics properties.

You may also need to use controls on the monitor itself to adjust the image or select the appropriate input channel. For example, if there is no image on the screen, check that the monitor is set to use the HDMI port that the computer is connected to, rather than an empty DVI port. These **On-Screen Display (OSD)** menus are operated using buttons on the monitor case. As well as input control, you can usually find settings for brightness, color/contrast, and power saving.

MULTIPLE DISPLAYS

Show Slide(s)

Multiple Displays (2 slides)

Interaction Opportunity

Ask learners what they like about using multiple display devices on their PCs.

A computer can be set up to use two (or more) display devices. In terms of hardware, the PC requires a graphics adapter with multiple display ports, multiple graphics adapters, or monitors with input and output DisplayPort or Thunderbolt connectors for daisy-chaining.

 Note: The adapter and monitors must support Multi-Stream Transport (MST) to use daisy chaining. To set up the chain, connect the first cable from the graphics adapter port to the "IN" port on the first monitor. Connect a second cable from the "OUT" port on the first monitor to the "IN" port on the second monitor.

Dual monitors can be used in one of three modes, configured via Windows display properties:

- Display the same image on both devices—select the **Duplicate these displays** option (this mode is useful for delivering presentations).

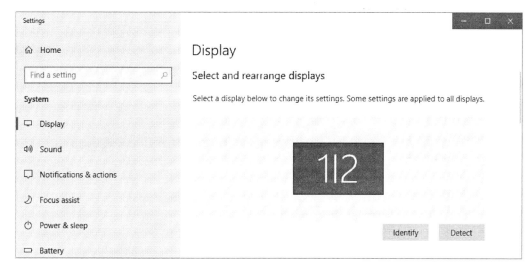

Configuring dual monitors in Windows 10 to duplicate the display. (Screenshot used with permission from Microsoft.)

- Display the desktop over both devices—select **Extend these displays** (this mode makes more screen "real estate" available and is useful for design, publishing, and programming work). Drag the displays in the box to position them correctly. You can put them to the left and right or above and below one another.

Configuring dual monitors in Windows 10 to extend the display. (Screenshot used with permission from Microsoft.)

- Display the desktop on one device only—select either **Show only on 1** or **Show only on 2**.

*Note: In Windows 10, you can select a multi-monitor mode quickly using **Windows** + **P**. This causes a prompt to appear on the right side of the primary display listing the options **PC screen only**, **Duplicate**, **Extend**, and **Second screen only**.*

*Note: To learn more, check the **Video** tile on the CHOICE Course screen for any videos that supplement the content for this lesson.*

Access the Checklist tile on your CHOICE Course screen for reference information and job aids on How to Install and Configure Display Devices.

Activity 3-1

Discussing Display Device Installation and Configuration

SCENARIO

Answer the following questions to check your understanding of the topic.

1. Look at the following exhibit.

   What two types of display cabling can be connected to this laptop?

   The image shows a VGA port and an HDMI port (with an RJ-45 network port between them). The USB ports could be used for a portable monitor.

2. **Which ports are present on the graphics card shown below?**

   The port on the left is DVI-I and the one on the right is DisplayPort.

3. **Which interfaces does the adapter cable shown below support?**

   DVI-I (left) and HDMI.

4. **A customer is shopping for a computer game for her daughter and wants to know if you can explain the reference to "DirectX" on the packaging?**

DirectX is Microsoft's API (Application Programming Interface) for 3D and multimedia applications. Software such as a computer game will specify a minimum DirectX version. The graphics card must support this version to run the game. Vendors often provide support through driver updates, even for older card models.

5. You are configuring two monitors in extended desktop mode.

What should you configure in the Display dialog box?

Ensure the layout of the displays in the dialog box matches their physical location.

Activity 3-2
Installing a Graphics Adapter

Show Slide(s)

Activity: Installing a Graphics Adapter

Teaching Tip

Run whichever of the tasks are best suited to the equipment you have available.

If you have the equipment available, ask learners to look at multi-monitor configuration options, such as daisy-chaining monitors.

BEFORE YOU BEGIN

What you do in this activity will depend on the components available to you. Check with your instructor which of the following steps you should perform.

You will perform this activity on your WORKBENCH PC.

SCENARIO

A common upgrade on machines used for playing games or doing Computer Aided Design or graphics intensive work is to upgrade the graphics adapter. Another upgrade that can be performed is to add a second adapter to the system so that two monitors can be used. This requires that both adapters support dual displays.

---

1. Record information about the graphics adapter make and model currently installed, including the driver version.

    a) Start and log on to the PC then press the **Windows+X** keys and select **Device Manager**.

    b) In **Device Manager**, expand the **Display adapters** node, and record the installed adapter name.

    • Adapter make and model: _____

    If there are multiple display adapters, record information about all of them.

    c) Right-click the adapter and select **Properties**. Select the **Driver** tab, then record the **Driver Provider** and **Driver Version** information.

    • Driver provider: _____

    • Driver version: _____

    Again, if there are multiple display adapters, do this for each of them.

2. Access the PC's internal components safely.

    a) Shut down the PC and then disconnect the power cable and all peripheral cables. Take the usual ESD precautions.

    b) Remove the system case cover.

3. Complete this step or one of the next two steps, as suggested by your instructor.

    a) If your system has onboard graphics, identify a free expansion slot that will accommodate the type of adapter you are installing.

    b) Remove the blanking plate from the slot.

    c) Insert the card into the slot, checking carefully to make sure that it is properly seated and that any locking catches are in place.

4. Complete this step, the previous step, or the next step, as suggested by your instructor.

    a) Remove your existing adapter (remember that there may be a plastic clip to release as well as the mounting screw).

    b) Swap adapters with a classmate, and install the new one.

5. Complete either this step or one of the previous steps, as suggested by your instructor.

a) Install a second graphics adapter alongside your existing one.

A second graphics adapter can be installed so that two monitors can be used at the same time. This type of setup is favored by graphics professionals where having lots of screen "real estate" is extremely productive. It can also be used with presenting software.

 Note: Another use for twin adapters is for high performance gaming systems where two cards are installed to double performance. Another dual-monitor option is to obtain a "multi-head" card with two or more outputs.

6. Verify the installation and configure display settings.

a) Close the system case.

b) Reconnect the peripheral devices. When connecting the display, make sure you connect the cable to a display port on the new adapter, if you installed a second adapter alongside an integrated one or existing card.

c) Reconnect the power cable and start the PC.

d) When the PC reboots, the new adapter should be detected automatically. If it is not, install the driver software that comes with the card.

e) Right-click the **Desktop** and select **Display settings**. Select the **Advanced display settings** link, and record the following information:

- Refresh rate: _____
- Bit depth: _____

f) Select the **Display adapter properties** link. Record the following information:

- Chip type: _____
- Total Available Graphics Memory: _____
- Dedicated Video Memory: _____

g) Select **List All Modes** to list the combinations of resolution and refresh rate supported by the monitor.

h) Select **Cancel** to close each dialog box.

i) In the **Settings** app, select the **Back** button.

j) Experiment with different text DPI settings by using the **Change the size of text** list box.

These are useful on very high resolution monitors where the on-screen menus can look very small as the default setting (96 dpi).

k) If you installed a second display adapter, configure the display across the two monitors, experimenting with the options available. When you have finished, set the display back to one monitor. Disconnect the second monitor and connect it back onto the other PC.

7. At the end of the activity, if you installed a second adapter, open the computer and remove it then hand it back to your instructor. Revert any other changes as suggested by your instructor.

Topic B

Troubleshoot Display Devices

EXAM OBJECTIVES COVERED
1001-5.4 Given a scenario, troubleshoot video, projector, and display issues.

As well as installing and configuring display devices, you also need to know how to identify and resolve issues related to using them.

COMMON DISPLAY ISSUES

Show Slide(s)
Common Display Issues

Interaction Opportunity
Ask learners to share other examples of display issues.

Common display issues include:

- No image is displayed on the monitor.
- Image is dim.
- Image flickers or is distorted.
- Images have low resolution or color depth.
- Images and icons are oversized.
- Incorrect color patterns.
- Dead pixels.
- Image is burned into the monitor.
- Unexpected objects or patterns appear on the monitor.
- Overheating.
- Protected content.

GUIDELINES FOR TROUBLESHOOTING DISPLAY DEVICES

Show Slide(s)
Guidelines for Troubleshooting Display Devices (3 slides)

*Note: All of the Guidelines for this lesson are available as checklists from the **Checklist** tile on the CHOICE Course screen.*

Here are some guidelines to follow to help troubleshoot display devices.

TROUBLESHOOT DISPLAY CONFIGURATION ISSUES

Follow these guidelines when you are troubleshooting display device configuration issues:

- **No image.** If no image is displayed on the monitor, try these actions:
  - Make sure that the monitor is plugged in and turned on. Check that the monitor is not in standby mode (press a key or cycle the power to the monitor to activate it).
  - Check the connection between the video card and monitor. Make sure the cable is connected securely at both ends and is not loose. Make sure that the cable has not become stretched or crimped. If there are dual display ports, check that the cable is connected to the right port.
  - If the monitor supports different display inputs (VGA and HDMI, for instance), check that it is switched to the correct one using the On-Screen Display (OSD) controls.
  - Try the monitor with a different PC and see if it works.

- **Dim image.** If the image is dim, check the brightness and contrast controls to make sure they are not turned all the way down. It is possible that a power saving mode is dimming the display. It is also possible that an adaptive brightness, auto-brightness, or eye-saving feature of the device or operating system has been enabled. These reduce brightness and contrast and can use lower blue light levels. This type of feature might activate automatically at a certain time of day or could use an ambient light sensor to trigger when the room is dark.
- **Image quality.** If there is a problem with image quality, such as a flickering or misshapen image or missing colors, try these actions:
  - Check the video cable and connector. If the connector is not securely inserted at both ends, this could cause flickering. If a pin is bent and not lining up with the video card connector, this can cause a missing color. If the cable is poor quality, higher resolutions may not be supported.
  - If video playback does not work, try lowering or disabling hardware acceleration (using the slider on the **Troubleshoot** tab). If this solves the problem, check for an updated display driver.

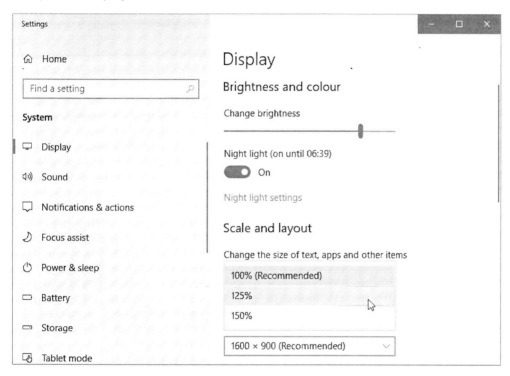

Configuring scaling on a Windows 10 PC. (Screenshot used with permission from Microsoft.)

- Increasing DPI makes text larger at a particular resolution. This is useful for flat panels that support high native resolutions (using a lower interpolated resolution would make the display "fuzzy"). However, this can cause graphics rendering problems with older software. Also, Windows may set a high DPI automatically when using a high resolution display device.
- If using a CRT monitor, check refresh rate and resolution settings for the video driver. If resolution is too high or refresh rate is too low this can cause the screen to flicker. On a TFT, check that there is no problem with the backlight.

The screen refresh rate setting is located under Advanced Display Properties on the Monitor tab. (Screenshot used with permission from Microsoft.)

- If a CRT image geometry is distorted (a pincushion effect where the edges appear to bulge, for instance), try adjusting the monitor's image control knobs.
- If a TFT image is distorted, check that the panel has not been bent or physically damaged.
- If a projector image is distorted, try to ensure the projector lens is lined up with the display screen or whiteboard. The position of the lens within the projector may be adjustable using a knob or dial. If the lens is above or below the screen, there may be a keystone effect where the top of the image is wider or narrower than the bottom. If the projector or lens cannot be repositioned, there may be a keystone correction control, accessed via the OSD menu, that allows you to adjust the digital image to compensate for this.
- **VGA mode.** If there is a problem with low resolution or color depth:
  - Low resolution or color depth (VGA rather than SVGA) can make the image look blocky or grainy.
  - If a computer boots in VGA mode without this being specified in the boot configuration, check the display driver.

Note: Windows 10 does not actually support VGA resolution anymore. The minimum resolution is SVGA (800x600).

- **Oversized images and icons.** If images and icons appear oversized:
  - One way for screen objects to look "too large" is to use a low resolution, such as VGA.
  - Another way is to use a high DPI scaling setting, as described previously.
  - You should also check whether a zoom tool is in use. Windows comes with accessibility features to allow the screen to be magnified. A user might unwittingly activate the screen magnifier (especially if it is configured with a hot key activation) and not know how to turn it off.

A user may not realize that the Magnifier tool is activated. (Screenshot used with permission from Microsoft.)

- **Color issues.** If there is a problem with color:
  - If a computer is used to produce digital art, it is very important that the display be calibrated to scanning devices and print output. **Color calibration** (or workflow) refers to a process of adjusting screen and scanner settings so that color input and output are balanced. Color settings should be configured with the assistance of a color profile. You can use the **Color Management** applet in Control Panel along with test card color patterns and spectrophotometers to define a color profile and verify that the display matches it.

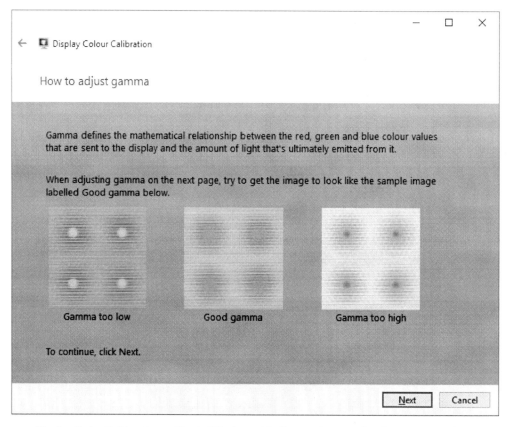

Display Color Calibration utility in Windows 10. (Screenshot used with permission from Microsoft.)

- You may also come across color glitches, such as purple or green horizontal lines or colors changing unexpectedly. These are usually caused by a faulty or loose connector or cabling that is either faulty or insufficient quality for the current image resolution. Try replacing the cable. If this does not fix the issue, there could be a hardware fault.

 Note: On a laptop, one simple test is to check whether the problem manifests on both the built-in display and on an external monitor. If the problem only appears on the external monitor, suspect the cable or connector/port.

TROUBLESHOOT ADAPTER AND MONITOR FAULTS

Many display problems are caused by errors in configuration, but you must also be alert to the possibility of hardware faults in the graphics adapter or monitor. In addition to the possible effects of a faulty cable or connector, be aware of these issues and possible solutions:

- **Dead pixels.** If you have dead pixels:
  - Defects in a flat panel monitor may cause individual pixels to be "stuck" or "dead." If a TFT panel has stuck (constantly bright) pixels, and the panel cannot be replaced under warranty, there are software utilities available to cycle the pixel through a series of relatively extreme color states to try to reactivate it.

     Note: Many vendors stipulate that they will only replace a screen if the number of manufacturing defects exceeds a stated threshold.

  - Fixed pixels can also sometimes be reactivated by gently pressing or tapping the affected area of the screen with a stylus or pencil eraser, though there is the risk of causing further damage or scratching the screen. Dead pixels (solid black) cannot usually be fixed.

- **Burn-In.** If you have burn-in:
  - Burn-in is where a static image is displayed for so long that the monitor's picture elements are damaged and a ghost image is "burned" permanently onto the display. Older monitors were highly prone to burn-in, which is why most operating systems include the option for an automatic screen saver to activate after so many minutes inactivity.
  - Modern flat panel monitors are not so susceptible to burn-in, though it is still worth using a screen saver or power saving mode just in case. Some plasma screens are vulnerable to burn-in and additional care should be taken when using a consumer TV device as display screen.
- **Artifacts.** There are two main sources of unexpected objects or patterns appearing on the screen.
  - If the artifacts are "static" and completely out of context with their surroundings, the likelihood is that the cause is a faulty adapter.
  - Some TFTs can suffer from "image persistence," where the crystals become slightly less responsive because they have been left in the same state for an extended period. The problem can usually be solved by turning off the display for a few hours.
  - In terms of 3D graphics performance and possible motion trails or slowdown (especially with computer games), you need to ensure the card is one that is capable of playing the game and that the latest driver and version of DirectX are installed.
  - If there are still issues with frame rates (the speed at which images are displayed), try disabling video effects or using a lower resolution.
  - Make sure that you are using the correct (and latest) drivers for your video card. The FAQs will list any issues with particular applications that the driver addresses.
- **Unexpected shutdowns.** If you are experiencing unexpected shutdowns:
  - A faulty display adapter or display adapter driver is a common cause of STOP errors, or Blue Screens of Death (BSoD). If the problem occurs only in specific circumstances, the fault could lie in some sort of compatibility between the driver and a particular program (typically a 3D game).
  - If the problem occurs more randomly or at bootup, the issue is more likely to be a fault in the adapter itself. 3D graphics cards come bundled with high performance GPUs and memory and as such are prone to overheating, especially in laptops. Make sure the system is being adequately cooled as prolonged overheating will cause permanent damage to the card.
- **Protected content.** If you encounter an error that indicates unauthorized content or an HDCP error:
  - DVI, HDMI, DisplayPort, and Thunderbolt all provide support for the Digital Rights Management (DRM) mechanism High-bandwidth Digital Content Protection (HDCP). HDCP allows a content source (such as a Blu-ray disc) to disable itself if the display adapter and monitor and/or speaker system do not support HDCP and fail to authenticate themselves with the playback source. There have been various iterations of HDCP (at time of writing the current version is 2.2) and backward-compatibility can be problematic as authentication may fail between devices that support different versions of the standard.

Activity 3-3

Discussing Display Device Troubleshooting

Show Slide(s)

Activity: Discussing Display Device Troubleshooting

SCENARIO
Answer the following questions to check your understanding of the topic.

1. Imagine that the display you installed is not showing the color blue.

    Which component(s) would you prioritize for fault-finding?

    The first thing to test is the display cable. If the original cable is properly inserted at the computer and monitor ends, try replacing it with a known good version. If this does not fix the problem, inspect the ports for signs of damage.

2. **What is the most likely cause of a flickering display?**

    On a CRT, flickering can occur if the refresh rate is set too low. On a TFT it could indicate a problem with the backlight. You should also verify that the connectors are secure and rule out other potential cabling problems.

3. **What would you do if the image from a projector appeared narrower at the top than at the bottom?**

    Ensure the projector lens is lined up with the whiteboard. You might be able to adjust the lens position using a knob or have to move the projector. If the projector or lens cannot be repositioned, there may be a digital keystone correction control.

4. You need to set up a system to show content-protected video.

    Which display connector types would be suitable?

    DVI, HDMI, DisplayPort, and Thunderbolt.

Activity 3-4
Troubleshooting Monitor Issues

 Show Slide(s)

Activity: Troubleshooting Monitor Issues

BEFORE YOU BEGIN

Your instructor has altered the display settings for your monitor. The computer is running and the lock screen is displayed.

This activity will be performed on your WORKBENCH PC.

 Teaching Tip

Before having learners begin this activity, you might want to send them on break so that you can adjust the following settings on their monitors so they are not correct:

SCENARIO

An employee recently had to move the location of his workstation. The employee reports that, since the move, the display does not appear in the center of the monitor. The images are too dark, making them difficult to see, and he cannot see as much on the screen as he would like. The employee needs you to resolve these issues so that he can get back to work.

- Brightness
- Contrast
- Vertical and horizontal display position
- Height and width of image
- Screen resolution

Then, restart the computers.

1. Log on to Windows, and examine the video output.

2. Adjust the monitor display.
   a) Referring to the monitor's documentation as necessary, locate the physical controls or On Screen Display (OSD) menu to adjust the brightness of the display image.
   b) Adjust the brightness so that the monitor is comfortable to view.
   c) Adjust the contrast so that you can view all the screen elements easily.

3. Change the resolution.
   a) To open the **Screen Resolution** window, if you are using a Windows 7 computer, right-click the desktop and select **Screen resolution**. If you are using a Windows 10 computer, right-click the desktop and select **Display settings**.
   b) In the **Resolution** section, select the current resolution to display the drop-down list.
   c) In the **Screen Resolution** window, select the appropriate resolution.
   d) If you are using Windows 7, select **OK**.
   e) In the **Display Settings** message box, select **Keep changes** to set the new resolution.

4. Adjust the horizontal and vertical positions of the image.
   a) Referring to the documentation as necessary, locate the controls to adjust the size and centering of the display image.
   b) Adjust the vertical display position so that the display is centered top-to-bottom on the screen.
   c) Adjust the horizontal display position so that the display is centered side-to-side on the screen.
   d) Adjust the height and width of the image so that there is either no border or the smallest border allowed.

Topic C

Install and Configure Multimedia Devices

 EXAM OBJECTIVES COVERED
1001-3.6 Explain the purposes and uses of various peripheral types.

Multimedia refers to devices used to play and record audio and video from different inputs and outputs. You will need to be able to support a wide range of multimedia devices, including speakers, microphones, headsets, and cameras.

AUDIO SUBSYSTEMS

 Show Slide(s)

Audio Subsystems (4 slides)

A computer's **audio subsystem** is made up of a **sound card** (to process audio signals and provide interfaces for connecting equipment) and one or more input (microphone) and output (speaker) devices.

SOUND CARDS

 Teaching Tip

Be sure to describe the purposes and uses of each device covered in this topic.

The basis of a sound (or audio) card is the **Digital Signal Processor (DSP) chip**, which contains one or more **Digital-to-Analog Converters (DACs)**. DACs convert the digital signals generated by the CPU to an analog electrical signal that can drive the speakers. The DSP also provides functions for playing digital sound (synthesis) and driving MIDI compatible devices. The quality of audio playback is determined by the card's **frequency response**, which is the volume that can be produced at different frequencies.

A basic sound chip may be provided as part of the motherboard chipset, but better quality audio functions can be provided as a PCI or PCIe expansion card, or as an external adapter connected by USB. Pro-level cards may also feature onboard memory, flash memory storing sound samples (wavetables), and multiple jacks for different input sources.

 Note: Locating recording functions within the computer case creates lots of problems with noise. Consequently, most audio interfaces designed for professional use are now external units connected via USB or Thunderbolt.

As with graphics cards, sound cards are designed to support sound APIs. Cards designed for use with Windows should support Microsoft's DirectSound3D (part of DirectX). Cards designed for use with games should also support Open AL and EAX, which provide extensions to DS3D for special sound effects.

Creative, Terratec, RealTek, and Turtle Beach are the most notable vendors of consumer sound cards, while M-Audio, RME, and Apogee are noted for their professional-level cards.

AUDIO CONNECTORS

Most audio connectors are 3.5 mm (⅛ inch) mono or stereo jacks (also referred to as phone plugs or mini TRS [Tip, Ring, Sleeve] connectors). A standard sound card will have several of these for different equipment.

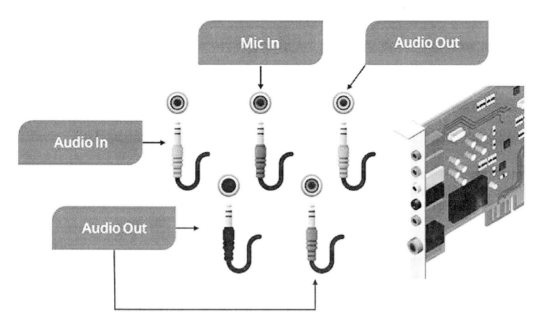

Audio jacks on a sound card. (Image © 123RF.com.)

Jack	Description
Audio in (light blue)	Audio in (or line in) is a low-level (1V) stereo signal as supplied by most tape decks, video players, tuners, CD players, and so on.
Microphone input (pink)	This is generally a mono-only analog input.
Audio out (lime)	Audio out (or line out) is a low-level (1V) analog stereo signal suitable for feeding into amplified speakers or headphones.
Audio out (black)	Carries the signal for rear speakers in a surround sound system.
Audio out (orange)	Carries the signal for the subwoofer in a surround sound system.

Higher end sound cards will include an **Sony/Phillips Digital Interface (S/PDIF) jack**. S/PDIF can either use coax cabling with RCA (or phono) connectors or fiber optic cabling and connectors, which can either be in a square form factor (TOSLINK) or use 3.5mm jacks. S/PDIF is most often used to carry digital data for surround-sound speaker systems.

A TOSLINK connector and port. (Image © 123RF.com.)

Note: *RCA connectors are distinguished by a collar surrounding the connector, which makes the fit between plug and socket more secure.*

AUDIO OUTPUT DEVICES

Show Slide(s)

Audio Output Devices (2 slides)

Audio playback is achieved via speakers or headphones, which are connected to the sound card via an analog or digital audio jack. Both analog and digital speakers are available (or speakers may support both analog and digital inputs).

Sound cards supporting multiple output channels with an appropriate speaker system can provide various levels of playback, from mono (on legacy systems) or stereo to some type of **surround sound**. Surround sound uses multiple speakers positioned around the listener to provide a "cinematic" audio experience.

- A 5.1 digital system (Dolby Digital or Digital Theater System [DTS]) has three front center, left, and right speakers, two left and right rear speakers, and a subwoofer for bass sounds.
- A 7.1 system (Dolby Digital Plus or DTS-HD) has two extra side speakers. A speaker system will usually have controls for adjusting volume, bass, and treble plus optionally EQ or preset sound effects.

 Note: *A sound card will also feature internal channels (or voices). These represent the number of sounds that the card can play and mix at once (polyphony). This is important for music recording and working with sound effects used by some games.*

 Note: *Most graphics adapters support audio over HDMI (or Thunderbolt), allowing surround sound output without a separate connection to a sound card. An HDMI cable would be connected from the graphics adapter port to the TV and then the TV would be connected to the surround sound speaker system.*

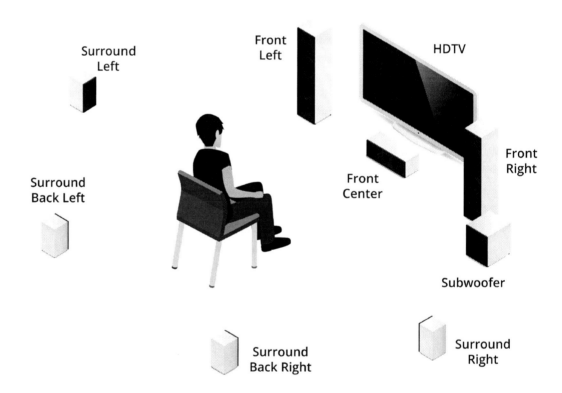

Surround sound configuration for a home theater. (Image © 123RF.com.)

MIDI EQUIPMENT

As well as playing sound via speakers, a card supporting **Musical Instrument Digital Interface (MIDI)** functions can be used to control MIDI equipment (such as a synthesizer or drum machine).

Show Slide(s)

MIDI Equipment

Instead of exchanging the sound wave, the devices exchange information about how to play a sound, in terms of sample (a sound pattern stored in a wavetable), volume, pitch, tempo, and so on. For example, you could use a keyboard to play with samples stored on the PC or use sequencing software to program a drum machine.

MIDI devices use 5-pin DIN connectors or USB connectors.

SOUND RECORDING EQUIPMENT

To record an analog sound wave, the sound card must **sample** the wave. The sampler divides the wave up into a number of slices per second (sampling rate) and records information about each slice (resolution). The higher the sampling rate (measured in Kilohertz [KHz]) and resolution (measured in bits), the better the representation of the source is. CD-quality audio is sampled at 16-bit/44.1 KHz, but professional cards may sample at 24-bit/192 KHz or better.

Show Slide(s)

Sound Recording Equipment

The card's circuitry and cabling introduce some degree of noise or distortion into the sampled audio. Noise levels are measured using **Total Harmonic Distortion (THD)** and **Signal-to-Noise Ratio (SNR)**. THD is measured as a percentage and SNR in decibels (dB). For both, smaller values represent better performance.

> *Note: When using a PC to record music, the acoustic performance of components such as the hard drive and fans is very important, so as not to cause interference with analog inputs. Locate an internal sound card in the slot farthest from any other components.*

A sound card can be fitted with several ports to connect different types of recording equipment.

HEADSETS

A **headset** combines headphones and a microphone in a single device. They are mostly used with Voice over IP (VoIP) calling, meeting, and conferencing applications. Most headsets are connected to the computer via a USB port or via a wireless interface, such as Bluetooth®.

Show Slide(s)

Headsets

AUDIO SETTINGS

To set up the audio subsystem, connect the microphone, headset, or speakers to the appropriate ports on the card or motherboard. Use the **Sound** applet in Control Panel or Windows Settings to test the hardware and configure settings.

Show Slide(s)

Audio Settings

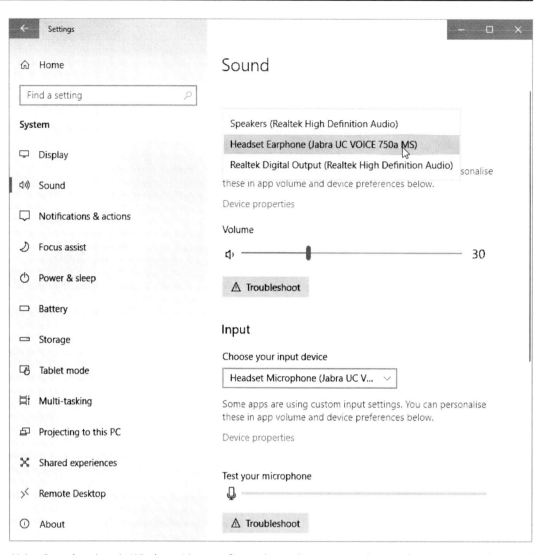

Using Sound settings in Windows 10 to configure the audio output and input devices. (Screenshot used with permission from Microsoft.)

If you have multiple devices connected at the same time, you can choose the defaults here and test levels for audio input and output.

If you have a multimedia keyboard, there are usually keys on that for adjusting the volume. Also, laptops have push-buttons and special function (Fn) keys to adjust the volume.

In Windows, use the **Speakers** icon in the Notification Area to control the volume and switch between playback devices.

Windows volume control. (Screenshot used with permission from Microsoft.)

WEBCAMS

Webcams record video images using a CMOS or CCD sensor and usually feature a microphone to record audio. Most webcams now support HD recording but may come with quite low quality lenses and records at up to about 30 frames per second (fps). Higher quality devices for professional recording and 4K resolution are available. Webcams are used for online video conferencing, as feeds for websites, and as surveillance devices.

Show
Slide(s)
Webcams (2 slides)

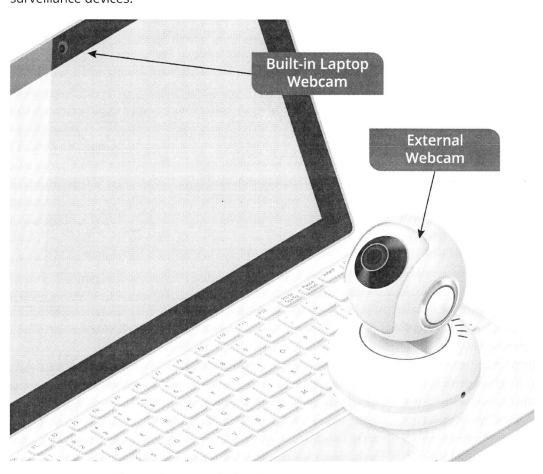

Built-in Laptop Webcam

External Webcam

Built-in and USB-attached webcam options. (Image © 123RF.com.)

Webcams can be built into a laptop computer chassis or connected as a peripheral device via an external USB port. Some webcams may come with Wi-Fi networking functionality.

 Note: *With webcams—and especially built-in webcams—it is important to enforce app permissions to prevent privacy abuses. While an application such as a browser might need to use the webcam for video conferencing from a particular service provider, that does not mean that other websites should be able to activate the camera.*

DIGITAL CAMERAS

Digital cameras are primarily still cameras, though many can record HD video too. They record an image using a light-sensitive CCD or CMOS array and store it on digital media (a flash memory card). Properties of 35 mm film, such as ISO sensitivity, can be set through software. Digital compact cameras dispense with traditional viewfinders and allow the user to compose each shot using a preview image on an LCD display

Show
Slide(s)
Digital Cameras (2 slides)

screen. In other respects, digital cameras have the same features and functions as film cameras.

From left to right: A compact action camera, a DSLR digital camera. (Image © 123RF.com.)

The digicam market is divided into consumer models (replicating the features of compact 35 mm film cameras), professional **Digital Single Lens Reflex (DSLR)** models (preserving the traditional viewfinder method of picture composition and supporting replaceable lenses and manual adjustments), and **prosumer** models (ranging from high end compacts to entry-level DSLRs). Additionally, smartphones and tablets now come with a camera function.

 Note: There are also mirrorless cameras, which support interchangeable lenses but do not use an optical viewfinder.

Apart from its lens, shutter speed, and feature set, the basic quality measurement of a digital camera is its **resolution**, expressed in **megapixels** (MP). The following table lists the best output that can be expected from images of a particular resolution.

Resolution	Uses
Less than 1 MP	On-screen viewing only.
1 to 2 MP	On-screen viewing and small prints (up to about 7 inches).
3 MP	Larger prints (up to about 12 inches, or letter sized).
4 to 8 MP and higher	Poster prints (30 inches and larger).

 Note: In point of fact, image resolution is now less important than the physical size of the sensor. Compact digicams support high resolution but have tiny sensors, while DSLRs have high resolution and larger sensors (the best quality have a "full frame" sensor; the same size as a frame of 35 mm film).

Another important factor is the type of memory card used by the camera. Cameras can only use one type of card. Most cameras convert images to compressed (JPEG) file format to save space. JPEG is a lossy compression algorithm, meaning that even at the highest quality setting, some image information is discarded. Professional and prosumer models can typically record uncompressed (RAW) data, but this requires about 2-3 times as much space per picture.

Picture files can be transferred to a PC using the removable memory card or the camera can be connected directly using USB or (on some models) over Wi-Fi wireless networking. Many printers also support memory card slots or connectivity for direct printing from a camera without requiring a PC.

Activity 3-5

Discussing Multimedia Device Installation and Configuration

Show Slide(s)

Activity: Discussing Multimedia Device Installation and Configuration

SCENARIO

Answer the following questions to check your understanding of the topic.

1. **What size and color connector would you look for to plug a basic microphone into a PC?**

   3.5mm jack, which is often color coded pink.

2. **You have installed a new sound card in a computer designed for home entertainment. What type of connector would you use to connect a digital surround sound speaker system to the new card?**

   S/PDIF—optical or coax. Coax for audio uses RCA connectors. An optical S/PDIF connector is also sometimes referred to as TOSLINK. Note that a lot of home entertainment setups might just output audio over HDMI with the signal from the graphics adapter.

3. **What type of speaker unit is the ".1" in a 5.1 or 7.1 surround sound system and where do you suggest this speaker be placed?**

   Subwoofer for bass (low frequency) response. Start with placing it in the front of the room, but consider trying other locations to see where you get the best base response for the space in which the surround sound system is set up.

4. **What type of interface would allow a software program running on the PC to operate a synthesizer connected as a peripheral device?**

   MIDI (Musical Instrument Digital Interface).

5. **What sampling rate from a sound card would you require if you want to be able to record CD-quality sound?**

   16-bit @ 44.1 KHz.

Summary

In this lesson, you supported display and multimedia devices by installing, configuring, and troubleshooting them. It is likely that you will be called upon to support display devices often as a computer technician.

What types of monitors do you have experience with? What types of connections have you used to connect those monitors to computers?

A: Answers will vary, but are likely to include LCD monitors with VGA, HDMI, or DVI connectors.

In your current job role, have you had to troubleshoot display device problems? If so, what did you do and how did you resolve the issues?

A: Answers will vary, but may include fixing a display output issue, adjusting display settings to resolve picture issues, or fixing some basic problems with connections, cables, or ports.

 Practice Question: Additional practice questions are available on the CompTIA CHOICE platform within the Assessments tile.

Lesson 4

Installing, Configuring, and Troubleshooting Storage Devices

LESSON INTRODUCTION

As a computer technician, your responsibilities are likely to include installing and maintaining many different types of computer components, including storage devices. By identifying the various types of storage devices that can be found in most personal computers, you will be better prepared to select, install, and maintain storage devices in personal computers.

Data storage comes in a variety of types and sizes and for different purposes. Temporary data storage in RAM and permanent storage on hard disk drives, optical drives (CD/DVD/Blu-ray™), and flash memory drives and cards are the main types of storage you will encounter.

LESSON OBJECTIVES

In this lesson, you will:

- Install system memory.
- Install and configure mass storage devices.
- Install and configure removable storage devices.
- Configure RAID.
- Troubleshoot storage device issues.

Topic A

Install System Memory

EXAM OBJECTIVES COVERED
1001-3.3 Given a scenario, install RAM types.

Just as some people say you can never be too rich, you can never have too much memory. Adding memory is one of the simplest and most cost-effective ways to increase a computer's performance, whether it is on a brand-new system loaded with high-performance applications or an older system that performs a few basic tasks.

SYSTEM MEMORY

 Show Slide(s)

System Memory (2 slides)

Teaching Tip

As you present this topic's content, point out that learners might need to distinguish between old and new technologies for the certification exam.

System memory is the main storage area for programs and data when the computer is running. System memory is a type of volatile memory called Random Access Memory (RAM). System memory is necessary because it is much faster than accessing data in a mass storage system, such as a hard disk. System memory provides a fast storage medium for the operating system and applications but it is **volatile**, meaning that data cannot be stored without a power supply.

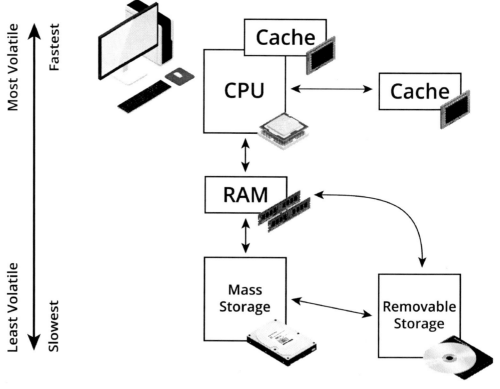

CPU, cache, and RAM are fast but volatile; mass storage and removable storage devices provide slower but permanent data retrieval. (Image © 123RF.com.)

Note: *Non-volatile memory does not require a constant power source to store data. Examples include read-only memory (ROM) and flash memory.*

A large quantity of system memory is essential for running a PC. It determines its ability to work with multiple applications at the same time and larger files. Each new generation of software tends to take up more memory space. If there is not enough system RAM, the memory space can be extended by using disk space (virtual memory), but as noted previously, accessing the disk is very slow compared to accessing RAM.

RAM TYPES

Several different RAM technologies have been used for system memory in PCs over the years.

 Show Slide(s)
RAM Types

RAM Type	Description
Dynamic RAM (DRAM)	DRAM stores each data bit as an electrical charge within a single bit cell. A bit cell consists of a capacitor to hold a charge (the cell represents 1 if there is a charge and 0 if there is not) and a transistor to read the contents of the capacitor.
	The electrical charge gradually dissipates, causing the memory cell to lose its information. In order to preserve the information, dynamic memory has to be refreshed periodically by accessing each bit cell at regular intervals. The refresh cycles slow down the operation of DRAM but it supports high densities (more MB per memory module) and is relatively low cost.
	Many types of DRAM have been developed and become obsolete.
Synchronous DRAM (SDRAM)	In the mid-1990s, variants of SDRAM were used for system memory. SDRAM is so-called because it is synchronized to the system clock. It has a 64-bit data bus. Consequently, if the bus is running at 66 MHz, the bandwidth available to an SDRAM memory controller is 66.6*64 or 4266 megabits per second. Dividing by 8 gives the bandwidth in megabytes per second (533 MBps).

Some notable RAM vendors include Kingston®, Crucial™ (Micron), Corsair, PNY, and Integral™.

DDR SDRAM

Double Data Rate SDRAM (DDR SDRAM) is an updated type of SDRAM (released to market in 2001) where data is transferred twice in one cycle ("double-pumped"). There are four DDR standards, matching different system clock speeds.

 Show Slide(s)
DDR SDRAM

 Teaching Tip
Emphasize that exam candidates must know the information in these tables, or be able to derive the type or a characteristic when provided with other characteristics.

RAM Type	Memory Clock (MHz)	Bus Clock (MHz)	Data Rate MT/s	Transfer Rate (Gbps)
DDR-200/ PC-1600	100	100	200	1.6
DDR-266/ PC-2100	133	133	266	2.1
DDR-333/ PC-2700	167	167	333	2.7

RAM Type	Memory Clock (MHz)	Bus Clock (MHz)	Data Rate MT/s	Transfer Rate (Gbps)
DDR-400/ PC-3200	200	200	400	3.2

SDRAM is referred to by the bus clock speed (PC100, PC133, and so forth). DDR chips are labeled using the maximum theoretical bandwidth (PC1600, PC2100, and so on) largely for marketing reasons. For example, consider DDR-200 PC-1600 memory:

- The internal memory clock speed and I/O bus speed are both 100 MHz.
- The data rate is double this as there are two operations per clock "tick." This is expressed in units called MegaTransfers per Second (200 MT/s). This gives the DDR-200 designation.
- The peak transfer rate is 1600 MBps (200 MT/s x 8 bytes per transfer). This gives the "PC-1600" designation. 1600 MBps is equivalent to 1.6 GBps. Note that the peak transfer rate does not represent "real world" performance; it is a maximum theoretical rate.

DDR2/DDR3/DDR4 SDRAM

Show Slide(s)

DDR2/DDR3/DDR4 SDRAM (3 slides)

DDR has been superseded by DDR2 (from 2003), DDR3 (from 2007), and DDR4 (from 2014) SDRAM. These increase bandwidth by multiplying the bus speed, as opposed to the speed at which the actual memory chips work. This produces scalable speed improvements without making the chips too unreliable or too hot.

The drawback is increased latency, as data takes longer to access on each chip. Latency is offset by improving the memory circuitry.

RAM Type	Memory Clock (MHz)	Bus Clock (MHz)	Data Rate (MT/s)	Transfer Rate (Gbps)
DDR2	100 to 266	200 to 533	400 to 1066	3.2 to 8.533
DDR3	100 to 266	400 to 1066	800 to 2133	6.4 to 17.066
DDR4	200 to 400	800 to 1600	1600 to 3200	12.8 to 25.6

The following represent specific examples of DDR standards:

- DDR2-1066/PC28500—the memory works at 266 MHz and the bus at 533 MHz, which with the double data rate gives 1066 MT/s and nominal transfer rate of 8.533 GBps. This is the best available DDR2 standard.
- DDR3-1600/PC312800—the memory works at 200 MHz and the bus at 800 MHz, which with the double data rate gives 1600 MT/s and nominal transfer rate of 12.8 GBps.
- DDR4-1600/PC4-12800—the memory works at 200 MHz and the bus at 800 MHz, which with the double data rate gives 1600 MT/s and nominal transfer rate of 12.8 GBps. The only advantage over DDR3-1600 is the lower voltage, reducing power consumption.
- DDR4-2400/PC4-19200—the memory works at 300 MHz and the bus at 1200 MHz, which with the double data rate gives 2400 MT/s and nominal transfer rate of 19.2 GBps, exceeding anything available for DDR3.

Note: Clock speeds ending 33 or 66 are usually rounded down; technically they are 33⅓ and 66⅔. In the case of DDR2-667, the memory manufacturers just didn't like the look of "DDR2-666" so they rounded up.

Note: *When specifying high performance RAM you may want to compare the performance timings. These are quoted as a series of numbers in the form 5-5-5-15. Each number represents a different timing statistic. The lower the numbers, the better the performance. Each DDR standard has timing variants. For example, DDR3-1333G has 8-8-8-12 timing, whereas DDR3-1600G8 has 8-8-8-10 and DDR3-1600K has 11-11-11-13. More information on SDRAM standards can be obtained from **jedec.org**.*

 Note: *You may also come across GDDRx memory, which is a type of DDRx optimized for use on graphics cards.*

MEMORY MODULES

A RAM module, or **memory module**, is a printed circuit board that holds a group of memory chips that act as a single unit. Memory modules reside in slots on the motherboard, and they are removable and replaceable. Memory modules are defined by their design and by the number and type of chips they contain.

 **Show Slide(s)**
Memory Modules (3 slides)

DUAL INLINE MEMORY MODULES

DDR for desktop system memory is packaged in 184-pin **Dual Inline Memory Module (DIMMs)**. The notches (keys) on the module prevent it from being inserted into a slot the wrong way around.

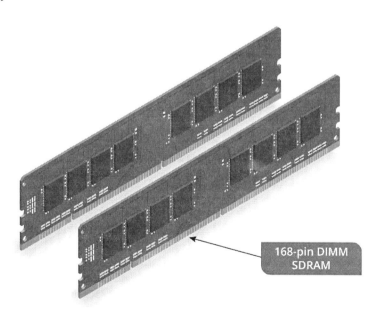

SDRAM packaged in 168-pin DIMMs. (Image © 123RF.com.)

 Note: *Memory slots look similar to expansion slots but have catches on each end to secure the memory modules.*

DDR2 and DDR3 are both packaged in 240-pin DIMMs but are not compatible. The modules and slots are keyed differently to prevent a module from being inserted into an incompatible slot. Faster modules typically feature heatsinks, because of the higher clock speeds.

DDR4 DIMMs have 288 pins. The modules are the same size as previous standards but the pins are more closely spaced. Again, the key position prevents a DDR4 module from being inserted into an incompatible DDR3 or DDR2 motherboard slot. DDR4 works at 1.2 V so is more power-efficient than previous standards.

RAM Type	Pins	Voltage
DDR	184	2.5 to 2.6V
DDR2	240	1.8 to 1.9V
DDR3	240	1.35 to 1.5V
DDR4	288	1.2V

LAPTOP MEMORY

Laptop RAM is packaged in a smaller module called **Small Outline DIMM (SODIMM)**. Both DDR and DDR2 use 200-pin packages, but the key position for DDR2 is slightly different to prevent insertion in a slot designed for DDR. DDR3 uses a 204-pin package while DDR4 is 260-pin.

The memory is typically fitted into slots that pop-up at a 45° angle to allow the chips to be inserted or removed.

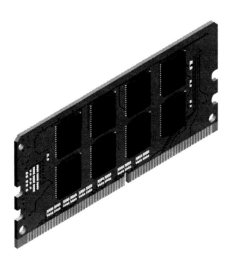

SODIMM. (Image © 123RF.com.)

DUAL-CHANNEL MEMORY

Show Slide(s)

Dual-Channel Memory (2 slides)

Teaching Tip

Point out that it is the motherboard that is dual-channel, rather than the memory modules themselves.

In the 2000s, the increasing speed and architectural improvements of CPU technologies led to memory becoming a bottleneck to system performance. To address this, Intel® and AMD developed a dual-channel memory architecture for DDRx RAM. Dual-channel was originally used primarily on server-level hardware but is commonly being employed on desktop systems and laptops too.

Single-channel memory means that there is one 64-bit bus between the CPU and RAM. With a **dual-channel memory** controller, there can effectively be two pathways through the bus to the CPU, meaning that 128 bits of data can be transferred per "transaction" rather than 64 bits. In fact, in most configurations they continue to operate as two independent 64-bit pathways, but this still increases the bandwidth available. Ordinary RAM modules are used (that is, there are no "dual-channel" DDR memory modules).

 Note: DDRx memory is sold in "kits" for dual-channel applications but there is nothing special about the modules themselves, other than being identical.

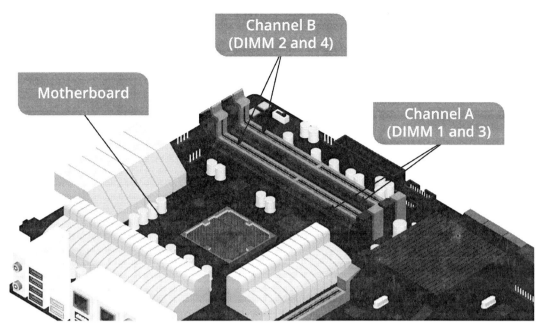

Motherboard DIMM slots (dual channel). Slots 1 and 3 (black slots) make up one channel, while slots 2 and 4 (grey slots) make up a separate channel. (Image © 123RF.com.)

For example, a dual-channel motherboard might have four DIMM slots arranged in color-coded pairs. Each pair represents one channel; each slot represents one of the two sockets in each channel. The memory modules installed should be identical in terms of speed and capacity. If only two slots are used, to enable dual-channel, the modules must be installed in socket 1 of each channel. You will need to consult the system documentation carefully to identify the appropriate slots to use. For motherboards supporting Intel CPUs and some AMD CPUs, the first sockets in both channels are slots 1 and 3. For most AMD CPU-based motherboards, it would mean filling slots 1 and 2. Unfortunately, there is no standardized color-coding. As well as using different colors, some motherboard manufacturers use the same color for the same channel; others use the same color for the same socket. Check the documentation carefully.

Adding an odd number of modules or adding mismatched DIMMs will cause the system to operate in single-channel mode. Dual-channel mode may also need to be enabled via the PC firmware's system setup program.

Some of Intel's CPUs and supporting chipsets have triple- or quadruple-channel memory controllers. AMD is starting to release quadruple-channel controllers too. In these architectures, if the full complement of modules is not installed, the system will revert to dual- or single-channel operation.

PARITY AND ECC RAM

Motherboards used to use a simple error detection method called **parity checking**. Each byte of data in memory is accompanied by a ninth bit. This bit is set to 1 or 0 to make the total number of bits set to 1 in the byte an odd or even number, depending on the type of parity checking being performed. When the byte is read, its parity is checked to ensure that the parity value is still odd (or even). If this is not the case, a bit must have become corrupted.

System memory for most desktops is **non-parity**; that is, it does not perform error checking (except for the startup memory count). For systems that require a high level of reliability (such as workstations and servers), **Error Checking and Correcting (ECC)**

 Show Slide(s)
Parity and ECC RAM

 Teaching Tip
ECC is more likely to be found on server systems than desktops, but it might be used in workstations.

memory is available. ECC memory is enhanced parity circuitry that can detect internal data errors and make corrections. ECC will detect and correct single-bit errors and allow the system to continue functioning normally. It will also detect errors of 2, 3 or 4 bits but will not correct them; instead, it will generate an error message and halt the system.

ECC memory has an extra chip and a 72-bit data bus rather than 64-bit. The motherboard must support the use of ECC memory modules (and the option to use them must typically be enabled in system setup). ECC memory cannot be mixed with non-ECC modules.

 Note: An ECC DIMM will have an odd number of memory chips, whereas non-parity DIMMs will have an even number of memory chips.

 Show Slide(s)

Memory Installation and Upgrade

MEMORY INSTALLATION AND UPGRADE

Upgrading the memory is a common task for any PC technician. If the motherboard supports it but the system is not configured to use it, enabling a dual-channel configuration is the best way of extracting more performance from existing components. Increasing the bus speed would require purchasing a new motherboard and memory modules (and possibly CPU).

 Note: When you are purchasing a computer, it is a good idea to get the fastest memory bus you can afford, as this is the component that is most difficult to upgrade later.

 Show Slide(s)

Memory Compatibility Issues (2 slides)

 Teaching Tip

Point out that Windows tools such as Device Manager or msinfo32 do not report detailed information about memory modules (or the motherboard or CPU). You need to install third-party software to view this.

 Interaction Opportunity

Ask learners to view the **System Summary** in msinfo32 to confirm the amount of installed RAM on their HOST or WORKBENCH PC.

MEMORY COMPATIBILITY ISSUES

In terms of compatibility, always consult the motherboard user guide, but consider the following general guidelines:

- The DIMM format must match the motherboard (you cannot install DDR modules in DDR2 slots, for instance).
- Different capacity modules can be installed (with the exception of most multi-channel configurations). Most vendors recommend installing the largest module in the lowest numbered slot.
- Modules from different vendors can be mixed, though this may cause problems with multi-channel configurations.
- For best performance, the modules should be the same speed as the motherboard. Different speeds can be mixed; that is, you can add modules that are faster or slower than the motherboard slots or mix modules of different speeds. The system will only operate at the best speed supported by all installed components (memory modules and controller), so this is not generally a good idea.
- For best performance and reliability, configure multi-channel systems with identical memory modules for each channel.
- ECC memory cannot be mixed with non-parity memory and must be supported by the motherboard. Similarly, registered memory cannot be mixed with unbuffered modules and must be supported by the motherboard.

Memory modules are quite easy to insert and remove (unless cabling within the case makes them inaccessible). The key point here is to ensure that the memory is suitable for the system and in the correct configuration.

Note: *To learn more, check the* **Video** *tile on the CHOICE Course screen for any videos that supplement the content for this lesson.*

Access the Checklist tile on your CHOICE Course screen for reference information and job aids on How to Install and Upgrade Memory.

Activity 4-1
Discussing System Memory Installation

SCENARIO
Answer the following questions to check your understanding of the content presented in this topic.

1. **What are the principal characteristics of DRAM technology?**

   Each cell in Dynamic RAM must be refreshed periodically to preserve its charge. It is high density and low cost.

2. **Why is Synchronous DRAM so-called?**

   Because it works at the same speed as the motherboard.

3. **What is the clock speed of PC2100 DDR SDRAM?**

   133 MHz.

4. **How many pins are there on a DIMM stick of DDR2 SDRAM?**

   240

5. **How can you distinguish memory slots on the motherboard?**

   They have plastic clips at either end.

6. **How is laptop system memory typically packaged?**

   SODIMM.

7. You are configuring a system with dual-channel memory. You have two modules and there are four slots.

   How would you determine which slots to use?

   Check the system guide—most Intel boards would require the use of slots 1 and 3 to use both channels, but it's best not to proceed without consulting the vendor's documentation.

8. **Your PC's system bus is 800 MHz. You have one 1 GB stick of PC3-12800 installed already. You have a 1 GB stick of PC3-8500 available. Should you add it to the system?**

   You should realize that the whole memory bus will operate at the slower speed, but otherwise there is no definitive answer—it does depend on how the PC is used. The performance benefits of more RAM probably outweigh the speed penalty in most circumstances, though.

9. Additional memory was installed in a user's system, and now it will not boot.

What steps would you take to resolve this job ticket?

First, verify that the correct memory type was installed on the system and in the correct configuration (consider whether dual-channel memory was installed in the correct slots). Check that the new memory module is seated properly in its slot. Try swapping memory around in the memory slots.

Activity 4-2
Upgrading Memory

Show Slide(s)

Activity: Upgrading Memory

Teaching Tip

If you haven't preinstalled CPU-Z, point learners to the installer in C:\comptia-labs\labfiles.

Some trainers have mentioned that CPU-Z can be tagged as adware by security software. Learners should not select options from the **Tools** menu.

Distribute the extra memory modules to learners (optionally, if there are a mix of systems and modules, ask them to request what type of memory they need from the "pile").

Ensure that learners take anti-static precautions when they handle and store the modules.

Help learners troubleshoot any installation problems.

BEFORE YOU BEGIN

Your instructor will give you a system memory module or kit to install. Remember that memory modules are particularly susceptible to ESD, so handle the modules carefully by the plastic edges and avoid touching the chips.

Perform this activity on your WORKBENCH PC.

SCENARIO

Adding extra system memory is one of the simplest (and cheapest) means of improving system performance. More memory means less slow pagefile access when multiple applications are running or when large files are being manipulated.

---

1. Use the Windows **System Properties** page and the CPUID CPU-Z utility to report system information and configuration.

   a) Open **System Properties** to confirm the amount of RAM currently installed.

   b) Run the **CPUID CPU-Z** utility by using its desktop shortcut and select **Yes** when prompted by User Account Control (UAC).

      The first tab shows information about the CPU.

   c) Select the **Memory** tab.

This tab shows the total amount of system memory, its type and timings as well as whether it is configured in dual-channel mode.

d)   Make a note of the DRAM frequency:
e)   Select the **SPD** tab.

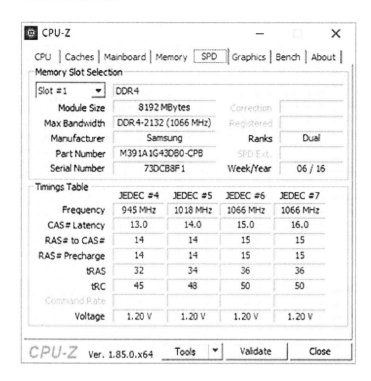

SPD stands for **Serial Presence Detect**. This chip reports the configuration of a memory module installed in a particular slot on the motherboard. You can use this to find out if there are spare slots available for upgrade; useful if your system documentation has not been kept up-to-date.

f)   Note which slot(s) the memory module(s) are installed in, and if the system is in dual-channel mode which slots comprise sockets in different channels.

  •   Slots where memory installed: _____
  •   Slots comprising sockets in different channels: _____

g)   Optionally, select the **Graphics** tab to view information about the video adapter and any graphics memory it might have installed.

h)   Select **Close**.

2.   Perform a memory module upgrade, and verify the procedure.

Teaching Tip
Be prepared to provide RAM modules to learners or assist them in removing the existing module so they can reinstall it. Also, remind them about using ESD protection when they work with RAM modules.

a)   Power down the PC, disconnect the power cable, and take the usual ESD precautions.

b)   Remove the case cover.

c)   Confirm that there is a free memory slot and that the memory you have been given is of the correct type.

 Note: *If your instructor has additional memory available for you to install in the PC, they will give it to you now. If not, you can remove the existing memory module and reinstall it. Be sure to follow ESD best practices when you work with RAM modules.*

d)   Release the clips on the memory slot, and push the module into place, taking care to handle it by the plastic parts, rather than touching the chips.

The clips should snap back into place when the module is properly inserted.

e)   Double-check that the module is seated correctly, and then close the system case.

f)   Reconnect the power cable and start the PC. As the PC boots, look to see if there is a memory check (most computers skip this sort of check these days). If there is an error, power off the PC again, and check that you have seated the module correctly.

g)   Log on to Windows and double-check in **System Properties** that the RAM has been recognized.

     h)   Run the **CPUID CPU-Z** utility again and check the memory configuration. Is it still running at the same speed?

           Answers will vary depending on the DIMM used to upgrade the PC.

     i)   Close the **System Information** and **CPU-Z** windows.

3.   If necessary, uninstall the added memory and return it to your instructor.

     a)   Power down the PC, disconnect the power cable, and take the usual ESD precautions.

     b)   Uninstall the extra module and hand it back to your instructor.

     c)   Close the system case, reconnect the power cable, and restart the PC.

     d)   Log in to Windows.

Topic B

Install and Configure Mass Storage Devices

EXAM OBJECTIVES COVERED
1001-3.1 Explain basic cable types, features, and their purposes.
1001-3.4 Given a scenario, select, install and configure storage devices.

Mass storage devices such as hard disks are one of the most common system components you will install. In this topic, you will install and configure hard disk drives (HDDs) and solid state drives (SSDs). Users rely on local persistent storage devices to keep their applications and data current and available. As a CompTIA® A+® technician, your responsibilities are likely to include installing and configuring different types of storage devices to provide your users with the data-storage capabilities that they need to perform their jobs.

STORAGE DEVICES

System memory provides a fast storage medium for the operating system and applications but is volatile, meaning that data cannot be stored without a power supply. Non-volatile storage devices (or **mass storage devices**) hold data when the system is powered off. Removable mass storage devices and removable media allow data to be archived from the PC and transferred between PCs.

Show Slide(s)

Storage Devices

Mass storage devices use magnetic, optical, or solid state technology to store data. At least some storage devices are fitted as internal components. In the case of internal devices that use removable storage media, the drive is positioned at the front of the case so that the media can be inserted and removed. Hard drives do not need user access and so do not need to be positioned near a faceplate.

External storage devices are also popular for backup and data transfer or to provide a drive type not available as an internal unit. A device such as an external hard drive would typically be connected to the computer via a USB port.

HARD DISK DRIVES

Even with the advances in the speed and capacity of other types of storage technology, the **hard disk drive (HDD)** remains the primary method of persistent storage for PC data. On a workstation PC, the hard disk drive will store the operating system files, application program files, system software files (such as drivers), and user data. On a server PC, the hard disks will store individual user files and shared sources of information, such as databases. Advances in hard disk technology have enabled disks of up to 8 terabytes (8000 GB) to be produced, although smaller capacities are more common for performance and reliability reasons.

Show Slide(s)

Hard Disk Drives (2 slides)

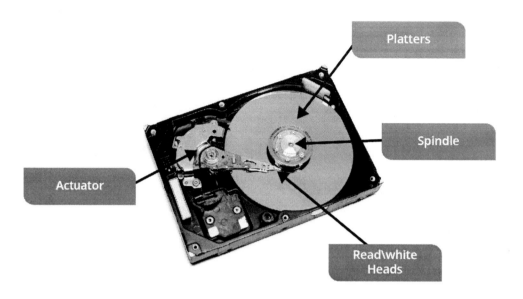

HDD with drive circuitry and casing removed showing 1) Platters; 2) Spindle; 3) Read/write heads; 4) Actuator. (Image by mkphotoshu © 123RF.com.)

In an HDD, data is stored on several metal or glass platters that are coated with a magnetic substance. The top and bottom of each platter is accessed by its own read/write head, moved by an actuator mechanism.

These heads do not actually touch the surface of the platters. The platters are mounted on a spindle and spun at high speed and the heads "float" above them at a distance of less than a millionth of an inch. The disk unit is kept sealed to maintain a constant air pressure (important for keeping the drive heads at the correct distance from the platters) and to prevent the entry of dust.

Each side of each platter is divided into circular **tracks** and each track contains several **sectors**, each with a capacity of 512 bytes. This low-level formatting is also referred to as the drive geometry.

There are two main formats for HDDs. 3.5" units are the mainstream type used in PCs. 2.5" form factors are used for laptops and as portable external drives. There is also a 1.8" form factor but it is not widely used. 2.5" HDDs can also vary in height, with 15 mm, 9.5 mm, 7 mm, and 5 mm form factors available.

DRIVE BAYS AND CADDIES

A drive can be fitted using a caddy. You screw the drive into the caddy and then screw the caddy into the case. A caddy can also allow you to fit a drive of a different size to the bay. For example, you can fit a 2.5" drive in a 3.5" bay by using an adapter caddy. Some caddies use rails so that you can pull the drive out without having to open the case.

HDD PERFORMANCE FACTORS

Several factors determine overall hard disk performance. One factor is the speed at which the disks can spin, measured in Revolutions Per Minute (RPM). The higher the RPM, the faster the drive is. High performance drives are rated at 15,000 or 10,000 rpm; average performance is 7,200 or 5,400 rpm.

Teaching Tip

You might want to mention the term Zoned Bit Recording (ZBR). Modern drives do not use tracks with the same number of sectors. To increase capacity, outer tracks contain more sectors.

Show Slide(s)

HDD Performance Factors (2 slides)

RPM is one factor determining **access time** (measured in milliseconds), which is the delay that occurs as the read/write head locates a particular track position (**seek time**) and sector location (**rotational latency**) on the drive. A high performance drive will have an access time below 3 ms; a typical drive might have an access time of around 6 ms.

The **internal transfer rate** (or data or disk transfer rate) of a drive is a measure of how fast read/write operations are performed on the disk platters. A 15 K drive should support an internal transfer rate of up to about 180 MBps, while 7.2 K drives will be around 110 MBps. The **external transfer rate** (often simply described as the transfer rate) measures how fast data can be transferred to the CPU across the bus. Cache memory can help to sustain better transfer rates. A high performance disk may feature an 8 MB or better cache.

 Note: Generally, the burst transfer rate is quoted. This is the maximum possible transfer rate under ideal conditions and cannot be sustained over a long period.

The other crucial factor that impacts HDD performance is reliability. Reliability is rated by various statistics, including **Early-life Failure Rate**, **Mean Time Between Failure (MTBF)**, which is the number of hours that a device should operate (under optimum conditions) before a critical incident can be expected, and **life expectancy**, which is the duration for which the device can be expected to remain reliable. All drives now feature **Self-Monitoring Analysis and Reporting Technology (S.M.A.R.T.)** to pass status information and alerts back to monitoring software. This can provide advance warning that a drive is about to fail.

Some of the major hard drive vendors include Seagate, Western Digital, Maxtor, Hitachi, Fujitsu, Toshiba, and Samsung.

STORAGE ADAPTERS AND CABLES

Host Bus Adapters (HBAs) provide a connection point for internal mass storage devices, such as hard drives, optical drives, and tape drives. The interface between the drive, host adapter, and the rest of the system is a type of bus. There used to be two main bus standards for attaching internal storage devices to a PC—Parallel ATA (PATA) and Small Computer System Interface (SCSI)—but these have now largely been replaced by SATA.

Show Slide(s)
Storage Adapters and Cables

 *Note: HBAs are also commonly referred to as **drive controllers**. Technically, the controller is the circuitry in the disk unit that allows it to put data on the bus, which the HBA shuttles to the CPU or RAM.*

SATA

Serial Advanced Technology Attachment (SATA) is the standard means of attaching internal storage drives to a desktop PC. It has superseded the legacy Parallel ATA (PATA) technology.

As the name suggests, SATA transfers data in serial format. This allows for thin, flexible cables of up to 1 m (39"). The cables are terminated with compact 7-pin connectors. Each SATA host adapter port supports a single device. SATA is a **hot swappable** interface. This means that a compatible drive can be connected or disconnected while the system is running.

Show Slide(s)
SATA (3 slides)

Teaching Tip
Although the exam objectives refer to SATA1, SATA2, and so on, this terminology has been deprecated by SATA IO in favor of either SATA Revision x.x or (in marketing products to consumers) SATA xGbps.

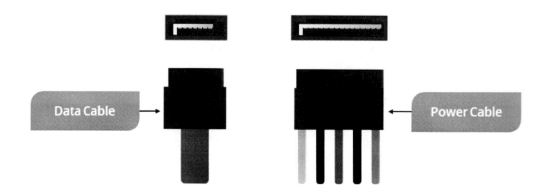

SATA connectors and ports (from left to right): SATA data, SATA power (with 3.3V orange wire). (Image © 123RF.com.)

The first commercially available SATA standard supported speeds of up to 1.5 Gbps. This standard was quickly augmented by SATA revision 2 (3 Gbps) and then SATA revision 3 (6 Gbps).

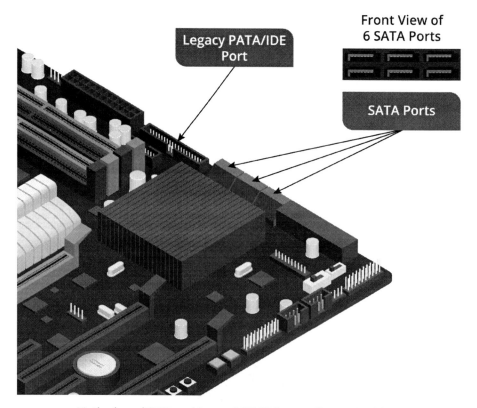

Motherboard SATA and legacy PATA/IDE ports. (Image © 123RF.com.)

More information on SATA standards can be obtained from **www.sata-io.org**.

 *Note: While SATA dominates the PC market, **Serial Attached SCSI (SAS)** is also very popular in the server market. It supports over 16,000 devices, offers point-to-point links (as opposed to shared bandwidth), has none of the termination issues that complicated legacy SCSI, and supports higher bandwidths (up to 12 Gbps).*

SOLID STATE DRIVES

Flash memory is being incorporated onto a new generation of **Solid State Drives (SSDs)** designed to replicate or supplement the function of the hard drive.

Show Slide(s)
Solid State Drives

Teaching Tip
SSD interfaces can be confusing, so be sure you allow time to cover this section in detail.

A 2.5" form factor solid state drive with SATA interface. (Image © 123RF.com.)

The advantages of flash memory-based SSDs are:

- The lack of moving parts makes them quieter, more power efficient, and less prone to catastrophic failure or damage due to shock (dropping or moving a device rapidly, for instance).
- Read times are better because seek time and consequently the effect of file fragmentation is eliminated.
- They are less susceptible to data loss in the event of power failure.
- Most drives still feature DRAM-based write cache to improve performance. In the event of a power failure, unwritten cache would be lost. However, the DRAM cache may be backed up by a battery to cover this eventuality.

The main disadvantage is the high cost; a 64 GB SSD costs a bit more than a 2 TB HDD (a 1 TB SSD can cost the same as a top-end server).

SSD INTERFACES AND FORM FACTORS

An SSD might be installed as the computer's only internal drive or as a system drive for use with an additional hard drive. The SSD would normally be used to install the OS and software applications, whereas the HDD would be used for user data files. In this configuration, both drives are available to the user.

Show Slide(s)
SSD Interfaces and Form Factors (2 slides)

An SSD might be installed to a SATA port as with a mechanical HDD. This is any easy way to upgrade the 2.5" drive in a laptop as the device form factor is exactly the same. The main drawback is that the 6 Gbps SATA interface can be a bottleneck to the best performing SSDs. Consequently, modern SSDs often use the PCI Express (PCIe) bus directly. Where SATA uses the **Advanced Host Controller Interface (AHCI)** logical interface to communicate with the bus, PCIe-based SSDs use the **Non-Volatile Memory Host Controller Interface Specification (NVMHCI)** or **NVM Express (NVMe)** for short.

A PCIe-based SSD can either be implemented as a regular PCIe adapter card or Add-in Card (AiC) or it can use the M.2 adapter interface. M.2 can use up to 4 PCIe **lanes**. Note that M.2 adapters are not hot-swappable or hot-pluggable. An M.2 adapter is considerably smaller than a PCIe adapter so the interface is often used on laptops as well as PC motherboards. M.2 supplies power over the bus so there is no need for a separate power cable. M.2 adapters can be different lengths (42 mm, 60 mm, 80 mm, or 110 mm), so you should check that any given adapter will fit on your motherboard. Labels indicate the adapter sizes supported.

Note: Note that M.2 is a physical form factor and so you can obtain M.2 SSDs that use the SATA/AHCI bus. These will not perform as well as NVMe-based M.2 SSDs. On the motherboard, an M.2 socket may be able to support both types of drive or only one; check the documentation. The key position on the connector is different for SATA and NVMe models. Also note that M.2 can be used for wireless adapters too.

Note: SATA 3.2 defines SATA Express (SATAe) as a means of interfacing with a 2-lane PCI Express bus. It uses a different connector, but the port is backwards-compatible with "ordinary" SATA cabling. You might also come across the U.2 (or SFF-8369) interface. U.2 uses the same physical interface as SATA Express and is hot-swappable, but supports up to 4 PCIe lanes, like M.2.

SSD PERFORMANCE FACTORS

Show Slide(s)

SSD Performance Factors (2 slides)

SSDs normally outperform HDDs but there are situations where they can perform worse than HDDs; when serving large (GB) files, for example.

When making a detailed comparison between different types of storage technology, you need to compare performance against different types of data transfer. For example, read and write performance are not equivalent. There are also differences between sequential access (reading data from the same "block" as might happen when transferring a large file) and random access (reading data from different locations on the drive or transferring lots of small files for instance). Along with the data throughput and latency/access time, you may need to consider the number of Input/Output Operations per Second (IOPS) that can be achieved by a device for different kinds of data transfer operation.

Flash chips are also susceptible to their own type of degradation over the course of many write operations, so the drive firmware and operating system must use **wear leveling** routines to prevent any single storage location from being overused and optimize the life of the device.

HYBRID DRIVES

Show Slide(s)

Hybrid Drives

Teaching Tip

You might also want to mention Intel's Optane "cache bridge" modules.

Solid state storage may also be incorporated on a **hybrid drive**. In a hybrid drive, the SSD portion functions as a large cache, containing data that is accessed frequently. The magnetic disc is only spun up when non-cached data is accessed. Version 3.2 of the SATA standard defines a set of commands to allow the host computer to specify how the cache should be used (also referred to as **host-hinted mode**). Alternatively, the drive firmware can run self-optimizing routines. The user does not have direct control over files stored on the cache.

DUAL-DRIVE CONFIGURATIONS

Show Slide(s)

Dual-Drive Configurations

Another option is for separate SSD and HDD units to be installed in a dual-drive configuration. In this case, the system chipset and storage drivers, usually based on Intel Smart Response Technology (SRT), make the caching decisions. Again, the user does not have control over the use of the SSD.

Note: SRT can only use caches up to 64 GB (at the time of writing). If the SSD is larger, SRT can reserve part of the drive for caching and the remainder of the capacity is then available to the user and can be manipulated via the OS disk and file management tools.

LEGACY STORAGE TECHNOLOGIES

Show Slide(s)

Legacy Storage Technologies (8 slides)

While SATA is the dominant connection method for most drive types, you may come across systems using much older host bus adapters, such as IDE and SCSI. It is important that you know how to configure these older technologies.

IDE/PATA

The **Parallel Advanced Technology Attachment (PATA)** interface was the principal mass storage interface for desktop PCs for many years. The interface was (and still is) also referred to as IDE (Integrated Drive Electronics) or EIDE (Extended IDE). As the name suggests, an EIDE bus uses parallel data transfers, meaning 16 bits is transferred for each clock tick.

A motherboard supporting PATA may come with one or two host adapters or **channels**, called IDE1 and IDE2 or primary (PRI IDE) and secondary (SEC IDE). A single PATA channel is now more typical if the motherboard also supports SATA. Each PATA channel supports two devices, 0 and 1, though they are usually labeled master and slave.

A PATA drive features a 40-pin port but typically uses 80-wire shielded cables, which are required for UDMA4 or better transfer modes. PATA cable is supposed to be up to 46 cm (18") long. Each PATA cable typically has three connectors, one for the motherboard and one for each device. Most cables are "Cable Select," allowing the master and slave device to be identified by the position of the connector on the cable. Pin 1 on the cable must be oriented with pin 1 on the connector. On the cable, pin 1 is identified with a red stripe. The connectors are also keyed to prevent them from being inserted the wrong way around.

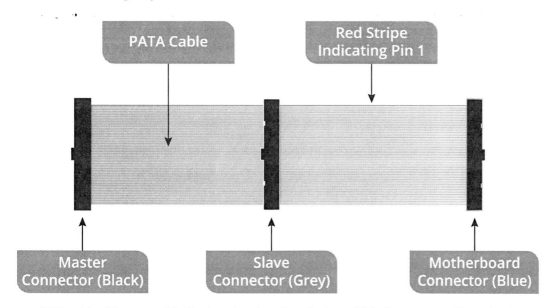

PATA cable with master (black), slave (grey), and motherboard (blue) connectors. The red strip indicates pin 1 on the cable. Note: There is currently a movement to generally rename the "master/slave" terminology to combinations like "parent/child" or "leader/follower." (Image © 123RF.com.)

PATA standards have evolved over the years. This table lists some of the later ATA standards.

Interface Standard	DMA Mode	Max. Transfer Rate (MBps)	Special Features
ATA/ATAPI-4	UDMA 2 (Ultra ATA/33)	33	Ultra DMA, 80-conductor cable, and cyclic redundancy checking
ATA/ATAPI-5	UDMA 4 (Ultra ATA/66)	66	

Interface Standard	DMA Mode	Max. Transfer Rate (MBps)	Special Features
ATA/ATAPI-6	UDMA 5 (Ultra ATA/ 100)	100	48-bit LBA expansion, and disk noise reduction
ATA/ATAPI-7	UDMA 6 (Ultra ATA/ 133)	133	Multimedia streaming

Table notes:

- ATAPI stands for ATA Packet Interface and is an extension to ATA to support CD/DVD drives and tape drives.
- DMA (Direct Memory Access) mode refers to the way that data is transferred to and from system memory.
- In the early days of the EIDE interface, BIOS versions severely restricted maximum drive capacity. Driver software in the OS now handles drive addressing. Logical Block Addressing (LBA) is a method of telling the drive how to address a particular place on the disk surface. 48-bit LBA supports drives up to a (theoretical) 144 Petabytes.

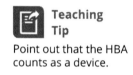

Teaching Tip

Point out that the HBA counts as a device.

SCSI

Small Computer Systems Interface (SCSI) is another parallel bus. One SCSI Host Bus Adapter (HBA) can control multiple devices, attached by internal ribbon cables or external SCSI cables. The SCSI standard also defines a command language that allows the host adapter to identify which devices are connected to the bus and how they are accessed.

SCSI was used to connect peripherals of different types but is now only associated with the connection of storage devices. As with IDE, you will not find SCSI on new systems, but should know how to configure it in case you encounter any legacy systems still

depending on it. A SCSI port is denoted by the following symbol:

The main SCSI standards are described in this table.

Interface Protocol	Standard	Bandwidth (MBps)	Bus Width (bits)	Max. Cable Length (meters)
SCSI-1	SCSI-1	5	8	• SE: 6 • LVD: NA • HVD: 25
Fast SCSI	SCSI-2	10	8	• SE: 3 • LVD: NA • HVD: 25
Fast-Wide SCSI	SCSI-2	20	16	• SE: 3 • LVD: NA • HVD: 25
Ultra SCSI	SCSI-3	20	8	• SE: 1.5 • LVD: NA • HVD: 25
Ultra Wide SCSI	SCSI-3	40	16	• SE: NA • LVD: NA • HVD: 25

Interface Protocol	Standard	Bandwidth (MBps)	Bus Width (bits)	Max. Cable Length (meters)
Ultra2 SCSI	SCSI-3	40	8	• SE: NA • LVD: 12 • HVD: 25
Ultra2 Wide SCSI	SCSI-3	80	16	• SE: NA • LVD: 12 • HVD: 25
Ultra3 SCSI (Ultra160 SCSI)	SCSI-3	160	16	• SE: NA • LVD: 12 • HVD: NA
Ultra 320 SCSI	SCSI-3	320	16	• SE: NA • LVD: 12 • HVD: NA

Given the number of different versions of the standard, SCSI configuration is relatively complex. SCSI devices were typically used on server-class hardware rather than on desktop PCs.

- Host adapter—the SCSI host adapter must be installed and recognized by the system for devices to be detected. A third-party driver might have to be installed for the host adapter to be recognized.
- Bus width—SCSI originally supported 8 devices (the host adapter counts as a device). Wide SCSI supports up to 16 devices.
- Signaling—SCSI specifies three signaling methods. Most buses and devices use Low Voltage Differential (LVD). Single Ended (SE) devices can be added to an LVD bus, but it reduces the performance of the whole bus. H(igh)VD is incompatible with the other two and must not be mixed.
- Termination—a SCSI bus must be terminated at both ends, usually by enabling termination on the first and last devices in the chain. Termination may either be enabled internally on the device by setting a switch or by physically connecting a terminator pack to a device or the host adapter.

 Note: There are passive and active terminators. Passive terminators are generally used with older devices (pre-Ultra SCSI). When installing a terminator pack, the terminator must match the signaling type (SE, LVD, HVD, or SE/LVD). Termination is also made more complex if there is a mix of narrow (8-bit) and wide (16-bit) devices on the bus.

- ID—each SCSI device must be allocated a unique ID, from 0 to 7 (or 15 for wide SCSI). IDs may be allocated automatically or by setting a jumper or click-wheel on the device itself. The order of SCSI ID priorities (from highest to lowest) is 7 through to 0 then 15 through to 8.

 Note: The host adapter is usually set to 7 or 15. A bootable hard disk is usually allocated ID 0.

There were numerous SCSI connectors. Some of the most common were:

- HD68—68-pin connectors used for internal and external ports. 68-pin adapters support Wide SCSI.
- Single Connector Attachment (SCA)—an 80-pin connector that incorporates both a power connector and configuration wires, allowing for hot swappable drives.

Show Slide(s)

Guidelines for Installing Mass Storage Devices

GUIDELINES FOR INSTALLING MASS STORAGE DEVICES

*Note: All of the Guidelines for this lesson are available as checklists from the **Checklist** tile on the CHOICE Course screen.*

Consider these guidelines when installing mass storage devices.

INSTALL MASS STORAGE DEVICES

There are several things to consider when you are installing an internal storage device in a computer system. It is not as simple as just plugging the device into the slot inside the case. Make sure you consider each factor before installation:

- **Does the computer have existing internal storage devices?** Do you need to plan for the addition of another controller for an additional device? You might need to purchase an additional SATA controller before you can add another SATA device. In addition, make sure that the computer has an available slot for the controller.
- **Does the device need additional drivers installed?** Make sure that you have the appropriate operating system device drivers to install the new storage device on the computer. If necessary, download the device drivers from the device manufacturer's website.
- **Does the computer have an available power supply cable to supply power to the device?** If not, you can purchase splitters to enable two (or more) devices to be connected to a single power connection, but be aware of power consumption. The number of connectors approximates the available power, so make sure that the storage device will not cause the computer to exceed the capacity of its power supply.
- **Does the computer have an available drive bay for the storage device?** Most hard drives require a 3.5-inch drive bay; most tape drives and optical drives require a 5.25-inch drive bay. If you want to install a hard drive in a 5.25-inch drive bay, you will need drive rails. Make sure you place the storage device where it will get good air flow to avoid overheating the device. Consider the placement of the drives inside the bays with the cable configurations. You may need to adjust the placement of the drives to match the order of cable connectors.
- **Do you have the necessary data cables to connect the storage device to the controller?** You will need a SATA data cable for each hard drive in the PC. Other types of storage devices might require different types of data cables.
- **Does the placement of the device interrupt the air flow of the case?** Make sure there is enough total air flow to handle whatever heat the new storage device will add to the computer.

Note: When adding or removing storage devices (or performing any type of work inside the PC case), make sure that you take a backup of any data stored on local drives.

*Note: To learn more, check the **Video** tile on the CHOICE Course screen for any videos that supplement the content for this lesson.*

Access the Checklist tile on your CHOICE Course screen for reference information and job aids on How to Install and Configure Mass Storage Devices.

Activity 4-3

Discussing Mass Storage Device Installation and Configuration

SCENARIO

Answer these questions to check your understanding of the content presented in this topic.

Show Slide(s)

Activity: Discussing Mass Storage Device Installation and Configuration

1. **True or false? The read/write heads on an HDD require regular cleaning to obtain optimum performance from the disk.**

    False.

2. **What basic factor might you look at in selecting a high-performance drive?**

    RPM—the speed at which it spins. Other factors to consider include the access and seek times, rotational latency, internal and external rater rates, and reliability.

3. **What is a S.M.A.R.T. hard disk?**

    One with Self Monitoring Analysis and Reporting Technology. This means that it can provide status reports to diagnostic software.

4. **True or false? SATA is an interface for hard drives only.**

    False.

5. **How many storage devices can be attached to a single SATA port?**

    One.

6. **In what two ways could a PC be configured to use an SSD cache?**

    Using a hybrid drive unit with both SSD and magnetic HDD devices or using a dual-drive configuration (with separate SSD / eMMC and HDD units).

7. **You are upgrading a drive. You have removed the main panel from the PC, disconnected the data and power cables, and removed the screws holding the drive to the cage, but it will not slide out. What is your next step?**

    Remove the second panel and check whether there are screws on the other side.

Activity 4-4
Installing Storage Devices

Show Slide(s)

Activity: Installing Storage Devices

Teaching Tip

Be prepared to supply additional storage devices for learners to install into their classroom PCs. Also be ready to assist the class as they work through the activity steps.

Optionally, provision a mix of interface types (SATA, IDE, SCSI, M.2).

If you have sufficient devices and motherboard RAID (or even a controller card), you may also want to ask learners to look at the options for creating a redundant volume (create a mirror, for instance).

BEFORE YOU BEGIN

To complete this activity, you will need the following hardware components for your workbench PC. If you do not have these available, you can remove and reinstall the existing hardware:

- A second hard drive or an optical drive and an empty drive bay.
- An available power connection for the device you are adding to the system.
- Optionally, rails to allow smaller drives to fit into larger drive bays.

You will perform this activity on your WORKBENCH PC.

SCENARIO

In this activity, you will install an additional disk drive into your system. The type of disk you install will depend on the components available, so check with your instructor to see which of the following steps you should complete and for any additional instructions.

---

1. List the type of removable storage devices in your PC and details such as model name or slot types.

Drive Type	Details
_____ Drive	
_____ Drive	
_____ Drive	
_____ Memory Card Reader	
_____ Memory Card Reader	

 Note: You're likely to have an optical drive, one or more memory card readers, and one or more USB drives, as well as possible eSATA ports. Revise the left column as needed to distinctly identify each drive.

2. Add a SATA hard drive and/or optical drive to your system. Depending on the motherboard, you may also need to install a host adapter.

    a) Power off the system, unplug all the peripherals and power cord, and open the computer case.

    b) Examine the motherboard to determine whether there are any SATA ports.

    c) If there are no SATA ports, locate a free adapter slot, and remove the blanking plate. Install the SATA host adapter and screw it down.

    d) Locate an available drive bay, and determine if the bay is the same form factor as the drive. Secure the drive to it, using a caddy and rails if necessary.

    e) Connect the drive to an available SATA port using a SATA cable.

f) Attach a power connector to the drive. You may need to obtain a Molex-SATA power converter from your instructor.

g) Replace the cover on your PC and reboot it.

h) Observe startup messages to check that the drive is detected. If the drive is not detected, check either that the onboard controller is enabled (through system setup) or that the host adapter has been recognized.

3. If you installed a hard disk, complete the following steps to make a partition and format it so that the disk is usable. If you installed a removable storage device, just check that you can read some removable media using it.

a) Reboot the PC into Windows and log on. Press the **Windows+X** keys and select **Computer Management**. Select the **Disk Management** tool.

Your new disk should appear as Disk 1.

b) In the **Initialize Disk** dialog box, select **GPT** and then select **OK**.

c) Right-click the area of **Unallocated Space** and select **New Simple Volume**.

d) Select **Next**.

e) Select **Primary Partition** and select **Next**.

f) Use the maximum amount of disk space. Select **Next**.

g) Assign drive letter **H**. Select **Next**.

h) Select the **NTFS** file system and use the partition label *HOME*. Check the box to perform a **quick format.** Select **Next**, and then select **Finish**.

i) After the format is complete and the partition is marked healthy, test that it is accessible by copying some files to it from your **C:** drive.

j) In **Disk Management**, right-click the volume and select **Delete Volume**. Select **Yes** to confirm.

4. Reverse the steps above to uninstall the extra drive(s) plus any adapter cards that you installed and return them to your instructor.

 Note: Your instructor will let you know if you need to perform this step.

 Teaching Tip

This step is optional - it can just help for the next class to get the learners to reset the PCs to the original configuration.

Topic C

Install and Configure Removable Storage

 EXAM OBJECTIVES COVERED
1001-3.4 Given a scenario, select, install, and configure storage devices.
1001-3.6 Explain the purposes and uses of various peripheral types.

Sometimes, the needs of the user are such that providing additional system memory and mass storage devices is not enough. Consider a situation where raw data is supplied to a user via a DVD, thumb drive, or flash memory card. How will the user get the information off the media and into their PC where they can work with it? In this topic, you will install and configure removable storage.

REMOVABLE STORAGE

 Show Slide(s)
Removable Storage

 Teaching Tip

Point out that this topic deals with not only the removable storage devices that are installed on a PC, but also the removable media that stores portable data.

Removable storage can refer to either a storage device that can be removed, or storage media that is removable.

Internal hard drives and Solid State Drives provide persistent storage for the computer's OS files, software applications, and user data files. Other types of persistent storage can be used as removable media. A removable disk or drive can be attached to a different computer to move or copy data files. Removable media is also used to make a backup.

OPTICAL MEDIA

 Show Slide(s)
Optical Media (9 slides)

 Teaching Tip

You should not have to spend a lot of time on this topic. Just be sure to distinguish the different storage types.

Compact discs (CDs) and **digital versatile discs (DVDs)** are mainstream storage formats for consumer multimedia, such as music and video. Both formats have been adapted for data storage with PC systems. The CD/DVD drives used with PCs can also play consumer versions of the discs.

- The data version of the **CD-ROM (CD)** became ubiquitous on PC systems as it has sufficient capacity (700 MB) to deliver most software applications.
- DVD is an improvement on CD technology and delivers substantially more capacity (up to about 17 GB). DVDs are used for software installs and for games and multimedia.

COMPACT DISCS

A CD is a layer of aluminum foil encased in protective plastic, which can also incorporate a label or screen-printed image on the non-playing side. The foil layer contains a series of **pits** and spaces in-between (called **lands**) arranged in a spiral. The changes between pits and lands are used to encode each bit. A standard CD is 120 mm in diameter and 1.2 mm thick. There are also 80 mm discs, which are playable in most CD-ROM drives.

A recordable version of the CD **(CD-R)** was developed in 1999. Rather than a premastered layer of foil with pits and lands, CD-Rs feature a layer of photosensitive dye. A special laser is used to transform the dye, mimicking the pits and lands of a normal CD, in a process called **burning**. Most ordinary CD players and drives can read CD-Rs but they may not play back properly on older equipment. CD-R is a type of Write Once Read Many (WORM) media. Data areas once written cannot be overwritten. If there is space, a new session can be started on the disc. However, this makes the disc unreadable in older CD-ROM drives.

A rewritable (or multisession) disc format (**CD-RW**) has also been developed. This uses a heat sensitive compound whose properties can be changed between crystalline and amorphous by a special laser. There is some concern over the longevity of recordable CD (and DVD) media. Cheaply manufactured discs have shown a tendency to degrade and become unusable (sometimes over the space of just a few years).

> **Note:** *While the regular capacity of a CD is 700 MB, there are high capacity 800 MB (90 minute) and 860 MB (99 minute) discs that can be used with a CD writer that supports overburning. Note that overburning is more likely to produce disks with data or playback errors.*

DIGITAL VERSATILE DISCS

Compared to CDs, DVDs have higher densities. DVDs are also thinner and can be dual-layer (DVD DL) and/or double-sided (DVD DS). Double-sided discs need to be turned over to play or record to the second side.

DVDs also feature a higher transfer rate, with multiples of 1.32 MBps (equivalent to 9x CD speed). The fastest models feature 24x read and write speeds.

Like CDs, there are recordable and rewritable versions of DVDs, some of which support dual layer recording. There are two slightly different standards for recordable and rewritable DVDs, referred to as DVD-R/DVD-RW versus DVD+R/DVD+RW. Most drives can read all formats but write in either + or - format. Many consumer DVD players can play DVD±R discs. An additional format, Panasonic's DVD-RAM, is not widely supported by computer DVD drives but is optimized for multiple write operations and so well suited to data storage. DVD±R supports dual layer and double-sided media, whereas DVD±RW supports double-sided media only.

BLU-RAY DISCS

Blu-ray Discs (BDs) have emerged as the next generation format for distributing consumer multimedia and can be used to distribute large applications, such as video games. Blu-ray is principally required to cope with the demands of High Definition video recording and playback. HD requires more bandwidth and storage space because it uses a much higher resolution picture (1920x1080 compared to 720x480 [NTSC] or 720x576 [PAL]) and better quality audio (digital surround sound).

A Blu-ray Disc works on fundamentally the same principle as DVD but with a shorter wavelength laser (a 405 nm blue laser compared to DVD's 650 nm red laser). This means discs can be higher density, although the cost of components to make the drives is greater. The base speed for Blu-ray is 4.5 MBps and the maximum theoretical rate is 16x (72 MBps). 2x is the minimum required for movie playback.

A standard BD has a capacity of 25 GB per layer; mini-discs (8 cm) can store 7.8 GB per layer. Dual-layer discs can store up to 50 GB and are readable in ordinary BD drives. Triple-layer 100 GB and quad-layer 128 GB (not currently re-recordable) discs are defined in the BD-XL specification. These require BD-XL compatible drives for writing and reading. There are currently no double-sided formats.

STANDARDS

Standards for the different types of CDs are published by Phillips and Sony as differently colored books.

Standard	CD Type
Red book	Audio CDs (16-bit sampled at 44.1 Hz).

Standard	CD Type
Yellow book	Data CDs with error correction (Mode 1) or without (Mode 2). Mode 2 makes more space available but is only suitable for use with audio and video where small errors can be tolerated.
Orange book	Defines the unused CD-MO and the more popular CD-R and CD-RW.

Standards for DVDs include the following.

Standard	Capacity (GB)	Description
DVD-5	4.7	Single layer, single-sided.
DVD-9	8.5	Dual layer, single-sided.
DVD-10	9.4	Single layer, double-sided.
DVD-18	17.1	Dual layer, double-sided.
DVD-Video	Up to 17.1	Commercially produced DVDs using mpeg encoding and chapters for navigation (can be single or dual layer and single or double-sided).
DVD-Audio	8.5	Format for high quality audio (superior sampling rates and 5.1 surround sound, for instance).

DRM AND REGION CODING

Consumer DVDs feature copy protection mechanisms such as Digital Rights Management (DRM) and region coding. Region coding, if enforced, means that a disc can only be used on a player from the same region.

Here are the DVD region codes in use:

- Region 0: No coding (playback is not restricted).
- Region 1: Canada and the US.
- Region 2: Europe, the Middle East, Japan, South Africa, and Egypt.
- Region 3: SE Asia.
- Region 4: South America, Australia, and New Zealand.
- Region 5: Russia, parts of Africa, and parts of Asia.
- Region 6: China.

 Note: The DVD drive region can be set via Device Manager.

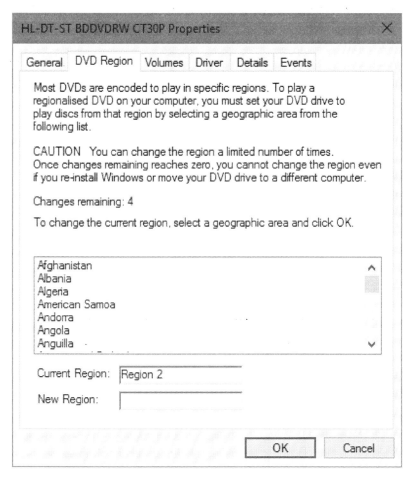

The DVD region supported by a PC DVD drive can be changed via Device Manager—though the firmware only permits a limited number of changes. (Screenshot used with permission from Microsoft.)

Some DVD players are multi-region, but some discs feature protection mechanisms to disable playback in such machines. PC software is not usually region coded, with the exception of some PC game discs.

Like DVDs, consumer Blu-ray Discs (BD-ROMs) are likely to be DRM-protected and may be region coded:

- Region A: America, Japan, and SE Asia.
- Region B: EMEA, Africa, Australia, and New Zealand.
- Region C: Russia and Central Asia (including China).

OPTICAL DRIVES

Optical drives include CD drives, DVD drives, and Blu-Ray drives.

Show Slide(s)

Optical Drives (2 slides)

Optical drives are considerably larger than hard disks (5.25" form factor). An internal unit would be installed to a 5.25" drive bay and connected to the motherboard via SATA data and power connectors. An external unit would be connected via USB (or possibly eSATA or Thunderbolt). External optical drives typically require their own power supply, provided via a supplied AC adapter. CD drives are rated according to their data transfer speed. The original drives had a data transfer rate of 150 KBps. Subsequently, drives have been available that offer multiples of the original rate; this would be around 52x for new models, offering transfer rates in excess of 7 MBps.

Optical disc drive. (Image © 123RF.com.)

Many optical drives also function as recordable/rewritable CD burners (or writers). Such drives feature three speeds, always expressed as the Record/Rewrite/Read speed (for example, 24x/16x/52x). One feature to look out for on such drives is BURN-proof technology, which prevents discs being ruined by buffer under-run errors (where the software cannot supply the drive the data to write quickly enough).

A **CD drive** consists of a spindle motor (to spin the disc), a laser and lens (to read the disc), and a tracking system to move the laser and lens assembly. The mechanism for inserting a CD is either tray or slot based. Slot-loading mechanisms have rollers that grab the disc. Sometimes, these cannot handle non-standard disc sizes. A drive may feature audio play and volume controls and a headphone jack.

 Note: Drives also feature a small hole that accesses a disc eject mechanism (insert a paper clip to activate the mechanism). This is useful if the standard eject button will not work or if the drive does not have power.

A **DVD drive** is similar to a CD drive, but with a different encoding method and a shorter wavelength laser. DVD drives also feature a higher transfer rate, with multiples of 1.32 MBps (equivalent to 9x CD speed). The fastest models feature 24x read and write speeds.

 Note: Most DVD drives can read and burn both DVD and CD media. When DVD was first introduced, drives that could burn CDs but only read DVDs were referred to as combo drives.

Generally speaking, **Blu-ray drives** are also capable of CD and DVD playback and burning. Recordable (BD-R) and re-recordable (BD-RE) drives and discs are also available. BD-R is often available at the same speed as playback while BD-RE is usually half playback speed.

FLASH MEMORY DEVICES

Solid state storage is any type of persistent digital storage technology that does not use mechanical parts. Most solid state devices used with modern PCs are based on **flash memory**. Flash memory is a type of non-volatile Electrically Erasable Programmable Read-Only Memory (EEPROM), also referred to as NAND flash. Flash memory is non-volatile because it does not need a power source to retain information.

Compared to other types of storage, flash memory is very small and light. Mass manufacturing has seen prices fall to affordable levels. Storage capacity ranges from 512 MB to 256 GB. Larger drives than this are available but (at the time of writing) are prohibitively expensive.

As the costs of producing flash memory have fallen, it has become a very popular removable storage technology.

 Show Slide(s)

Flash Memory Devices (3 slides)

 Teaching Tip

Flash memory is overtaking most applications of older storage technology. You might also want to mention the XQD and CFast formats.

NAND flash is named after the type of logic gate (NOT AND) used to design the memory cells. EEPROM uses a different logic gate (NOR). The main practical difference is that EEPROMs erase small blocks of one byte, while NAND flash erases block sizes similar to a disk sector (512 bytes or larger) per operation, making NAND flash faster. EEPROMs suffer less from write wearing, though.

USB thumb drive (left) and SD memory card (right). (Image © 123RF.com.)

There are many ways of packaging flash memory for external storage use. One of the most popular is the USB drive (or thumb or pen drive). This type of drive simply plugs into any spare USB port.

Another popular type of packaging is the **memory card**, used extensively in consumer digital imaging products, such as digital still and video cameras. There are several proprietary types of memory card.

- Secure Digital (SD)—this full-size card comes in three capacity variants. The original SD cards have a 2 GB maximum capacity, whereas SDHC is up to 32 GB and SDXC is up to 2 TB. There are also four speed variants. The original specification is up to 25 MBps, UHS allows up to 108 MBps, UHS-II is rated at up to 156 MBps full duplex or 312 MBps half duplex, while UHS-III specifies two full duplex rates of 312 MBps (FD312) and 624 MBps (FD624).
- Mini-SD—this is a smaller version of the SD card, using the same capacity and speed designations.
- Micro-SD—this is the smallest version of the SD card, using the same capacity and speed designations.
- Compact Flash (CF)—nominally supports 512 GB, though no cards larger than 256 GB were ever made. The speed of CF cards is rated on the same system as CDs, using multiples of 150 KBps. The fastest devices work at up to 1066x read speeds (or 160 MBps).
- xD—this format was used on Olympus cameras but has been discontinued.

 Note: The speeds quoted are "max burst speed." Sustained read and write speeds will be much lower. Cards also have a speed class rating indicating their minimum write speed capability.

 Note: The smaller form factors can be used with regular size readers using a caddy to hold the card.

MEMORY CARD READERS

Many PCs are fitted with **memory card readers** with slots that will accommodate most of the sticks on the market.

A memory card reader is usually designed to fit in a front-facing 3.5" drive bay, though some can be fitted to a 5.25" bay.

Show Slide(s)
Memory Card Readers (2 slides)

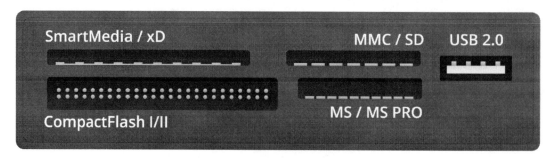

Multi-card reader. (Image © 123RF.com.)

The reader then needs to be connected to a USB hub. Most motherboards have at least one spare 9-pin USB header for making internal connections, or the reader may come with an expansion card (as with the HP model shown below). Alternatively, you may be able to run a USB converter cable from the reader to one of the external USB ports.

 Note: *To support the fast speeds of modern card types, the reader must be connected to a USB 3 port.*

Another option is an external USB memory card reader.

EXTERNAL STORAGE DRIVES

Show Slide(s)
External Storage Drives

External hard disks and portable SSDs have become very popular for backup, additional storage, and as a means of transferring files. External drives are packaged in a **drive enclosure**. The drive enclosure usually provides USB, Thunderbolt, and/or eSATAp ports. The enclosure also provides for an external power supply, if the drive is too large to be powered over USB, and the casing protects the drive from damage.

External storage device. (Image © 123RF.com.)

Some enclosures support Ethernet network connections, referred to as **Network Attached Storage (NAS)**. Advanced enclosures are designed to host multiple disk units, possibly configured in a RAID array to provide better data security.

Activity 4-5

Discussing Removable Storage Device Installation and Configuration

SCENARIO

Answer the following questions to check your understanding of the topic.

1. **What is the primary benefit of using removable solid state storage?**

   Answers will vary, but should include the portability of thumb drives and flash memory cards plus easier and faster rewriting compared to optical media.

2. **Which two media types allow you to write to an optical disc only once?**

   ☐ CD-ROM

   ☑ CD-R

   ☐ CD+RW

   ☑ DVD+R

   ☐ DVD-RW

3. **If a CD writer is 12x8x32x, what is the maximum transfer rate when creating a CD-R?**

   1.8 MBps (1800 KBps).

4. **True or false? DVD-RW media allows double-layer recording.**

   False. Only DVD, DVD-R, or DVD+R media can be double layer.

5. **What is the transfer rate of a 10x DVD drive?**

   13.21 MBps

6. **What is the capacity of a single Blu-ray dual-layer recordable disc?**

   50 GB (25 GB per layer).

7. **True or false? A memory card reader is needed to attach a USB flash memory drive to a PC.**

   False—the "drive" will plug into any USB port.

Show Slide(s)
Activity: Discussing Removable Storage Device Installation and Configuration

Teaching Tip
Consider displaying various examples of storage devices, including both drives and discs or other media, and ask participants to identify them. This can be an opportunity to generate discussion on the differences between the various types of devices and the media that they use, as well as the common practice of treating the drive and the medium as identical entities.

8. **Name the two main specifications for currently available memory card formats.**

Secure Digital (SD) and Compact Flash (CF).

Topic D

Configure RAID

EXAM OBJECTIVES COVERED

1001-3.4 Given a scenario, select, install and configure storage devices.

Whether it is the system files required to run the OS or data files generated by users, an HDD or SSD stores critical data. If a boot drive fails, the system will crash, and if a data drive fails, users will lose access to files and there may be permanent data loss if those files have not been backed up. To mitigate these risks, the drives that underpin critical systems can be provisioned in a redundant configuration. Redundancy sacrifices some disk capacity but provides fault tolerance for the mission-critical volume. As a PC technician, you will have to configure and support such systems very often, so it is important that you understand the types of redundant drive configurations available.

RAID

With **Redundant Array of Independent Disks (RAID)**, many hard disks can act as backups for each other to increase reliability and fault tolerance, or they can act together as one very large drive.

> *Note: RAID can also be said to stand for "Redundant Array of Inexpensive Disks" and the "D" can also stand for "devices."*

RAID LEVELS

The RAID advisory board defines RAID levels. The most common levels are numbered from 0 to 6, where each level corresponds to a specific type of fault tolerance. Only levels 0, 1, and 5 are of much relevance at the desktop, however.

- **RAID 0 (Striping without Parity). Disk striping** is a technique where data is divided into blocks and spread in a fixed order among all the disks in the array. RAID 0 requires at least two disks. Its principal advantage is to improve performance by spreading disk I/O over multiple drives.

  The logical volume size is the combined total of the smallest capacity physical disk in the array. When building a RAID array, all the disks should normally be identical in terms of capacity and ideally in terms of type and performance, though this is not mandatory. If disks are different sizes, the size of the smallest disk in the array determines the maximum amount of space that can be used on the larger drives. RAID 0 adds no storage overhead and is a means of obtaining a large logical volume from multiple, low capacity disks.

  However, because it provides no redundancy, this method cannot be said to be a true RAID implementation. If any physical disk in the array fails, the whole logical volume will fail, causing the computer to crash and requiring data to be recovered from backup. Consequently, RAID 0 would never be used for live data storage.

Show Slide(s)

RAID

Interaction Opportunity

We've mentioned configuring "software" RAID using the Windows Dynamic Disks and Storage Spaces features. Most workstations and servers use hardware RAID, with a dedicated RAID-capable disk controller. Emphasize what is meant by RAID 0, RAID 1, and RAID 5.

Show Slide(s)

RAID Levels (9 slides)

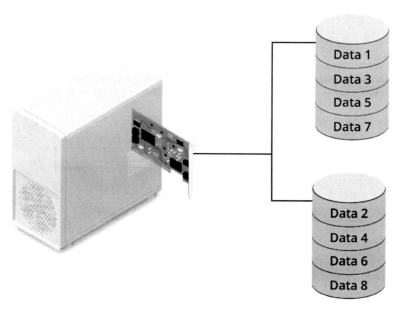

RAID 0 (striping) - data is spread across the array. (Image © 123RF.com.)

- **RAID 1 (Mirroring). Mirroring** requires two hard disks. The mirror disk is a duplicate of the data disk. Each write operation is duplicated on the second disk in the set, introducing a small performance overhead. A read operation can use either disk, boosting performance somewhat.

  This strategy is the simplest way of protecting a single disk against failure. If one disk fails (degrading the array), the other takes over. There is little impact on performance during this time (obviously the boost of having two drives available for read operations is lost), so availability remains good, but the failed disk should be replaced as quickly as possible as there is no longer any redundancy. When the disk is replaced, it must be populated with data from the other disk (resynching). Performance while rebuilding is reduced, though RAID 1 is better than other levels in that respect and the rebuilding process is generally shorter than parity-based RAID.

  In terms of cost per gigabyte, disk mirroring is more expensive than other forms of fault tolerance because disk space utilization is only 50 percent. Also the total volume size cannot exceed the available capacity of the physical disks. However, disk mirroring usually has a lower entry cost because it requires only two disks and a relatively cheap RAID controller (or software RAID). The availability of cheap, large HDDs makes the 50% overhead less of a drawback.

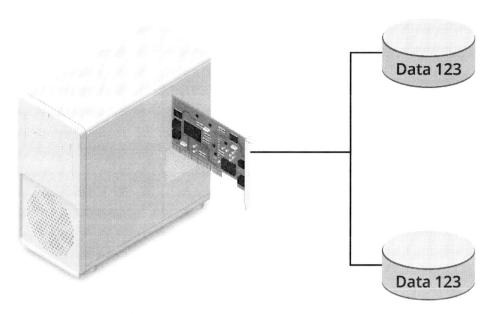

RAID 1 (mirroring) - data is written to both disks simultaneously. (Image © 123RF.com.)

- **RAID 5 (Striping with Distributed Parity)** Striping with distributed parity (RAID 5) writes error checking information across all the disks in the array. The data and parity information is managed so that the two are always on different disks. If a single disk fails, enough information is spread across the remaining disks to allow the data to be completely reconstructed. Stripe sets with parity offer the best performance for read operations. However, when a disk has failed, the read performance is degraded by the need to recover the data using the parity information. Also, all normal write operations suffer reduced performance due to the parity calculation.

RAID 5 requires a minimum of three drives but can be configured with more. This allows more flexibility in determining the overall capacity of the array than is possible with RAID 1. A "hard" maximum number of devices is set by the controller or OS support, but the number of drives used is more likely to be determined by practicalities such as cost and risk. Remember that adding more disks increases the chance of failure.

The level of fault tolerance and available disk space is inverse. As you add disks to the set, fault tolerance decreases but usable disk space increases. If you configure a RAID 5 set using 3 disks, a third of each disk is set aside for parity. If four are used, one quarter is reserved on each disk. Using a three 80 GB disk configuration, you would have a 160 GB usable volume.

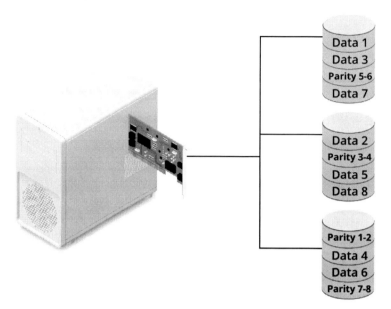

RAID 5 (striping with parity). (Image © 123RF.com.)

Note: *If the disks are different sizes, the size used is that of the smallest disk. Extra disk space on larger drives is wasted.*

- **RAID 1+0 (RAID 10).** As described previously, RAID 0 is striping with no parity (that is, no fault tolerance is provided). This provides high throughput, but leaves the volume at risk. RAID 1 provides mirroring; the highest achievable disk fault tolerance. RAID 1+0 (also called RAID 10) is a combination of both these configurations (nested RAID). A logical striped volume is configured with two mirrored arrays. This configuration offers excellent fault tolerance as one disk in each mirror can fail and the array will still function.

  You will need at least four disks to create this configuration and there must be an even number of disks. Note that it carries the same 50% disk overhead that mirroring does.

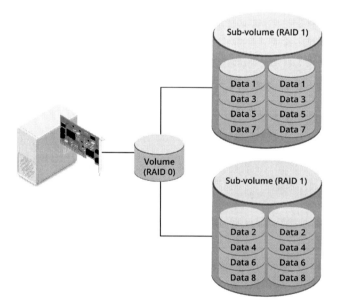

RAID 10 - either disk in each of the sub-volumes can fail without bringing down the mail volume. (Image © 123RF.com.)

RAID CONFIGURATION OPTIONS

It is possible to implement RAID using either hardware or software.

Show Slide(s)

RAID Configuration Options (4 slides)

HARDWARE RAID

A **hardware RAID solution** means that creating volumes from an array of physical disks is an operation supported by a plug-in controller card or by the motherboard, independently of the installed operating system. Hardware solutions are principally differentiated by their support for RAID levels. Entry-level controllers might support only RAID 0 or RAID 1, whereas mid-level controllers might add support for RAID 5 and RAID 10.

In addition, hardware RAID is often able to hot swap a damaged disk (replace the failed unit without shutting down Windows), thereby keeping the system operational all the time. Hot swapping is a feature of high-end hardware RAID solutions and requires a compatible controller and disk units. When the new disk is installed, the RAID controller transparently synchronizes it with the remaining disks in the set.

On the downside, hardware RAID is more expensive than a software solution and may lock you into a single vendor solution.

Modern low cost RAID solutions may use the SATA interface whereas Serial Attached SCSI (SAS) is a popular technology for server-class machines.

The array is normally configured by launching the firmware configuration utility by pressing the appropriate key combination during startup. Sometimes a RAID controller configuration tool is available from within the OS, too.

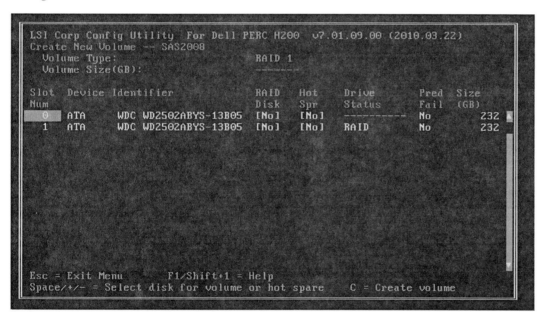

Configuring a volume using RAID controller firmware.

SOFTWARE RAID

Windows provides the option to set up software-based RAID using standard disks and controllers. Windows Server and Windows client Professional/Enterprise editions support fault tolerant mirroring (RAID 1) and striping with parity (RAID 5) arrays. In a software solution, internal disks using different types of interface can be combined in an array but USB- or Thunderbolt-connected external drives are usually not supported. All editions of Windows 10, however, come with the Storage Spaces feature, which provides mirroring and parity-based RAID-like functionality with USB-connected and other external drive types. Linux® can use the Logical Volume Manager (LVM) to implement most RAID levels.

HOT SWAP

A system configured for RAID might support **hot swappable** drives. While this is usually a server-level feature, it might be implemented on high-end workstations. Rather than using cabled connectors, hot swappable drives plug (or "mate") into a combined data and power port on the enclosure. This means that drives can be easily added and removed from the front of the case without having to open the chassis. The drives are secured and released from the enclosure using a latch.

Media server with hot swappable hard drives. (Image © 123RF.com.)

Activity 4-6
Discussing RAID Configuration

Show Slide(s)

Activity: Discussing RAID Configuration

SCENARIO

Answer the following questions to check your understanding of the topic.

---

1. **If you have a computer with three hard disks, what type of RAID fault-tolerant configuration will make best use of them?**

   RAID 5 (striping with parity); RAID 0 is not fault-tolerant and RAID 1 and RAID 10 require an even number of disks.

2. You are configuring four 120 GB drives in a RAID 5 array.

   How much space will be available?

   360 GB.

3. **What is the minimum number of disks required to implement RAID 10 and how much of the disks' total capacity will be available for the volume?**

   RAID 10 requires at least four disks (two mirrored pairs) and comes with a 50% capacity overhead so the volume will only be half the total disk capacity.

Topic E
Troubleshoot Storage Devices

EXAM OBJECTIVES COVERED
1001-5.3 Given a scenario, troubleshoot hard drives and RAID arrays.

End users rely on the hard drives in their PCs to store important system information and personal or professional data and files. Without a hard drive that works properly, the computer system is essentially worthless. As a CompTIA A+ technician, you will likely be called upon to fix or troubleshoot common problems with hard drives and other storage devices.

DISK FAILURES

Hard disk drives are most likely to fail due to mechanical problems either in the first few months of operation or after a few years, when they begin to reach the end of their useful life. Sudden loss of power can also damage a disk, especially if it is in the middle of a read/write operation.

A hard drive that is failing might display the following symptoms:

- **Read/write failure**. When you are trying to open or save a file, an error message such as "Cannot read from the source disk" is displayed.
- **Blue Screen of Death (BSoD)**. A failing hard disk and file corruption may cause a particularly severe read/write failure, resulting in system STOP errors (a crash screen).
- **Bad sectors**. When you run the `chkdsk /r` program it can test the surface of the hard disk. If more bad sectors are located each time the test is run, it is a sure sign that the disk is about to fail.

 Note: Use the Check Disk utility regularly to check that the drive is in good condition. `chkdsk /f` will fix file system errors but will not identify bad sectors.

- **Constant LED activity**. **Disk thrashing** can be a sign that there is not enough system RAM as data is continually moved between RAM and the pagefile.
- **Noise**. A healthy hard disk makes a certain low-level noise when accessing the platters. A loud or grinding noise or any sort of clicking is a sign of a problem.

When experiencing any of these symptoms, replace the disk as soon as possible to minimize the risk of data loss.

DISK INTEGRITY TESTING

You can use the Windows `chkdsk` utility to verify the integrity of a formatted disk. Most hard drives run a self-diagnostic program called **S.M.A.R.T (Self-Monitoring, Analysis, and Reporting Technology)** that can alert the operating system if reliability is compromised. In Windows, you can run the following command to perform a S.M.A.R.T check:

```
wmic /node:localhost diskdrive get status
```

Teaching Tip

Be sure you allocate sufficient time to cover this content. Stress the importance of data and the need to back it up, especially if troubleshooting efforts are not successful.

Show Slide(s)

Disk Failures

Interaction Opportunity

As you present this content, ask learners if they have experience with any of these issues and discuss the appropriate responses.

Interaction Opportunity

Ask learners to listen to their PCs to detect normal disk noise (hopefully) and to observe any disk status indicator lights.

Show Slide(s)

Disk Integrity Testing (2 slides)

Interaction Opportunity

If you have SpeedFan installed on the HOST or WORKBENCH PCs, ask learners to start it and view the output for disk information.

If you suspect that a drive is failing, you should try to run more advanced diagnostic tests on the drive. Most hard drive vendors supply utilities for testing drives or there may be a system diagnostics program supplied with the computer system.

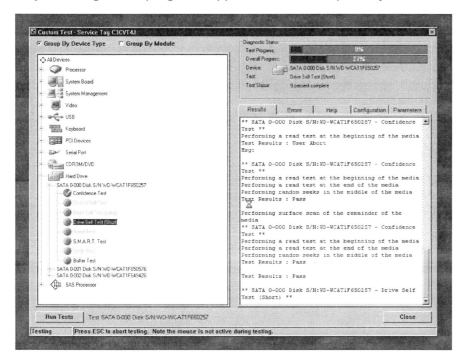

Using system diagnostics software to test a hard drive.

You can also use Windows utilities to query S.M.A.R.T. and run manual tests.

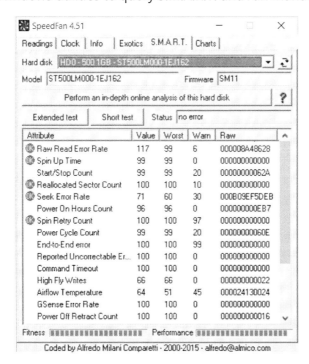

Viewing S.M.A.R.T. information via the SpeedFan utility.

Show
Slide(s)

Boot Failures (2 slides)

BOOT FAILURES

If the hard drive is not detected at boot (or if a second hard drive is not shown under Windows), first check that it is powering up. Drive activity is usually indicated by an LED on the front panel of the system unit case. If this is inactive, check that the drive has a power connector attached. If the PC has no LEDs, or you suspect that they may be faulty, it is usually possible to hear the hard drive spinning up. Once you have determined that the drive is powering up, try the following:

- If the system is not booting correctly from the hard drive, check that the boot sequence is set correctly in the PC firmware system setup program and that there are no removable disks in floppy or optical drives.
- Check that data cables are not damaged and that they are correctly connected to the drive.
- If the drives are connected to a motherboard port, check that it has not been disabled by a jumper or via system setup.

Once you have determined that the drive configuration is correct, try the following. If a boot hard drive is detected by the firmware hardware check (**Power On Self-Test [POST]**) but not by Windows (for example, if you get an error such as "OS not found"), there is probably a problem with the file system. Boot into the recovery environment using the Windows setup disc and enter C: at the command prompt. If this produces the error message **Invalid media type**, the disk has no valid file system structure on it. This may be caused by surface errors or by a virus. You may be able to recover from this by running the bootrec tool at a boot command prompt or by reformatting the disk (at the expense of any data, of course).

If you enter C: at the command prompt and you see the error message **Invalid drive specification**, the drive may have an invalid partition structure. You can check the drive's partition structure with diskpart.

Show
Slide(s)

Boot Block Repair (2 slides)

BOOT BLOCK REPAIR

One of the unwelcome actions that malware can perform is to damage the boot information on the hard drive. There are two ways of formatting the boot information: **MBR** and **GPT**.

- In the Master Boot Record (MBR) scheme, the MBR is located in the first sector of the first partition. It contains information about the partitions on the disk plus some code that points to the location of the active boot sector. The Boot Sector is located either on the sector after the MBR or the first sector of each other partition. It describes the partition file system and contains the code that points to the method of booting the OS (the Boot Configuration Data store for a Windows system, or GRUB or LILO Linux boot managers). Each primary partition can contain a boot sector, but only one of them can be marked active.
- With the Globally Unique ID (GUID) Partition Table (GPT) boot scheme, the boot information is not restricted to a single sector, but still serves the same basic purpose of identifying partitions and boot loaders. GPT is associated with UEFI firmware, but can also be used by most legacy BIOS firmware if supported by the OS (32-bit Windows has problems booting from a combination of GPT and BIOS). GPT is not subject to the restrictions on number and size of partitions that limit MBR; there are still limits, but not ones that are likely to be reached in practice.

 Note: GPT often uses a "protective" MBR to prevent disk tools from overwriting the GPT.

Whether the disk is using an MBR or GPT partitioning scheme, damage to these records results in boot errors such as "OS not found" or "Invalid drive specification." If this problem has been caused by a virus (it can also occur due to disk corruption or installing operating systems with conflicting boot loaders in multiboot configurations), the best way to resolve it is to use the boot disk option in your antivirus software. This will include a basic antivirus scanner that may detect the virus that caused the problem in the first place.

If you don't have the option of using a recovery disk created by the antivirus software, you can try to use the repair options that come with the Windows product disk. Be aware that these may not work completely reliably if the system is still infected with a virus.

1. Boot from the product disk and select the **Repair** option.
2. First, try to use the **Startup Repair** option. If this does not work, select the **Command Prompt** option.
    *   Enter `bootrec /fixmbr` to attempt repair of the MBR.
    *   Enter `bootrec /fixboot` to attempt repair of the boot sector.
    *   Enter `bootrec /rebuildbcd` to add missing Windows installations to the Boot Configuration Database (BCD).
3. Restart the PC.

 Note: These tools may not be suitable for use with multiboot configurations if one of the other OSes has created a non-standard partition table.

FILE RECOVERY OPTIONS

If the computer will not boot from a hard disk, you may want to try to recover data from it. To do this, you will usually need to remove the drive from its internal enclosure and connect it to another PC. Use a driver that matches the type (flat, crosshead/ crosspoint/Phillips, or star/Torx) and size of screw to avoid damaging the screw heads or threads.

 **Show Slide(s)** File Recovery Options (2 slides)

External enclosure kits are available to provide the data and power connectors required. The enclosure will then generally be interfaced to the PC via a USB port and the disk can be mounted using **Disk Management** (if it is in a state to be recognized by Windows) or analyzed using file recovery software.

If a file is corrupted, it may be possible to use software to rebuild it (or at least, to recover some data from it). `chkdsk` restores file fragments from bad sectors to the root of the volume (as filennnn.chk files), but these are rarely directly usable. Third-party file recovery software is available and can be more successful.

Using file recovery software to scan a disk.

DISK PERFORMANCE ISSUES

Show Slide(s)

Disk Performance Issues

Slow disk performance is often a bottleneck for modern computer systems. In this case, the best solution may be to add more RAM rather than replace the disk or to upgrade the disk to an SSD or hybrid drive.

Disk performance can be improved by ensuring that file fragmentation is minimized. **Disk defragmentation** is a process whereby the contents of a disk are moved around to optimize disk access times. The components of a file (known as clusters) are placed adjacent on the disk surface (they are said to be contiguous). Windows normally tries to run the defragmenter periodically as a scheduled task, but this process can be interrupted by user file access requests. It may be necessary to run the tool manually during a "downtime" period.

Teaching Tip

The low disk space threshold is still set at 200 MB.

Low disk capacity can also be a cause of slow performance. When a disk is 90% full, its capacity meter is shown in red in Explorer. Windows warns the user via the notification area when disk space is critically low (below 200 MB). If the disk continues to be filled up, system performance will be very severely impacted. You can use the Disk Cleanup program to free up space, but the user may have to take manual steps, such as moving or deleting files, uninstalling unnecessary applications, and so on.

GUIDELINES FOR TROUBLESHOOTING OPTICAL DRIVES

Consider these guidelines when troubleshooting optical drives.

Show Slide(s)

Guidelines for Troubleshooting Optical Drives (2 slides)

GENERAL TROUBLESHOOTING TIPS FOR OPTICAL DRIVES

Here are some general guidelines for troubleshooting optical drives:

- Optical drives such as CD, DVD, and Blu-ray drives can generally go for a very long time between failures. This is because the part of the drive that reads the disc does not actually touch the disc. All reading (and writing with recordable and re-writable media) is done using lasers. This means that the read/write "heads" are not as likely to get dirty as with magnetic media drives such as floppy drives, where the read/

write heads commonly touch the disc. However, discs do get dirty and carry that dirt inside the optical drive. Special cleaning kits are available for cleaning optical drives if read/write problems are experienced. Most problems related to dirt, though, are caused by dirt on the disc itself.

- Support for CD drives is built into Windows. If your CD drive is not able to read CDs at all, it is likely to be a hardware problem.
- DVD-Video requires MPEG decoding hardware or software (codecs) to be installed for playback. This is supplied with Vista Home Premium and Ultimate editions and in each edition of Windows 7 except Starter and Home Basic. Windows 8 requires third-party software to be installed. Remember also that a DVD-ROM cannot be read from a CD-ROM drive.
- There is currently no native support for Blu-ray in any version of Windows, but the drive should be bundled with the appropriate codecs and software.

TROUBLESHOOTING CD/DVD/BD WRITING

Here are some guidelines for troubleshooting write errors on optical discs:

- Where Windows does not support a particular recordable or rewritable format directly, third-party software is required.
- Some writable media are not manufactured to the highest possible standards, so errors during CD or DVD write operations can be quite common. Check that you are using the write speed recommended for the brand of discs you have purchased. If the error is persistent, however, it is not due to the media.
- Most problems are connected to buffer underruns. On older devices, once the writing process starts, it cannot be paused. Therefore, if the OS does not supply data to the burner's buffer quickly enough, errors will be introduced into the disc's layout. The following solutions can usually be applied:
  - Try burning discs at a lower write speed.
  - Copy source files to the local hard disk (rather than removable or network drives).
  - Do not use other applications when burning a disc.
- The latest CD and DVD writers usually ship with buffer underrun protection.

COMMON RAID CONFIGURATION ISSUES

RAID is usually a means of protecting data against the risk of a hard disk drive failing. The data is either copied to a second drive (mirroring) or additional information is recorded on multiple drives to enable them to recover from a device failure (parity). RAID can be implemented using hardware controllers or features of the operating system. However, you might encounter the following issues with RAID systems:

Show Slide(s)

Common RAID Configuration Issues

- RAID not found.
- RAID stops working.

*Note: To learn more, check the **Video** tile on the CHOICE Course screen for any videos that supplement the content for this lesson.*

GUIDELINES FOR TROUBLESHOOTING RAID ISSUES

Here are some guidelines to consider when you are troubleshooting RAID issues.

Show Slide(s)

Guidelines for Troubleshooting RAID Issues (2 slides)

TROUBLESHOOT RAID ISSUES

Consider these guidelines as you troubleshoot RAID issues:

- If Windows does not detect a RAID array during setup or at boot time:

- Check that the drivers for the RAID controller are installed and use the RAID configuration utility to verify its status.

```
                                                    F10 = System Services
                                                    F11 = BIOS Boot Manager
                                                          F12 = PXE Boot
One 2.40 GHz Quad-core Processor, Bus Speed:4.80 GT/s, L2/L3 Cache:1 MB/8 MB

System Memory Size: 4.0 GB, System Memory Speed: 1067 MHz



Broadcom NetXtreme II Ethernet Boot Agent v5.0.5
Copyright (C) 2000-2009 Broadcom Corporation
All rights reserved.
Press Ctrl-S to Configure Device (MAC Address - 842B2B19E291)



Dell PERC H200/6Gbps SAS HBA BIOS
MPT2BIOS-7.01.09.00 (2010.03.22)
Copyright 2000-2009 LSI Corporation.

Integrated RAID exception detected:
    Volume (Hd1:079) is currently in state INACTIVE/OPTIMAL
Enter the Dell PERC H200/HBA Configuration Utility to investigate!

Press Ctrl-C to start Dell PERC H200/HBA Configuration Utility..
```

Boot message indicating a problem with the RAID volume—press Ctrl+C to start the utility and troubleshoot.

- If you cannot access the configuration utility, then the controller itself could have failed.
- If RAID stops working:
  - One of the purposes of using RAID (or at least RAID 1/5/10) is that it is much less likely than a simple disk system to just "stop working." If one of the underlying disks fails, the volume will be listed as "degraded," but the data on the volume will still be accessible.

 Note: *RAID 0 has no redundancy, so if one of the disks fails, it will stop working. In this scenario, you had better hope that you have a recent data backup.*

  - The precise process for managing a disk failure with an array will be dependent on the vendor that supplied the array and the configuration being supported. All array controllers will be capable of generating an event to the OS system log and perhaps of generating an alert message for the administrator.

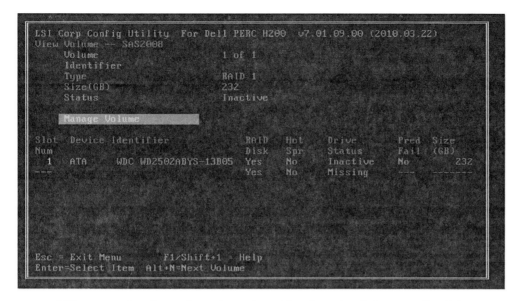

```
LSI Corp Config Utility  For Dell PERC H200  v7.01.09.00 (2010.03.22)
View Volume -- SAS2008
    Volume                    1 of 1
    Identifier
    Type                      RAID 1
    Size(GB)                  232
    Status                    Inactive

    Manage Volume

Slot  Device Identifier          RAID  Hot  Drive      Pred  Size
Num                              Disk  Spr  Status      Fail  (GB)
  1   ATA      WDC WD2502ABYS-13B05  Yes   No   Inactive    No       232
                                   Yes   No   Missing

Esc = Exit Menu        F1/Shift+1 = Help
Enter=Select Item  Alt+N=Next Volume
```

RAID errors using the configuration utility - this volume is missing one of its disks.

- Most desktop-level RAID solutions can tolerate the loss of only one disk, so it should be replaced as soon as possible. If the array supports hot swapping, then the new disk can simply be inserted into the chassis of the computer or disk chassis. Once this is done, the array can be rebuilt using the RAID configuration utility (if a hardware RAID controller is used) or Disk Management (if you are using dynamic disks to implement "software" RAID). Note that the rebuilding process is likely to severely affect performance as the controller is likely to be writing multiple gigabytes of data to the new disk.

> **Note:** *When hot swapping a faulty disk out, take extreme caution not to remove a healthy disk from the array as making a mistake could cause the array to fail, depending on the configuration. Disk failure is normally indicated by a red LED. Always make a backup beforehand.*

- If a volume is not available, either more than the tolerated number of disks has failed or the controller has failed. If the boot volume is affected, then the operating system will not start. If too many disks have failed, you will have to turn to the latest backup or try to use file recovery solutions. If the issue is controller failure, then data on the volume should be recoverable, though there may be file corruption if a write operation was interrupted by the failure. Either install a new controller or import the disks into another system.

> **Note:** *To learn more, check the **Video** tile on the CHOICE Course screen for any videos that supplement the content for this lesson.*

Activity 4-7
Discussing Storage Device Troubleshooting

Show Slide(s)

Activity: Discussing Storage Device Troubleshooting

SCENARIO

Answer the following questions to check your understanding of the topic.

1. A user complains that a "Buffer underrun" error keeps occurring when they try to write to recordable DVDs.

   What would you suggest?

   Do not use other applications at the same time as DVD writing, make sure that the source files are on the local hard disk (not a removable or network drive), or try using a slower write speed.

2. You are trying to install Windows from the setup disc, but the computer will not boot from the CD.

   What should you do?

   Check the boot order in system setup is set correctly; check that the disc is not dirty or scratched.

3. **If you experience an error such as "BCD missing" when booting the computer, what action could you take?**

   Use the Startup Repair tool or run `bootrec /rebuildbcd`.

4. **A user reports hearing noises from the hard disk—does this indicate it is failing and should be replaced?**

   Not necessarily—hard disks do make noises but they are not all indicators of a problem. Question the user to find out what sort of noises are occurring or inspect the system yourself.

5. A PC displays the message "Invalid media type" when you try to access it from a command prompt.

   What is the likely cause and how might you attempt to fix it?

   The file system is corrupt. You can try using the Startup Repair tool or run bootrec /fixboot to recover it without losing data.

6. A user reports that there is a loud clicking noise when she tries to save a file.

   What should be your first troubleshooting step?

   Determine whether a data backup has been made. If not, try to make one.

7. You are investigating a disk problem. The system can no longer access the C: drive.

What command could you use to try to repair the error?

bootrec /fixmbr

8. A RAID utility reports that the volume is degraded.

What should you do?

A degraded volume is still working but has lost one of its disks. In most RAID configurations, another disk failure would cause the volume to fail so you should add a new disk as soon as possible (though do note that rebuilding the array will reduce performance).

Activity 4-8
Troubleshooting Storage Devices

Show Slide(s)

Activity:
Troubleshooting
Storage Devices

Teaching Tip

For this activity, you will need to dismiss learners from the room so that you can introduce the issue in the first scenario to all of their PCs. To engage remote participants, consider demonstrating the step. Alternatively, if you have a system with a hard drive problem, you can have learners work as a group to troubleshoot and resolve the problem.

To create the issue, you could replace the drive with a non-functioning one or loosen the cables on the drive. If you introduce different causes to different PCs, you can have participants observe as each symptom is resolved.

BEFORE YOU BEGIN
To simulate the first issue, your instructor will introduce a drive problem on your system.

SCENARIO
In this activity, you will troubleshoot different issues relating to hard drives.

---

1. A user has reported that her computer cannot boot and is getting an error message at POST. Diagnose and correct the issue.
   a) Reproduce the problem by booting the computer and observing the error. Listen to determine if the drive is spinning up during POST.
   b) Access the firmware setup program to check that the drive port is enabled.
   c) Power off the computer, disconnect any cabling, and then open the case. Verify that the drive data cable and power cable are properly connected.
   d) If nothing else corrects the problem, replace the drive.

2. Another user has reported that there are grinding noises coming from her computer case. Once you take a closer look, you suspect that it is the hard drive.

   What is the possible cause and solution to this type of issue?

   ● The hard drive is physically damaged, so the drive must be replaced.

   ○ A virus has attacked the hard drive, so you can use antivirus software to mitigate the issues.

   ○ Data is corrupt on the drive, and the PC has not been shut down correctly.

3. When a user tries to access the hard drive containing his data, the system locks up and makes a clicking sound. From the command prompt, he can change to drive D, but when he tries to access a file or list the files on the drive, it locks up and begins clicking again.

   What is the most likely cause of the problem?

   The most likely cause of this problem is a bad hard drive—some of the sectors on the hard drive are probably damaged. You will probably need to replace the hard drive. If you do continue to use the drive, monitor it closely and ensure that the user backs up file data often.

4. **What steps might you take to attempt to resolve this problem?**

You could try running the Windows error-checking option in the **Tools** pane of the **Local Disk Properties** dialog box. Definitely back up the data if you can get to any of it. You can try using other software utilities to recover the data or take the drive to a data recovery facility.

5. A user reports that some of his folders have begun disappearing and some folder and file names are scrambled with strange characters in their names.

What is the most likely cause of the problem?

If it is not caused by a virus, the most likely cause of this problem is a bad hard drive, and you will probably need to replace it. If you do continue to use the drive, monitor it closely and ensure that the user backs up file data often.

6. **What steps might you take to attempt to resolve this problem?**

You should isolate the system or drive and check for viruses, because the result of some infections looks like this problem. If you do not identify a security issue, use error checking tools, such as Windows `chkdsk`, to scan the file system. Back up the data if you can get to any of it. You can try using other software utilities to recover the data or take the drive to a data recovery facility.

Summary

In this lesson, you installed, configured, and performed troubleshooting on various types of storage devices. The ability to support users in their need to store and retrieve essential data is an integral part of an A+ technician's job duties.

Which types of storage devices have you worked with? Have you installed additional hard drives or replaced hard drives?

A: Answers will vary. Most systems today use SATA or solid state drives. Additional drives can be installed to provide more storage space or as part of a RAID array.

What sorts of issues have you experienced with storage devices? How will the troubleshooting tools and guidelines presented in this lesson help with future issues?

A: Answers will vary, but might include hard drive failure, boot issues, lost or corrupted files, poor performance, or misconfiguration of RAID or other storage solutions. The tools and guidelines presented here should help make detecting and resolving these issues easier in the future.

 Practice Question: *Additional practice questions are available on the CompTIA CHOICE platform within the **Assessments** tile.*

Lesson 5

Installing, Configuring, and Troubleshooting Internal System Components

LESSON INTRODUCTION

As a CompTIA® A+® technician, you are not only responsible for the components outside the system unit, but all the internal components as well. On the job, you may be asked to connect peripheral components for a user, or you may be asked to swap out a motherboard.

Having the knowledge and skills to properly install and configure the internal system components is crucial because, in most cases, users will not have the knowledge or the experience to install the components themselves. It will be your professional responsibility to know the technical specifications for these components and how to manage them appropriately.

LESSON OBJECTIVES

In this lesson, you will:

- Select and install a CPU to upgrade or repair a computer system.

- Configure and update BIOS and UEFI.

- Install power supplies.

- Troubleshoot internal system components.

- Configure a custom PC.

Topic A

Install and Upgrade CPUs

EXAM OBJECTIVES COVERED
1001-3.5 Given a scenario, install and configure motherboards, CPUs, and add-on cards.

In this topic, you will examine the types and features of CPUs and cooling systems. Much like the motherboard, the CPU is another important component of the computer system that actually carries out all the tasks requested by the applications installed in the computer. The CPU is a heat generator, so part of understanding the CPU includes understanding how to manage heat inside the computer case by managing the airflow and temperature. Keeping the system cool is an easy but important way to maintain or even increase its productivity. A computer that runs too hot risks damaging its own components. As an A+ technician, you need to be familiar with these essential components of the computer system.

CPU

Show Slide(s)

CPU

Teaching Tip

Explain the various features of CPUs.

The **Central Processing Unit (CPU)**, or simply the **processor**, executes program instruction code, performs mathematical and logical calculations, and controls Input/Output (I/O) functions. The CPU is commonly described as the "brains" of a computer; in fact, it is better thought of as a very efficient sorting office. The CPU cannot think, but it can process simple instructions very, very quickly and efficiently. A computer is only as "clever" as its software.

PC processors are produced by Intel® or other manufacturers who use the Intel instruction set and whose processors are, therefore, IBM® PC (or x86) compatible. Currently, only AMD (Advanced Micro Devices) falls into this category.

CPU MANUFACTURING PROCESS

Note: *This information is provided for reference; it is not part of the exam objectives.*

A **microprocessor** is a programmable **integrated circuit (IC)**. An IC is a silicon chip embedded on a ceramic plate. A **silicon chip** is a wafer of purified silicon doped with a metal oxide (typically copper or aluminum). This doping process creates millions of transistors and signal pathways within an area called the **die**. These transistors provide the electrical on/off states that are the basis of binary computer systems.

The process used to create the transistors is referred to as an n-micron or n-nanometer (nm) process, reflecting the size of the features (a transistor for instance) that can be created. A micron is a millionth of a meter; a nanometer is a billionth of a meter. This process has developed from 1 micron (80486) to 0.014 micron (or 14 nm).

Scaling down the process allows reduced voltages and therefore more speed with less heat. It also allows more components to be added to the same package, which has enabled innovations such as on-die cache, multicore CPUs, and on-die graphics processors.

CPU ARCHITECTURES

The CPU is designed to run software programs. When a software program runs (whether it be an operating system, BIOS firmware, antivirus utility, or word processing application), it is assembled into instructions utilizing the fundamental **instruction set** of the CPU and loaded into system memory. The CPU then performs the following operations on these instructions:

1. The control unit fetches the next instruction in sequence from system memory to the pipeline.
2. The control unit decodes each instruction in turn and either executes it itself or passes it to the **Arithmetic Logic Unit (ALU)** or **Floating Point Unit (FPU)** for execution.
3. The result of the executed instruction is written back to a register or to system memory. A **register** is a temporary storage area available to the different units within the CPU.

This overview is grossly simplified, of course. Over the years, many different internal architectures have been developed to optimize the process of fetch, decode, execute, and writeback, while retaining compatibility with the basic x86 instruction set, which defines a CPU as IBM PC compatible.

Show Slide(s)

CPU Architectures

Teaching Tip

Emphasize that a CPU is not making any clever decisions; it is merely processing many, many instructions very quickly. Cleverness and decision-making occur at the software level.

INSTRUCTION SETS

The instruction set used by IBM PC compatible CPUs is called **x86-32** or **IA-32** (Intel Architecture). The way the instructions are processed internally has been modified and optimized by various different CPU architectures, but otherwise the same platform has been in use for the last 30 years (IA-32 updated the 16-bit x86 instruction set, first launched in 1978).

Up until a few years ago, CPUs were designed to run 32-bit code. This means that each instruction can be up to 32-bits in length. A 32-bit CPU's **General Purpose (GP) registers** are also 32-bits wide. However, since 2004, most desktop CPUs (and from 2006, most laptop CPUs) released to the market have been capable of running 64-bit code.

Show Slide(s)

Instruction Sets

Teaching Tip

The main advantage of 64-bit instruction sets is greater memory addressing capabilities.

 Note: 32-bit Pentium compatible CPUs feature additional larger registers for floating point calculations (80-bit) and SIMD processing (64- or 128-bit). They also feature a 64-bit data bus. It is the GP register size that makes a CPU 32- or 64-bit.

Intel first developed a 64-bit instruction set for its Itanium server CPU platform in 2001. This platform (**IA-64**) has never gained acceptance in the PC market, however. AMD's 64-bit instruction set (**AMD64**) has proved more popular and was adopted by Intel for its 64-bit desktop and mobile line. Intel refers to it as EM64T or Intel 64. The same instruction set is also called **x86-64** or **x64**.

The utilization of 64-bit CPU features by installing 64-bit operating systems took some time to grow, principally because of the lack of 64-bit drivers for peripheral devices. However, at this point, it is estimated that well over half of the Windows install base is 64-bit.

Show Slide(s)

Addressing

Teaching Tip

Point out that memory includes paged memory, not just RAM.

ADDRESSING

The system bus between the CPU and memory consists of a data bus and an address bus. The width of the data bus (64-bit on all current CPUs) determines how much data can be transferred per clock cycle; the width of the address bus determines how many memory locations the PC can access.

Teaching Tip

On Wikipedia, there is a claim that all words ever spoken by human beings amount to around 5 exabytes of data. Whether or not this claim is true, 16 exabytes is a lot of data.

Note: In modern CPU designs, the bus is double or quad "pumped," meaning that there are two or four 64-bit transfers per clock cycle. Also, the memory architecture is likely to be multi-channel, meaning that there are two, three, or four 64-bit data paths operating simultaneously.

The address bus for most 32-bit CPUs is either 32- or 36-bits wide. A 32-bit address bus can access a 4 GB address space; 36-bit expands that to 64 GB. In theory, a 64-bit CPU could implement a 64-bit address space (16 Exabytes). In practice, the current generation of x64 CPUs are "restricted" to 48-bit address spaces (256 TB) to reduce the complexity in remaining compatible with 32-bit software.

CACHE

Show Slide(s)

Cache

A computer stores the data for the programs and files currently open in *system memory*. The CPU has *registers* to store instructions and data that it is processing. Instructions are moved in and out of these registers to the system memory.

Cache is a small block of high-speed memory that enhances performance by pre-loading (caching) code and data from relatively slow system memory and passing it to the CPU on demand. Essentially, cache stores instructions and data that the CPU is using regularly.

In early CPU designs, cache was implemented as a separate chip on the motherboard, but almost all new CPUs incorporate most types of cache as features on the CPU itself (on die). Cache is designed in multiple levels. Level 1 cache is "closest" to the CPU and supports the fastest access. Level 2 cache is typically larger and a bit slower while Level 3 and Level 4 cache, if used, are larger and possibly a bit slower still.

HYPERTHREADING

Show Slide(s)

Hyperthreading

Teaching Tip

This section covers a lot of technologies doing similar things with long names, so be sure to distinguish among them clearly to help keep learners oriented.

Point out that software has to be written or rewritten to use these improvements.

As a crude example, having a 64-bit CPU doesn't offer much of a benefit if you are running 32-bit software. It doesn't make 32-bit software run twice as fast; in fact, it might run it a bit slower than a 32-bit CPU would.

One way to make instruction execution more efficient is to improve the way the pipeline works. The basic approach is to do the most amount of work possible in a single clock cycle (**multitasking**). There are various ways to achieve this goal, though.

- **Superpipelining.** CPUs process multiple instructions at the same time (for example, while one instruction is fetched, another is being decoded, another is being executed, and another is being written back to memory). This is referred to as a **superscalar architecture**, as multiple execution units are required. Superscalar architectures also feature longer pipelines with multiple stages but shorter actions (micro-ops) at each stage, referred to as **superpipelining**.

  The original Pentium® had a 5-stage pipeline; by contrast, the Pentium 4 has up to 31 stages (NetBurst® architecture). NetBurst actually proved relatively inefficient in terms of power and thermal performance, so Intel reverted to a modified form of the P6 architecture it used in Pentium IIs and IIIs for its "Core" brand CPUs (with around 14 stages).

- **Multithreading.** Another approach is **Simultaneous Multithreading (SMT)**, called **HyperThreading (HT)** or **HyperThreading Technology (HTT)** by Intel.

  A **thread** is a stream of instructions generated by a software application. Most applications run a single process in a single thread; software that runs multiple parallel threads within a process is said to be **multithreaded**. SMT allows the threads to run through the CPU at the same time. It duplicates many of the registers of the CPU. This reduces the amount of "idle time" the CPU spends waiting for new instructions to process. To the OS, it seems as though there are two or more CPUs installed.

  The main drawback of SMT is that it works best with multithreaded software. As this software is more difficult to design, it tends to be restricted to programs designed to run on servers. Desktop applications software often cannot take full advantage.

MULTIPROCESSING AND MULTICORE PROCESSORS

Yet another approach to making a computer system faster is to use two or more physical CPUs, referred to as **Symmetric Multiprocessing (SMP)**. An SMP-aware OS can then make efficient use of the processing resources available to run application processes on whichever CPU is "available." This approach is not dependent on software applications being multithreaded to deliver performance benefits. Traditionally, SMP was provided by physically installing two or more CPUs in a multi-socket motherboard. Obviously, this adds significantly to the cost and so is implemented more often on servers and high-end workstations.

However, improvements in CPU manufacturing techniques have led to another solution: dual-core CPUs, or **Chip Level Multiprocessing (CMP)**. A dual-core CPU is essentially two processors combined on the same die. The market has quickly moved beyond dual-core CPUs to multicore packages with 3, 4, 8, or more processors.

 Note: Most mainstream CPU models are now multicore. Single-core CPUs are still produced for the lowest budget models but manufacturing volumes mean that multicore CPUs are at the point of being cheaper to produce than single-core ones.

 Show Slide(s)

Multiprocessing and Multicore Processors

 Teaching Tip

Dual core is now considered mainstream, with single core processors restricted to use in netbooks.

Teaching Tip

Emphasize that multicore technology suffers from the law of diminishing returns.

CLOCK SPEED

Despite the architectural features just discussed, the speed at which the CPU runs is generally seen as a key indicator of performance. This is certainly true when comparing CPUs with the same architecture but is not necessarily the case otherwise. Intel Core 2 CPUs run slower than Pentium 4s, but deliver better performance. Budget and low power models will work at around 1-2 GHz while premium models will run at 3-4 GHz.

The **core clock speed** is the speed at which the CPU runs internal processes and accesses L1 and L2 cache (L2 cache access speed actually depends on the CPU architecture, but full-speed access to L2 cache has been standard for some time). The Front Side Bus (FSB) speed is the interface between the CPU and system memory.

 Show Slide(s)

Clock Speed

OVERCLOCKING

When a manufacturer releases a new chip, it sets an optimum clock speed based on systems testing. This clock speed will be set at a level where damage to the chip is not likely to occur during normal operation. Increasing this speed (**overclocking**) is done using the system setup firmware program by adjusting the **CPU Speed** or **Advanced Chipset Features** properties. You can either increase the core clock speed (multiplier) or the FSB speed (overclocking the memory chips) or both. Increasing the clock speed requires more power and generates more heat. Therefore, an overclocked system must have a suitable power supply and sufficient cooling. The operating environment (the warmth of the room and build-up of dust) must also be quite carefully controlled.

Overclocking is generally performed by hobbyists and games enthusiasts but it is also a means to build a PC more cheaply by specifying lower cost components, then boosting their performance.

Without cooling, overclocking increases the risk of thermal damage to components and may increase the frequency of system lockups. It also invalidates the warranty. Original Equipment Manufacturers (OEM) generally try to prevent overclocking in their PC systems by disabling custom settings in the computer's system setup program.

A CPU may also run at a lower actual speed than it is capable of if it is put in a power saving mode.

 Show Slide(s)

Overclocking

 Teaching Tip

Overclocking is mainly a consideration for hobbyists and gamers.

Show Slide(s)

Power Management (Throttling)

Teaching Tip

Point out that power consumption and green computing are hot topics for IT buyers.

Show Slide(s)

Other CPU Features (2 slides)

Teaching Tip

VT is generally disabled on budget CPU models.

POWER MANAGEMENT (THROTTLING)

Rising energy costs and environmental legislation are placing power efficiency at the top of the agenda for IT buyers. In terms of CPU performance, more speed means greater power consumption and heat production. To deal with these issues, CPUs can implement power management to enter lower power states, referred to as **throttling**.

Another aspect of power management is protection for the CPU. If a processor runs too hot, the system can become unstable or damage can occur. CPUs provide routines to reduce performance to protect against overheating.

OTHER CPU FEATURES

Two other features of modern CPUs need to be covered here. These support the use of virtualization and power-efficient graphics capability.

- **Virtualization extensions.** Virtualization software allows a single computer to run multiple operating systems or **Virtual Machines (VM)**. Intel's Virtualization Technology (VT) and AMD's AMD-V provide processor extensions to support virtualization, also referred to as **hardware-assisted virtualization**. This makes the VMs run much more quickly. These extensions are usually features of premium models in a given processor range.

    There is also a second generation of virtualization extensions to support **Second Level Address Translation (SLAT)**, a feature of virtualization software designed to improve the management of virtual (paged) memory. These extensions are referred to as **Extended Page Table (EPT)** by Intel and **Rapid Virtualization Indexing (RVI)** by AMD.

- **Integrated GPU.** Most computer systems provide some sort of built-in graphics adapter. Initially, an **integrated GPU** would be implemented as part of the motherboard chipset; Intel's Graphics Media Accelerator, for instance. Nowadays, it is more likely that an integrated GPU, or Integrated Graphics Processor (IGP), will be part of the CPU (Intel HD Graphics, for example).

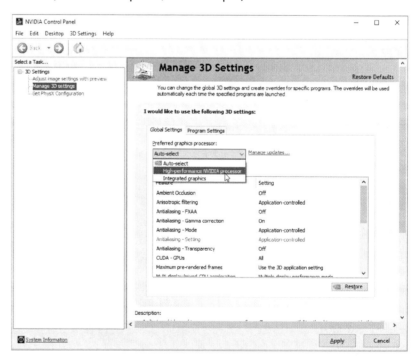

NVIDIA's control panel allows the system to select a graphics processor depending on application requirements.

Apart from cost, an IGP is more power-efficient than a dedicated card. Some laptop systems with both an IGP and a dedicated card are capable of switching automatically between them (NVIDIA Optimus and ATI Hybrid Graphics technologies), depending on whether an application requires advanced 3D performance or not, to conserve battery life.

CPU PACKAGING AND COMPATIBILITY

There have been numerous CPU architectures, and within each architecture, a number of different models, and for each set of models, a brand to position them within a particular market segment. CPU packaging refers to the **CPU's form factor** and how it is connected to the motherboard. Intel and AMD use different socket types so you will never be able to install an AMD CPU in a motherboard designed for an Intel CPU (and vice versa). Additionally, within Intel's and AMD's own ranges, a given CPU socket type will only be compatible with a fairly limited number of CPU models.

The following tables summarize some of the various CPU models and socket types that have been used over the years. Note that the supported desktop processors and memory are illustrative rather than definitive. For more up-to-date information, visit a site such as CPU World, Tom's Hardware, or AnandTech.

Show Slide(s)
CPU Packaging and Compatibility (2 slides)

Teaching Tip
For the certification exam, candidates will need to distinguish between sockets and slots, and between PGA and LGA.

INTEL CPU RANGES AND SOCKET TYPES

Brand Name	Description
Core®	This is Intel's flagship desktop and mobile CPU series. The earliest models (Core Solo and Core Duo) were laptop-only chips. The Core 2 series introduced desktop versions plus 64-bit and multicore support. The current range is divided into Core i3, i5, and i7 brands, with i7 representing the best performing models. The Core iX range has been based on successive generations of microarchitectures, named Nehalem, Sandy Bridge, Ivy Bridge, Haswell, Broadwell, and Skylake.
Pentium®	The Pentium used to be Intel's premium 32-bit CPU brand and you may still find Pentium 4-based computers in use. The Pentium brand has been reintroduced to represent "mid-range" CPU models based on the Core microarchitecture
Celeron®	This has long been Intel's budget brand.
Atom®	This brand designates chips designed for low-power portable devices (smartphones and tablets).
Xeon®	This brand is aimed at the server/workstation market. Current Xeons are often differentiated from their Core counterparts by supporting n-way multiprocessing and ECC memory and coming with larger caches.

Intel uses **Land Grid Array (LGA)** form factor CPUs. In LGA, the pins that connect the CPU and socket are located on the socket. This reduces the likelihood of damage to the CPU but increases the chance of damaging the motherboard.

GIGA-BYTE Z97X Gaming motherboard with Intel Socket 1150. (Image © Gigabyte.)

AMD CPU RANGES AND SOCKET TYPES

Older AMD brands such as Athlon™, Phenom™, Sempron™, and Turion™ have been phased out over the last few years. The following brands represent the company's Zen microarchitecture in different segments:

- Ryzen™/Threadripper™ and Ryzen Mobile—this brand now represents AMD's pitch for the high-end enthusiast segment, replacing older AMD FX chips.
- Epyc™—AMD's server-class CPU brand, replacing its long-standing Opteron series of chips.

AMD uses **Pin Grid Array (PGA)** form factor chips, designed to fit in a **Zero Insertion Force (ZIF) socket** on the motherboard. As the name suggests, a PGA chip has a number of pins on the underside of the processor. These plug into corresponding holes in the socket. Care must be taken to orient the CPU correctly with the socket and to insert it so as not to bend or break any of the pins.

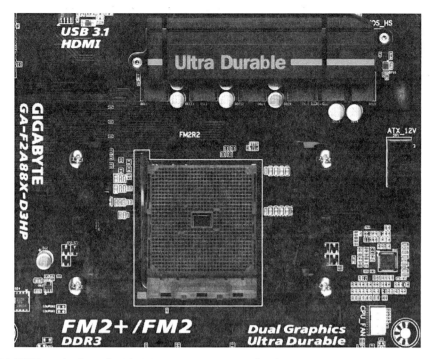

GIGA-BYTE motherboard with ZIF-type FM2+/FM2 socket for AMD CPUs. (Image © Gigabyte.)

COOLING MECHANISMS

Heat is a by-product of pushing electric current through the various electronic components in the computer. The faster the components work, the more heat is produced. Excessive temperatures can cause the components to malfunction or even damage them. One of the most significant problems with CPUs (and graphics cards) is their thermal output. While Intel and AMD are both focusing on making new CPU designs more thermally efficient, all CPUs require cooling. Also, a specific CPU model requires a specific cooling system as some run hotter than others (later Pentium 4s being a good example).

HEAT SINKS AND THERMAL PASTE

A **heat sink** is a block of copper or aluminum with fins. As the fins expose a larger surface area to the air around the component, a greater cooling effect by convection is achieved. Before attaching the heat sink, dots of **thermal paste** (also referred to as thermal grease or thermal compound) should be applied to the surface of the CPU so that placing the heat sink spreads the paste into a thin layer. At the microscopic level, when two solids touch, there are actually air gaps between them that act as insulation; the liquid thermally conductive compound gel fills these gaps to permit a more efficient transference of heat from the processor to the heat sink.

A heat sink is a **passive cooling device**. Passive cooling means that it does not require extra energy (electricity) to work. In order to work well, a heat sink requires good airflow around the PC. It is important to try to keep "cable clutter" to a minimum.

 Show Slide(s)
Cooling Mechanisms (3 slides)

 Teaching Tip
Point out the various cooling methods used on the PCs in the classroom. Liquid-based systems are quieter than fans. Exam candidates need to know where thermal compound is applied, and why.

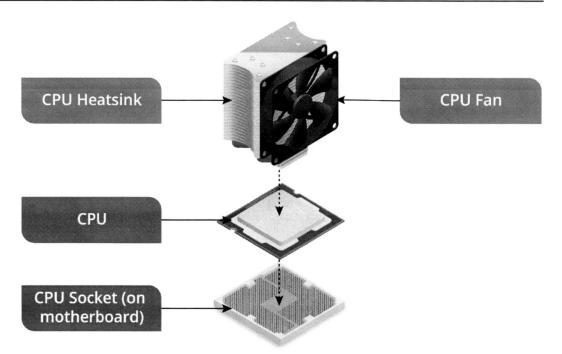

CPU heatsink and fan assembly. Note: When purchasing a CPU, most CPU fans included already have thermal paste applied to the bottom of the CPU fan. If there is no thermal paste applied or the CPU didn't come with a CPU fan, then you'll need to purchase a separate tube of thermal paste. (Image © 123RF.com.)

There are various mechanisms for clamping a CPU heat sink to the motherboard. There may be a retaining clip or push pins. Push pins can be released and reset for insertion by making a half turn with a screwdriver.

FANS

Many PCs have components that generate more heat than can be removed by passive cooling. A fan improves air flow and so helps to dissipate heat. Fans are used for the power supply and chassis exhaust points. The fan system will be designed to draw cool air from vents in the front of the case over the motherboard and expel warmed air from the back of the case.

 Note: *A common implementation is to include air vents near the bottom of the front of the case and to place a fan near the top of the rear of the case to pull cooler air through the system.*

Typically, the speed of the fan is varied according to the temperature, and sensors are used to detect whether a fan has failed. Smaller fans may be used to improve the performance of the heat sink on the CPU, GPUs, and even hard disks.

A fan is an active cooling device. It requires power to run.

The main problem with fans, especially at the lower end of the market, is that they generate noise. A fan also needs to be matched to the CPU model to ensure that it is powerful enough to cope with the processor's thermal output.

Most CPU fans are designed to be removed without the use of tools. Usually the fan assembly will have clips and a power connector.

Some chassis designs incorporate a plastic shroud or system of baffles to cover the CPU and channel the flow of air. The shroud is usually attached to the case using plastic clips.

HEAT PIPES AND SPREADERS

A **heat pipe** is a sealed tube containing some type of coolant (water or ethanol). The liquid close to the heat source evaporates then condenses at a cooler point in the pipe and flows back towards the heat source. The cool parts of the pipe are kept so by convection. This mechanism is more effective than a simple heat sink and fan assembly. It is necessary for a CPU that runs particularly hot or where there is not much space for airflow within the chassis. A **dual heat pipe** has two tubes, providing better cooling.

A **heat spreader** uses the same design but is a flat container rather than a pipe. This design is better suited to portable computers. If used without fans, heat pipes and spreaders are classed as passive cooling.

LIQUID-BASED COOLING SYSTEMS

PCs used for high-end gaming (those with twin graphics cards, for instance) and with overclocked components may generate more heat than basic thermal management can cope with. PCs used where the ambient temperature is very high may also require exceptional cooling measures.

A liquid-cooled PC. (Image by Olivér Svéd © 123RF.com.)

Liquid-based cooling refers to a system of pumping water around the chassis. Water is a much more effective coolant than air convection and a good pump can run more quietly than numerous fans. On the downside, liquid cooling makes maintenance and upgrades more difficult, requires comparatively more power to run, and is costly. Liquid cooling is an active cooling technology as the pump requires power to run.

FANS AND POWER

Power is supplied to a CPU or case fan by connecting its power connector to an appropriate header on the motherboard (make sure you plug the CPU fan into the header marked "CPU Fan" to ensure that the chipset can run the fan at an appropriate speed). Power connectors and headers for fans are 3-pin or 4-pin.

- 3-pin models control fan speed by varying the voltage.
- 4-pin models control fan speed by switching the voltage on and off (using a Pulse Width Module [PWM] signal carried by the fourth wire). This gives better control over fan speed.

Fans with a 3-pin connector can usually be used with 4-pin headers but the system may not be able to vary the fan speed (or may need special configuration to be able to do so). A fan with a 4-pin connector will usually work with a 3-pin header but will not be able to use PWM.

CPU INSTALLATION CONSIDERATIONS

Show Slide(s)

CPU Installation Considerations

Before you replace a processor, you need to make sure you select a processor that matches the type of socket on the system board. Not all processors that use a particular socket will be compatible with your system; this is just one of several items you will need to check for compatibility. Also, when it comes to removing the CPU, there are several cooling device designs and socket types to deal with.

If you are upgrading the CPU, check that the new model is supported by the motherboard. Use the motherboard manufacturer's website to get up-to-date information (for example, to find out about CPU models that were released after the motherboard's documentation was written).

> **Note:** *Just because a motherboard has the correct socket type does not mean that a CPU model will be compatible. The motherboard must have a compatible chipset and voltage regulators, too.*

Pin 1 on the processor MUST match pin 1 on the processor socket. Both the processor and the socket carry distinguishing markings to indicate pin 1. On a processor, this may be:

- A beveled corner or a white dot printed in one corner of the processor.
- A square, rather than round, joint where one of the pins is connected to the underside of the processor.
- A "spur" on one corner of the gold patch on the underside of the processor.

On a processor socket, this may be:

- A difference in the pattern of pin holes in one corner.
- A "1" printed on the motherboard next to one corner.

> **Note:** *To learn more, check the **Video** tile on the CHOICE Course screen for any videos that supplement the content for this lesson.*

> **Access the Checklist tile on your CHOICE Course screen for reference information and job aids on How to Install and Upgrade Processors.**

Activity 5-1

Discussing CPU Upgrades

**Show
Slide(s)**

Activity: Discussing
CPU Upgrades

SCENARIO

Answer the following questions to check your understanding of the topic.

1. **What limits upgrade potential for the system processor?**

   The type of CPU socket and chipset provided on the motherboard.

2. **How can CPU performance be improved?**

   Overclocking—setting the processor to run at a higher clock speed than it was designed for.

3. **Why can cache improve performance?**

   A CPU tends to repeat the same routines and access the same data over-and-over again. If these routines are stored in fast cache RAM, they can be accessed more quickly than instructions and data stored in system memory.

4. **What does SMP mean?**

   Symmetric Multiprocessing—installing more than one CPU. This requires a motherboard with multiple CPU sockets.

5. **How is the heat sink and fan assembly attached, and what problems can occur releasing it?**

   The heat sink is attached to the motherboard via a clip or push pins. There will also be a power connector for the fan. Clip mechanisms can be difficult to release; push pins are now more common and just require a half turn on each pin with a screwdriver to release. Another issue can arise where too much thermal paste has been applied, causing the heat sink to stick to the processor.

6. **What must you check when inserting a PGA CPU chip?**

   That pin 1 is aligned properly and that the pins on the package are aligned with the holes in the socket. Otherwise, you risk damaging the pins when the ZIF lever is lowered.

7. **What is the difference between a heat sink and a heat pipe?**

   A heat sink uses solid metal fins to dissipate heat through convection (often assisted by using fans to move air across the fins). A heat pipe contains fluid that evaporates in the area over the CPU, cools and condenses in a another part of the pipe, and then flows back to the area over the CPU to continue the cycle.

Activity 5-2
Planning for a CPU Upgrade

Show Slide(s)

Activity: Planning for a CPU Upgrade

Teaching Tip

If you haven't preinstalled CPU-Z, point learners to the installer in C:\comptia-labs\labfiles.

Note that some trainers have mentioned that CPU-Z can be tagged as adware by security software. Learners should not select options from the Tools menu.

BEFORE YOU BEGIN
You will perform this activity at your WORKBENCH PC.

SCENARIO
You want to upgrade the CPU in your home PC. You need to make sure that the CPU you are installing will perform better than the one currently installed, and that it will work with the existing motherboard and other components.

---

1. Use the **Windows System Properties** page and the CPUID CPU-Z utility to report system information and configuration.

   a) Check **System Properties** to confirm the type of CPU currently installed.

   b) Run the **CPUID CPU-Z** utility using its desktop shortcut and click **Yes** when prompted by User Account Control (UAC).

   The first tab shows information about the CPU.

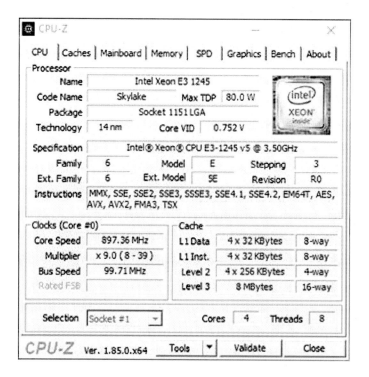

c) Select the **Caches** tab. Cache helps the CPU "smooth" the flow of instructions fetched from system memory and make processing more efficient. Different CPU models come with different amounts of cache, arranged in levels. Level 1 cache is the fastest and usually the smallest.

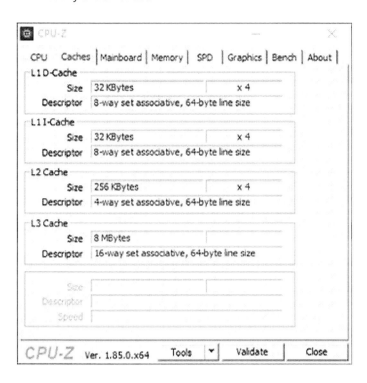

d) Select the **Mainboard** tab. This shows information about the motherboard and system firmware vendor and model.

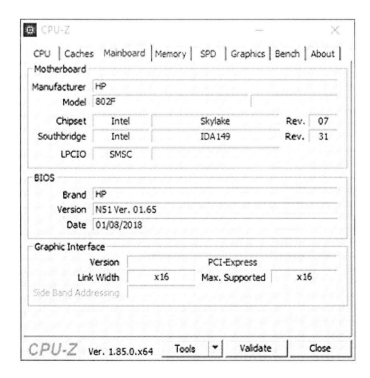

2. Determine which CPUs would provide better performance in the PC.

a) Using a vendor site such as **http://processormatch.intel.com/**, locate CPUs that are compatible with the motherboard and chipset.

b) If available, review installation instructions for the replacement CPU.

Teaching Tip

Optionally, ask learners to download and run an automated vendor compatibility tool as well.

Topic B
Configure and Update BIOS/UEFI

EXAM OBJECTIVES COVERED
1001-3.5 Given a scenario, install and configure motherboards, CPUs, and add-on cards.

In PC support, you will often need to use the system setup program to check or modify firmware settings and to perform firmware updates.

SYSTEM FIRMWARE

Firmware straddles a gray area between hardware and software. Firmware is specialized software stored in memory chips that store information whether or not power to the computer is on. It is most often written on an electronically reprogrammable chip so that it can be updated with a special program to fix any errors that might be discovered after a computer is purchased, or to support updated hardware components.

System firmware provides low-level code to allow the computer components to be initialized and load the main operating system software.

BIOS

For many years, the system firmware for a PC was called the **BIOS** (Basic Input/Output System). BIOS provides the industry standard program code that initializes the essential components of the PC and ensures that the design of each manufacturer's motherboard is PC compatible.

UEFI

Newer motherboards may use a different kind of firmware called **Unified Extensible Firmware Interface (UEFI)**. UEFI provides support for 64-bit CPU operation at boot, a full GUI and mouse operation at boot, networking functionality at boot, and better boot security. A computer with UEFI may also support booting in a legacy BIOS mode.

SYSTEM FIRMWARE SETUP PROGRAMS

System settings can be configured via the system firmware setup program. This may also be referred to as **CMOS setup**, **BIOS setup**, or **UEFI setup**.

> *Note: The term CMOS Setup is still widely used, even though the setup configuration is no longer stored within the CMOS RAM component.*

You can normally access the system setup program with a keystroke during the power-on (boot) process. The key combination used will vary from system to system; typical examples are **Esc**, **Del**, **F1**, **F2**, or **F10**. The PC's documentation will explain how to access the setup program; often a message with the required key is displayed when you boot the PC.

Show Slide(s)
System Firmware

Teaching Tip
Emphasize how to access the system startup program and the types of settings that can be configured from it.

Show Slide(s)
BIOS

Interaction Opportunity
Ask learners to access the system setup and try to locate each of the settings pages as you discuss them. Explain that not all systems will have the same configuration options—some may have fewer options, while others might have more options.

Show Slide(s)
UEFI

Show Slide(s)
System Firmware Setup Programs

Interaction Opportunity
Consider having learners view the firmware settings on their classroom PCs as you present this content.

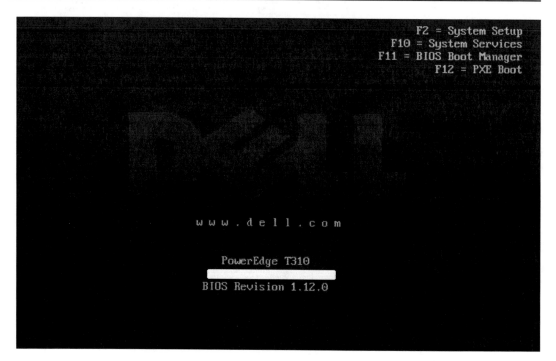

Bootup access to system firmware setup.

*Note: One issue with modern computers is that the boot process can be very quick. If this is the case, you can **Shift**-click the **Restart** button from the Windows logon screen to access UEFI boot options. Alternatively, the motherboard vendor may supply a tool for disabling fast boot or accessing the setup program.*

You navigate a legacy BIOS setup program using the keyboard arrow keys. Pressing **Esc** generally returns to the previous screen. When closing setup, there will be an option to exit and discard changes or exit and save changes. Sometimes this is done with a key (**Esc** versus **F10**, for instance), but more often there is a prompt. There will also be an option for reloading the default settings, in case you want to discard any customizations you have made.

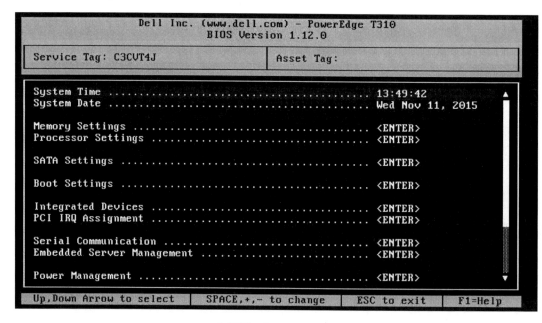

A BIOS setup program.

UEFI setup programs might feature a graphical interface and mouse support.

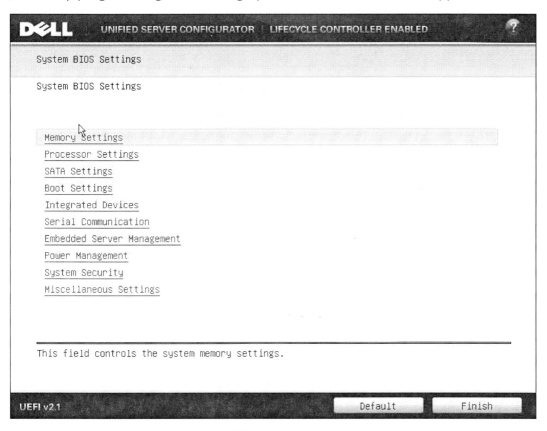

A UEFI setup program.

SYSTEM COMPONENT SETTINGS

The system firmware setup program will contain information about core components such as the CPU, chipset, RAM, hard drive(s), optical drive(s), and the battery (on a laptop).

CPU FEATURES

There will be options for configuring features of the CPU, such as number of cores, cache, power performance, support for instruction set extensions that speed up virtualization (running multiple guest operating systems in a hypervisor), and so on.

In most cases, these features will be detected and enabled by default. You may want to disable them to perform troubleshooting, however.

Show Slide(s)
System Component Settings (3 slides)

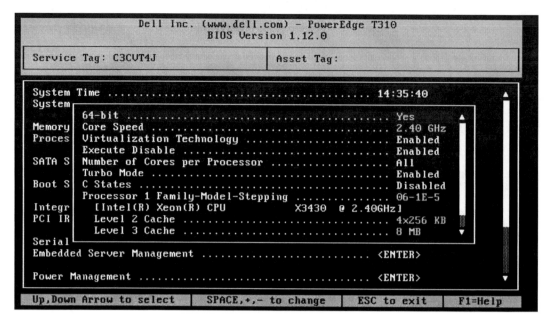

CPU feature menu.

RAM

The system software detects installed memory modules via a Serial Presence Detect (SPD) chip in the modules. The system software will allow you to enable or disable a boot-time memory check. There may also be options for configuring multi-channel memory modes. There may also be the option to overclock system memory modules.

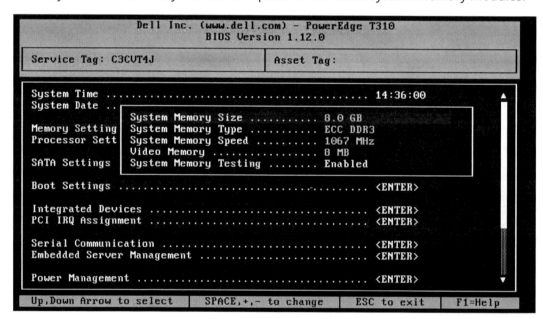

System memory properties and settings.

POWER MANAGEMENT

Power management enables features such as soft power on/off (enabling the Windows Shut Down routine to power off the computer), power saving modes, hibernation, and so on. This option should normally be enabled.

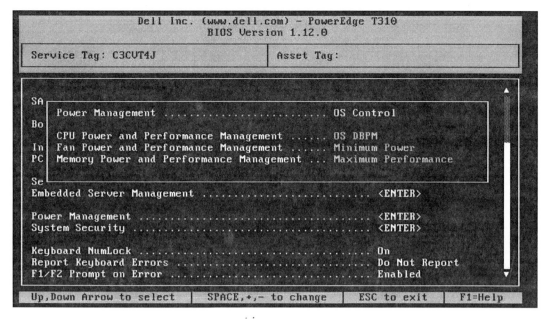

Power management profile configuration.

DATE, TIME, AND DAYLIGHT SAVINGS

Sometimes known as the **real time**, this is simply the calendar date and time. The PC's Real Time Clock (RTC) can be automatically adjusted back or forward one hour as appropriate, within the time zone under Windows. If the real time clock starts to lose the correct date or time, the RTC battery could be failing.

BOOT OPTIONS

One of the most important parameters in system setup is the **boot sequence** or **boot device priority**. This defines the sequence in which the system firmware searches devices for a boot manager. You will usually be able to set 3 or 4 options in priority order.

 **Show Slide(s)**

Boot Options (2 slides)

 Teaching Tip

As PATA and SCSI have returned to the exam objectives, you might want to point out that options for IDE/ATA Mode and SCSI will appear separately from SATA (AHCI), if they are supported as boot devices. Older SATA devices could work in either IDE or AHCI mode.

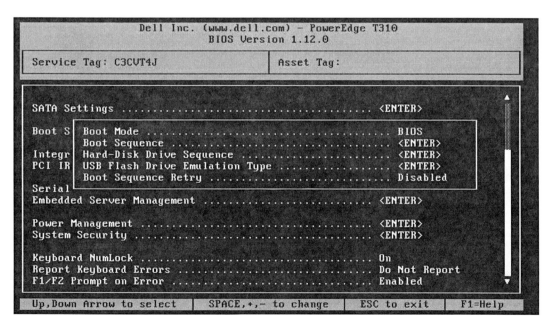

Boot parameters.

Typical choices include:

- **Hard drive.** A SATA boot disk should generally be connected to the lowest numbered port but it is usually possible to select the hard drive sequence if multiple fixed drives are installed.
- **Solid State Drive (SSD).** An SSD attached using SATA will be listed with other SATA/AHCI devices. An SSD installed as a PCIe Add-in Card (AIC) or on the M.2 interface can be used as a boot device if the firmware supports NVMe.
- **Optical drive (CD/DVD/Blu-ray).** If you are performing a repair install, you might need to make this device highest priority.
- **USB.** Most modern systems can boot from USB drives.
- **Network/PXE.** Uses the network adapter to obtain boot settings from a specially configured server.

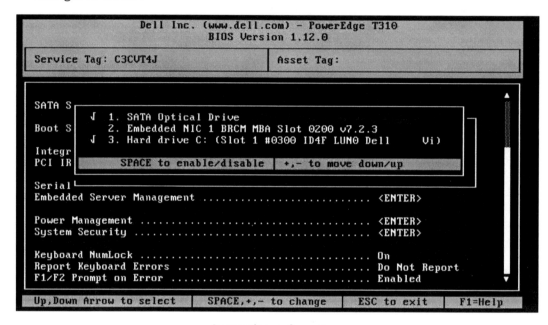

Boot order configuration.

INTERFACE CONFIGURATION SETTINGS

Show Slide(s)

Interface Configuration Settings

There will be options for enabling/disabling and configuring any controllers and adapters provided on the motherboard. This will include storage adapters and possibly features such as USB, network adapter, graphics adapter, and sound adapter.

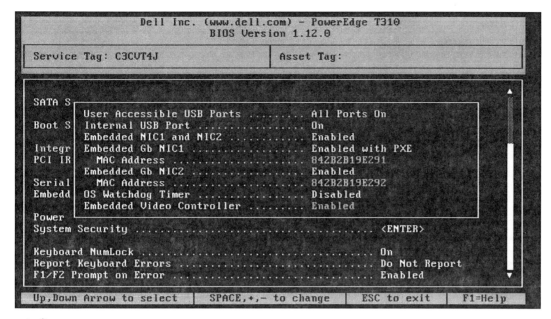

Onboard device configuration.

SECURITY SETTINGS

Several categories of security settings can be configured in system firmware setup programs.

Show Slide(s)
Security Settings (2 slides)

AUTHENTICATION

Different system software will provide different support for authentication methods. There are usually at least two passwords, though some systems may allow for more:

- Supervisor/Administrator/Setup—protect access to the system setup program.
- User/System—lock access to the whole computer. This is a very secure way of protecting an entire PC as nothing can be done until the POST has taken place. The only real way of getting around this would be to open the PC and reset the system setup configuration, which isn't very easy to do.

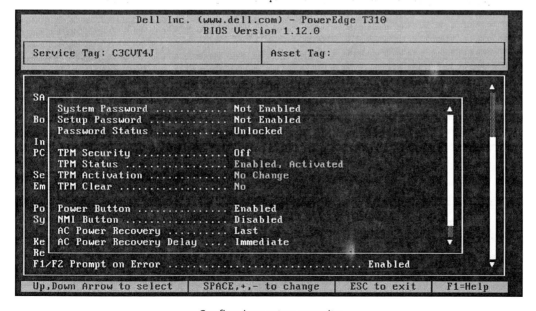

Configuring system security.

Note: For user/system authentication, you have to tell everyone who uses the PC the password, which weakens the security considerably. This option would be used only on workstations and servers that aren't used for interactive logon (a computer running monitoring or management software, for instance).

DRIVE LOCKS

There are generally three options for securing access to the disk specifically (rather than the PC generally):

- Configure and store the password in the PC firmware; this means that the disk is unusable except with the designated computer.
- Store the password in the disk firmware; this is configured in conjunction with a compatible PC firmware and means that the disk is transferable between computers with a compatible firmware.
- Use **Full Disk Encryption (FDE)** to encode the contents of the drive as well as password-protecting it. The selected password is used as the basis of the encryption key. Again, this requires a hard drive and firmware compatible with the same FDE product.

Note: In most cases, there is some sort of recovery mechanism. This might involve the supervisor password or a password recovery disk.

DRIVE ENCRYPTION

Teaching Tip

Point out that you will come back to drive encryption later in the course.

Drive encryption means that the entire contents of the drive (or volume), including system files and folders, are encrypted. OS security measures are quite simple to circumvent if you can get hold of the drive itself. Drive encryption allays this security concern by making the contents of the drive accessible only in combination with the correct encryption key.

Windows supports drive encryption in the BitLocker product, bundled with the Professional/Enterprise/Ultimate editions.

Note: Third-party disk encryption products are available for other versions and editions of Windows.

TPM

BitLocker® requires the secure storage of the key used to encrypt the drive contents. Normally, this is stored in a **Trusted Platform Module (TPM)** chip on the computer motherboard. TPM is a specification for hardware-based storage of digital certificates, keys, hashed passwords, and other user and platform identification information. Essentially, it functions as an embedded smart card. Each TPM microprocessor is hard-coded with a unique, unchangeable key (the endorsement key). During the boot process, the TPM compares hashes of key system state data (system firmware, boot loader, and OS kernel) to ensure they have not been tampered with. The TPM chip has a secure storage area that a disk encryption program such as Windows BitLocker can write its keys to.

It is also possible to use a removable USB drive (if USB is a boot device option). As part of the setup process, you also create a recovery password or key. This can be used if the disk is moved to another computer or the TPM is damaged.

Note: You may need to enable the TPM chip via the system setup before it can be used. Many vendors ship the computer with TPM disabled.

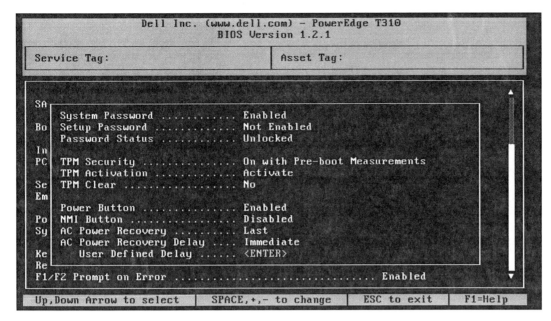

Configuring a TPM.

LoJack

Some laptop firmware is bundled with **LoJack tracking software** (developed by Absolute Software), essentially a security rootkit designed to prevent theft. If enabled (and the user has subscribed to LoJack®), a "dialer" is activated that attempts to contact Absolute Software's authorization servers each day. If the laptop is reported stolen, the authorization servers can force the laptop into a locked down mode (require a boot password or remotely wipe data, for instance). The software can also attempt to locate the laptop, either using GPS data if the laptop has a GPS chip or using information about nearby wireless networks. It can also try to identify the thief by installing forensic tools (a key logger and screen capture utility).

INTRUSION DETECTION

A computer chassis can be installed with sensors to report intrusion detection (if the chassis or lockable faceplate is opened) to management software or display an alert at boot time. Some setup programs can lock the workstation automatically if an intrusion is detected, requiring a supervisor to log on with the relevant password to unlock it again.

SECURE BOOT

Secure boot is a security system offered by UEFI. It is designed to prevent a computer from being hijacked by malware. Under secure boot, UEFI is configured with digital certificates from valid OS vendors. The system firmware checks the operating system boot loader using the stored certificate to ensure that it has been digitally signed by the OS vendor. This prevents a boot loader that has been modified by malware (or an OS installed without authorization) from being used.

 Teaching Tip

Point out that Secure Boot does not support the installation of Windows 7.

Note: Certificates from vendors such as Microsoft (Windows 8/10 and Windows Server 2012 and later) and Linux distributions (Fedora, openSUSE, and Ubuntu) will be pre-loaded. Additional certificates for other boot loaders can be installed (or the pre-loaded ones removed) via the system setup software. It is also possible to disable secure boot.

FIRMWARE UPDATES

System vendors and motherboard manufacturers may regularly update their system firmware in order to fix bugs, solve incompatibilities with operating systems, or to add

 **Show Slide(s)**

Firmware Updates

new features. You should visit the relevant support website regularly to check whether upgrades are available. As upgrading the firmware is relatively risky (a failed motherboard update can leave the computer unbootable, for instance), it is only worth doing if the update fixes a specific problem that you are encountering or if it is regarded as a **critical update**.

 Note: *Performing a firmware update is often referred to as "flashing."*

 Note: *To learn more, check the **Video** tile on the CHOICE Course screen for any videos that supplement the content for this lesson.*

 Access the Checklist tile on your CHOICE Course screen for reference information and job aids on How to Configure and Update System Firmware.

Activity 5-3

Discussing BIOS/UEFI Configuration and Updates

SCENARIO

Answer the following questions to check your understanding of the topic.

Show Slide(s)

Activity: Discussing BIOS/UEFI Configuration and Updates

1. **What advantages does UEFI have over BIOS?**

   UEFI supports 64-bit CPU operation and better hardware support at boot. UEFI also allows for full GUI system utilities and mouse support plus better system startup security options (such as pre-OS boot authentication).

2. **Name three keys commonly used to run a PC's BIOS/UEFI system setup program.**

   Esc, Del, F1, F2, F10.

3. **What widely supported boot method is missing from the following list? HDD, FDD, Optical, USB.**

   Network/PXE (Pre-eXecution Environment)—obtaining boot information from a specially configured server over the network.

4. **Where should you launch a typical firmware upgrade utility—from system setup or from Windows?**

   If the option is available, it is safer to run a firmware upgrade from the system setup program as it reduces the risk of some other process interfering with the update.

5. **If you want to enforce TPM system security, what other BIOS feature should you enable?**

   A supervisor password to prevent the TPM keys from being accessed or cleared.

6. **True or false? Processor extensions such as VT are set by the vendor depending on the CPU model and cannot be enabled or disabled by the user.**

   Mostly false. A feature such as VT is sometimes disabled on some low-end models, but if it is available as a feature of that model, the user can choose whether it is enabled or disabled.

7. **A user's computer was recently installed with a new optical drive. The user now reports a "chassis" error message after the POST sequence. What might be the cause?**

   Intrusion detection is enabled in the BIOS.

8. **When you are configuring BIOS security, what is the difference between a supervisor password and a user password?**

    The user password allows the boot sequence to continue, while a supervisor password controls access to the firmware setup program.

9. **What security system allows system boot to be disabled if the computer is reported stolen?**

    LoJack for Laptops (other tracking software suites are available).

Topic C
Install Power Supplies

EXAM OBJECTIVES COVERED
1001-3.7 Summarize power supply types and features.

In this topic, you will take a closer look at the computer's power supply and its connections to the other system components. The computer's power supply is the main source of power for all components installed within the system unit. Understanding the power requirements of all the components and the maximum power supplied is crucial in managing the overall computer system power needs. Whether you are upgrading or replacing faulty components, you need to effectively manage the capacity of the current power supply.

ELECTRICAL CIRCUITS

Electricity is the flow of electrons through a conductor. The characteristics of the electricity supply are measured as voltage, current (amperage), resistance, and power.

- **Voltage**—the potential difference between two points (often likened to pressure in a water pipe) measured in Volts (V).
- **Current**—the actual flow of electrons, measured in Amps (I). A current flows in a circuit, which is made when conductors form a continuous path between the positive and negative terminals of a power source. The size of the current is determined by the conductivity of the circuit (for example, a higher current can flow in a thicker wire than can in a thinner one).
- **Resistance**—a degree of opposition to the current caused by characteristics of the conductor, measured in Ohms (Ω or R).
- **Power**—the rate at which electricity is drawn from the supply by the device using it, measured in Watts. Power is equal to the Voltage multiplied by the Current (W=V*I).
- **Energy**—the amount of power consumed by a device over time. This is measured in Watt-hours (or more typically, Kilowatt-hours [kWh]).

In a **Direct Current (DC)** circuit, the charge flows in one direction from the positive to negative terminals of the power source at a constant voltage. DC is used for electronic circuits, which require stable voltages. Grid power is supplied as **Alternating Current (AC)**, which means that the current flows in both directions around the circuit and the voltage alternates between low and high values. AC is a cheap way to distribute electrical power over long distances, but is incompatible with PC electronics. Transformers in the PC's power supply are used to convert AC to DC voltages.

In the US, grid power is supplied at 120 VAC with a tolerance of ±5 percent, giving a range of 114 VAC to 126 VAC. Historically, US grid power has been supplied at 110 VAC and 115 VAC, and these values are still widely referred to. In continental Europe and Ireland, mains electricity is supplied at 220 VAC, while in the UK it is 240 VAC; however, there are tolerances that mean most devices designed for IT use in the European market can work with a supply of 220-240 VAC.

Here are the electrical components used in a PC's electronic circuits:

- **Conductor**—a material that is good at conducting electricity, such as gold, copper, or tin. These are used for wires and contacts.

Show Slide(s)

Electrical Circuits (3 slides)

Teaching Tip

It's not necessary to go into extensive detail; just be sure to point out the differences between AC and DC, and the relationship between voltage and current.

- **Insulator**—a material that does not conduct electricity, such as rubber or plastic. These are used as sheaths for wires to prevent short circuits or electric shocks.

 Note: Some materials are better conductors or insulators than others. Most materials have some degree of resistance, which creates heat as a current passes through it.

- **Semiconductor**—a material that can act as both a conductor and an insulator. This provides switch-like functionality, where a circuit can be opened and closed, used to represent binary (on/off) digits.
- **Resistor**—these oppose the flow of current without blocking it completely and are used to manage electronic circuits.
- **Diode**—a valve, allowing current to flow in one direction only. These are used in a computer's power supply and as protection for components.
- **Fuse**—this is a safety device. The flow of electricity creates heat. A fuse is designed so that if the current is too high, the heat will cause the fuse wire to melt and break, breaking the circuit and shutting off the current.
- **Transistor**—in computers, these are semiconductor switches used to create logic devices. Typically, a type called a Field Effect Transistor (FET) is used to make components such as CPUs and memory.
- **Capacitor**—this stores electrical energy and is often used to regulate voltages. Note that a capacitor can hold a charge after the power is removed.

PSU

Show Slide(s)

PSU

Teaching Tip

Focus on explaining PSU and motherboard compatibility and ensuring that the PSU is powerful enough to meet the demands of the CPU, GPU, and ultra-fast drives contained in the PC.

Show Slide(s)

PSU Form Factors

The **Power Supply Unit (PSU)** delivers Direct Current (DC) low voltage power to the PC components.

The PSU contains transformers (to step down to lower voltages), rectifiers (to convert AC to DC), and filters and regulators (to ensure a "clean" output or steady voltage). The other important component in the PSU is the fan, which dissipates the heat generated. Better quality models feature low noise fans.

PSU FORM FACTORS

The power supply's size and shape (or form factor) determines its compatibility with the system case, in terms of available room plus screw and fan locations. The form factor also determines compatibility with the motherboard, in terms of power connectors.

- Most PSUs are based on the ATX form factor. An ATX PSU should be 150 mm wide by 86 mm high by 140 mm deep. The "server-class" EPS12V specification allows PSUs to be 180 mm or 230 mm deep. These will usually fit ATX cases though obviously they protrude farther into the case so the available space should be measured first.
- For Small Form Factor (SFF) PCs such as those based on the Micro-ATX motherboard form factor, an ATX PSU may fit. If the case is a slimline type, a smaller form factor may be required. Although there is no definition of a Micro-ATX PSU, the standards documentation refers to the following:
  - SFX12V—100 mm wide by 50 mm high by 125 mm deep with a 40 mm fan or 63.5 mm high with a 60 mm fan. There is an option to use a top-mounted 80 mm fan, making the unit 80 mm high.
  - TFX12V (Thin Form Factor)—this is narrower and longer compared to the "boxy" ATX and SFX formats. It measures 85 mm wide by 65 mm high by 175 mm deep. The part that fits the case slot is 61 mm high but there is a 4 mm bevel to accommodate the top-mounted fan.

- SFF PSUs are rarely rated above 300 W. You can check **formfactors.org** for complete descriptions of the Intel specifications.

INPUT VOLTAGE

A PSU is plugged into an electrical outlet using a suitable power cable. The plug should always be fitted with a working fuse of the correct rating (typically 3 A or 5 A). The plug should suit the outlet type of the country you are in, though "travel plug" converters are commonly available.

Show Slide(s)
Input Voltage

A critical point to recognize if you are taking a computer to a different country is to ensure that the PSU is set to the correct **input voltage**. A PSU designed only for use in North America, with an input voltage of 115 V, will not work in the UK, where the voltage is 240 V. Some PSUs are dual voltage and are auto-switching (or auto-sensing); some have a switch to select the correct voltage; others can only accept one type of input voltage (fixed).

The input operating voltages should be clearly marked on the unit and accompanying documentation.

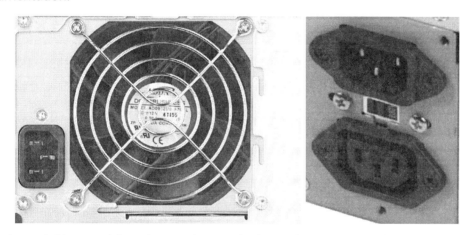

Autoswitching PSU (left) and PSU with manual voltage selector (between the power points).

PSU POWER RATINGS

A PSU must be able to supply adequate power to all the PC's components. The maximum power output (**power rating**) available from a PC power supply is measured in watts, calculated as voltage multiplied by current (V*I). This can be referred to as the power rating or wattage rating.

Show Slide(s)
PSU Power Ratings

The PSU found in a standard desktop PC is typically rated at around 200-300 W. This is normally sufficient for a full range of expansion cards and peripherals. Slimline desktop PCs may be fitted with 100-200 W power supplies. Tower systems and servers often have units rated over 300 W; enough to power many more disk drives, tape units, and other storage devices than would be fitted in a desktop PC. Gaming PCs might require 500 W or better power supplies to cope with the high specification CPU and graphics card(s).

> **Note:** *The power requirement of different components varies widely (for example, CPUs can range from 17 W to over 100 W, depending on the model). If you are building or upgrading a system, the simplest way to work out the power requirement is to use an online calculator such as the one found at **outervision.com**.*

Show Slide(s)

Output Voltages

OUTPUT VOLTAGES

When specifying a PSU for a system that needs a lot of power, it is also important to look closely at the power distribution of each unit. Power distribution refers to how much power is supplied over each rail. A rail is a wire providing current at a particular voltage.

Output Rail (V)	Maximum Load (A)	Maximum Output (W)
+3.3	20	130
+5	20	130
+12	33	396
-12	0.8	9.6
+5 (standby)	2.5	12.5

The output of +3.3 V and +5 V has a combined limit. No combination of values actually adds up to 450 W, but PSU outputs are self-certified by the manufacturers, so this situation is not uncommon.

For a modern computer, the output rating of the +12 V rail (or rails) is the most important factor, as +12 V is the most heavily used. A PSU with two +12 V rails can be referred to as **dual rail**. Each rail has a safety feature called **Overcurrent Protection (OCP)**, which cuts the circuit if the current exceeds a safe limit. Some PSU vendors prefer single +12 V rail designs while others use multi-rail designs, and it is one factor in determining overall PSU performance and safety. The internal design of the PSU has no effect on the way you make the connections to the motherboard.

Also note that peak output is only achieved under optimum conditions; sustained (or continuous) power output represents "real world" performance.

The power output is not the same as the power the PSU draws from grid power. If a PSU works at around 75% efficiency, a 300 W supply would draw 400 W from the outlet. The extra energy is lost mainly as heat.

Note: As power becomes more expensive, power efficiency is an increasingly important criterion to use when selecting a PSU. An ENERGY STAR compliant PSU must be 80% efficient at 20-100% of load (many vendors only display the efficiency obtained under low load). 80 PLUS is a similar rating scheme.

PSU ADAPTER TYPES

Show Slide(s)

PSU Adapter Types (3 slides)

Teaching Tip

The exam objective specifically mention only the 24-pin connector, but you should also consider covering the other adapter and connector types to provide additional practical knowledge.

The power adapters supply various combinations of 3.3 V, 5 V, and 12 V positive and negative current. Not all components use power at precisely these voltages. **Voltage regulators** on the motherboard are used to correct the voltage supplied from the PSU to the voltage required by the component.

The ATX PSU standard has gone through several revisions, specifying different adapter types.

- **P1 adapter.** In the original ATX specification, the 20-pin P1 (2x10) adapter (also called the **main connector**) supplies power to the motherboard. Black wires are ground, yellow wires are +12 V, red wires are +5 V, and orange wires are +3.3 V.

   Most systems are now based on the ATX12V version 2 specification. This defines a 24-pin (2x12) P1 adapter to replace the 20-pin one. This is sometimes implemented as 20+4-pin P1 cable for compatibility with older ATX motherboards that have 20-pin adapters.

A 24-pin main motherboard power cable and port. (Image © 123RF.com.)

- **Molex and SATA connectors.** The 4-pin (1x4) **Molex connectors** and 15-pin (1x15) SATA (Serial ATA) connectors supply +12 V and +5 V power for peripheral devices housed within the system case. The number of connectors determines the number and type of devices (such as hard drives and optical drives) that can be supported.

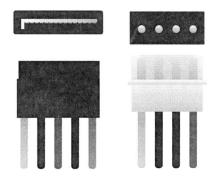

From left to right, SATA and Molex power adapters. (Image © 123RF.com.)

 Note: *Modular PSUs have cables that are detachable from the PSU unit, allowing only the connectors actually required to be used. This reduces clutter within the chassis, improving air flow and cooling.*

If there are insufficient adapters, it is possible to obtain splitters (also called y-adapters) so that two devices can be connected to the same cable. You can also obtain conversion adapters (Molex to SATA, for instance).

- **PCIe connectors.** A 6-pin (2x3) connector is used to supply an extra 75 W power (+12 V) to PCIe graphics cards. This was updated to an 8-pin (2x4) connector delivering 150 W in the ATX12V v2.2 specification. Some adapters or dual-card systems will require the use of multiple PCIe auxiliary power connectors.

A PCIe 6-pin power adapter. (Image © 123RF.com.)

P4 and EPS 12V connectors. The ATX12V standard specifies an additional 4-pin (2x2) +12 V connector (often labeled P4) to support the operation of the CPU.

You may also come across 8-pin +12 V connectors. The **Entry-level Power Supply (EPS) specification** was developed initially for server-class hardware. Many of its features were incorporated in ATX12V. EPS12V defines an 8-pin +12 V connector. This is often wired as two 2x2-pin connectors so that an EPS12V PSU can be connected to an ATX motherboard with a 4-pin +12 V port.

An EPS 12V connector. (Image © 123RF.com.)

POWER NEEDS CALCULATION

Show Slide(s)

Power Needs
Calculation (2 slides)

Calculating the amount of power needed for a PC helps ensure that you have enough power available for all the devices on the PC. The process is fairly simple:

1. List the devices that need to have power served by the PSU. Be sure to include the following:
   - Motherboard
   - CPU
   - RAM
   - Hard drives
   - CD drives
   - DVD drives
   - Floppy drives (if any)
   - Expansion cards

2. Determine the power requirements for each device.
3. Add up the power requirements for the existing total power load.
4. Consider adding a buffer of 20 to 30 percent for future power needs.
5. Examine the details on the PSU currently installed, paying particular attention to the maximum output.
    - If you have not exceeded the power available, you do not need to upgrade the PSU.
    - If you have, you will need to obtain a PSU with a higher output and install it.

*Note: To learn more, check the **Video** tile on the CHOICE Course screen for any videos that supplement the content for this lesson.*

Access the Checklist tile on your CHOICE Course screen for reference information and job aids on How to Install a Power Supply Unit.

Activity 5-4
Discussing Power Supply Installation

 Show Slide(s)

Activity: Discussing Power Supply Installation

SCENARIO
Answer the following questions to check your understanding of the topic.

1. **How would you calculate the power used by a component?**

   Multiply its voltage by the current it draws (W=V*I).

2. **What causes a fuse to blow—excessive voltage or excessive current?**

   Excess current.

3. **What is the significance of a PSU's power output when you are designing a custom build PC?**

   It determines the number of drives, expansion cards, and peripherals that the PC can support (assuming the peripherals do not have their own power supplies).

4. **Are you able to use a standard ATX12V PSU with a Mini-ITX motherboard?**

   Yes (assuming it fits in the case you have chosen).

5. **You have a power supply with an 8-pin connector on it. What is this for?**

   It supplies power to a PCI Express graphics card.

6. **You are connecting a new PSU. The PSU has a square 4-pin P4 cable but there is no square 4-pin receptacle on the motherboard. Should you leave the cable disconnected?**

   No; it will plug into an 8-pin EPS12V receptacle near the CPU. You should check the motherboard documentation for advice about which pins to plug the cable into.

7. **What setting should you check before installing a PSU?**

   That the voltage selector is set to the correct voltage (or if there is no selector, that the PSU is suitable for the voltage used by the building power).

8. Another technician replaced the PSU on a PC. Later the same day the PC's owner contacts you to say that the system has been displaying numerous alerts about high temperature.

What do you think might be the cause?

You would need to open the case to investigate the problem. Perhaps when the upgrade was performed, one of the fan power connectors was not attached properly. If the PSU cabling was not secured with cable ties, it could disrupt air flow within the case, reducing the effectiveness of fans. There could be a fault with the fan on the new PSU.

Activity 5-5

Calculating Power Requirements and Installing a PSU

Show Slide(s)

Activity: Calculating Power Requirements and Installing a PSU

BEFORE YOU BEGIN

You will perform this activity at your WORKBENCH PC.

SCENARIO

In the first part of this activity, you will calculate the power required by your workbench PC. As a guide, you can refer to the following table that includes common component types, example specifications, and required wattages.

Component Type	Example Specification	Example Wattage Required
CPU	Intel Core i7-970, 3.2 GHz	130
Memory	4 GB DDR3-1600	8
Video card	NVIDIA GeForce 8800 GTS	220
Motherboard	ASUS P6X58D Premium LGA	36
Hard drive	1 TB SATAII 7200 RPM	6
Optical drive	6x Blu-ray	32
NIC	10/100/1000 Mbps PCI-Express	14
Sound card	SoundBlaster X-Fi Titanium	23
USB wired keyboard	Yes/No	4
USB wired mouse	Yes/No	4
USB flash drive	Yes/No	5
Other external devices	External DVD+R drive	5

Teaching Tip

There are several free power-supply calculators available on the web, such as the calculator at **https:// outervision.com/ power-supply- calculator**. You can have participants access this calculator, or another online power-supply calculator that you might be familiar with, to help them complete this activity.

1. Examine your PC, and complete the **Specification** column of the following table. If you have different or additional components in your PC, revise the table accordingly.

Component Type	Specification	Wattage Required
CPU		
Memory		
Video card		
Motherboard		
Hard drive		
Optical drive		
NIC		
Sound card		
USB wired keyboard		

Component Type	Specification	Wattage Required
USB wired mouse		
USB flash drive		
Other external devices		

2. If you can, determine the power required by each component, and complete the table. Again, example values have been provided for your reference.

3. Calculate the total wattage required for your PC. Compare this value with the maximum wattage output listed on the power supply. Does this power supply need to be upgraded?

4. Add a buffer of 30 percent to the total wattage required for your PC. Will the existing power supply continue to supply enough power if additional components are added to the system?

5. After calculating the power load for all the components and future needs, you have determined that it exceeds the capacity of the installed power supply. Remove the existing power supply.

   a) Shut down the computer.
   b) Unplug the power cord from the electrical outlet.
   c) On ATX systems, to discharge any remaining electricity stored in the computer's capacitors, toggle the power switch on the computer on and off.
   d) Remove any components necessary in order to access the power supply and its connection to the system board.
   e) Unplug all power connections from devices, marking where each connection went to as you go.
   f) Unplug the power supply from the motherboard.
   g) Unscrew the power supply from the case.
   h) Remove the power supply from the case.

Teaching Tip

In most cases, you will not have extra power supplies for learners to install in their PCs, so you can just have them uninstall and reinstall the one they have (or consider swapping PSUs with a partner if they are compatible).

6. Install the replacement power supply.

   Note: *If you don't have another power supply, reinstall the power supply you just removed.*

   a) Insert the power supply into the case. Align the guides on the base of the supply with the base.
   b) Secure the power supply to the case.
   c) Plug all power connections into the devices.
   d) Plug the power supply into the system board.
   e) Reinstall any components you removed to access the power supply.
   f) Plug the power cord from the power supply to the electrical outlet.

7. Test the power supply.
   a) Turn on the system.
   b) Test all components.

Topic D

Troubleshoot Internal System Components

 EXAM OBJECTIVES COVERED

1001-5.2 Given a scenario, troubleshoot problems related to motherboards, RAM, CPUs, and power.

As a CompTIA A+ technician, it is essential for you to be comfortable working with system components, whether you are installing them, configuring them, or trying to figure out how to resolve issues with them. It is only a matter of time before a personal computer's internal system hardware components experience problems, and generally these are problems users themselves cannot fix. As a CompTIA A+ technician, many of the service calls that you respond to will involve troubleshooting system hardware components, and your ability to quickly and effectively diagnose and solve the problems will be essential in maintaining the satisfaction level of the users you support.

BASIC HARDWARE PROBLEMS

Show Slide(s)

Basic Hardware Problems

Teaching Tip

This topic covers troubleshooting the core PC components such as the motherboard, CPU, memory, and power. Exam candidates will need to be able to recognize typical symptoms and their likely causes.

When you are troubleshooting suspected problems, look for simple solutions first.

- Find out if anything has changed.
- Eliminate hardware issues as a cause first.
- Try one thing at a time.
- Take care to ensure that a user's data is backed up before proceeding.

There are several externally observable symptoms that may help you to diagnose a hardware problem without having to open the computer chassis.

INDICATOR LIGHTS

Most devices have a status **Light Emitting Diode (LED)** to indicate that the device is switched on and receiving power.

Some devices may have additional status indicators or show other functions. For example, a hard drive LED shows activity; normally this should flicker periodically. If a hard drive LED is solid for extended periods it can indicate a problem, especially if the PC is not doing any obvious processing.

Similarly, network adapters often have LEDs to indicate the connection speed and activity on the network.

ALERTS

Most PC systems now have quite good internal monitoring systems (such as the internal thermometers). When these systems detect problems, they can display an administrative alert, either on the local system or to some sort of network management system. The operating system may also be able to detect some kinds of hardware failure and display an appropriate alert.

OVERHEATING

Excessive heat damages the sensitive circuitry of a computer very easily. If a system feels hot to the touch you should check that the fans are operating and are not clogged by dirt or dust.

> **Note:** *PCs and laptops can get very warm without there being a specific problem.*

As mentioned above, many systems now come with internal temperature sensors that you can check via driver or management software. Use the vendor documentation to confirm that the system is operating within acceptable limits.

Unusual odors, such as a burning smell, or smoke will almost always indicate something (probably the power supply) overheating. The system should be shut down immediately and the problem investigated.

Thermal problems are also likely to cause symptoms such as spontaneous reboots, blue screens, lockups, and so on. These will typically be cyclic—if you turn the system off and allow it to cool, the problem will only reappear once it has been running long enough for heat to build up again.

LOUD NOISES

Devices may also start to fail over time. Drives of most types are most prone to failure, but sensitive chips such as memory and graphics adapters can also develop problems (often caused by some underlying thermal issue).

Loud or unusual noises can often indicate that a device such as a fan or hard drive is failing. Note that these may not be caused by hardware problems alone. For example, a fan that sounds noisy may be spinning too fast because its driver software is not controlling it properly.

You also need to be able to distinguish between "healthy" noises and "unhealthy" ones. For example, a hard disk may make a certain "whirring whine" when first spinning up and a "chattering" noise when data is being written, but clicking, squealing, loud noise, or continual noise can all indicate problems.

> **Note:** *Newer and more expensive models make very little noise. There may also be a setting in system setup to optimize disk performance to reduce noise.*

VISIBLE DAMAGE

If a system has had liquid spilled on it or if fans or the keyboard are clogged by dust or dirt, there may be visible signs of this.

Actual physical damage to a computer system is usually caused to peripherals, ports, and cables. Damage to other components is only really likely if the unit has been in transit somewhere. Inspect a unit closely for damage to the case; even a small crack or dent may indicate a fall or knock that could have caused worse damage to the internal components than is obvious from outside.

If a peripheral device does not work, examine the port and the end of the cable closely for bent, broken, or dirty pins and connectors. Examine the length of the cable for damage.

POWER PROBLEMS

PC components need a constant, stable supply of power to run. If the computer will not start, it is likely to be due to a power problem. If the PC suddenly turns off or restarts, power problems are also likely.

Show Slide(s)
Power Problems (2 slides)

Teaching Tip
Remind learners to check for the obvious things first, such as disconnected cables or blown fuses.

In the normal course of operations, the PSU converts the AC mains supply to DC voltages. DC voltage is used to power the internal drives and motherboard components. The PSU continually draws standby power from the mains (unless the PSU has its own on/off switch and it has been switched off). When the PC is switched on, the PSU starts supplying 12 V power and fans and disks should spin up. The PSU tests its 5 V and 3.3 V supplies, and when it is sure that it is providing a stable supply, it sends a "Power Good" signal to the processor.

The processor then begins to run the Power On Self-Test (POST) program. POST will not run without a CPU. Some motherboards may be able to sound an alert or light a status LED if the CPU is not present or not working.

If none of the LEDs on the front panel of the system case are lit up and you cannot hear the fans or hard drives spinning, the computer is not getting power. This is likely to be a fault in the PSU, incoming mains electricity supply, power cables/connectors, or fuses.

To isolate the cause of no power, try the following tests:

- Check that other equipment in the area is working; there may be a blackout.
- Check that the PSU cabling is connected to the PC and the wall socket correctly and that all switches are in the "on" position.
- Try another power cable—there may be a problem with the plug or fuse. Check that all of the wires are connected to the correct terminals in the plug. Check the fuse resistance with a multimeter.
- Try plugging another piece of "known-good" equipment (such as a lamp) into the wall socket. If it does not work, the wall socket is faulty. Use another socket and get an electrician to investigate the fault.
- Try disconnecting extra devices, such as optical drives. If this solves the problem, the PSU is underpowered and you need to fit one with a higher power rating.

Teaching Tip

Exam candidates should be able to use a multimeter to check the voltage on a pin connector and to test a fuse.

Show Slide(s)

Multimeter Use (3 slides)

MULTIMETER USE

A **multimeter** can be used to measure voltage, current, and resistance. Voltage readings can be used to determine whether, for example, a power supply unit is functioning correctly. Resistance readings can be used to determine whether a fuse or network cable is functioning correctly.

- To test a fuse, set the multimeter to measure resistance and touch the probes to each end of the fuse. A good fuse should have virtually zero Ohms of resistance; a blown fuse will have virtually infinite resistance.
- Power supply problems can be indicated by otherwise inexplicable system lockups or unprompted reboots.

> *Caution: PC power supplies are NOT user-serviceable. Do NOT attempt any maintenance beyond the simple tests described. Never remove the cover of a power supply.*

- When you measure the voltage for each pin in a connector, be aware that a degree of tolerance is allowed:

Supply Line	Color Code	Tolerance	Minimum Voltage	Maximum Voltage
+5 V	Red	±5%	+4.75 V	+5.25 V
+12 V	Yellow	±5%	+11.4 V	+12.6 V
-12 V	Blue	±10%	-10.8 V	-13.2 V
+3.3 V	Orange	±5%	+3.135 V	+3.465 V
+5 V Standby	Purple	±5%	+4.75 V	+5.25 V

Supply Line	Color Code	Tolerance	Minimum Voltage	Maximum Voltage
PSU On	Green	Higher than +3 V when PC is off; less than 0.9 V when the PC is on.		
Power Good	Gray	Less than 0.9 V when the PC is off; higher than 2.5 V when the PC is on.		
Ground	Black	-	-	-

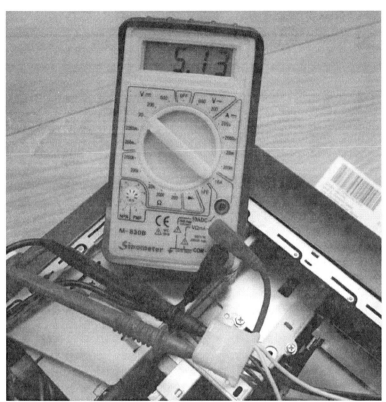

Testing a Molex connector with a multimeter.

If it seems that the PSU voltages are correct and that all power connectors are properly in place, then there may be a fault or overload on one of the peripheral devices (for example, the optical drive or the hard disk). Remove one peripheral device at a time (turn OFF when removing and reconnecting devices) to confirm whether the fault lies with one of these units. If you still cannot identify the fault, then the problem is likely to be a faulty motherboard or adapter card.

If you suspect that a power supply is faulty, do not leave it turned on for longer than absolutely necessary and do not leave it unattended. Keep an eye out for external signs of a problem (for example, smoke or fire). Turn off immediately if there are any unusual sights, smells, or noises.

 Note: *It is usually easier (and safer) to test the power supply by substitution (install a known good PSU) than to test with a multimeter.*

POWER SUPPLY TESTER

A **Power Supply Tester** is a device designed (unsurprisingly) with the sole purpose of testing PSUs. It is much simpler to use than a multimeter as you do not have to test each pin in turn.

 Show Slide(s)

Power Supply Tester

Typical models come with ports for the 20/24-pin P1, Molex, SATA, plus 8-pin, 6-pin, and 4-pin connectors found on different models of PSU. Usually each pin on each port has an LED to indicate whether the voltage supplied is good or (in more advanced models) a reading of the voltage supplied.

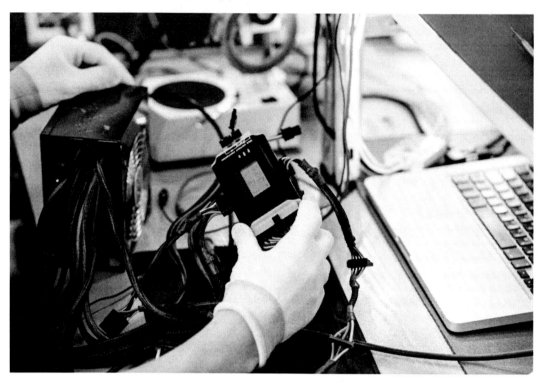

Technician working with a power supply tester. (Image by Konstantin Malkov © 123RF.com.)

POST AND BOOT PROBLEMS

Show Slide(s)

POST and Boot Problems (6 slides)

Once the CPU has been given the power good signal, the system firmware performs the **Power On Self Test (POST)**. The POST is a built-in diagnostic program that checks the hardware to ensure the components required to boot the PC are present and functioning correctly. This is the general process for the POST:

1. The POST starts by locating video card firmware at the address C000 in memory. If found, the video card is initialized from its own firmware. Information from the card manufacturer may also be displayed at this point.
2. A startup screen is displayed. More tests on the system, including counting through system RAM, are performed. If any errors are found, a text error message is displayed. Explanations of these messages are usually found in the system guide. Once numeric codes, these messages now tend to be descriptive, such as "key stuck."
3. You should be able to access the system setup routine from this point. This allows you to reconfigure the settings stored in system setup. The key used to invoke system setup varies according to the firmware, but is usually **Delete**, **F2**, **Esc**, **F10**, or **F1**.
4. Some PCs indicate that system checks have been successfully completed at this point with a single short beep, but the trend for modern computers is to boot silently.
5. A search is made for further interfaces that may have firmware chips on them. This could include storage adapters and network cards. Further information about these cards may be displayed at this point and their memory addresses reserved.

6. The firmware may display a summary screen about the system configuration. This may scroll by quite quickly. Use the **Pause** key if you want to analyze it.
7. The operating system load sequence starts.

 Note: On modern computers, the POST happens very quickly to improve boot times so you are unlikely to see any POST messages. A modern POST is unlikely to perform thorough checks such as a memory count.

POST NOT RUNNING

If power is present (for example, if you can hear the fans spinning) but the computer does not start or the screen is blank and there are no beeps from the speaker, it is likely that the POST procedure is not executing.

If the screen is blank, check that the monitor cable is connected and undamaged and that the monitor is powered on. If the monitor has separate inputs (for example, HDMI and DVI), make sure it is switched to the correct one. If possible, test with another monitor to confirm that there is no problem with the display.

If you can rule out a problem with the display itself, other likely causes are faulty cabling or a damaged or mis-seated CPU or other motherboard component. To troubleshoot, try the following tests and solutions:

- Ask what has changed—if the system firmware has been flashed and the PC has not booted since, the system firmware update may have failed. Use the reset procedure.
- Check cabling and connections, especially if maintenance work has just been performed on the PC. An incorrectly oriented storage adapter cable or a badly seated adapter card can stop the POST from running. Correct any errors, reset adapter cards, and then reboot the PC.
- Check for faulty interfaces and devices—it is possible that a faulty adapter card or device is halting the POST. Try removing one device at a time to see if this solves the problem (or remove all non-essential devices then add them back one-by-one).
- Check the PSU—even though the fans are receiving power, there may be a fault that is preventing the Power Good signal from being sent to the CPU, preventing POST.
- Check for a faulty CPU or system firmware. If possible, replace the CPU chip with a known good one or update the system firmware.
- Some motherboards have jumpers to configure modes (such as firmware recovery) or processor settings. If the jumpers are set incorrectly it could cause the computer not to boot. If a computer will not work after being serviced, check that the jumpers have not been changed.

 Note: Remember to ask "What has changed" when troubleshooting. For example, it is best practice to check that a system works properly after performing any sort of servicing work (such as updating the firmware) but not all technicians are so diligent. If a user complains that their previously working PC will not boot, find out what happened to it in the intervening period.

POST BEEP CODES

If POST detects a problem, it generates an error message. As the error may prevent the computer from displaying anything on the screen, the error is often indicated by a series of beeps.

 Teaching Tip
Exam candidates might want to memorize these codes.

For a beep code, you must decode the pattern of beeps and take the appropriate action. Use resources such as the manufacturer's website to determine the meaning of the beep code. Examples of manufacturer websites include **ami.com**, **phoenix.com** (Award), **compaq.com**, and **dell.com**. Websites such as **bioscentral.com** provide a good summary and can be located easily through Internet search engines.

The codes for the original IBM PC are listed in this table.

Code	Meaning
1 short beep	Normal POST—system is OK.
2 short beeps	POST error—error code shown on screen.
No beep	Power supply or motherboard problem (use a multimeter to check the onboard speaker is functioning).
Continuous beep	Power supply, motherboard, or system memory problem.
Repeating short beeps	Power supply, motherboard, or keyboard problem.
1 long, 1 short beep	Motherboard problem.
1 long, 2 or 3 short beeps	Display adapter error.
3 long beeps	3270 keyboard card.

Error messages on the screen are usually descriptive of the problem. In each case, take the appropriate action.

 Note: *If the screen is blank on bootup but you hear a single beep, check the monitor is turned on and connected properly. Try testing the monitor with a different computer. If the monitor is OK, try replacing the graphics adapter.*

BIOS TIME AND SETTINGS RESET

While modern computers do not rely on the CMOS battery to store system settings, if the computer is losing the correct time, it can be a sign that the Real Time Clock battery is failing. On older computers, the failure of the battery may lead to system setup settings being lost or corrupted. You may see a "CMOS Checksum" error or similar. To replace the CMOS battery:

1. Obtain a coin cell battery that is compatible with your motherboard.
2. Unclip the existing battery and take it out.
3. Plug in the new battery.
4. Switch the computer back on.

OPERATING SYSTEM SEARCH/BOOTS TO INCORRECT DEVICE

Once the POST tests are complete, the firmware searches the devices as specified in the boot sequence. If the first drive in the sequence is not found, it then moves on to the next. For example, if there is no fixed disk, the boot sequence checks for a USB-attached drive. If no disk-based boot device is found, the system might attempt to boot from the network. If no boot device is found, the system displays an error message and halts the boot process.

If the system attempts to boot to an incorrect device, check that the removable drives do not contain media that are interfering with the boot process and that the boot device order is correctly configured.

OS BOOT TROUBLESHOOTING AND LOG ENTRIES

Show Slide(s)
OS Boot Troubleshooting and Log Entries (2 slides)

If a boot device is located, the code from the boot sector on the selected device is loaded into memory and takes over from the system firmware. The boot sector code loads the rest of the operating system files into system memory. Error messages received after this point can usually be attributed to software (or driver) problems rather than issues with hardware devices.

Viewing startup messages on a Linux server.

> **Note:** *In Windows 7, you can use the Startup Configuration utility (`msconfig`) to show boot messages (select OS boot information on the Boot tab). In Windows 10, this setting does not work and you need to enable verbose boot messages via the registry.*

If no error message is displayed at startup, issues with the operating system can often be diagnosed by checking for log entries.

- In Windows, boot messages are written to the C:\Windows\ntbtlog.txt file. You should also use Event Viewer to analyze the **System** and **Application** logs for any errors.
- In Linux, you can review the boot messages using the `dmesg | less` command.

MOTHERBOARD COMPONENT PROBLEMS

Few problems are actually caused by the motherboard itself, but there are a few things to be aware of.

Show Slide(s)

Motherboard Component Problems (4 slides)

- The motherboard does contain soldered chips and components, which could be damaged by Electrostatic Discharge (ESD), electrical spikes, or overheating.
- The pins on integrated connectors can also be damaged by careless insertion of plugs.
- In some cases, errors may be caused by dirt (clean the contacts on connectors) or **chip creep**, where an adapter works loose from its socket over time, perhaps because of temperature changes.

> **Note:** *Remember to ask "What has changed?" Check job logs to find out whether any maintenance or upgrades were carried out recently.*

- **Unstable operation.** Symptoms of intermittent device failure such as the system locking up, unexpected shutdown, displaying a Blue Screen of Death (BSoD) crash screen, or continuous rebooting are difficult to diagnose with a specific cause, especially if you are not able to witness the events directly. The most likely causes are software, disk problems, or malware.

 Note: *A blue screen is a system crash screen proprietary to Windows. A macOS system that suffers catastrophic process failure shows a spinning pinwheel (of death), also called a spinning wait cursor.*

If you can discount these, try to establish whether the problem is truly intermittent or whether there is a pattern to the errors. If they occur when the PC has been running for some time, it could be a thermal problem.

Next, check that the power supply is providing good, stable voltages to the system. If you can discount the power supply, you must start to suspect a problem with memory, CPU, or motherboard.

- **Visual inspection.** Inspect the motherboard for any sign of damage. If a component has "blown" it can leave scorch marks. You could also look for **distended capacitors**. The capacitors are barrel-like components that regulate the flow of electricity to the system chips. If they are swollen or bulging or emitting any kind of residue they could have been damaged or could have failed due to a manufacturing defect.

If there is physical damage to the motherboard you will almost certainly need diagnostic software to run tests to confirm whether there is a problem. Testing by substituting "known good" components would be too time consuming and expensive. The most likely causes of physical damage are heat, ESD, or a power surge or spike. It is worth investigating any environmental problems or maintenance procedures that could be the "root cause" of the error.

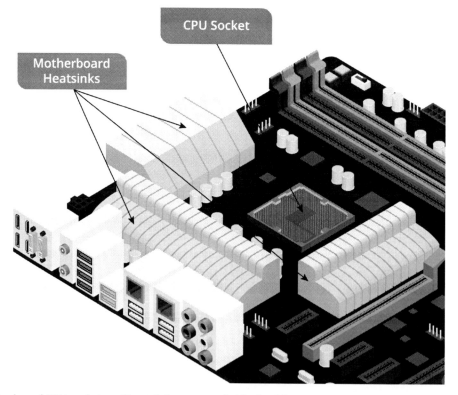

Motherboard CPU socket and heatsinks surrounded by healthy capacitors. (Image © 123RF.com.)

- **Overheating.** Insufficient cooling is the main cause of processor, memory, and motherboard problems. Thermal faults are normally cyclic: a system works for some time, crashes, and then works again later because powering down allows the processor to cool. To check for overheating issues:

- Ensure that the CPU fan is working. Proper cooling is vital to the lifespan and performance of the processor. If the processor is running too hot, it can decrease performance. A processor that is overheating can cause crashes or reboot the machine.

    Is the fan's power cable properly connected? Is the fan jammed, clogged, or too small? If a processor upgrade is installed, the fan from the original CPU may not be suitable for the new device.

     Note: *Pro-actively optimize the existing cooling system by clearing dust from chips, heat sinks, and fans. Also verify that there is sufficient space around the PC's vents to allow for adequate air flow. If the PC is positioned too closely to a wall, it might prevent effective cooling.*

- Make sure the heatsink is properly fitted. It should be snug against the processor. Heatsinks are usually "stuck" to the processor using a special heat conductive paste. Some manufacturers use lower quality paste. In these cases, it is possible to clean away the old paste and replace it with better paste, which will help the processor to run at a lower temperature.
- Always use blanking plates to cover up holes in the back or front of the PC. Holes can disrupt the airflow and decrease the effectiveness of the cooling systems.
- Speed—is the processor running at the correct speed? Running a processor at a higher clock speed can cause overheating. Double-check the voltage and timing settings in CMOS Setup.
- Environment—is the room unusually warm or dusty or is the PC positioned near a radiator or in direct sunlight?

Thermal problems may also affect system operation by causing loose connectors to drift apart, components to move in their sockets, or circuit board defects such as hairline cracks to widen and break connections. Some of these faults can be detected by visual inspection.

 Note: *CPUs and other system components heat up while running. Take care not to burn yourself when handling internal components.*

Activity 5-6

Discussing System Component Troubleshooting

Show Slide(s)

Activity: Discussing System Component Troubleshooting

SCENARIO
Answer the following questions to check your understanding of the topic.

1. **What cause might you suspect if a PC experiences intermittent lockups?**

    Assuming the cause is not recent installation of faulty software or hardware, then thermal or power problems are most likely. Loose connections or faulty memory or CPU are also possibilities.

2. **How might you diagnose a thermal problem?**

    Feel if the system is hot to touch, check temperature gauges, watch for cyclic lockup/reboot problems.

3. **What measurement would you expect from a multimeter if a fuse is good?**

    Zero ohms.

4. **What might stop a POST from executing?**

    Faulty cabling and connections, poorly-seated chips, faulty interfaces and devices, logic errors, faulty CPU, motherboard, or PSU.

Activity 5-7

Diagnosing Power Problems

Show Slide(s)

Activity: Diagnosing Power Problems

Teaching Tip

Hand out one multimeter and one good and one "blown" fuse per student. Remember to collect this kit at the end of the activity.

It is probably a good idea to demonstrate the main exercise (measuring PSU voltages) first so that learners are confident that they will do this exercise safely.

Monitor learners carefully to ensure they are performing the exercise safely.

If any learners feel unsure about working with electricity, do not force them to do so!!!

BEFORE YOU BEGIN

Your instructor will provide you with a multimeter or power supply tester to use to test the output voltages from the PSU. This involves working with a live system. Follow the instructions carefully and do not touch parts of the computer when it is switched on.

You will perform this activity at your WORKBENCH PC.

SCENARIO

You have been assigned several power problems to solve.

---

1. **Problem #1** When the user turns on the PC, it does not always come on and sometimes it just shuts itself down abruptly, with no warning. When she turns on the system again, there is no fan noise. She is using a legacy database application and the data is being corrupted during the improper shutdowns.

    What would you do to resolve this problem?

    Unplug the power cord. Remove the system cover. Using compressed air, remove the dust from around the fan spindle. Verify that there is no obvious reason the fan is not spinning. Replace the power cord and restart the computer. Verify that the computer starts properly. If these actions did not fix the problem, you would need to replace the power supply. Leaving the problem alone would allow heat to build up to dangerous levels, causing serious damage to the system.

2. **Problem #2** A user is reporting an odor coming out of his computer. You have serviced this machine recently and replaced the computer's power supply unit.

    What would you do to resolve this problem?

    An odor coming from the power supply could be a sign that there is something wrong. Because you have just replaced the unit, verify that all the connections are secure and that the fan is functioning. Restart the machine and verify that the power supply is running as it should. Once the functionality of the unit is verified, then odor is probably a result of installing a new power supply unit. If the odor does not go away in a few days, then contact the power supply manufacturer.

Teaching Tip

Refer students to the table of voltage tolerances in the Multimeter Use section to check their readings.

Teaching Tip

If you have power supply testers available, you can have learners use them instead of multimeters. You will need to lead them through the testing process.

3. **Problem #3** One of the other hardware technicians has been trying to troubleshoot a power problem. The system will not come on when the user turns on the power switch. He determined that the user has an ATX motherboard and power supply. You have been assigned to take over this trouble ticket.

    a)   You will be using a multimeter to measure 5 and 12 Volts DC. Set your multimeter accordingly and attach its probes if required.

    b)   Remove the PC from the electrical supply, then remove the case cover.

Teaching Tip

As an alternative to this step, if you have a PC with a power supply problem, have learners work as a team to troubleshoot and resolve the issue.

c) Find a spare Molex connector, or remove a Molex connector from a optical drive or hard disk drive.

d) Insert the black (REF) probe into a black cable connector and the other probe into the yellow cable connector in the Molex.

e) Turn on your multimeter.

f) Reconnect the power cord to your PC and to building power, and turn it on.

g) Take a reading and record the results here.

_____

h) Turn off your PC and repeat the above process for the red cable and write the result here:

_____

i) Are these recordings acceptable?

4. **Problem #4** The user turns on the power switch, but the PC does not come on. He does not hear the fan, there is no power light on, and he hears no beeps or other sounds coming from the system. His system is plugged into a surge protector.

What would you do to resolve this problem?

Verify that the power cord is securely connected to the power supply and to the electrical outlet on the surge protector. Verify that the surge protector is turned on and plugged in. Verify that the surge protector is working by plugging in a known good electrical device and turning it on. If the device did not turn on, check to see whether any reset buttons need to be reset on the surge protector, or check the electric outlet's circuit breaker. Restart the computer. If these actions did not solve the problem, you would need to replace the power supply.

5. You also need to perform some routine testing of safety equipment. Using your multimeter, measure the resistance of your ESD kit's wrist strap cable, connecting the crocodile clip to the black probe and touching the red probe to the metal plate that makes contact with your skin.

Why is it so high?

A wrist strap must allow high voltage charges to leak from your body and clothing through the ground, but prevent large currents from flowing into your body and causing an electric shock. This is accomplished by a megaohm resistor.

6. Using your multimeter, measure the resistance of a fuse—your instructor will provide you with these.

What does it mean if the reading is zero or over range?

The fuse has blown and must be replaced.

Activity 5-8
Diagnosing System Errors

BEFORE YOU BEGIN
You will perform this activity at your WORKBENCH PC.

SCENARIO
You are attempting to resolve problems for a user who has been reporting intermittent but severe system errors, such as frequent unexpected shutdowns. The problems have been getting more frequent, and you have been unable to pinpoint a cause within the system software, power supply, memory, or any adapter cards. You are starting to suspect that there is a bad CPU, and you need to proceed accordingly to get the user back to work with as little downtime and cost as possible.

1. **What initial steps should you take to identify and resolve a potential CPU problem?**

    ☐ Replace the CPU with a known-good processor.

    ☑ Verify that the CPU fan and other cooling systems are installed and functional.

    ☐ Replace the motherboard.

    ☑ If the CPU is overclocked, throttle it down to the manufacturer-rated clock speed.

2. **All other diagnostic and corrective steps have failed. You need to verify that it is the CPU itself that is defective. What should you do?**

    ⬤ Replace the CPU with a known-good chip.

    ◯ Remove all the adapter cards.

    ◯ Reinstall the operating system.

    ◯ Replace the motherboard.

3. A colleague suggests that you might want to view the symptoms of some different system errors. For each following components:
    1. Prepare to work inside the computer case.
    2. Remove or alter the component as described in the following steps.
    3. Restore power to the PC.
    4. Examine and record what happens. You can use Notepad or a separate sheet of paper if you like.
    5. Shut down and cut power to the PC.
    6. Reinstall or otherwise restore the component.

4. Remove the system RAM from the motherboard. What happens?

Show Slide(s)

Activity: Diagnosing System Errors

Teaching Tip

After learners have done the main exercise, see if they can troubleshoot some errors that you create for them. You could send them on a break and then introduce any or all of the following problems:

- Use a plug with a faulty fuse.
- Change system setup to say that there are no hard drives installed.
- Connect a monitor with a bent pin in the connector so that a color is missing from the display.
- Unseat an adapter card.
- Remove a blanking plate (will not cause an error, but learners should observe that PC is set up in way that will cause maintenance issues over time).

5. Disconnect the hard disk drive from the motherboard. What happens?

6. Rearrange the memory cards by putting them in different slots or removing one of them. What happens?

7. Your instructor will now create a problem on your PC. Use your troubleshooting skills to try and solve it. Record what you found during the troubleshooting process.

Topic E

Configure a Custom PC

 EXAM OBJECTIVES COVERED

1001-3.8 Given a scenario, select and configure appropriate components for a custom PC configuration to meet customer specifications or needs.
1001-3.9 Given a scenario, install and configure common devices.

As a CompTIA A+ technician, you must be knowledgeable in many different areas of information technology. This may include supporting a wide variety of client configurations, such as gaming or audio and video workstations. You must be prepared to fully support any type of environment, including more specialized hardware and software configurations based on job roles and tasks.

CLIENT PERSONAL COMPUTERS

When installing and configuring user workstations, it is important to identify what the specific needs are of the user that will be using the workstation to perform job tasks. Standard clients are a good starting point for any installation and must be examined to verify that they fit the requirements of the job function.

Standard business client computers are end-user computers that are administered and managed centrally by a server.

You might be called on to set up or service any of the following client types:

- **Standard (thick) clients.** A **standard client** (sometimes referred to as **thick client** to distinguish it from a thin client) is an ordinary office PC. It will be used to run locally installed desktop applications, such as office productivity (word processor, spreadsheet, and presentation) plus Line of Business software, email/calendaring/contact management, and a web browser.

  When you are configuring a standard client, it is important to pay attention to the *recommended* Windows or Linux system requirements and to the software application requirements. Using the minimum OS requirements is likely to lead to poor performance.

  A standard client might be configured with multiple user accounts. These user accounts might be defined locally on each computer (a workgroup) or on a network directory server (a domain). Windows 10 also supports the use of Microsoft accounts, which use cloud services to synchronize settings and data across each of the Windows-based devices that a user signs in to. Each standard user account is allocated its own private data storage folders. Each account can be configured with different desktop settings and (if applicable) network permissions and privileges.

  If data is stored locally, then access to storage locations is required with a consistent pathway to data. Similarly, if data is stored on a network, then a consistent path should be established to the storage location with proper security implementations.

- **Thin clients.** A **thin client** is a PC or appliance designed to act as an interface to applications that run on a network server. The client may be interfacing with particular software applications or with an entire Windows Desktop. This is referred to as **Virtual Desktop Infrastructure (VDI)**. In this scenario, the only really important performance criteria for the thin client is the network link. The client PC does no application processing. It just transfers mouse and keyboard input to the

 Teaching Tip
This topic can be assigned as self-study if time is short.

 Show Slide(s)
Client Personal Computers (2 slides)

 Teaching Tip
Account setup is covered in more detail elsewhere in the course.

server and processes video and audio output coming back. The applications do not get installed on the computer and do not use up any hard drive space. RAM is used to run the application from the server.

 Note: Virtualization is covered in greater detail later in the course.

The client may be interfacing with particular software applications or with an entire Windows or Linux desktop. The client will have to meet the minimum requirements for installing the selected OS, but that is all. The computer might require specialized software in order to access the applications hosted by the server. The computer may also require a specific browser or browser version in order to run any web-based applications.

 Note: Microsoft has a Thin Client version of Windows 7 but its minimum spec is actually the same as any other Windows 7 edition. It's worth noting that Microsoft stopped distinguishing between "minimum" and "recommended" system requirements.

When the thin client starts, it boots a minimal OS, allowing the user to log on to a **Virtual Machine (VM)** stored on the company server infrastructure. The user makes a connection to the VM using some sort of remote desktop protocol (Microsoft Remote Desktop or Citrix ICA, for instance). The thin client has to find the correct image and use an appropriate authentication mechanism. There may be a 1:1 mapping based on machine name or IP address or the process of finding an image may be handled by a connection broker. Consequently, to configure a thin client you need only install the thin client OS and configure the connection manager/broker. User accounts are created on the server rather than directly on the thin client itself.

BUSINESS WORKSTATIONS

Show Slide(s)

Business Workstations (5 slides)

The term **workstation** is sometimes used to describe a computer that runs more demanding applications than standard office suites. These systems typically have faster processors, more memory, and faster and larger drives than standard desktop systems.

Most computers deployed for business use will fit one of the following profiles.

- **Programming, development, and virtualization workstations.** A workstation used to develop software or games will run one or more **Integrated Development Environments (IDEs)**. It may also run a local database server application for testing. Consequently, these workstations require fast CPUs and mass storage access, plus plenty of system memory.

  Development work is also likely to require virtualization, so that the developer has access to multiple operating system environments for testing. Virtualization requires a lot of system memory. Each guest OS would typically need at least 1—2 GB even for average performance. It also benefits from multiple CPU cores and multi-channel memory as well as a large, fast disk subsystem.

- **Graphics and CAD/CAM design workstations.** Media design workstations are configured to support the needs of graphic designers, engineers, architects, 3D media developers, and other design-driven job roles. A workstation used for different types of design will have to support applications with high CPU, GPU, and memory requirements. Such workstations also need a fast storage subsystem and are typically provisioned with Solid State Drives (SSDs), rather than older hard disks.

  Typical design applications include:

  - Image editing and illustration tools.

Teaching Tip

If you have examples of other graphic design or CAD/CAM workstations, either via photo or as actual setups, consider sharing them with learners.

- **Desktop Publishing (DTP)** and web design.
- **Computer Aided Design (CAD).**
- **Computer Aided Manufacturing (CAM).**

 Note: CAM workstations can control machine tools found in manufacturing environments. Specialized controller cards may be required as well as specialized connections and software. CAM machines may be installed in harsh environments —such as manufacturing buildings and automotive factories—so the workstations may need to be hardened machines that will not be adversely affected by their working environments.

Design work will also often require specialist peripherals, such as a digitizer and styluses. Vendors often produce graphics adapters specially designed for use with CAD software.

- **Audio/Video editing workstations.** A workstation used to edit Audio/Video (A/V) files, create animations, or produce music will have high performance requirements. These computers must be able to support the demanding editing programs that audio/video technicians use in post-production editing functions. Most professional videos taken today include special effects and CGI (computer generated imagery) that is all applied after the digital video is taken.

Again, it is important not to overlook the disk subsystem, which can become a performance bottleneck as media files will often have to be streamed from the disk. Workstations will generally need 10 K or 15 K disks to perform well. Multimedia files are also extremely large, so the disk subsystem will have to be very high capacity. This means that the best performing Solid State Drive (SSD) storage may not be affordable at the capacities required.

These workstations require specialized adapters to capture audio and video from a variety of sources.

- An input/output (I/O) card allows audio/video input to be sampled and saved as a digital file. As with a consumer-level video capture card, an I/O card can use an HDMI or Thunderbolt connection to a recording device, but Serial Data Interface (SDI) over 75 ohm coax cabling is a more likely option for broadcast-quality equipment.
- For music recording and production, professional-level sound cards, referred to as audio interfaces, feature numerous inputs, including ¼" phone plugs to connect microphone and amplifier equipment, S/PDIF ports, and 5-pin DIN ports for MIDI equipment. Audio interfaces are usually provisioned as external units, connected to the PC over USB or Thunderbolt, to avoid the problem of electrical interference from PC components when making recordings.

OTHER REQUIREMENTS

You will also find other equipment might be required, such as:

- **Dual monitors.** With all types of workstation, screen "real estate" is often at a premium. This means that they are often provisioned with two or more monitors.
- **RAID.** As they are used to process critical data, where losing even an hour's work might represent a huge loss to the business, most workstations will be configured with a RAID disk system, to provide insurance against disk failure.

COMPUTERS FOR HOME USE

When not used solely for school homework, web browsing, and email, home computers are often specified as **media centers** or **gaming rigs**. When used for media streaming or gaming, these systems often require fast video, storage, and network

 Teaching Tip

Mention that the power needed to run these computers will not only come from AC power, but from digital power as well, so it's important to check the requirements of all the computing components within the environment.

 Show Slide(s)

Computers for Home Use (6 slides)

 Interaction Opportunity

Poll learners to see who has experience with any of the custom clients presented in this topic. Ask how they have used them and what they expect to be doing with them in the future.

connections. A home network might also have network attached storage or servers from which files can be shared.

Most media center or gaming computers deployed for home use will fit one of the following profiles.

- **Home theater PCs, home server PCs, and NAS.**
  - A **home theater PC (HTPC)** can be used in place of consumer appliances such as **personal video recorders (PVR)** to watch and record TV broadcasts and play movies and music, either from local files or from streaming Internet services. The PC will need to be equipped with an appropriate TV tuner card to process the incoming TV signal (broadcast, cable, or satellite) and usually comes with a remote control (and peripherals such as the mouse and keyboard would normally be wireless). The HTPC is usually equipped with specific entertainment software that can be used to manage the music and video files stored on the computer. The PCs are generally located near the TV and other home entertainment devices and have a HTPC form factor, which is aesthetically appealing and designed to look similar to other home entertainment devices. They are also designed to be less noisy than a traditional PC, with more compact quieter cooling methods and the addition of sound dampening foam or padding to limit excessive noise generated by the fan and hard drive.
  - A **home server PC** is either an HTPC with a slightly expanded role or a repurposed desktop or low-end PC server used primarily for file storage, media streaming, and printer sharing. Such PCs do not need to be particularly powerful in terms of CPU and memory, but they will need a good network link. Most would also be configured with RAID storage to reduce the risk of losing valuable movie and audio files, even though there should be a backup system in place to protect against theft, fire, or accidental deletion.
  - There are also purpose-built devices to fill a home server role. A **Network Attached Storage (NAS)** appliance is a hard drive (or RAID array) with a cut-down server board, usually running some form of Linux, that provides network access, various file sharing protocols, and a web management interface. The appliance is accessed over the network, either using a wired Ethernet port or Wi-Fi. In a SOHO network you would plug the NAS device into an Ethernet port on the Internet router.

 Note: Most network adapters (or Network Interface Cards [NIC]) in machines from the last few years will be Gigabit Ethernet capable. It may be worth upgrading the adapter on an older machine but you need to bear in mind that many of the SOHO Internet router appliances come with Fast Ethernet switch ports (100 Mbps) rather than Gigabit ones. It will usually make more sense to install two adapters and bond them. The vast majority of homes will be using Wi-Fi streaming in any case and the most useful upgrade will be to 802.11n or 802.11ac.

As well as sharing the disk resource, a NAS box will usually be able to share a printer. It will also be able to make files available over the Internet, using HTTP or FTP. Care needs to be taken to secure the device and the router/firewall properly if this is the case.

Some NAS devices and home server PCs can stream media files to wireless speakers or an IP-enabled TV (or various other types of media player). A streaming media server will have higher demand for CPU, memory, and bandwidth than an ordinary file server.

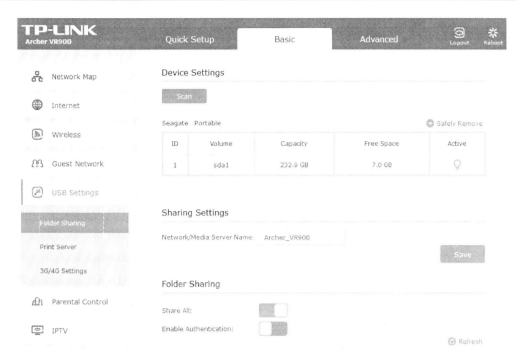

Most SOHO Internet router appliances can perform a basic file and printer sharing function, using USB-attached storage. (Screenshot courtesy of TP-Link.)

- **Gaming PCs.**
  - A PC built for gaming is almost always based around the latest graphics adapter technology. Of course, the latest games tend to be able to make the latest graphics technology obsolete within a few months of release, so upgrade potential is a key characteristic of these systems. PC games feature lots of media assets that must be loaded from permanent storage so a fast drive technology such as a Solid State Drive (SSD) is preferable to slower hard disks (HDD).

    Gaming PCs will share some of the traits of a home theater PC: surround sound audio and a high quality display. There are also gaming-oriented peripherals, such as keyboards and mice. Many games also benefit from headsets, so that players can bark instructions at one another as they eliminate enemies over the Internet. Low-latency, high bandwidth Internet access is almost as important to the average gamer as the frame rate the system's GPU can achieve.

    The addictive nature of PC games means that the processors are very highly utilized, or **thrashed** for considerable periods of time. Some gamers are also fond of overclocking components to obtain better performance. All this means that a gaming PC will generate more heat than most other types of computer. It is not unusual for them to use more powerful fans (which must run silently of course) or liquid cooling.

- There are many different peripherals used within the gaming world. The most common ones include the mouse and keyboard, but there are others that may be used depending on the type of game played. These might include:
  - Gaming mice that are either wired or wireless and include many buttons and different ergonomic form factors.
  - Customized keypads, with moveable keys.
  - Steering wheels used for auto racing games.
  - 3D glasses.
  - Specialized gaming mouse pads.
  - Specialized audio system.
  - PC video camera.

GUIDELINES FOR SELECTING COMPONENTS FOR A CUSTOM PERSONAL COMPUTER

Show Slide(s)

Guidelines for Selecting Components for a Custom Personal Computer (2 slides)

*Note: All of the Guidelines for this lesson are available as checklists from the **Checklist** tile on the CHOICE Course screen.*

Here are some guidelines to consider when selecting components for custom personal computers.

SELECT COMPONENTS FOR A CUSTOM COMPUTER

Follow these guidelines when selecting components for a custom computer:

- Verify that the computer meets or exceeds the operating system and application requirements. This should include the fastest and most reliable:
  - RAM
  - CPU
  - Storage subsystem
  - Video subsystem, including a fast refresh rate on the monitor
- Verify you know what the main intention of the computer will be for. It might be for CAD/CAM, A/V editing, watching TV and movies, or gaming. While each of these types of custom computers require better performance than the average PC, each will likely have specific requirements that should be verified with the end user.
- Consider installing additional cooling mechanisms to keep the system from overheating.
- Verify that the network card, the router, and the network cabling or WiFi signal are all capable of the highest possible speed.
- Consider purchasing specialized devices for the work that will be performed on the custom computer. This might include specialized keyboards, mice, or other adapters to connect specific devices such as MIDI instruments, video cameras, or manufacturing machines, to name just a few.
- Implement a RAID system to help ensure data is not lost. This should be in addition to performing regular backups that are securely stored off site.

*Note: To learn more, check the **Video** tile on the CHOICE Course screen for any videos that supplement the content for this lesson.*

Access the Checklist tile on your CHOICE Course screen for reference information and job aids on How to Configure Thick and Thin Client Personal Computers.

Activity 5-9

Discussing Custom PC Configuration

Show Slide(s)

Activity: Discussing Custom PC Configuration

SCENARIO

Answer the following questions to check your understanding of the topic.

---

1. **Which component is likely to be a performance bottleneck on a workstation used to edit digital movies?**

   The disk subsystem is most likely to cause the performance bottleneck. The files will be too large to be stored completely in system memory and so must be streamed from the disk, which will need to be both large and fast.

2. **For what type of workstation is a CPU with 4 or more cores particularly well suited?**

   Multiple cores benefit software that can take advantage of multi-threading. Examples include virtualization software and Rapid Application Development (RAD) tools.

3. **You are specifying a PC to act as a home theater. What multimedia outputs should it support?**

   Surround sound audio outputs to the speaker system and HDMI to the TV screen.

4. **Which factors are most likely to make a PC used for gaming require high-end cooling?**

   These PCs use at least two heavyweight processors: the CPU and GPU. Also, gamers are more likely than most other users to overclock components to improve performance. Overclocking requires very effective thermal management solutions.

5. **On a thin client, which component is more important: NIC or HDD?**

   Thin clients do not need much permanent storage at all—some can make do without any mass storage. They do not generate that much network traffic either but that said, the NIC is the more important component here.

6. **Why might high-spec components (CPU, memory, RAID) not be a good idea in a home theater PC?**

   These devices need to operate as quietly as possible and using high-spec components means heat, heat requires cooling, cooling usually means fans, and fans mean noise.

Activity 5-10
Selecting Components for Custom Workstations

Show Slide(s)

Activity: Selecting Components for Custom Workstations

SCENARIO

You have been asked by your manager to evaluate the hardware and software needs for all the clients within the Human Resources (HR) department of your organization. There was a recent reorganization of the department, and some of the job roles and functions have changed. Based on the recent changes, you need to review the job functions and identify what type of client workstation will meet those needs.

---

1. **A user needs to be able to access the central employee data repository to run reports, but does not need access to any local applications used to create, edit, and manage the employee data. The employee data is managed on a server that can be accessed with a log in. What type of client is best in this case?**

   ● Thin client

   ○ Virtualization workstation

   ○ Thick client

2. **June has recently been put in charge of making updates to the Human Resource employee benefits website. She will be publishing a monthly newsletter and posting company-wide announcements, among other small updates and changes, on a regular basis. All changes to the website must be tested on a number of platforms and web browsers to verify that the changes are correct regardless of the operating system and browser. What type of client setup would you suggest for her?**

   Answers will vary, but will most likely include a virtualization workstation so that she can switch from different operating systems and test any website changes quickly.

3. **In order to properly support the HR employee benefits website, a new server running client VMs has been installed so that the environment that the application requires can be strictly administered by IT staff. Current PCs will be used to access the Client VM environment that is configured on the VM Server. What needs to be present at all PCs that will be accessing this new server and application?**

   ☑ Appropriately configured VM Client.

   ☑ Fast network connection to server hosting the VM environment.

   ☐ Upgrade to video cards.

·4. **True or False? The HR manager's client computer must meet the recommended requirements to run Windows 10 so that she can access and use all of the HR-related applications used by the organization. In this case, the best client option is a thick client.**

True

Activity 5-11

Selecting Components for Custom Personal Computers

Show Slide(s)

Activity: Selecting Components for Custom Personal Computers

SCENARIO

You are a support technician for a local business that specializes in consulting, purchasing, and installing home computing solutions for consumers. You are responsible for fulfilling all the orders that have come in overnight through the business' website.

1. Customer 1 is using a desktop PC to play home movies and to set up slide shows to show his family their vacation photos and is having difficulty with the computer freezing during the movies. He is looking for a solution that will allow him to store and play his movies seamlessly through a computer. He also wants his wife to be able to access the pictures and movies from her laptop within the house.

    What type of computer setup would you suggest for this customer? What specific questions might you ask this customer about additional component needs?

    Answers may vary, but will most likely include setting up a home server PC for easy file sharing among the household computing devices and to provide more speed to play movies from the PC. You may ask if they are in need of additional storage space and if they are looking for redundancy through a RAID array in the PC.

2. Customer 2 is from a small real estate office who has recently hired a graphic designer to produce informational pamphlets and other marketing materials for the agency, such as property drop sheets and circular layout designs. The office manager has asked your company to determine the hardware and software needs for the designer's workstation so that it can be ordered and set up before their scheduled start date in two weeks.

    What hardware and software requirements would you suggest for the graphic designer's workstation?

    Answers may vary, but will most likely include a PC with a high-end, multicore processor, a high end video card, and the maximum RAM that the motherboard can handle. In addition, the motherboard should contain multiple high-speed ports for peripherals such as external hard drives or additional video cards. The applications will most likely include Adobe's Creative Cloud or similar graphic-design software.

3. Customer 3 is looking to make the switch from a traditional TV cable box and DVD player to a home theater PC, so that she can stream Netflix and record shows and movies from her TV. She already purchased a computer from a local home entertainment store but cannot figure out why she cannot connect the cable TV wire into the computer.

What would you check for first?

She needs to have a TV tuner card installed in the computer. The tuner card provides the port to connect the cable from the provider to the computer. You would also want to verify that the tuner card is correctly configured, and that all device drivers are installed and up-to-date.

Summary

In this lesson, you installed, configured, and performed troubleshooting on internal system components such as CPUs, system firmware, and power supplies, You also examined the requirements for configuring custom PCs for specific uses. Your ability and comfort level in performing these types of hardware support will make you a valuable asset to your IT team.

Which system firmware have you worked with, if any? What types of configuration did you perform?

A: Answers will vary. BIOS is the traditional system firmware, but current computers are more apt to have UEFI. Some of the configuration that might be performed includes setting the boot device, performing diagnostics, and flashing the firmware.

What types of custom client setups do you think you will encounter the most in your role as an A+ technician?

A: Answers will vary, but may include gaming PCs due to the rise in the gaming systems sold to consumers in the last few years, and also home theater PCs and home server PCs.

 Practice Question: Additional practice questions are available on the CompTIA CHOICE platform within the **Assessments** *tile.*

Lesson 6

Installing, Configuring, and Maintaining Operating Systems

LESSON INTRODUCTION

So far in this course, you worked with the Microsoft® Windows® operating system. As you know, a CompTIA® A+® technician will probably also be responsible for setting up, maintaining, and troubleshooting computers and devices that have other operating systems installed. Familiarity with other desktop operating systems, such as Linux® and macOS®, will enable you to support more of your user base.

Since so many computers today come with operating system software installed by the vendor, an ordinary user might never need to install an operating system. As an IT professional, however, you might be called upon to install operating systems for a variety of reasons: if the original installation does not meet a user's needs; if the system needs to be upgraded; if you are redeploying a system from one user to another; or even if you need to complete a brand new build and construct a computer entirely from scratch. In all of these cases, you will need to be able to install, configure, and maintain the computer's operating system.

LESSON OBJECTIVES

In this lesson, you will:

- Configure and use Linux.
- Configure and use macOS.
- Install and upgrade operating systems.
- Perform OS maintenance tasks.

Topic A

Configure and Use Linux

EXAM OBJECTIVES COVERED
1002-1.3 Summarize general OS installation considerations and upgrade methods.
1002-1.9 Given a scenario, use features and tools of the Mac OS and Linux client/desktop operating systems.

The various operating systems you might encounter use different tools, but the functionality of those tools is common across all types of systems. You will need to configure disks and file systems, user accounts, and software applications.

Many individuals and organizations have adopted Linux as a desktop and server OS because of its high security, low cost, and ease of licensing. In this topic, you will examine the basics of Linux so that you can begin to understand and appreciate its benefits.

Show Slide(s)

The Linux Operating System

THE LINUX OPERATING SYSTEM

Like all operating systems, **Linux** enables the most basic common system operations, such as file management, user account management, and so forth. It provides a means for users to interact with their computer's hardware and software.

Show Slide(s)

Distributions (4 slides)

DISTRIBUTIONS

The core of Linux is called the **kernel** and this is the same on all versions or **distributions** (**distros**). The kernel is the software component that provides the core set of operating system functions. These include features for managing system hardware and for communicating between software and hardware. A Linux distribution is a complete Linux implementation, including kernel, shell, applications, utilities, and installation media, that is packaged, distributed, and supported by a software vendor. Common distributions include:

- **Red Hat/CentOS**—the most commercially successful distribution. Also, the CentOS distribution is a stable, predictable, manageable, and reproducible platform derived from the sources of Red Hat® Enterprise Linux® (RHEL). CentOS is maintained by The CentOS Project, a community-driven free software effort that is modeled on the structure of the Apache® Foundation and has its own governing board. CentOS benefits from Red Hat's ongoing contributions and investment.
- **SUSE®**—originally developed in Germany, the company was bought out by US networking company Novell.
- **Debian/Ubuntu®**—one of the many volunteer-driven distributions. Ubuntu is one of most widely used versions of Debian.
- **Knoppix**—another popular Debian derivative.

These are some of the more popular distributions for PCs. There are a huge number of flavors, many of which have been developed for specialist applications such as running routers, set-top boxes, smart TVs, Internet of Things (IoT) devices, and so on. The smartphone OS, Android™, is based on Linux.

LINUX DESKTOP OPTIONS

Linux was originally developed with a **Command-Line Interface (CLI)** or **shell** very much like **UNIX**.

Today many users of Linux still use the **bash** shell and server-based editions will often only have the command-line environment installed. For this reason, it is important that support technicians are comfortable with using Linux shell commands. Many system tasks still require the use of the command even if a GUI environment is running. Within a GUI, you can open a **terminal window** to run shell commands.

> *Note: There are other CLI shells, include Bourne (sh), C Shell (csh), and Korn (ksh).*

For ease of use, many distributions aimed at end user PCs have a graphical shell loaded. Some popular GUI shells include:

- **Gnome (GNU Object Model Environment)**—the oldest and most widely deployed GUI. Used by default on Fedora® and Debian.

> *Note: **GNU** is a recursive acronym standing for "GNU is Not UNIX." Many of the non-kernel bits of software developed under the open source GNU license to replace their proprietary UNIX equivalents can be used with Linux.*

- **KDE® (K Desktop Environment)**—a very popular GUI often used by SUSE.
- **Cinnamon**—based on the MINT GUI.
- **Xfce**—one of the many lightweight GUIs, designed for systems with less RAM and CPU power.

A typical Linux GUI desktop looks like the image in the following figure.

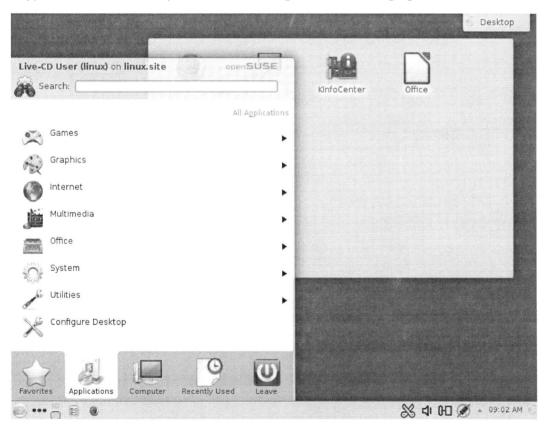

Linux GUI desktop.

It is worth noting that although the desktop can vary from distro to distro, most will have a common theme, with a start menu, taskbar, system tray, and so on, in a similar fashion to Windows and macOS. It should also be noted that unlike Windows and Mac, the default GUI shell can be swapped for a different one. Many GUIs, including **Gnome**, will support features like **virtual desktop** (Mission Control on macOS).

Many distros will come with a range of open source applications pre-installed such as Firefox® Browser and office applications such as Libre.

One thing that does vary from one distro to another is system tools. **SUSE**, for example, comes with a tool called **YaST** which provides a Control Panel style utility for Linux. Other similar tools are **webmin** and **Yumix**. However, it should be noted that all these tools simply update the standard Linux configuration files stored in the **/etc** folder.

YaST Control Center.

LINUX COMMANDS

Show Slide(s)

Linux Commands (2 slides)

Linux commands are entered in a standard format, featuring the command followed by a space then a number of options (or switches) and/or arguments, depending on the function of the command. Wildcards (* and ?) can be used in the same way as at the Windows command line.

- The first "word" input is interpreted as the command. This could be a full or relative path to the executable or just the name of an executable stored in a directory identified by a **PATH** environment variable. The command "word" is completed by the first space character.
- **Options** (or **switches**) are used to change the operation of a command. They can be single letters (preceded by a single hyphen) or words (preceded by a double hyphen). The order the options are placed on the command is not important.
- **Arguments** are values supplied to the command for it to operate on, such as file names. Arguments should be supplied in the correct order for the command's syntax.

You can send or redirect the results of one command to another command. Pipes are used to combine Linux tools on a single command line, enabling you to use the output of one command as the input to another. The **pipe symbol** is a vertical bar (|), which you type between two commands.

You can issue more than one command before pressing **Enter**. Place a semicolon (;) between the commands and they will be issued one after the other.

CASE SENSITIVITY

Commands, parameters, and file and directory names are all case sensitive in Linux. For example, `ls -l file.data` and `ls -L File.data` would produce completely different results. Using capitals in the command name would generate an error message.

GETTING HELP

Any Linux command will generally give a reasonably detailed explanation of its function and syntax when the `--help` parameter is used. The help is often several pages long so use of the `| more` (pipe) at the end of the command is recommended on any command that generates large amounts of output. It shows the results a page at a time. For example: `ls --help | more`

Alternatively, you can use `man` to view the help pages for a particular command. For example, use `man man` to view the help pages for the `man` command.

> **Note:** *Also note that Linux terminals support* **Tab completion** *to help in entering commands. You can use* **Shift+Page Up** *or* **Shift+Page Down** *and* **Ctrl+Shift+Up Arrow** *or* **Ctrl+Shift+Down Arrow** *to scroll. Use the* **Up** *and* **Down** *arrow keys to scroll through previously used commands. Use* `q` *to quit a command.*

LINUX DISK AND FILE MANAGEMENT

In Linux, the directory structure is defined as a **File System Hierarchy**. Unlike Windows, drive letters like C: or D: are not used. The file system starts at the root, represented by /. Directories and subdirectories can be created from the root to store files.

It is important to realize that everything available to the Linux OS is represented as a file in the file system, including devices. This is referred to as the **unified file system**. For example, a single hard drive attached to a SATA port would normally be represented in the file system by /dev/sda. A second storage device—perhaps one attached to a USB port—would be represented as /dev/sdb.

When Linux boots, a system kernel and **virtual file system** are loaded to a RAM drive. The virtual file system identifies the location of the persistent root partition from the appropriate storage device and loads the file system stored on the disk.

MOUNTING PARTITIONS

A file system configured on a partition on a particular storage device is attached to a particular directory (**mount point**) within the unified file system using the `mount` command. For example, the following command mounts partition 1 on the mass storage device **sda** to the directory **/mnt/diskC**.

```
mount /dev/sda1 /mnt/diskC
```

Mountable file systems are listed in the **/etc/fstab** file.

> **Note:** *Think of the root file system representing everything on the computer as "THE" file system and a file system for a particular partition as just "A" file system.*

Show Slide(s)
Linux Disk and File Management (5 slides)

Teaching Tip
Learners really need to grasp the concept of the unified file system and its recursive nature.

LINUX FILE SYSTEMS

Most Linux distributions use some version of the **ext** file system to format partitions on mass storage devices. **ext3** is a 64-bit file system with support for journaling, which means that the file system tracks changes, giving better reliability and less chance of file corruption in the event of crashes or power outages. Support for journaling is the main difference between ext3 and its predecessor (ext2). **ext4** delivers significantly better performance than **ext3** and would usually represent the best choice for new systems.

Linux can also support FAT/FAT32, though it is designated as **VFAT**. Additional protocols, such as the **Network File System (NFS)**, can be used to mount remote storage devices into the local file system.

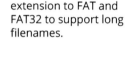

Teaching Tip

VFAT was developed by Microsoft for Windows 95 as an extension to FAT and FAT32 to support long filenames.

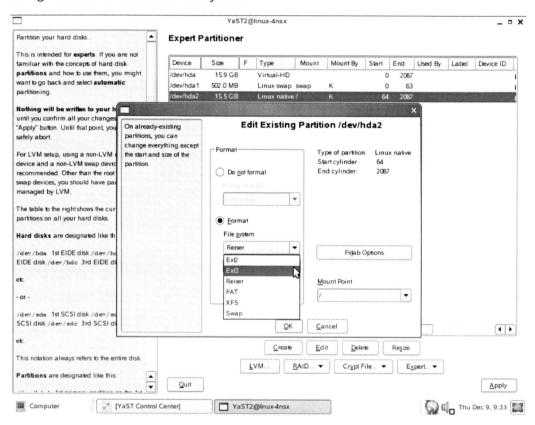

Using YaST to format a partition.

SWAP PARTITION

Virtual memory allows a computer to use disk space to supplement the amount of system RAM installed. If applications or data files use up the available physical memory, "pages" of data from RAM can be written to swap space on a disk to free up some space. If the paged data is required again, it is transferred from the swap space back to RAM.

Most default installations of Linux create a **swap partition** to use as swap space. The swap partition is formatted with a minimal kind of file system. It can only be used by the memory manager and not for storage of ordinary data files.

DISK MANAGEMENT COMMANDS

The file system choice can be made when the disk has been partitioned. Most Linux distros provide GUI tools for managing disks and file systems, but the following represent the main command-line options:

* `fdisk`—used to create and manage partitions on a hard disk.

- `mkfs`—used to format a partition.
- `mkswap`—used to format a swap partition. The `swapon` command is used to activate the partition as swap space.
- `dd`—make a copy of an input file (`if=`) to an output file (`of=`) and apply optional conversions to the file data. One notable use of dd is to clone a disk (in the following, **sda** might be the fixed drive and **sdb** a removable drive): `dd if=/dev/sda of=/dev/sdb`
  - You would need to boot from a live CD so that the file system was not mounted at the time of cloning. You can also clone a disk to a disk image (.img) file: `dd if=/dev/sda of=/mnt/usbstick/backup.img`
  - To restore, you could simply reverse the input and output files: `dd if=/mnt/usbstick/backup.img of=/dev/sda`

NAVIGATION IN THE LINUX DIRECTORY STRUCTURE

The core commands that a technician should know to navigate the Linux file structure include `ls`, `cp`, `mv`, `rm`, and `cd`, along with many more. This table describes these commands and how to use them.

Show Slide(s)

Navigation in the Linux Directory Structure

Command	Used to	Description and Examples
`ls`	List files	The `ls` command is used to display a folder in the same way as `dir` at the Windows command prompt. Popular parameters include `-l` to display a detailed (long) list and `-a` to display all files including hidden or system files. The following example shows the entire contents of the **/etc** directory in a detailed format: `ls -l -a /etc`
`pwd`	Print working directory	The `pwd` command simply displays the current directory you are working in. Any commands you use which don't specify a directory will assume your current one. The prompt on some distros will show your **current working directory** or a ~ symbol, which indicates you are in your **home directory**.
`cd`	Change directory	The `cd` command is used to change your working directory. Typical syntax would be: • `cd /etc`—change directory to **/etc**. This is an **absolute path** (begins with /) so will work regardless of your current directory. • `cd documents`—change your directory to a subdirectory called **documents**. This is a **relative path**. The **documents** directory must exist below the current directory. • `cd ..`—change your directory to the **parent directory** of the one you are currently working in.

Command	Used to	Description and Examples
cp	Copy files	The `cp` command is used to create a copy of files either in the same or different folder with the same or different name. For example: • `cp file1.txt file1.old`—copy **file1.txt** in the current working directory to a new file called **file1.old** in the same directory. • `cp /etc/hosts /tmp`—copy the file **hosts** from the directory **/etc** into the directory **/tmp**, keeping the file name the same. • `cp -v /var/log/message* /home/usera`—copy all files beginning with the name **message** from the **/var/log** directory into **/home/usera**. The **-v** option displays the files copied.
mv	Move files	The `mv` command is used to either move files from one directory to another or rename a file. For example: • `mv /home/usera/data.txt /tmp`—move the file **data.txt** from the **/home/usera** directory to the **/tmp** directory, keeping the file name the same. • `mv alarm.dat /tmp/alarm.bak`—move and rename the file **alarm.dat** in the current directory to **alarm.bak** in **/tmp**. • `mv /var/log/app1.log /var/log/app1.old`—rename the file **app1.dat** in the **/var/log** folder to **app1.old**.
rm	Remove files	The `rm` command is potentially very dangerous if used incorrectly. Although its main role is to delete files, with an additional parameter (`-r`) it can also be used to delete directories. For example: • `rm data.old`—remove the single file data.old from the current working directory. • `rm /var/log/*.bak`—remove all files ending in **.bak** from the **/var/log** directory. • `-r /home/usera/data`—remove the contents of the entire directory tree underneath the folder **/home/usera/data**.

Caution: *Use the `-r` switch with caution!*

Note: *Remember that Linux commands operate without prompts, allowing you to cancel.*

Command	Used to	Description and Examples
`grep`	Filter files	The `grep` (Globally search a Regular Expression and Print) command is used to search and filter the contents of files, displaying the lines that match the search string. The search string can be a simple text value to match (a **literal**) or can use a sophisticated pattern-matching system called **regular expressions (regex)**. `grep` is especially useful for searching long files such as system logs. For example, the following command displays only the lines in the Linux system log file for messages that contain the text **uid=1003**, ignoring the case of the text:

- `grep -I "uid=1003" /var/log/messages`

The `grep` command can also be used to search a directory for a certain file. The `ls -l | grep audit` command returns a long listing of any files in the current directory whose name contains **audit**.

LINUX FILE EDITORS

vi or **vim** is a text file editor derived from a UNIX original. Although this tool is very powerful, it is based on letter- and number-based commands to modify the text. For example, **dd** when pressed will delete the whole line the cursor is on; **5dd** would delete 5 whole lines. When **vi** is in **command mode**, input such as this is interpreted as a command.

Show Slide(s)

Linux File Editors (2 slides)

To enter text, you need to switch to **insert mode** by pressing an appropriate command key. For example, **i** switches to insert mode at the current cursor position, **a** appends text at the end of the current line, and **o** inserts text on a new line below the current line. The **Esc** key switches from insert mode back to command mode.

To save a file, use **:w** from command mode. To save and quit, use **:wq**. **:q!** quits without saving.

There are other command-line editors, such as **mcedit**, **nano**, **pico**, or **joe**, that are easier to learn to use.

LINUX USER ACCOUNTS

Linux, like most operating systems, supports multiple users. The **root user**, also known as the **superuser**, is the default administrative account on a Linux system. This account can do anything on the system. You should only use this account when absolutely necessary. For most Linux distributions, you create a regular user when you are installing Linux. This is the user you should log on as for day-to-day tasks. Even many administrative tasks can be performed more safely under the regular user account.

Show Slide(s)

Linux User Accounts (2 slides)

User accounts are linked to a **primary group**, which determines many aspects of security in Linux. User settings are stored in the **/etc/passwd** file and group settings are stored in the **/etc/group** file. The user password is typically stored as an encrypted hash in the **/etc/shadow** file, along with other password settings, such as age and expiration date. The command-line utilities `useradd`, `usermod`, and `userdel` can be used to add, modify, and delete user information. The `groupadd`, `groupmod`, and `groupdel` commands can be used to manage groups.

A user can belong to many groups but can only have one **effective group ID** at any one time. The effective group ID is listed for the user account in **etc/passwd** and can be changed using the `newgrp` command.

Many distros have GUI-based utilities that allow user and group management. YaST is an example of one of these.

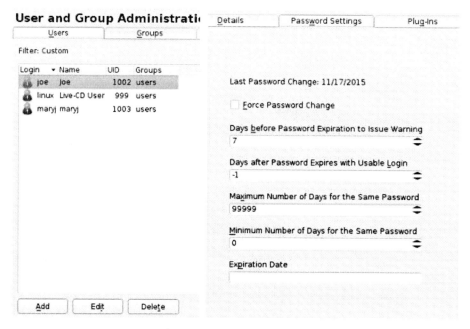

User and group Administration tool in YaST.

su (Superuser)

The su command allows a normal Linux user to become superuser (or root). The command will prompt the user for the root user's password. Additionally, it is possible to put a different user name after the su command and become that user, assuming the password is known.

Using su without an option retains the original user's profile and variables. The switched user also remains in the home directory of the original user. Using su - changes users and launches a new shell under the context of that new user. This is a much better practice.

sudo (Superuser Do)

The sudo command allows a normal user to run specified commands with superuser privilege level. The superuser first has to edit the **/etc/sudoers** file listing the commands and users that are allowed to run them. The user enters the sudo command followed by the path of the command they wish to run. The user might be asked to confirm his or her password, if it has not been cached recently.

passwd (Password Utility)

The passwd command allows a user to change their own password or superuser (root) to change or reset someone else's. When a user runs the command, Linux will prompt first for the existing password then the new one, twice. The superuser can reset another user's password by typing the user name after the command. The existing password is not required in this case. To reset the password for the user **fredb**, the superuser would enter the command passwd fredb

Note: *Don't confuse* passwd *with* pwd *(Print Working Directory).*

LINUX FILE SYSTEM PERMISSIONS

The Linux file system has a relatively simple security system compared to Windows NTFS. There are just three different rights, as shown in the following table.

Show Slide(s)

Linux File System Permissions (2 slides)

Access Right	Enables You To:
Read (r)	View the contents of a file or directory.
Write (w)	Modify or delete the object (in the case of directories, allows adding, deleting, or renaming files within the directory).
Execute (x)	Run an executable file or script. For directories, execute allows the user to do things like change the focus to the directory and access or search items within it.

For each object, these permissions are set for the **owner**, for the **group** the owner belongs to or that the object has been assigned to, and for **other users** ("the world"). Using symbolic notation, each permission is allowed (**r** or **w** or **x**) or denied (**-**). If you run `ls -l` to obtain a directory listing, directory or file object permissions will be shown as follows:

- **drwxr-xr-x 2 administrator administrator Desktop**
- **-rw-rw-r-- 1 administrator administrator MEMO.txt**

The leading character designates the file type. For example, **-** represents a regular file and **d** indicates a directory. The permissions for the **Desktop** directory show that the **owner** (administrator) has full (**rwx**) permissions, whereas the **group** (also administrator) and **others** have read and execute (**r-x**). For the **MEMO.txt** file, the **user** and **group** have read/write (**rw-**) permissions, whereas **others** has read permissions only (**r--**).

Permissions can also be expressed numerically, using the octal value format shown in the following table. An octal value can represent up to eight digits (0-7):

Digit	Permission	Binary Value	Rights
0	- - -	0000	Deny all
1	- - x	0001	Execute
2	- w -	0010	Write
3	- w x	0011	Write and execute
4	r - -	0100	Read-only
5	r - x	0101	Read and execute
6	r w -	0110	Read and write
7	r w x	0111	Allow all

So, for example, a file with numeric permission **0775** (the leading zero identifies the value as an octal, but can often be omitted) grants all rights to the owner and the owner's group and Read/Execute rights to everyone else.

Note: Remember that Execute=1, Write=2, and Read=4—add those values together to get a particular combination of permissions.

From the shell, the `chmod` command can be used to secure files and directories, using either symbolic or octal notation. Only the owner can change permissions. The command `chown` allows the superuser to change the owner of a file or directory, whereas `chgrp` can be used to change the group.

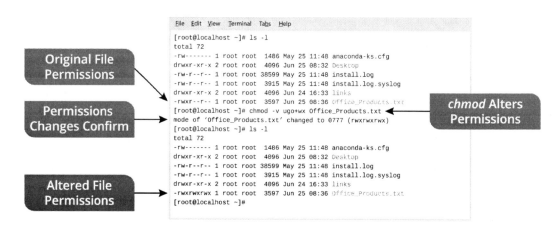

Modifying permissions using the chmod command.

LINUX SOFTWARE MANAGEMENT

A distribution contains any software packages the distribution vendor or sponsor considers appropriate. Copies of these packages (including any updates) will be posted to a software repository. Often the vendor will maintain different repositories. For example, there may be one for officially supported package versions, one for beta/untested versions, and one for "at own risk" unsupported packages.

The integrity of a package is usually tested by making a cryptographic hash of the compiled package, using a function such as **MD5** or SHA-256. The hash value and function is published on the package vendor's site. When you download a package, you can run the same function on the package file (using a command such as **md5sum** or **sha256sum**) and compare the output with the published value. If they do not match, you should not proceed with the installation.

PACKAGE MANAGERS (APT-GET)

Linux software is made available both as source code and as pre-compiled applications. A source code package needs to be run through the appropriate compiler with the preferred options. Pre-compiled packages can be installed using various tools, such as **rpm** (Red Hat Package Manager), **apt** (Debian), or **yum** (Fedora). Many distributions also provide GUI package manager front-ends to these command-line tools.

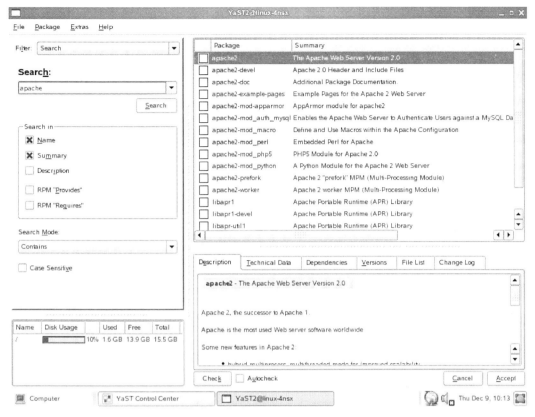

YaST package manager in SUSE.

The following uses of `apt-get` provide some examples of how packages are managed at the command line:

- `apt-get update`—refresh the local database with information about the packages available from the repository.
- `apt-get upgrade`—update all packages with the latest versions.
- `apt-get install` *PackageName*—install a new application.

LINUX SYSTEM COMMANDS

There are many tools and techniques available to troubleshoot issues with applications or update the network configuration. You should also know how to shut down or reboot a Linux PC.

Show Slide(s)

Linux System Commands

Command	Description
`ps` and `kill`	The `ps` command displays the **Linux processes** (programs) that are currently running. Each process has a system generated **process ID** which can be used with the `kill` command to end the process. The parameter `-ef` displays processes being run by all users along with a more detailed display.
`ifconfig` and `iwconfig`	The `ifconfig` and `iwconfig` tools display the current state of the network interfaces within Linux. `ifconfig` is the original tool designed for cabled Ethernet interfaces, whereas `iwconfig` displays information about the wireless adapters configured within the system.

Command	Description
shutdown	Linux is designed to be a very stable operating system and the server versions often run non-stop for months or even years at a time. However, the desktop versions are likely to be powered on and off much more often. The shutdown command has two main parameters: -h to halt or -r to reboot the system followed by when the event should take place. Examples of this could be now, +10 (+10 meaning ten minutes from now), or 17:30 (to specify an exact time).

*Note: To learn more, check the **Video** tile on the CHOICE Course screen for any videos that supplement the content for this lesson.*

Access the Checklist tile on your CHOICE Course screen for reference information and job aids on How to Configure and Use Linux.

Activity 6-1
Discussing Linux Configuration and Use

Show Slide(s)

Activity: Discussing Linux Configuration and Use

SCENARIO
Answer the following questions to check your understanding of the topic.

1. **What type of file system is usually used for the Linux boot partition?**

   A version of ext (ext4 or ext3).

2. **What command would you normally need to run in order to access the contents of a USB memory stick inserted into Linux?**

   ```
   mount
   ```

3. **Which Linux command will display detailed information about all files and directories in the current directory, including system files?**

   ```
   ls -la
   ```

4. A command has generated a large amount of data on the screen.

   What could you add to the command to make the output more readable?

   Either | `more` or | `less`.

5. **What command would allow you to use delete the contents of the folder /home/fred/junk and all its subdirectories?**

   ```
   rm -r /home/fred/junk
   ```

6. **What command could you use to move a file names.doc from your current directory to the USB stick linked to folder /mnt/usb?**

   ```
   mv names.doc /mnt/usb
   ```

7. A file is secured with the numeric permissions **0774**.

   What rights does another user account have over the file?

   Read-only.

8. **What command allows file and directory permissions to be changed?**

   ```
   chmod
   ```

9. **Which Linux command allows a user to run a specific command or program with superuser/root privileges?**

   ```
   sudo
   ```

10. Which file contains the list of user accounts created on Linux?

/etc/passwd.

11. You want your Linux PC to close gracefully at 9:00 p.m., as a scheduled power outage is planned at 12:00 midnight.

How could you do this?

```
shutdown -h 21:00
```

Activity 6-2
Configuring and Using Linux

Show Slide(s)

Activity: Configuring and Using Linux

BEFORE YOU BEGIN

Complete this activity by using Hyper-V Manager and the LX1 (Cent OS Linux) VM.

Remember that all commands and input in Linux are case-sensitive.

Whenever you are prompted for a password, use *Pa$$w0rd*.

SCENARIO

In this activity, you will investigate some of the features of the Linux GNOME desktop environment, plus some command-line tools.

1. Use Hyper-V Manager to start the **LX1** VM and sign on using the account **centos** and password *Pa$$w0rd*. Identify the main elements of the desktop environment.

    a) In **Hyper-V Manager**, right-click **LX1** and select **Start**. Double-click the VM to open the connection window.

    b) When the VM has booted, select the **centos** account icon.

    c) Type *Pa$$w0rd* and then press **Enter** to sign on.

    Note: The first time users log in, they are prompted to configure localization settings. If a Welcome screen is displayed, accept the defaults or other settings as your instructor suggests.

    d) View the desktop.

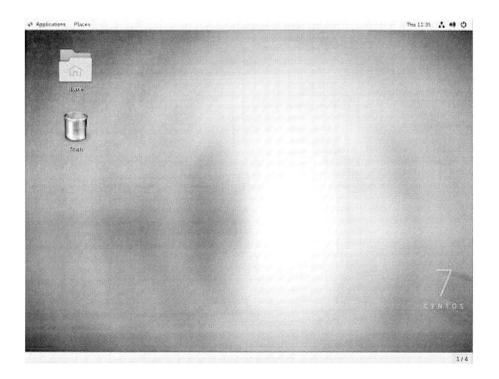

e) Note the following features of the desktop.
- The **Applications** menu contains shortcuts to software, while **Places** contains shortcuts to file system locations.
- The right-hand icon on the menu bar accesses settings, plus options for signing out or shutting down the PC.
- The bottom taskbar shows open windows. You can switch between workspaces (multiple desktops) using the "1/4" icon at the bottom right.

f) Select the **power** icon and then select the **Settings** icon. ※ Browse some of the options, such as **Network**.

The **Settings** page contains configuration options similar to Windows Control Panel.

g) Close the Settings window.

2. Use the file browser to identify some of the principal directories in the Linux file system.

a) Double-click the **Home** icon on the desktop.
This starts in the current user's home directory.

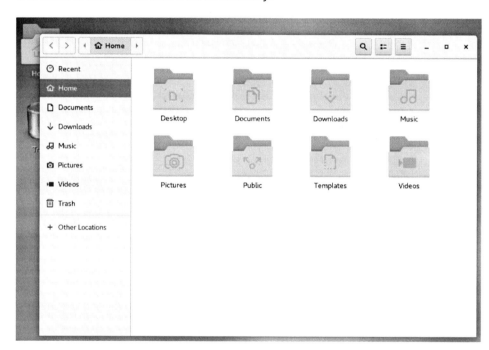

b) Select **Other Locations** and then **Computer** to view the File System Hierarchy (FSH).

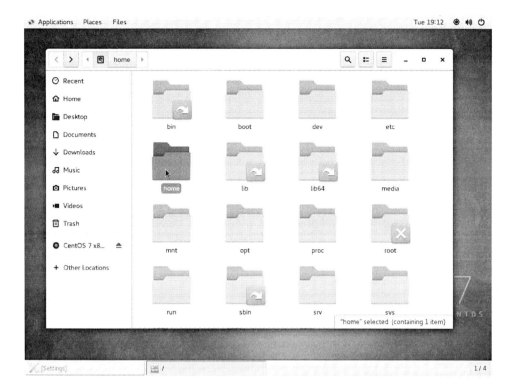

c) Note some of the key root directories.
- /boot—boot loader files.
- /etc—computer-level configuration files.
- /var—variable files, such as logs, print spoolers, and cache.
- /usr—shareable and read-only data and binaries.
- /bin and /sbin—core and system binary files (applications).
- /mnt—location for temporary file systems.
- /dev—files representing devices.

d) You can see the top-level **home** directory here. If you open this you will see the directory for the **centos** user.

3. Linux is predominantly configured via commands operating on text-based configuration files.

a) Right-click the desktop and select **Open Terminal**.

b) In the terminal window, type `ls  -l` and press **Enter**.

This displays a detailed list of files in the current folder (with permissions, modified date, and so on).

c) Type `cd desktop` and press **Enter**. Why does this return an error message?

The directory is **Desktop**, not **desktop**. Remember that the Linux file system is case-sensitive.

d) Use the correct command to change to the Desktop directory then use **ls** to return a file list. Is the directory empty?

e) In the terminal window, type `vi` and press **Enter**.

This text editor opens in command mode.

> **Note:** *For users familiar with Microsoft Windows editors such as Notepad, **vi** can seem challenging at first. With a little practice and memorizing some of the important modes and commands, it becomes easier to use.*

f)   Type i to switch to insert mode at the current cursor position. Notice that the bottom of the window now shows **-- INSERT --** to indicate that you are in insert mode. Type the following lines:

```
I'm learning to use vi
It's easy when you know how
```

g)   Press **Esc** to exit insert mode and return to command mode, and then type ***dd***

Whenever you are about to issue a command, always use **Esc** first.

h)   Press **Esc**, and then type :w hello-vi.txt and press **Enter** to save the file as "hello-vi.txt" in the current directory.

The **:w** is the command to write the file to the current directory. Linux doesn't require or use filename extensions, but adding a file extension helps users to identify the file type and makes it easier to share files with Windows users.

i)   Press **Esc**, and then type G followed by o.

The **G** moves to the last line of the file. The lower case **o** opens a new line after the current line and places you in **Insert** mode. If you typed a capital **O**, it would open a new line before the current line.

j)   Type the following line:

```
It could take a while
```

k)   Press **Esc**, type :q! and press **Enter** to quit the editor without saving changes.

If you typed **:q** without the **!**, you would see an error message that the file was not written since the last change and be prompted to issue the command with the **!** to override and close without saving.

l)   Type cp hello-vi.txt ../Documents/ and press **Enter** to copy the file to the **Documents** directory.

m)   Type cd / and press **Enter** to switch to the root directory.

4.   You can use the **find** and **grep** tools to search for files and file contents. Try to locate the **httpd.conf** file within the **/etc** directory, extract specific messages from the boot log (**dmesg**), and locate references to the network adapter (**eth**) in the system log (**/var/log/messages**).

a)   At the terminal, run the following command to get help on the find command.

```
man find
```

If you want to see more of the man page than fits on the screen, press **Spacebar** to view the next page, or press **Enter** to display the next line.

b)   Press ***q*** to quit the help file.

c)   Run the following command to locate **httpd.conf** (the principal configuration file for the Apache web server).

```
find /etc -name 'httpd.conf'
```

Observe that a lot of "Permission Denied" errors are returned. You can prefix the command with sudo so that the search can access those directories. Alternatively, you can filter out the errors by using grep.

```
find /etc -name 'httpd.conf' 2>&1 | grep -v 'Permission
denied'
```

 Note: *If this prints with a break in the command, enter it as a single command (ignoring the line break).*

The **-v** switch is a way of specifying NOT the matched string. The parameter **2>&1** ensures that the error output is included in the string piped to grep.

d)   Run the command dmesg to show the contents of the boot log.

You can see that this is a long list of output so using a search tool will be very helpful.

e) Run the following command to filter for events relating to initializing the disks:

```
dmesg | grep 'sd\|mount'
```

Within the match expression, the pipe character (|) works as a logical OR. It must be escaped using \| however. The effect is to search for the keywords **sd** OR **mount**.

f) To search the system log for references to the network adapter, use the following command—confirm with ***Pa$$w0rd*** when you are prompted:

```
sudo grep 'eth' /var/log/messages | less
```

Note that **less** is similar to **more**. It allows you to view the output one page at a time but also to scroll back up through the output.

g) Press q to quit viewing the output.

5. Next, create a new user account named ***Sam*** with the password ***Pa$$w0rd***. Create a group named ***SharedDisk*** and add **Sam** to the group.

a) Create the new group first, by running the following command:

```
sudo groupadd SharedDisk
```

b) Create the new user account, and add it to the group with the following command:

```
sudo useradd -G SharedDisk Sam
```

c) Configure the user password by running the following command:

```
sudo passwd Sam
```

When prompted, enter and confirm the password as ***Pa$$w0rd***

Note that CentOS correctly advises you that this is a bad password to use. It is especially bad to use it for each user account, including root.

d) To test the account, press **Ctrl+Alt+F2** to open a new console. Enter the user name ***Sam*** and confirm the password when prompted.

e) Switch back to the centos user console by pressing **Ctrl+Alt+F1**.

6. The **LX1** VM has a second virtual disk attached. For the next step, list the disks attached to the system, and then configure and format a file system on the second device.

a) In the terminal window, type `sudo fdisk -l` and press **Enter**.

```
[administrator@lx5 ~]$ sudo fdisk -l
WARNING: fdisk GPT support is currently new, and therefore in an experimental ph
ase. Use at your own discretion.

Disk /dev/sda: 68.7 GB, 68719476736 bytes, 134217728 sectors
Units = sectors of 1 * 512 = 512 bytes
Sector size (logical/physical): 512 bytes / 4096 bytes
I/O size (minimum/optimal): 4096 bytes / 4096 bytes
Disk label type: gpt
Disk identifier: BE17ECA1-B2EE-4873-B33F-5C867E3EB67E

#         Start         End     Size  Type            Name
 1          2048      411647     200M  EFI System      EFI System Partition
 2        411648     2508799      1G  Microsoft basic
 3       2508800   134215679   62.8G  Linux LVM

Disk /dev/sdb: 10.7 GB, 10737418240 bytes, 20971520 sectors
Units = sectors of 1 * 512 = 512 bytes
Sector size (logical/physical): 512 bytes / 4096 bytes
I/O size (minimum/optimal): 4096 bytes / 4096 bytes


Disk /dev/mapper/centos-root: 42.6 GB, 42601545728 bytes, 83206144 sectors
```

b) Examine the results.

fdisk shows information about the disk. **sda** is the disk that CentOS is installed to while **sdb** is the unformatted disk. On **sda**, you can see three partitions, for the EFI system, boot files (note that **fdisk** reports XFS as "Microsoft basic"), and an LVM partition. Logical Volume Manager (LVM) is used to divide this partition into logical block devices, hosting volumes for root and home storage areas plus a swap partition. The advantage of using LVM, rather than basic partitions, is that the volumes can be shrunk or expanded or configured with some sort of RAID protection as required.

c) Run `sudo parted -l` and compare the output to fdisk.

Note that `parted` correctly reports the file system type as XFS. Most other Linux distributions use ext3 or ext4, but XFS is the default in CentOS and RedHat.

d) To use `parted` to initialize the disk and create a new partition using all the available disk space, run the following commands in sequence (press **Enter** after each command):

```
sudo parted /dev/sdb
print free
mklabel gpt
mkpart primary
```

e) Respond to the prompts with the following input to choose a file system type and set the start and end of the partition:

```
fat32
0%
100%
```

f) Run the following commands to check the new partition was created successfully and quit `parted`:

```
print
quit
```

Note the warning about updating **/etc/fstab**. While you have created a partition, you have not yet mounted it to make it available for file storage. **/etc/fstab** is a file containing a list of file systems to mount at boot time.

g) Run `lsblk` to view the new disk and partition structure.

h) Run the following command to format the new partition, using FAT32:

```
sudo mkfs.vfat -n SharedDisk /dev/sdb1
```

7. Create a directory to host the new partition and then mount it to that directory. See if you can set permissions to restrict use to the **SharedDisk** group. Use `man mount` to research the command syntax.

a) Create a directory for the mount point, and then mount the partition using the following commands (ignore the line break in the `mount` command):

```
sudo mkdir /media/disk1
sudo mount -t vfat /dev/sdb1 /media/disk1 -o
rw,umask=0007,gid=SharedDisk,uid=Sam
```

The `mount` options set the disk to read/write mode and configure the default permissions (`umask`). The mask contains values to subtract from the permissions granted, so this mask means files and folders are created on the partition with **0770** (**rwx** for the owner and group but no permissions for "world"). If you were to set the mask to **0022**, the default permissions would be **0755** (**rwx** for the owner, **rx** for the group and world). The **gid** and **uid** parameters set the default group and user.

b) Run the following command to view the file systems formatted with XFS or FAT that are currently mounted:

```
mount | grep 'xfs\|fat'
```

Note that the partition is only mounted temporarily. To mount at boot, the partition must be added to /etc/fstab. You won't attempt that in this activity.

c) Run `nano /media/disk1/hello.txt` to try to create a text file on the new partition. Add some text then use **Ctrl+O** plus **Enter** to try to save the file. Permission is denied. Only the user account **Sam** and members of the group **SharedDisk** have access.

d) Press **Ctrl+X** to close nano, responding with **n** to the prompt.

e) Run the following commands to add the centos user account to the SharedDisk group and then to make that group current.

```
sudo usermod -a -G SharedDisk centos
newgrp SharedDisk
```

f) Run `nano /media/disk1/hello.txt` to create a text file on the new partition. Add some text then use **Ctrl+O** and then press **Enter** to save the file.

This should work.

g) Press **Ctrl+X** to close nano.

h) Press **Ctrl+Alt+F2** to switch to the Sam user's console. Run the following command to view the partition and open the file:

```
cd /media/disk1
ls -l
nano hello.txt
```

i) Check that you can modify the file then save and close it.

8. Use the **du** and **df** commands to check disk space and usage, and then unmount the **SharedDisk** partition and run an integrity check using `fsck`.

a) Press **Ctrl+Alt+F1** to switch back to the centos user's console.

b) Run the following command to show available space on all file systems except temporary ones:

```
df | grep -v 'tmpfs'
```

c) Run the following command to check how much space files in your home profile are using:

```
du /home/centos
```

d) Try to unmount the SharedDisk partition by running the following command:

```
sudo umount /dev/sdb1
```

Note the error.

e) Switch to Sam's console and change focus to the default directory by running `cd` without arguments.

f) Switch back to the administrator console and run `umount` again—it should work this time:

```
sudo umount /dev/sdb1
```

g) Use the following command to run an integrity check on the disk:

```
sudo fsck.vfat /dev/sdb1
```

9. Finally, use the **ps** and **top** utilities to report on process usage.

a) Run `ps -ef` to show extended information (**-f**) about processes started by all users (**-e**).
In the output, you can see the user and Process ID (PID). The "C" column shows an index of CPU usage. Note also the processes running in tty2 (Sam's console).

b) Run the `top` command. This is a simple means of showing which processes are most active.

c) Press **q** to quit.

10. Use the command line to shut down the VM.

   a) Run the following command to try to shut down the VM.

   ```
   shutdown -h now
   ```

   b) Scroll up to locate the PID (the number in the second column of the ps-ef output) for Sam (or rerun the **ps -ef** command) and record the PID for `login-Sam`. Run the following commands to kill Sam's session and shut down:

   ```
   sudo kill SamPID
   shutdown -h now
   ```

   Note that you are just using the `kill` command for this activity. This is not a good way to end a user's session.

11. At the end of each activity, you need to close the VM. You will always discard any changes you made.

   a) From the connection window, select **Action→Revert**.

   b) If you are prompted to confirm, select the **Revert** button.

Topic B

Configure and Use macOS

EXAM OBJECTIVES COVERED
1002-1.3 Summarize general OS installation considerations and upgrade methods.
1002-1.9 Given a scenario, use features and tools of the Mac OS and Linux client/desktop operating systems.

Mac® computers from Apple® use the macOS® operating system. Mac users tend to be found in art, music, graphic design, and education because macOS includes apps geared to those audiences. In this topic, you will examine some of the important features and functions of macOS.

APPLE MACS AND macOS

macOS is the generic name for the operating system that powers Apple Mac computers. It was formerly known as **Mac OS** (from launch until 2001) and then **OS X** (from 2001 through to 2016). All macOS versions are based on UNIX technology, and many "under the hood" commands are shared between the two operating systems.

Show Slide(s)

Apple Macs and macOS (2 slides)

Whereas Microsoft Windows can be installed and used on any PC with Intel architecture, macOS may only be installed on Apple's own hardware. By creating what has become known as a "walled garden" for their computers and software, Apple has been able to impose strict quality controls on the apps and devices that are available for the Mac. This has ensured that, compared to Windows, there are fewer outbreaks of viruses and malware and fewer system stability issues caused by faulty drivers or application/device conflicts.

Note: You might hear the term "Hackintosh," which refers to installing macOS on non-Apple hardware, often as a virtual machine. Apple's license agreement only permits installation on Apple hardware.

Note that macOS and iOS are separate operating systems. There are several visual and operational similarities between macOS and iOS and there are utilities to exchange information between the two, but it is not possible to run programs built for macOS on iOS and vice versa. iOS® is purely an OS for the iPhone® and iPad®, whereas macOS is only used for desktop and laptop computers.

OS X AND macOS VERSIONS

Since its release in 2001, OS X (and now macOS) has undergone regular 10.x updates and revisions to keep pace with updates to Apple Mac hardware. Updates and new versions are distributed free of charge through the App Store. OS X versions were originally named after big cats and then places in California; something that continues with the latest macOS releases.

Teaching Tip

Apple did produce a macOS Server version but development on this seems to be winding down.

Unless the hardware is particularly old and can't be upgraded, most Apple Mac computers will now be running macOS High Sierra (10.13) or macOS Mojave (10.14). OS X 10.7 (Lion) is the earliest release that is still supported by Apple. If your Macintosh computer meets the minimum requirements for OS X installation, the hardware should all be compatible with the latest version of macOS. You can verify that your hardware is supported by examining the technical specifications at **support.apple.com/specs**.

APPLE INPUT DEVICES

You should be aware of some differences between the input devices used for Macs and those used for PCs.

Apple Keyboards and Mice

Although a Windows keyboard can be used on an Apple Mac (and vice versa), there are a number of differences between the keys:

- **Command**—the equivalent of **Ctrl** on a Windows keyboard. For example, **command+C** will copy to the clipboard as **Ctrl+C** does on a Windows computer. If you're using a Windows keyboard on a Mac, use the **Windows** key as the **command** key.
- **Option**—equivalent of the **Alt** key.
- **Control**—*not* the equivalent of **Ctrl** on a Windows keyboard!

Apple mice do not feature obvious buttons. Older mice have five sensors that can be set to different actions via **System Preferences**. The later **Magic Mouse** models have a **touchpad** surface with **gesture** support. The **Magic Trackpad** has a larger working surface.

 *Note: You can set up right-click in **System Preferences** or use **Control+click**.*

APPLE MAGIC TRACKPAD AND GESTURE SUPPORT

Like the Magic Mouse®, the Magic Trackpad® supports gestures to control the user interface. Apple introduced gestures as a simple way to control macOS from a Magic Trackpad or built-in trackpad of a MacBook®. To see what gestures are available on the Mac or to change any of the settings, go to **System Preferences→Trackpad**.

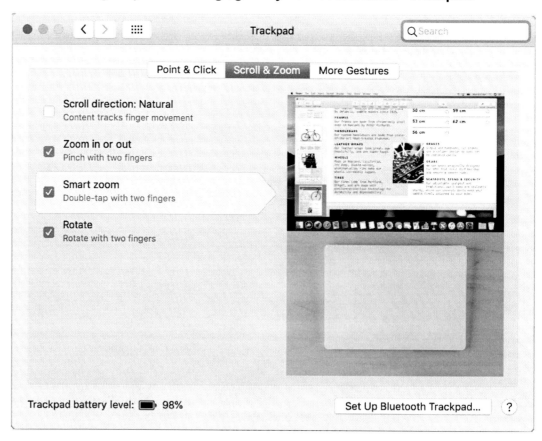

Configuring the trackpad. (Screenshot courtesy of Apple.)

macOS FEATURES

If you are using an Apple Mac computer for the first time, you will notice that the desktop and user interface is similar to a Windows-based PC in some respects but very different in others. As with Windows, a Mac boots to a graphical desktop environment. Any apps that have been installed and configured to launch at boot will also start.

At the top of the screen is the menu bar. This is always present with all apps, but the menu titles shown will vary between different software.

Menu bars with different apps running. (Screenshot courtesy of Apple.)

To the left of the menu bar is the Apple menu, represented by the Apple icon . The items are consistent on this menu for all apps. Some of the key menu items are:

- **About this Mac**: Displays basic support information about the computer.

About this Mac. (Screenshot courtesy of Apple.)

- **Displays**: Shows the current display and its configuration. Click **Displays Preferences** to change the display resolution of the screen, to calibrate the color settings, or to **AirPlay** the display to a device such as an Apple TV.
- **Storage**: Shows the capacity and current usage of the internal hard drive as well as any external drives that are connected to the Mac.
- **Service**: If the computer is under warranty or is protected by the AppleCare Protection Plan, clicking on the relevant links will bring up more information about the available support options. If there is a significant fault with the computer and it is covered by warranty or AppleCare, it is recommended that you follow the

Show Slide(s)

macOS Features (6 slides)

Teaching Tip

For users familiar with Windows, they can think of Finder as the equivalent of File Explorer and Dock as the equivalent of the taskbar. Also, point out the menu changes based on the currently selected window.

instructions and obtain help and support through an Apple Authorized Service Provider.

In the top-right corner of the menu bar is the **Status** menu. This gives quick access to important key features of the computer.

Status menu options vary according to the software that is installed (from left to right: Dropbox, Adobe Creative Cloud, Google Drive, Wacom Tablet, Evernote, Ring, Todoist, Skype, Arq, Skyfonts, Displays, Bluetooth, Wi-Fi, Drives, Keyboard Preferences and Day/Time). (Screenshot courtesy of Apple.)

THE DOCK

The **dock** at the bottom of the screen gives one-click access to your favorite apps and files, similar to the taskbar in Windows. You can change the way the dock behaves—to configure autohide or position it at another edge of the screen—by right-clicking near the vertical line at the right of the dock.

The dock contains the Finder and Trash icons by default. (Screenshot courtesy of Apple.)

To add a new app or file to the dock, click and drag the icon of the app/file into the dock. The **Finder** and **Trash** icons are always available in the dock. Apps that are open in the dock display a dot below the icon.

Right-click any dock icon to change how that app/file behaves. In the options menu, you can remove that icon from the dock, select **Open at login** to start the app when the computer boots, and **Show in Finder** to find the location of the target file.

SPOTLIGHT SEARCH

Spotlight Search can be used to find almost anything on macOS. To start a new search, click the magnifying glass in the menu bar or press **Command+Space** to bring up the search box. You can change the document types that are searched in **Preferences**. If you wish to specifically exclude locations from **Spotlight** search, click the **Privacy** button to add a folder or drive to the excluded results.

SYSTEM PREFERENCES

The **System Preferences** panel is the equivalent of the Windows **Control Panel**. It is the central "go-to" place for changing settings and network options, and optimizing a macOS configuration.

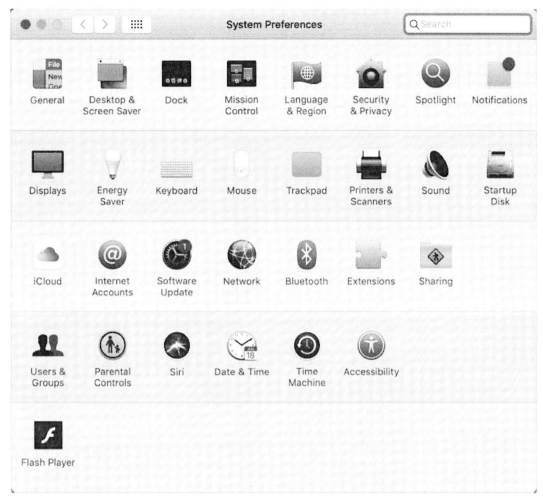

System Preferences. (Screenshot courtesy of Apple.)

You can access the **System Preferences** panel from the **Apple menu**, from the **System Preferences** icon in the dock, or by entering *system preferences* from **Spotlight Search**.

 Note: *If you are not sure where you would change a specific option, just start typing its name in the search box. For example, typing password in the search box will highlight all the options where a password may be set.*

MISSION CONTROL AND MULTIPLE DESKTOPS

It is possible to configure macOS with **multiple desktops** (or spaces) using the **Mission Control** feature. This enables the user to set up one or more desktops with different sets of apps, backgrounds, and so on, which is an easy way of managing tasks more effectively.

To set up a new desktop, activate **Mission Control** with the **F3** key. At the top of the screen, it will display a small image of the current desktop with all the open apps below. Move your cursor to the top-right corner of this screen. A tab with a plus symbol will appear from the right. Click on it and a second desktop (Desktop 2; the original will have been renamed Desktop 1) will appear at the top. The open apps shown will still be running on Desktop 1. If you want an app to only run on Desktop 2, click its window and drag it on to the Desktop 2 screen at the top.

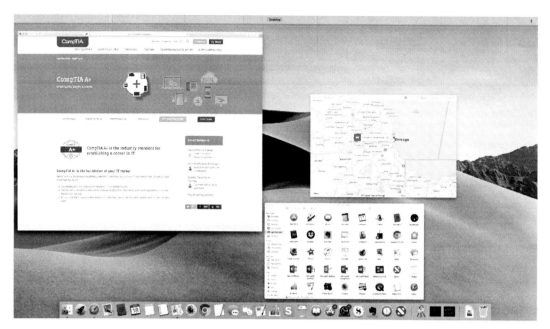

Mission Control. (Screenshot courtesy of Apple.)

It's possible to configure this further from the app menu in the dock. Right-click on an app and you will see the following menu:

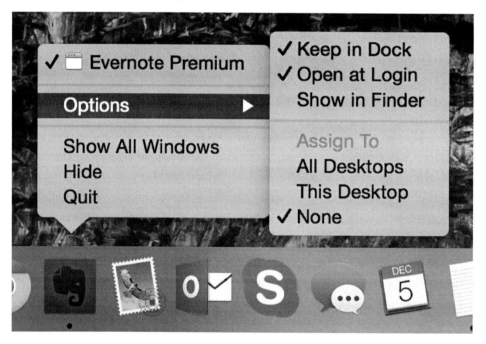

Configuring Mission Control. (Screenshot courtesy of Apple.)

As well as the standard options in the top half of this menu, you can choose to make an app available to all desktops, the currently displayed desktop, or no desktops at all.

To switch between desktops, press the **F3** key and choose a desktop. Alternatively, press **control+left** or **Control+right** to cycle between screens. You can also swipe left or right with three/four fingers on the trackpad, depending on how it is configured.

To remove a desktop, press **F3** and hover the cursor over the desktop to be deleted, then click its **Close** icon. All apps associated with that (now deleted) desktop will revert to the main desktop.

macOS FILE MANAGEMENT

The **Finder** is the **macOS** equivalent of **Explorer** in Windows. It lets the user navigate all the files and folders on a Mac. It is always present and open in the dock.

Show Slide(s)

macOS File Management (3 slides)

The Finder icon. (Screenshot courtesy of Apple.)

When you first select **Finder**, it displays your most recently used files under **Recents**. Selecting one of the favorites in the sidebar will change that view. For example, selecting **Applications** will show the apps within that default macOS folder.

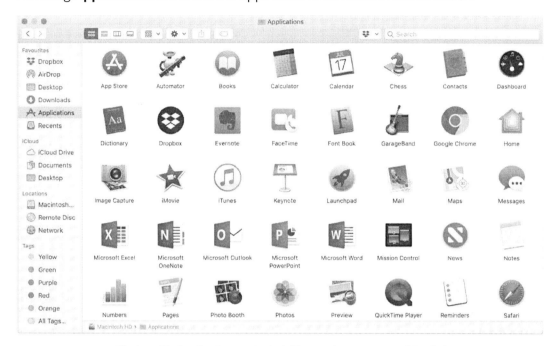

Finder with Applications selected. (Screenshot courtesy of Apple.)

HFS PLUS AND APFS

Where Windows uses NTFS and Linux typically uses ext3 or ext4, Apple Mac workstations and laptops use the **Extended Hierarchical File System (HFS Plus)**. HFS Plus supports many of the same features as NTFS but cannot perform native file/folder encryption. The maximum volume and file size is 8 ExaBytes. The only reserved characters are **:** and **/**.

In macOS High Sierra and later, HFS Plus updated to the Apple File System (APFS), which does support native file encryption. It also provides better support for SSDs. Upgrading to High Sierra (or later) automatically converts the startup volume from HFS Plus to APFS if the disk is an SSD. Otherwise, the file system can be converted without data loss using the Disk Utility.

> **Note:** *While data loss is not expected, always make a backup before performing this type of operation.*

OPTICAL DRIVES AND REMOTE DISC

Since 2016, no Apple Mac has been sold with an internal optical drive. While an external USB drive can be used, another option is the **Remote Disc** app, which lets the user access a CD/DVD drive on another Mac or Windows computer. This isn't suitable for audio CDs, DVD movies, recordable CDs/DVDs, or Windows installation disks, however.

To set up Remote Disc sharing on a Mac, open **System Preferences→Sharing** then make sure the check box is ticked next to **DVD or CD sharing**. To access the optical drive, click **Remote Disc** in **Finder**. The Mac with the drive that has just been configured will be displayed. Click its icon to access the drive.

iCloud

iCloud is Apple's online storage solution for its users. It provides a central, shared location for mail, contacts, calendar, photos, notes, reminders, and so on, across macOS and iOS devices. By default, each user is provided with 5 GB of storage (at the time of writing), although it is possible to upgrade to more space for an additional monthly fee. This space is shared across all iCloud® components and devices.

A **keychain** password cache can also be stored in iCloud to enable easy login to websites across macOS and iOS devices.

To manage iCloud, open **icloud.com** and sign in using an Apple ID. To see usage, click the user name in the top-right of the browser window and select **Settings**. This will show the amount of storage used and the devices that are linked to this account.

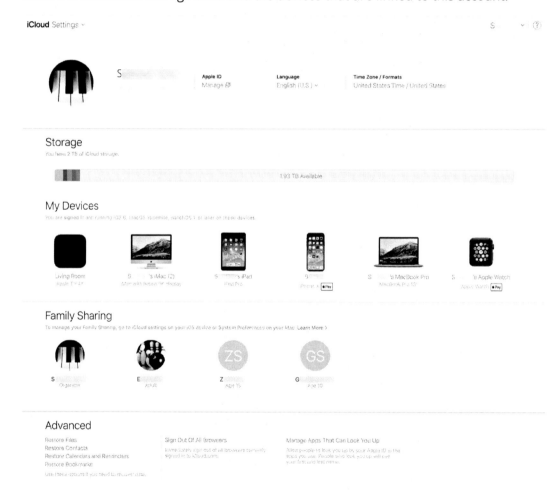

Configuring iCloud. (Screenshot courtesy of Apple.)

macOS USERS AND PASSWORDS

An **Administrator** account and an optional **Guest User** account are created when macOS is installed. To add a new account, open **System Preferences→Users & Groups**. Four types of account are available: **Administrator**, **Standard**, **Managed with Parental Controls**, and **Sharing Only**. The user's password can either be from iCloud or a separate password.

Show Slide(s)

macOS Users and Passwords (3 slides)

- **Administrator**: This is the user type created when you set up your Mac computer. From this user, additional administrator users or other user types can be created. An administrator user can convert users between standard and administrator user types. This user type should never be configured for automatic login as this could result in someone restarting the computer and gaining access to the user with administrator privileges.
- **Standard**: This type of user can change their own settings, but not those of other users. They can also install apps for their own account. This user cannot create additional users or change the settings of other user accounts.
- **Managed with Parental Controls**: The administrator specifies which apps and other content can be accessed by this user type. The websites that can be accessed can also be restricted by the administrator. In addition, time limits can be implemented for when the user can use the computer.
- **Sharing Only**: This type of user is created to give someone permission to access your shared files or to share your screen. The user cannot log in to the computer and cannot make changes to any settings on the computer. In order to give someone sharing permission, configure settings in the Sharing preferences.

APPLE ID

When first setting up an Apple Mac, the user will be assigned an **Apple ID** that is based on the sign-in email address. This Apple ID is used for purchases from the App Store, accessing iCloud and other functions. A user may already have an Apple ID from previous iTunes purchases or an iOS device.

KEYCHAIN

The Keychain® in macOS helps you to manage passwords for websites and Wi-Fi networks. This feature is also available as **iCloud Keychain**, which makes the same passwords securely available across all macOS and iOS devices. The Keychain makes password management much easier, but occasionally problems can happen. If there are any problems, they will be identified by the **Keychain Access** app (in **Utilities**).

If warning messages are displayed, it's possible to attempt a repair with **Keychain First Aid**. Launch this from the **Keychain Access** menu. After entering an administrator password, select either **Verify** or **Repair**. If the problem persists, try resetting the Keychain itself. Select **Keychain Access→Preferences**. Select **Reset My Default Keychains** to create a new empty keychain.

If you have forgotten a password, search for the website by typing into the search box. From the results, select the password that you want to view or change. Check the box for **Show password** and enter an administrator password to reveal the password for that device or service.

Keychain Access tool. (Screenshot courtesy of Apple.)

If other people have access to the Mac, it is wise to restrict access to the Keychain. To do this, select the Keychain, then under the **Edit** menu, select **Change settings for Keychain *Name***, where *Name* is the Keychain selected.

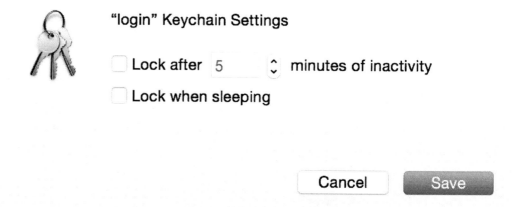

Securing a Keychain. (Screenshot courtesy of Apple.)

macOS SOFTWARE MANAGEMENT

There are two main distribution mechanisms for macOS apps: the App Store and app downloads.

APP STORE

Much like the store for iOS devices, the App Store provides a central portal for Apple and developers to distribute free and paid-for software. It is also used to distribute updates to macOS and new releases of the operating system. The icon for the App Store is .

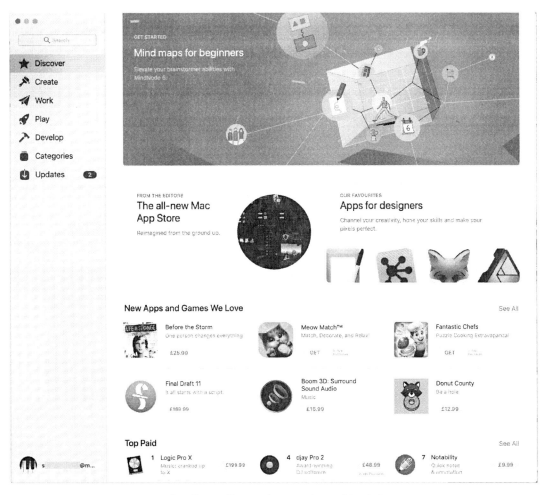

App Store. (Screenshot courtesy of Apple.)

DOWNLOAD APPS

Microsoft Office, Adobe® Creative Cloud®, and Skype® are just three examples of apps that are not available in the App Store. To install any of these apps, it is necessary to download them from the vendor site, ensuring that you select the macOS version. macOS download apps are normally distributed as **.DMG** (disk image) installer files. Follow the on-screen instructions to install the app. The last step will almost certainly ask you to copy the file to the **Applications** folder.

Skype_7.17.377.dmg
41.5 MB

Disk Image file. (Screenshot courtesy of Apple.)

By default, macOS will only allow apps to be installed that have been downloaded from the Mac App Store. To allow the installation of download apps, go to **System Preferences→Security & Privacy**. Click the padlock to make changes to the settings—you will need to enter the Administrator password to continue.

Always use the installer package to remove apps that are no longer required.

Updates for apps that have been downloaded outside of the App Store are usually managed within the app itself. For example, Microsoft Office runs a regular auto-update to check for new versions and security updates.

APPLICATION COMPATIBILITY

If you need to use Mac OS 9 applications on an OS X/macOS system, you can do so in the Classic environment. To use the Classic environment, you must have a Mac OS 9 System Folder installed on your computer, either on the same hard disk as macOS, or on another disk or disk partition.

BOOT CAMP AND WINDOWS

Boot Camp is a utility supplied with macOS that allows a full Windows installation to be made on a Mac. Once installed and Windows set up, the user has a choice of either operating system when booting the computer. In summary, the installation process for Windows on macOS is as follows:

1. Ensure that the Apple Mac meets the system requirements for the version of Windows that is to be installed.
2. Obtain an ISO disk image of Microsoft Windows.
3. Run **Boot Camp Assistant** from the **Applications→Utilities** folder.

 *Note: More comprehensive information about running Boot Camp Assistant can be found at **support.apple.com/HT201468**.*

4. Follow the on-screen instructions to repartition the hard drive on the Mac.
5. Format the new Windows partition and install Windows on it.

To boot into the Windows partition, press and hold the **OPTION** key as the Mac boots. Select the Windows partition from the **Startup Manager**.

APP CRASHES AND FORCE QUIT

When an app is busy or processing a complex request, the spinning wait cursor will appear and usually disappear again within a few seconds. Should it remain visible for longer, it is possible that the app has gone into an endless loop or entered a state where it is not possible to complete its process.

 Note: The spinning wait cursor is also known as the spinning wheel, spinning pinwheel, and the spinning beach ball of death!

If a macOS app stops responding, it should be possible to close it down and restart without having to restart the computer. Run **Force Quit** from the **Apple menu** (always available in the Menu Bar) or press **command+option+esc**. You will probably need to switch into another app or window to be able to do this.

Select the app that isn't responding—Mail in the example shown in the following figure—then click **Force Quit** to close it down.

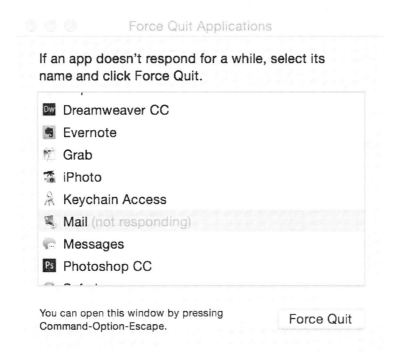

Using Force Quit to stop an app that is not responding. (Screenshot courtesy of Apple.)

It will prompt for a confirmation that you really want to force the app to quit, then show a dialog box enabling you to send a troubleshooting report to Apple.

Clicking **Report** will produce diagnostic information and a crash dump. It is always useful to report errors as they may point to an **undocumented feature** in macOS that needs to be addressed in a future update.

TROUBLESHOOTING AN APP
If an app constantly crashes, take the following steps:

- Ensure the latest version of the app is installed.
- If the crash only happens with a specific document or file, try recreating that file from scratch in case it is corrupt.
- Uninstall the app by dragging it to **Trash** and reinstall from either the App Store or the third-party vendor's site.

macOS DIAGNOSTIC UTILITIES
macOS has several utilities that are provided as part of a default installation. You can find these utility apps in the **Other** folder in **Launchpad**, and in the **Utilities** folder under **Applications**.

Show Slide(s)

macOS Diagnostic Utilities (3 slides)

SYSTEM INFORMATION
The **System Information** app provides detailed diagnostic information about your Mac.

SCREEN SHARING
Screen Sharing allows another user to view your macOS desktop and operate the computer from another Apple Mac or a computer or device installed with **VNC Viewer**. Configure **Screen Sharing** via **System Preferences→Sharing**. Enable screen sharing, then choose how users are authorized to connect. You can restrict access to specific Mac accounts or groups or a subset of those users as well as allow users to connect by requesting permission. **VNC** users can be configured to access the computer using a

password. Connect to another macOS computer with screen sharing enabled by opening it via the **Shared** folder in **Finder**.

ACTIVITY MONITOR

Activity Monitor is used to watch CPU, memory, energy, disk, and network usage. Use this app if you want to track unusual activity or patterns on the Mac and to try and establish if a specific app or process is causing overload of resources.

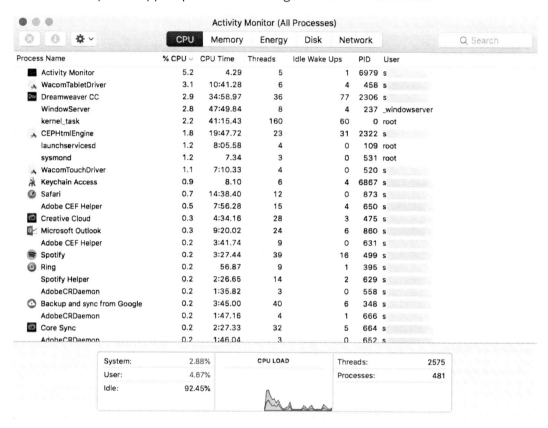

Activity Monitor. (Screenshot courtesy of Apple.)

CONSOLE

The console records error and log messages and helps you to diagnose problems within macOS.

Use the console to view the log and diagnostic reports. (Screenshot courtesy of Apple.)

TERMINAL

The **Terminal** is the equivalent to the Windows **Command Prompt** window. Use **Terminal** to run network troubleshooting utilities such as the ping command, or enter advanced commands to modify the macOS environment—with care!

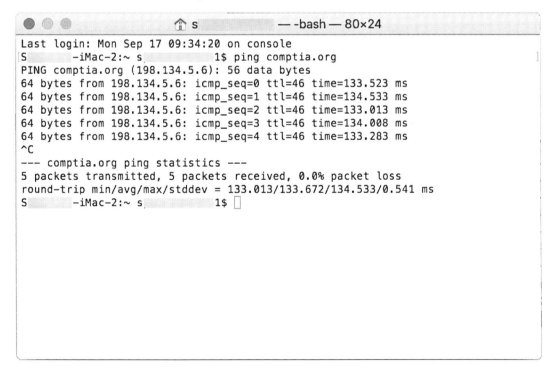

Terminal. (Screenshot courtesy of Apple.)

Show
Slide(s)

macOS Recovery

macOS RECOVERY

macOS includes a set of utilities that you can use to restore a Mac from the **Time Machine** backup program, to reinstall macOS from a system image, or to reformat or repair the system disk.

To access the **Recovery** menu, as you power up the Apple Mac hold down the **command+R** keys until you see the Apple logo. After selecting your language, it will boot into macOS Recovery, enabling you to select from the options shown in the following figure.

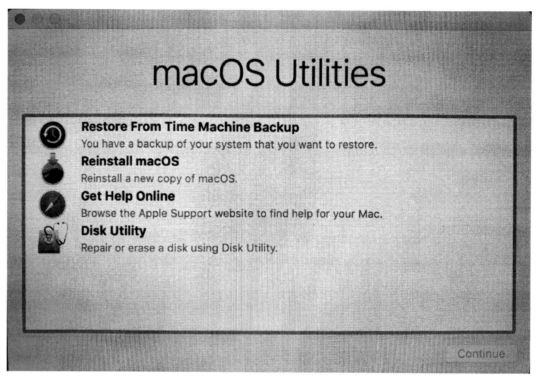

macOS Recovery menu. (Screenshot courtesy of Apple.)

When you reboot an Apple Mac, if the startup drive is not available for any reason and it's connected to the Internet, the computer will try to boot from a web-based drive.

Use a **Time Machine** snapshot backup if you want to restore the Mac to a specific point in time; for example, if you have replaced or reformatted the hard drive. Alternatively, if you have created a disk image (**.DMG**) as a restore point, use the **Disk Utility** option to restore from that file. It's also possible to restore disk images from a web link.

*Note: To learn more, check the **Video** tile on the CHOICE Course screen for any videos that supplement the content for this lesson.*

Access the Checklist tile on your CHOICE Course screen for reference information and job aids on How to Configure and Use macOS.

Activity 6-3
Discussing macOS Features and Tools

Show Slide(s)

Activity: Discussing macOS Features and Tools

SCENARIO
Answer the following questions to check your understanding of the topic.

1. **Where would you look for the option to view and configure wireless adapter status in macOS?**

   In the **Status** menu on the Menu bar, in the top-right of the screen.

2. **How do you activate Spotlight Search using the keyboard?**

   Command+Spacebar.

3. **Where would you change the default gestures on a Magic Trackpad?**

   Under **System Preferences→Trackpad**.

4. **What is the name of Apple's multiple desktop management feature?**

   Mission Control.

5. **What is the equivalent of Explorer in macOS?**

   The Finder.

6. **What app would you use to install Windows 10 on a Mac?**

   Boot Camp Assistant lets you create a new partition and install a fresh version of Windows.

7. **What is the correct name for the spinning beach ball of death?**

   Spinning wait cursor.

Topic C

Install and Upgrade Operating Systems

 EXAM OBJECTIVES COVERED
1002-1.3 Summarize general OS installation considerations and upgrade methods.
1002-1.4 Given a scenario, use appropriate Microsoft command-line tools.

 Teaching Tip

The objective is for general OS considerations, so while you focus on Windows, point out the features of Linux and macOS install/upgrade procedures, too.

 Show Slide(s)

OS Installation Types (3 slides)

Being able to install or upgrade an operating system can be important if you have built a custom computer system from scratch, if the system you purchased from a vendor did not have the correct system installed, or if you are completely redeploying existing hardware from one system to another.

The skills and information in this topic will help you plan and perform an OS installation properly, for whatever your technical and business requirements might be.

OS INSTALLATION TYPES

An operating system installation copies the OS system and bundled application files from the installation media to a partition on the target computer's fixed disk. OS setup scans the computer for hardware devices and loads appropriate drivers. The user may be prompted for information about the computer name, network settings, and the primary user account.

OS INSTALLATION OVERVIEW

The installation of an operating system should be carefully planned. It will consist of the following phases:

1. Select an installation method—attended or unattended, and clean install or in-place upgrade, for example.
2. Check compatibility—that the core components of the computer are sufficient to run the OS and that peripheral devices have drivers suitable for use with the OS. If upgrading, you also need to check application compatibility and establish the upgrade path.
3. If upgrading, back up any existing user data or settings.

    This is obviously not necessary if installing to a new computer, but is a vital step if you are replacing (rather than upgrading) an existing installation. While it takes more time, performance and reliability can be improved by performing a clean install.

     Note: If you are performing an in-place upgrade, you should also make a full system backup before proceeding so that the upgrade can be rolled back should anything go wrong.

4. Choose a boot method to use to load the OS setup files.
5. Prepare the fixed disk and copy setup files to the target.
6. Configure installation options.
7. Verify installation—check logs and complete tests to confirm that installation has succeeded.

ATTENDED AND UNATTENDED INSTALLATIONS

An installation where the installer inputs the configuration information in response to prompts from a setup program is called an **attended installation**, whereas an installation that derives configuration information from a file designed for that purpose is called an **unattended installation**.

CLEAN INSTALL OR IN-PLACE UPGRADE

There are two main approaches to performing an attended installation:

- **Clean install**—means installing the OS to a new computer or completely replacing the OS software on an old one. Any existing user data or settings would be deleted during the setup process.
- **In-place upgrade**—means installing on top of an existing version of the OS, retaining applications, user settings, and data files.

A clean install is generally seen as more reliable than upgrading. In a corporate network environment, installations are completed using **images** (a template containing the OS and required software) so that machines use a consistent set of software and configuration options. PC vendors also use images to install new systems for sale.

Upgrades are generally designed for home users. Upgrade software can be purchased at a discount.

*Note: To learn more, check the **Video** tile on the CHOICE Course screen for any videos that supplement the content for this lesson.*

Access the Checklist tile on your CHOICE Course screen for reference information and job aids on How to Back Up Data and Settings.

COMPATIBILITY CONSIDERATIONS

Show Slide(s)

Compatibility Considerations

Before you install or upgrade the OS on a computer, you must make sure that the computer hardware supports the new OS version. You may also need to check that any existing software applications will run under the new version.

OS COMPATIBILITY/UPGRADE PATH

If you are considering upgrading, you must check that the current OS version is supported as an upgrade path to the intended version. The OS vendor should publish supported upgrade paths on their website. For example, the upgrade paths for Windows 10 are published here: **docs.microsoft.com/en-us/windows/deployment/ upgrade/windows-10-upgrade-paths** while the upgrade support documents for macOS are here: **support.apple.com/macos/high-sierra**.

With Windows, you also have to consider the edition when upgrading. You can usually upgrade to the same or higher edition (Windows 7 Home Premium to Windows 10 Home or Professional or Windows 10 Home to Windows 10 Professional, for instance), but you cannot upgrade from a home to an enterprise edition. Downgrading the edition is supported in some circumstances (Windows 7 Professional to Windows 10 Home, for instance) but this only retains documents and other data, not apps and settings. Downgrading from an Enterprise edition is not supported.

Note that you can only upgrade the same type of operating system. You cannot "upgrade" from Windows to Linux, for instance.

HARDWARE COMPATIBILITY AND APPLICATION COMPATIBILITY

The first step in checking hardware compatibility is to verify that the system exceeds the recommended requirements or prerequisites. The minimum requirements will not usually deliver adequate performance.

The second step is to verify that peripheral devices and expansion cards will work under the OS. Effectively this means, "Has the manufacturer released a stable driver for the OS?" Microsoft maintains a **Windows Logo'd Product List (LPL) catalog**, previously called the **Hardware Compatibility List (HCL)**. This is a catalog of tested devices and drivers. If a device has not passed Windows logo testing, you should check the device vendor's website to confirm whether there is a driver available.

If you are performing an in-place upgrade or if you are planning a clean install and need to know whether you will be able to reinstall a particular app, you also need to check with each application vendor whether the new OS version is supported. In some cases, you may need to purchase an application upgrade, too.

> *Note: You can sometimes use automated **Upgrade Advisor** software to check whether the existing computer hardware (and software applications) will be compatible with a new version of Windows. An **Upgrade Advisor** might be bundled with the setup program or available from the vendor website.*

Unsupported hardware or software can cause problems during an in-place upgrade and should be physically uninstalled from the PC. It is also worth obtaining the latest drivers for various devices from the vendor's website. The Windows setup media ships with default drivers for a number of products, but these are often not up-to-date nor are they comprehensive.

> *Note: Store the latest drivers for your hardware on a USB drive or network location so that you can update hardware efficiently.*

LINUX INSTALLATION AND COMPATIBILITY

The hardware requirements for installing Linux will depend upon the distribution of Linux you choose. Linux is a portable operating system, which means it can run on a variety of hardware platforms. There are versions available for many different processor types, including Intel x86, Itanium, DEC Alpha, Sun Sparc, Motorola, and others. In general, a basic installation of Linux on a workstation might require as little as 16 or 32 MB of memory and 250 MB of disk space, but you might need several gigabytes of disk space for a complete installation, including all utilities.

Because Linux is a portable operating system, it is compatible with a wide range of hardware. You will need to check with the vendor or provider of your Linux distribution to verify if your particular system hardware is supported by that distribution.

A site that works well for this is **linux.com**. They have a yearly comparison of the Linux distributions and what they feel are the best distributions for various purposes.

Some web resources you can use to research general Linux hardware support include:

- The Linux Hardware Compatibility HOWTO website at **tldp.org/HOWTO/Hardware-HOWTO/index.html**.
- The Linux Questions website's hardware compatibility list at **linuxquestions.org/hcl**.
- Linux hardware and driver support lists at **linux-drivers.org**.

Check your Linux vendor's website and read the technical documentation for the distribution of Linux you plan to install or upgrade to in order to determine if your existing applications will be supported under the new version.

*Note: To learn more, check the **Video** tile on the CHOICE Course screen for any videos that supplement the content for this lesson.*

Access the Checklist tile on your CHOICE Course screen for reference information and job aids on How to Check Compatibility for OS Installation or Upgrade.

INSTALLATION BOOT METHODS

The **installation boot method** refers to the way in which the installation program and settings are loaded onto the PC. You may need to access the computer's firmware setup program to ensure that a particular boot method is available, enabled, and set to the highest priority.

Show Slide(s)

Installation Boot Methods (2 slides)

Teaching Tip

Discuss which method is appropriate for a given scenario.

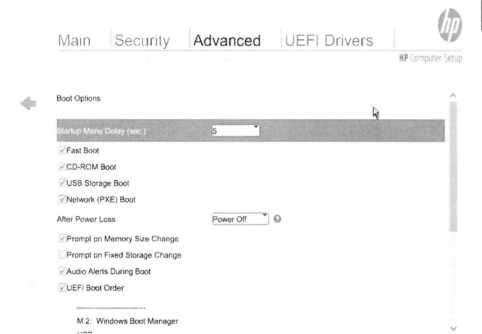

Configuring boot devices and priority in a computer's firmware setup program. (Screenshot courtesy of Hewlett-Packard, Inc.)

OPTICAL DISC (CD-ROM/DVD/BLU-RAY)

Most attended installations and upgrades are run by booting from the setup CD-ROM or DVD. This might be listed as Optical Drive in the firmware setup program. You can also run a clean install or upgrade from an existing Windows installation.

An **ISO file** contains all of the contents from an optical disc in a single file. ISO files stored on removable media or a host system are often used to install virtual machine operating systems. An ISO file can be mounted to the file system as though it were a physical optical drive.

EXTERNAL DRIVE/FLASH DRIVE (USB/ESATA)

One problem with disc-based installs is that the setup disc quickly becomes out-of-date and post-installation tasks for installing drivers, updates, and service packs can take longer than the original installation. One way around this is to build **slipstreamed media**, with all the various patches and drivers already applied. The media could be CD-ROM, DVD, or USB-attached flash drive or external drive connected by USB or by eSATA. The computer firmware must also support USB or eSATA as a boot method.

 *Note: Microsoft provides a tool to create installation media from an ISO of the product setup files (**support.microsoft.com/en-us/help/15088/windows-create-installation-media**).*

NETWORK BOOT (PXE)

A remote network installation means connecting to a shared folder containing the installation files (which could be slipstreamed). The target PC must have a usable partition on the hard disk in which to store temporary files. There also needs to be some means of booting with networking software. Most computers now come with a **Preboot eXecution Environment (PXE)** compliant firmware and network adapter, which supports booting from a network with a suitably configured server.

 *Note: macOS supports a similar network boot method to **PXE** called **NetBoot**.*

INTERNAL FIXED DISK (HDD/SSD)/INTERNAL HARD DRIVE (PARTITION)

Once the OS has been installed, you will usually want to set the internal fixed disk (or the boot partition on the internal fixed disk) as the default (highest priority) boot device and disable any other boot devices. This ensures the system doesn't try to boot to the setup media again. If access to the firmware setup program is secured, it also prevents someone from trying to install a new OS without authorization.

An OS can be installed to a Hard Disk Drive (HDD) or Solid State Drive (SSD). Note that in the firmware setup program, the HDD will probably be on a SATA port while an SSD might be on a SATA, M.2, or PCIe port.

There may be some circumstances where you have to copy the installation media to the computer's fixed disk. To do this, you would remove the disk from the target PC and attach it to another machine. Use the other machine to partition the disk as appropriate and copy the setup files to it. Use the **diskpart** tool to set the partition as active. Use the **bootsect** tool to copy code to make the partition bootable. Finally, reinstall the disk to the target computer and boot to the partition containing your setup files.

SECURE BOOT

Motherboards now use a type of system firmware called **Unified Extensible Firmware Interface (UEFI)**. In UEFI, there is an option called **secure boot**, which restricts OS installation to trusted software. This will prevent installation of Windows 7 and some distributions of Linux if enabled because the setup files for these operating systems are not digitally signed in a way that the firmware is able to trust.

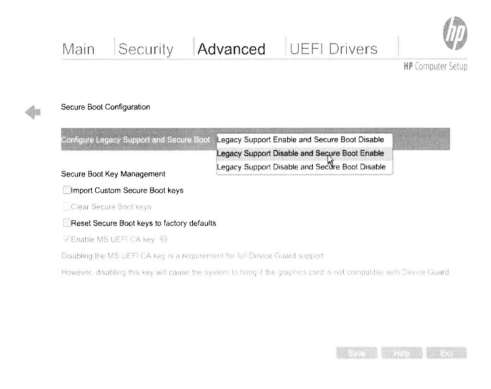

Configuring the Secure Boot option in the system firmware setup program. (Screenshot courtesy of Hewlett-Packard, Inc.)

Also, a 32-bit edition of Windows needs to be installed in legacy BIOS mode. You can also choose to install using legacy BIOS mode if you do not want to use EFI boot for some reason.

*Note: To learn more, check the **Video** tile on the CHOICE Course screen for any videos that supplement the content for this lesson.*

Access the Checklist tile on your CHOICE Course screen for reference information and job aids on How to Select an Installation Boot Method.

DISK FORMATTING AND PARTITIONING

The operating system must be installed to a partition that is of a suitable size and formatted with an appropriate file system. In Windows, the **boot partition** and **system partition** cannot be changed (except by using third-party tools), so it is important to plan the disk partition scheme in accordance with the way the computer will be used:

Show Slide(s)

Disk Formatting and Partitioning (5 slides)

- Will the computer have multiple operating systems installed (multiboot)? If so, it is best practice to create a partition for each OS.

- Does the boot partition have spare capacity for growth? Running out of space will cause serious problems, so leave plenty of overhead.

  Windows must be installed to a boot partition formatted with NTFS.

- Is some sort of hardware RAID being used? If so, the RAID utility must be used to configure the RAID level and create volumes before the OS can be installed. A RAID

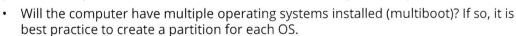

configuration utility is invoked by pressing a key combo such as **Ctrl+F** during startup (when the RAID firmware BIOS is processed).

- Is an SSD or hybrid SSD being used? The SSD should be used for the boot partition as this will improve performance.

 Note: Remember that in Microsoft's terminology, the system partition is where the boot files are and the boot partition is where the operating system is installed.

MULTIBOOT

If a user needs multiple operating systems, they can be set up on the same computer in a **multiboot** environment. Most operating systems can be run in this way, with the following caveats:

- Each OS should be installed to a separate boot partition.
- The system partition must be accessible to each OS. This means that, typically, it must be formatted using FAT or FAT32).
- New operating systems should not overwrite the boot manager. The general principle is to install the older operating system first, as an older OS is less likely to recognize a multiboot environment. Alternatively, the boot manager may need to be reconfigured manually following installation of an OS.

Multiboot is seldom used anymore as virtualization represents a simpler way of achieving the same aim, with the major advantage that the different operating systems can be used concurrently.

DISK FORMATTING

 **Teaching Tip**

Emphasize the use of the different partitions.

The easiest way to ensure a properly formatted boot drive with the correct partitions and format is to install to a blank hard disk. If you are using a disk with existing data that you do not want to keep, you can choose to delete existing partitions using the disk setup tool.

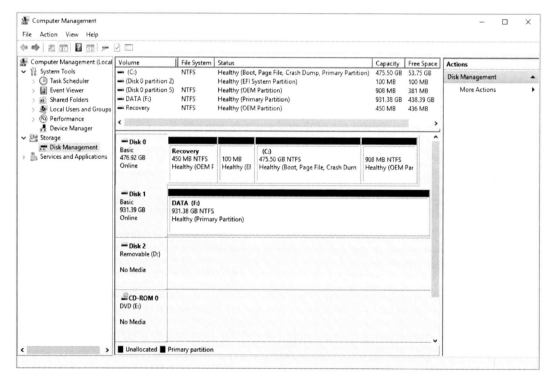

Partition layout for a GPT-style disk and Windows 10. (Screenshot used with permission from Microsoft.)

The previous figure shows the typical partition layout for an OEM-formatted PC with UEFI-type firmware:

- Disk 0 is a Solid State Drive (SSD) hosting the boot and system partitions. There are also two OEM partitions used for OS recovery and vendor diagnostic tools. The boot partition has been assigned drive letter C: and the other partitions have no drive letter.
- Disk 1 is a second fixed disk. More accurately, it is a RAID volume comprising two mirrored HDDs, but because this is hardware RAID, it appears as a single disk to the OS.
- Disk 2 is a flash memory card reader and you can also see the optical disc drive.
- All the partitions except the EFI system partition are formatted using NTFS. The Extensible Firmware Interface (EFI) system partition uses a type of FAT but isn't listed as such in the drive management tool.

By contrast, the following screenshot shows the partitions created by the CentOS Linux setup tool if automatic partitioning is selected.

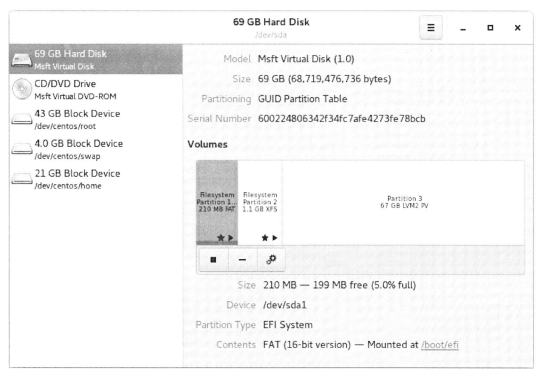

CentOS Linux default partitions.

The fixed disk is divided into three partitions: an EFI system partition, one for the Linux boot loader, and a Logical Volume Manager (LVM) partition. The LVM software is used to divide this last partition into three volumes (block devices)—one for the OS system files (root), one for a swap partition, and one for user data (home).

OS SETUP DISK FORMATTING TOOLS

While you can inspect and configure disks, partitions, and file systems using the Disk Management console once Windows is installed, a different tool is used from the Setup program to prepare the disk.

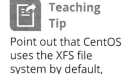

Teaching Tip

Point out that CentOS uses the XFS file system by default, rather than ext4.

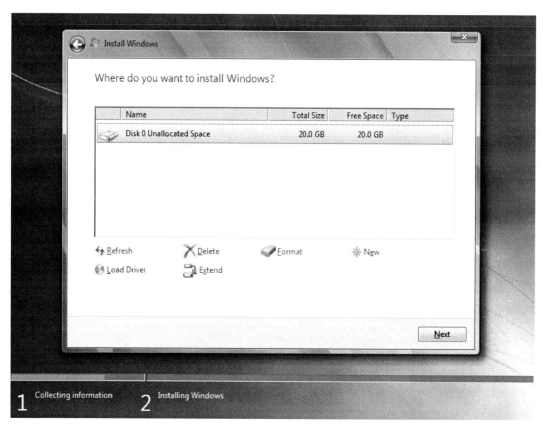

Windows disk setup options. (Screenshot used with permission from Microsoft.)

If you are performing a clean install but the target disk already has a partition structure, you can use the setup tool to delete the existing partitions. You can use the **New** button to create a custom partition structure or just select a disk with enough unallocated space and allow setup to create the required partitions automatically.

LOADING DISK DRIVERS

In order to manage the hard disk, the setup program must have an appropriate driver for it. Most of the time the setup media will include a suitable driver. If you are installing to a RAID volume or to a computer with legacy firmware, it is possible that the disk or volume may not be recognized. If this is the case, you will have to load the disk or RAID vendor's driver via the **Load Driver** option on the **Where do you want to install Windows** dialog box in setup.

LOCALE SETTINGS AND SOFTWARE SELECTION

Show Slide(s)

Locale Settings and Software Selection (2 slides)

When you perform an attended installation, you need to manually configure setup at various points in the process. Windows setup is much better streamlined than in the past, with all the configuration options at the beginning and end of the process.

Note: You are focusing on the Windows setup program here, but other operating systems present similar choices.

The first step in a Windows attended installation is to choose the language, regional format settings, time zone, and keyboard type. You should also check that the date and time are displayed correctly.

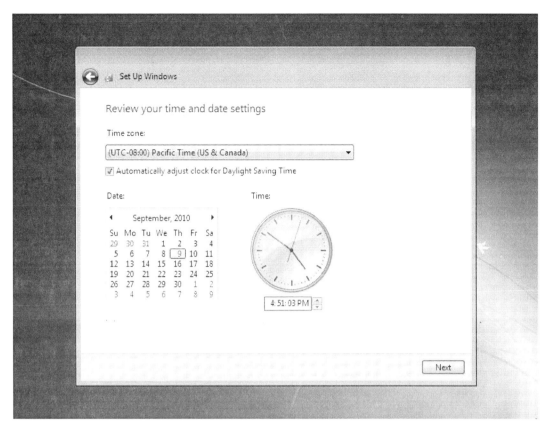

Configuring the time zone during Windows 7 setup. (Screenshot used with permission from Microsoft.)

Having done that, you can initialize setup by entering the product key, accepting the End User License Agreement (EULA), choosing the install type—upgrade or custom (clean install)—and partitioning and formatting the disk. Setup then proceeds without requiring any intervention. During this time, setup copies the OS files to the system folder, detects hardware devices, and loads appropriate drivers. Once this process is complete, the PC will restart.

SOFTWARE SELECTIONS

In Windows setup, there is no opportunity to install additional software as such, though you can choose options such as linking the installation to a Microsoft user account and syncing files to OneDrive. When you install Linux, however, there is typically a setup option prompting you to select the type of installation and choose specific software packages to use.

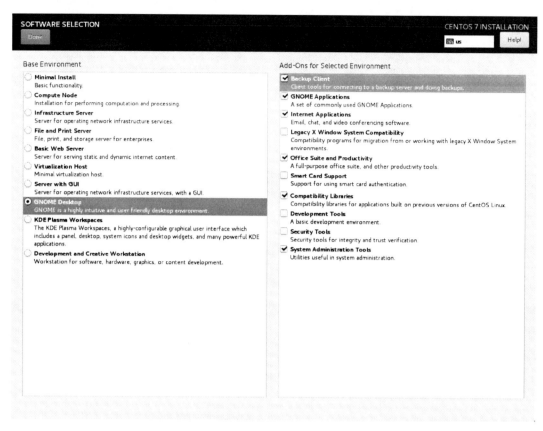

Selecting a computer environment/role and software add-ons during CentOS setup.

NETWORKING CONSIDERATIONS

There are some network-related things you will want to consider during installation.

WINDOWS UPDATE

If the setup program detects that a network connection is present, it may present an option to use **Windows Update** to download the latest installation files from the Internet. If no Internet connection is available or you want to skip this step, you can use **Windows Update** after setup is complete.

> **Note:** *In Windows 7, you could disable* **Windows Update** *automatic updating during setup if desired. This option is not available when installing Windows 10.*

WORKGROUP VS. DOMAIN SETUP

A **workgroup** is a Microsoft peer-to-peer network model in which computers are grouped together with access to shared resources for organizational purposes. A **domain** is a Microsoft client/server network model that groups computers together for security and to centralize administration. Computers that are members of a domain have access to a shared central user account database, which means that an individual can use a single user account to log on at any computer within the domain.

Windows does not support joining a domain during an attended installation. The computer can be joined by reconfiguring **System** properties in **Control Panel**, via the **Settings** interface, or can be joined during an unattended installation by using an answer file or script.

There is no option to change the default workgroup name (**WORKGROUP**) either. In Windows networking, the workgroup name is now entirely cosmetic.

Show Slide(s)

Networking Considerations (2 slides)

Teaching Tip

Note that patch management is covered in another part of the course.

Teaching Tip

You might want to note that Windows 10 **can** join an Azure AD domain (using the **Set up for an organization** option).

There is a **Domain join instead** option, but this just prompts for the creation of a local account. You can then join a domain using Windows **Settings** or the **System** applet.

In Windows 7, you are prompted to configure the computer's host name and choose a user name and password for the local administrator account. In Windows 8/10, you can choose to use a **Microsoft account** rather than creating a **local account**.

If the computer is not connected to the Internet, you will just be prompted to create a local account. You can convert a local account to a Microsoft account (or vice versa) using Windows **Settings**.

*Note: To learn more, check the **Video** tile on the CHOICE Course screen for any videos that supplement the content for this lesson.*

Access the Checklist tile on your CHOICE Course screen for reference information and job aids on How to Select a Network Type During Windows Installation.

POST-INSTALLATION TASKS

Windows should detect all supported hardware and load the appropriate drivers during setup. When you have gotten to the final configuration screens, it is a good sign that the installation has succeeded. You might want to check the log files, check Device Manager to confirm all hardware has been recognized, and test each hardware device to verify functionality. You can use Programs and Features (in Control Panel) or the Microsoft Store to install any optional Windows components or third-party software applications.

Post-Installation Tasks

Update the system documentation with details of the installation. Keeping up-to-date documentation is important for system maintenance and troubleshooting.

MICROSOFT PRODUCT ACTIVATION

Microsoft Product Activation or **Volume Activation for Windows** operating system is an antipiracy technology that verifies that software products are legitimately purchased. Product activation reduces a form of piracy known as casual copying. For example, you must activate the Windows operating systems within a given number of days after installation. After the grace period, users cannot access the system until they activate Windows. Volume Activation automates the activation process.

For individual installations of Windows, you can activate the installation over the Internet. If you do not have an Internet connection, you can activate over the phone, although this takes a little longer. If you wish, you can postpone product activation and activate later in the activation grace period.

In large organizations, you can use a Volume License Product Key, which eliminates the need to individually activate each installation of Windows. You can also activate Windows as part of an automated installation.

REPAIR INSTALLATIONS

If a Windows computer will not boot or if you are troubleshooting a problem such as slow performance and cannot find a single cause, it may be necessary to perform some sort of "repair installation." There are several means of accomplishing this.

Show Slide(s)
Repair Installations

Note: A repair install will only work if you are replacing the same version of the operating system; you cannot upgrade in this manner.

Teaching Tip
Stress that a recovery partition is usually "concealed" (not given a drive letter). You access the partition via the boot screens before Windows loads.

FACTORY RECOVERY PARTITION

A **recovery disc** or **factory recovery partition** (also called a **Rescue Disk**) is a tool used by OEMs to restore the OS environment to the same state on which it was shipped. The disc or recovery partition is used to boot the system, then a simple wizard-driven process replaces the damaged installation with an image stored on a separate partition on the hard disk. The recovery process can be started by pressing a key during startup (**F11** or **Ctrl+F11** are often used; a message is usually shown on-screen).

OEM media will not usually recover user data or settings or applications installed—everything gets set back to the state in which the PC was shipped from the factory. User data should be recovered from backup, which obviously has to be made before the computer becomes unbootable.

You could also create recovery media manually or using backup software or drive imaging. In this scenario, you can create images that reflect all the software and service packs that a typical machine should include. Most backup suites have a simple wizard-driven routine for creating recovery media.

The advantages of using a recovery partition are that less time is required to re-build the machine and from a technical support point-of-view, recovery is much easier for end-users than re-installing Windows.

The main disadvantages with OEM recovery media are that the tool only works if the original hard disk is still installed in the machine and will not include patches or service packs applied between the ship date and recovery date. The recovery image also takes up quite a lot of space and users may not feel that they are getting the hard disk capacity that they have paid for!

 Note: A recovery partition is not usually allocated a drive letter so will not be obvious to the user. You can make the partition visible to Explorer through the Disk Management program.

REFRESH/RESTORE INSTALLATION

An in-place upgrade repair install is a "last gasp" method of restoring a Windows 7 installation that will not boot. The install process is run over the top of an existing installation. This can preserve some settings, application software installation, and data files while restoring system files. In Windows 8 and Windows 10, there are officially supported refresh and reset options to try to repair the installation. Using refresh (called **Just remove my files** in Windows 10) recopies the system files and reverts most system settings to the default, but can preserve user personalization settings, data files, and apps installed via Windows Store. Desktop applications are removed.

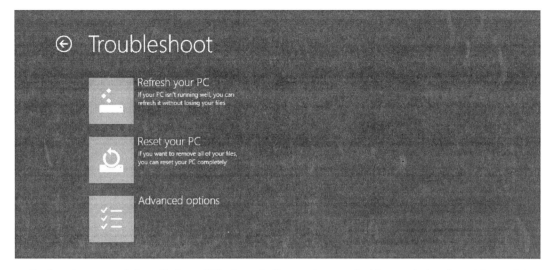

Performing a repair installation of Windows 8. (Screenshot used with permission from Microsoft.)

Using the **Reset** option (called **Fully clean the drive**) deletes the existing OS plus apps, settings, and data ready for the OS to be reinstalled.

UNATTENDED INSTALLATIONS

Performing an attended installation is time-consuming. Although the setup process has been streamlined since the early versions of Windows, an attended installation still requires the installer to monitor the setup program and input information. When it comes to deploying large numbers of installations (whether at the same time or over a period of months), there are several options for completing fully or partially unattended installations. As with ordinary installs, these can be completed using a variety of media but most would be based on the remote network installation boot method (PXE).

Show Slide(s)

Unattended Installations (2 slides)

IMAGE DEPLOYMENT

Any installation involving more than a few PCs makes using imaging technology worthwhile. An image is a clone of an existing installation stored in one file. The image can contain the base OS and configuration settings, service packs and updates, applications software, and whatever else is required. An image can be stored on DVD or USB media or can be accessed over a network.

Windows supports the use of **answer files**, allowing for fully or partially unattended installations. An answer file is an **eXtensible Markup Language (XML)** text file that contains all of the instructions that the Windows **Setup** program will need to install and configure the OS without any administrator intervention.

Using unattended installation allows for multiple installations to occur simultaneously, can prevent errors during installation, and creates more consistency between installations in a large-scale rollout, all while lowering overhead costs and decreasing installation time and effort.

WINDOWS SYSTEM IMAGE MANAGER

The **Windows System Image Manager** is used to configure answer files. An answer file contains the information input during setup, such as product key, disk partitions, computer name, language and network settings (including whether to join a domain or workgroup), and so on. This file is accessed automatically during setup, meaning that an installer does not have to be present. The **System Image Manager** is packaged with the **Windows Assessment and Deployment Kit (ADK)**, formerly the **Windows Automated Installation Kit (WAIK)**, available from Microsoft's website.

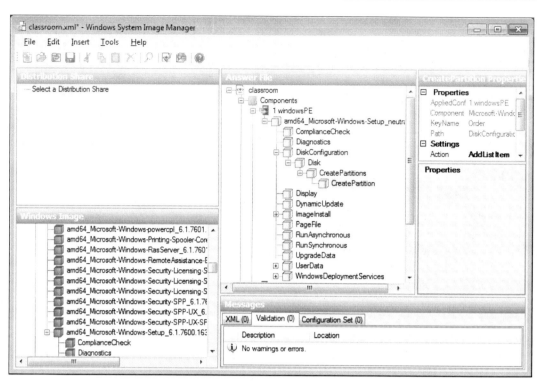

Windows System Image Manager. (Screenshot used with permission from Microsoft.)

DRIVE CLONING AND SYSPREP

If Windows is to be deployed to multiple machines with similar hardware specifications, the most common method of deployment is to use disk imaging software to clone an installation from one PC (the **reference machine**) to the rest. This has the advantage that a full system can be built, including applications, service packs and patches, and default user settings.

 Note: You need different images for 32- and 64-bit platforms.

Microsoft's **Deployment Image Servicing and Management** tool (**dism**, part of the ADK) is used to duplicate the disk contents. **Dism** reads the contents of a drive and writes the output to a **.WIM** (Windows Image File) format file.

However, duplicating an existing installation exactly can cause problems, as it repeats the **Security ID** (**SID**; a unique identifier for each machine) and assumes that the machines have exactly the same hardware configuration, which may not be the case.

Microsoft's System Preparation Tool (Sysprep) utility should be run before imaging the disk to side-step these problems. You can run the tool from **%SystemRoot% \System32\Sysprep\sysprep.exe**.

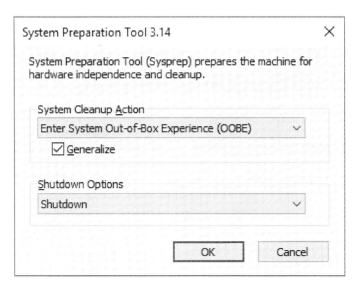

Resealing your computer using sysprep. (Screenshot used with permission from Microsoft.)

*Note: The **Sysprep** utility has gone through several updates with different Windows versions and service packs.*

WINDOWS DEPLOYMENT SERVICES

A basic network installation can be set up by putting the installation files in a network share, booting the machine to the network, then accessing the installation program from the share.

Windows Deployment Services is a Windows Server component used to implement network installs more effectively for **.WIM** images and answer files.

To support network deployments, clients must have a PXE compatible firmware and network adapter.

Activity 6-4
Discussing OS Installation

Show Slide(s)

Activity: Discussing OS Installation

SCENARIO
Answer the following questions to check your understanding of the topic.

1. **When should you use FAT32 for the system partition?**

   When using UEFI system firmware, the EFI system partition should be formatted with a FAT file system. Another scenario is when you are configuring a multiboot system with an older version of Windows or with Linux.

2. **If you want to use PXE as an installation method, what type of compatible component would you require?**

   Network adapter/NIC and system firmware support.

3. **What is the advantage of using a USB thumb drive to install Windows?**

   You can install images larger than will fit on a DVD. This might be useful if you want to install multiple software applications at the same time as Windows itself.

4. **What is a recovery partition?**

   A partition containing a backup of the system configuration at a particular point in time. These are often used on OEM PCs to enable the PC to be restored to its factory settings.

5. **What should you configure in order to perform an unattended installation?**

   An answer file containing the setup configuration.

6. **What is meant by disk imaging?**

   Cloning an installation from one PC to another.

7. **How would you configure a PC to join a domain during installation of Windows 7?**

   Use an answer file with the appropriate settings, and ensure that a domain controller is available to the PC during setup. You cannot join a domain during attended setup (though you could immediately after setup finishes).

Activity 6-5

Deploying a Windows Image

BEFORE YOU BEGIN

Complete this activity using Hyper-V Manager and the PC1 (Windows 10) VM.

You normally create answer files by using the Windows System Image Manager. As that process is quite complex, there is an answer file supplied for use in this activity.

SCENARIO

When you want to deploy Windows to multiple workstations, you will usually image a reference system containing all the system updates, applications, and Windows features that you want to use on each workstation. Before you can use the reference system as an image, however, you need to run the `sysprep` utility so that Windows generates a new unique system ID when installed to a new workstation. In this activity, you will practice performing a Windows unattended installation by using an image and answer file.

1. On the **PC1 VM**, examine the contents of the answer file in **C:\LABFILES \unattend.xml**.

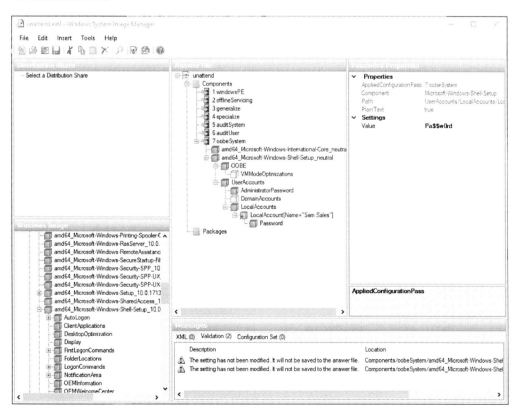

This answer file was created by using Windows System Image Manager. (Screenshot used with permission from Microsoft.)

Show Slide(s)

Activity: Deploying a Windows Image

Teaching Tip

Optionally, if you have time, ask learners to create VMs and perform attended installations of other operating systems (such as Windows 7, Windows 10, and CentOS). Choose the **C: \COMPTIA-LABS \TEMP** folder as the storage location. Ask learners to delete any VMs they create and empty the **TEMP** folder at the end of the activity.

You can use Generation 2 VMs for each of these, but remember that Secure Boot must be disabled for Windows 7 and CentOS.

If you are installing CentOS and it hangs at reboot, have learners turn off and turn back on to complete setup.

a) Start **PC1**, and sign on to the **Admin** account with the ***Pa$$w0rd*** credential.

b) Open **File Explorer** and browse to **C:\LABLFILES.**

c) Right-click the **Unattend** file, and select **Edit with Notepad++**.

d) Identify some of the features of this answer file.

```
 2  ☐<unattend xmlns="urn:schemas-microsoft-com:unattend">
 3  ☐   <settings pass="oobeSystem">
 4  ☐      <component name="Microsoft-Windows-International-Core" processorArchitecture="amd64" publicKeyTo
 5             <InputLocale>en-us</InputLocale>
 6             <SystemLocale>en-us</SystemLocale>
 7             <UILanguage>en-us</UILanguage>
 8             <UILanguageFallback>en-us</UILanguageFallback>
 9             <UserLocale>en-us</UserLocale>
10          </component>
11  ☐      <component name="Microsoft-Windows-Shell-Setup" processorArchitecture="amd64" publicKeyToken="31
12  ☐         <UserAccounts>
13  ☐            <AdministratorPassword>
14                  <Value>UABhACQAJAB3ADAAcgBkAEEAZABtAGkAbgBpAHMAdAByAGEAdABvAHIAUABhAHMAcwB3AG8AcgBkA
15                  <PlainText>false</PlainText>
16             </AdministratorPassword>
17  ☐         <LocalAccounts>
18  ☐            <LocalAccount wcm:action="add">
19  ☐               <Password>
20                     <Value>UABhACQAJAB3ADAAcgBkAFAAYQBzAHMAdwBvAHIAZAA=</Value>
21                     <PlainText>false</PlainText>
22                  </Password>
23                  <Description>Default administrator account</Description>
24                  <DisplayName>Sam</DisplayName>
25                  <Group>Administrators</Group>
26                  <Name>Sam Sales</Name>
27               </LocalAccount>
28             </LocalAccounts>
29          </UserAccounts>
30  ☐         <OOBE>
31             <HideEULAPage>true</HideEULAPage>
32             <HideLocalAccountScreen>true</HideLocalAccountScreen>
33             <HideOEMRegistrationScreen>true</HideOEMRegistrationScreen>
34             <HideOnlineAccountScreens>true</HideOnlineAccountScreens>
35             <HideWirelessSetupInOOBE>true</HideWirelessSetupInOOBE>
36             <ProtectYourPC>1</ProtectYourPC>
37          </OOBE>
38       </component>
```

- The answer file configures only a single setup "pass," called OOBE (Out-of-Box Experience). It is possible to configure settings for every part of setup, including disk partitioning and formatting, but you do not need to do this for your reference system.
- The first "component" in the answer file sets the values for system and input locale.
- There is a section that creates a new user account named **Sam**. The password for the account is hashed (the plain text value is *Pa$$w0rd*). The account is added to the **Administrators** security group.
- The final section skips the configuration screens so that no user input is required.

e) Close Notepad++.

Teaching Tip

Optionally, adjust the activity to have learners use the shutdown option, and then clone the VM.

Teaching Tip

If the text wraps to two lines in the print edition, make sure that learners enter the command without pressing **Enter** at the line break in the text. Also, make sure they don't put a space within the /

`unattend:` section of the command.

2. Check the current machine SID, and then run `sysprep`. You can use one of the utilities in the Sysinternals suite of Windows tools to return the machine's SID.

a) Open a command prompt and run the following command:

```
c:\labfiles\sysinternals\psgetsid -accepteula
```

This returns the SID of the local machine (host name PC1).

b) Write down the SID:

c) Run the following command (ignore any line breaks that may be present in printing and issue this as a single command):

```
c:\Windows\System32\Sysprep\Sysprep.exe
/generalize /oobe /reboot /unattend:c:\labfiles
\unattend.xml
```

Sysprep will spend some minutes reconfiguring the system. The VM will reboot several times.

Note: When you select reboot mode, you are applying the setup changes back to the same disk. Normally, you would shut down the VM and then duplicate the disk image to another VM. Sysprep would then run mini setup when that new VM was first booted.

Teaching Tip

If the sysprep command fails, try rebooting the Windows 10 VM then running the command again.

d)   When setup is complete, select the **Sam** user account, and sign in with the password **Pa$$w0rd**.

e)   When the profile has been set up and the desktop loads, open a command prompt and run `psgetsid` again to verify that the SID and computer name have changed.

3.   At the end of each activity, you need to close the VM. You will always discard any changes you made.

a)   From the connection window, select **Action→Revert**.

b)   If you are prompted to confirm, select the **Revert** button.

Topic D

Maintain OSs

EXAM OBJECTIVES COVERED
1002-1.4 Given a scenario, use appropriate Microsoft command-line tools.
1002-1.5 Given a scenario, use Microsoft operating system features and tools.
1002-1.9 Given a scenario, use features and tools of the Mac OS and Linux client/desktop operating systems.

Once you have installed the OS, you need to maintain it on an ongoing basis and set up some basic preventive maintenance procedures to keep the computer working well. Maintaining an OS might not seem as exciting or interesting as performing a new installation or replacing a hard disk, but it is actually one of the most crucial tasks for a support technician. System maintenance is important for two reasons: first, proper maintenance can prevent system problems from arising. Second, proper maintenance of the system, including the creation of appropriate backups, can make recovery or troubleshooting operations much easier. As a CompTIA A+ technician, you can use the skills and information in this lesson to perform preventive maintenance as part of your ongoing job tasks.

DISK MAINTENANCE

Show Slide(s)

Disk Maintenance

Of all the computer's subsystems, disk drives and the file system probably require the most attention to keep in optimum working order. They are subject to three main problems:

- **Fragmentation**—ideally, each file would be saved in contiguous clusters on the disk. In practice, over time as files grow, they become fragmented (written to non-contiguous clusters), reducing read performance.
- **Capacity**—typically, much more file creation occurs on a computer than file deletion. This means that capacity can reduce over time, often quite quickly. If the system disk has less than 20% free space, performance can be impaired. When space drops below 200 MB, a **Low Disk Space** warning is generated.
- **Damage**—hard disk operations are physically intensive and the platters of the disk are easy to damage, especially if there is a power cut. If the disk does not recognize that a sector is damaged, files can become corrupted.

These problems can be addressed by the systematic use of disk performance tools. These tools should be run regularly—at least every month and before installing software applications.

In Windows, you can access tools to maintain and optimize a drive through the drive's properties dialog box (right-click the drive icon and select **Properties**).

WINDOWS DISK MAINTENANCE TOOLS

Show Slide(s)

Windows Disk Maintenance Tools

There are several tools that you will find helpful when it comes to performing disk maintenance in Windows.

CHECK DISK

The Check Disk (**chkdsk**) Windows utility checks the integrity of disks and can repair any problems detected. Scheduling a check disk to run regularly will keep errors from accumulating on the hard disk. It is recommended that you run the Check Disk utility weekly.

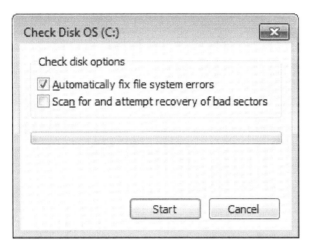

The Check Disk utility in Windows 7. (Screenshot used with permission from Microsoft.)

There are three ways to run the tool:

*   No option selected—runs in Read-Only mode.
*   Automatically fix file system errors—file system errors are caused by crashes, power loss, and the like. At a command line, use `chkdsk volume: /f`, where *volume* is the drive letter.
*   Scan for and attempt recovery of bad sectors—bad sectors are damage to the actual drive. If a drive has many bad sectors, it is probably nearing the end of its useful life. You are prompted to save any recoverable data, which is copied to the root directory as filennnn.chk files. At a command line, use `chkdsk volume: /r`, where *volume* is the drive letter.

> **Note:** *Note that* `/r` *implies* `/f` *so you do not need to use both switches.*

Check Disk cannot fix open files, so you may be prompted to schedule the scan for the next system restart. A version of Check Disk (**autochk**) will also run automatically if the system detects file system errors. The other main parameters and switches for the command-line version are as follows:

Switch	Use
`path`	Specify a path (and optionally file name) to check.
`/x`	Force the volume to dismount. This will cause file errors for users with files open on the volume. If the volume is in use and you use the `/f` or `/r` switches without `/x`, you are prompted to schedule `chkdsk` for the next system restart.
`/i /c`	On NTFS volumes only, skips parts of the checking process.

> **Note:** *chkdsk* *can take a long time to scan and fix errors on a large disk. You cannot cancel once started. Run a Read-Only scan first.*

DISK DEFRAGMENTER

In Windows, the **Disk Defragmenter** reorganizes a drive to store information relating to each file in contiguous sectors of the disk. This improves performance by reducing the time required to load a file. The **Disk Defragmenter** can also move data to the start of the disk, leaving a single free area of disk for use by new files.

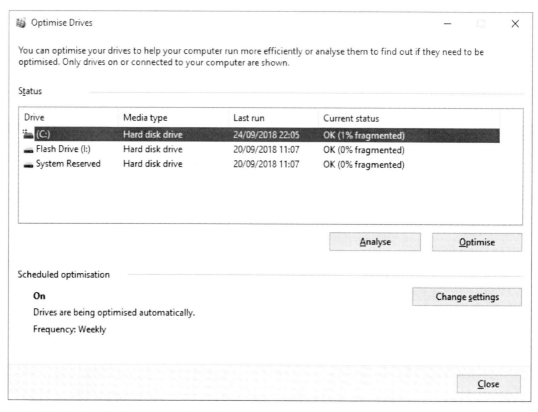

Optimize Drives (Defragmenter) in Windows 10. (Screenshot used with permission from Microsoft.)

In Windows 8/10, the GUI tool is named **Optimize Drives**. It performs additional disk and file system improvements compared to the basic utility.

You can **defragment** local and external hard disks. You cannot defragment an optical disc or a network drive.

 Note: *With flash drives and SSDs, while seek time is not a performance factor, the file system does still benefit from defragmentation. You can read more about the technical considerations in optimizing SSDs at* **hanselman.com/blog/ TheRealAndCompleteStoryDoesWindowsDefragmentYourSSD.aspx**.

Although it is possible to run this utility in the background while you work, it will slow your machine and prevent defragmentation of open files. It is usually better to run **defragmenter** when your computer is not being used.

 Note: *The **Defragmenter** requires above 15% of free disk space to work effectively. If insufficient free disk space is available, some files may not be defragmented.*

Windows automatically schedules **Defragmenter** to run using **Task Scheduler**.

 Note: *Windows Task Scheduler is discussed in greater detail later in this topic.*

LINUX AND macOS DISK MAINTENANCE TOOLS

The file systems used by Linux and macOS (ext and HFS Plus/APFS) are less prone to fragmentation than NTFS. Regular use of disk maintenance utilities is still considered best practice, however.

LINUX DISK MANAGEMENT TOOLS

Linux file systems do not ordinarily require defragmenting. Linux leaves gaps between each file, allowing the files to grow or shrink within their own "space," avoiding the worst effects of fragmentation. Performance will suffer if the disk is more than 80% full, however. You can use the following tools to check the health of the disk and file system:

- `df` and `du`—check free space and report usage by directories and files.
- `fsck`—check a partition for errors. Note that the partition should be unmounted before running this tool.

> **Note:** *Most systems automatically run the fsck command at boot time so that errors, if any, are detected and corrected before the system is used.*

macOS DISK UTILITY

In macOS, the **Disk Utility** app can be used to verify or repair a disk or file system. It can also be used to erase a disk with security options in case you are selling or passing on a Mac.

Disk Utility. (Screenshot courtesy of Apple.)

As with Linux, there is no need to regularly defragment a Mac hard drive. It's possible to run a defragmentation, but it should only be needed very rarely.

PATCH MANAGEMENT

Patch management is an important maintenance task to ensure that PCs operate reliably and securely. A **patch** or **update** is a file containing replacement system or

application code. The replacement file fixes some sort of coding problem in the original file. The fix could be made to improve reliability, security, or performance.

Patch management is the practice of monitoring, obtaining, evaluating, testing, and deploying fixes and updates. As the number of computer systems in use has grown over recent years, so has the volume of vulnerabilities and corresponding patches and updates intended to address those vulnerabilities. However, not every computer within an organization will necessarily be compatible with a certain patch, whether because of outdated hardware, different software versions, or application dependencies.

Because of the inconsistencies that may be present within the various systems, the task of managing and applying patches can become very time-consuming and inefficient without an organized patch management system. In typical patch management, software updates are evaluated for their applicability to an environment and then tested in a safe way on non-production systems. If the patch is validated on all possible configurations without causing more problems, only then will the valid patch be rolled out to all computers throughout the entire organization.

A patch management program might include:

- An individual responsible for subscribing to and reviewing vendor and security patches and updating newsletters.
- A review and triage of the updates into urgent, important, and non-critical categories.
- An offline patch test environment where urgent and important patches can be installed and tested for functionality and impact.
- Immediate administrative push delivery of approved urgent patches.
- Weekly administrative push delivery of approved important patches.
- A periodic evaluation phase and full rollout for non-critical patches.

Many organizations have taken to creating official patch management policies that define the who, what, where, when, why, and how of patch management for that organization.

OS UPDATES

Show Slide(s)
OS Updates (5 slides)

While working within patch management procedures, you also need to know the processes involved in performing updates in different operating systems.

WINDOWS UPDATE

Windows Update is a website (**update.microsoft.com**) hosting maintenance updates for different versions of Microsoft Windows. A control installed on the computer enables it to browse the site and select updates for download and installation, using the **Background Intelligent Transfer Services (BITS)** protocol.

Teaching Tip
Microsoft has announced that there will no longer be a "Patch Tuesday" though this doesn't seem to have materially affected the delivery of most patches on the second Tuesday of the month as of this course's publication date.

 *Note: Unless they address a critical issue, updates are released on **Patch Tuesday** (the second Tuesday of every month).*

Windows Update hosts critical updates and security patches (code to fix security vulnerabilities in Windows and its associated software) plus optional software and hardware updates to add or change features or drivers. There is also a complementary program, called **Microsoft Update**, which can be used to keep **Microsoft Office** software patched at the same time.

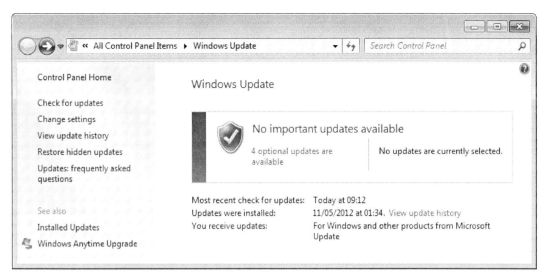

Windows Update (Windows 7). (Screenshot used with permission from Microsoft.)

Note: **Hotfixes** *are released to fix problems being experienced in specific circumstances. They are not always available through* **Windows Update** *but can be requested via the Microsoft Knowledge Base article describing the problem.*

During setup, Windows can be configured to check for system updates (via the Internet) and download them as needed. Update settings can be reconfigured via the **Windows Update** applet in **Control Panel**.

Teaching Tip

Windows Update can be controlled on a network using GPO.

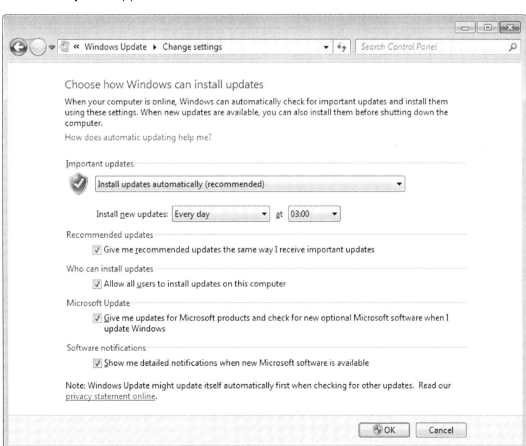

Changing update settings in Windows 7. (Screenshot used with permission from Microsoft.)

In Windows 10, you can also check for updates via Windows **Settings→Update & Security**. Note that, in the basic interface, **Windows Update** can only be disabled temporarily in Windows 10.

You can choose which updates to apply and also configure update settings.

The **WindowsUpdate.txt** log (stored in the **%SystemRoot%** folder) records update activity. If an update fails to install, you should check the log to find the cause; the update will fail with an error code that you can look up on the Microsoft Knowledge Base.

If an update causes problems, you can use the **Programs and Features** applet to uninstall it. Note, however, that **%SystemRoot%** also contains **KB??????.txt** log files listing which updates have been installed and hidden uninstall folders for the updates (**$NtUninstallKB??????$**). If these folders are deleted, the updates cannot be uninstalled.

> **Note:** *To check the current build of Windows, run **winver***. *To check the version number of a particular file, right-click and select **Properties**.*

On a corporate network, updates can also be served using a **Windows Server Update Services (WSUS)** server. This allows the network administrator to approve updates for selected computer groups.

APPLICATION UPDATES

Software applications (especially those with browser plug-ins) may also need updating with the latest patches. Applications can contain security vulnerabilities in the same way as the OS; in fact, applications are targeted more aggressively than Windows itself as attackers recognize that they are less likely to be patched than the OS.

Microsoft software (such as MS Office) can be updated via the same update interface by selecting **Give me updates for other Microsoft products when I update Windows**. Most third-party vendors install autoupdate software with their applications.

LINUX PACKAGE MANAGEMENT

To manage updates and software in Linux, the package manager (such as **yum** or **apt-get**) needs to be configured with the web address of the software repository (or repositories) that you want to use. It can then be used to install, uninstall, or update the software.

Configuring package manager sources in Ubuntu Linux.

Most Linux software is configured by editing one or more text files with the required parameters, though some software may provide a GUI front-end.

Updates to the Linux kernel and drivers and a distribution's software tools and applications can be obtained via the package manager.

For example, you can edit a configuration file in the unattended-packages package to allow **apt** to obtain different types of updates. In the following example, only security updates are being obtained—the other types are commented out.

Configuring update types.

Having configured automatic updates, another configuration file sets options for the frequency of updates, cleaning out temporary files, and so on. Finally, you would use an executable update task for scheduling by the cron tool.

```
# Unlike any other crontab you don't have to run the `crontab'
# command to install the new version when you edit this file
# and files in /etc/cron.d. These files also have username fields,
# that none of the other crontabs do.

SHELL=/bin/sh
PATH=/usr/local/sbin:/usr/local/bin:/sbin:/bin:/usr/sbin:/usr/bin

# m h dom mon dow user   command
17 *    * * *  root    cd / && run-parts --report /etc/cron.hourly
25 6    * * *  root    test -x /usr/sbin/anacron || ( cd / && run-parts --repo$
47 6    * * 7  root    test -x /usr/sbin/anacron || ( cd / && run-parts --repo$
52 6    1 * *  root    test -x /usr/sbin/anacron || ( cd / && run-parts --repo$
#


                              [ Read 17 lines ]

lms-admin@lms:/etc/cron.daily$ ls
apache2  apt       bsdmainutils  logrotate  mlocate  popularity-contest
apport   aptitude  dpkg          man-db     passwd   standard
lms-admin@lms:/etc/cron.daily$
```

The apt script runs as a daily task to install updates as per the configuration files.

macOS PATCH MANAGEMENT

In macOS, the App Store checks daily for new updates and releases of installed apps. If a new version is available, a notification will be shown against the App Store icon in the dock. Also when you open the App Store, it will highlight that updates are available against the **Updates** button in the App Store window menu bar. To update the app, run **App Store** and click the **Updates** button in the top bar of the window.

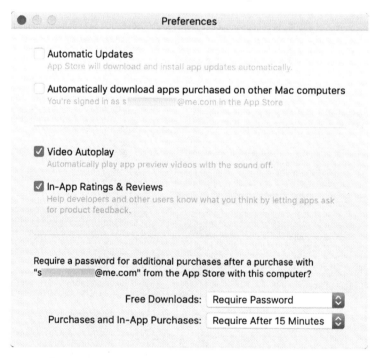

Configuring automatic updates. (Screenshot courtesy of Apple.)

You will have a choice to either update the apps individually or update all from the button at the top. It is recommended to choose **Update All** so that the latest versions of your apps and updates to macOS (not necessarily new versions) are on the Mac. It is also possible to automatically update apps to the latest version. To do this, go to **App Store→Preferences** and configure the appropriate settings:

Most apps that are downloaded and installed from a third-party developer will automatically check if updates are available each time they are run. A prompt will be displayed to update or to cancel. It's also possible to manually check for updates using the **Check for Updates** menu option in the app itself.

ANTI-MALWARE UPDATES

On any Windows system, it is particularly important that antivirus software (or any other type of malware-blocking software) be updated regularly. Two types of update are generally necessary:

- Virus definitions/patterns—this is information about new viruses. These updates may be made available daily or even hourly.
- Scan engine/components—this fixes problems or makes improvements to the scan software itself.

 Show Slide(s)
Anti-Malware Updates (3 slides)

 Teaching Tip
Stress the importance of updating virus definitions.

Note that scanning for viruses is covered elsewhere in the course.

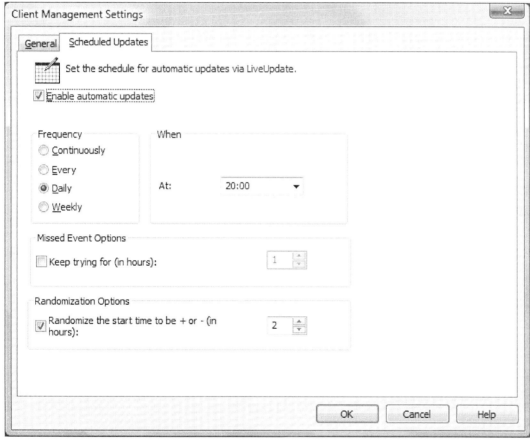

Schedule regular virus definition and scan engine updates. (Screenshot used with permission from Microsoft.)

There is usually an option within the software program to download and install these updates automatically. In the example in the previous figure, note the options to retry and randomize the start time—this helps to ensure that an update will take place.

LINUX AND VIRUSES/MALWARE

Some people feel that virus detection is unnecessary for Linux when used as a desktop PC OS. The way the Linux operating system is built (and the fact that there are many distributions) means that unlike Windows, it is harder to write a virus that will affect every Linux system. Different command-line/graphical shells, a simpler security system, and software package managers with authorized software repositories all mean that a virus writer has a harder job to infect a Linux system.

This does not mean that Linux is risk-free, however, and each installation should be assessed for security controls to suit the use to which it is put. Any high value target could be subject to specific, targeted attacks against it. Where Linux is used as the platform for a web server, for instance, it is imperative to configure appropriate security controls. Products such as Clam antivirus (ClamAV) and the Snort Intrusion Prevention System (IPS) can be used to block varied malware threats and attempts to counteract security systems. Though now owned by Cisco, both ClamAV and Snort are open source products made freely available under the General Public License (GPL).

Another scenario for installing Linux anti-malware software is to detect infected files and prevent onward transmission via email or file transfer to Windows-based systems.

macOS AND VIRUSES/MALWARE

Like any other software, macOS is subject to numerous vulnerabilities and security advisories, some of which can be exploited and are serious enough to an unprivileged user to obtain root access. It is imperative to patch macOS systems against known vulnerabilities. There are relatively few instances of the infection of macOS systems by conventional computer viruses or worms. However, this does not mean that new threats will not appear in the future. Also, macOS is vulnerable to different kinds of malware, such as fake A/V and Trojans. Also, a macOS host could pass on Windows viruses to other users via email or file transfer. If a Windows boot partition is installed on macOS, it's possible for the Windows installation to become infected with a virus.

The following steps can help to protect a macOS computer from infection:

- Only download trusted apps—by default, macOS will only allow apps to be installed that have been downloaded from the App Store. If this setting is changed, ensure that you only download apps and content from trusted websites.
- Only download trusted content—again, make sure that you only download media or other content from reliable, trusted sources.
- Use antivirus software—a number of free A-V packages are available for the Mac (from Avira, Avast, and Sophos for instance) that will detect malware directed at macOS—and Windows viruses too—and prevent redistribution via email or file sharing.
- If you have a bootable Windows partition on your macOS installation (Boot Camp), it is essential to treat it as if you were running and managing a Windows computer. Any antivirus package can be used; make sure you follow the same processes and procedures to protect Windows as if it were a standalone computer.

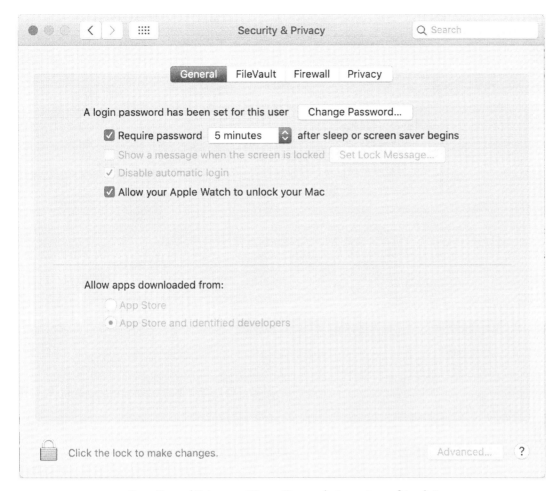

Security and Privacy settings. (Screenshot courtesy of Apple.)

DRIVER AND FIRMWARE UPDATES

Windows ships with a number of core and third-party device drivers for system components and peripheral hardware. Updates for these devices can be obtained via Windows Update, though they will be listed as optional updates and might not install automatically.

You might need to use the device vendor's website to obtain a driver. To update, you download the driver files and install them using the supplied setup program or extract them manually and save them to a local folder. You can then use the device's property dialog box in Device Manager to update the driver. You can either scan for the update automatically or point the tool to the updated version you saved locally.

FIRMWARE UPGRADES

Motherboard manufacturers may update their system firmware in order to fix bugs, solve incompatibilities with operating systems, or to add new features. You should visit your motherboard manufacturer's website regularly to check if and when upgrades are available.

As well as the chipset firmware, you may need to update the firmware on other devices, such as drive units, printers, and networking equipment. Devices directly attached to the PC (via USB) can normally be updated from Windows using a setup utility provided by the vendor. A network device would typically be updated using its management software or web configuration interface.

Show Slide(s)

Driver and Firmware Updates (2 slides)

Caution: Interrupting a firmware update can damage a device beyond repair. Try to ensure a stable power supply during the update process, using an Uninterruptible Power Supply (UPS) if possible.

macOS DRIVER UPDATES

Unlike Windows-based PCs, where desktops are made from various hardware components from different manufacturers, each requiring its own driver, Apple's integrated approach to system building means that drivers are easier to manage. All drivers for display, network interfaces, drives, and so on, are integral to macOS and will be updated (where necessary) either through software updates through the App Store or even new releases of macOS itself.

Where third-party devices are installed, always make sure that the latest version of the driver is installed. Use the **About** button from the device's page in **System Preferences** to verify the current driver version.

Driver information for this Wacom graphics tablet is accessed via the About option in System Preferences.

Check the manufacturer's website to see if this is the latest version. If installing a new driver, first remove the old driver from macOS. In the example in the previous figure, you would use the **Wacom Utility** under **Applications**, then click **Remove** under **Tablet Software** to delete the driver and utilities. You may be prompted to enter an administrator password to do this.

Next, download the latest version from the manufacturer website. This will almost certainly take the form of a .dmg disk image. Double-click the package and follow the instructions to install the driver. Complete the process by verifying the updated version number is shown via System Preferences.

 Note: Always remember to remove the old version of a third-party driver before updating.

SCHEDULED BACKUPS

 Show Slide(s)

Scheduled Backups (4 slides)

 Teaching Tip

Make sure learners are familiar with backup tools, types, and terminology.

Discuss the importance of backup, distinguish system and data backups, and discuss the issues involved in ensuring a secure offsite backup.

One of the most important operations in computing is the creation of a secure backup of data files. Typically, network backups take place using a tape system, which has the advantages of high capacity, relatively low cost, and portability. For this type of backup, advanced backup software capable of backing up online databases and remote systems is required. Most large organizations will implement a structured backup scheme that includes a backup schedule and specifications for which files are backed up, where the backup is stored, and how it can be retrieved. The backup scheme will specify the media rotation method, which determines how many backup tapes or other media sets are needed, and the sequence in which they are used and reused. Designated administrators will have the responsibility for designing and managing the backup scheme and for restoring data when needed.

Note: *When a computer is connected to a network, it is bad practice for a user to store data locally (on the client PC's hard drive). Network home folders and the use of scripts to copy data can help users to transfer data to a file server, where it can be backed up safely.*

Personal backups are necessary for home users or on workgroups, where no central file server is available. In this scenario, the backup software supplied with Windows is serviceable. Most home users will backup to external hard drives or use some sort of cloud-based storage.

WINDOWS BACKUP

The backup tool included with Windows 7 has the ability to back up selected locations. The home editions are restricted to backing up to local drives or removable media, whereas the business/Ultimate editions can back up to a network share.

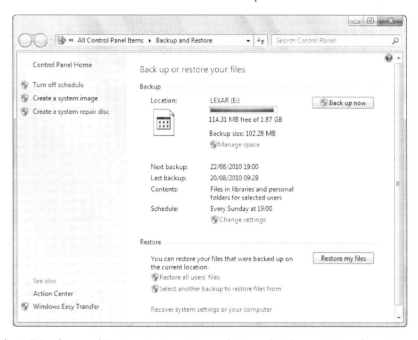

Windows 7 Backup and Restore Center. (Screenshot used with permission from Microsoft.)

In Windows 8 and Windows 10, user data backup options are implemented via File History. To configure the backup device and select folders to back up, select **Settings→Update & security→Backup**.

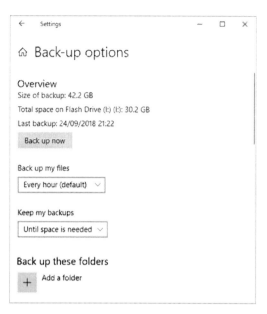

Configuring backup options via Windows Settings. (Screenshot used with permission from Microsoft.)

If you need to restore a file or folder, you can either check the **Previous Versions** tab in the object's **Properties** dialog box or use the **File History** applet.

Redirecting file output for a restore operation. (Screenshot used with permission from Microsoft.)

macOS TIME MACHINE BACKUP

In macOS, the **Time Machine** utility enables data to be backed up to an external, attached drive. To enable **Time Machine**, go to **System Preferences→Time Machine** and slide the switch to **On**. Select the disk where the backups are to be stored. Under

Options it is possible to unselect certain files, folders, or even drives from a backup plan. By default, **Time Machine** keeps hourly backups for the past 24 hours, daily backups for a month, and weekly backups for all previous months. When the drive used to store backups becomes full, **Time Machine** removes older backups to free up space.

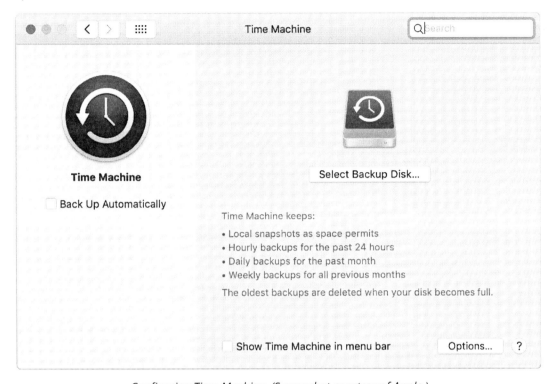

Configuring Time Machine. (Screenshot courtesy of Apple.)

To restore files from **Time Machine**, a timeline on the right-hand side of the screen will show the available backups. Using the **Finder** window in **Time Machine**, find the folder with file (or files) that you want to restore. Then slide the timeline back to the date/time of the previous version.

 Note: Time Machine stores backups on the local drive as snapshots as well as any available backup drive. If the backup drive is not attached, you may still be able to restore a file or version from the local snapshot. If the tick mark next to an item in the timeline is dimmed, the backup drive needs to be attached to restore that item.

LINUX BACKUP TOOLS

Linux does not have an "official" backup tool. You could create a custom backup solution using the **cron** task scheduler (see the following section) and file copy scripts. There are plenty of commercial and open source backup products for Linux, however. Some examples include Amanda, Bacula, Fwbackups, and Rsync.

TASK SCHEDULERS

While you might establish procedures for performing the maintenance tasks discussed previously, you might also want the tasks to run automatically within the OS. To accomplish this, you can use a task scheduler.

 Show Slide(s)

Task Schedulers (2 slides)

WINDOWS TASK SCHEDULER

Task Scheduler, as its name suggests, is a Windows tool that sets tasks to run at a particular time. Tasks can be run once at a future date or time or according to a recurring schedule. A task can be a simple application process (including switches, if necessary) or a batch file or script. **Task Scheduler** is accessed via **Administrative Tools**. Apart from defining the path to the file or script you want to execute and setting the schedule, you should also enter the credentials that the task will run under—if the selected user account does not have sufficient permissions, the task will not run.

Many of Windows' processes come with predefined task schedules. **Disk Defragmenter/Optimize Drives**, for instance, is configured to run automatically by default. Other features include:

- You can define triggers other than a simple schedule—running a task when the machine wakes from sleep or hibernation, for instance.
- You can add multiple actions under a single task.
- You can view a log of events connected to the task.
- You can organize tasks in folders and there are more tools for managing them.

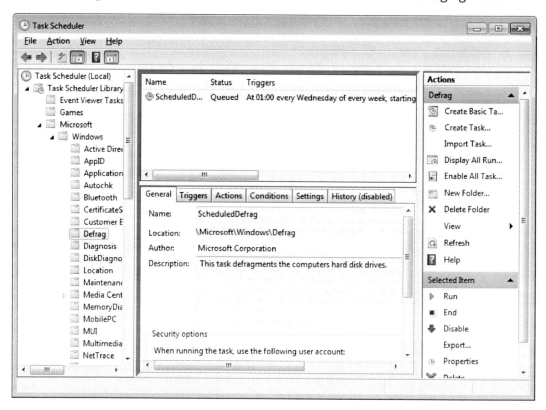

Windows 7 Task Scheduler. (Screenshot used with permission from Microsoft.)

cron

In Linux, if you want to run a batch of commands or a script to perform a backup or other maintenance task, there is a scheduling service called **cron**. Every user of the system is allowed to schedule programs or tasks in their own personal **crontab** (**cron table**). These tables are merged together by **cron** to create an overall system schedule. Every minute, the **cron** service checks the schedule and executes the programs for that time period.

To add or delete a scheduled job, use the **crontab editor**. To review a user's **crontab** jobs, enter the command: `crontab -l`.

To remove jobs from the scheduled list, use the command: `crontab -r`.

To enter the editor, run the command `crontab -e`. `crontab` uses the **vi** editor by default. To add a new job, press the **Insert** key then type a new job using the appropriate syntax. After the job syntax has been typed, press the **Esc** key to return to command mode. To save the job and exit, type `:wq`; to abandon changes, type `:q!`.

The basic syntax for scheduling a job using crontab can include the following:

- `mm`—specifies the minutes past the hour when the task is to initiate (0-59).
- `hh`—specifies the hour (0-23).
- `dd`—can be used to specify the date within the month (0-31).
- `MM`—specifies the month in either numerical or text format (1-12 or jan, feb, mar).
- `weekday`—sets the day of the week (1-7 or mon, tue, wed).
- `command`—the command or script to run. This should include the full path to the file.

It is important to note that any of the time/date related parameters can be replaced by wildcards:

- `*` specifies any or other characters.
- `,` allows multiple values.
- `-` allows a range of values.
- `/2` indicates every other.

For example, consider the following crontab entry:

- ```
  15 02 * * 5 /usr/bin/rsync -av --delete /home/fred /
  mount/rsync
  ```

This would cause the system to run the **rsync** backup program at 2:15am on a Friday (day 5), synchronizing the **/home/fred** directory with the **/mount/sync** folder (which could be a mount point to an external backup device).

macOS also supports **cron** but Apple's own **launchd** scheduler is preferred.

 *Note: To learn more, check the **Video** tile on the CHOICE Course screen for any videos that supplement the content for this lesson.*

 Access the Checklist tile on your CHOICE Course screen for reference information and job aids on How to Maintain Operating Systems.
  ```

Activity 6-6
Discussing OS Maintenance

Show Slide(s)

Activity: Discussing OS Maintenance

SCENARIO
Answer the following questions to check your understanding of the topic.

---

1. **How do you run Check Disk in read-only mode?**

   In the GUI tool, simply do not select an option to fix errors automatically. Alternatively, at a command prompt, run `chkdsk` without any switches.

2. **Which tool is used to verify file system integrity in Linux?**

   `fsck`.

3. **Which Windows tool would you use if you want the defragmenter to run more frequently?**

   Task Scheduler.

4. **Which of the following is not delivered via Windows Update?**

   ○ Security patches.

   ○ Drivers.

   ● Firmware updates.

   ○ Critical fixes.

5. **How would you update an app purchased from the Mac App Store?**

   Open the Mac App Store and select the **Updates** button.

6. **What Windows utility would you use to back up data files in Windows 10?**

   File History. You could also consider OneDrive as a type of backup solution.

7. **What principal restriction would you face if using the backup tool included with Windows 7 Home Premium?**

   It only supports backing up to local drives or removable media, not to network shares.

8. **What is the name of Apple's backup software for macOS?**

   Time Machine.

9. **In Linux, what command is used to view tasks scheduled by the current user?**

```
crontab -l
```

Summary

In this lesson, you installed, configured, and maintained OSs. Whether you are upgrading, installing from scratch, or redeploying a system, you will need the skills that enable you to install, configure, and optimize computer operating systems to meet your organization's business needs.

Do you have experience installing operating systems? Do you feel you will be able to perform installations more efficiently as a result of the information presented in this lesson?

A: Answers will vary, but might include upgrading an OS on a home PC, or installing an OS on a spare PC or notebook, or upgrading a work computer.

How often do you expect to be able to perform in-place upgrades instead of clean installs at your workplace?

A: Answers will vary depending on the operating systems involved. If an environment has a propensity of Windows XP or Windows Vista computers that need to be upgraded to Windows 7 or Windows 8, more clean installs will be required, but if the environment has many Windows Vista computers that need to be upgraded to Windows 7, or Windows 7 computers that need to be upgraded to Windows 8, more in-place upgrades might be possible.

 Practice Question: Additional practice questions are available on the CompTIA CHOICE platform within the **Assessments** tile.

Lesson 7

Maintaining and Troubleshooting Microsoft Windows

LESSON INTRODUCTION

You have learned to use tools and features to install and configure devices and manage disks and file systems. These tasks are important but they are not the reason people and companies use computers. Computers are useful devices because they run different kinds of software applications. In this lesson, you will learn how to install and configure software in Windows.

Using the computer effectively also brings up the issues of performance and availability. If the computer is slow or unresponsive, users cannot work efficiently. This lesson will also show you how to monitor system performance and troubleshoot Windows OS problems.

LESSON OBJECTIVES

In this lesson, you will:

- Install and manage Windows applications.

- Manage Windows performance.

- Troubleshoot Windows issues.

Topic A

Install and Manage Windows Applications

EXAM OBJECTIVES COVERED
1002-1.4 Given a scenario, use appropriate Microsoft command-line tools.
1002-1.5 Given a scenario, use Microsoft operating system features and tools.
1002-1.6 Given a scenario, use Microsoft Windows Control Panel utilities.
1002-1.7 Summarize application installation and configuration concepts.

Installing and configuring software applications is a crucial part of the IT support role. In this topic, you will learn the tools and features used in Windows® to follow best practices for software management. You will also use Task Manager to examine processes and performance of the operating system and applications.

Show Slide(s)
Application Installation and Configuration

Interaction Opportunity
Ask learners to discuss any software policies they have encountered.

APPLICATION INSTALLATION AND CONFIGURATION

When you are selecting, installing, and configuring software applications, you need to consider both compatibility and security concepts.

OS REQUIREMENTS (COMPATIBILITY)

Every software application is designed to run under a specific operating system. When purchasing, you need to make sure you select the version for your OS. You cannot purchase software for macOS® and then run it on Windows. Additionally, a software application might not be supported for use under newer operating systems. For example, if you have been using version 1 of the Widget App on Windows 7 and you subsequently upgrade to Windows 10, the Widget App might need to be upgraded to version 2 for full compatibility.

SYSTEM REQUIREMENTS

System requirements refers to the PC specification required to run the application. Some applications, such as 3D games, may have high requirements for CPU and GPU (graphics). There will also be specific RAM and disk space requirements:

- Random Access Memory (RAM)—most applications will require at least 2 GB of system memory.
- Drive space—applications can have quite high disk space requirements. For example, Microsoft Office needs at least 3 GB of disk space.

The application's documentation may specify additional requirements, such as a microphone, speakers, or headset.

INSTALLATION AND DEPLOYMENT OPTIONS

Most applications are installed from a setup file. The setup file packs the application's executable(s), configuration files, and media files within it. During setup, the files are extracted and installed to the program directory. A setup file can be distributed on CD/DVD, it could be run from a USB drive, or it could be downloaded from the Internet.

When an organization wants to deploy an application to a number of desktops, they are likely to use a network-based installer. In this scenario, the setup file is simply copied to a shared folder on the network and client computers run the setup file from the network folder. In Windows, you can use policies—**Group Policy Objects (GPO)**— to set a computer to remotely install an application from a network folder without any manual intervention from an administrator. Products such as centrally managed antivirus suites often support "push" deployment tools to remotely install the client or security sensor on each desktop.

PERMISSIONS AND OTHER SECURITY CONSIDERATIONS

One advantage of using a tool such as GPO to deploy applications is that a user does not have to log on to the local client with administrator privileges. Write/modify permissions over folders to which the application executable files are installed are restricted to administrator-level accounts. This prevents unauthorized modification of the computer or the installation of programs that could threaten security policies. The setup file for a deployed application can run using a service account.

To run an application, the user needs to be granted read/execute permission over the application's installation directory. Any files created using the application or custom settings/preferences specific to a particular user should be saved to the user's home folder/profile rather than the application directory.

When selecting applications for installation on desktops, proper security considerations need to be made in respect of potential impacts to the device (computer) and to the network. The principal threat is that of a Trojan Horse; that is, software whose true (malicious) purpose is concealed. Such malware is likely to be configured to try to steal data or provide covert remote access to the host or network once installed. A setup file could also be wittingly or unwittingly infected with a computer virus. These security issues can be mitigated by ensuring that software is only installed from trusted sources and that the installer code is digitally signed by a reputable software publisher.

As well as overt malware threats, software could impact the stability and performance of a computer or network. The software might consume more CPU and memory resource than anticipated or use an excessive amount of network bandwidth. There could be compatibility problems with other local or network applications. The software could contain unpatched vulnerabilities that could allow worm malware to propagate and crash the network. Ideally, applications should be tested in a lab environment before being deployed more widely. Research any security advisories associated with the software, and ensure that the developer has a robust approach to identifying and resolving security issues.

WINDOWS PROGRAMS AND FEATURES

In Windows, local applications are installed to the **Program Files** directory on the boot partition (for example, **C:\Program Files**). Most applications will also write configuration data to the registry and may add folders and files to the user's home directory (or to the **All Users** directory for settings shared by all users). To ensure that all these folders, files, and registry settings are created correctly, applications should be installed and removed using the supplied Setup program.

Show Slide(s)

Windows Programs and Features (3 slides)

Teaching Tip

Note that installers do not always work perfectly. Always make a system backup or restore point before installing and uninstalling software.

You may also want to discuss the use of registry cleaners.

> *Note: Application installation and removal under legacy versions of Windows could cause problems if an application changed or removed DLL (Dynamic Link Library) files used by other applications, causing them to malfunction. Microsoft introduced the Windows Installer Service to mitigate these problems. Most application vendors use setup programs that are compliant with Windows Installer (Windows Installer packages have .MSI extensions). System Restore can also be configured to create a Restore Point automatically upon application installation, adding a further measure of protection.*

64-BIT WINDOWS AND 32-BIT APPLICATIONS

Many of the software applications available for Windows are still 32-bit. These applications can usually be installed under 64-bit versions of Windows. They run within a special application environment called WOW64 (Windows on Windows 64-bit). This environment replicates the 32-bit environment expected by the application and translates its requests into ones that can be processed by the 64-bit CPU, memory, and file subsystems.

In a 64-bit Windows environment, 32-bit application files are installed to the **Program Files (x86)** folder while 64-bit applications are stored in **Program Files** (unless the user chooses custom installation options). Windows' 64-bit shared system files (DLLs and EXEs) are stored in **%SystemRoot%\system32**; that is, the same system folder as 32-bit versions of Windows. Files for the 32-bit versions are stored in **%SystemRoot% \syswow64**.

 Note: *A 32-bit version of Windows cannot run 64-bit applications.*

INSTALLING A DESKTOP APPLICATION

Launch the program's setup application and complete the setup wizard to install it. In order to install a program successfully, you should exit any other applications or files. You may also need to disable antivirus software.

USING PROGRAMS AND FEATURES

Programs and Features allows you to uninstall a program or add or remove component features of software such as Microsoft Office. There is also usually a repair option, which will reinstall the components of the program.

 **Interaction Opportunity**

Ask learners to open **Programs and Features** to view installed applications and to check which Windows features are enabled.

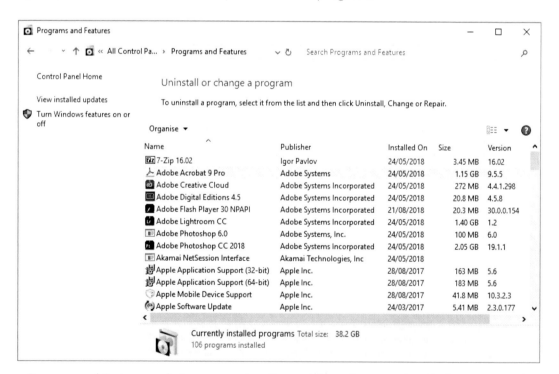

Programs and Features—select a program icon then use the options to uninstall, change, or repair. (Screenshot used with permission from Microsoft.)

Note: In order to uninstall a program successfully, you should exit any applications or files that might lock files installed by the application or the PC will need to be restarted. You may also need to disable antivirus software. If the uninstall program cannot remove locked files, it will normally prompt you to check its log file for details (the files and directories can then be deleted manually).

ENABLING WINDOWS FEATURES

You can use **Programs and Features** to enable or disable optional Windows components. Click the **Turn Windows features on or off** link then check the boxes for the features you want to enable (or uncheck boxes to remove those features).

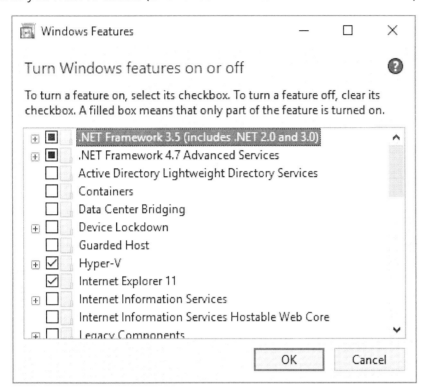

Enabling and disabling Windows Features. (Screenshot used with permission from Microsoft.)

SOFTWARE CONFIGURATION

Most configuration options for software are quite specific to each program. You can use menus such as **File→Options**, **Edit→Preferences**, or the **Help** menu to change the configuration settings.

DEFAULT PROGRAMS

Use the **Default Programs** applet to set the programs you wish to use for particular tasks or to configure individual file associations (choosing which application is used to open files with a particular extension).

Show Slide(s)

Software Configuration (3 slides)

Interaction Opportunity

Ask learners to open this applet to check the current configuration.

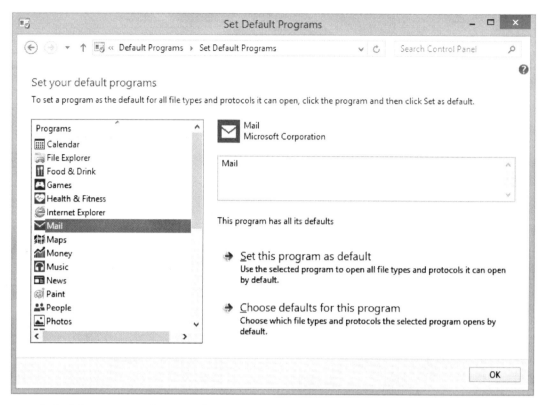

Default Programs applet in Windows 8.1. (Screenshot used with permission from Microsoft.)

Note: In Windows 10, select **Windows Settings→Apps→Default apps**.

COMPATIBILITY MODE

One of the challenges for Microsoft in releasing a new version of Windows is to provide compatibility for hardware and software developed for previous versions.

Windows provides a degree of support for legacy DOS and Windows 9x programs, and each version provides support for earlier 2000/XP/Vista/7/8 versions. The **Properties** dialog box for executable files and the shortcuts to such programs have a **Compatibility** tab. It allows you to configure the program's original operating system environment and force it to use compatible display settings.

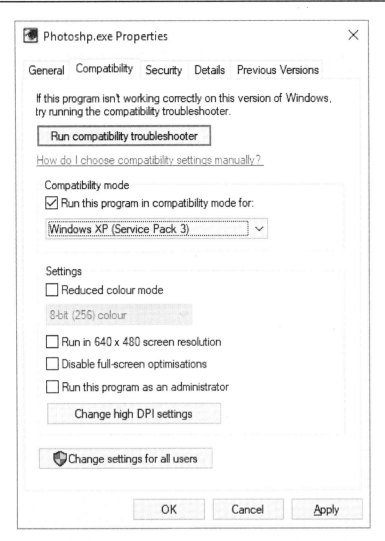

Access program compatibility options via the application's executable or shortcut file properties. (Screenshot used with permission from Microsoft.)

Features such as User Account Control and its greater protection for system folders (Program Files and the system root), the Aero desktop compositing engine, and 64-bit Windows versions have made application compatibility even more challenging. UAC problems can be solved by running the program as an administrator, and there is an option to turn off advanced desktop compositing effects. There is a **Program Compatibility Troubleshooter** wizard (right-click the shortcut or executable) to help.

MICROSOFT STORE APPS

Windows 8 introduces support for a different kind of program, referred to variously as a Windows app, Store app, Universal app, or Modern/Metro app. These apps run across any kind of Windows device, including Windows-based smartphones and tablets. Windows apps are not installed via **Programs and Features** but via the **Microsoft Store**.

Users must sign into the Microsoft Store using a Microsoft account. Apps can be transferred between any Windows device where the user signs in with that Microsoft account.

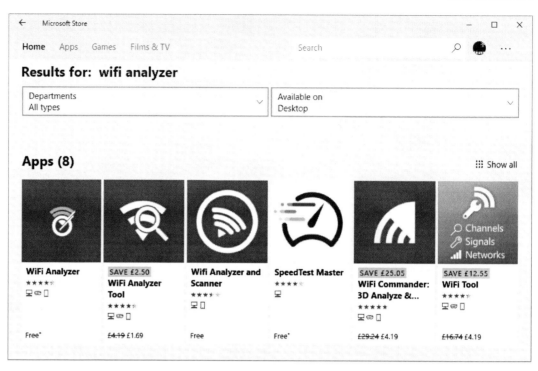

Microsoft Store. (Screenshot used with permission from Microsoft.)

Unlike desktop applications, store apps run in a restrictive sandbox. This sandbox is designed to prevent a store app from making system-wide changes and prevent a faulty store app from "crashing" the whole OS or interfering with other apps and applications. This extra level of protection means that users with only standard permissions are allowed to install store apps. Installing a store app does not require confirmation with UAC or computer administrator-level privileges.

Apps can be uninstalled via the app's shortcut menu on the **Start Screen**. You can choose to uninstall an app from that device only or from all devices, wiping any data stored by the app in your account in the process.

APPLICATION AND PRINT SERVICES

Show Slide(s)

Application and Print Services (4 slides)

A **service** is a Windows process that does not require any sort of user interaction and so runs in the **background** (without a window). Services provide functionality for many parts of the Windows OS, such as allowing logon, browsing the network, or indexing file details to optimize searches. Services may be installed by Windows and by other applications, such as antivirus, database, or backup software.

SERVICES CONSOLE

You might want to disable non-essential services to improve performance or security. You can prevent a service from running at startup by setting it to **Manual** or prevent it from running completely by setting it to **Disabled**. Note that this may cause problems if other services depend upon it. If something is not working properly, you should check that any services it depends upon are started.

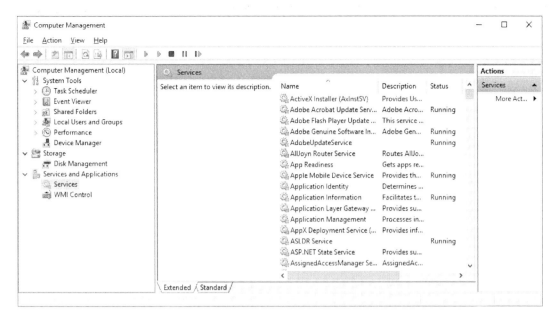

Managing services using the Computer Management console. (Screenshot used with permission from Microsoft.)

To configure services, open the **Computer Management** console, then expand **Services and Applications** from the tree and click the **Services** icon. Alternatively, you can run the **services.msc** command. The services snap-in displays a list of installed services in the right-hand panel. Clicking a service displays information about it in the left-hand panel. The shortcut menu for a service allows you to start, stop, pause/ resume, or restart (stop then start).

PRINT MANAGEMENT

If you use Windows to host a printer (acting as a print server), you need to make drivers available for the different client operating systems that may be connecting to the printer. Windows comes with a **Print Management** snap-in (in **Administrative Tools**), where you can manage drivers and monitor the status of printers.

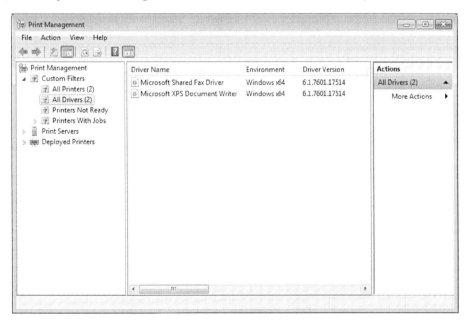

Print Management (Windows 7). (Screenshot used with permission from Microsoft.)

*Note: Note that **Print Management** is not available in the Home editions.*

COMPONENT SERVICES

The **Component Object Model** (**COM+, Distributed COM [DCOM]**, and **ActiveX**) is a means for developers to link software applications and leverage Windows services. For example, **COM OLE** (Object Linking and Embedding) allows an Excel® spreadsheet to be saved within a Word document or a custom software application could use COM to write to the event log. The **Component Services** snap-in (accessed via **Administrative Tools**) enables you to register new server applications or reconfigure security permissions for existing services.

DATA SOURCES

The **Data Sources** or **ODBC Data Sources** snap-in (from **Administrative Tools**) enables you to control data connections set up on the local computer. A data source allows a client application to share data from a server application. For example, an Excel spreadsheet could be set up with a data connection to an SQL Server®.

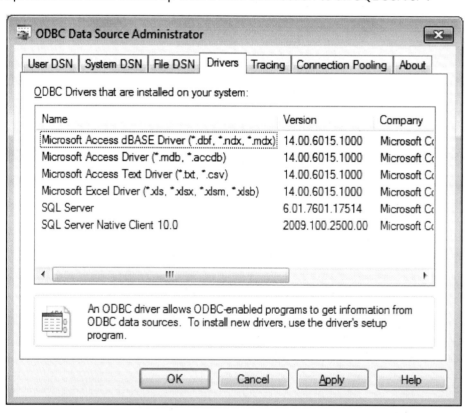

Checking available drivers using the Data Sources snap-in. (Screenshot used with permission from Microsoft.)

An Open Database Connectivity (ODBC) data source consists of a driver for the server application plus the location of the data (a file or a server). You may also need to supply the table name and logon credentials. Typically, drivers get added when an application is installed.

Users can set up new data sources using the **My Data Sources** folder that gets added within their **Documents** folder in their profile.

TASK MANAGER

The **Task Manager** utility (`taskmgr.exe`) allows the user to shut down applications that are not responding. An ordinary user can end an unresponsive application that they ran initially, but administrative rights are required to end processes that were not started by the user. This protects the system by ensuring malware cannot disable antivirus software or other protections. In addition to this functionality, **Task Manager** can be used to monitor the PC's key resources. The quickest way to open **Task Manager** is to press **Ctrl+Shift+Esc**.

*Note: Other ways to open **Task Manager** include pressing **Ctrl+Alt+Del** and selecting **Task Manager**, right-clicking the taskbar, and running `taskmgr.exe`.*

 Show Slide(s)

Task Manager (7 slides)

 Teaching Tip

Task Manager is a vital tool so make sure you allocate plenty of time to this subject.

Task Manager has been significantly overhauled in Windows 8 and Windows 10. First we examine the Windows 7 version and the Windows 10 version follows after.

APPLICATIONS TAB

The **Applications** tab shows applications currently running in a desktop window. The shortcut menu for each allows you to force the application to close (**End Task**), manage its window, and show the process associated with the application.

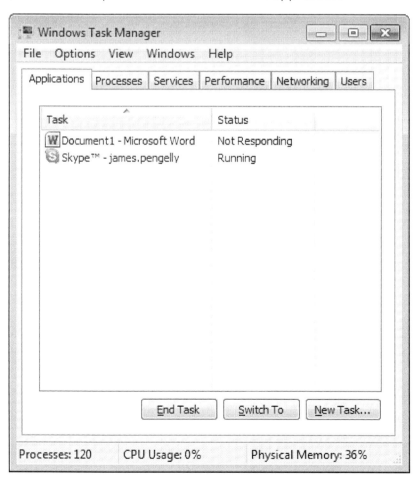

Windows 7 Task Manager—Applications tab. (Screenshot used with permission from Microsoft.)

If an application is not responding, forcing it to close may result in the loss of any unsaved data. You are prompted to confirm what you want to do.

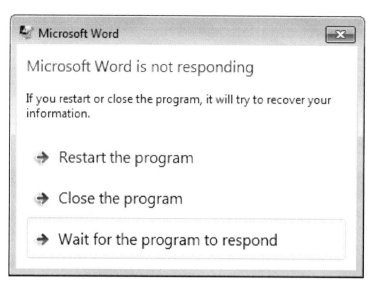

Program not responding dialog box. (Screenshot used with permission from Microsoft.)

Some applications, including Microsoft Office ones, can try to recover unsaved information from autosave and temp files.

PROCESSES TAB

The **Processes** tab shows CPU utilization and memory usage for each process.

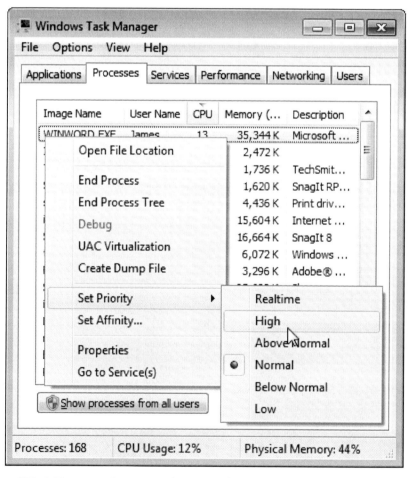

Windows 7 Task Manager—Processes tab. (Screenshot used with permission from Microsoft.)

To view system-level processes (those not running under the logged-on user account), you must select the **Show processes from all users** option.

You would examine these values to discover whether a particular application was misbehaving. For example, an application may "leak" memory by not freeing it up when it has finished using it. To show more than the default CPU and Memory Usage, select **View→Select Columns** and check the items that you want to look at.

If a process is not responding or if you suspect it is faulty, you can right-click and select **End Process** to terminate it.

In some circumstances, you may want to privilege one task over another, or conversely, set one task to have fewer resources than others. You can do this by right-clicking the process and choosing an option from the **Set Priority** submenu. For example, if you had a Voice over IP application and its priority was not already set to **Above normal**, changing its priority might improve call quality as the CPU would privilege that process over ones set to any other level.

*Note: As with other administrative tools, some settings in **Task Manager** (such as showing system level processes) are not available unless you run the tool with administrative privileges.*

You can choose to open the folder containing the process and inspect its file properties. This can be useful if you suspect a malware infection—you should check that the process is installed to a valid location. Sometimes a single process (such as svchost.exe) will "host" multiple services; conversely, there may be multiple versions of the process running. You can use the **Go to Service(s)** option in the process's shortcut menu to view them.

*Note: Use the **File** menu to launch a new process. You can choose to launch the process with administrative privileges by checking the box.*

SERVICES TAB

You can use the **Services** tab to show which services are running, start and stop services, or open the services management console. Each running service is associated with a host process through its **Process ID (PID)**. You can use the **Go to Process** option in the process's shortcut menu to view it.

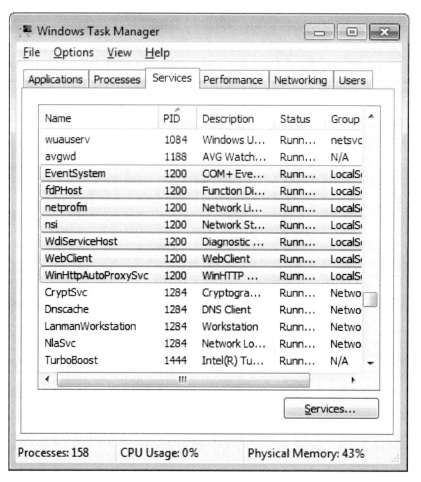

Windows 7 Task Manager—Services tab. (Screenshot used with permission from Microsoft.)

PERFORMANCE TAB

The **Processes** tab shows which applications might be using (or over-using) system resources. You can also use Task Manager to get a snapshot of overall system performance. Select the **Performance** tab to view resource usage. On a system with multiple processors, you should see multiple graphs for CPU Usage (one for each CPU). If this is not the case, select **View→CPU History→One Graph per CPU**. Note that physical, multicore, and HyperThreaded processors are all represented.

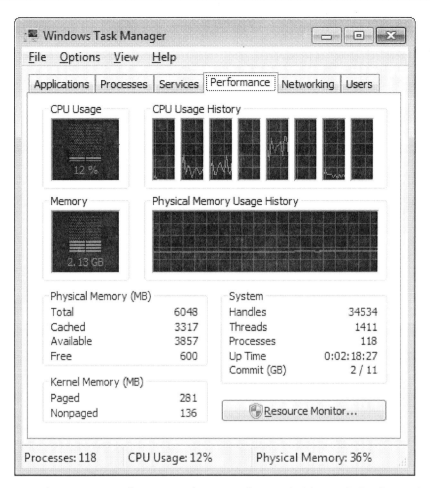

Windows 7 Task Manager—Performance tab. (Screenshot used with permission from Microsoft.)

The following memory usage is displayed:

- **Physical Memory**—usage of system RAM (not including the pagefile).
- **Kernel Memory**—physical and paged memory used by Windows core files.
- **System summary**—showing handles, threads, and processes (software objects being managed by the CPU), system uptime, and the commit charge (overall memory usage, including physical memory and pagefile).

High peak values are nothing to worry about, but consistently high utilization means that you should consider adding more resources to the system (or run fewer processes!). CPU and physical memory obviously require physical upgrades. Windows will normally change the **pagefile** dynamically if it is running out of space. If it has been set manually, you should increase it using the **Performance Settings** button on the **Advanced** page of **System Properties**.

 Note: If the commit charge exceeds total physical memory, then performance will suffer as the system will be using the disk-based pagefile extensively. You need to multiply the commit charge (measured here in gigabytes) by 1024 to compare to physical memory (measured in megabytes).

There is also a link to **Resource Monitor**, which shows additional live performance information.

NETWORKING TAB

The **Networking** tab shows the status and utilization of the network adapter(s). Utilization is expressed as a percentage, so if the link is 10 Gbps (as shown), 10% utilization shows that the computer is transferring about 1 Gbps currently.

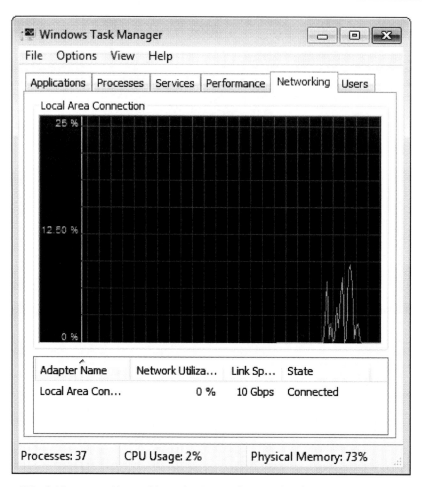

Windows 7 Task Manager—Networking tab. (Screenshot used with permission from Microsoft.)

USERS TAB

The **Users** tab shows who is logged on to the machine. An administrator can disconnect or log off other users or send them a notification (to inform them that the computer will be shut down, for instance).

WINDOWS 10 TASK MANAGER

In Windows 10, you can open **Task Manager** via the **Ctrl+Shift+Esc** key combo, by right-clicking the taskbar, or by using the **Windows+X** menu. **Task Manager** may start in a "compact" mode; click the **Show details** button to expand it.

*Note: **Task Manager** in Windows 8 is essentially the same as in Windows 10.*

Interaction Opportunity

Ask learners to start **Task Manager** and view each tab as you describe them.

In Windows 10, the functions of the **Applications** and **Processes** tabs are consolidated across the **Processes** and **Details** tabs. On the **Processes** tab, you can expand each app or background process to view its sub-processes and view more clearly what resources each is taking up.

The shortcut menu allows you to end a task. There is also an option to search for information about the process online. Another option is to view more information about a process via the **Details** tab. You can identify services associated with a process via the shortcut menu on the **Details** tab.

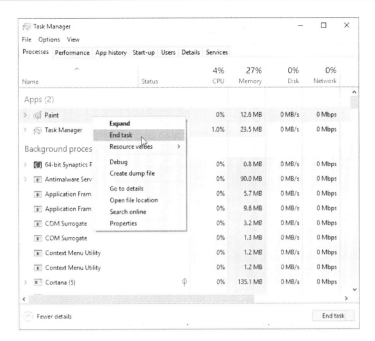

Windows 10 Task Manager—Processes tab. (Screenshot used with permission from Microsoft.)

The **Performance** tab provides more information about the CPU, memory, disk, and network subsystems, while the **App History** tab shows usage information for Windows Store apps.

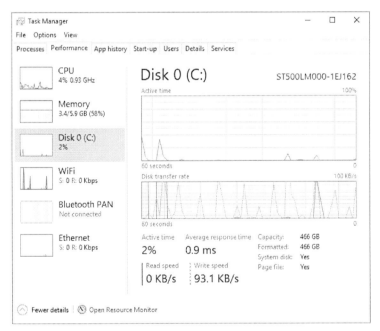

Windows 10 Task Manager—Performance tab. (Screenshot used with permission from Microsoft.)

The **Users** tab lets you see who is logged on (and allows you to send them a message or sign them out) plus information about the processes they are running and the resource utilization associated with their account.

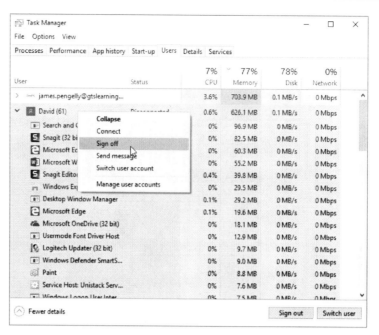

Windows 10 Task Manager—Users tab. (Screenshot used with permission from Microsoft.)

The **Startup** tab lets you disable programs added to the Startup folder (type `shell:startup` at the **Run** dialog box to access this) or set to run using the registry. Right-click the headers and select **Startup type** to show how the program is launched. It also shows how much impact each item has on boot times.

The tasklist and taskkill Commands

You can also identify which service is running in which process (and vice versa) at a command line using the `tasklist` command. `tasklist` shows a list of processes (images) along with a PID, session name and number, and memory usage (in kilobytes). You can run the command with the `/fi` switch to apply various filters (for example, `tasklist /fi "memusage gt 150000"` shows processes using more than 150 MB)—check the online help for details. Using `tasklist /svc` shows a list of services within each process.

The `taskkill` command can be used to end processes and services. Use `taskkill /pid processid` or `taskkill /im ImageName` to end a task by PID or image name respectively. Use the **/t** switch to also halt any child processes.

The `/f` switch terminates the process without any user notification (for the user to save changes, for instance) and will also terminate it even if it is currently displaying a dialog box. You can run the command with an appropriate filter (`/fi "Criteria"`). You can use a PID, image name, service name, or window title or target multiple images using a filter for CPU time, memory usage, or status ("Not Responding," for instance).

*Note: There may be circumstances when you need to run Explorer with administrative privileges. To do this, open a command prompt using **Run as administrator**. Use `taskkill /f /im explorer.exe` to terminate the existing **Explorer** process, then run `explorer.exe` again from the same command prompt.*

Note: *On a network, you can use* `taskkill` *and* `tasklist` *to manage processes on a remote computer using the* `/s` *switch to identify the remote host (by IP address or host name) and the* `/u` *and* `/p` *switches to specify credentials (user name and password).*

Note: *To learn more, check the* **Video** *tile on the CHOICE Course screen for any videos that supplement the content for this lesson.*

Access the Checklist tile on your CHOICE Course screen for reference information and job aids on How to Install and Manage Windows Applications.

Activity 7-1

Discussing Windows Application Management

SCENARIO

Answer the following questions to check your understanding of the topic.

1. You need to install a desktop application across a network of 500 Windows PCs.

    What is the most efficient means of doing this, and what security considerations should you make?

    Rather than try to install the application by logging on locally to each PC to run the setup file, you can put the installer file on a network share and use Windows Group Policy Objects (GPO) or some sort of script to "push" deploy the application. You can use a service account with appropriate permissions to install the software on the local machine. You should test this process and the application first in a lab environment to identify potential impacts to the local device and/or network. You must also ensure that the application vendor provides a digitally signed installer file, to prove that the code has not been tampered with.

2. An installer program may present up to three options in Programs and Features. Two are **Uninstall** and **Change**.

    What is the third?

    Repair.

3. **How would you configure a legacy Windows 98 application to work with Windows 10?**

    Open the application's property sheet and select the **Compatibility** tab to select the appropriate mode. You can also run the **Program Compatibility Troubleshooter**.

4. You take a support call where the user doesn't understand why a program runs at startup when the **Startup** folder is empty.

    What is the likely cause and how could you verify this?

    The program has added a registry entry to run at startup. You could check this (and optionally disable the program) by using **Task Manager**.

5. **What additional information is shown on the Users tab in Windows 10 Task Manager compared to Windows 7?**

    It shows user-initiated processes and resource utilization.

6. You are watching **CPU Usage** and notice that it often jumps to 100% and then falls back.

   Does this indicate a problem?

   Probably not—**CPU Usage** usually peaks and falls. If it stays over 80-90%, the system could require a faster CPU or if it spikes continually, there could be a faulty application.

Activity 7-2

Configuring Windows Applications and Services

 Show Slide(s)

Activity: Configuring Windows Applications and Services

BEFORE YOU BEGIN

Complete this activity on the Hyper-V Manager and the PC1 (Windows 10) and PC2 (Windows 7) VMs.

SCENARIO

In this activity, you will explore a software compatibility issue and look at the **Services** snap-in and **Task Manager** tools.

---

1. Windows can run software in an environment that simulates older versions of Windows to try to solve compatibility problems. On the **PC2 VM**, use the **C:\LABFILES\pgpfreeware.exe** program to explore compatibility troubleshooting options.

    a) Open the **Hyper-V Manager** window. In the **Virtual Machines** panel, right-click **PC2** and select **Start**. Double-click the VM to open the connection window.

    b) Press **Ctrl+Alt+End** to show the sign-on screen. Select **Switch User→Other User** to use a different account to the one shown initially. In the **User name** box, type **.\Admin**. Type **Pa$$w0rd** in the other box, and then press **Enter**.

    c) Start **Windows Explorer** and open the **C:\LABFILES** folder.

    d) Double-click the **PGPfreeware.exe** file to run it.

    e) Select **OK** to dismiss the error message. On the taskbar, select the **Program Compatibility Assistant** window icon, and then select the **Close** button.

    f) Right-click the executable and select **Troubleshoot compatibility**.

    g) Select **Try recommended settings**, and then select **Start the program**.

    h) At the **UAC** prompt, select **Yes** to continue with the installation.

    In this instance it is safe to proceed, but on a production network you should be much more cautious about installing unsigned software.

    i) Cancel any error messages, but leave the troubleshooter open.

    j) In the **Program Compatibility** troubleshooter, select **Next**, and then select **No, try again using different settings**.

    k) Check **The program worked in earlier versions of Windows but won't install or run now**, and then select **Next**.

    l) Select **Windows 95** and select **Next**.

    m) Select **Start the program**.

    n) At the **UAC** prompt, select **Yes** to continue with the installation.

    The program will still not install.

    o) Cancel the error messages.

    p) In the **Program Compatibility** troubleshooter, select **Next**, then select **No, report the problem to Microsoft and check online for a solution**.

    q) Select the **Close** button.

    In this instance, the software is just not compatible with Windows 7, and you would have to look at the vendor's site for an updated version or create a Windows 9x Virtual Machine (VM) to use to run the program.

---

2. Open Task Manager, and observe the status information as you run the HeavyLoad PC "stress test" tool. HeavyLoad is developed by JAM Software (jam-software.com).

a) Right-click the taskbar and select **Start Task Manager**. Observe the **Applications** tab. You might have some **Explorer** instances running.

b) Select the **Processes** tab, and observe the background processes running under the user account.

c) Select the **Performance** tab, and observe how much of the VM's resources are committed just to running Windows itself.

d) Select **Options→Always On Top**.

e) On the desktop, double-click the **HeavyLoad** icon.

f) In HeavyLoad, use the **Test Options** menu or the toolbar buttons to use the following tests:

- **Write Temp File** - Enabled.
- **Allocate Memory** - Enabled.
- **Start TreeSize** - Disabled.
- **Stress GPU** - Disabled

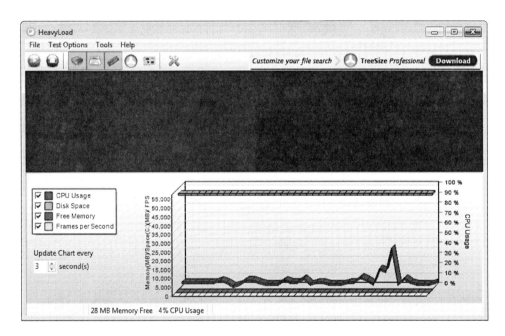

g) Select **File→Start Selected Tests**.

h) In **Task Manager**, verify that **CPU Usage** graph shows the point at which **HeavyLoad** was launched.

i) Check the **Applications** and **Processes** tabs in **Task Manager**, and observe the CPU and memory utilization for the **HeavyLoad.exe** process.

j) Optionally, try starting some of the installed applications, such as Thunderbird or Nmap, using the desktop shortcuts. Observe if there is any effect on performance, such as taking a long time to display a window (there may not be).

k) Watch for a **Low Disk Space Warning** notification as the HeavyLoad temp file reduces spare disk capacity.

l) In **HeavyLoad**, select **File→Stop Tests**. Observe **Task Manager** as **CPU utilization** drops and more memory is made available.

m) Exit the HeavyLoad application.

3. Use **Task Manager** to list running services and identify the processes that are hosting services.

a) Select the **Services** tab and sort by **Status**.

Note the number of services is far higher than the number of processes seen previously. Also note that each service has a PID (Process ID).

b) Select the **Processes** tab then select the **Show processes from all users** button.

Services running under the system, local service, and network service machine accounts are shown.

c) Select **View→Select Columns**. Check **PID** and select **OK**.

Note the number of **svchost.exe** processes running and that these have the same PID as many of the services you looked at. Svchost is a generic process for running many Windows services.

d) Right-click a **svchost.exe** process and select **Go to Service(s)** to switch back to the **Services** tab. Services running within that svchost.exe process image are selected. Note that they have the same PID.

4. Some services are essential but others can be disabled to reduce startup time or make more system memory available. Practice managing services by disabling the **Themes** service.

a) In **Task Manager**, on the **Services** tab, locate the **Themes** service. Right-click it and select **Stop Service**.

Note the change to the desktop when the service is not running.

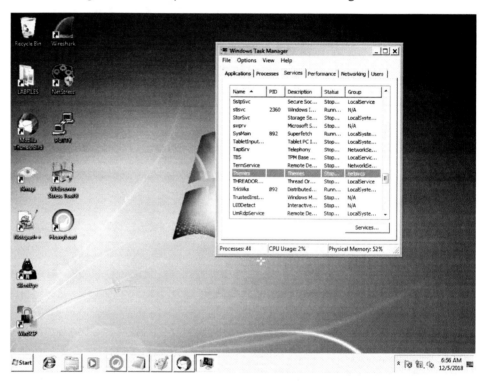

With the Themes service disabled, desktop compositing effects are not available, so the taskbar and window borders look much plainer. (Screenshot used with permission from Microsoft.)

b) Minimize Task Manager.

c) Open the **Computer Management** console, expand **Services and Applications**, and then select **Services** in the left pane.

This snap-in lets you manage services. These are Windows and third-party processes that run in the background to support functions of Windows and third-party applications. You may choose to disable or enable services to improve performance or to troubleshoot a problem.

d) Right-click **Themes** and select **Properties**.

Note the options available here.

- On the **General** tab—start, stop, pause, and resume a service and change its startup type (whether the service runs when Windows starts).

- On the **Log On** tab—specify the user account used to run the service.
- On the **Recovery** tab—options for troubleshooting if the service does not start.
- On the **Dependencies** tab—any relationships to other services.

 *Note: If the **Startup type** is **Disabled**, you cannot start the service. You must change the **Startup type** to **Automatic** or **Manual** first.*

e)   On the **General** tab, select **Start**, and then select **OK**.

f)   Close any open windows.

5.   Start the **PC1 VM**, and compare the version of **Task Manager** running on Windows 10 to the Windows 7 version you have just looked at.

a)   Start **PC1** and sign on to the **Admin** account with the ***Pa$$w0rd*** credential.

b)   Right-click **Start** and select **Task Manager**.

c)   In Task Manager, select **More details**.

d)   On the **Processes** tab, examine the list of **Apps**, **Background processes**, and **Windows processes** running.

e)   Select the **Memory** column to list the apps and processes by memory usage.

f)   Select the **CPU** column to list the apps and processes by CPU usage.

g)   Right-click the app or process using the most CPU resource and then select **Go to details**.

h)   On the **Details** tab, observe the list of apps and processes listed by executable name.

The highlighted executable is for the process you selected from the **Processes** tab. Information includes the status of a process, its PID (process ID), and resource usage. To end a process, you can right-click it and then select **End task**, or **End process tree**. The latter closes not only the selected task, but all related tasks started by the selected task. You can add additional columns by right-clicking the column header and then selecting **Select columns**.

i)   Select the **Performance** tab.

You can view the current system performance on this tab in terms of CPU usage, memory consumption, disk usage, and network throughput.

j)   On the left, select **Disk 0 (C:)**.

You can see detailed information about the disk resources.

k)   Select the **App history** tab.

This tab shows the usage history of installed Windows Store apps.

l)   Select the **Startup** tab.

This shows information about items configured to run at startup. There may be nothing showing here, but typically it shows at least OneDrive and Windows Defender.

m)   Select the **Users** tab.

This shows information about resource usage on a per-user basis.

n)   Select the **Services** tab.

This is a list of all services in the computer, and shows the status (running, stopped) of each. Also shown is the PID.

6.   At the end of each activity, you need to close the VMs. You will always discard any changes you made.

a)   From the connection window, select **Action→Revert**. If you are prompted to confirm, select the **Revert** button.

b)   Repeat to revert the PC2 VM.

Topic B

Manage Windows Performance

EXAM OBJECTIVES COVERED
1002-1.5 Given a scenario, use Microsoft operating system features and tools.
1002-1.6 Given a scenario, use Microsoft Windows Control Panel utilities.

Diagnosing the cause of slow performance can be a difficult and frustrating task. You need to be able to use the system configuration and monitoring/logging tools to capture utilization of system components over time.

SYSTEM PROPERTIES

Show Slide(s)

System Properties (2 slides)

You can obtain a brief overview of some key system information from the **System Properties** applet. You can access this via **Control Panel** or by right-clicking the **Computer/This PC** object and selecting **Properties**. The **System Properties** home page displays summary information about the computer, including the processor type and installed RAM, plus the Windows edition, product key, and activation status. The system settings include network identification and domain membership, hardware settings and configuration, user profiles, and performance and recovery options. Select the **Tasks** or **Advanced system settings** links to access the configuration dialog boxes.

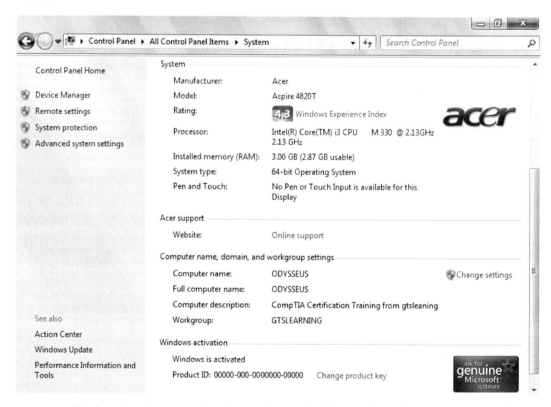

Windows 7 system properties. (Screenshot used with permission from Microsoft.)

In Windows 10, the **System** applet shown in the previous graphic is still available, though the **Performance Information** tool has been discontinued, but there is also a system category within Windows **Settings**. Some of the system information is available on the **About** page.

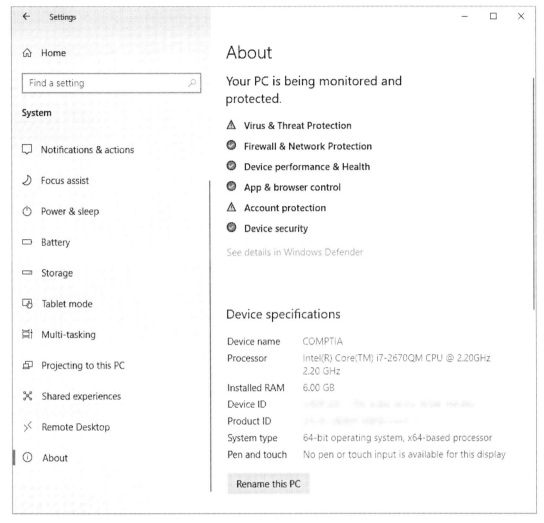

Windows 10 Settings app showing the About page. (Screenshot used with permission from Microsoft.)

Interaction Opportunity

Ask learners to open the **Settings** app and view the information for the classroom PC. They can then open **System Info** and the **Advanced System Properties** dialog boxes to follow along with your presentation.

ADVANCED SYSTEM PROPERTIES

From the **System** applet, clicking **Advanced system settings** opens the **System Properties** dialog box. This allows you to configure remote settings, system protection, and advanced settings.

REMOTE SETTINGS

The **Remote Settings** tab enables (or disables) connections to the local PC from another PC on the network. There are two types of remote connection:

*   **Remote Assistance** means that the local user sends a request to another user on a remote computer inviting them to view or control their desktop.
*   **Remote Desktop** means that the remote user can initiate a connection at any time. The remote user needs to sign on to the local machine using an authorized account (configured via this dialog box).

Show Slide(s)

Advanced System Properties (3 slides)

Teaching Tip

System Restore and Remote Desktop are discussed in more detail elsewhere in the course.

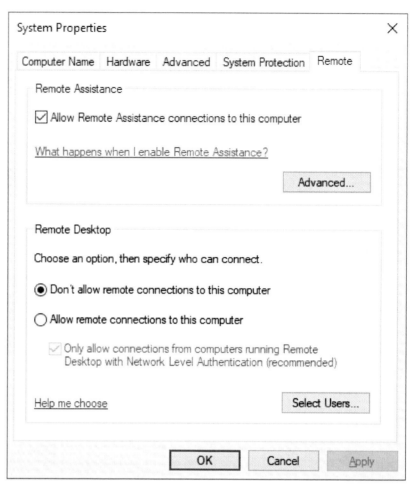

System Properties dialog box—Remote Settings tab in Windows 10. (Screenshot used with permission from Microsoft.)

SYSTEM PROTECTION

The **System Protection** tab provides options for configuring the **System Restore** feature. **System Restore** creates configuration backups. If there are changes or file corruptions that damage information in the registry or you want to reverse changes made when installing an application or device driver, you can use **System Restore** to reset the system configuration to an earlier point in time. Click **Configure** to enable or disable **System Protection** and set how much disk space the tool is allowed to use.

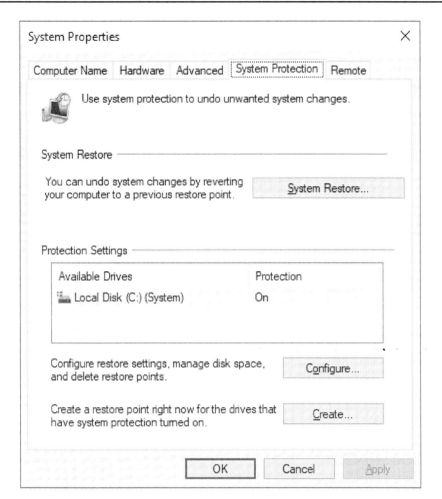

System Properties dialog box—System Protection tab in Windows 10. (Screenshot used with permission from Microsoft.)

ADVANCED SETTINGS

Upgrading the hardware resources on a system is fine if you have the budget and you can find compatible parts, but the rapid changes in computer technology mean that PCs and laptops can be very quickly left behind in terms of upgrade potential. There are various tweaks that can be made to improve the performance of an older system without specifying new hardware. The options on the **Advanced** tab include the following:

- Performance options, including:
  - Configure desktop visual effects for best appearance or best performance.
  - Virtual Memory (paging).
  - Foreground/Background processing priority (a desktop PC should always be left optimized for programs).
- Startup and recovery options.
- Environment variables.
- User Profiles.

Teaching Tip

You might also want to discuss the use of pagefiles on SSDs. There is often-expressed concern that paging could diminish SSD lifetime through excessive writes. Most desktop users are unlikely to hit these limits, but there are circumstances where paging to an SSD might be more risky (development workstations running lots of VMs or A-V editing, for instance). But even then the performance benefit is likely to outweigh the risk anyway—you buy these things to use them.

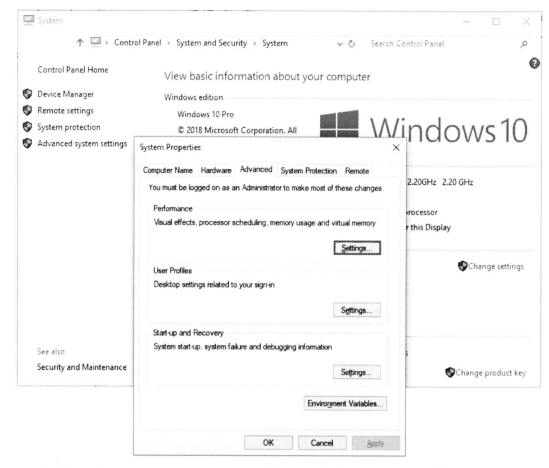

System Properties dialog box—Advanced tab in Windows 10. (Screenshot used with permission from Microsoft.)

VIRTUAL MEMORY

Show Slide(s)

Virtual Memory (2 slides)

Using **virtual memory** is a way for the computer to accomplish more than the limits of what its physical memory can perform. The computer system uses a portion of the hard disk as if it was physical RAM. When all physical memory is filled, the OS can transfer some of the least-recently used data from memory to a file on the hard disk called the **pagefile**, thereby freeing up an equivalent amount of space in the memory chips for other purposes. When the original data is needed again, the next least-recently used data is moved out of RAM onto the hard drive to make room to reimport the needed data.

In Windows systems, the **Virtual Memory Manager (VMM)** manages the memory mappings and assignments .Running out of memory would mean that a process might not be able to start or could crash.

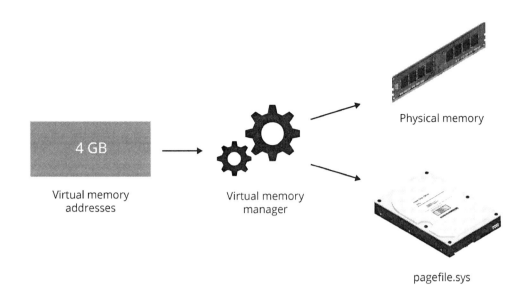

Physical memory

4 GB

Virtual memory
addresses

Virtual memory
manager

pagefile.sys

Virtual memory. (Image © 123RF.com.)

Virtual memory is not nearly as fast as actual memory. Modern DDRx SDRAM DIMMs read/write speeds are measured in nanoseconds, whereas hard drive seek, read, and write times are measured in milliseconds. If your computer is frequently exceeding its physical RAM and having to resort to using a pagefile on disk, adding more physical RAM may be the most economical way of effecting a noticeable change in performance.

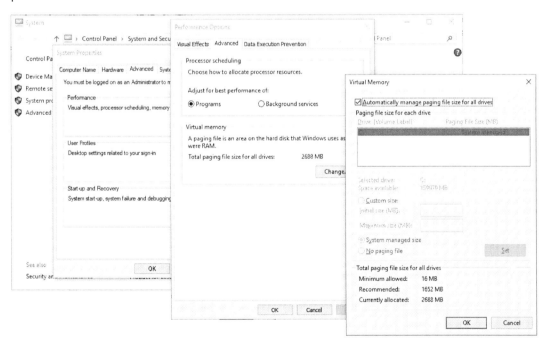

Configuring virtual memory in Windows 10. (Screenshot used with permission from Microsoft.)

When tuning the pagefile, keep the following in mind:

• Windows can manage the pagefile and set an appropriate level. There is very little point in setting custom values unless you have a specific performance goal or requirement in mind.

- Each physical disk can have a pagefile of its own. This will allow Windows, depending on hardware, to concurrently access the paging files and, therefore, increase performance.
- The pagefile does not have to use contiguous disk space, although performance can be further enhanced if it does. To ensure that the pagefile uses contiguous space, you will need to defragment your disk then set the maximum and minimum sizes of the pagefile to the same value.

 Note: If the pagefile is a fixed size but too small, Windows might run out of memory, which could cause programs to crash. Also, if the pagefile is too small, the system may not be able to generate a complete crash dump of the memory contents, which will hamper efforts to troubleshoot system errors.

For more information on pagefile tuning considerations, view Microsoft's Knowledge Base article (**support.microsoft.com/en-us/help/2860880/how-to-determine-the-appropriate-page-file-size-for-64-bit-versions-of**).

WINDOWS PERFORMANCE MANAGEMENT TOOLS

 Show Slide(s)
Windows Performance Management Tools (4 slides)

Windows provides numerous Administrative Tools to monitor system performance.

- **Task Manager**—as you have seen, you can use the **Performance** tab in **Task Manager** to monitor utilization statistics in real time.
- **Resource Monitor**—shows an enhanced version of the sort of snapshot monitoring provided by **Task Manager**. You can see graphs of resource performance along with key statistics, such as threads started by a process or hard page faults/second. Continually rising numbers of either of these can indicate a problem.

 Teaching Tip
Make sure learners are familiar with the terminology of objects, instances, and counters.

- **Reliability Monitor**—displays a log of "system stability" events, so you can see at a glance whether a particular application has stopped responding frequently.
- **Performance Monitor**—configure detailed reports on different system statistics and log performance over time.

PERFORMANCE MONITOR

Windows **Performance Monitor** can be used to provide real-time charts of system resources or can be used to log information to a file for long-term analysis. You can run the tool from the **Administrative Tools** folder or **Computer Management**; you can also run `perfmon.exe`.

By monitoring different resources at different times of the day, you can detect bottlenecks in a system that are causing problems. It may be that a particular application starts freezing for longer and longer periods. This could be caused by a number of things. Perhaps it is that the processor is too slow, which would cause the requests to take longer; perhaps the hard disk is too slow, which would mean that it takes too long for the computer to open and save files; perhaps the application uses a network link that has become faulty or congested.

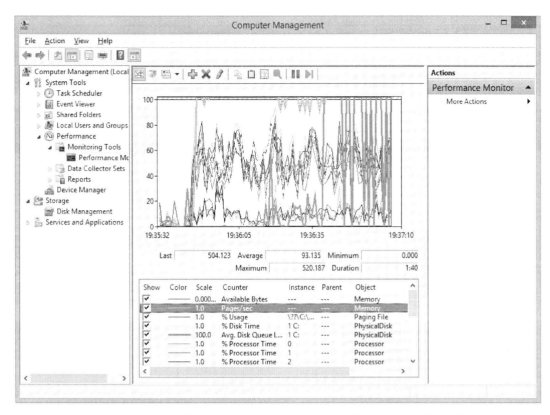

Performance Monitor in Windows 8.1. (Screenshot used with permission from Microsoft.)

The performance of the computer could be increased by upgrading any or all of these components, but **Performance Monitor** will help you decide which is critical.

ADDING OBJECTS, COUNTERS, AND INSTANCES

Resources, such as memory and disk, are collected into **objects**. Objects have counters, representing different performance statistics, and there can be multiple instances of the same type of object. For example, disk performance can be measured using the **Physical Disk Object**, and a useful counter is the **Average Queue Length**. If there are two disks, three instances of this object can be viewed: disk 0, disk 1, and disks Total.

Some of the most commonly used counters are listed here:

Object	Counter	Description
Processor	% Processor Time	The percentage of time that the processor is executing a non-idle thread. In general terms, this should be low. If it is greater than 85% for a sustained period, you may have a processor bottleneck.

Object	Counter	Description
	% Privileged Time % User Time	If overall processor time is very high (over 85% for sustained periods), it can be helpful to compare these. Privileged time represents system processes, whereas user time is software applications. If privileged time is much higher, it is likely that the CPU is underpowered (it can barely run Windows core processes efficiently).
Physical Disk	% Disk Time	The percentage of elapsed time that the selected disk drive is busy servicing read or write requests. This is a good overall indicator of how busy the disk is. Again, if the average exceeds 85% for a sustained period, you may have a disk problem.
	Average Disk Queue Length	The number of requests outstanding on the disk at the time the performance data is collected. Taken with the preceding counter, this gives a better indicator of disk problems. For example, if the disk queue length is increasing and disk time is high, then you have a disk problem.
Memory	Available Bytes	The amount of memory available—this should not be below about 10% of total system RAM. If available bytes falls continuously, there could be a memory leak (that is, a process that allocates memory but does not release it again).

Object	Counter	Description
	Pages/sec	The number of pages read from or written to disk to resolve hard page faults. This means your system is using the paging file. Nothing wrong as long as this is not excessive (averaging above about 50). You probably also want to check the paging file's usage by viewing the paging object itself.
Paging File	% Usage	The amount of the pagefile instance in use in percent. If your paging file is currently 1000 MB on the disk and this figure averages 50%, then it means you might benefit from adding memory (about 500 MB, in fact). Don't forget that if your system pages excessively, then disk performance will suffer—paging is disk intensive.

Notice that it is not always immediately apparent which component is causing a problem. Many counters are interrelated and must be viewed with other counters in mind. For instance, if your system memory is low, then the disk will likely be slow because of excessive paging.

LOGGING PERFORMANCE

In **Performance Monitor**, you can create log files, referred to as **Data Collector Sets**, to record information for viewing at a later date. You can generate a library of performance measurements taken at different times of the day, week, or even year. This information can provide a system baseline and then be used to give a longer-term view of system performance. There are two types of logs: counter and trace:

- **Counter logs** allow you to collect statistics about resources, such as memory, disk, and processor. These can be used to determine system health and performance.
- **Trace logs** can collect statistics about services, providing you with detailed reports about resource behavior. In essence, trace logs provide extensions to the Event Viewer, logging data that would otherwise be inaccessible.

Saved log files can be loaded into **Performance Monitor** from the **Reports** folder for analysis or exported to other programs.

*Note: To learn more, check the **Video** tile on the CHOICE Course screen for any videos that supplement the content for this lesson.*

Access the Checklist tile on your CHOICE Course screen for reference information and job aids on How to Manage Windows Performance.

Activity 7-3
Discussing Windows Performance Management

SCENARIO
Answer the following questions to check your understanding of the topic.

1. **How do you enable a Windows 7 computer to function as a Remote Desktop Server?**

    Open **System properties**, select **Change settings**, then select the **Remote** tab and check the **Allow remote connections to this computer** option on the **Remote** tab. You can also specify the user accounts permitted to connect to the server.

2. **Why isn't the System Protection feature a substitute for making a backup?**

    System Protection restore points are stored on the local disk and so would not allow recovery from the failure, loss, or destruction of the disk. System Protection is designed only to allow the rollback of configuration changes.

3. **What is the advantage of setting the pagefile to the same minimum and maximum sizes?**

    The pagefile will not become fragmented (assuming you defragmented the disk before doing this).

4. You have a computer with two SATA disks. You want to evaluate the performance of the primary disk.

    How would you select this in Performance Monitor and what might be appropriate counters to use?

    Open the **Add Counter** dialog box, select the **Physical Disk** object, select the counter, then select the **0 C:** instance. Useful counters to use to evaluate performance include **% Disk Time** and **Average Disk Queue Length**.

5. You are monitoring system performance and notice that a substantial number of page faults are occurring.

    Does this indicate that a memory module is faulty?

    No—it shows the system is using the pagefile intensively and could benefit from more system RAM being installed.

Topic C

Troubleshoot Windows

EXAM OBJECTIVES COVERED

1002-1.4 Given a scenario, use appropriate Microsoft command-line tools.
1002-1.5 Given a scenario, use Microsoft operating system features and tools.
1002-3.1 Given a scenario, troubleshoot Microsoft Windows OS problems.

An operating system like Windows provides a lot of information to assist troubleshooting, through configuration utilities and event logs. Plenty of tools are available to diagnose and recover from different kinds of problems. In this topic, you will learn which tools and techniques can help to resolve some of the common Windows OS problem symptoms.

EVENT VIEWER

When a problem is related to Windows or a software application rather than the computer hardware, there will often be an error message associated with the problem. This makes troubleshooting simpler as you may only need to find out what the error message means using product documentation, the Microsoft Knowledge Base, or useful websites and newsgroups.

The **Event Viewer** (`eventvwr.msc`) is a management console snap-in for viewing and managing system logs. It can also be accessed via **Computer Management** or **Administrative Tools**. The default page shows a summary of system status, with recent error and warning events collected for viewing.

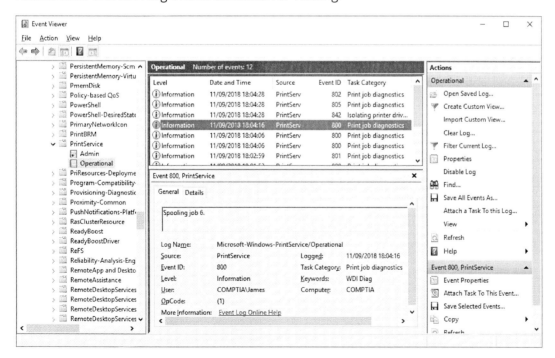

Windows 10 Event Viewer. (Screenshot used with permission from Microsoft.)

Teaching Tip

Learners should be prepared to apply their knowledge and demonstrate that they understand the importance attached to the proper sequence of actions, as described in the exam objectives.

Make sure learners understand which tools and procedures are available for which versions of Windows.

Show Slide(s)

Event Viewer (2 slides)

Teaching Tip

Learners should learn which log to look at for particular error types.

The three-part pane view lets you see the details of the selected event in the bottom pane without having to open a separate dialog box. The third pane contains useful tools for opening log files, filtering, creating a task from an event, and so on.

DEFAULT LOG FILES
The principal Windows log files are shown in this table.

Log File	Description
System Log	Contains information about service load failures, hardware conflicts, driver load failures, and so on.
Security Log	This log holds the audit data for the system.
Application Log	Contains information regarding application errors.
Setup	Records events generated during installation.

The files (**application.evtx**, **security.evtx**, **system.evtx**, and **setup.evtx**) are stored (by default) in the **%SystemRoot%\System32\Winevt\Logs** folder.

 Note: You can also log boot events by using `msconfig`. *This boot log file is saved to* **%SystemRoot%\ntbtlog.txt**. *It is not shown in* **Event Viewer**, *though.*

Each log file has a default maximum size (usually about 20 MB), but you can change this by selecting **Properties** on the appropriate log. This option also allows the overwrite option to be set either as overwrite, do not overwrite, or archive (close the current file and start a new one).

 Note: Be careful about preserving logs. Many computers have ample free disk space, but archive logs can grow very large if left unmonitored.

There are many other logs, stored under the **Applications and Services Logs** node. You would investigate these when troubleshooting a particular Windows service or third-party application.

EVENT TYPES
The **Event Viewer** displays each line or item in the source log file as an event and categorizes each event. The types of events are shown here.

Event	Description
Information	Significant events that describe successful operations, such as a driver or service starting or a document printing.
Warning	Events that may indicate future problems, such as when the system runs low on disk space.
Error	Significant problems, such as service failures and device conflicts.
Critical	An unrecoverable error that made the application or Windows close unexpectedly.

Event	Description
Successful Audit	Security access attempts that were successful.
Failure Audit	Security access attempts that were unsuccessful. This may indicate a possible security breach or simply a user mistyping a password.

More information for each event can be displayed by double-clicking the event in question. This displays a screen that contains the date and time of the event, the user and computer name, an event ID, source, type, and category, and a description of the event and the data in bytes and words.

THE SYSTEM CONFIGURATION UTILITY

The **System Configuration Utility** (`msconfig`) is used to modify various settings and files that affect the way the computer boots and loads Windows.

 *Note: The `msconfig` tool is frequently used to test various configurations for diagnostic purposes, rather than to permanently make configuration changes. Following diagnostic testing, permanent changes would typically be made with more appropriate tools, such as **Services**, to change the startup settings of various system services.*

GENERAL TAB

The **General** tab allows you to configure the startup mode, choosing between **Normal**, **Diagnostic**, and a **Selective** startup, where each portion of the boot sequence can be selected.

 Show Slide(s)

The System Configuration Utility (5 slides)

 Teaching Tip

The `msconfig` command can be used to configure boot parameters and startup programs and services.

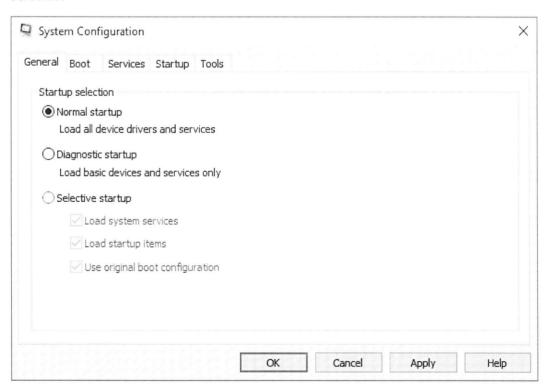

System Configuration Utility—General tab. (Screenshot used with permission from Microsoft.)

BOOT TAB

The **Boot** tab lets you configure basic settings in the **Boot Configuration Data (BCD)** store.

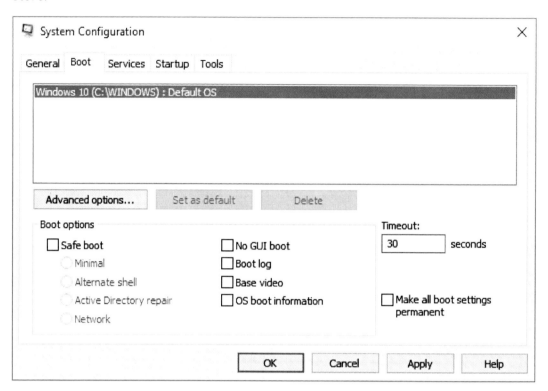

System Configuration Utility—Boot tab. (Screenshot used with permission from Microsoft.)

You can change the default OS, add boot options, such as Safe boot, with minimal drivers and services, and set the timeout value—the duration for which the boot options menu is displayed. To add boot paths you have to use the `bcdedit` command.

Note: *If you are troubleshooting a system that keeps using Safe boot or boots to a command prompt, check that one of the previous options has not been made permanent in **System Configuration**.*

SERVICES TAB

The **Services** tab lets you choose specifically which services are configured to run at startup. The date that a service was disabled is also shown, to make troubleshooting easier.

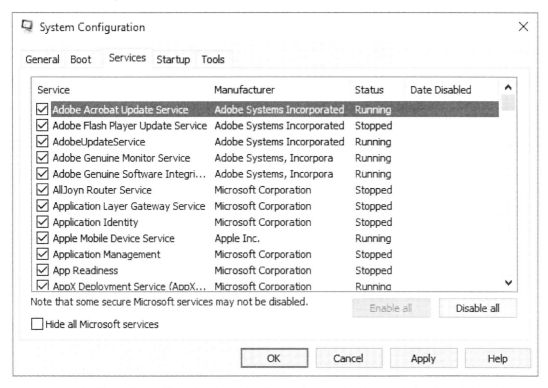

System Configuration Utility—Services tab. (Screenshot used with permission from Microsoft.)

STARTUP TAB

In Windows 7, the **Startup** tab controls the shortcuts that have been placed in the **Startup** folder of the **Start Menu** and startup items that have been written to the registry.

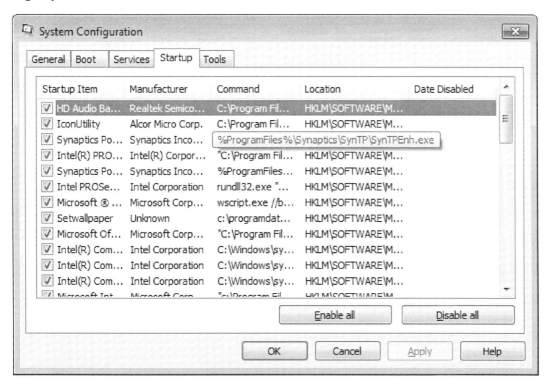

System Configuration Utility—Startup tab (Windows 7). (Screenshot used with permission from Microsoft.)

The **Start Menu** is built from a template containing settings for all users plus shortcuts customized for the current user profile. The template is stored in **C:\ProgramData \Microsoft\Windows\Start Menu\Programs** and the user-specific shortcuts are in **C: \Users\UserName\AppData\Roaming\Microsoft\Windows\Start Menu**.

 Note: If the computer's performance is sluggish, try disabling startup items, as long as they are not providing key services, such as virus protection.

Windows 8 and Windows 10 use **Task Manager** as the means of disabling startup items.

TOOLS TAB

The **Tools** tab contains shortcuts to various administrative utilities including System Information, Configuring UAC, Registry Editor, and so on.

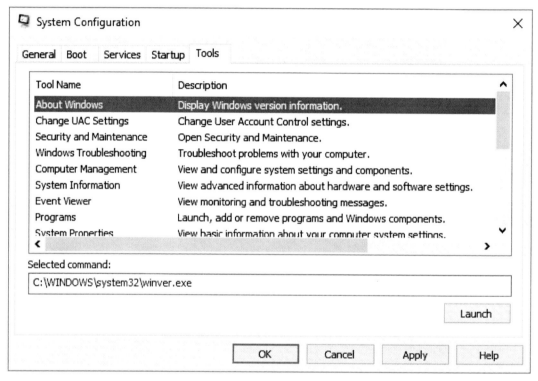

System Configuration Utility—Tools tab. (Screenshot used with permission from Microsoft.)

TROUBLESHOOTING TIPS FOR WINDOWS SYSTEM ISSUES

This section discusses some typical Windows error messages and conditions.

SLOW SYSTEM PERFORMANCE

Slow system performance can have many causes. Use **Task Manager** to determine if any resources are at 90-100% utilization and then note which process is most active. You may need to identify a particular Windows service running within a svchost.exe process (use the PID). **Windows Update/Installer**, the Superfetch/ Prefetch caching engine, and **Windows Defender** (or third-party security software) are often the culprits.

1. Wait for these processes to complete—if there is a mix of CPU, memory, and disk activity, then the process is probably operating normally, if slowly. If there is no disk activity or conversely if disk activity does not drop from 100%, the process could have stalled.

 Show Slide(s)

Troubleshooting Tips for Windows System Issues (3 slides)

Teaching Tip

Defragmentation is covered in the maintenance topic.

2. If the process or system continues to be unresponsive, you can either restart the service or kill the task process.
3. If killing the process doesn't restore system performance, try restarting the computer (reboot). The problem could be transitory and might not reoccur.
4. If the service or process becomes unresponsive again after restarting, disable it and check with the software vendor for any known problems.

If you can't identify any overutilization, consider the following troubleshooting techniques and solutions:

- Apply updates—check for any missing Windows and application updates and install the latest drivers for hardware devices.
- Defragment the hard drive—running defrag regularly on a Hard Disk Drive (HDD) improves file I/O by putting files into contiguous clusters. Also make sure there is sufficient free disk space.
- Power management issues—if the user has been closing sessions using sleep or hibernate, try restarting the computer. Verify that the system is not operating in a power-saving mode (CPU throttling).
- Check for underpowered components—check resource utilization using **Task Manager**, **Resource Monitor**, or (for more extended periods) **Performance Monitor**. If CPU, system memory, disk, or network resources are continually stretched then the system will have to be upgraded.
- Disable application startup—use the **System Configuration Utility** (`msconfig`) or **Task Manager** to prevent unnecessary services and programs from running at startup. If you need to run the services, consider setting them to delayed startup or manual startup to avoid slowing down boot times too much.
- Disable Windows services/applications—if a service is not required and is causing problems, you can set it to Disabled to prevent it from being started. Note that some security-critical services (such as Windows Update) can be re-enabled automatically by the OS.
- Security scan—scan the computer for viruses and other malware.
- Check the configuration of antivirus software—while necessary to keep users as safe as possible from malware, A-V software can have a very harmful effect on performance. Try disabling scanning temporarily to test whether performance improves. Make sure the software is configured to exclude Windows system files it shouldn't scan and configure any exceptions for software applications recommended by the vendor. These typically include database files and the image files used for virtual hard disks.

SERVICE FAILS TO START

If you see a message such as **One or more services failed to start** during the Windows load sequence, check **Event Viewer** and/or the **Services** snap-in to identify which service has failed. Troubleshooting services can be complex, but bear the following general advice in mind:

- Try to start the service manually—as most computers run a lot of services at startup, some can sometimes become "stuck." If a service is not required "immediately," it may help to set it to delayed start.
- Services depend on account permissions to run—make sure that the service has sufficient privileges. Check that the service is associated with a valid user or system account and that the password configured for the account is correct.
- Some services depend on other services to run—verify that disabling one service has not inadvertently affected others.
- If a core Windows service is affected, check system files and scan the disk for errors and malware.
- If an application service is affected, try reinstalling the application.

- You may be able to use **regsvr32** to re-register the software component (Dynamic Link Library [DLL]) that the service relies upon. In 64-bit versions of Windows, there are two versions of **regsvr32**. The 64-bit version (located in **%SystemRoot% \System32\regsvr32.exe**) is called by default and used with 64-bit DLLs. The 32-bit version is in **%SystemRoot%\SysWOW64\regsvr32**. Run this version to re-register 32-bit DLLs.
- Check whether the service is supposed to run—faulty software uninstall routines can leave "orphan" registry entries and startup shortcuts. Use the **System Configuration Utility** (**msconfig**) or **Registry Editor** (`regedit`) to look for orphaned items.

TROUBLESHOOTING TIPS FOR APPLICATION ISSUES

Show Slide(s)

Troubleshooting Tips for Application Issues (2 slides)

Teaching Tip

Printing is covered in detail in the printing topics for the Core 1 objectives.

As well as system-wide issues, some errors may be isolated to a particular application or file type.

APPLICATION CRASHES

If an application crashes, the first priority is to try to preserve any data that was being processed. Users should be trained to save regularly, but modern suites such as Microsoft Office are configured to save recovery files regularly, minimizing the chance of data loss.

Try to give the process time to become responsive again and try to establish if you need to try to recover data from temporary files or folders. When you have done all you can to preserve data, kill the task process. If the application crashes continually, check the event logs for any possible causes. Try to identify whether the cause lies in processing a particular data file or not.

If you cannot identify a specific cause of a problem, the generic solution to this type of problem is to uninstall then reinstall. Sometimes the Windows installer fails to remove every file and registry setting; if this is the case, then following manual uninstall instructions might help.

An uninstall followed by a reinstall can be a lengthy process. Many installers offer a **Repair** option (accessed via **Programs and Features**).

PRINTING ISSUES

Printing issues can involve the printer hardware, network connectivity, or Windows settings. If you can discount hardware and network problems, make the following checks in Windows:

1. Use the printer's property dialog box to try printing a test page. If this is successful, there must be an application or file-specific problem.
2. Open the print queue and check for stalled print jobs.
3. Restart the print spooler service.
4. Check for any driver updates or known issues.
5. Check permissions configured on the printer.
6. Check for disk problems on the partition hosting the spool folder.

BLUE SCREENS AND SPONTANEOUS SHUTDOWNS

Show Slide(s)

Blue Screens and Spontaneous Shutdowns (2 slides)

A **Blue Screen of Death (BSoD)** displays a Windows **STOP** error. A **STOP** error is one that causes Windows to halt. **STOP** errors can occur when Windows loads or while it is running. Most BSoDs, especially those that occur during startup, are caused by faulty hardware or hardware drivers.

- Use **System Restore**, or (if you can boot to **Safe Mode**), **Rollback Driver** to restore the system to a working state.

- Remove a recently added hardware device or uninstall a recently installed program.
- Check seating of hardware components and cables.
- Run hardware diagnostics, `chkdsk`, and scan for malware.
- Make a note of the stop error code (which will be in the form: Stop: 0x0...) and search the Microsoft Knowledge Base (**support.microsoft.com/search**) for known fixes and troubleshooting tips. The various newsgroups accessible from this site offer another valuable source of assistance.

```
A problem has been detected and windows has been shut down to prevent damage
to your computer.

A process or thread crucial to system operation has unexpectedly exited or been
terminated.

If this is the first time you've seen this stop error screen,
restart your computer. If this screen appears again, follow
these steps:

Check to make sure any new hardware or software is properly installed.
If this is a new installation, ask your hardware or software manufacturer
for any windows updates you might need.

If problems continue, disable or remove any newly installed hardware
or software. Disable BIOS memory options such as caching or shadowing.
If you need to use Safe Mode to remove or disable components, restart
your computer, press F8 to select Advanced Startup Options, and then
select Safe Mode.

Technical information:

*** STOP: 0x000000F4 (0x0000000000000003,0xFFFFFA800275F060,0xFFFFFA800275F340,0
xFFFFF80002984DB0)


Collecting data for crash dump ...
Initializing disk for crash dump ...
Beginning dump of physical memory.
Dumping physical memory to disk:  10
```

Blue Screen (of Death or BSoD). (Screenshot used with permission from Microsoft.)

Note: *If the system autorestarts after a blue screen and you cannot read the error, press* **F8** *after POST to open the* **Advanced Options** *menu and select the* **Disable automatic restarts** *option. This option can also be set from* **Advanced System Properties→Startup and Recovery Settings***.*

If a system halts without any sort of error message, there is likely to be a power problem or a problem with the CPU.

TROUBLESHOOTING TIPS FOR FILE AND MEMORY CORRUPTION

Problems with slow performance, application crashes, and blue screens could be caused by some sort of file corruption occurring on the disk or in system memory. You can use the following tools to verify the integrity of system files and memory hardware.

SYSTEM FILE CHECKER

Windows comes with a **Windows Resource Protection** mechanism to prevent damage to or malicious use of system files and registry keys and files.

Show Slide(s)

Troubleshooting Tips for File and Memory Corruption (3 slides)

Teaching Tip

Note that these tools can be used to detect and recover from virus and spyware infection, though they are not a substitute for antivirus software.

The **System File Checker** utility (`sfc`) provides a manual interface for verifying system files and restoring them from cache if they are found to be corrupt or damaged. System files (and shared program files) are maintained and version controlled in the **WINSxS** system folder. This means that the product media is not called upon, but the **WINSxS** folder can consume quite a lot of disk space.

The program can be used from a command line (as Administrator) in the following modes:

- `sfc /scannow`—runs a scan immediately.
- `sfc /scanonce`—schedules a scan when the computer is next restarted.
- `sfc /scanboot`—schedules scans whenever the PC boots.

```
Administrator: Command Prompt                                    —    □    ×

C:\WINDOWS\system32>sfc

Microsoft (R) Windows (R) Resource Checker Version 6.0
Copyright (C) Microsoft Corporation. All rights reserved.

Scans the integrity of all protected system files and replaces incorrect versions with
correct Microsoft versions.

SFC [/SCANNOW] [/VERIFYONLY] [/SCANFILE=<file>] [/VERIFYFILE=<file>]
    [/OFFWINDIR=<offline windows directory> /OFFBOOTDIR=<offline boot directory> [/OFFLOGF
ILE=<log file path>]]

/SCANNOW       Scans integrity of all protected system files and repairs files with
               problems when possible.
/VERIFYONLY    Scans integrity of all protected system files. No repair operation is
               performed.
/SCANFILE      Scans integrity of the referenced file, repairs file if problems are
               identified. Specify full path <file>
/VERIFYFILE    Verifies the integrity of the file with full path <file>.  No repair
               operation is performed.
/OFFBOOTDIR    For offline repair, specify the location of the offline boot directory
/OFFWINDIR     For offline repair, specify the location of the offline windows directory
/OFFLOGFILE    For offline repair, optionally enable logging by specifying a log file pat
h

e.g.

       sfc /SCANNOW
       sfc /VERIFYFILE=c:\windows\system32\kernel32.dll
       sfc /SCANFILE=d:\windows\system32\kernel32.dll /OFFBOOTDIR=d:\ /OFFWINDIR=d:\windo
ws
       sfc /SCANFILE=d:\windows\system32\kernel32.dll /OFFBOOTDIR=d:\ /OFFWINDIR=d:\windo
ws /OFFLOGFILE=c:\log.txt
       sfc /VERIFYONLY
```

System File Checker utility. (Screenshot used with permission from Microsoft.)

WINDOWS MEMORY DIAGNOSTICS

Windows includes a **Windows Memory Diagnostics** tool to test memory chips for errors. You can either run the tool from **Administrative Tools** or boot to **Windows Preinstallation/Recovery Environment** and select **Windows Memory Diagnostic**. Select **Restart now** and check for problems. The computer will restart and run the test. Press **F1** if you want to configure test options.

If errors are found, first check that all the memory modules are correctly seated. Remove all the memory modules but one and retest. You should be able to identify the faulty board by a process of elimination. If a known-good board is reported faulty, the problem is likely to lie in the motherboard.

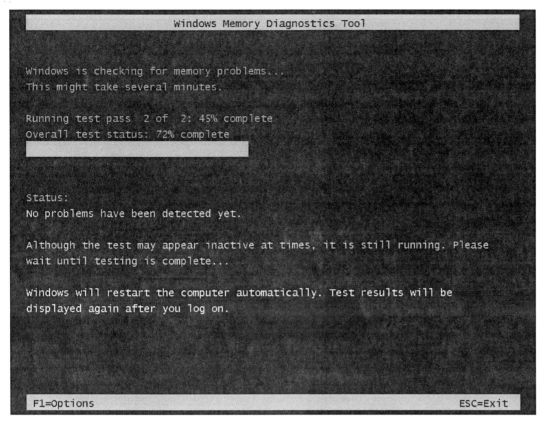

```
                    Windows Memory Diagnostics Tool

Windows is checking for memory problems...
This might take several minutes.

Running test pass  2 of  2: 45% complete
Overall test status: 72% complete



Status:
No problems have been detected yet.

Although the test may appear inactive at times, it is still running. Please
wait until testing is complete...

Windows will restart the computer automatically. Test results will be
displayed again after you log on.




F1=Options                                                     ESC=Exit
```

Windows Memory Diagnostics. (Screenshot used with permission from Microsoft.)

TROUBLESHOOTING TIPS FOR BOOT PROBLEMS

Assuming there is no underlying hardware issue, the general technique for troubleshooting boot problems is to determine the failure point, and therefore the missing or corrupt file. This can then be replaced, either from the source files or using some sort of recovery disk.

BOOT PROCESS

When a computer starts, the firmware runs a **Power On Self Test (POST)** to verify that the system components are present and functioning correctly. It then identifies a boot device and passes control to the operating system's boot loader process.

With a legacy BIOS, the firmware scans the disk identified as the boot device and reads the **Master Boot Record (MBR)** in the first sector of the disk. The MBR identifies the **boot sector** or **Volume Boot Record (VBR)** for the partition marked as active. The VBR loads the boot manager, which for Windows is **bootmgr.exe**. The boot manager reads information from the **Boot Configuration Data (BCD)** file, which identifies operating systems installed on the computer. bootmgr and the BCD are normally installed to a hidden **System Reserved** partition. This partition can be formatted as either FAT32 or NTFS.

Assuming there is only a single Windows installation, the boot manager loads the Windows boot loader **winload.exe** in the system root folder.

 Note: If there is more than one OS installation, the boot manager shows a boot menu allowing the user to select the installation to boot.

winload then continues the Windows boot process by loading the kernel (**ntoskrnl.exe**), the Hardware Abstraction Layer (**hal.dll**), and boot device drivers.

 Show Slide(s)
Troubleshooting Tips for Boot Problems (2 slides)

 Teaching Tip
Make sure learners are aware of which recovery tool is suitable for different situations and in what order you might try using these tools.

Control is then passed to the kernel, which initializes and starts loading the required processes. When complete, the **winlogon** process waits for the user to authenticate.

With an EFI boot, the initial part of the boot process is different. Following POST, the firmware reads the **GUID Partition Table (GPT)** on the boot device.

The GPT identifies the EFI System Partition, which is always formatted with FAT. The EFI system partition contains the **bootmgr.efi** boot manager and the BCD. In point-of-fact, Windows uses its own implementation of the boot manager called **bootmgfw.efi** (**bootmgr.efi** is configured to time out quickly and **bootmgfw.efi** loads instead). Each Windows installation has a subfolder under **\EFI\Microsoft** that contains a BCD and **bootmgfw.efi**.

bootmgfw.efi reads the BCD to identify whether to show a boot menu and for the location of **winload.efi**. From this point, the Windows boot loader continues the boot process by loading the kernel, as described previously.

FAILURE TO BOOT/INVALID BOOT DISK

If the system firmware returns an error message such as **No boot device found** or **Invalid boot disk**, then the system has completely failed to boot. The most common cause of this error used to be leaving a floppy disk in the drive on a restart. A modern cause is for the system firmware to be set to use USB for boot. Check for any removable disks and change the boot device priority/boot order if necessary. If this message occurs when booting from a hard disk or SSD, check the connections to the drive. If the error is transitory (for example, if the message occurs a few times then the PC starts to boot OK), it could be a sign that the hard disk is failing. On an older system, it could be that the system firmware is having trouble detecting the drive.

NO OS FOUND

An **OS missing** type message can appear when a disk drive is identified as the boot device but does not report the location of the OS loader. This could indicate a faulty disk, so try running disk diagnostics (if available) then use a recovery option to run `chkdsk`.

If the disk cannot be detected, enter system setup and try modifying settings (or even resetting the default settings). If the disk's presence is reported by the system firmware but Windows still will not boot, use a startup repair tool to open a recovery mode command prompt and use the `bootrec` tool to try to repair the drive's boot information.

1. Enter `bootrec /fixmbr` to attempt repair of the MBR.
2. Enter `bootrec /fixboot` to attempt repair of the boot sector.
3. Enter `bootrec /rebuildbcd` to add missing Windows installations to the Boot Configuration Database (BCD).

You could also use `diskpart` to ensure that the system partition is marked as active and that no other partitions have been marked as active.

GRAPHICAL INTERFACE FAILS TO LOAD/BLACK SCREEN

If Windows appears to boot but does not display the logon dialog box or does not load the desktop following logon, the likely causes are malware infection or corruption of drivers or other system files. If the system will boot to a GUI in Safe Mode, then replace the graphics adapter driver. If the system will not boot to a GUI at all, then the Windows installation will probably have to be repaired or recovered from backup. It is also possible that the boot configuration has been changed through `msconfig` and just needs to be set back.

Windows is also sporadically prone to black screen issues, where nothing appears on the screen. This will often occur during update installs, where the best course of action is to give the system time to complete the update. Look for signs of continuing disk activity and spinning dots appearing on the screen. If the system does not recover from a black screen, then try searching for any currently known issues on support and troubleshooting sites (**support.microsoft.com/en-ph/help/14106/windows-10-troubleshoot-black-screen-problems**). You can use the key sequence **Windows+Ctrl+Shift+B** to test whether the system is responsive. There should be a beep and the display may reinitialize.

If the problem occurs frequently, use `sfc` to verify system file integrity and check video drivers.

SLOW BOOT/SLOW PROFILE LOAD

If Windows does boot, but only very slowly, you need to try to identify what is happening to slow the process down. You can enable verbose status messages during the Windows load sequence by configuring a system policy or applying a registry setting. In Windows 7, enable **Verbose vs normal status messages** or in Windows 8/10, enable **Display highly detailed status messages**.

Delays affecting the system prior to logon are caused by loading drivers and services. Quite often the culprit will be some type of network service or configuration not working optimally, but there could be some sort of file corruption, too.

If the system is slow to load the desktop following logon, the issue could be a corrupt user profile. The registry settings file **ntuser.dat** is particularly prone to this. Rebuilding a local user profile means creating a new account and then copying files from the old, corrupt profile to the new one, but excluding the following files:

- **Ntuser.dat**
- **Ntuser.dat.log**
- **Ntuser.ini**

SAFE BOOT

Safe Mode loads only basic drivers and services required to start the system. This is a useful troubleshooting mode as it isolates reliability or performance problems to add-in drivers or application services and rules out having to fully reinstall Windows. It may also be a means of running analysis and recovery tools, such as `chkdsk`, **System Restore**, or antivirus utilities.

Safe Mode defaults to SVGA resolution (800x600). Higher resolutions may be available if the basic driver supports them.

You can boot to Safe Mode using the System Configuration utility, but this option is only useful if you can sign in to Windows anyway. If you cannot sign in, there are different startup repair options for Windows 7 and Windows 8/10.

WINDOWS 7 ADVANCED BOOT OPTIONS

In Windows 7, the **Advanced Boot Options** menu allows the selection of different startup modes for troubleshooting. To show the menu, press **F8** during startup—after the memory count; try tapping repeatedly if the menu doesn't get displayed.

Teaching Tip

We're not going to attempt to discuss how to configure policies here. There will be a section on it later in the course (though the exam objectives focuses on security-related policies). Learners can search on either term for detailed instructions.

Show Slide(s)

Safe Boot (4 slides)

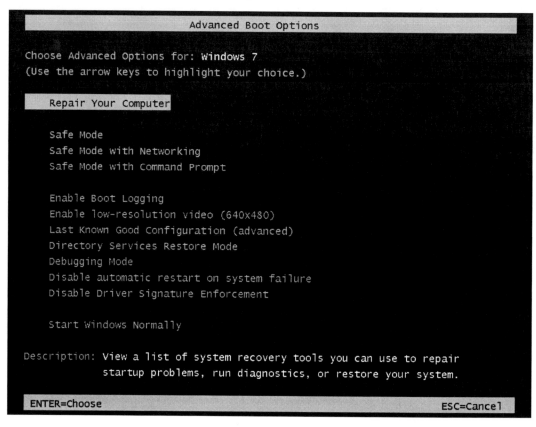

Advanced Boot Options in Windows 7. (Screenshot used with permission from Microsoft.)

Apart from Safe Mode, some of the other options include:

- **Safe Mode with Networking**—includes drivers and services required to access the network.
- **Safe Mode with Command Prompt**—runs the command shell rather than Explorer.
- **Last Known Good**—boots with the last registry configuration that was used to log on successfully.

WINDOWS 8/10 STARTUP SETTINGS

In Windows 8 and Windows 10, the boot process happens too quickly to use **F8**. You can hold the **Shift** key when selecting the **Restart** option from the **Power** menu to display troubleshooting options—note that you don't have to sign in to view the power menu.

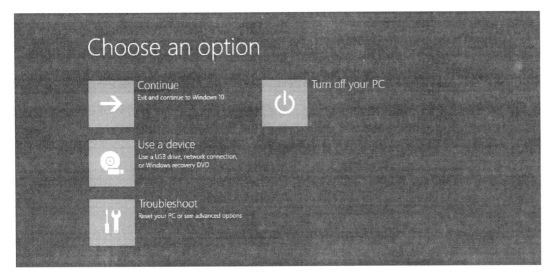

Windows 10 Startup options. (Screenshot used with permission from Microsoft.)

From the first **Choose an option** screen, select **Troubleshoot**. From the next screen, select **Advanced options**. Select **Startup Settings**, then on the next screen, select **Restart**.

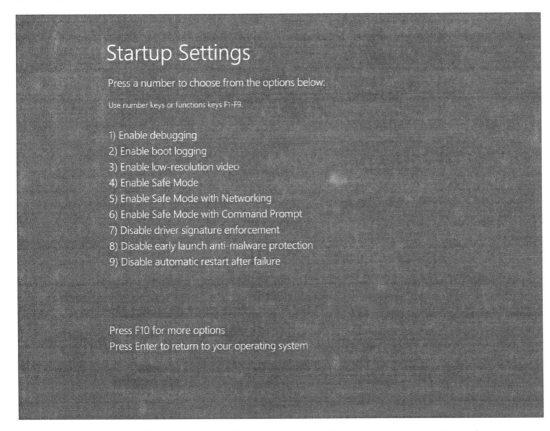

Windows 10 Startup Settings. (Screenshot used with permission from Microsoft.)

Press **F4** to select **Safe Mode**, or choose another option as necessary.

WinRE AND STARTUP REPAIR

Show Slide(s)

WinRE and Startup Repair (2 slides)

Teaching Tip

Make sure learners know the difference between Windows 7 and Windows 8/10 on this topic.

If you cannot boot the computer from the local installation, you can try booting from the product media, a repair disk, or a recovery partition. You may have to access BIOS or UEFI setup to configure the boot device to the recovery media.

If you don't have the product media, you can make a system repair disk from Windows using the `recdisc` tool. Obviously, you need to have done this before the computer starts failing to boot or create one using a working Windows installation.

Once in the recovery environment, if the boot files are damaged, you can use the **Startup Repair** option to try to fix them. You can also launch **System Restore** or restore from an image backup from here. The last two options are to run a memory diagnostic and to drop into the **Recovery Environment** command prompt, where you could run startup recovery commands such as `diskpart`, `sfc`, `chkdsk`, `bootrec`, `bcdedit`, or `regedit` manually.

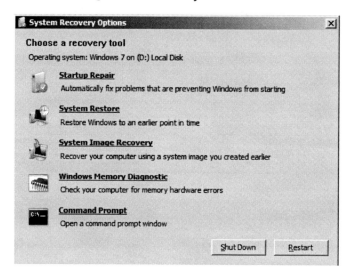

Windows 7 System Recovery Options. (Screenshot used with permission from Microsoft.)

 Note: *The Recovery Environment is an extended version of the Preinstallation Environment (PE) used to set up Windows in the first place.*

In Windows 8/10, as well as `recdisc`, you can use the **Recovery Media Creator** to create a USB-based repair disk and optionally include any recovery partition from the local disk. Boot using the recovery media, then from the first **Choose an option** screen, select **Troubleshoot**. From the next screen, select **Advanced options**.

Advanced options let you run system restore, reinstall from a system image backup, run the automated startup repair tool, or drop to a command prompt. On a UEFI-based install, there is also an option to reboot to the system firmware setup program. In Windows 10, you may also be able to use **See more recovery options** to revert to a previous build, following a feature update.

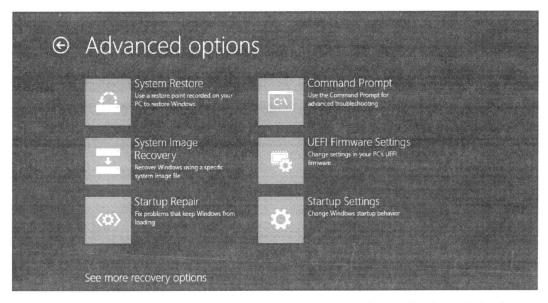

Windows 10 Startup Troubleshooting—Advanced options. (Screenshot used with permission from Microsoft.)

SYSTEM RESTORE

System Restore allows you to roll back from system configuration changes. **System Restore** allows for multiple restore points to be maintained (some are created automatically) and to roll back from changes to the whole registry and reverse program installations and updates.

 Note: System Restore does not restore (or delete) user data files. Files stored in users' Documents folders will be preserved. Also, the contents of settings folders such as Recent and Favorite links and Temporary Internet Files will not be rolled back.

CONFIGURING SYSTEM PROTECTION

The **System Protection** tab (opened via the **System Properties** applet) lets you select which disk(s) to enable for system restore and configure how much disk capacity is used. The disk must be formatted with NTFS, have a minimum of 300 MB free space, and be over 1 GB in size.

Restore points are created automatically in response to application and update installs. They are also created periodically by the **Scheduled Tasks** applet. Windows will try to create one when it detects the PC is idle if no other restore points have been created in the last 7 days. You can also create a restore point manually from this dialog box.

 Show Slide(s)
System Restore (4 slides)

 Teaching Tip
Stress the key facts of System Restore:

* Doesn't change data files.

* Can be run from the product disk.

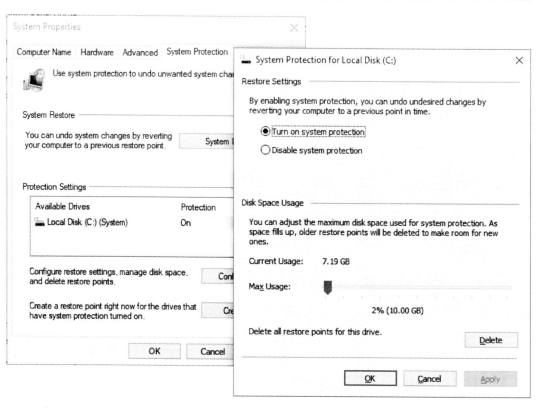

Configuring System Protection in Windows 10. (Screenshot used with permission from Microsoft.)

USING SYSTEM RESTORE

To restore the system, open the **System Restore** tool (`rstrui`), or run it by booting from the product disk or selecting the **Repair Your Computer** from the **Advanced Options** boot menu (Windows 7) or the Startup Recovery tools in Windows 8/10.

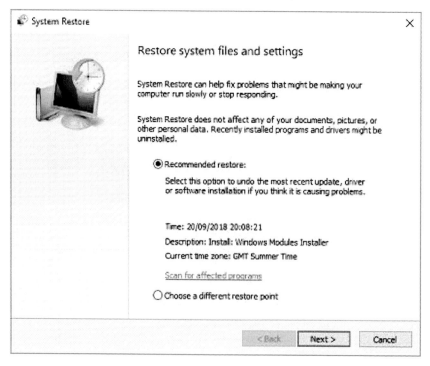

Using System Restore to apply a previous system configuration. (Screenshot used with permission from Microsoft.)

*Note: **System Restore** does not usually reset passwords (that is, passwords will remain as they were before you ran the restore tool), but **System Restore** does reset passwords to what they were at the time the restore point was created if you run it from the product disk. This can be used to recover from a forgotten administrator password (refer to **https://support.microsoft.com/en-us/help/940765/how-to-use-system-restore-to-log-on-to-windows-7-or-windows-vista-when** for more details).*

ROLL BACK UPDATES

If an update causes problems, you can try to uninstall it. You might be able to use **System Restore** to do this. Otherwise, open the **Programs and Features** applet and click **View installed updates**. Select the update then click the **Uninstall** button.

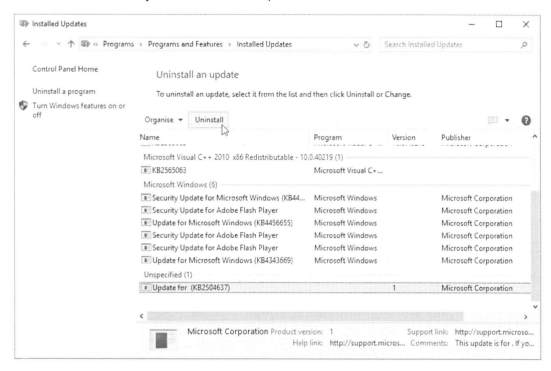

Using Programs and Features to uninstall an update. (Screenshot used with permission from Microsoft.)

ROLL BACK DEVICE DRIVERS

If you are experiencing problems with a device and you have recently updated the driver, Windows also provides a **Roll Back Driver** feature. A new driver may not work properly because it has not been fully tested or it may not work on your particular system. Driver roll back can recover a system speedily and easily where this has occurred. You can use **Device Manager** to revert to the previous driver. Right-click the device and select **Properties**. Click the **Driver** tab then click the **Roll Back Driver** button.

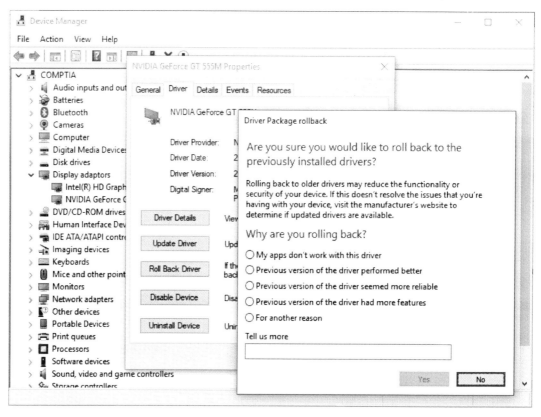

Using driver rollback via Device Manager. (Screenshot used with permission from Microsoft.)

Show Slide(s)

System Repair and Reinstall (4 slides)

SYSTEM REPAIR AND REINSTALL

If **System Restore** or **Startup Repair** do not work and you cannot boot to a log on, try to boot in **Safe Mode**. If this works, you should then be able to pinpoint the problem to a particular driver or service. **Safe Mode** loads Windows with a minimal set of drivers and services, so if this works it tells you that something is going wrong later on in the OS load. If the computer will not boot at all, you will have to resort to a system repair tool or possibly a reinstall option and restore from data backup (presuming you have made one). The various versions of Windows use different system recovery tools and backup processes.

CREATING AND USING A RECOVERY IMAGE

You can make a complete backup of the system configuration and data files. This is called an **image**. This method is simple, but you do need a backup device with large capacity. The best option is usually a removable hard drive. The best compression ratio you can hope for is 2:1—so a 20 GB system will create a 10 GB image—but if the system contains a lot of files that are already heavily compressed, the ratio could be a lot lower. You do have to keep the image up-to-date or make a separate data backup.

You create a system image using the **Backup and Restore** applet in **Control Panel**. Click the **Create a system image** link in the tasks pane. Select a backup device and give the image a suitable name.

To recover the system using the backup image, use the **Advanced Boot Option** or the **System Image Recovery** option off a repair disk or recovery environment.

REINSTALLING WINDOWS

If you do not have an up-to-date image, the last option is to reinstall Windows. You can try reinstalling Windows 7 over the top of an existing installation. This will preserve the

---

previous data in a **Windows.old** folder and might allow you to recover data files, if you do not have a data backup. You will need to reinstall software applications and reconfigure user accounts and settings.

In Windows 8 and Windows 10, there is a **reset** option to try to repair the installation. This recopies the system files and reverts all PC settings to the default, but can preserve user personalization settings, data files, and apps installed via Windows Store. Desktop applications are removed.

Restart to the recovery environment (or use a repair disk). From the first **Choose an option** screen, select **Troubleshoot**. Select **Reset this PC**.

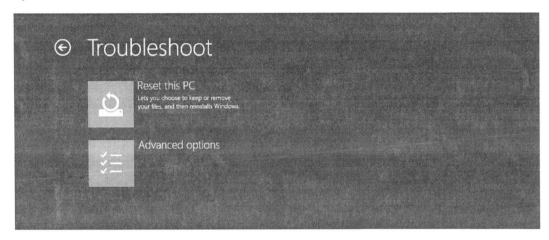

Windows 10 startup recovery. (Screenshot used with permission from Microsoft.)

Reset this PC options. (Screenshot used with permission from Microsoft.)

Select **Keep my files** or **Remove everything** as appropriate. The computer will restart and you will be prompted to sign on using an administrator account to authorize the reinstallation. Select **Reset** to continue (or **Cancel** if you have changed your mind).

If you choose to remove everything, there is a further option to securely delete information from the drive. This will take several hours but is recommended if you are giving up ownership of the PC.

Choosing whether to securely erase the drive. (Screenshot used with permission from Microsoft.)

GUIDELINES FOR TROUBLESHOOTING WINDOWS ISSUES

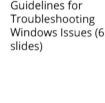

Show Slide(s)

Guidelines for Troubleshooting Windows Issues (6 slides)

 Note: *All of the Guidelines for this lesson are available as checklists from the **Checklist** tile on the CHOICE Course screen.*

Consider the following guidelines when troubleshooting issues on a Windows machine.

TROUBLESHOOT WINDOWS ISSUES

Follow these guidelines for troubleshooting Windows issues:

- Examine log files and **Event Viewer** to get information about what has happened on the system.
- Use the **System Configuration Utility** to modify system settings and files that affect the way the computer boots and loads Windows.
- Use **Task Manager** to attempt to locate a reason for slow system performance.
- Use **Event Viewer** to attempt to determine why a service fails to start.
- If an application crashes:
  - Try to preserve any data that was being processed.
  - See if the process will become responsive again or if you need to kill the process.
  - Attempt to recover data from temporary files or folders if the process was killed.
  - Examine **Event Viewer** logs.
  - If the application repeatedly crashes, uninstall then reinstall the application, or if available, use the **Repair** option in **Programs and Features**.
- If there are printing issues, determine whether the issue is with the printer hardware or network connectivity. If it isn't those issues, examine Windows settings and check the following:
  1. Use the printer's property dialog box to try printing a test page. If this is successful, there must be an application or file-specific problem.
  2. Open the print queue and check for stalled print jobs.
  3. Restart the print spooler service.
  4. Check for any driver updates or known issues.
  5. Check permissions configured on the printer.
  6. Check for disk problems on the partition hosting the spool folder.
- If the user experiences frequent BSoDs:

- Use **System Restore**, or (if you can boot to **Safe Mode**), **Rollback Driver** to restore the system to a working state.
- Remove a recently added hardware device or uninstall a recently installed program.
- Check seating of hardware components and cables.
- Run hardware diagnostics, **chkdsk**, and scan for malware.
- Make a note of the stop error code (which will be in the form: Stop: 0x0...) and search the Microsoft Knowledge Base (**support.microsoft.com/search**) for known fixes and troubleshooting tips. The various newsgroups accessible from this site offer another valuable source of assistance.

- If the user experiences file or memory corruption:

  - Use **sfc** to verify system files and restore them from cache if corrupt or damaged.
  - Use the **Windows Memory Diagnostics** tool to test memory chips for errors.
- If the user is experiencing boot problems, determine the failure point, and therefore the missing or corrupt file. This can then be replaced, either from the source files or using some sort of recovery disk.
- Try booting into **Safe Mode** to troubleshoot by loading only minimal required components.
- If you cannot boot the computer from the local installation, you can try booting from the product media, a repair disk, or a recovery partition. You may have to access BIOS or UEFI setup to configure the boot device to the recovery media.
- Use **System Restore** to rollback system configuration changes.
- Rollback updates that are causing issues by uninstalling them.

  1. Open **Programs and Features**.
  2. Select **View installed updates**.
  3. Select the update that is causing the problem, then select the **Uninstall** button.
- Rollback troublesome device drivers:

  1. Open **Device Manager**.
  2. Right-click the device having the problem and select **Properties**.
  3. Select the **Driver** tab.
  4. Select the **Roll Back Driver** button.
- If all else fails, determine whether you need to perform a system restore or reinstall Windows.

*Note: To learn more, check the **Video** tile on the CHOICE Course screen for any videos that supplement the content for this lesson.*

Activity 7-4
Discussing Windows Troubleshooting

Show Slide(s)

Activity: Discussing Windows Troubleshooting

SCENARIO
Answer the following questions to check your understanding of the topic.

1. **What is the full path to the Windows system log?**

    %SystemRoot%\System32\Winevt\Logs\System.evtx

2. **What are the tab headings in `msconfig`, and which tab is not in the Windows 8/10 version?**

    General, **Boot**, **Services**, **Startup**, and **Tools**. In Windows 8/10, the functionality of the **Startup** tab has moved to Task Manager.

3. **What device optimization settings could you check to mitigate slow performance problems?**

    Defragment the hard disk, and ensure there is sufficient free space. Verify that the power management configuration is not throttling components such as the CPU or GPU. You can also use performance monitoring to check device utilization and determine whether upgrades are required.

4. A user calls saying that her screen occasionally goes blue and the system shuts down.

    What should you advise her to do?

    Record as much information from the blue screen, especially the STOP error number, as she can so that you can research the particular error.

5. A program is continually using 99-100% of processor time.

    What should you do?

    Try to end the application or the process using Task Manager, then contact the application vendor to find out why the problem is occurring.

6. **Where would you start to investigate a "Service failed to start" error?**

    Check the event log for more information.

Teaching Tip

You might also mention System Restore as a method of reverting from a known faulty driver update.

7. **Which troubleshooting tool is most likely to identify whether a problem is related to a device driver or to a faulty system component?**

Using **Safe Mode** boots with a minimal set of drivers and services. If **Safe Mode** boot is successful but normal boot is not, the issue is likely to be with driver software. Re-enable each driver in turn to identify the culprit. If the problem also manifests in **Safe Mode**, it is more likely to have an underlying hardware cause.

8. You are assisting a user whose application is in the state shown in the exhibit.

How would you troubleshoot this problem?

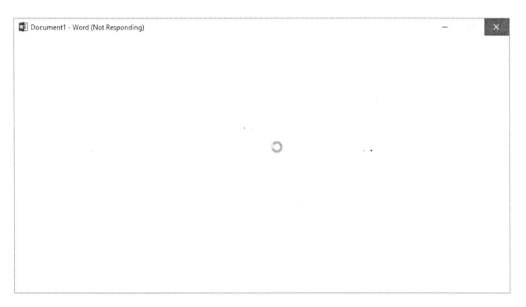

The user will be concerned about losing any unsaved work. Ask the user to describe what he or she was doing at the time of the crash to try to diagnose what might have caused it. Give the program a few minutes to finish processing —check Task Manager for ongoing disk activity. If the application does not start responding, check autosave and temp folders for a recent copy of the file data. Use Task Manager to end the process. Restart the application and try to open any file data you might have recovered. Check the log files and online resources to try to diagnose the cause of the crash. If the problem persists, consider solutions such as disabling add-ons or reinstalling. Demonstrate to the user how to set up autosave (if it is not already configured) and how to save regularly.

9. A system is experiencing intermittent boot errors. The issue can be fixed temporarily by repairing the boot files.

What should you do to fix the problem in the longer term?

Run diagnostic software to rule out a disk problem. Recurrent file errors/ corruption are a sign the disk is failing. You might also consider malware as a cause.

10. A computer is caught in a reboot loop. It starts, shows a BSoD, then reboots.

What should you do?

Boot using a recovery tool, such as the product disc, and attempt startup repair.

11. **If you suspect improper handling during installation has caused damage to a RAM module, how could you test that suspicion?**

    Run a Memory Diagnostic. This tests each RAM cell and so should uncover any fault.

Activity 7-5
Using Windows Troubleshooting Tools

Show Slide(s)

Activity: Using Windows Troubleshooting Tools

BEFORE YOU BEGIN

Complete this activity by using Hyper-V Manager and the PC1 (Windows 10) and PC2 (Windows 7) VMs. You need to adjust some of the VM settings to facilitate some of the troubleshooting actions you will perform in the activity.

1. In **Hyper-V Manager**, right-click the **PC2** VM and select **Settings**.
2. Select the **BIOS** node, then in the **Startup order** box, select **IDE** and select the **Move Up** button. This prevents the option to boot from the product disc (interfering with selecting the **Advanced Boot** Options menu).
3. Select **OK**.

SCENARIO

In this lab, you will use some of the startup troubleshooting modes for Windows 7 and Windows 10.

---

1. On **PC2**, run the **C:\LABFILES\crash.ps1** script to simulate a BSoD stop error.
   a) Start the **PC2** VM and sign on using the account **Admin** and password **Pa$$w0rd**.
   b) Press the **Windows** key and type *powershell*.
   c) Right-click the **Windows Powershell** link and select **Run as administrator**.
   d) At the **UAC** prompt, select **Yes**.
   e) Type *C:\LABFILES\crash* and press **Enter**.

   The system will go to a bluescreen and start a memory dump.

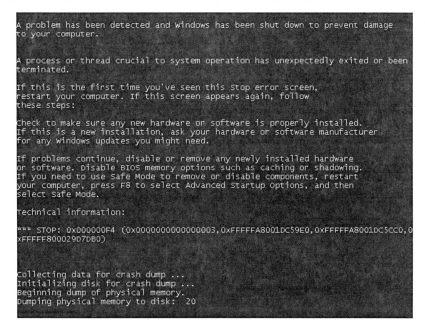

BSoD. (Screenshot used with permission from Microsoft.)

f)   Once this is complete, the system will reboot to Windows Error Recovery.

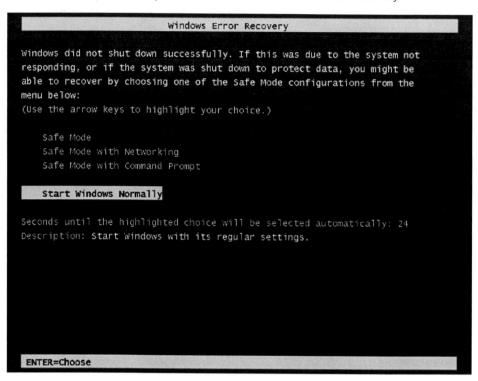

Windows Error Recovery. (Screenshot used with permission from Microsoft.)

g)   Use the arrow keys to select **Safe Mode**. Press **Enter**.

Notice that the device driver names are listed as the computer starts up.

h)   Sign in as **Admin**.

Windows Help and Support opens. This explains what Safe Mode is. Also, you can see Safe Mode in the corners of the computer's display.

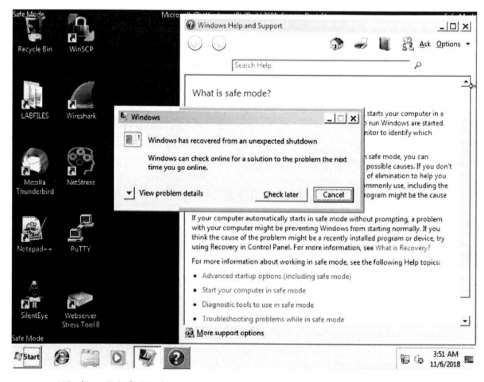

Windows 7 Safe Mode. (Screenshot used with permission from Microsoft.)

2. Use **Event Viewer** to examine logs related to the crash event and using Safe Mode.

    a) When you sign back in, the message **Windows has recovered from an unexpected shutdown** is displayed. Select **View problem details**.

       This shows the location of the memory dump. Analyzing the information in system memory at the time of a crash can help a developer identify the cause of the problem. If there were an actual problem with an application or driver, you would send the dump file to the developer for analysis.

    b) Select the **Cancel** button.

    c) Open **Computer Management**, expand the **Event Viewer** folder, expand **Windows Logs**, and then select the **System** log.

       Note that there are numerous service failure events. These are generated because the system is running in Safe Mode.

    d) Open a couple of items to view the descriptions of the events.

    e) In the **Actions** pane, select **Filter Current Log**.

    f) In the **Filter Current Log** dialog box, check the **Critical** and **Warning** boxes and then select **OK**.

    g) Examine the critical kernel power event.

    h) Open the **Application** log. Filter for any **Warning** or **Error** messages. Are there any serious problems?

       Most of the errors and warnings you see will relate to not being able to contact domain services or use the Internet to obtain updates. The WMI errors are of no concern.

    i) Close the Computer Management console.

    j) Select **Start**, select the arrow on the **Shut down** button, and then select **Restart**. Windows restarts normally.

Teaching Tip

Encourage students to run a web search on any of the errors (such as "WMI error 10"). They will have to use the HOST PC's browser of course (assuming there is classroom Internet access).

3. **Last Known Good** resets the computer to the configuration that was last used successfully to log on. It can be a simple way of recovering the system if installation of a driver causes startup problems. Disable a device such as the network adapter, and then use the LKG boot option to revert the change.

    a) In the **Virtual Machine Connect** window, from the **View** menu, select **Full Screen Mode**.

       You need to use this mode for the VM to recognize keyboard input during the boot sequence.

    b) Sign back into Windows. Open **Computer Management** and select the **Device Manager** snap-in.

    c) Locate a device such as the network adapter that has a **Disable** option when you right-click it.

    d) Right-click the device and select **Disable**. Select **Yes** to confirm.

    e) Select **Start→Shut Down→Restart**.

    f) When the screen turns black, start pressing **F8** to display the **Advanced Boot Options** menu.

       *Note: If you miss it, wait for Windows to boot, press **Ctrl+Alt+End**, and then use the power icon on the logon screen to restart the VM and try again—do not try to log on!*

    g) Use the arrow keys to select **Last Known Good Configuration (advanced)**. Press **Enter**.

       Windows starts normally, but the configuration control set which was last used to sign in successfully is used to startup Windows. Note that using Last Known Good for recovery is only ever successful when, following a device driver system change, you do NOT log on. The logon process overwrites the Last Known Good configuration.

    h) Log on as **Admin**. When the desktop has been initialized, check Device Manager and verify that the device is no longer disabled.

    i) You can now use the **Restore** icon to exit full screen mode if you wish.

4. Both Windows 7 and Windows 10 support the System Restore recovery tool, and on both platforms, it works in a similar way. For the last part of this activity, you will use Windows 10. In this step, enable system protection and create a restore point on PC1.

   a) Start **PC1** and sign on to the **Admin** account with the *Pa$$w0rd* credential.

   b) Click in the search box and type *restore*. Select the **Create a restore point** link.

   c) In **System Properties**, select the **Configure** button.

   d) Under **Restore Settings**, select **Turn on system protection**.

   e) Under **Disk Space Usage**, move the slider bar to the right about a quarter of the way along the **Max Usage** gauge and then select **OK**.

   f) In the **System Properties** dialog box, select the **Create** button.

   g) In the **System Protection** dialog box, type *Initial restore point*, and then select **Create**.

   h) When the confirmation prompt is displayed, select **Close**, and then select **OK** to close the **System Properties** dialog box.

5. Make some configuration changes, such as enabling some Windows Features and changing the account password.

   a) In the Instant Search box, type *windows features*, and select the **Turn Windows features on or off** link from the search results.

   b) In the **Windows Features** dialog box, select the **Internet Information Services** and **Telnet Client** boxes. Select **OK**.

   c) When the feature installation process has completed, if prompted, select **Don't restart**.

   d) Optionally, use **Apps & features** to uninstall one of the applications, such as **Microsoft Baseline Security Analyzer**.

   e) Press **Ctrl+Alt+End** then click **Change a password**.

   f) Type the old password (*Pa$$w0rd*) and a new password of *Trojan01* then press **Enter**. Select **OK**.

   g) Sign out of the VM.

6. Now, imagine that the changes you just made were in fact made by a malicious Trojan, which has now locked you out of your machine. How useful will System Restore be in removing the "Trojan" Windows Features, recovering your password, and recovering your programs? First, try restarting to the Recovery Environment.

   a) At the accounts screen, confirm that you cannot sign in with the password **Pa$$w0rd**.

   b) Select the power icon, then hold down the **Shift** key and select **Restart**.

   c) When the recovery environment is opened at restart, on the **Choose an option** page, select **Troubleshoot**.

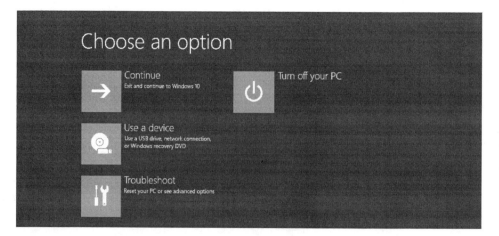

Windows 10 Recovery Environment. (Screenshot used with permission from Microsoft.)

d) Select **Advanced options** and then select **System Restore**.

e) Select the option for the **Admin** account and try to sign on with the password **Pa$ $w0rd**.

This will not work as the "Trojan" changed the account password.

7. Try booting from the product disc to use System Restore.

a) If necessary, in the **Virtual Machine Connect** window for **PC1**, select **Media→DVD Drive→ Insert Disk**.

b) If necessary, browse and select the file **C:\COMPTIA-LABS\win10.iso** (or use the file suggested by your instructor). Select **Open**.

c) From the menu bar, select **File→Settings**.

d) Select the **Firmware** node. In the **Boot order** box, select **DVD Drive** and then select **Move Up**. Select **OK**.

e) In the **Virtual Machine Connect** window, select **Action→Turn Off**.

f) In the **Turn Off Machine** dialog box, select **Turn Off**. If prompted, confirm by selecting **Turn Off**.

g) In the **Virtual Machine Connect** window for **PC1**, select **Start**.

h) When prompted to boot from the DVD, press **Enter**.

Windows starts from the product disc image.

i) Select **Next**.

Windows 10 Setup. (Screenshot used with permission from Microsoft.)

j) Select **Repair your computer**.

k) When the recovery environment is opened, from the **Choose an option** page, select **Troubleshoot**.

l) Select **System Restore**.

m) Under **Choose a target operating system**, select **Windows 10**.

n)   In the **System Restore** wizard, select **Next**.

Using Windows 10 System Restore. (Screenshot used with permission from Microsoft.)

o)   Select the **Initial restore point** row and then select **Next**.

p)   Select **Finish**, and then select **Yes**.

q)   When the restore operation is complete, select **Restart**. Do *not* boot from the disc this time.

r)   When Windows restarts, log on as **Admin**. Which password do you need to use?

   The password should be Pa$$w0rd.

s)   At the **System Restore** prompt, select **Close**.

t)   Open the **Windows Features** dialog box, and verify that the **Internet Information Services** and **Telnet Client** features are not installed.

u)   Optionally, open **Apps & features** to verify that the application is still present.

8.   At the end of each activity, you need to close the VMs. You will always discard any changes you made.

a)   From the connection window, select **Action→Revert**.

b)   If you are prompted to confirm, select the **Revert** button.

c)   Repeat to revert the PC2 VM.

Summary

In this lesson, you maintained and performed troubleshooting on Windows PCs. In your role as an A+ technician, you will be advising and supporting users in a number of areas surrounding computing devices, so using the guidelines and procedures provided in this lesson will enable you to provide the required level of support to users.

Which Windows performance management tools would you expect to use most in your workplace?

A: Answers will vary, but might include Task Manager and Performance Monitor.

Have you ever recovered a severely compromised Windows system? If so, then describe your experience.

A: Answers will vary, but may include having to use Last Known Good Configuration or Safe Mode to identify issues and recover systems. You might need to resort to performing a factory reset if the damage is too severe.

 *Practice Question: Additional practice questions are available on the CompTIA CHOICE platform within the **Assessments** tile.*

Lesson 8

Network Infrastructure Concepts

LESSON INTRODUCTION

In this lesson, you will learn about the technologies underpinning networking infrastructure, such as network cables, wireless standards, switches, routers, and protocols. Having a basic background in networking fundamentals is a vital prerequisite for providing IT support. In today's environment, standalone computing is a rarity. Just about every digital device on the planet today is connected to external resources via some kind of network, whether it is a small office/home office network, a corporate Wide Area Network (WAN), or directly to the Internet itself.

The ability to connect, share, and communicate using a network is crucial for running a business and staying connected to everything in the world, so as a CompTIA® A+® support technician, you will need to understand the technologies that underlie both local and global network communications to ensure that the organization you support stays connected.

LESSON OBJECTIVES

In this lesson, you will:

- Use appropriate tools to select, install, and test network cabling for a given network type.

- Compare and contrast the functions and features of networking hardware devices.

- Compare and contrast wireless networking protocols.

- Compare and contrast Internet connection types.

- Describe the properties and characteristics of Internet Protocol (IP) addressing and network configuration.

- Identify the protocols and ports underpinning Internet applications and local network services.

Topic A
Wired Networks

EXAM OBJECTIVES COVERED
1001-2.2 Compare and contrast common networking hardware devices.
1001-2.7 Compare and contrast Internet connection types, network types, and their features.
1001-2.8 Given a scenario, use appropriate networking tools.
1001-3.1 Explain basic cable types, features, and their purposes.
1001-3.2 Identify common connector types.

Teaching Tip

Learners need to be able to relate different cable and connector types to one another and know the capabilities of different media.

Show Slide(s)

Network Types (4 slides)

Teaching Tip

Learners need to know what LAN, WAN, and MAN mean.

In this topic, you will identify types of wired networks. Recognizing network types and suitable cabling options for them will help you determine the best approach for customer needs. In order to properly and safely work with networking components, you must also understand how networking tools are used and how they can be used to fix common issues found in networks.

NETWORK TYPES

A **network** is two or more computer systems linked together by some form of transmission medium that enables them to share information. The network technology is what connects the computers, but the purpose of the network is to provide services or resources to its users. Historically, these services have included access to shared files, folders, and printers plus email and database applications. Modern networks are evolving to provide more diverse services, including web applications, social networking, Voice over IP, multimedia conferencing, and Internet of Things connectivity for household devices and appliances.

To categorize the size and nature of individual networks, the industry has developed terms that broadly define the scope of different types of network.

LOCAL AREA NETWORKS

One basic distinction between types of network is between **Local Area Networks (LANs)** and Wide Area Networks (WANs). A LAN is a self-contained network that spans a small area, such as a single building, floor, or room. In a LAN, all the nodes or hosts participating in the network are directly connected with cables or short-range wireless media. A LAN is typically a single site or possibly several sites in close proximity connected by high-speed backbones. The term **campus area network (CAN)** is sometimes used for a LAN that spans multiple nearby buildings. Any network where the nodes are within about 1 or 2 km (or about 1 mile) of one another can be thought of as "local."

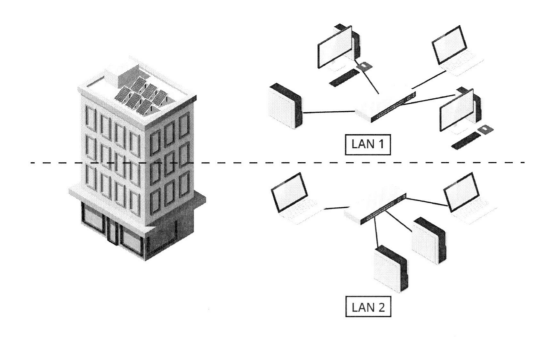

LANs within a building. (Image © 123RF.com.)

WIDE AREA NETWORKS

A **Wide Area Network (WAN)** spans multiple geographic locations. WANs typically connect multiple LANs using long-range transmission media. WANs are usually thought of as relying on some intermediate network, such as the Internet or phone system, to connect geographically diverse LANs. A network where remote users "dial-in" is also a type of WAN.

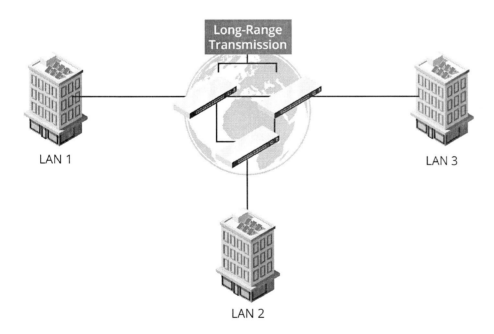

Wide Area Network (WAN). (Image © 123RF.com.)

METROPOLITAN AREA NETWORKS

The term Metropolitan Area Network (MAN) is sometimes used, though it doesn't really have a clear definition other than an area equivalent to a city or other municipality. It could mean a company with multiple connected networks within the same metropolitan area—so, larger than a LAN but smaller than a WAN.

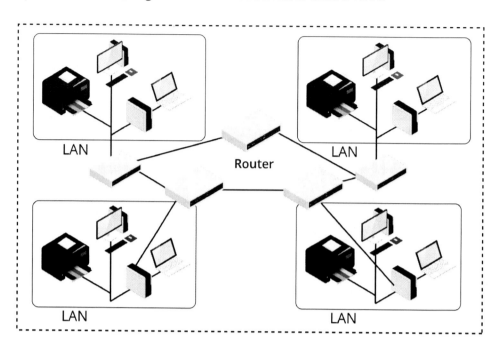

Metropolitan Area Network (MAN). (Image © 123RF.com.)

ETHERNET TYPES AND STANDARDS

Show Slide(s)

Ethernet Types and Standards

Teaching Tip

Learners should know what Ethernet standards relate to in terms of speed and media.

Note that 10G components are expensive. It is used in data centers and possibly for backbone links.

You might also want to note that Ethernet is increasingly widely deployed on WANs, too (Metro Ethernet).

Most cabled LANs are based on the **Ethernet** networking product, developed by the DIX consortium (Digital Equipment Corporation [DEC], Intel, and Xerox). Ethernet standards are now maintained by the Institute of Electrical and Electronics Engineers (IEEE). Ethernet is technically known by the series of standards produced by the IEEE 802.3 working group. Although the product name is not used in 802.3 standards documentation, it is otherwise universally referred to as Ethernet.

There are four broad "types" of Ethernet:

- 10 Mbps (10BASE-)—this is the original standard, specifying cabling and connectors for copper wire and fiber optic products.
- Fast Ethernet (100BASE-)—copper wire and fiber optic implementations of 100 Mbps LANs.
- Gigabit Ethernet (1000BASE-)—1000 Mbps LANs. This has replaced Fast Ethernet as the "standard" for a typical LAN.
- 10G Ethernet (10GBASE-)—10 Gbps links for LANs and WANs, mostly using fiber optic media. 10G Ethernet is widely used in data centers.

The **IEEE 802.11** series of standards (Wi-Fi) are used to implement Wireless Local Area Networks (WLAN) so the technologies complement one another and are often used together in the same network.

Ethernet is a very flexible technology. It can support a wide range of different types and sizes of LAN. While a LAN is self-contained, that does not mean that it has to be small. LANs can range from networks with three or four nodes to networks with thousands of nodes. We are going to focus on two particular classes of LAN: SOHO and enterprise.

COMMON ETHERNET NETWORK IMPLEMENTATIONS

Networks can range in size from just a few connected devices in a home environment, to thousands of devices in a large worldwide enterprise.

Show Slide(s)

Common Ethernet Network Implementations (3 slides)

SOHO NETWORKS

A **SOHO** (Small Office Home Office) LAN is a business-oriented network possibly using a centralized server in addition to client devices and printers, but often using a single Internet appliance to provide connectivity. Home and residential networks may also be classed as SOHO.

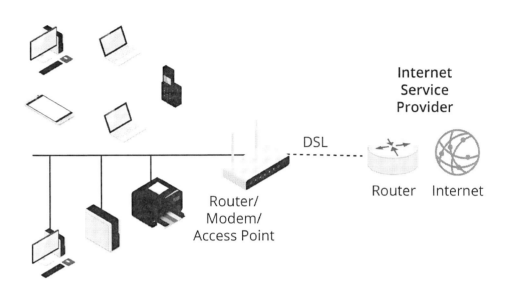

A typical SOHO network layout. (Image © 123RF.com.)

These Internet appliances provide the following functions:

- Access point—allows clients with wireless radio adapters to connect to the network.
- Ethernet switch—connects wired client devices and printers with RJ-45 cables.
- Internet modem—interfaces with the physical link to the ISP's routers (DSL or cable, for instance).
- Internet router—forwards communications to and from the Internet Service Provider (ISP) routers to provide Internet access.

ENTERPRISE NETWORK ARCHITECTURE

Networks supporting larger businesses or academic institutions use the same switch, access point, router, and modem functions as are present in SOHO networks, but because they must support more clients with a greater degree of reliability, each function is performed by a separate network device. You could think of these larger networks as falling into two categories:

Teaching Tip

Point out that while the functions are the same, enterprise-class devices provide reliability and scalability.

- **SME (Small and Medium Sized Enterprise)**—A network supporting tens of users. Such networks would use structured cabling and multiple switches, access points, and routers to provide connectivity.
- **Enterprise LAN**—A larger network with hundreds or thousands of servers and clients. Such networks would require multiple enterprise-class switch, access point, and router appliances to maintain performance levels.

The term Campus Area Network (CAN) is sometimes used for a LAN that spans multiple nearby buildings.

The following graphic illustrates how network appliances might be positioned in an enterprise LAN. Client devices are located in work areas, which are connected to the network by cabling running through wall conduit and patch panel or by wireless access points. Workgroup switches connect these devices to core/distribution switches and routers, which provide access to network servers, printers, and Internet services. Internet services run in protected Demilitarized Zones (DMZ) to provide Internet access for employees, email and communications, remote access via Virtual Private Networks (VPNs), and web services for external clients and customers.

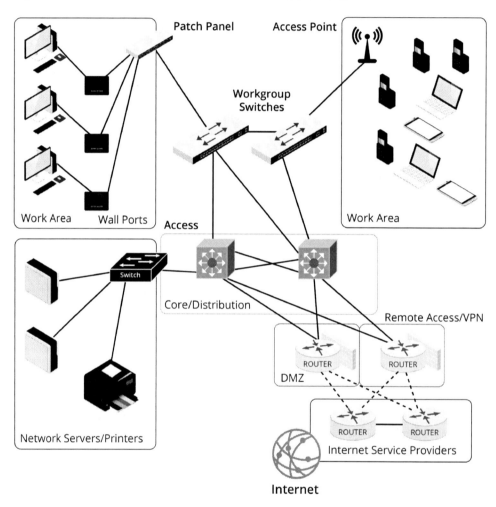

Positioning network components. (Image © 123RF.com.)

 Show Slide(s)

Twisted Pair Cabling and Connectors (4 slides)

 Teaching Tip

Exam candidates will need to know the data rates for all of the different categories of network cable.

TWISTED PAIR CABLING AND CONNECTORS

Most cabled LANs use a type of copper wire called twisted pair as transmission media.

UNSHIELDED TWISTED PAIR (UTP) CABLE

Unshielded Twisted Pair (UTP) is the type of cabling most widely used for computer networking. With the type of UTP used for Ethernet, the cable contains four copper conductor "pairs." Each conductor has an insulating sheath. Each pair of conductors is twisted, which reduces interference between the wires (crosstalk) and interference from other electromagnetic sources, referred to as Electromagnetic Interference (EMI). Each pair is twisted at a different rate to further reduce interference. The signals sent over each pair are balanced. This means that each wire carries an equal but opposite signal to its pair. This is another factor helping to identify the signal more strongly against any source of interference.

The four pairs are covered by a protective outer jacket. The insulation sheaths and jacket are usually made of (PVC).

UTP works well where there are no powerful interference sources, but the electrical signaling method has limited range. The signal is said to suffer from attenuation, meaning that it loses power quickly over long ranges (above 100 m).

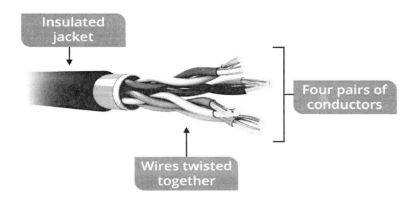

UTP cable. (Image © 123RF.com.)

CAT STANDARDS

The number of twists is one factor in determining the speed and transmission limitations of the cable. Twisted pair cable is rated for different Ethernet applications according to "Cat" specifications, defined in the TIA/EIA-568-C Commercial Building Telecommunications Cabling Standards.

Cat	Frequency	Capacity	Max. Distance	Network Application
5	100 MHz	100 Mbps	100 m (328 ft)	100BASE-TX
5e	100 MHz	1 Gbps	100 m (328 ft)	1000BASE-T
6	250 MHz	1 Gbps	100 m (328 ft)	1000BASE-T
6	250 MHz	10 Gbps	55 m (180 ft)	10GBASE-T
6A	500 MHz	10 Gbps	100 m (328 ft)	10GBASE-T

 Note: *Vendors sometimes label Cat 6A cable as "Cat 6e" because Cat 5e followed Cat 5. The "A" stands for "augmented."*

Cat 5 cable is no longer available. Cat 5e is tested at 100 MHz—as Cat 5 was—but to higher overall specifications for attenuation and crosstalk, meaning that the cable is rated to handle Gigabit Ethernet throughput. Cat 5e would still be an acceptable choice for providing network links for workstations. Cat 6 can support 10 Gbps, but over shorter distances. Cat 6A is an improved specification cable with the ability to support 10 Gbps over 100 m. It is mostly deployed in data centers or as backbone cabling between servers and network appliances.

 Note: *Cabling is not the only part of the wiring system that must be rated to the appropriate category. For faster network applications (Gigabit Ethernet and better), the performance of connectors becomes increasingly critical. For example, if you are installing Cat 6A wiring, you must also install Cat 6A patch panels, wall plates, and connectors.*

SHIELDED TWISTED PAIR (STP)

When twisted pair cabling was first used in networks based on IBM's Token Ring product, it was usually shielded to make it less susceptible to interference and crosstalk. Each pair was surrounded by a braided shield. This cable construction is referred to as **Shielded Twisted Pair (STP)**. STP is bulky and difficult to install, so where a degree of protection from interference is required, modern twisted pair cabling installations use screened cables, meaning a shield positioned around all pairs. There are many different ways of designating different types of shielding. Most Cat 5e/6/6A cable is available in shielded variants, notably F/UTP and U/FTP:

- F/UTP—with a foil screen around all pairs, often also designated ScTP.
- U/FTP—with foil shielding for each pair.

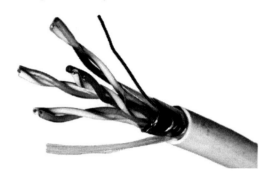

F/UTP cable with a foil screen surrounding unshielded pairs. (Image by Baran Ivo and released to public domain.)

Legacy STP cable could be more complex to install as it required bonding each element to ground manually but modern screened and shielded solutions (using appropriate cable, connectors, jacks, and patch panels) reduce this complexity by incorporating grounding within the design of each element.

PLENUM CABLE

A **plenum** space is a void in a building designed to carry Heating, Ventilation, and Air Conditioning (**HVAC**) systems. Plenum space is typically a false ceiling, though it could also be constructed as a raised floor. As it makes installation simpler, this space has also been used for communications wiring in some building designs. Plenum space is an effective conduit for fire, as there is plenty of airflow and no fire breaks, such as walls and doors. If the plenum space is used for heating, there may also be higher temperatures. Therefore, building regulations require the use of fire-retardant plenum cable in such spaces. **Plenum cable** must not emit large amounts of smoke when burned, be self-extinguishing, and meet other strict fire safety standards.

General purpose (non-plenum) cabling uses PVC (polyvinyl chloride) jackets and insulation. Plenum-rated cable uses treated PVC or Fluorinated Ethylene Polymer (FEP). This can make the cable less flexible but the different materials used have no effect on bandwidth. Data cable rated for plenum use under the US National Electrical Code (NEC) is marked CMP/MMP. General purpose cables are marked CMG/MMG or CM/MP.

WIRING STANDARDS FOR TWISTED PAIR

Twisted pair cabling for Ethernet is terminated using modular **RJ-45** connectors. RJ-45 connectors are also referred to as 8P8C, standing for 8-position/8-contact. Each conductor in 4-pair Ethernet cable is color-coded. Each pair is assigned a color (Blue, Orange, Green, or Brown). The first conductor in each pair has a predominantly white insulator with stripes of the color; the second conductor has an insulator with the solid color.

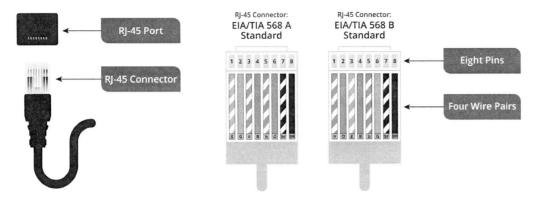

Twisted pair RJ-45 connectors. (Image © 123RF.com.)

The ANSI/TIA/EIA 568 standard defines two methods for terminating RJ-45 connectors: **T568A** and **T568B**. The wiring for T568A is shown in the previous figure. In T568B, pin 1 is wired to Orange/White, pin 2 is wired to Orange, pin 3 is wired to Green/White, and pin 6 is wired to Green or, put another way, the orange and green pairs are swapped over.

A normal—or straight through—Ethernet cable is wired with the same type of termination at both ends. Using T568A at one end and T568B at the other creates a **crossover cable**. Crossover cables were once used to connect computers directly, but Gigabit Ethernet interfaces can perform the crossover automatically, even if standard cable is used.

Organizations should try to avoid using a mixture of the two standards. It is difficult to say whether one is more prevalent than the other. T568A is mandated for US government premises and by the residential cabling standard (TIA 570).

PATCH PANELS AND STRUCTURED CABLING

A Gigabit Ethernet link using twisted pair cabling can be up to 100 m (328 feet) long. This means there must be no more than 100 m of cabling between the switch and the computer. There is also a distinction between solid and stranded cabling.

Solid cabling uses a single thick wire for each conductor. Solid cable is used for "permanent" links, such as cable running through walls. This is often also called **drop cable**, as the installer drops the cable through the wall void to the hole cut out for the port. This cable links the RJ-45 port on a wall plate with a patch panel. Rather than using modular RJ-45 connectors, solid cable terminates in Insulation Displacement Connectors (IDC) at the back of the wall plate and patch panel, as shown here.

The other side of the patch panel has pre-wired RJ-45 ports. A patch cord is used to connect a port on the patch panel to a port on the switch. A patch cord is made using stranded cable, which comprises lots of very thin wires twisted to make a single conductor. This makes the cable much more flexible but less efficient. A patch cord is not supposed to be longer than 5 m.

 Show Slide(s)
Patch Panels and Structured Cabling (2 slides)

 Teaching Tip
Note that these restrictions apply if the installation needs to be standards-compliant.

Point out the importance of labeling ports and cables in patch panels.

You might also want to refer to the term "flood wiring." This means overprovisioning ports in a building because you are not quite sure what the exact requirement or desk layout is going to be. Flood wiring allows for subsequent changes to the room layout.

Patch panel with pre-wired RJ-45 ports. (Image by Svetlana Kurochkina © 123RF.com.)

A second patch cord is used between the computer's network adapter and the wall port. This use of patch cords, permanent links, and patch panels is referred to as a **structured cabling system**.

> **Note:** *It is vital to use an effective labeling system when installing this type of network so that you know which patch panel port is connected to which wall port.*

CABLE INSTALLATION AND TESTING TOOLS

Show Slide(s)
Cable Installation and Testing Tools (7 slides)

Teaching Tip
If you have cable connectors and crimpers or IDCs and punch-down tools, consider having learners use them to create cables they can use. If you follow this suggestion, be sure to test the cables that they make.

You could fill a small van and spend a not-so-small fortune on the various tools available for installing and maintaining data cabling. The range of tools you require will of course depend on the cabling work you do, but the following can be considered typical.

WIRE STRIPPER/CUTTER

Electrician's scissors (snips) are designed for cutting copper wire and stripping insulation and cable jackets. Alternatively, there are dedicated tools or tools that have replaceable blades for different data cable types. Cable cutting blades should be rounded to preserve the wire geometry. Stripping tools should have the correct diameter to score a cable jacket without damaging the insulation around each wire.

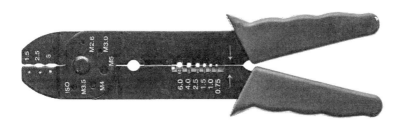

A cable stripper. (Image by gasparij © 123RF.com.)

PUNCH-DOWN TOOL

These tools fix conductors into an IDC. The wire pairs are untwisted and laid in the terminals in the IDC in the appropriate termination order (T568A or T568B). It is important not to untwist the pairs too much, however. The punch-down tool then presses the wire into the terminal, cutting through the insulation to make an electrical contact. There are different IDC formats (66, 110, and Krone) and these require different blades. Many punch-down tools have replaceable blades.

A punch-down tool. (Image by gasparij © 123RF.com.)

CRIMPERS

These tools fix a jack to a cable. As with an IDC, the wires are laid in the appropriate terminals in the jack and the crimper tool then closes and seals the jack. The tools are specific to a particular type of connector and cable, though some may have modular dies to support a range of RJ-type jacks.

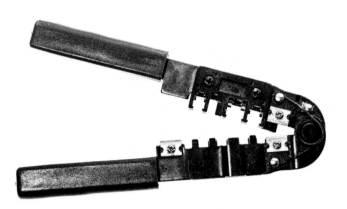

A wire crimper. (Image by gasparij © 123RF.com.)

 Note: *It is best to use prefabricated patch cords where possible. These are far less likely to create problems.*

CABLE TESTING TOOLS

The best time to verify wiring installation and termination is just after you have made all the connections. This means you should still have access to the cable runs. Identifying and correcting errors at this point will be much simpler than when you are trying to set up end user devices. When troubleshooting a cabled network link, you may need to consider:

- The patch cord between the PC and the wall port.
- The wall port and the cabling in the wall.
- The port on the patch panel and the patch cord to the switch port.

Test patch cords by substitution with a "known good" one. If the problem is not caused by the patch cord and you can rule out configuration errors, you need to start testing the structured links. There are a number of network cabling and infrastructure troubleshooting devices to assist with this process.

A **multimeter** can be used as a basic cable testing tool. The primary purpose of a multimeter is for testing electrical circuits, but you can use one to test for the continuity of any sort of copper wire, the existence of a short, and the integrity of a terminator. To perform useful tests, you need to know the readings that are expected from a particular test. For example, if the resistance measured across UTP Ethernet cable is found to be 100 ohms, then the cable is OK, but if the resistance between the two ends of a cable is infinity, then the cable has a break. Many multimeters designed for ICT use incorporate the function of a wire map tester. These are also available as dedicated devices. Wire map testers can identify wiring problems that a simple continuity test will not detect, such as transpositions and reversed pairs.

Multimeter. (Image by Norasit Kaewsai © 123RF.com.)

More advanced cable testers provide detailed information on the physical and electrical properties of the cable. For example, they test and report on cable conditions, crosstalk, attenuation, noise, resistance, and other characteristics of a cable run. Devices classed as certifiers can be used to test and certify cable installations to a particular performance category (for example, that a network is TIA/EIA 568-C Category 6 compliant). They use defined transport performance specifications to ensure an installation exceeds the required performance characteristics for parameters such as attenuation and crosstalk.

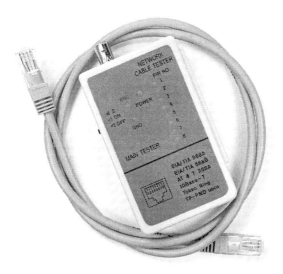

A cable tester. (Image by Vladimir Zhupanenko © 123RF.com.)

TONE GENERATOR AND PROBE

A **tone generator and probe** tool is used to trace a cable from one end to the other. This may be necessary when the cables are bundled and have not been labeled properly. This device is also known as a "Fox and Hound" or "toner and probe." The tone generator is used to apply a signal on the cable. The probe is used to detect the signal and follow the cable over ceilings and through ducts or identify it from within the rest of the bundle.

To locate a cable in a group of cables, connect the tone generator to the copper ends of the wires, then move the tone locator over the group of cables. A soft beeping tone indicates that you are close to the correct wire set; when the beeping is loudest, you have found the cable.

 Note: *Do not connect a tone generator to a cable that is connected to a NIC. The signal sent by the tone generator can destroy network equipment.*

LOOPBACK PLUGS

A **loopback plug** is used to test a port. It involves connecting pin 1 to pin 3 and pin 2 to pin 6. You can do this either by rewiring the jack or twisting the relevant pairs together on a cable stub. Alternatively, you can purchase a prefabricated loopback plug. When you connect a loopback plug to a port, you should see a solid connection LED. You can also use the plug in conjunction with diagnostic software.

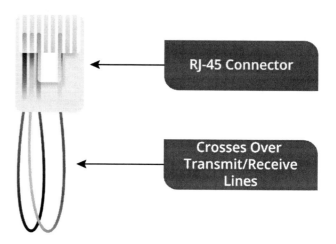

A loopback plug. (Image © 123RF.com.)

FIBER OPTIC CABLING AND CONNECTORS

Copper wire carries electrical signals, which are subject to interference and attenuation. Light signals are not susceptible to interference, cannot easily be intercepted (eavesdropped), and suffer less from attenuation. Consequently, fiber optic cabling can support much higher bandwidth, measured in multiple gigabits or terabits per second, and longer cable runs, measured in miles rather than feet.

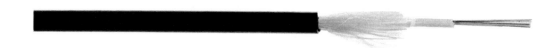

A fiber optic strand. (Image by artush © 123RF.com.)

An optical fiber consists of an ultra-fine core of glass to carry the light signals surrounded by glass or plastic cladding, which guides the light pulses along the core, and a protective coating called the buffer. The fiber optic cable is contained in a protective jacket and terminated by a connector.

Fiber optic cables fall into two broad categories: single-mode and multi-mode:

- **Single-Mode Fiber (SMF)** has a small core (8-10 microns) and is designed to carry a long wavelength, near infrared (1310 or 1550 nm) light signal, generated by a laser. Single-mode cables support data rates up to 10 Gbps or better and cable runs of many kilometers, depending on the quality of the cable and optics.
- **Multi-mode (MMF)** has a larger core (62.5 or 50 microns) and is designed to carry a shorter wavelength light (850 nm or 1300 nm) transmitted in multiple waves of varying length. MMF uses less expensive optics and consequently is less expensive to deploy than SMF. However, it does not support such high signaling speeds or long distances as single-mode and so is more suitable for LANs than WANs.

A number of connectors have been designed for use with fiber optic cabling. Some types are more popular for multi-mode and some for single-mode. Connectors for MMF are usually color-coded beige while those for SMF are blue. The core of each connector is a ceramic or plastic ferrule that ensures continuous reception of the light signals.

- **Straight Tip (ST)**—A bayonet-style connector that uses a push-and-twist locking mechanism; used mostly for multi-mode networks.
- **Subscriber Connector (SC)**—Connector with a push/pull design that allows for simpler insertion and removal than FC. There are simplex and duplex versions, though the duplex version is just two connectors clipped together. It can be used for single- or multi-mode.
- Lucent or **Local Connector (LC)**—A small form factor connector with a tabbed push/pull design. LC is similar to SC but the smaller size allows for higher port density.

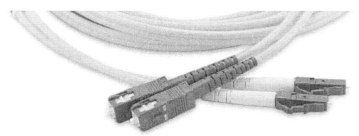

Patch cord with duplex SC format connectors (left) and LC connectors (right). (Image by YANAWUT SUNTORNKIJ © 123RF.com.)

Patch cords for fiber optic can come with the same connector on each end (ST-ST, for instance) or a mix of connectors (ST-SC, for instance). Fiber optic connectors are quite easy to damage and should not be repeatedly plugged in and unplugged.

 Note: *To protect your eyesight, do not look directly into a fiber optic port.*

COAXIAL CABLING AND CONNECTORS

Coaxial, or **coax cable** is a different type of copper cabling, also carrying electrical signals. Where twisted pair uses balancing to cancel out interference, coax uses two conductors that share the same axis. The core signal conductor is enclosed by plastic insulation (dielectric) then a second wire mesh conductor serves both as shielding from EMI and as a ground.

 Show Slide(s)

Coaxial Cabling and Connectors (4 slides)

Detailed layers of a coaxial cable. (Image by destinacigdem © 123RF.com.)

Coax cables are categorized using the Radio Grade (RG) "standard." The Radio Grade (or Radio Guide) classifications were developed by the US military but are no longer actively maintained by any sort of standards body. They do not prescribe the quality of coax cabling but categorize it by the thickness of the core conductor and the cable's characteristic impedance.

- RG-6 cable has a thicker core conductor for better signal quality and is often used as a drop/patch cable for modern Cable Access TV (CATV) and broadband cable modems.
- RG-59 cable has a thinner core conductor and was used as a drop cable for older CATV/cable modem installs and is also used for CCTV cabling.

Coax cabling is also available with tri- or quad-shielding for better resistance to EMI and eavesdropping.

In most cases, BNC (alternately Bayonet-Neill-Concelman, British Naval Connector, or Barrel Nut Connector) connectors are crimped to the ends of the cable. The impedance of the connector must match the cable type (50 or 75 ohm).

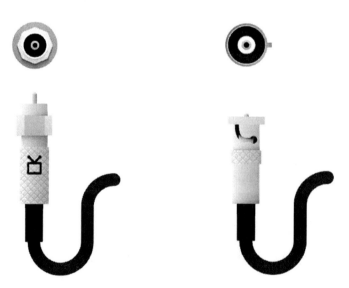

An example of a coaxial F-connector (left) and a BNC connector (right). (Image © 123RF.com.)

Coax installations also use screw-down F-connectors. A broadband cable service, for example, is likely to use the F-connector for drop cables.

As an Ethernet LAN media product (10BASE-5/Thicknet and 10BASE-2/Thinnet), coax could support 10 Mbps with cable lengths of up to 500 m and 185 m, respectively. Coax is considered obsolete in terms of LAN applications but is still widely used for CCTV networks and as drop cables for cable TV (CATV) and Internet access, where it can support higher bandwidths but at reduced range. In a Hybrid Fiber Coax (HFC) network, coax cable links the fiber optic trunk serving the whole street to the cable "modem" installed in the customer's premises. Coax suffers less from attenuation than twisted pair but is generally bulkier and more difficult to install.

Activity 8-1
Discussing Wired Networks

 Show Slide(s)

Activity: Discussing Wired Networks

 Teaching Tip

As an optional practical exercise, consider handing out examples of different cable types with various connectors, and ask learners to identify them. For example, Cat5e vs. Cat6, regular cable vs. plenum cable, straight-through vs. crossover wiring, and examples of different fiber optic patch cables.

SCENARIO

Answer the following questions to check your understanding of the topic.

1. Your company has a global presence, and all locations can communicate. At each site, there is a network, and that network connects to the overall organizational network. In some locations, there are multiple sites within a city.

   Identify each type of network described here.

   The global network is a WAN. The network at each site is a LAN. The sites within a city comprise a MAN.

2. You are performing a wiring job, but the company wants to purchase the media and components from another preferred supplier. The plan is to install a network using copper cabling that will support Gigabit Ethernet. The customer is about to purchase Cat5e cable spools.

   Is this the best choice?

   Cat5e will meet the requirement and will cost the least. Cat6 might offer better performance without adding too much cost. Cat6A would be the best choice for supporting future requirements, but it is likely to cost more than the customer is budgeting for. You should also notify the customer if plenum-rated cabling will be required.

3. **What is the significance of network cabling marked "CMP/MMP"?**

   The cable is plenum cable, rated for use in plenum spaces (building voids used with HVAC systems).

4. You need to connect cable wires to a patch panel.

   Which networking tool might help you?

   A punch down tool. Remember that punch down tools are used to terminate solid core cabling to Insulation Displacement Connector (IDC) blocks in patch panels and wall plates, while crimpers are used to attach RJ-45 jacks to stranded patch cord cabling

5. **What type of tool provides comprehensive information about the properties of a network cable installation?**

   A cable certifier.

6. **What features of fiber optic cable make it more suitable for WANs than copper cabling?**

It suffers less attenuation (and therefore longer range) and is immune to EMI and eavesdropping.

7. **What types of connector are often used with coaxial cable?**

BNC connectors and F-connectors.

Topic B
Network Hardware Devices

EXAM OBJECTIVES COVERED
1001-2.2 Compare and contrast common networking hardware devices.

In this topic, you will identify several types of network devices and other components. Network adapters, Internet modems, switches, and routers are fundamental network connectivity devices, and you will often encounter them in the network environments that you support. Understanding the functions and capabilities of these devices will prepare you to support a wide variety of network environments.

NETWORK INTERFACE CARDS

Communications are transported over an Ethernet cable by electrical signaling in the case of twisted pair, or light signaling in the case of fiber optic. The physical connection to the network media is made using a port in the computer's network adapter or **Network Interface Card (NIC)**. For the NIC to be able to transmit and receive the signals and process them as digital data, they must be divided into regular units with a consistent format. There must also be a means for each node on the local network to address communications to another node. Ethernet provides a data link protocol to perform these framing and addressing functions.

The signaling mechanism uses various encoding methods to represent the 1s and 0s of computer data as electrical or light pulses. The transceiver in the NIC is responsible for transmitting and receiving these pulses in the agreed frame format.

FRAMES

Each frame is identified by a preamble sequence, which is basically a warning to the NIC to expect a new frame. A frame is formatted with control information in the form of header fields, each of a fixed size and presented in a fixed order. The most important fields are the destination and source addresses of the adapter to which the frame is being directed and the adapter from which it was sent. Other information (not shown in the following simplified figure) includes the frame length and network layer protocol identifier.

Following these fields comes the payload. This is the data that is being transported over the network. It will normally consist of a network packet, such as an Internet Protocol (IP) packet, with its own headers and payload. Putting layers of packets within one another like this is called encapsulation.

The frame finishes with a checksum. The receiving computer can calculate its own checksum and compare it to this value. If they do not match, the receiving host rejects the frame as damaged.

Teaching Tip

Relating devices to layers is not an objective at the A+ level, but the layer terminology may help learners understand it better. You may want to refer to the simpler TCP/IP layer model rather than OSI.

Continue to draw a distinction between SOHO equipment (where one device performs lots of functions) and enterprise equipment.

Show Slide(s)

Network Interface Cards (2 slides)

Teaching Tip

Optionally, show learners some captured packets. Identify the frame and show them the contents of an actual frame.

Don't go into detail; just show them the header and basic format. Help them to understand the process of encapsulation by showing how the protocols are stacked in layers.

Construction of a frame.

ETHERNET NIC FEATURES

Most motherboards come with an onboard Ethernet network adapter. An additional or replacement NIC could also be installed as a PCIe expansion card if the onboard adapter is not suitable for a particular network implementation.

Show Slide(s)

Ethernet NIC Features (4 slides)

All onboard cards support copper-based Ethernet with RJ-45 ports. You might use an add-in card to support other types of Ethernet, notably fiber optic. Some cards support more than one type of connector. You can also purchase cards with multiple ports of the same type—two or four Gigabit RJ-45 Ethernet ports, for instance. The multiple ports can be bonded to create a higher speed link. Four Gigabit Ethernet ports could be bonded to give a nominal link speed of 4 Gbps.

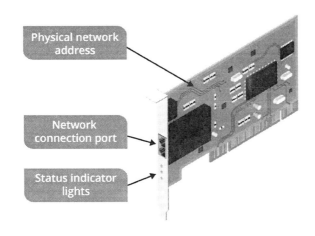

Physical network address

Network connection port

Status indicator lights

A network interface card. (Image © 123RF.com.)

MEDIA ACCESS CONTROL (MAC) ADDRESS

Each Ethernet network adapter port has a unique hardware or physical address known as the **Media Access Control (MAC)** address. MAC addresses provide the value used in a frame's source and destination address fields. A MAC address consists of 48 binary digits (6 bytes). This is typically represented as 12 digits of hexadecimal with colon or hyphen separators or no separators at all—for example, 00:60:8c:12:3a:bc or 00608c123abc.

Teaching Tip

Note that a NIC with more than one port will have more than one MAC address.

Hopefully learners will understand what is meant by hexadecimal. It is a content example on IT Fundamentals+ so learners should have previous knowledge of it. If not, the format is explained in the topic on IPv6.

NIC LED STATUS DIODES

Network adapters typically have one or more Light Emitting Diode (LED) status lights that can provide information on the state of the network connection.

- Most adapters have a link light that indicates if there is a signal from the network. If the link light is not lit, there is generally a problem with the cable or the physical connection.

- Most adapters also have an activity light that flickers when packets are received or sent. If the light flickers constantly, the network might be overused or there might be a device generating network noise.

- Some multi-speed adapters have a speed light to show whether the adapter is operating at 10 Mbps (Ethernet), 100 Mbps (Fast Ethernet), or 1000 Mbps (Gigabit Ethernet).

- Some types of equipment combine the functions of more than one light into dual-color LEDs. For example, a green flickering light might indicate normal activity, whereas an orange flickering light indicates network traffic collisions.

LEGACY NETWORKING DEVICES

In a structured cabling system, the computer is connected to a wall port and—via cabling running through the walls—to some sort of patch panel. The port on the patch panel is then connected to a port on the switch. The switch is the network appliance that "ties" the whole local network together. However, while switches are the appliances at the core of most modern Ethernet networks, you should also be aware of the basic function of legacy appliances, such as hubs and bridges.

HUBS AND REPEATERS

A **hub** is an early type of device used to implement the Ethernet cabling design, referred to as a star topology. The hub contains a number of ports—typically between 4 and 48—to provide connections for network devices. A hub simply ensures that all devices receive signals put on the network, working as a **multiport repeater**.

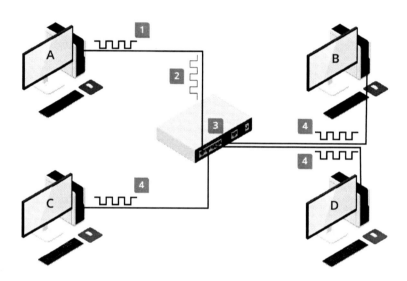

Using a hub to implement a physical star topology. Node A transmits a signal, which is received by the hub and forwarded out of each other port for reception by all the other nodes. (Image © 123RF.com.)

A **repeater** is a device used to overcome the distance limitations imposed by network cabling. It receives a transmission arriving over one cable segment and then regenerates and retransmits it at the original strength over another cable segment.

 Note: Standalone repeater devices are still widely used. On fiber optic networks it is often necessary to use repeaters on long-distance communications cabling.

BRIDGES

A **bridge** is a device that divides a local network into two or more segments. Hosts on one segment are able to communicate with those on another segment only via the bridge. **Contention** arises in hub-based Ethernet because all communications are received by all computers connected to the hub. The hub just repeats all transmissions across all ports. A lot of the communications are unnecessary and a lot of them "collide." When there is a collision, all the nodes have to stop and resend frames, slowing the network down. The network segment in which these collisions occur is called a **collision domain**. Any nodes attached to a hub are in a single collision domain.

A bridge can be used to divide an overloaded network into separate collision domains. The bridge keeps track of the MAC addresses attached to each segment. The bridge only passes signals from one segment to another if there is a match to the destination MAC address, reducing traffic loads in any one segment. The network should be designed so that relatively little traffic actually needs to pass over the bridge.

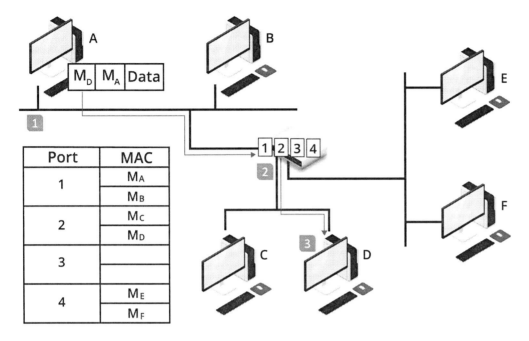

Port	MAC
1	M_A
	M_B
2	M_C
	M_D
3	
4	M_E
	M_F

Bridge operation—the bridge tracks MAC addresses associated with each port and only forwards communications out of the port associated with the destination MAC address. (Image © 123RF.com.)

SWITCHES

Neither hub nor bridge appliances are widely used on networks anymore. Their functions have been replaced by Ethernet **switches**. Like hubs, switches can connect nodes together in a single network, repeating and regenerating signals over multiple ports. Like bridges, switches are used to reduce the effect of contention on network performance.

Show Slide(s)

Switches (3 slides)

A workgroup switch. (Image © 123RF.com.)

MICROSEGMENTATION

An Ethernet switch performs the same sort of function as a bridge but can provide many more ports. Bridges only came with up to 4 ports. A single switch might have up to 48 ports and multiple switches can be connected together to create a switched fabric with thousands of ports. Each switch port is a separate collision domain. In effect, the switch establishes a point-to-point link called a virtual circuit between any two network nodes. This is referred to as **microsegmentation**. It works as follows:

1. Computer A transmits a frame intended for Computer B.
2. The switch receives the frame into a port buffer and reads the destination MAC address from the Ethernet frame.
3. The switch uses its MAC address table to look up the port connected to the destination MAC address.
4. The switch uses its high speed backplane to send the frame out on port 3 for computer B to receive.
5. None of the other connected devices, such as host C, observe any activity on the network while this process takes place. Therefore, these other devices are able to transmit and receive at the same time.

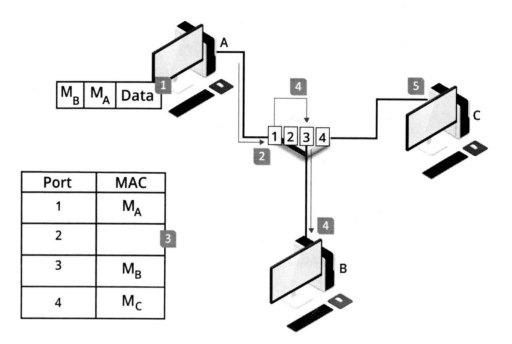

Switch operation. (Image © 123RF.com.)

Because each port is in a separate collision domain, collisions can only occur if the port is operating in half-duplex mode. This would only occur if a legacy network card or a hub is attached to it. Even then, collisions only affect the segment between the port and that adapter—they do not slow down the whole network. For other devices, the network appears free, so they are able to send communications at the same time using the full bandwidth of the network media.

 Note: Half duplex means that a port can either send or receive but cannot do both at the same time. Ports supporting Gigabit Ethernet can send and receive at the same time (full duplex).

 Note: You are very unlikely to come across hub or bridge appliances. The vast majority of Ethernet networks are implemented using switches. Gigabit Ethernet can only run using switches. Note that the function of a bridge is still an important one, though. For example, a PC might use a software bridge between network adapters (for network connectivity when the host is running virtualization software, for instance).

MANAGED AND UNMANAGED SWITCHES

An **unmanaged switch** performs the microsegmentation function described previously without requiring any sort of configuration. You just power it on, connect some hosts to it, and it works without any more intervention. You might find unmanaged switches with four or eight ports used in small networks. There is also an unmanaged switch embedded in most of the Internet router/modems supplied by Internet Service Providers (ISP) to connect to their networks.

Larger workgroups and corporate networks require additional functionality in their switches. Switches designed for larger LANs are called **managed switches**. A managed switch will work as an unmanaged switch out-of-the-box, but an administrator can connect to it over a management port, configure security settings, and then choose options for the switch's more advanced functionality.

Show Slide(s)

Managed and Unmanaged Switches (3 slides)

Teaching Tip

There is a very wide range of enterprise switch models. You might want to call out the distinction between access and distribution switch models. Refer learners to Cisco's website for more information.

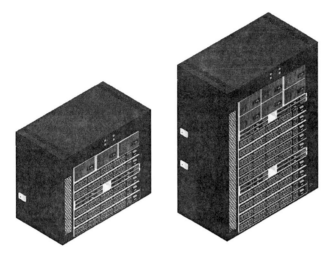

Modular chassis allows provisioning multiple access switches. (Image © 123RF.com.)

One of the main reasons for using managed switches is that enterprise networks might have to provide hundreds or thousands of access ports. This is accomplished by linking multiple switches together. Having that many ports on the same network creates its own performance and security issues, so managed switches support a method of dividing the ports into separate Virtual LANs (VLANs).

Configuration of a managed switch can either be performed over a web interface or some sort of command line.

```
FastEthernet1/0/1 is up, line protocol is up (connected)
  Hardware is Fast Ethernet, address is f41f.c253.7103 (bia f41f.c253.7103)
  MTU 1500 bytes, BW 100000 Kbit/sec, DLY 100 usec,
     reliability 255/255, txload 1/255, rxload 1/255
  Encapsulation ARPA, loopback not set
  Keepalive set (10 sec)
  Full-duplex, 100Mb/s, media type is 10/100BaseTX
  input flow-control is off, output flow-control is unsupported
  ARP type: ARPA, ARP Timeout 04:00:00
  Last input 00:00:51, output 00:00:00, output hang never
  Last clearing of "show interface" counters never
  Input queue: 0/75/0/0 (size/max/drops/flushes); Total output drops: 0
  Queueing strategy: fifo
  Output queue: 0/40 (size/max)
  5 minute input rate 0 bits/sec, 0 packets/sec
  5 minute output rate 0 bits/sec, 0 packets/sec
     18 packets input, 1758 bytes, 0 no buffer
     Received 4 broadcasts (2 multicasts)
     0 runts, 0 giants, 0 throttles
     0 input errors, 0 CRC, 0 frame, 0 overrun, 0 ignored
     0 watchdog, 2 multicast, 0 pause input
     0 input packets with dribble condition detected
     111 packets output, 13828 bytes, 0 underruns
     0 output errors, 0 collisions, 1 interface resets
     0 unknown protocol drops
```

Viewing interface configuration on a Cisco switch.

POWER OVER ETHERNET

Show Slide(s)

Power Over Ethernet

Teaching Tip

Emphasize what sort of devices can use PoE: access points, VoIP handsets, etc. You couldn't, for instance, run a laptop or printer off PoE, but you might be able to run a netbook.

Power over Ethernet (PoE) is a means of supplying electrical power from a switch port over Cat 5 or better data cabling to a connected powered device, such as a tablet computer, VoIP handset, security camera, or wireless access point. PoE is defined in two IEEE standards (now both rolled into 802.3-2012):

- **802.3af**—powered devices can draw up to about 13 W over the link. Power is supplied as 350mA@48V and limited to 15.4 W, but the voltage drop over the maximum 100 feet of cable results in usable power of around 13 W.
- **802.3at (PoE+)**—powered devices can draw up to about 25 W. PoE+ allows for a broader range of devices to be powered such as cameras with pan/tilt/zoom capabilities, door controllers, and thin client computers.

PoE-enabled switches are referred to as end-span (or end-point) **Power Sourcing Equipment (PSE)**. If an existing switch does not support PoE, a device called a **power injector** can be used. When a device is connected to a port on a PoE switch, the switch goes through a detection phase to determine whether the device is PoE-enabled. If not, it does not supply power over the port and therefore does not damage non-PoE devices. If so, it determines the device's power consumption and sets the supply voltage level appropriately.

Powering these devices through a switch is more efficient than using a wall-socket AC adapter for each appliance. It also allows network management software to control the devices and apply power schemes, such as making unused devices go into sleep states and power capping.

ETHERNET OVER POWER

Show Slide(s)

Ethernet Over Power (2 slides)

SOHO networks are unlikely to use a structured cabling scheme, with cable conduit and patch panels. Many SOHO networks will be based around a single Internet router, server computer, and several workstations, possibly all located within the same room. A residential network might also require connectivity for smart appliances, such as

Smart TVs and game consoles. The main challenge is usually joining up the location selected for the majority of the equipment with the location of the Internet access line.

An obvious solution for connecting SOHO devices is wireless. For many SOHO networks, the bandwidth available for WLANs will be adequate. There may be interference issues, however, and some home appliances, such as set-top boxes, might not support Wi-Fi. As an alternative to installing new data cabling, Ethernet over Powerline products can make use of building power circuits. Power is typically delivered as a 50-60 Hz alternating current, at between 100-240 volts, varying from country to country. Powerline overlays a higher frequency carrier signal on the lines and uses this to transfer Ethernet frames.

Teaching Tip

Power outlet configurations can vary according to location, and learners might want to search for images of *power over ethernet* to see the many different configurations that are available.

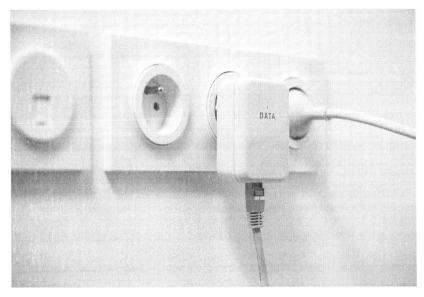

Powerline adapter provides an Ethernet port from a power outlet. (Image by Le Moal Olivier © 123RF.com.)

A network connection is established via a Powerline adapter plugged directly into an electrical outlet. Note that strip sockets are generally not supported. The adapter provides one or two Ethernet RJ-45 ports to connect network equipment. The adapters automatically detect and communicate with one another over the electrical wiring with no configuration needed, though optionally a security key can be enabled to encrypt transmissions. A pass-through adapter also features an electrical outlet, allowing continued use of the socket.

Standards for Ethernet over Powerline are defined by IEEE 1901 and products are managed by the HomePlug Powerline Alliance. Most products on the market conform to the HomePlug AV or AV2 standards, which are interoperable (older HomePlug 1.0 devices are not compatible). Within this, products are rated according to the maximum (theoretical) bandwidth, from AV200 (200 Mbps) to AV1200. If a mix of adapters is used, the network will operate only at the highest speed supported by all of the adapters.

Note: Most Powerline installations will not achieve more than half the theoretical bandwidth.

Activity 8-2
Discussing Network Hardware Devices

Show Slide(s)

Activity: Discussing Network Hardware Devices

Interaction Opportunity

Ask learners to observe the link lights on the HOST computer's network adapter. Optionally, arrange for learners to view the communications room to see how patch panels and switches are interconnected.

SCENARIO
Answer the following questions to check your understanding of the topic.

1. **What is a MAC address?**

   A unique 48-bit identifier coded into every network interface. This is also referred to as the physical or hardware address. A MAC address is expressed as 12 hex digits, usually with colon or hyphen delimiters between each byte value. For example: aa:bb:cc:00:11:22. Each hex digit expresses a 4-bit value using the characters 0 to 9 plus A, B, C, D, E, and F.

2. **What feature(s) should you check when ordering an Ethernet network card?**

   That it supports the correct speed (for example, Gigabit or 10GbE) and media type/connector (for example, RJ-45 for copper cabling or LC for fiber optic).

3. A technician has discovered an 8-port Ethernet hub appliance in a store.

   Can this device be usefully deployed on a modern network?

   No. Hubs support only half duplex mode and limited speed. There could be very specific circumstances in which you need to deploy a hub (to support some sort of legacy server equipment, for instance) but in general terms, using a hub along with modern switches and network adapters is likely to cause configuration errors and performance problems.

4. Your manager is resisting the use of an unmanaged switch to support a network of up to a dozen computers at a branch office.

   What are the arguments for and against proceeding?

   As it requires no configuration, an unmanaged switch should be simpler (and cheaper) to deploy. An unmanaged switch will not support configuration features such as Virtual LANs (VLANs), but these would not be required on such a small network. A managed switch would support a remote configuration and monitoring interface and security features that might be useful, however. You might also mention traffic prioritization as a good reason to deploy a managed switch (though the scenario does not specify supporting VoIP handsets).

5. You are assisting a customer looking to purchase switches that support powering VoIP handset devices directly. The customer is confused between Power over Ethernet and Ethernet over Power.

Can you explain the difference and identify which technology the customer needs?

The customer needs a switch supporting Power over Ethernet (PoE). This means that the switch sends power over the data cabling and RJ-45 port to the device. Ethernet over Power (or Powerline) is a means of networking devices by using building power outlets and circuits, rather than data cabling.

Topic C
Wireless Networks

EXAM OBJECTIVES COVERED
1001-2.2 Compare and contrast common networking hardware devices.
1001-2.4 Compare and contrast wireless networking protocols.
1001-2.7 Compare and contrast Internet connection types, network types, and their features.

Teaching Tip

There is a lot of emphasis on wireless connections and security in the exam objectives. Try to allocate as much time as possible to this topic.

Show Slide(s)

What is Wireless Networking?

Show Slide(s)

Wireless Frequencies and Channels (4 slides)

Teaching Tip

Point out the relationship between frequency, power, range, and bandwidth. A low frequency signal, such as VHF, can travel a long way but can carry relatively little information because lots of broadcasters want to use this bit of the spectrum, so they are allocated only narrow portions of it.

A Wi-Fi signal needs a lot of power to travel even a fairly short distance but it can use wider "channels" with a higher range of frequencies in them to carry more information.

Teaching Tip

Exam candidates should memorize the key facts about Wi-Fi standards.

Wireless technologies can now achieve sufficient bandwidth to replace wired ports for many types of clients in a typical office. It is also more convenient for SOHO networks to use wireless as the primary access method for computers, laptops, smartphones, and tablets. Wireless can provide connectivity for desktops or even servers in places where it is difficult or expensive to run network cabling. As a CompTIA A+ technician, you will often be called upon to install, configure, and troubleshoot wireless technologies, so it is imperative that you understand the basics.

WHAT IS WIRELESS NETWORKING?

"Wireless" encompasses a whole range of connectivity products and technologies, from personal area networking to Internet connectivity. Most wireless technologies use radio waves as transmission media. Radio systems use transmission and reception antennas tuned to a specific frequency for the transfer of signals.

WIRELESS FREQUENCIES AND CHANNELS

The range of broadcast radio frequencies (RF) extends from 3 KHz to 300 GHz. Frequencies are subdivided into bands such as very low and ultra high. FM radio and television signals are broadcast in the Very High Frequency (VHF) band (30-300 MHz).

The use of the radio spectrum is regulated by national governments and (to some extent) standardized internationally by the International Telecommunications Union (ITU). Use of a frequency usually requires a license from the relevant government agency. The license ensures no one else can transmit that frequency within a particular area.

There are however, unregulated frequencies—Industrial, Scientific, and Medical (ISM) bands—that do not require a license, such as the 2.4 GHz and 5 GHz bands. The wireless networking products operate in these unregulated ultra high frequencies. There is a limit on power output, which means range is restricted.

802.11 (WIRELESS LAN STANDARDS)

When talking about "wireless networking" for desktops, laptops, smartphones, and tablets, the term is generally understood to mean the IEEE's 802.11 standards for Wireless LANs (WLANs), also called **Wi-Fi**. There are five main versions of the standard, as summarized here:

Standard	Maximum Transfer Rate	Band
802.11a (1999)	54 Mbps	5 GHz
802.11b (1999)	11 Mbps	2.4 GHz
802.11g (2003)	54 Mbps	2.4 GHz

Standard	Maximum Transfer Rate	Band
802.11n (2009)	288.8 Mbps/stream (Single Channel)	2.4/5 GHz
	600 Mbps/stream (Bonded Channels)	
802.11ac (2013)	1.7 Gbps (at time of writing)	5 GHz

Note that the transfer rates quoted are illustrative of an optimal installation and are heavily dependent on the quality of the access point, the number of clients connecting simultaneously, and interference and obstructions in the environment. The frequencies used by Wi-Fi lack penetrating power and there can be interference from nearby unregulated devices, such as baby monitors and cordless phones. Microwave ovens can also cause interference.

The actual data rate will drop with distance and in the presence of interference, with the preference being for a slower, stable connection over a faster, error-prone one.

FREQUENCIES

Every wireless device operates on a specific radio frequency within an overall frequency band. It is important to understand the difference between the two most common frequency bands in the IEEE 802.11 standards: 2.4 GHz and 5.0 GHz.

Teaching Tip

Note that wavelength is inversely proportional to frequency.

- 2.4 GHz is the longer wavelength, which gives it longer range (given the same power output) and makes it better at propagating through solid surfaces. However, the 2.4 GHz band does not support a high number of individual channels and is often congested, both with other Wi-Fi networks and other types of wireless technology, such as Bluetooth. Consequently, with the 2.4 GHz band there is increased risk of interference and the maximum achievable data rates are typically lower than with a 5 GHz channel.
- 5 GHz is less effective at penetrating solid surfaces and so does not support the maximum ranges achieved with 2.4 GHz standards. Nonetheless, the band supports more individual channels and suffers less from congestion and interference, meaning it supports higher data rates.

RANGE

Products working in the 2.4 GHz band can be quoted as having a maximum indoor range of anywhere from 30 to 45 m (100 - 150 feet). Products using 5 GHz are usually quoted as having a maximum range of about one third less (up to about 30 m, say). For most wireless networks, however, absolute range is less important than the number of clients that have to be supported and the construction of walls and ceilings.

CHANNELS

The 2. band is subdivided into up to 14 channels, spaced at 5 MHz intervals from 2412 MHz up to 2484 MHz. Wi-Fi requires bandwidth of approximately 20 MHz, not 5 MHz. Consequently, a site designer needs to choose the channels that do not overlap. On a WLAN where only the first 11 channels are available, channels 1, 6, and 11 can be selected as non-overlapping.

Note: *In the Americas, regulations permit the use of channels 1-11 only, while in Europe, channels 1-13 are permitted. In Japan, all 14 channels are permitted.*

The limited number of non-overlapping channels means that co-channel interference is a real possibility. Special codes embedded in the signal give each transmitting node a distinguishing pattern, so that nearby networks can share the same channel at once. At some point, however, the channel becomes saturated with too many WLANs.

The 5 GHz band is subdivided into 23 non-overlapping channels each ~20 MHz-wide. The greater number of non-overlapping channels means that co-channel interference is less of a problem for the 5 GHz band. This means that more WLANs can occupy the same area or that you can provision more access points closer together to support a greater density of client devices.

> **Note:** *Initially there were 11 channels in the 5 GHz band, but the subsequent 802.11h standard added another 12. 802.11h also adds the Dynamic Frequency Selection (DFS) method to prevent access points working in the 5 GHz band from interfering with radar and satellite signals. The exact use of channels can be subject to different regulations in different countries.*

WIRELESS NETWORK STANDARDS

Show Slide(s)

Wireless Network Standards (2 slides)

Use of the legacy standards—802.11a/b/g—is now limited to quite old equipment. You are relatively unlikely to come across networks still supporting them. As 802.11nb and g both worked at 2.4 GHz, 802.11g provided an upgrade path for 802.11b WLANs. Working in the 5 GHz band, 802.11a is incompatible with the other two and was not as widely adopted.

IEEE 802.11n

The 802.11n standard provides substantially more bandwidth than the legacy standards. It multiplexes the signals from 2-4 separate antennas in a process called **Multiple-Input-Multiple-Output (MIMO)**. The configuration of 802.11n devices is identified by AxB:C notation, where A is the number of transmit antennas, B is the number of receive antennas, and C is the number of simultaneous transmit and receive streams. The maximum possible is 4x4:4 but common configurations are 2x2:2, 3x3:2, or 3x3:3. Both the transmitter and receiver must support the same number of streams.

802.11n can deliver even more bandwidth with the option to use two adjacent 20 MHz channels as a single 40 MHz channel (channel bonding). 802.11n products can use channels in the 2.4 GHz band or the 5 GHz band. The 5 GHz band is preferred for optimal bandwidth and to avoid interference with existing 2.4 GHz networks and devices. Channel bonding is only a practical option in the 5 GHz band. Assuming the maximum number of spatial streams and optimum conditions, the nominal data rates for 802.11n are 288.8 Mbps for a single channel and 600 Mbps for bonded channels.

> **Note:** *Cheaper adapters may only support the 2.4 GHz band. Many smartphone models only support 2.4 GHz. An access point or adapter that can support both is referred to as dual band. A dual band access point can support both 2.4 GHz and 5 GHz bands simultaneously. This allows legacy clients to be allocated to the 2.4 GHz band.*

IEEE 802.11ac

The 802.11ac standard continues the development of 802.11n technologies. The main distinction is that 802.11ac works only in the 5 GHz band. The 2.4 GHz band can be used for legacy standards (802.11b/g/n) in mixed mode. The aim for 802.11ac is to get throughput similar to that of Gigabit Ethernet or better. It supports more channel bonding (up to 80 or 160 MHz channels), up to 8 spatial streams rather than 4, and denser modulation (at close ranges).

As with 802.11n, only high-end equipment will be equipped with sufficient antennas to make use of up to 8 streams. At the time of writing, no devices actually support more than 4x4:4 streams. The maximum theoretical data rate with 8 streams and 160 MHz channel bonding is about 6.93 Gbps. Cisco's Aironet 1850e 4x4:4 access points support up to 1.7 Gbps with 80 MHz channels.

ACCESS POINTS AND WIRELESS NETWORK MODES

Show Slide(s)

Access Points and Wireless Network Modes (3 slides)

Most Wi-Fi networks are configured in what is technically referred to as **infrastructure mode**. Infrastructure mode means that each client device (or station) is configured to connect to the network via an **Access Point (AP)**. In 802.11 documentation, this is referred to as a Basic Service Set (BSS). The MAC address of the AP is used as the **Basic Service Set Identifier (BSSID)**. More than one BSS can be grouped together in an **Extended Service Set (ESS)**.

The **access point** works as a bridge, forwarding communications between the wireless stations and the wired network, referred to as a Distribution System (DS). The access point will be joined to the network in much the same way as a host computer is—via a wall port and cabling to an Ethernet switch.

An access point. (Image © 123RF.com.)

Access Points can also be configured to forward frames between one another, functioning in a Wireless Distribution System (WDS) to extend the network without using a cabled backbone. A WDS can be configured in bridge mode, where the access points only forward communications between one another, and repeater mode, where they also communicate with stations.

A WDS can be complex to set up and can suffer from compatibility problems when devices from multiple vendors are used. For residential users, a **range extender** is a simpler device for regenerating a signal from an access point to a more remote location, such as an upstairs room. Another option is a range extender that works with a powerline adapter to communicate with the access point over the electrical wiring.

AD-HOC AND WI-FI DIRECT

Stations can also be configured to connect directly to one another. With older network standards, this is referred to as **ad-hoc mode**. Such peer-to-peer connections are now more likely to be implemented as Wi-Fi Direct, which has the advantage of automatically configuring a secure link between the stations.

WIRELESS MESH NETWORK (WMN) TOPOLOGY

The 802.11s standard defines a **Wireless Mesh Network (WMN)**. Unlike an ad hoc network, nodes in a WMN (called Mesh Stations) are capable of discovering one another and peering, forming a Mesh Basic Service Set (MBSS). The mesh stations can perform path discovery and forwarding between peers, using a routing protocol, such as the Hybrid Wireless Mesh Protocol (HWMP).

PERSONAL AREA NETWORKS

The concept of a **Personal Area Network (PAN)** has gained some currency with the profusion of wireless and cellular connection technologies in the last few years. A PAN refers to using wireless connectivity to connect to devices within a few meters—printers, smartphones, headsets, speakers, video displays, and so on.

WIRELESS NETWORK CARDS

Show Slide(s)

Wireless Network Cards

Each station in a Wi-Fi network needs to be installed with a Wi-Fi adapter supporting the 802.11 standard(s) used on the network. A Wi-Fi adapter can be installed if the function is not available on the motherboard. Both internally installed adapter cards and USB-connected adapters are available. A Wi-Fi card may also need to be installed to support the latest standard (upgrading from 802.11g to 802.11n or 802.11ac, for instance). Like an Ethernet card, a Wi-Fi adapter is identified at the data link layer by a MAC address.

Activity 8-3

Discussing Wireless Networks

Show Slide(s)
Activity: Discussing Wireless Networks

SCENARIO

Answer the following questions to check your understanding of the topic.

---

1. **What is the maximum transfer rate of an 802.11g Wi-Fi adapter?**

    54 Mbps.

2. **Why are 2.4 GHz networks more susceptible to interference than 5 GHz networks?**

    Each channel in a 2.4 GHz network is only 5 MHz wide while Wi-Fi requires about 20 MHz. Consequently, there is not much "space" for separate networks and the chances of overlap are high. There are also numerous other product types that work in the 2.4 GHz band.

3. **How does 802.11n achieve greater speeds than previous Wi-Fi standards?**

    Largely through using multiple reception and transmission antennas (MIMO) and channel bonding.

4. **Can 802.11ac achieve higher throughput by multiplexing the signals from both 2.4 and 5 GHz frequency bands? Why or why not?**

    No, because 802.11ac works only at 5 GHz.

5. **Why might a wireless mesh network topology be used?**

    Each station in a wireless mesh can be made capable of discovering other nodes on the network and forwarding traffic. This can be used to create a network that covers a wide area without deploying numerous access points or extenders.

Topic D
Internet Connection Types

EXAM OBJECTIVES COVERED
1001-2.2 Compare and contrast common networking hardware devices.
1001-2.4 Compare and contrast wireless networking protocols.
1001-2.7 Compare and contrast Internet connection types, network types, and their features.

In the previous topics, you identified the network cabling and devices used to implement different types of Local Area Networks (LANs). A key component of any network is the ability to communicate with remote hosts over the Internet. In this topic, you will learn to compare and contrasts methods of Internet access, as provided for typical SOHO network types.

Show Slide(s)

Internet Connections

Interaction Opportunity

Ask learners if they can think of any businesses that don't require Internet access, and discuss their responses.

INTERNET CONNECTIONS

The major infrastructure of the Internet, also referred to as the **Internet backbone**, consists of very high bandwidth trunks connecting **Internet eXchange Points (IXPs)**. These trunks and IXPs are mostly created by telecommunications companies and academic institutions. They are typically organized on national and international levels. Within the data center supporting any given IXP, **Internet Service Providers (ISPs)** establish high-speed links between their networks, using transit and peering arrangements to carry traffic to and from parts of the Internet they do not physically own. There is a tiered hierarchy of ISPs that reflects to what extent they depend on transit arrangements with other ISPs.

Customers connect to an ISP's network via a local **Point of Presence (PoP)**. The ISP uses a **backhaul** link (or a transit arrangement with another ISP) to connect each POP to their core network infrastructure and one or more IXPs.

INTERNET SERVICE PROVIDERS

Show Slide(s)

Internet Service Providers (2 slides)

Most home users and businesses rely on an Internet Service Provider (ISP) to facilitate the link between their SOHO network and the Internet. Internet access is then a question of how you join your local network to the ISP's PoP.

The consumer and small business technologies for doing this are dial-up, "broadband" (DSL, FTTx, or cable), and wireless (radio or satellite). Each has its advantages and disadvantages depending on the type of access and frequency of use required.

Most SOHO Internet access methods makes use of the **Public Switched Telephone Network (PSTN)**. The PSTN is the national and global telecommunications network. The voice-grade copper wire part of this network (between subscribers and the telecom provider's switches) is sometimes referred to as the **Plain Old Telephone Service (POTS)**, "local loop," or "last mile."

The ISP handles the business of allocating one or more public Internet Protocol (IP) addresses that will work on the Internet and other services, such as domain name registration, web and email hosting, and so on.

Enterprise ISP solutions will offer much higher bandwidth links, often using fiber optic cabling.

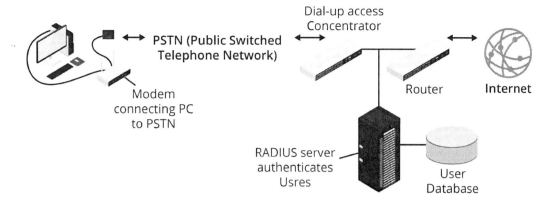

Internet access for a standalone PC via an ISP. (Image © 123RF.com.)

POINT-TO-POINT PROTOCOL

The **Point-to-Point Protocol (PPP)** is typically used to encapsulate the network protocol, which will usually be TCP/IP, over the link to the ISP. PPP also provides a mechanism to authenticate the user and manage the connection between the local computer or network and the ISP's router.

BROADBAND INTERNET ACCESS

Broadband covers a range of different connection technologies. The main characteristics are that they are "always-on" (that is, the connection does not need to be re-established for each session) and data transfer rates are (a lot) higher than analog dial-up.

DSL

Digital Subscriber Line (DSL) uses the higher frequencies available in a copper telephone line as a communications channel. The use of a filter prevents the DSL signals from contaminating voice traffic. The use of advanced modulation and echo canceling techniques enable high bandwidth, full duplex transmissions.

A DSL "modem" makes the connection to the phone system. Typically, the modem function will be part of a DSL router/modem/access point appliance that can provide access to a small network of computers. The phone line makes the connection to a bank of DSL modems in the exchange, called a **DSL Access Multiplier (DSLAM)**. The DSLAM channels voice and data traffic to the appropriate network. Depending on the equipment used by the ISP, the data link protocol used for DSL may be **PPP over ATM (PPPoA)** or **PPP over Ethernet (PPPoE)**.

There are various "flavors" of DSL, notably asymmetrical and symmetrical types:

- **Asymmetrical DSL (ADSL)** is a "consumer" version of DSL that provides a fast downlink but a slow uplink. There are various iterations of ADSL, with the latest (ADSL2+) offering downlink rates up to about 24 Mbps and uplink rates up to 1.4 Mbps, or 3.3 Mbps upstream if the provider supports Annex M/ADSL2+ M.

  Often service providers impose usage restrictions to limit the amount of data downloaded per month. Actual speed may be affected by the quality of the cabling in the consumer's premises and between the premises and the exchange and also by the number of users connected to the same DSLAM (contention). The maximum range of an ADSL modem is typically about 10,000 feet (2 miles or 3 km), but the longer the connection, the greater the deterioration in data rate.

Show Slide(s)

Broadband Internet Access

Interaction Opportunity

Poll learners to measure which Internet access methods they use at home.

Show Slide(s)

DSL (2 slides)

Teaching Tip

Note that while learners may be most familiar with DSL router/modems, a DSL modem can be supplied as a separate device. You may also want to note that a modem may be supplied as an add-in card for an enterprise router.

Stress the point that the modem has to be matched to the DSL type. You cannot use an ADSL modem for VDSL.

- Symmetric versions of DSL offer the same uplink and downlink speeds. These are of more use to businesses and for branch office links, where more data is transferred upstream than with normal Internet use.
- **Very High Bitrate DSL (VDSL)** achieves higher bit rates at the expense of range. It allows for both symmetric and asymmetric modes. Over 300 m (1000 feet), an asymmetric link supports 52 Mbps downstream and 6 Mbps upstream, whereas a symmetric link supports 26 Mbps in both directions. VDSL2 also specifies a very short range (100 m/300 feet) rate of 100 Mbps (bi-directional).

FIBER OPTIC INTERNET ACCESS

Show Slide(s)

Fiber Optic Internet Access (3 slides)

Fiber optic cabling supports much higher bandwidth and lower distance limitations than copper cabling. Fiber optic cabling has replaced copper cabling within the "core" of telecommunications networks. Extending fiber optic cabling to individual subscriber homes and businesses is slowly taking place. There are two principal types of businesses operating fiber optic networks for SOHO Internet access—companies with their roots in cable TV on one hand and the telecommunications providers with their roots in telephone services on the other.

HYBRID FIBER COAX (HFC)/CABLE

A cable Internet connection is usually available along with a **Cable Access TV (CATV)** service. These networks are often described as **Hybrid Fiber Coax (HFC)** as they combine a fiber optic core network with coax links to customer premises equipment, but are more simply just described as "broadband cable" or just as "cable."

The cable modem is interfaced to the local network or computer through an Ethernet adapter and with the cable network by a short segment of coax. More coax then links all the premises in a street with a **Cable Modem Termination System (CMTS)**, which routes data traffic via the fiber backbone to the ISP's Point of Presence (PoP) and from there to the Internet. Cable based on the **Data Over Cable Service Interface Specification (DOCSIS)** supports downlink speeds of up to 38 Mbps (North America) or 50 Mbps (Europe) and uplinks of up to 27 Mbps. DOCSIS version 3 allows the use of multiplexed channels to achieve higher bandwidth.

FIBER TO THE CURB (FTTC)

For the telecommunications companies, the major obstacle to providing really high bandwidth to consumers and small businesses is in the last mile of the telephone network. Copper cabling infrastructure in the last mile is often of poor quality as it was only designed to service a telephone line. The projects to update this wiring to use fiber optic links are referred to by the umbrella term "Fiber to the X" (FTTx).

The most expensive solution is **Fiber to the Premises (FTTP)** or its domestic variant **Fiber to the Home (FTTH)**. The essential point about both these implementations is that the fiber link is terminated on customer premises equipment. Such "pure" fiber solutions are not widespread and generally carry a price premium above other types of Internet access.

Show Slide(s)

Dial-Up Internet Access (2 slides)

Teaching Tip

Discuss why dial-up access might still be relevant to PC support. (Dial-up links can still be prevalent in rural areas.)

Other solutions can variously be described as **Fiber to the Node (FTTN)** or **Fiber to the Curb/Cabinet (FTTC)**. These extend the fiber link to a communications cabinet in the street servicing multiple subscribers. This is similar model to HFC, but instead of the coax segment, each subscriber is linked to the fiber service by running Very High Bitrate DSL (VDSL) over the existing telephone wiring.

DIAL-UP INTERNET ACCESS

Dial-up is simply a telephone conversation between two computers. Whereas with DSL this "conversation" is pushed to the higher frequency parts of the phone line, with dial-up it occupies the whole frequency range, but not very efficiently. Ordinary telephone charges apply for the duration of each session and the phone line cannot be used for voice calls at the same time. A dial-up link is very low bandwidth.

A dial-up connection is facilitated by analog modems on each end of the line. A dial-up modem converts digital signals to an analog carrier signal (modulation) and transmits it over the telephone cable, making a distinctive screeching noise. The modem at the other end converts the analog signal back to digital (demodulation) and processes the data.

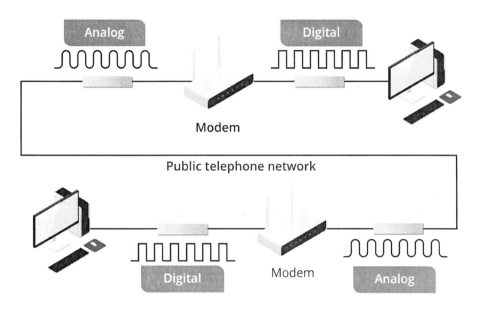

Dial-up modems. (Image © 123RF.com.)

The main disadvantages of this system are the low data transfer rates, the time it takes for the connection to be established, and error prone links. The fastest modems can only usually work at 33.6 Kbps (V.34+) and this speed is reaching the limitations of analog lines. Using the V.90 or V.92 digital signaling protocol, a downlink speed of up to 56 Kbps is possible in theory, though rarely achieved in practice. The use of compression can also improve the data transfer throughput, though as many of the files being transferred are likely to be compressed already (image files, for instance), the improvement will be variable.

Consequently, dial-up has been almost completely superseded by other technologies and would only be used as a backup method or in areas where no other access methods are supported.

ISDN INTERNET ACCESS

Integrated Services Digital Network (ISDN) is a digital circuit-switched technology for voice, video, and data (hence "integrated services"). ISDN makes use of existing copper telephone wiring, if the wiring is of sufficient quality. Unlike dial-up, however, it uses the line to transmit digital signatures for both voice and data. This means that there are no inefficient analog-to-digital conversions and so higher speeds can be supported.

Show Slide(s)

ISDN Internet Access

ISDN is a dial-up service billed for by line rental and per-minute usage. Although it is a dial-up technology, it is capable of establishing a circuit connection in less than 1 second—much faster than an analog modem.

The most common uses of ISDN are for interconnection of LANs and remote users (teleworkers) to businesses. There are two classes of ISDN:

- **Basic Rate Interface (BRI)** provides two 64 Kbps "B" channels for data and one 16 Kbps "D" channel for link management control signals. It is sometimes called 2B+D. One option is to use one B channel for data and leave the other for voice or fax; another is to provide a 128 Kbps link by concatenating the two B channels. This form of ISDN is intended for SOHO use.
- **Primary Rate Interface (PRI)** provides 23 or 30 "B" channels (or between about 1.5 and 2 Mbps), depending on location in the world, and one 64 Kbps D channel. This form of ISDN is intended for larger companies and is commonly used to provide a link between two company locations.

Much of the switching technology of ISDN remains in use in terms of the telecommunications core network, but as an Internet access method for subscribers, it has largely been superseded by DSL and cable. It remains a good solution outside metropolitan areas where these other services may not be available.

An ISDN connection would typically be facilitated through a **Terminal Adapter (TA)**. The TA may be an external appliance or a plug-in card for a PC or compatible router. The TA is connected to the ISDN network via an NT1 device (Network Terminator). The ISDN-enabled router may then either be connected to a switch or support direct connections from ISDN devices.

FIXED WIRELESS INTERNET ACCESS

Show Slide(s)

Fixed Wireless Internet Access (2 slides)

Wired broadband Internet access is not always available, especially in rural areas or in older building developments, where running new cable capable of supporting DSL or FTTC is problematic. In this scenario, some sort of fixed wireless Internet access might be an option.

SATELLITE INTERNET ACCESS

Satellite systems provide far bigger areas of coverage than can be achieved using other technologies. A **Very Small Aperture Terminal (VSAT)** microwave antenna is aligned to an orbital satellite that can either relay signals between sites directly or via another satellite. Satellites use frequency bands in the Super High Frequency range (3-30 GHz). The widespread use of satellite television receivers allows for domestic Internet connectivity services over satellite connections. Satellite services for business are also expanding, especially in rural areas where DSL or cable services are less likely to be available. The transfer rates available vary between providers and access packages, but 2 or 6 Mbps up and 15-20 Mbps down would be typical. There are also likely to be quite restrictive usage limits.

Satellite connections experience quite severe **latency** problems as the signal has to travel over thousands of miles more than terrestrial connections, introducing a delay of many times what might be expected over a land link. For example, if accessing a site over DSL involves a 15-50 ms delay on the link, accessing the same site over a satellite link could involve a 1000 ms delay. This is an issue for real-time applications, such as video-conferencing, VoIP, and multi-player gaming.

To create a satellite Internet connection, the ISP installs a satellite dish (antenna) at the customer's premises and aligns it with the orbital satellite. The satellites are in geostationary orbit above the equator, so in the northern hemisphere the dish will be pointing south. Because the satellite does not move relative to the dish, there should be no need for any realignment. The antenna is connected via coaxial cabling to a DVB-S (Digital Video Broadcast Satellite) modem. This can be installed in the PC as an adapter card or as an external box connected via a USB or Ethernet port.

LINE OF SIGHT WIRELESS INTERNET SERVICE PROVIDER (WISP)

Line of Sight (LoS) is a wireless connection method using ground-based microwave antennas aligned with one another. Endpoints can transmit signals to one another as long as they are unobstructed by physical objects. The antennas themselves are typically affixed to the top of tall buildings in order to reduce this interference. A line of sight service can cover great distances that typical wireless signals cannot, while at the same time saving the service provider from having to install cabling infrastructure. Additionally, the connection in an LoS service is often low latency, or at least, lower latency than satellite.

A disadvantage of LoS is that the actual unobstructed sight line can be difficult to maintain, especially if the area between the two endpoints is not owned by the client or the provider. Likewise, LoS services are usually more expensive than other methods.

A company specializing in LoS networks is referred to as a **Wireless Internet Service Provider (WISP)**. A WISP might use Wi-Fi type networking or proprietary equipment. The services can operate over a range of frequencies. The use of certain frequencies may be impacted by the deployment of 5G cellular services, which may involve changes to the way some frequency bands are licensed for use.

CELLULAR RADIO NETWORKS

The 2.4 GHz and 5 GHz frequency bands used by Wi-Fi have quite severely restricted range while fixed wireless Internet requires a large dish antenna. Cellular radio wireless networking facilitates communications over much larger distances using portable equipment like smartphones. Cellular networking is also used by some Internet of Things (IoT) devices, such as smart energy meters.

CELLULAR RADIO (GSM/TDMA AND CDMA)

A cellular radio makes a connection using the nearest available transmitter (cell or base station). Each base station has an effective range of up to 5 miles (8 km). The transmitter connects the phone to the mobile and landline telephone networks. Transmitter coverage in many countries is now very good, with the exception of remote rural areas. Cellular radio works in the 850 and 1900 MHz frequency bands (mostly in the Americas) and the 900 and 1800 MHz bands (rest of the world).

Cellular digital communications standards are described as belonging to a particular generation. For 2G, there were two competing formats, established in different markets:

- **Global System for Mobile Communication (GSM)**-based phones. GSM allows subscribers to use a **Subscriber Identity Module (SIM)** card to use an unlocked handset with their chosen network provider. GSM is adopted internationally and by AT&T and T-Mobile in the US.
- TIA/EIA IS-95 (cdmaOne)-based handsets. With **Code Division Multiple Access (CDMA)**, the handset is managed by the provider, not the SIM. CDMA adoption is largely restricted to the telecom providers Sprint® and Verizon.

In both cases, the cell network was built primarily to support voice calls, so 2G data access was provided on top, using Circuit Switched Data (CSD). CSD is somewhat similar to a dial-up modem, though no analog transmissions are involved. CSD requires a data connection to be established to the base station (incurring call charges) and is only capable of around 14.4 Kbps at best.

3G

The transition from 2G to 3G saw various packet-switched technologies deployed to mobiles:

- General Packet Radio Services/Enhanced Data Rates for GSM Evolution (GPRS/EDGE) is a precursor to 3G (2.5G) with GPRS offering up to about 48 Kbps and EDGE about 3-4 times that. Unlike CSD, GPRS and EDGE allow "always on" data connections, with usage billed by bandwidth consumption rather than connection time.

Show Slide(s)

Cellular Radio Networks (2 slides)

Teaching Tip

Note that speeds for these standards are almost impossible to specify precisely. The values here are given just for the basis of a comparison against other data communications standards. Learners shouldn't need to quote them for the exam.

- Evolved High Speed Packet Access (HSPA+) is a 3G standard developed via several iterations from the Universal Mobile Telecommunications System (UMTS) used on GSM networks. HSPA+ nominally supports download speeds up to 168 Mbps and upload speeds up to 34 Mbps. HSPA+-based services are often marketed as 4G if the nominal data rate is better than about 20 Mbps.
- CDMA2000/Evolution Data Optimized (EV-DO) are the main 3G standards deployed by CDMA network providers. EV-DO can support a 3.1 Mbps downlink and 1.8 Mbps uplink.

4G

Long Term Evolution (LTE) is a converged 4G standard supported by all network providers. Any device using a 4G connection needs a SIM card. LTE has a maximum downlink of 150 Mbps in theory, but no provider networks can deliver that sort of speed at the time of writing. Around 20 Mbps is more typical of real-word performance.

LTE Advanced (LTE-A) is intended to provide a 300 Mbps downlink, but again this aspiration is not matched by real-world performance. Current typical performance for LTE-A is around 40 Mbps.

5G

According to the original specification, a 4G service was supposed to deliver 1 Gbps for stationary or slow-moving users (including pedestrians) and 100 Mbps for access from a fast-moving vehicle. Those data rates are now the minimum hoped-for standards for 5G. 5G is currently only available in trial areas. Speeds of up to 70 Gbps have been achieved under test conditions, but commercial products and service standards are not likely to appear until 2020.

Activity 8-4

Discussing Internet Connection Types

 Show Slide(s)

Activity: Discussing Internet Connection Types

SCENARIO

Answer the following questions to check your understanding of the topic.

1. **If you have remote employees who need to connect to the corporate network but they are located in a remote area with no access to high-speed Internet service, what do you think is the best Internet connection method to use?**

   Satellite is the most likely option. A dial-up link is unlikely to provide sufficient bandwidth for a remote access VPN. In some cases, tethering to a cell phone or connecting to a wireless network device is an option, but this will depend on how remote the employees' location is and if they can get a strong cellular signal.

2. **True or false? Analog modems are required for dial-up and ISDN Internet access services.**

   False. Dial-up uses an analog modem but Integrated Services Digital Network (ISDN) uses digital not analog transmissions. The link is created via an adapter called an NT1. This may loosely be referred to as an "ISDN modem," but it is not an analog modem.

3. **What type of SOHO Internet access method offers the best bandwidth?**

   Fiber to the Premises is the best, but it is not always available. Fiber to the Curb and Hybrid Fiber Coax (cable) are the best options for the majority of residential subscribers.

4. **Which protocol enables a dial-up user to exchange frames of data with an ISP's access server?**

   Point-to-Point Protocol (PPP).

5. **What type of cabling is used with the WAN port of a cable modem?**

   Coax.

6. **What Internet access method would be suitable for a business requiring a high bandwidth connection where no cabled options exist?**

   Line-of-sight microwave radio from a Wireless Internet Service Provider (WISP).

Topic E

Network Configuration Concepts

EXAM OBJECTIVES COVERED
1001-2.2 Compare and contrast common networking hardware devices.
1001-2.6 Explain common network configuration concepts.

Teaching Tip

Learners are likely to find this topic challenging so try to allocate plenty of time.

Now that you are familiar with the basic components that make up a network, you can start to take a look at Transmission Control Protocol/Internet Protocol (TCP/IP) addressing and data delivery. In this topic, you will identify the properties and characteristics of TCP/IP.

As a CompTIA A+ technician, you must be able to identify how protocols work together and with the network hardware to provide services. Understanding how everything is connected and functioning within the network will allow you to properly support TCP/IP within a network.

Show Slide(s)

Routers (2 slides)

Teaching Tip

Clearly differentiate between the separate functions of modems, switches, and routers.

Note that the term "unmanaged switch" is used here only to delay the topic of VLANs momentarily.

ROUTERS

Ethernet switches connect nodes on the basis of local or hardware (MAC) addresses. Everything connected to an unmanaged switch is part of the same physical and logical network. When you want to connect such a network to the Internet or when you want to divide a large local network into logical subnetworks, you need to use one or more routers.

A **router** is responsible for moving data around a network of networks, known as an internetwork or internet. While a switch forwards frames using hardware (MAC) addresses within a single network segment, a router forwards packets around an internetwork using logical network and host IDs.

A router. (Image © 123RF.com.)

There are many different types and uses of routers, but on an enterprise network, a router tends to perform one of the following two tasks:

- LAN router—divide a single physical network into multiple logical networks. This is useful for security and performance reasons.

- WAN or edge/border router—join a network using one type of media with a network using different media. A typical example is to join a LAN to a WAN, such as the Internet.

Selection of the path or route to the destination network is determined dynamically or statically. The packet moves, hop by hop, through the internetwork to the target network. Once it has reached the destination network, the hardware address can be used to move the packet to the target node. This process requires each logically separate network to have a unique network address.

ROUTERS VERSUS MODEMS

Make sure you understand the separate functions of modems and routers when connecting to the Internet. A **modem** works at the same level as a switch, making a physical network link with the ISP's network. The type of modem must be matched to the type of link (dial-up, DSL, cable, and so on). A router makes decisions about forwarding between the two logical networks. For SOHO networks, this is usually a simple choice between the local network and the Internet. On a SOHO network, the modem and the router are typically bundled in the same appliance.

VIRTUAL LAN (VLAN)

The switches on an enterprise network can provide thousands of ports. It is inefficient to have that many connections to the same "logical" network. The ports are divided into groups using a feature of managed switches called **Virtual LAN (VLAN)**. Each VLAN is associated with a different logical subnetwork address. Communications between different VLANs therefore have to go through a router. As well as improving performance, this is a security benefit too. Traffic passing between VLANs can be easily filtered and monitored to ensure it meets security policies.

THE TCP/IP PROTOCOL SUITE

Protocols are procedures or rules used by networked hosts to communicate. For communication to take place, the two hosts must have a protocol in common. Often, several protocols used for networking are designed to work together. This collection of protocols is known as a **protocol suite**.

A number of protocol suites have been used for LAN and WAN communications over the years. However, the overwhelming majority of networks have now converged on the use of the **Transmission Control Protocol/Internet Protocol (TCP/IP)** suite. Most network implementations you will be required to install and support will depend on the use of TCP/IP.

TCP/IP was originally developed by the US Department of Defense but is now an open standard to which anyone may contribute. Developments are implemented through the Internet Engineering Task Force (IETF), which is split into a number of working groups. Standards are published as Request For Comments (RFCs). The official repository for RFCs is at **www.rfc-editor.org** and they are also published in HTML format at **tools.ietf.org/html**.

TCP/IP protocols are packet-based. This means that rather than sending a data message as a single large whole, it is split into numerous small packets. Smaller packets have a better chance of being delivered successfully and are easier to resend if lost or damaged.

Routers choose the paths that packets take around the network from source to destination.

Show Slide(s)

The TCP/IP Protocol Suite (3 slides)

Teaching Tip

You are using the layer model to help learners understand the function of the protocols, although matching protocols to layers is not an A+ exam objective.

TCP/IP PROTOCOLS

The main protocols in the suite provide addressing and transport services. The function of these protocols can be better understood by dividing them into layers. The TCP/IP suite uses a model with four distinct layers.

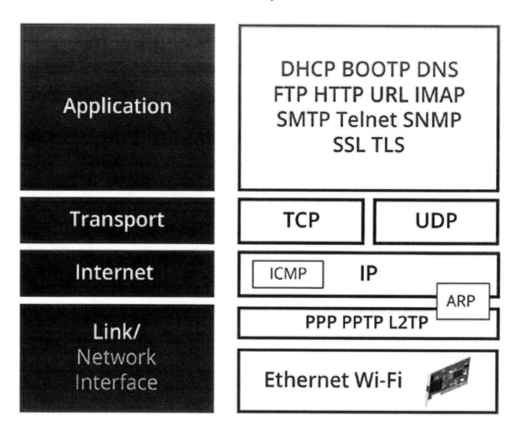

TCP/IP model. (Image © 123RF.com.)

The layers and main protocols working at each layer are as follows:

- **Link or Network Interface layer**—responsible for putting frames onto the physical network. This layer does not contain TCP/IP protocols as such. At this layer, different networking products and media can be used, such as Ethernet or Wi-Fi. Communications on this layer take place only on a local network segment and not between different networks. Data at the link layer is packaged in a unit called a frame and nodes are identified by a MAC address (assuming Ethernet or Wi-Fi).
- **Internet Protocol (IP)**—provides packet addressing and routing at the network layer. IP provides best effort delivery of an unreliable and connectionless nature. A packet might be lost, delivered out of sequence, duplicated, or delayed.
- **Transmission Control Protocol (TCP)**—guarantees orderly transmission of packets at the transport layer. TCP can identify and recover from lost or out-of-order packets. This is used by most TCP/IP application protocols as failing to receive a packet or processing it incorrectly can cause serious data errors.
- **User Datagram Protocol (UDP)**—provides unreliable, non-guaranteed transfer of packets. UDP is an alternative way of implementing the transport layer to TCP. UDP is faster and comes with less of a transmission overhead because it does not need to send extra information to establish reliable connections. It is used in time-sensitive applications, such as speech or video, where a few missing or out-of-order packets can be tolerated. Rather than causing the application to crash, they would just manifest as a glitch in video or a squeak in audio.

- **Application protocols**—there are numerous protocols used for network configuration, management, and services. Application protocols use a TCP or UDP port to connect the client and server.

ADDRESS RESOLUTION PROTOCOL (ARP)

When IP is being used with a physical/data link specification such as Ethernet or Wi-Fi, there must be a mechanism to deliver messages from IP at the network layer to computers addressed at the link layer. **Address Resolution Protocol (ARP)** finds the MAC (network adapter) address associated with an IP address.

ICMP

Additionally, you should be aware of the **Internet Control Message Protocol (ICMP),** which works at the network layer. ICMP delivers status and error messages and is used by diagnostic utilities such as **ping** and **tracert**.

Teaching Tip

ARP and ICMP are not called out on the exam objectives, but it would be worth taking a minute or two to discuss their importance.

INTERNET PROTOCOL AND IP ADDRESSING

The core protocol in TCP/IP is the Internet Protocol (IP), which provides network and host addressing and packet forwarding between networks.

Show Slide(s)

Internet Protocol and IP Addressing (4 slides)

IPv4 PACKET STRUCTURE

As with a frame, an IP packet adds some headers to whatever transport/application layer data it is carrying in its payload. There are two versions of IP: IPv4 and IPv6. We will discuss IPv6 later. The main IPv4 headers are as follows:

Teaching Tip

You might want to note that TTL was originally conceived as a measure of time (seconds) but is only used as a hop count now.

Field	Description
Source IP address	Identifies the sender of the datagram by IP address.
Destination IP address	Identifies the destination of the datagram by IP address.
Protocol	Indicates whether the data should be passed to UDP or TCP at the destination host.
Checksum	Verifies the packet's integrity upon arrival at the destination.
Time to Live	The number of hops a datagram is allowed to stay on the network before being discarded, otherwise packets could endlessly loop around an internet. A router will decrease the TTL by at least one when it handles the packet.

IPv4 ADDRESS FORMAT

An IPv4 address is 32 bits long and is used within an IPv4 packet to define the source and destination of the packet. In its raw form it appears as:

```
11000110000101001000100000001001
```

The 32 bits are subdivided into four groups of 8 bits (1 byte) known as **octets**. The above IP address could therefore be rearranged as:

```
11000110   00101001   00010000   00001001
```

This representation of an IP address makes human memorizing of the number almost impossible (much less entering it correctly into configuration dialogs). To make IP addresses easier to use, they are usually displayed in **dotted decimal notation**. This notation requires each octet to be converted to a decimal value. The decimal numbers are separated using a period. Converting the previous number to this notation gives:

```
198 . 41 . 16 . 9
```

CONVERTING BETWEEN BINARY AND DECIMAL FORMAT

Teaching Tip

Mention that odd numbers end in a binary 1. Even numbers end in a zero.

Encourage learners to perform the calculations in their heads, and use the calculator to check the answer.

The following examples demonstrate the process of converting between binary and decimal notation. The base of any number system tells us two things: how many different values any given digit can have and the factor by which the value of a digit increases as we move from right to left in a number. Thus, in normal base 10 (or decimal) numbers, a digit can take any one of ten different values (0 through 9), and the values of the different place positions within a number, moving from right to left, are units (ones), tens, hundreds, thousands, and so on.

In base 2 (binary), digits can only take one of two different values (0 and 1). The place values are powers of 2 ($2^1=2$, $2^2=4$, $2^3=8$, $2^4=16$, and so on). Consider the octet "11101101" represented in base 2. The following figure shows the place value of each digit in the octet:

```
   128       64       32       16        8        4        2        1
    1         1        1        0        1        1        0        1
  128*1     64*1     32*1     16*0      8*1      4*1      2*0      1*1
```

Therefore, the decimal equivalent is:

```
   128   +   64   +   32   +    0   +    8   +    4   +    0   +    1   =  237
```

You can use the same sort of method to convert from decimal to binary. For example, the number 199 can be converted as follows:

```
199  =
128   +   64   +    0   +    0   +    0   +    4   +    2   +    1
128       64        32       16        8        4        2        1
128*1     64*1     32*0     16*0      8*0      4*1      2*1      1*1
 1         1         0        0        0        1        1        1
```

If all the bits in an octet are set to 1, the number obtained is 255 (the maximum possible value). Similarly, if all the bits are set to 0, the number obtained is 0 (the minimum possible value). Therefore, theoretically an IPv4 address may be any value between 0.0.0.0 and 255.255.255.255. However, some addresses are not permitted or are reserved for special use.

Show Slide(s)

Subnet Masks (4 slides)

Teaching Tip

Tell learners that all masks use high order contiguous bits. If they look blankly at you, say that means the mask consists of a variable number of binary 1s, starting on the left and working right until you have enough for your needs. When the first zero is encountered, there will be no more 1s.

What this means is that in decimal, the mask will always be one of the following values in the least significant octet:

128, 192, 224, 240

248, 252, 254, 255

SUBNET MASKS

An IP address provides two pieces of information encoded within the same value:

- The network number (**network ID**)—this number is common to all hosts on the same IP network.
- The host number (**host ID**)—this unique number identifies a host on a particular IP network.

A **subnet mask** (or netmask) is used to distinguish these two components within a single IP address. It is used to "mask" the host ID portion of the IP address and thereby reveal the network ID portion.

Where there is a binary 1 in the mask, the corresponding binary digit in the IP address is part of the network ID. The relative sizes of the network and host portions determines the number of networks and hosts per network a particular addressing scheme can support.

Many subnetting schemes use one of the **default masks**. These are masks comprising whole octets only. Each default mask is known by a particular "class."

Class	Dotted Decimal Mask	Network Prefix	Binary Mask
A	255.0.0.0	/8	11111111 00000000 00000000 00000000
B	255.255.0.0	/16	11111111 11111111 00000000 00000000

Class	Dotted Decimal Mask	Network Prefix	Binary Mask
C	255.255.255.0	/24	11111111 11111111 11111111 00000000

The mask can be expressed in dotted decimal format or as a network prefix. The network prefix is simply the number of ones that appear in the mask.

 Note: The 1s in the mask are always contiguous. For example, a mask 11111111 11110000 00000000 00000000 is valid but 11111111 00000000 11110000 00000000 is not.

MASKING AN IP ADDRESS (ANDing)

The network ID portion of an IP address is revealed by "ANDing" the subnet mask to the IP address. When two 1s are ANDed together, the result is a 1. Any other combination produces a 0.

```
1   AND   1   =   1
1   AND   0   =   0
0   AND   1   =   0
0   AND   0   =   0
```

For example, to determine the network ID of the IP address 172.30.15.12 with a subnet mask of 255.255.0.0, the dotted decimal notation of the IP address and subnet mask must first be converted to binary notation. The next step is to AND the two binary numbers. The result can be converted back to dotted decimal notation to provide the network ID (172.30.0.0).

```
172. 30. 15. 12    10101100 00011110 00001111 00001100
255.255.  0.  0    11111111 11111111 00000000 00000000
172. 30.  0.  0    10101100 00011110 00000000 00000000
```

Instead of quoting the mask each time, you could express that network ID with a prefix instead: 172.30.0.0/16.

ROUTING DECISION

A host can communicate directly on the local network segment with any other host that has the same network ID. Communications with a host that has a different network ID must be sent via a router.

When two hosts attempt to communicate via IPv4, the protocol compares the source and destination address in each packet against a subnet mask. If the masked portions of the source and destination IP addresses match, then the destination interface is assumed to be on the same IP network. For example:

```
172. 30. 15. 12    10101100 00011110 00001111 00001100
255.255.  0.  0    11111111 11111111 00000000 00000000
172. 30. 16.101    10101100 00011110 00010000 01100101
```

In the example, IP concludes the destination IPv4 address is on the same IP network and would try to deliver the packet locally.

If the masked portion does not match, IP assumes the packet must be routed to another IP network. For example:

```
172. 30. 15. 12    10101100 00011110 00001111 00001100
255.255.  0.  0    11111111 11111111 00000000 00000000
172. 31. 16.101    10101100 00011111 00010000 01100101
```

In this case, IP concludes the destination IPv4 address is on a different IP network and would forward the packet to a router rather than trying to deliver it locally.

*Note: This describes **unicast addressing**, where a single host is addressed. An address where the host bits are all "1"s is the **broadcast address** for a network. A message sent to a broadcast address is received by all hosts on the network. The broadcast address of the previous example would be 172.16.255.255.*

HOST IP CONFIGURATION

 Show Slide(s)

Host IP Configuration

 Teaching Tip

Exam candidates should understand the function of each of these parameters, know what a DHCP server is for, know when APIPA is used, and be able to spot an APIPA address.

Each host must be configured with an IP address and subnet mask at a minimum in order to communicate on an IPv4 network. This minimum configuration will not prove very usable, however. Several other parameters must be configured for a host to make full use of a modern network or the Internet.

IPv4 ADDRESS AND SUBNET MASK

An IPv4 address and subnet mask can be set manually (static address). The IP address is entered as four decimal numbers separated by periods (e.g., 172.30.15.12). The IP address identifies both the network to which the interface is attached and also its unique identity on that network. An interface must be configured with an IP address.

The subnet mask is used in conjunction with the IP address to determine whether another interface is located on a local or remote network. An interface must be configured with a subnet mask.

DEFAULT GATEWAY

The **default gateway** parameter is the IP address of a router to which packets destined for a remote network should be sent by default. This setting is not compulsory but failure to enter a gateway would limit the interface to communication on the local network only.

CLIENT-SIDE DNS

Another important part of IP configuration is specifying the IP address of one or more **Domain Name System (DNS)** servers. These servers provide resolution of host and domain names to their IP addresses and are essential for locating resources on the Internet. Most local networks also use DNS for name resolution. Typically, the DNS server would be the gateway address, though this may not be the case on all networks. Often two DNS server addresses (preferred and alternate) are specified for redundancy.

STATIC AND DYNAMIC IP ADDRESSES

 Show Slide(s)

Static and Dynamic IP Addresses (3 slides)

Using static addressing requires that an administrator visit each computer to manually enter the configuration information for that host. If the host moves to a different subnet, the administrator must manually reconfigure it. The administrator must keep track of which IP addresses have been allocated to avoid issuing duplicates. In a large network, configuring IP statically on each node can be very time consuming and prone to errors that can potentially disrupt communication on the network.

Static addresses are typically only assigned to systems with a dedicated functionality, such as router interfaces, network-attached printers, or servers that host applications on a network.

DHCP

When an interface is given a static configuration manually, the installer may make a mistake with the address information—perhaps duplicating an existing IP address or entering the wrong subnet mask—or the configuration of the network may change, requiring the host to be manually configured with a new static address. To avoid these problems, a **Dynamic Host Configuration Protocol (DHCP)** Server can be used to allocate an IP address and subnet mask (plus other settings) dynamically.

The computer contacts the DHCP server as it starts up and is allocated a lease for an IP address. Settings such as default gateway and DNS server addresses may be passed to the computer at the same time. If the address information needs to change, this can be done on the DHCP server, and clients will update themselves automatically when they seek a new lease (or a new lease can be requested manually).

 Note: *The DHCP client communicates with the server using broadcast communications so there is no need to configure a DHCP server address.*

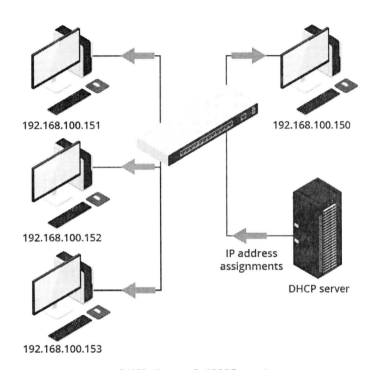

DHCP. (Image © 123RF.com.)

LINK LOCAL ADDRESSING/APIPA

Hosts also have a "fallback" mechanism for when the computer is configured to use a DHCP server but cannot contact one. In this scenario, the computer selects an address at random from the range 169.254.1.0 to 169.254.254.255. Microsoft calls this **Automatic Private IP Addressing (APIPA)**. When a host is using an APIPA address, it can communicate with other hosts on the same network that are using APIPA, but cannot reach other networks or communicate with hosts that have managed to obtain a valid DHCP lease.

 Note: *"APIPA" is Microsoft's term. Other vendors and open source products use the term "link local" instead.*

DHCP RESERVATIONS

It is often useful for a host to use the same IP address. Servers, routers, printers, and other network infrastructure can be easier to manage if their IP addresses are known. One option is to use static addressing for these appliances, but this is difficult to implement. Another option is to configure the DHCP server to **reserve** a particular IP address for that device. The DHCP server is configured with a list of the MAC addresses of hosts that should receive the same IP address. When it is contacted by a host with one of the listed MAC addresses, it issues a lease for the reserved IP address.

Note: The main drawback of this method is that if the DHCP server fails, then critical network devices might fail to obtain IP addresses.

PUBLIC AND PRIVATE IP ADDRESSES

Show Slide(s)

Public and Private IP Addresses (4 slides)

Teaching Tip

Public versus private addressing isn't called out as a content example, but NAT is, so you need to cover it at least briefly. Exam candidates shouldn't need to memorize the private ranges for A+ (apart from APIPA, which they should learn), but they'll have to learn them for future certification exams.

To communicate on the Internet, a host must obtain a unique public IP address. Typically this is allocated by an Internet Service Provider. Relatively few companies can obtain sufficient public IP addresses for all their computers to communicate over the Internet, however. There are various mechanisms to work around this issue.

PRIVATE ADDRESSING

The IP address scheme defines certain ranges as **private addresses**. These ranges are defined by RFC 1918 and are sometimes referred to as RFC 1918 addresses. Hosts with IP addresses from these ranges are not allowed to route traffic over the Internet. Use of the addresses is confined to private LANs. There are three private address ranges, each associated with one of the default subnet masks:

- 10.0.0.0 to 10.255.255.255 (Class A private address range).
- 172.16.0.0 to 172.31.255.255 (Class B private address range).
- 192.168.0.0 to 192.168.255.255 (Class C private address range).
- 169.254.0.0 to 169.254.255.255 (APIPA/link-local autoconfiguration). As discussed earlier, this range is used by hosts for autoconfiguration when a DHCP server cannot be contacted (selecting a link-local address).

Internet access can be facilitated for hosts using the private addressing scheme in two ways:

- Through a router configured with a single or block of valid public addresses; the router translates between the private and public addresses using Network Address Translation (NAT).
- Through a proxy server that fulfills requests for Internet resources on behalf of clients.

NETWORK ADDRESS TRANSLATION

Teaching Tip

Assure learners you will cover ports in depth in the next topic.

Most hosts on private networks are not configured with IP addresses that can communicate directly to the Internet. Instead, when clients on the local network connect via a router, the router converts the client's private IP address into a valid public address using **Network Address Translation (NAT)**.

A NAT address pool supports multiple simultaneous connections but is still limited by the number of available public IP addresses. Smaller companies may only be allocated a single or small block of addresses by their ISP. In this case, a means for multiple private IP addresses to be mapped onto a single public address would be useful, and this is exactly what is provided by **Network Address Port Translation (NAPT)**, which is also referred to as Port Address Translation (PAT) or as NAT overloading.

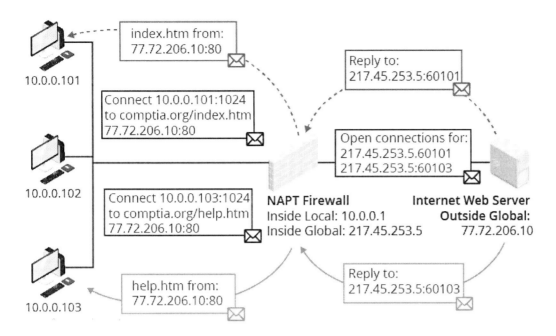

NAT overloading. (Image © 123RF.com.)

NAPT works by allocating each new connection a high level TCP or UDP port. For example, say two hosts (10.0.0.101 and 10.0.0.103) initiate a web connection at the same time, requesting responses on the client (or source) port 1024. The NAPT service creates two new client port mappings for these requests (10.0.0.101:60101 and 10.0.0.103:60103). It then substitutes the private source IPs for a single public source IP (217.45.253.5) and forwards the requests to the public Internet. It performs a reverse mapping on any traffic returned to those client ports, inserting the original private IP address and client port number, and forwarding the packets to the internal hosts.

VIRTUAL PRIVATE NETWORKS

A **Virtual Private Network (VPN)** connects the components and resources of two (private) networks over another (public) network. The Internet provides a cost effective way of connecting both users to networks and networks to networks. Rather than a user direct-dialing your server, which is private but expensive, the user connects to an ISP, which is cheap, but public.

A VPN is a "tunnel" through the Internet (or any other public network). It uses special connection protocols and encryption technology to ensure that the tunnel is secure and the user is properly authenticated. Once the connection has been established, to all intents and purposes, the remote computer becomes part of the local network (though it is still restricted by the bandwidth available over the WAN link).

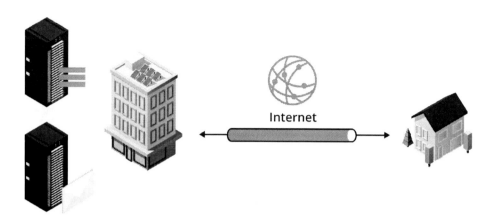

A typical VPN configuration. (Image © 123RF.com.)

IPv6

Show Slide(s)
IPv6 (5 slides)

Teaching Tip

Note that there is no such thing as IPv5 as the version field protocol ID "5" was assigned to another protocol (the Internet Stream Protocol) in the 1970s.

The addressing scheme discussed earlier is for IP version 4. Because it is feared the global supply of IPv4 addresses will run out, a new version of IP addressing, IP Version 6, has been developed. An IPv6 address is a 128-bit number (contrast with the 32-bit number used in v4). This massively increases the available pool of available addresses compared to IPv4.

IPv6 also includes new efficiency features, such as simplified address headers, hierarchical addressing, support for time-sensitive network traffic, and a new structure for unicast addressing.

BINARY AND HEXADECIMAL NOTATION

Network addresses are represented as binary values when processed by the computer but because binary has only two values for each position and the values for IPv6 addresses are very large, this would require a long string of characters to write out. This is difficult enough to read but even harder to type accurately into configuration dialogs.

Binary values are converted to decimal for IPv4 addresses but as IPv6 addresses are so much longer, hexadecimal notation is used. Hexadecimal has 16 characters (0...9 plus A, B, C, D, E, F). Therefore, it only takes 1 hexadecimal character to represent 4 binary characters. The following table summarizes the equivalent representations of decimal values from 0-15 in binary and hex.

Decimal	Hexadecimal	Binary
0	0	0000
1	1	0001
2	2	0010
3	3	0011
4	4	0100
5	5	0101
6	6	0110
7	7	0111
8	8	1000
9	9	1001

Decimal	Hexadecimal	Binary
10	A	1010
11	B	1011
12	C	1100
13	D	1101
14	E	1110
15	F	1111

IPv6 ADDRESS NOTATION

To express a 128-bit IPv6 address in hexadecimal notation, the binary address is divided into eight double-byte (16-bit) values delimited by colons. For example:

```
2001:0db8:0000:0000:0abc:0000:def0:1234
```

Even this is quite cumbersome, so where a double-byte contains leading zeros, they can be ignored. In addition, one contiguous series of zeroes can be replaced by a double colon place marker. Thus, the address above would become:

```
2001:db8::abc:0:def0:1234
```

Teaching Tip

Exam candidates should be able to identify validly constructed IPv6 addresses.

IPv6 ADDRESSING SCHEMES

An IPv6 address is divided into two main parts: the first 64 bits are used as a network ID while the second 64 bits designate a specific interface.

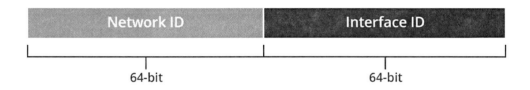

In IPv6, the interface identifier is always the last 64 bits; the first 64 bits are used for network addressing. (Image © 123RF.com.)

Teaching Tip

Relate the IPv6 address types to their IPv4 equivalents. You might want to mention that ARP is replaced by the Neighbor Discovery (ND) protocol.

As the network and host portions are fixed size, there is no need for a subnet mask. Network addresses are written using prefix notation, where /nn is the length of the routing prefix in bits. Within the 64-bit network ID, the length of any given network prefix is used to determine whether two addresses belong to the same IP network.

GLOBALLY UNIQUE UNICAST ADDRESSING

As with IPv4, a unicast address identifies a single network interface. The main types of unicast addressing are global and link-local. A **global address** is one that is unique on the Internet (equivalent to public addresses in IPv4). Global unicast addresses have the following format:

- The first 3 bits indicate that the address is within the global scope. In hex notation, a global unicast address will start with either "2" or "3."
- The next 45 bits are allocated in a hierarchical manner to regional registries and from them to ISPs and end users.
- The next 16 bits identity site-specific subnet addresses.
- The final 64 bits are the interface ID. The interface ID is either generated from the adapter's MAC address (padded with extra bits to make it 64 bits in length) or is randomly generated.

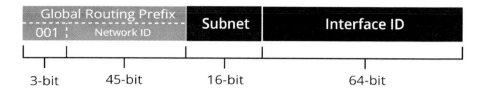

IPv6 global unicast address format. (Image © 123RF.com.)

In IPv6, address blocks are automatically assigned hierarchically by routers. Top-level routers have top-level address blocks, which are automatically divided and assigned as routers and segments are added. This divides the address space as a logical hierarchy, compared to the ad-hoc address-space management procedures that were developed for IPv4, making it easier to manage.

LINK-LOCAL ADDRESSING

Link-local addresses are used by IPv6 for network housekeeping traffic. Link-local addresses span a single subnet (they are not forwarded by routers). Nodes on the same link are referred to as neighbors. In hex notation, link-local addresses start with `fe80::`

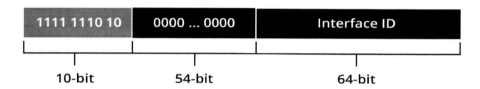

IPv6 link-local unicast address format. (Image © 123RF.com.)

The equivalent in IPv4 is Automatic Private IP Addressing (APIPA) and its 169.254.0.0 addresses. However, unlike IPv4, an IPv6 host is always configured with link-local addresses (one for each link), even if it also has a globally unique address.

Activity 8-5

Discussing Network Configuration Concepts

Show Slide(s)

Activity: Discussing Network Configuration Concepts

SCENARIO

Answer the following questions to check your understanding of the topic.

1. **What is the difference between a router and a modem?**

   A router is a device that can forward traffic between different logical networks. These networks might use different media and different ways of transporting frames across links. In an Ethernet network, a host interfaces with the local network (LAN) using a network adapter. When a link is point-to-point, using media such as a telephone line, a modem is used to convert the signals that can be carried over the media from the LAN format to the WAN format. Where a router is connected to such links, it may be installed with a modem, but the functions of the devices are separate. The modem makes a physical network link with the ISP network, functioning at the same level as a switch. The router can make decisions about forwarding between logical networks.

2. Protocols within the TCP/IP suite (and products supporting TCP/IP networks) are conceived as working at one of four layers.

   What are those four layers called?

   Link/Network Interface, Internet, Transport, and Application.

3. **What is meant by dotted decimal notation?**

   An IPv4 address is a 32-bit number expressed as four octets (bytes). A byte can be expressed as the decimal values 0 to 255, and these are used to represent the IP address, with dots between each decimal number. This scheme is easier for people to read than a binary number and reduces configuration errors.

4. **When is a default gateway required?**

   When a host needs to communicate with hosts located outside its own IP network.

5. A host is configured with the IP address 192.168.1.10/24.

   What is the host's subnet mask?

   255.255.255.0.

6. **What is the purpose of a DHCP server?**

   A Dynamic Host Configuration Protocol (DHCP) server automatically allocates a TCP/IP configuration (IP address, subnet mask, default gateway, and DNS servers) to hosts when they join the network.

7. **What is special about an IP address that starts 169.254?**

   It is an APIPA address—that is, one automatically selected if the interface is configured to use DHCP but cannot contact a DHCP server.

8. A host is configured with the IP address 172.29.0.101.

   What is significant about this address?

   It is a private address and cannot be reached directly over the Internet. The host must use a router with address translation or a proxy service to communicate on the Internet.

9. **What is the function of NAT?**

   Network Address Translation (NAT) enables a router to map private network IP addresses onto a public IP address. Private addressing keeps the local network more secure and reduces the demand for unique IP addresses.

10. **Apart from its length, what is the main difference between the structure of an IPv4 address and an IPv6 address?**

    Both types of IP address identify a host within a specific logical network. In an IPv4 address, the network ID portion is determined by applying a mask to the whole address. In an IPv6 address, the host portion is always the last 64 bits of the address. The first 64 bits are used with network prefixes to identify networks and subnetworks.

Topic F
Network Services

EXAM OBJECTIVES COVERED
1001-2.1 Compare and contrast TCP and UDP ports, protocols, and their purposes.
1001-2.5 Summarize the properties and purposes of services provided by networked hosts.

In the previous topics, you explored the network hardware and protocols that facilitate the process of making connections between hosts and networks, including Internet connections. In this topic, you will move on to examine the various ports and protocols that are used to provide application services.

Properly configuring the ports of a network device and selecting the right protocol will ensure that data gets transmitted over the network. As a CompTIA A+ technician, you must understand how ports and protocols are implemented within a network and how they function to provide the right level of data transmission while keeping data secure.

TCP AND UDP PORTS

The protocols we have looked at so far are primarily concerned with moving frames and packets between nodes and networks. At the link/physical layer, Ethernet allows nodes to send one another frames of data using MAC addresses. These frames would typically be transporting IP packets. At the network layer, IP provides addressing and routing functionality for a network of networks (or internetwork).

Protocols at the transport layer, one up from the network layer, are concerned with effective delivery. At the transport layer, the content of the packets starts to become significant.

Any given host on a network will be communicating with many other hosts using many different types of networking data. One of the critical functions of the transport layer is to identify each type of network application. It does this by assigning each application a **port number** between 0 and 65535. For example, data addressed to the HTTP web browsing application can be identified as port 80 while data requesting an email application service can be identified as port 143. At the transport layer, on the sending host, data from the upper layers is packaged as a series of segments and each segment is tagged with the application's port number. The segment is then passed to the network layer for delivery. The host could be transmitting multiple HTTP and email segments at the same time. These are multiplexed using the port numbers onto the same network link.

> *Note: In fact, each host assigns two port numbers. On the client, the destination port number is mapped to the service that the client is requesting (HTTP on port 80, for instance). The client also assigns a random source port number (47747, for instance). The server uses this client-assigned port number (47747) as the destination port number for its replies and its application port number (80 for HTTP) as its source port. This allows the hosts to track multiple "conversations" for the same application protocol.*

At the network and data link layers, the port number is not significant—it becomes part of the data payload and is "invisible" to routers and switches working at the network and data link layers. At the receiving host, each segment is extracted from its frame

Teaching Tip

Exam candidates need to know the basic function and port numbers of each of the application protocols listed.

Show Slide(s)

TCP and UDP Ports (2 slides)

Teaching Tip

Point out that this use of the term "segment" is completely different to a segment of a physical network topology.

and then identified by its port number and passed up to the relevant handler at the application layer.

TCP VERSUS UDP

Teaching Tip

Make sure learners are clear on the difference between TCP and UDP.

The transport layer is also responsible for ensuring reliable data delivery so that packets arrive error-free and without loss. The transport layer can overcome lack of reliability in the lower level protocols. This reliability is achieved by the **Transport Control Protocol (TCP)** using acknowledgement messages that inform the sender the data was successfully received.

The kinds of problems that may occur during the delivery of the data are non-delivery and delivery in a damaged state. In the first case, the lack of acknowledgement results in the retransmission of the data and, in the second case, a **Negative Acknowledgement (NACK)** forces retransmission. TCP is described as connection-oriented, because it ensures the reliability and sequencing of messages passing over the connection.

On the other hand, sometimes it is more important that communications be faster than they are reliable. The acknowledgements process of TCP adds a lot of overhead. The **User Datagram Protocol (UDP)** is a connectionless, non-guaranteed method of communication with no sequencing or flow control. There is no guarantee regarding the delivery of messages or the sequence in which packets are received. UDP is suitable for applications that do not require acknowledgement of receipt and can tolerate missing or out-of-order packets. It may be used for applications that transfer time-sensitive data but do not require complete reliability, such as voice or video. The reduced overhead means that delivery is faster. If necessary, the application layer can be used to control delivery reliability.

WELL-KNOWN PORTS

Show Slide(s)

Well-Known Ports

Teaching Tip

Exam candidates need to memorize these port numbers.

Any application or process that uses TCP or UDP for its transport, such as HTTP for web services or POP3 for email, is assigned a unique identification number called a port. The server and client applications use different ports. For example, a client may contact an HTTP server at IP address 77.72.206.10 on port 80 (77.72.206.10:80). The HTTP server would respond to the client on a temporary (or ephemeral) port number that the client has opened for that purpose (47747, for instance).

Server port numbers are assigned by the Internet Assigned Numbers Authority (IANA). Some of the "well-known" port numbers are listed in the following table.

Port #	TCP/UDP	Process	Description
20	TCP	ftp-data	File Transfer Protocol - Data
21	TCP	ftp	File Transfer Protocol - Control
22	TCP	ssh	Secure Shell
23	TCP	telnet	Telnet
25	TCP	smtp	Simple Mail Transfer Protocol
53	TCP/UDP	domain	Domain Name System
67	UDP	bootps	BOOTP/DHCP Server
68	UDP	bootpc	BOOTP/DHCP Client
80	TCP	http	HTTP
110	TCP	pop3	Post Office Protocol
123	UDP	ntp	Network Time Protocol
137-139	UDP/TCP	netbt	NetBIOS over TCP/IP
143	TCP	imap4	Internet Mail Access Protocol

Port #	TCP/UDP	Process	Description
161	UDP	snmp	Simple Network Management Protocol
162	UDP	snmp-trap	Simple Network Management Protocol Trap
389	TCP	ldap	Lightweight Directory Access Protocol
427	TCP	slp	Service Location Protocol
443	TCP	https	HTTP Secure
445	TCP	smb	Server Message Block/Common Internet File System
548	TCP	afp	Apple Filing Protocol
3389	TCP	rdp	Remote Desktop Protocol

IANA defines the ephemeral port range as 49152 to 65535, but some operating systems use different values.

Enabling and disabling ports is an important part of configuring a firewall, to ensure that only valid application protocols are allowed.

The TCP/IP suite encompasses a large number and wide range of protocols. Some of the principal protocols amongst these are discussed in the following sections.

DNS

The **Domain Name System (DNS)** is a hierarchical system for resolving names to IP addresses. It uses a distributed database that contains information on domains and hosts within those domains. The information is distributed among many name servers, each of which holds part of the database. The distributed nature of the system has the twin advantages that maintenance of the system is delegated and loss of one DNS server does not prevent name resolution from being performed.

At the top of the DNS hierarchy is the root, which is often represented by a period (.). There are 13 root level servers (A to M). Immediately below the root lie the **Top Level Domains (TLDs)**. There are several types of top level domain, but the most prevalent are generic (.com, .org, .net, .info, .biz), sponsored (.gov, .edu), and country code (.uk, .ca, .de).

The domain name system is operated by ICANN (**icann.org**), who also manage the generic top level domains. Country codes are generally managed by an organization appointed by the relevant government. Each domain name has to be registered with a Domain Name Registry for the appropriate top level domain.

Information about a domain is found by tracing records from the root down through the hierarchy. The root servers have complete information about the top level domain servers. In turn, these servers have information relating to servers for the second level domains.

No name server has complete information about all domains. Records within the DNS tell them where the missing information is found.

Show Slide(s)

DNS (4 slides)

Teaching Tip

DNS is a critical service on most networks.

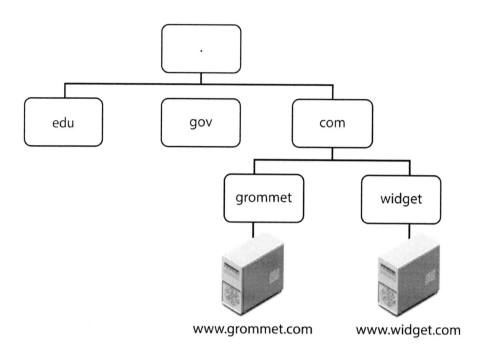

DNS hierarchy. (Image © 123RF.com.)

FULLY QUALIFIED DOMAIN NAME

The full name of any host is called its **Fully Qualified Domain Name (FQDN)**. FQDNs reflect the hierarchy, from most specific (the host) to least specific (the top level domain followed by the root). For example: www.widget.com.

The structure of a FQDN follows a fixed hierarchy, with the top level of the hierarchy shown to the right of the name. Each part of the name (a label) is separated by period characters (full stops). Any given label can consist of letters, numbers, and hyphens (though it cannot start with a hyphen).

The **domain name** identifies a company, organization, or even an individual. The name has to be unique and officially registered (a process that is normally handled by your ISP).

Host names and local domains are specified within the organization (for example, to identify a server located in the sales department of a company). The www host name is a common alias to indicate that the resource is a web server.

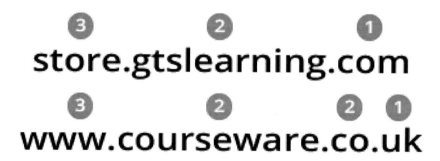

Parts of two FQDNs with 1) Top level domain; 2) Subdomain; 3) Host name. (Image © 123RF.com.)

DNS SERVERS

Different types of DNS servers are used by private organizations:

- **Authoritative name server**—this type of DNS server holds domain records and can respond authoritatively to requests for information about hosts in the domain(s) it manages. On a private network, such as an Active Directory (AD) domain, a name server must be running to host the AD DNS records. These records would not be made publicly available outside the LAN. On the Internet, public information about a domain, such as the location of its web and email servers, will be published to a name server. These are usually hosted by ISPs.
- **Recursive resolver**—when a client application wants to resolve a name or FQDN, it uses a recursive resolver to perform the query. The resolver contacts name servers in the DNS hierarchy until it either locates the requested record or times out. When you configure a DNS server on a client, it is usually the address of a resolver that you are entering.

 Note: On a private network, the same DNS server is likely to be identified for both functions. For example, an AD DNS server might both host the DNS records and provide name resolution for other Internet domain requests (typically by forwarding them to another server). Alternatively, the network might use client-facing forwarding-only servers whose only purpose is to select the best DNS server to answer a particular request and forward it on.

A DNS server is usually configured to listen for queries on UDP port 53.

WEB SERVERS AND HTTP/HTTPS

A **web server** is one that provides client access using the HyperText Transfer Protocol (HTTP) or its secure version (HTTPS).

HTTP AND HTML

HyperText Transfer Protocol (HTTP) is the basis of the World Wide Web. HTTP enables clients (typically web browsers) to request resources from an HTTP server. A client connects to the HTTP server using its TCP port (the default is port 80) and submits a request for a resource, using a **Uniform Resource Locator (URL)**. The server acknowledges the request and returns the data.

Typically, an organization will lease a server or space on a server from an ISP. Larger organizations with their own Internet Point-of-Presence may host websites themselves. Web servers are not only used on the Internet, however. Private networks using web technologies are described as **intranets** (if they permit only local access) or **extranets** (if they permit remote access).

HTTP is usually used to serve HyperText Markup Language (HTML) web pages, which are plain text files with coded tags describing how the page should be formatted. A web browser can interpret the tags and display the text and other resources associated with the page (such as picture or sound files). Another powerful feature is its ability to provide hyperlinks to other related documents. HTTP also features forms mechanisms (GET and POST) whereby a user can submit data from the client to the server.

The functionality of HTTP servers is often extended by support for scripting and programmable features (web applications).

UNIFORM RESOURCE LOCATOR

Resources on the Internet are accessed using an addressing scheme known as a Uniform Resource Locator (URL). A URL contains all the information necessary to identify and access an item. For example, a URL for an HTTP resource might contain the following elements:

 Show Slide(s)

Web Servers and HTTP/HTTPS (3 slides)

 Teaching Tip

Just make sure learners are familiar with the use of these protocols and some of the terminology.

- The protocol describes the access method or service type being used.
- The host location is usually represented by a Fully Qualified Domain Name (FQDN). The FQDN is not case sensitive. The host location can also be an IP address; an IPv6 address must be enclosed in square brackets.
- The file path specifies the directory and file name location of the resource (if required). The file path may or may not be case-sensitive, depending on how the server is configured.

http://store.gtslearning.com/comptia/index.htm

URL with 1) Protocol; 2) FQDN; 3) File path. (Image © 123RF.com.)

SSL/TLS

One of the critical problems for the provision of early e-commerce sites was the lack of security in HTTP. Under HTTP, all data is sent unencrypted and there is no authentication of client or server. **Secure Sockets Layer (SSL)** was developed by Netscape and released as version 3.0 in 1996 to address these problems. SSL proved very popular with the industry and is still in widespread use. **Transport Layer Security (TLS)** was developed from SSL and ratified as a standard by IETF. TLS is now the product in active development, with 1.2 as the latest version.

SSL/TLS is typically used with the HTTP application (referred to as **HTTPS** or HTTP Over SSL or HTTP Secure) but can also be used to secure other TCP/IP application protocols. TLS can also be used with UDP applications, referred to as **Datagram Transport Layer Security (DTLS)**. Some VPN solutions depend on the use of DTLS.

 Note: HTTPS operates over port 443 by default. HTTPS operation is indicated by using https:// for the URL and by a padlock icon shown in the browser.

The basic function of TLS is:

1. A server is assigned a digital certificate by some trusted Certificate Authority.
2. The certificate proves the identity of the server (assuming that the client trusts the Certificate Authority).
3. The server uses the digital certificate and the SSL/TLS protocol to encrypt communications between it and the client.

This means that the communications cannot be read or changed by a third party.

 Note: It is also possible to install a certificate on the client so that the server can trust the client. This is not often used on the web but is a feature of VPNs.

MAIL SERVERS

Email is a messaging system that can be used to transmit text messages and binary file attachments encoded using **Multipurpose Internet Mail Extensions (MIME)**. Email can involve the use of multiple protocols. The following process illustrates how an email message is sent from a typical corporate mail gateway (using the Microsoft Exchange mail server) to a recipient with subscriber Internet access:

1. The email client software on the sender's computer (sender@515support.com) sends the message to the Exchange email server using Microsoft's **Message Application Programming Interface (MAPI)** protocol. The mail server puts the message in a queue, waiting for the next **Simple Mail Transfer Protocol (SMTP)** session to be started. SMTP uses TCP port 25 by default.

 Show Slide(s)

Mail Servers (3 slides)

 Teaching Tip

Point out that while the client to server connection uses encrypted protocols (for message submission and retrieval), SMTP transfers between servers for different email domains are not usually encrypted. Put another way, the sender cannot depend on end-to-end encryption without using S/MIME or PGP.

 Interaction Opportunity

Ask learners to suggest why encryption is important (consider accessing a mailbox over an open access point or allowing a network password to be sniffed from email traffic).

2. When the Exchange SMTP server starts to process the queue, it first contacts a DNS server to resolve the recipient's address (for example, recipient@othercompany.com) to an IP address for the othercompany.com email server, listed as a Mail Exchanger (MX) record in DNS.

3. It then uses SMTP to deliver the message to this email server. The delivery usually requires several "hops"; for example, from the mail gateway to the sender's ISP, then to the recipient's ISP. The hops taken by a message as it is delivered over the Internet are recorded in the message header.

4. The message is put in the message store on the recipient's mail server. To retrieve it, the recipient uses his or her mail client software to connect with the mailbox on the server, using the **Post Office Protocol (POP3)** on TCP port 110 or **Internet Message Access Protocol (IMAP)** on TCP port 143. POP3 is more widely implemented, but IMAP provides extra features, such as support for mail folders other than inbox on the server and calendar functionality.

 Note: Email communications between a client and server would normally be protected with SSL/TLS security. The default port numbers for these are 587 (SMTPS), 993 (IMAPS), and 995 (POP3S).

To configure an email account, you need the username, password, and default email address, plus incoming and outgoing server addresses and protocol types from the ISP.

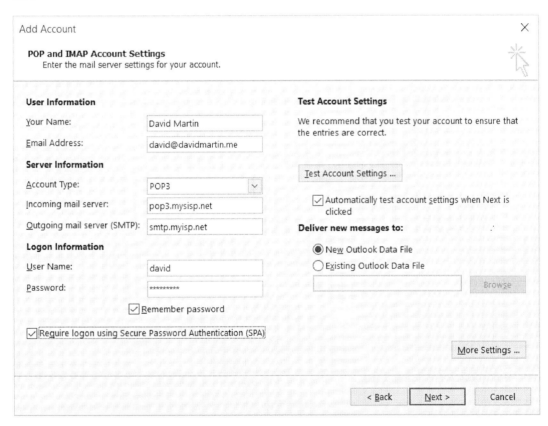

Configuring an email account. The incoming server is either POP3 or IMAP while the outgoing server is SMTP. (Screenshot used with permission from Microsoft.)

Internet email addresses follow the mailto URL scheme. An Internet email address comprises two parts—the username (local part) and the domain name, separated by an @ symbol. The domain name may refer to a company or an ISP; for example, david.martin@comptia.org or david.martin@aol.com.

Different mail systems have different requirements for allowed and disallowed characters in the local part. The local part is supposed to be case-sensitive, but most mail systems do not treat it as such. An incorrectly addressed email will be returned with a message notifying that it was undeliverable. Mail may also be rejected if it is identified as spam or if there is some other problem with the user mailbox (such as the mailbox being full).

Of course, there are many more network communication types than email. Network services are equally likely to support Voice over IP, videoconferencing, messaging, and integration with social media.

FILE AND PRINTER SHARING

Show Slide(s)
File and Printer Sharing (3 slides)

One of the core network functions is to provide shared access to disk and print resources. These services may be performed using proprietary protocols, such as File and Print Services for Windows Networks. A file server could also be implemented using standard protocols, such as File Transfer Protocol (FTP), though this lacks a lot of the functionality of Windows file services.

SERVER MESSAGE BLOCK (SMB)/COMMON INTERNET FILE SYSTEM (CIFS)

Server Message Block (SMB) is the application protocol underpinning file and printer sharing on Windows networks. In all supported versions of Windows, version 2 of the protocol is used (SMB2), though there is support for legacy Windows clients. SMB usually runs directly over TCP on port 445 but can also run as part of NetBIOS over TCP/IP, over UDP and TCP in the port range 137-139. The Samba software package implements the protocol for Linux computers, enabling them to share and access resources on an otherwise Windows-based network. SMB is also sometimes referred to as the **Common Internet File System (CIFS)**.

APPLE FILING PROTOCOL (AFP)

The **Apple Filing Protocol (AFP)** performs a similar file sharing function to SMB but for Apple networks running Mac OS. AFP is associated with the use of two ports:

- UDP or TCP port 427—this is a port running the Service Location Protocol, used to advertise the availability of file shares. It is not required by later versions of OS X (10.2 and up).
- TCP port 548—this is the main port used by AFP.

> *Note: Apple is phasing out support for AFP in favor of its own version of SMB2 (SMBX).*

FILE TRANSFER PROTOCOL (FTP)

The **File Transfer Protocol (FTP)** was one of the earliest protocols used on TCP/IP networks and the Internet. As its name suggests, it allows a client to upload and download files from a remote server. It is widely used to upload files to websites. Also, if you have existing files that you want to make available to remote users, FTP is a simple service to install and maintain. Files made available through FTP can be in any format, including document, multimedia, or application files.

FTP is associated with the use of TCP port 21 to establish a connection and either TCP port 20 to transfer data in "active" mode or a server-assigned port in "passive" mode.

The FTP client may take a number of forms:

- Most installations of TCP/IP include a command-line client interface. The commands `put` and `get` are used to upload and download files, respectively.

- Dedicated GUI clients allow you to connect to servers, browse directories, and upload and download files.
- Internet browsers allow you to connect to an FTP service and download files. You use another type of URL to connect to an FTP server; for example, *ftp:// ftp.microsoft.com/*.

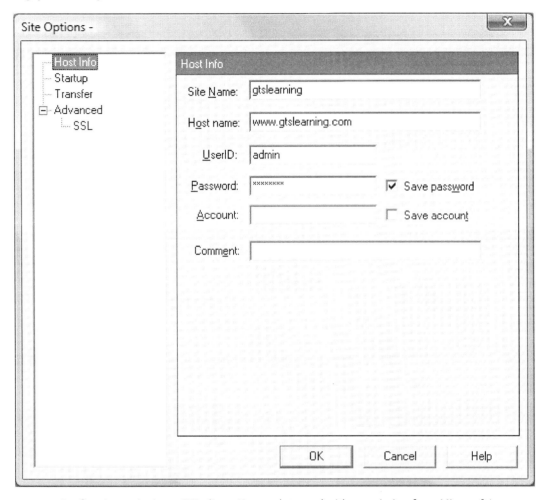

Configuring a site in an FTP client. (Screenshot used with permission from Microsoft.)

 Note: Plain FTP is unencrypted and so poses a high security risk. Passwords for sites are submitted in plaintext. There are ways of encrypting FTP sessions (FTPS and SFTP), however, and it is the encrypted services that are most widely used now.

NETWORK HOST SERVICES

The purpose of a network is to make host services available. There are many categories of network service, but some of the most important roles are described here.

AUTHENTICATION SERVER

Most networks have some sort of access control system to prevent unauthorized users (and devices) from connecting. In a Windows homegroup, for example, the access control method is a simple password, shared with all authorized users. Enterprise networks use authentication servers to configure user accounts and authenticate the subjects trying to use those accounts. On a Windows domain, the user database and authentication service is provided by Active Directory, using a mechanism based on the Kerberos protocol.

 Show Slide(s)
Network Host Services

 Teaching Tip

The important thing in this section is to define the roles, not to go into too much detail on each role. Learners can refer to this after class if they want more detail.

You are also likely to come across the terms AAA server and RADIUS server. An Authentication, Authorization, and Accounting (AAA) server is one that consolidates authentication services across multiple access devices, such as switches, routers, and access points. Remote Authentication Dial-in User Service (RADIUS) is an example of an AAA protocol.

DHCP AND DNS SERVERS

Authentication is just one part of providing network access. Hosts must also receive a suitable network configuration to be able to communicate on the network. DHCP and DNS are two of the services that facilitate this:

- Dynamic Host Configuration Protocol (DHCP) servers assign IP address information to host automatically when they connect to the network.
- Domain Name System (DNS) servers allow users to access resources using host names and Fully Qualified Domain Names (FQDN) by resolving those names to IP addresses.

LIGHTWEIGHT DIRECTORY ACCESS PROTOCOL (LDAP)

Network resources can be recorded as objects within a directory. A directory is like a database, where an object is like a record and things that you know about the object (attributes) are like fields. In order for products from different vendors to be interoperable, most directories are based on the same standard.

The main directory standard is the X.500 series of standards, developed by the International Telecommunications Union (ITU) in the 1980s.

The problem with X.500 is that the full set of standards specified the use of a complex protocol stack as a means of network access, at a time when most organizations were already opting to use TCP/IP. Researchers developed a means for clients to connect to an X.500 server over TCP/IP and this was standardized by the IETF as the **Lightweight Directory Access Protocol (LDAP)**. LDAP is a protocol used to query and update an X. 500 directory, or any type of directory that can present itself as an X.500 directory. It is widely supported in current directory products—Windows Active Directory, Apple OpenDirectory, or the open source OpenLDAP, for instance.

LDAP uses TCP and UDP port 389 by default.

A **Distinguished Name** is a unique identifier for any given resource within the directory. A distinguished name is made up of attribute-value pairs, separated by commas. Examples of attributes include Common Name (CN), Organizational Unit (OU), and Domain Component (DC). The most specific attribute is listed first and successive attributes become progressively broader. This most specific attribute is also referred to as the **Relative Distinguished Name**, as it uniquely identifies the object within the context of successive (parent) attribute values.

NetBIOS/NetBT

The very earliest Windows networks used network software called the **Network Basic Input/Output System (NetBIOS)**. NetBIOS allowed computers to address one another by name and establish sessions. As the TCP/IP suite became the standard for local networks, NetBIOS was re-engineered to work over the TCP and UDP protocols, referred to as **NetBIOS over TCP/IP (NetBT)**:

- Name service (UDP port 137).
- Datagram transmission service (UDP port 138).
- Session service (TCP port 139).

As you know, modern networks use IP, TCP/UDP, and DNS for these functions. NetBT should be disabled on most networks. It is only required if the network has to support pre-Windows 2000 legacy systems (plus some network applications).

INVENTORY MANAGEMENT SERVERS

Inventory management refers to keeping a record of the systems running on your network. This is not a simple task to try to perform manually, so a number of protocols have been developed to assist.

Show Slide(s)
Inventory Management Servers (2 slides)

SIMPLE NETWORK MANAGEMENT PROTOCOL (SNMP)

The **Simple Network Management Protocol (SNMP)** is a framework for management and monitoring network devices. SNMP consists of a management system and agents.

The **agent** is a process running on a switch, router, server, or other SNMP-compatible network device. This agent maintains a database called a **Management Information Base (MIB)** that holds statistics relating to the activity of the device. An example of such a statistic is the number of frames per second handled by a switch. The agent is also capable of initiating a trap operation where it informs the management system of a notable event (port failure, for instance). The threshold for triggering traps can be set for each value.

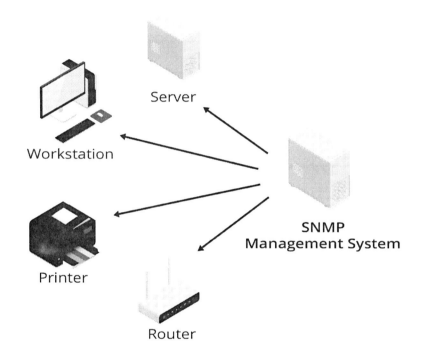

SNMP agents and management system. (Image © 123RF.com.)

The management system (a software program) provides a location from which network activity can be overseen. It monitors all agents by polling them at regular intervals for information from their MIBs and displays the information for review. It also displays any trap operations as alerts for the network administrator to assess and act upon as necessary.

SNMP device queries take place over UDP port 161; traps are communicated over UDP port 162.

ENDPOINT MANAGEMENT SERVER

Modern security models recognize that networks must not just apply security controls at the perimeter or border. A security principle called **defense in depth** calls for policies such as workstation hardening to ensure they cannot be compromised and used to attack the network from within. Of course, modern networks do not just consist of computer workstations—any type of endpoint computing device must be protected too, including laptops, smartphones, tablets, printers, and "smart" appliances.

An **Endpoint Management Server** facilitates this process by identifying computing devices running on the network and ensuring that they are securely configured. This might mean applying OS and antivirus updates automatically, cataloging software applications installed on each device, applying security policies, retrieving and analyzing log files, and monitoring performance and other status alerts.

Microsoft has the System Center and Configuration Manager (SCCM) for Windows (plus support for other device types). There are many other product examples.

syslog

Effective network management often entails capturing logs from different devices. It is much easier to review logs and respond to alerts if the logs are consolidated on a single system.

Prior to Windows 7, one limitation of Windows logs was that they only logged local events. This meant that third party tools were required in order to gain an overall view of messaging for the entire network. However, the development of event subscriptions allows logging to be configured to forward all events to a single computer, enabling a holistic view of network events.

The equivalent system in UNIX and Linux is usually **syslog**. This was designed to follow a client-server model and so allows for centralized collection of events from multiple sources. It also provides an open format for event logging messages and as such, has become a de facto standard for logging events from distributed systems. For example, syslog messages can be generated by Cisco routers and switches, as well as servers and workstations, and collected in a central database for viewing and analysis.

LEGACY AND EMBEDDED SYSTEMS

An **embedded system** is a computer system that is designed to perform a specific, dedicated function. These systems can be as small and simple as a microcontroller in an intravenous drip-rate meter or as large and complex as an industrial control system managing a water treatment plant. Embedded systems might typically have been designed to operate within a **closed network**; that is one where the elements of the network are all known to the system vendor and there is no connectivity to wider computer data networks. Where embedded systems need to interact within a computer data network, there are special considerations to make in terms of the network design, especially as regards security.

A **legacy system** is one that is no longer directly supported by its vendor. Networks often need to retain hosts running DOS or legacy versions of Windows (XP and earlier) or old-style mainframe computers to run services that are too complex or expensive to migrate to a more modern platform. Legacy systems usually work well for what they do (which is why they don't get prioritized for replacement) but they represent very severe risks in terms of security vulnerabilities. It is important to isolate them as far as possible from the rest of the network and ensure any network channels linking them are carefully protected and monitored.

Both legacy and embedded systems represent a risk in terms of maintenance and troubleshooting too, as they tend to require more specialist knowledge than modern, off-the-shelf, computing systems. Consultants with expertise in such systems can become highly sought after.

INTERNET SECURITY APPLIANCES AND SOFTWARE

Networks connected to the Internet need to be protected against malicious hosts and applications by a firewall and anti-malware scanners. Networks also need to scan for

Show Slide(s)

Legacy and Embedded Systems

Show Slide(s)

Internet Security Appliances and Software

Interaction Opportunity

This section discusses these systems in the context of Internet security appliances. There are also host-based IDS/IPS and firewalls. Emphasize that IDS software might run on a host to protect a network (as installed on a host-based router or as a sensor) or be installed on a host to protect just that host. Ask learners to browse some of the vendor sites mentioned to get a better feel for the capabilities and deployment options for UTM. You might also want to discuss the limitations of these devices and some of the challenges faced in using them (volume of alerts, analyzing traffic protected by end-to-end encryption, analyzing traffic in the cloud, and so on).

"unusual" host behavior or network traffic, using Intrusion Detection Systems (IDS) and Intrusion Prevention Systems (IPS). These services can be implemented on servers but enterprise networks are likely to use dedicated Internet security appliances.

INTRUSION DETECTION SYSTEM (IDS)

A network-based **Intrusion Detection System (IDS)** comprises a sensor plus an analysis engine that scans network traffic for signs of threats or other violations of security policy. The IDS can be programmed with signatures of known intrusion attempts. Like antivirus software, these intrusion signatures (usually called plug-ins in the context of IDS) must be kept up to date. Also like antivirus, IDS can use behavioral or **heuristic** techniques to identify potential threats. In contrast to a basic packet-filtering firewall, which can be configured with rules about IP addresses and application protocol ports, a network-based IDS examines the contents of the application layer payload in the packet.

When an IDS detects an intrusion event, it creates a log entry and can also send an alert to an administrator, if the event is considered important enough. One of the major drawbacks of IDS is the detection of too many innocuous events (false positives).

There are many vendors supplying IDS software and appliances. The underlying detection engine for most of these products is based either on **Snort** or on **Suricata**. Each IDS solution adds its own connectivity (options for sensor placement), configuration, and reporting tools.

INTRUSION PROTECTION SYSTEM (IPS)

An **Intrusion Protection System (IPS)** adds some sort of real-time blocking (or shunning) functionality on top of the basic IDS. An IPS may drop packets, reset connections, or run a script to trigger a response on another server or network device (firewall, switch, or router).

UNIFIED THREAT MANAGEMENT (UTM)

Network security applications include antivirus scanners, intrusion detection/prevention, and firewalls. These might be deployed as separate appliances or server applications, each with its own configuration and logging/reporting system. A **Unified Threat Management (UTM)** appliance is one that enforces a variety of security-related measures, combining the work of a firewall, malware scanner, and intrusion detection/prevention. A UTM centralizes the threat management service, providing simpler configuration and reporting compared to isolated applications spread across several servers or devices. Some of the major UTM vendors and products include Barracuda, Sophos, Check Point, Fortinet, Cisco Meraki, Juniper SRVX, and Dell SonicWall.

There are two basic ways of implementing network connectivity for IDS and IPS or UTM server services and appliances:

- **Install the appliance inline with the network**—this means that all network traffic passes through the server or appliance. This allows the appliance to block suspect traffic easily. The drawback is that a single appliance would represent a critical point of failure. If the forwarding function of the appliance were to fail, no traffic would be able to pass into or out of the network. This can be mitigated by using two or more appliances for redundancy.
- **Install the appliance as a sensor**—this means that the appliance has a tap or mirror that enables it to view the traffic passing over a network link or switch. This makes prevention slower and more complex as the appliance must trigger a script for the preventive action to be enacted by another device (switch, router, or firewall).

In both cases, the ability to deal with high traffic volumes is critical. If the device is overwhelmed by the traffic volume, it will not be inspecting all of that traffic and could be allowing malicious traffic to pass undetected. A dedicated security appliance should be able to perform better in this respect than running the security service on a server or router.

PROXY SERVER

On a SOHO network, devices on the LAN access the Internet via the router using a type of Network Address Translation (NAT), specifically Port-based Network Address Translation. This type of NAT device translates between the private IP addresses used on the LAN and the publicly addressable IP addresses used on the Internet.

Many enterprise networks use some sort of NAT too but another option is to use a proxy server. A **proxy server** does not just translate IP addresses. It takes a whole HTTP request from a client, checks it, then forwards it to the destination computer on the Internet. When the reply comes back, it checks it, and then shuttles it back to the LAN computer. A proxy can be used for other types of traffic too (email, for instance).

A proxy server can usually operate either as a transparent service, in which case the client requires no special configuration, or as non-transparent. For a non-transparent proxy, the client must be configured with the IP address and service port (often 8080 by convention) of the proxy server.

Activity 8-6

Discussing Network Services

Show
Slide(s)
Activity: Discussing
Network Services

SCENARIO

Answer the following questions to check your understanding of the topic.

1. **If a network application cannot tolerate a missing packet, what type of transport protocol should it use?**

   Transmission Control Protocol (TCP).

2. **True or false? Protocols that stream video and audio over the Internet are likely to be based on UDP.**

   True. UDP carries less overhead compared to Transmission Control Protocol (TCP), so is better suited to playing media files where small glitches due to lost packets are less of a problem than the whole video freezing.

3. **What is DNS?**

   Domain Name System—servers that map host and domain names to IP addresses.

4. **What configuration parameter must be entered to enable a client to use DNS?**

   The IP address of a DNS server on the local network or network reachable by the client.

5. **True or false? An HTTP application secured using the SSL/TLS protocol should use a different port to unencrypted HTTP.**

   True. By default HTTPS uses port 443. It is possible in theory to apply SSL/TLS to port 80 but most browsers would not support this configuration.

6. **What protocol would a mail client use to access the message store on a remote mail server?**

   Typically Post Office Protocol (POP3) or Internet Message Access Protocol (IMAP). A proprietary protocol such as MAPI (Microsoft Exchange) might also be used.

7. A firewall filters applications based on their port number.

If you want to configure a firewall on the mail server to allow clients to download email messages, which port(s) might you have to open?

Either TCP port 993 (IMAPS) or 995 (POP3S), depending on the mail access protocol in use (IMAP or POP). These are the default ports for secure connections. Unsecure default ports are TCP port 143 and TCP port 110. Port 25 (SMTP) is used to send mail between servers, not to access messages stored on a server. Port 587 is often used by a client to submit messages for delivery by an SMTP server.

8. You are configuring a Network Attached Storage (NAS) appliance.

What file sharing protocol(s) could you use to allow access to Windows, Linux, and Apple macOS clients?

Most clients should support Server Message Block (SMB)/Common Internet File System (CIFS). You might want to configure Apple Filing Protocol to support older macOS clients. Another option is to configure File Transfer Protocol (FTP).

9. **What is the difference between SNMP and syslog?**

The Simple Network Management Protocol (SNMP) provides a means for devices to report statistics to a management server. Syslog provides a means for devices to send log entries to a remote server.

10. You are advising a customer about types of security appliance.

What are the principal types and configuration options?

A network Intrusion Detection System (IDS) scans packet contents for signs of traffic that could violate security policies. An Intrusion Protection System (IPS) can effect some sort of action to block such traffic. An IPS is usually provisioned as a Unified Threat Management (UTM) appliance to include firewall, anti-malware, and other security functionality. Appliances with blocking functionality are typically deployed inline with the network, so that all traffic passes through the appliance. Alternatively, a tap or sensor can be attached to the network so that traffic is copied for the appliance to read.

Summary

In this lesson, you identified many different network concepts and technologies. Networking is at the heart of any type of business. Without it, a business simply cannot function in today's world. It is your job to help ensure that the networks behind the business are running properly and managed correctly.

What do you think are the most important network concepts covered in this lesson?

A: Answers will vary, depending on the setup of the work or home computing environments that learners use. For example, if an individual is a gamer, he or she might be drawn more toward issues of LANs and bandwidth. If a person has interest in one day being a system administrator, he or she might be drawn to technologies such as wireless connectivity.

What experience do you have with any of the technologies discussed in this lesson?

A: Answers will vary according to the backgrounds of different individuals. Possible experiences include: troubleshooting your own Internet connectivity problems, or setting up a home network for a friend or family member by using a router or switch.

 *Practice Question: Additional practice questions are available on the CompTIA CHOICE platform within the **Assessments** tile.*

Lesson 9

Configuring and Troubleshooting Networks

LESSON INTRODUCTION

In a previous lesson, you identified networking technologies. With that knowledge, you are now prepared to implement those technologies. In this lesson, you will install and configure networking capabilities.

As a CompTIA® A+® technician, your duties will include setting up and configuring computers so that they can connect to a network. By installing, configuring, and troubleshooting networking capabilities, you will be able to provide users with the connectivity they need to be able to perform their job duties.

LESSON OBJECTIVES

In this lesson, you will:

- Configure Windows settings for different types of Internet and VPN connections.

- Install and configure SOHO router/modems and set up secure wireless access.

- Configure firewall settings and browser options to ensure safe Internet use on a SOHO network.

- Use remote access technologies to connect to hosts over a network.

- Troubleshoot wired and wireless problems plus IP configuration issues using command-line tools.

- Select, install, and configure Internet of Things (IoT) home automation devices.

Topic A
Configure Network Connection Settings

EXAM OBJECTIVES COVERED
1001-2.3 Given a scenario, install and configure a basic wired/wireless SOHO network.
1002-1.6 Given a scenario, use Microsoft Windows Control Panel utilities.
1002-1.8 Given a scenario, configure Microsoft Windows networking on a client/desktop.

Teaching Tip

This topic covers objectives from both Core 1 and Core 2.

The Core 2 content examples refer to specific features of Windows adapter configuration.

The Core 1 examples are more vague. You might expect questions in Core 1 to focus more on the driver properties of NICs, but both exams demand knowledge of these settings.

Show Slide(s)

NIC Properties

Teaching Tip

Exam candidates need to know how to open these configuration pages.

Interaction Opportunity

Ask learners to open the dialog boxes on their classroom computers, and compare the settings available to the screenshots in the manual.

Show Slide(s)

Wired Network Cards

Once all the hardware connections are made in a networking environment, you will need to make sure that the operating system is configured to use the hardware successfully. It is important to fully understand not only the hardware and the connections within a network, but also how Windows will need to be setup and configured to accomplish connectivity with the resources of a network.

NIC PROPERTIES

A computer joins a network by connecting the network adapter—or Network Interface Card (NIC)—to a switch or wireless access point. For proper end user device configuration, the card settings should be configured to match the capabilities of the network appliance.

WIRED NETWORK CARDS

Almost all wired network adapters are based on some type of Ethernet. The adapter's media type must match that of the switch it is connected to. Most use copper wire cable (RJ-45 connectors), though installations in some corporate networks may use fiber optic connections. The adapter and switch must also use the same Ethernet settings. The main parameters are:

- **Signaling speed**—most devices you will see will support Gigabit Ethernet, working at a nominal data rate of 1 Gbps. Older standards include Fast Ethernet (100 Mbps) and "plain" Ethernet (10 Mbps). Most network adapters will work at all three speeds. There is also a 10 Gbps standard, though this is not often used for desktop machines as the adapters and switches are expensive.
- **Half or full duplex**—this determines whether the connection transfers data in both directions simultaneously (full duplex) or not (half duplex). The overwhelming majority of devices use full duplex. Gigabit Ethernet requires full duplex to work.

Most wired network adapters will autonegotiate network settings such as signaling speed and half- or full duplex operation with the switch. For this to work, both the port on the switch and the network adapter should be configured to use the "Autonegotiate" setting, which should be the default.

If these settings do need to be configured manually, locate the adapter in **Device Manager**, right-click and select **Properties**, then update settings using the **Advanced** tab.

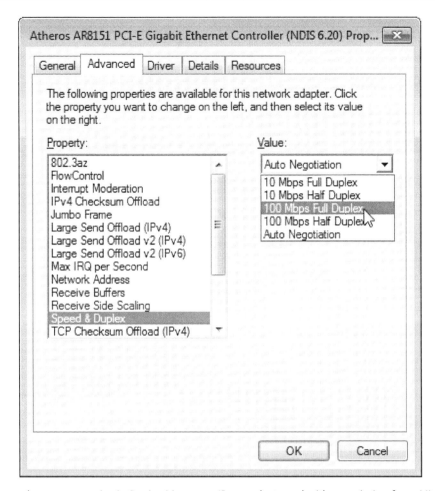

Ethernet adapter properties in Device Manager. (Screenshot used with permission from Microsoft.)

Most of the other settings can be left to the default. In some circumstances, you may be able to improve performance or troubleshoot connectivity problems by enabling or disabling or tweaking the parameters for settings such as jumbo frames, buffers, scaling, and offloads.

QOS

Quality of Service (QoS) means using a network protocol to prioritize certain types of traffic over others. Enterprise networks can use QoS protocols to make sure traffic such as Voice over IP calling or video conferencing is given higher priority than traffic where the timing of packets is less important, such as ordinary file downloads.

QoS parameters are usually configured on a managed switch. In the network adapter properties, you may need to enable the QoS protocol ("802.1p" or "QoS Packet Tagging," for instance). It is possible that QoS may also be controlled by a higher level protocol, which would be configured via the QoS Packet Scheduler client software installed by default on the OS's logical adapter.

Show Slide(s)
QoS

ONBOARD NETWORK CARDS

Most computers come with an onboard Gigabit Ethernet network adapter as part of the system chipset. The port will be an RJ-45 type for use with twisted-pair cabling. If there is any issue with the onboard NIC, the first step should be to use the BIOS/UEFI system setup program to find out whether it is enabled (look in the "Integrated Peripherals" or "Onboard Devices" section). You might disable the onboard adapter if installing a plug-in card.

Show Slide(s)
Onboard Network Cards

Show Slide(s)
Wireless Network Cards

Teaching Tip
The exception is 802.11a, which very few adapters support. 802.11b adapters should not really be allowed on a modern network either.

WIRELESS NETWORK CARDS

The most important setting on a wireless card is support for the 802.11 standard supported by the access point. Most cards are set to support any standard available. This means that a card that supports 802.11n will also be able to connect to 802.11g and 802.11b networks.

With the card shown in the following figure, for instance, you can enable or disable 802.11n Mode and select either mixed support for 802.11b/g or force use of either. For 802.11.n, you can also configure whether to use channel bonding.

Note: Making a network work in compatibility mode can reduce the performance of the whole network.

A couple of other settings are of interest:

- **Roaming Aggressiveness**—when the adapter starts to move out of range of one access point, it might try to connect to another one with a better signal. Roaming aggressiveness determines how tolerant the adapter is of weak signals. If you use multiple APs, tweaking this setting up or down might result in better performance.
- **Transmit Power**—this sets the radio power level. It is typically set to the highest possible by default.

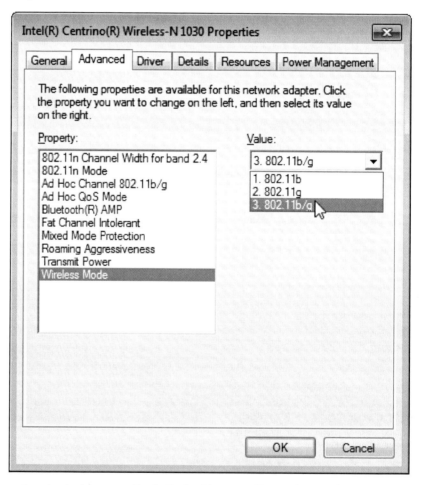

Wireless network adapter properties in Device Manager. (Screenshot used with permission from Microsoft.)

Note: *You might see a setting for "Ad hoc QoS Mode" on a wireless adapter. This enables Wireless Multimedia (WMM), which is a Wi-Fi specification for delivering QoS over wireless networks.*

WAKE ON LAN

Wake on LAN (WoL) allows you to start up a computer remotely. When the computer is switched off (but not unplugged), the network card can be kept active using standby power. The administrator would use network software to broadcast a "magic packet" to the NIC; when it receives it, the NIC initiates the computer's boot process.

Show Slide(s)

Wake on LAN

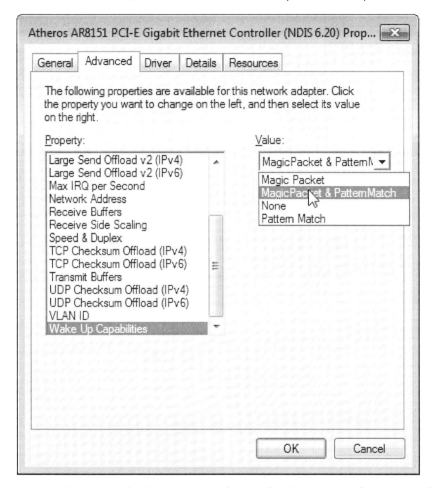

WoL settings for a network adapter. (Screenshot used with permission from Microsoft.)

Some devices with wireless chipsets come with **Wake-on-Wireless LAN (WoWLAN)**, but the technology is not so widely supported.

Note: *To learn more, check the* ***Video*** *tile on the CHOICE Course screen for any videos that supplement the content for this lesson.*

Access the Checklist tile on your CHOICE Course screen for reference information and job aids on How to Set Up Wake on LAN.

NETWORK CONNECTIONS IN WINDOWS 7 AND WINDOWS 8

Show Slide(s)

Network Connections in Windows 7 and Windows 8 (4 slides)

Interaction Opportunity

Ask learners to open Network and Settings, and to browse the classroom network via Explorer. Ask them to check the network location type.

Having verified connection properties of the Ethernet or Wi-Fi interface, you must also configure the card with the appropriate network client software and protocol, including addressing information relevant to the protocol.

Most Ethernet and Wi-Fi networks use the Internet Protocol (IP) with a DHCP server, which means that the card receives address parameters automatically.

NETWORK AND SHARING CENTER

In Windows® 7 and Windows 8, the Network and Sharing Center is used to provide an overview of network availability and configuration. Right-click the network status icon in the notification area and select **Open Network and Sharing Center** or open the applet via Control Panel.

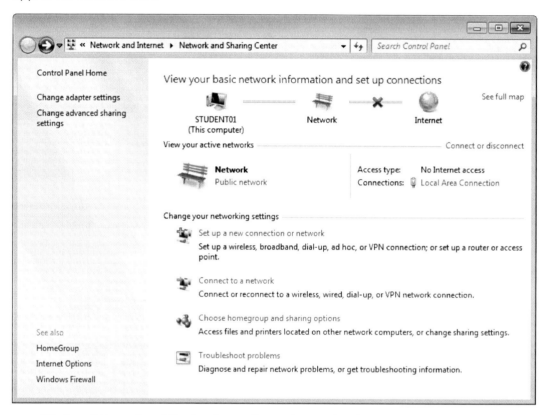

Windows 7 Network and Sharing Center. (Screenshot used with permission from Microsoft.)

WIRED NETWORK CONNECTIONS

To access the adapter property sheets, select **Change adapter settings**. In Windows 8, the option is labeled **Manage network connections**.

*Note: Alternatively, run `ncpa.cpl` from the **Instant Search** box or **Run** dialog box.*

Teaching Tip

Point out that Linux uses eth0, eth1,... and wlan0, wlan1,... as the default interface names. macOS, following BSD, uses en0, en1, ... for wired and wireless interfaces.

In Windows 7, the wired network adapter will be listed as **Local Area Connection** (though you can rename it if you prefer), whereas a wireless adapter will be listed as **Wireless Network Connection**. In Windows 8, the adapters are named **Ethernet** and **WiFi**.

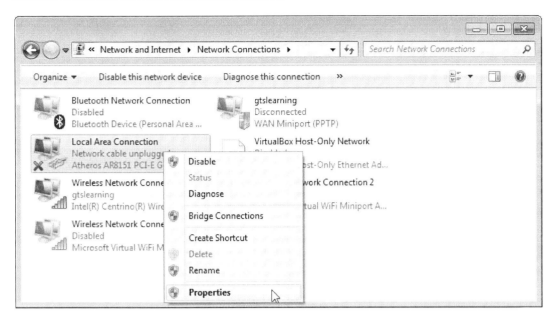

Network Connections in Windows 7. (Screenshot used with permission from Microsoft.)

ADAPTER PROPERTIES

Right-click an adapter and select **Properties** to configure settings or **Status** to view information about the connection. From the **Properties** dialog box, you can add or configure the appropriate service, protocol, or client.

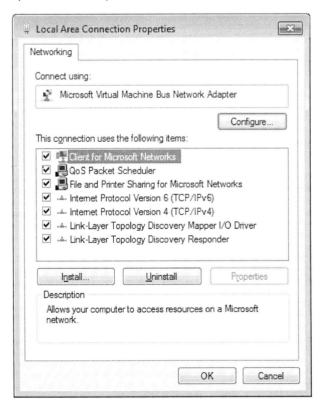

Local Area Network Adapter properties. (Screenshot used with permission from Microsoft.)

- **Clients** provide connections to types of file servers, such as Linux/UNIX or Windows.
- **Protocols** provide the format for addressing and delivering data messages between systems, the most widely adopted being TCP/IP.

- **Services** allow your machine to provide network functionality to other machines.

By default, the following clients, protocols, and services are installed on the default Ethernet adapter:

- Client for Microsoft Networks.
- File and Print Sharing for Microsoft Networks.
- Internet Protocol—both IP version 4 and IP version 6 will be installed. The network adapter automatically uses the appropriate version of the protocol depending on the network it is connected to.
- Link-layer Topology Discovery—provides the network mapping and discovery functions in the Network and Sharing Center.

Checked items are described as being "bound" to an adapter. When installing a new protocol or service, check that it is only bound to adapters that should be using that protocol or service.

WIRELESS NETWORK CONNECTIONS

To join a WLAN, click the network status icon in the notification area and select from the list of displayed networks. If the access point is set to broadcast the network name or Service Set ID (SSID), then the network will appear in the list of available networks. The bars show the strength of the signal and the lock icon indicates whether the network uses encryption. To connect, select the network then enter the pre-shared key (or log on in the specified way if using a network authentication server).

If you choose the **Connect automatically** option, Windows will use the network without prompting whenever it is in range.

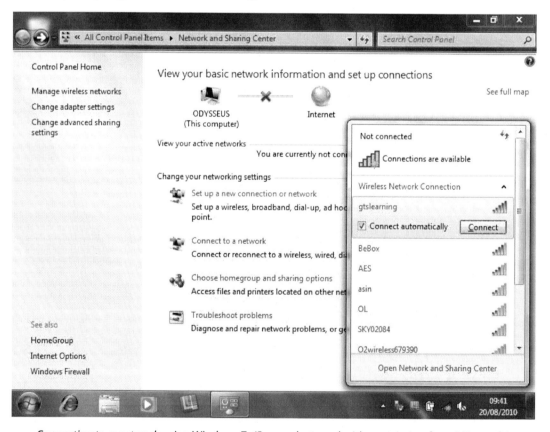

Connecting to a network using Windows 7. (Screenshot used with permission from Microsoft.)

If the WLAN is not shown (if SSID broadcast is disabled), click **Open Network and Sharing Center** then **Set up a new connection or network** and proceed by entering the network SSID, security information, and network location type.

NETWORK CONNECTIONS IN WINDOWS 10

Windows 10 manages network settings via the **Network & Internet** section in the Settings app. Use the **Status** page to monitor the current network connection. There are links to the **Network and Sharing Center** and **Network Connections** applets (via **Change adapter options**) from there.

Show Slide(s)

Network Connections in Windows 10

Interaction Opportunity

Ask learners to open **Settings** and view the current IP address (**View network properties**) and then open ncpa.cpl to view the adapter properties.

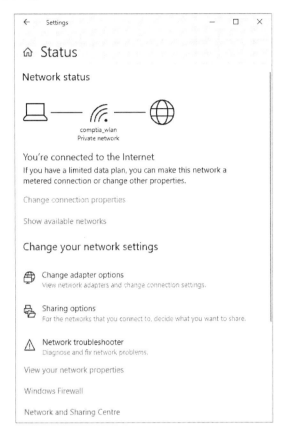

Windows 10 Network & Internet Settings app. (Screenshot used with permission from Microsoft.)

You can join a wireless network using the network status icon in the notification area. If you need to input WLAN settings manually, from the **Network & internet** page, select **WiFi →Manage known networks→Add a new network**.

IP ADDRESS CONFIGURATION

IP address properties can be configured through the network connection's **Properties** dialog box. Both wired and wireless adapters are configured in the same way. By default, Windows machines obtain an IP address dynamically, but you can configure a static IP address and other settings, such as DNS servers.

Show Slide(s)

IP Address Configuration (2 slides)

Teaching Tip

Exam candidates must be familiar with the layout of these dialog boxes.

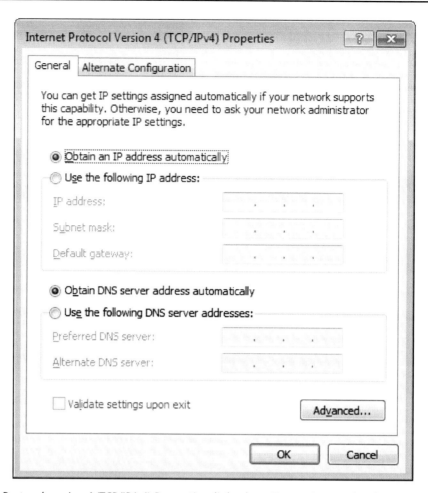

Internet Protocol version 4 (TCP/IP/v4) Properties dialog box. (Screenshot used with permission from Microsoft.)

 Note: A machine can communicate with local hosts with a valid IP address and subnet mask but cannot communicate with other networks unless a default gateway is specified.

 Note: A machine that cannot access a DNS server will not be able to resolve host names or web addresses. As DNS is a critical service, two server addresses are usually specified for redundancy.

 Note: In Windows 10, you can also configure IP via the Settings interface. Select **Network & Internet** then **Ethernet** or **WiFi** as appropriate. Click the adapter or WLAN SSID. Under "IP Settings," click the **Edit** button.

AUTOMATIC IP CONFIGURATION AND DHCP

Configuring IP addresses and other TCP/IP network information manually raises many difficult administrative issues and makes misconfiguration of one or more hosts more likely. A Dynamic Host Configuration Protocol (DHCP) service can be provided by a Windows Server or by a device such as a switch or router. DHCP can allocate an IP address to a new machine joining the network. To use DHCP, select the **Obtain an IP address automatically** option. If a Windows machine fails to obtain an IP address dynamically, it will utilize an Automatic Private IP Addressing (APIPA) address from a reserved range (169.254.x.y).

Teaching Tip

Be sure learners understand that Windows clients default to using APIPA in the absence of a DHCP Server. This results in their having an IP address in the range 169.254.x.y. These issues have a significant bearing on the troubleshooting process.

ALTERNATE CONFIGURATION

Windows allows you to define an alternative IP address configuration for a machine if it cannot contact a DHCP server and using APIPA is unsuitable. This is useful in the scenario where you have a laptop computer connecting to DHCP in a corporate network but that requires a static IP address on the user's home network.

Teaching Tip

Point out that the **Alternate Configuration** tab does not appear if a static configuration has been assigned on the **General** tab.

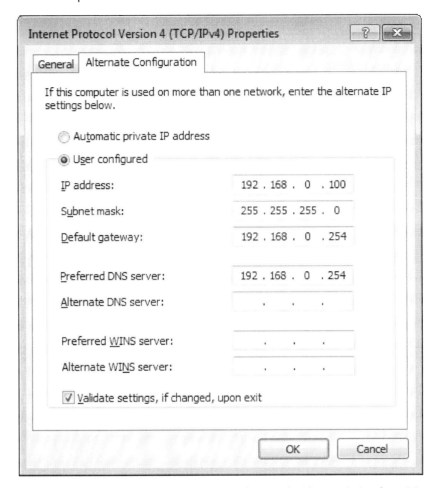

TCP/IP Alternate Configuration dialog box. (Screenshot used with permission from Microsoft.)

 *Note: The **Alternate Configuration** tab is not displayed unless the **Obtain an IP address automatically** option is selected.*

 *Note: To learn more, check the **Video** tile on the CHOICE Course screen for any videos that supplement the content for this lesson.*

 Access the Checklist tile on your CHOICE Course screen for reference information and job aids on How to Configure IP Addresses.

OTHER NETWORK CONNECTIONS

Most residential and small office networks connect to the Internet via a SOHO "router." These Internet appliances combine a 4-port switch and wireless access point with a router/modem that can connect to the ISP's network over DSL or Hybrid Fiber Coax (HFC) lines. The computers connect to the router by using the switch ports or access

Show Slide(s)

Other Network Connections (3 slides)

point and are assigned an IP configuration by a DHCP server running in the appliance. Correctly configuring the Ethernet or WiFi adapter in Network Connections will allow the computer to join this type of network.

There are a number of other ways of connecting to the Internet and other remote networks, however.

DIAL-UP

Teaching Tip

Discuss when dial-up might still be necessary.

If you do happen to be using a dial-up modem, check that the line is analog not digital, especially if connecting from a hotel.

A **dial-up connection** uses an analog modem to dial another modem on the ISP's remote access server, which then transfers the data onto the ISP's network and to and from the wider Internet. The call is placed in the same way as a voice call and may incur connection charges. The maximum link speed is just 56 Kbps.

Note: *Given perfect line conditions, modems can work at up to 56 Kbps downlink and 48 Kbps uplink. Line conditions are rarely perfect, however, and actual speeds may be a lot lower.*

To create a dial-up connection, a modem must be installed in the computer or an external modem can be connected via USB. The dial-up port on the modem should then be connected to the phone socket. This is typically done using a silver satin cable with an RJ-11 connector for the modem and a suitable connector for the phone point, depending on region. For example, in the US an RJ-11 connector is used, but in the UK, a BT connector is often required. Regardless of the physical interface, the modem must be installed to one of the computer's software COM ports. The modem must also be configured with the local dialing properties, such as access prefix for an outside line, area code, and so on.

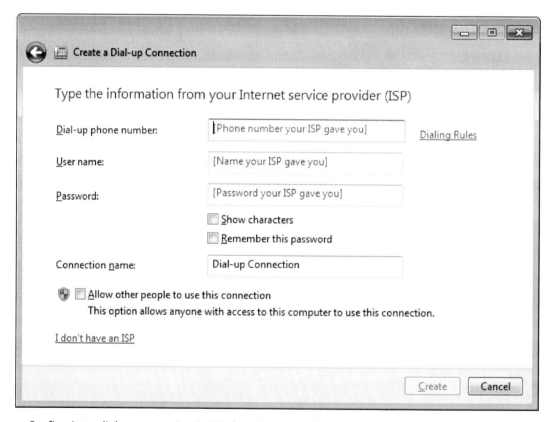

Configuring a dial-up connection in Windows 7. (Screenshot used with permission from Microsoft.)

You can use the **Set Up a Connection or Network** wizard to configure a link to the ISP's server.

You can connect or disconnect the link or reconfigure it using the network status icon.

WIRELESS WAN (CELLULAR)

Wireless Wide Area Network (WWAN or cellular) Internet access refers to using an adapter to link to a cellular phone provider's network via the nearest available transmitter (base station). The bandwidth depends on the technologies supported by the adapter and by the transmitter (3G or 4G, for instance).

The WWAN adapter can be fitted as a USB device or (on laptops) as an internal adapter. The advantage of the latter is that they do not protrude from the chassis; USB adapters are quite unwieldy.

Once the vendor's software has been installed, plug in the adapter and it will be detected and configured automatically. You can then use the software to open a connection, check signal strength, view usage, and so on.

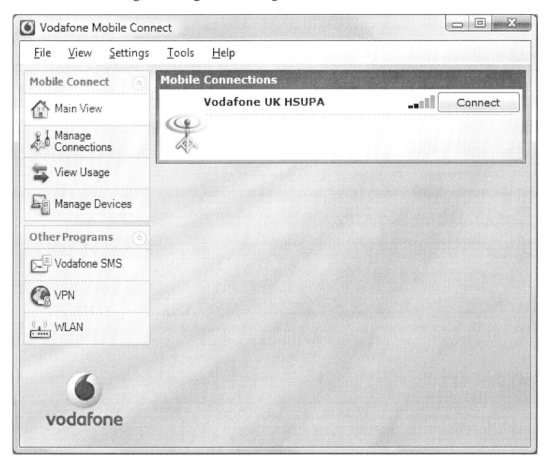

Vodafone Mobile Connect management software.

VIRTUAL PRIVATE NETWORK (VPN)

A Virtual Private Network (VPN) is a "tunnel" through the Internet. It allows a remote computer to join the local network securely. Windows supports a number of VPN types but you may need to obtain third-party software.

If the VPN type is supported, you can configure a connection using the Windows client from Network Connections.

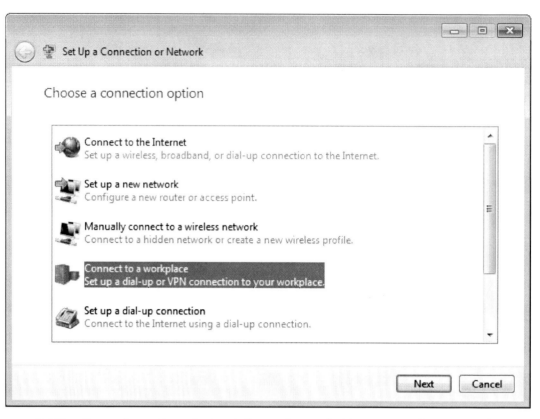

Set Up a Connection or Network wizard. (Screenshot used with permission from Microsoft.)

Subsequently, the network connection will be available by clicking the network status icon. Right-click the icon under "Dial-up and VPN" to **Connect** or **Disconnect** or modify the connection's Properties.

Accessing a VPN connection from the network status icon in Windows 7. (Screenshot used with permission from Microsoft.)

Note: *To learn more, check the* **Video** *tile on the CHOICE Course screen for any videos that supplement the content for this lesson.*

Access the Checklist tile on your CHOICE Course screen for reference information and job aids on How to Configure Other Network Connection Settings.

Activity 9-1

Discussing Network Connection Configuration Settings

 Show Slide(s)

Activity: Discussing Network Connection Configuration Settings

SCENARIO
Answer the following questions to check your understanding of the topic.

1. You need to configure duplex settings on a network adapter manually.

   What steps do you need to follow?

   Open **Device Manager** and the adapter's **Property** sheet. Select the **Advanced** tab and select the **Duplex** property (or **Speed and Duplex**). Change the value as required, and select **OK**.

2. **True or false? If you want a computer to be available through Wake-on-LAN, you can disconnect it from the power supply but must leave it connected to the network data port.**

   False. The network adapter must be connected to standby power, and the computer could not start anyway if it were disconnected from the power supply.

3. A Windows computer is configured to use DHCP, but no DHCP server is available. The computer is not using an APIPA address either.

   Why is this?

   It has been configured with an Alternate Configuration static IP address.

4. **Why are IP addresses entered under DNS, and why should there be two of them?**

   These are the IP addresses of DNS servers that will process client requests to resolve host and domain names to IP addresses. DNS is a critical service on Windows networks and on the Internet, so a second server should always be specified for redundancy

5. **What parameters do you need to specify to connect to a VPN?**

   Assuming you have a remote host topology, you need to establish a connection to a server over a public network such as the Internet. The VPN server then facilitates a connection to a local network. You need to specify the location of the VPN server as an IP address or Fully Qualified Domain Name (FQDN). If the VPN type is not detected automatically, you might need to configure extra settings or use third-party VPN client software. To connect to the VPN, the user must submit credentials, such as a user name and password.

Activity 9-2

Configuring Network Connection Settings

Show Slide(s)

Activity: Configuring Network Connection Settings

Teaching Tip

Emphasize that learners must perform these steps or the activity will not produce the intended results.

BEFORE YOU BEGIN

You need to stage a configuration error to discover as you work through this activity. Perform these steps to run the **C:\COMPTIA-LABS\LABFILES\unplug.ps1** PowerShell script:

1. On the HOST computer, activate the **Instant Search** box, and type `powershell`

2. Right-click the **Windows PowerShell** icon and select **Run as administrator**. Select **Yes** to accept the UAC prompt.

3. In the **Windows PowerShell** window, type `c:\comptia-labs\labfiles \unplug` and press **Enter**. Type **R** to run the script once.

> *Note: If you receive an error message about disabled scripts, run the* `Set-ExecutionPolicy Unrestricted` *cmdlet, and type* `A` *(for* **Yes to All***) when you are prompted. Then, try running the* `unplug` *script again.*

SCENARIO

In this activity, you will use five VMs and one virtual switch to create a complete LAN, all running within your HOST computer. The following network diagram is provided to assist you.

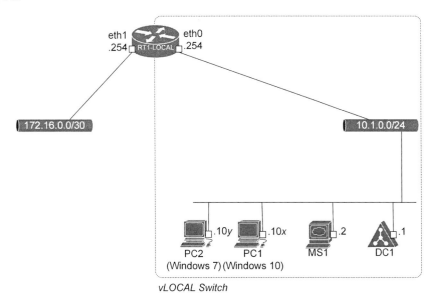

Network environment for configuring network connection settings.

Teaching Tip

Talk through each of these features as learners view the diagram.

1. Using the network diagram, observe and verify the following features:

   • The network interfaces shown within the **vLOCAL Switch** box are all connected to the same virtual switch. The virtual switch functionality is always running as part of the Hyper-V hypervisor. You do not need to start it at any point.

   • The round icon at the top shows a router VM that has two interfaces. This is configured at the default gateway for all the other VMs. You will only look at a single local network in this activity, so there is no actual connectivity through the external interface.

   • The "pipe" icon shows the IP addressing scheme used by the hosts connected to this switch. All addresses come from the range 10.1.0.0/24 (subnet mask: 255.255.255.0). The number on each host shows its static address. For example, the router's full IP address for the local interface is 10.1.0.254.

   • There are two Windows Server VMs. The **DC1** VM is running Active Directory and DNS and has the static IP address 10.1.0.1. The **MS1** VM is running DHCP and has the static address 10.1.0.2.

   • The **PC1** and **PC2** VMs are the Windows 10 and Windows 7 client workstations you have used previously. Their addresses are dynamically assigned by the DHCP server from the range 10.1.0.101 to 10.1.0.109.

2. Start the VMs to create the network.

   You do not need to open connection windows for the VMs unless you are specifically prompted to do so.

   a) In Hyper-V Manager, right-click **RT1-LOCAL** and select **Start**.

   b) Right-click **DC1** and select **Start**.

   c) Wait until the **DC1** thumbnail shows the logon screen, and then start **MS1**.

   d) Wait until the **MS1** thumbnail shows the logon screen, and then start **PC1** and **PC2**.

   e) Open a connection window for **PC2**.

   f) Sign on, using the account **515support\Administrator** and password **Pa$$w0rd**

Interaction Opportunity

If unexpected connectivity issues occur, ask learners to check that NLA on **DC1** has correctly identified the domain profile (have them point to the network status tooltip, and look for **corp. 515support.com**). If the network is unknown, learners should restart the activity. Boot **DC1** first, and sign on to check that NLA has functioned correctly.

This occurs if NLA runs before the domain services are properly loaded. Make sure learners allow DC1 to complete its boot process before starting MS1 and for MS1 to boot before starting PC1 and PC2. A script runs automatically in DC1 and MS1 to disable and reenable the network adapter at boot, but this is not always successful. Unfortunately, there is no way to hard code domain profile selection.

3. On the **PC2 VM**, view the adapter status, and open the **Network and Sharing Center**.

   a) On PC2, on the taskbar, point to the network status icon , and observe the tool tip.

   It should identify the network connection as **corp.515support.com** with the alert that there is no Internet access.

   b) Select the icon and select **Open Network and Sharing Center**.

c) Examine the information shown about the network layout and type. Also, note that under **Change your network settings**, there is an option to set up a new connection, such as a dial-up or VPN connection.

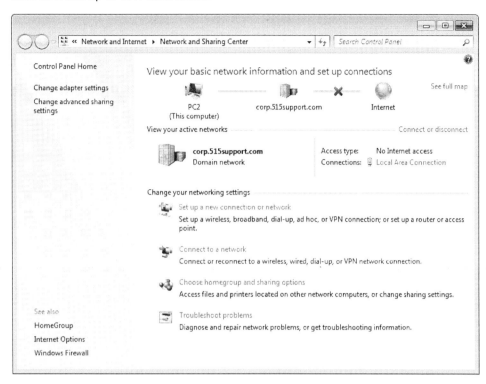

Network and Sharing Center in Windows 7. (Screenshot used with permission from Microsoft.)

4. View the adapter properties.

a) Select the **Local Area Connection** link.

b) In the **Local Area Connection Status** dialog box, examine the link speed, and then select the **Details** button.

c) In the **Network Connection Details** dialog box, examine the values for **IPv4 Address**, **IPv4 Subnet Mask**, **IPv4 Default Gateway**, **IPv4 DNS Server**, and **IPv4 DHCP Server**. Make sure you can relate them to the network topology diagram shown at the start of the activity.

d) Select **Close** to return to the **Local Area Connection** dialog box.

e) Select the **Properties** button.

You can bind and configure clients, services, and protocols in this dialog box.

f) Double-click **Internet Protocol Version 4 (TCP/IPv4)**.

The adapter is set to obtain its configuration automatically.

g) Select the **Alternate Configuration** tab.

You can use this to set a static IP address if no DHCP server is available. This address would be used instead of an APIPA address.

h) Select the **Cancel** button.

i) Select the **Configure** button. If prompted with **Do you wish to proceed?**, select **Yes**.

j) In the **Microsoft Virtual Machine Bus Network Adapter Properties** dialog box, select the **Advanced** tab.

This is the same **Properties** dialog box that would open if you selected the adapter via **Device Manager**. This emulated network adapter driver does not support many configurable settings. There are no options for Wake-on-LAN or QoS.

 Note: Optionally, open this dialog box on the HOST computer, and compare the difference.

    k) Select **Cancel**, and then select **Close**.

5. Browse the network to identify other hosts and resources.

    a) In the **Network and Sharing Center**, under **View your basic network information**, select the **corp.515support.com** link.

    b) If a **Network discovery is turned off** bar is shown, select it, and then select **Turn on network discovery and file sharing**.

    c) Double-click the **DC1** icon.

       The server is hosting several shared folders.

    d) Select the **Back** button.

       Notice that **PC1** is missing.

6. Open a connection window for **PC1**, and sign on as ***515support\Administrator***. Identify what network problem occurred, and remediate it.

    a) In Hyper-V Manager, double-click the **PC1** icon.

    b) Select **Other user**.

    c) In the **User name** dialog box, type ***515support\administrator***. Type ***Pa$$w0rd*** in the other box, and press **Enter**.

    d) Observe the network status icon.

       The red cross means that the network cable is not connected (or the adapter is faulty). Instead of checking the back of the computer for the cable, you need to look at the VM's configuration settings.

    e) In the VM connection window, select **File→Settings**.

    f) Select the **Network Adapter** node.

       It is listed as **Not connected**.

    g) From the **Virtual switch** list box, select **vLOCAL** and then select **OK**.

    h) Observe the network status icon change.

       It should connect to the **corp.515support.com** network, but still show an error status for Internet connectivity.

    i) Select the icon, and select **Network & Internet settings**.

    j) Scroll down and select **View your network properties**.

       This shows the same sort of information as the Windows 7 **Status** dialog box.

    k) Select the **Back** button.

    l) Select the **Network and Sharing Center** link.

       This interface is still available in Windows 10, though it does not show all of the same information as in Windows 7. The adapter is named **Ethernet**, rather than **Local Area Connection**.

    m) Close the Network and Sharing Center.

    n) If you have time, view the other nodes in **Network & Internet settings**. Note the different options under **Ethernet** compared to **Status**. Also note the options for configuring dial-up and VPN connections.

> **Note:** *The VM does not have a wireless adapter. If such an adapter were present however, there would be a WiFi node to use to configure it.*

7. At the end of each activity, you need to close the VMs and discard any changes you made.

    a) From the connection window, select **Action→Revert**.

    b) If you are prompted to confirm, select the **Revert** button.

    c) On the **HOST**, in the **Hyper-V Manager** console, right-click each VM that is still running and select **Revert**. At the end of the lab, the state of each VM should be listed as **Off**.

Teaching Tip

If learners ask about the pcap adapter, tell them this is a loopback adapter used by the Wireshark protocol analyzer that is installed on this VM.

Topic B

Install and Configure SOHO Networks

EXAM OBJECTIVES COVERED

1001-2.3 Given a scenario, install and configure a basic wired/wireless SOHO network.
1002-2.3 Compare and contrast wireless security protocols and authentication methods.
1002-2.10 Given a scenario, configure security on SOHO wireless and wired networks.

Previously in this course, you covered basic networking concepts, the Transmission Control Protocol/Internet Protocol (TCP/IP) addressing scheme, and how networks are connected. In this topic, you will use that knowledge to install and configure a SOHO network.

No matter what the size or location of the network, you are still responsible for understanding how it is structured and configured. A+ technicians must understand the needs and complexities of SOHO wired and wireless networks.

Teaching Tip

Wireless security objectives and content examples appear on both the Core 1 and Core 2 exams, so this is a very important topic.

SOHO NETWORKS

A Small Office Home Office (SOHO) LAN is a business-oriented network, possibly using a centralized server in addition to client devices and printers, but often using a single Internet appliance to provide connectivity. Home and residential networks may also be classed as SOHO.

Show Slide(s)

SOHO Networks

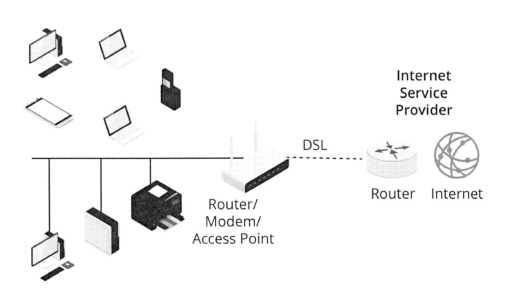

A typical SOHO network layout.

COMMON SOHO NETWORK HARDWARE

A DSL/cable modem is installed as Customer Premises Equipment (CPE), typically as some sort of combined router/modem. Make sure you understand the functions of the separate device types bundled within these appliances:

- **Modem**—connects to the service provider cabling and transfers frames over the link. The modem type must be matched to the network type (ADSL, VDSL, or cable).
- **Router**—forwards packets over the WAN (Internet) interface if they do not have a local destination IP address. Some appliances may provide the ability to configure local subnets, though this is not typical of the device's supplied by the service providers.
- **Switch**—allows local computers and other host types to connect to the network via RJ-45 ports. This will be an unmanaged switch so no configuration is necessary.
- **Access point**—allows hosts to connect to the network over Wi-Fi.

On a DSL modem, the RJ-11 port on the modem connects to the phone point. A microfilter (splitter) must be installed to separate voice and data signals. These can be self-installed on each phone point by the customer. Modern sockets are likely to feature a built-in splitter.

A self-installed DSL splitter.

 Note: *The modem might be provided as a separate device. If this is the case, it will provide an RJ-45 port to connect to the RJ-45 WAN port on the router.*

 Note: *The steps for most cable modems are the same except that you will be connecting to the provider network using a coax cable. Make sure the coax connector is secure (but do not overtighten it).*

SOHO NETWORK CONFIGURATION

You need to connect a computer (PC or laptop) to the device's built-in unmanaged switch so that you can configure the appliance. Make sure the computer is set to obtain an IP address automatically. Connect the computer to one of the RJ-45 LAN ports on the router/modem. These are usually color-coded yellow. Wait for the Dynamic Host Configuration Protocol (DHCP) server running on the router/modem to allocate a valid IP address to the computer.

Use a browser to open the device's management URL, as listed in the documentation. This could be an IP address or a host/domain name:

```
http://192.168.0.1
http://www.routerlogin.com
```

It might use HTTPS rather than unencrypted HTTP: If you cannot connect, check that the computer's IP address is in the same range as the device IP.

The management software will prompt you to choose a new administrator password. Enter the default password (as listed in the documentation or printed on a sticker accompanying the router/modem). Choose a long password (12 characters or more) with a mix of alphanumeric and symbol characters. If there is also an option to change the default username of the administrator account, this is also a little bit more secure than leaving the default configured.

CONFIGURING INTERNET ACCESS

Most appliances will use a wizard-based setup to connect to the Internet via the service provider's network. The DSL/cable link parameters are normally self-configuring. You might need to supply a username and password. If manual configuration is required, obtain the settings from your ISP.

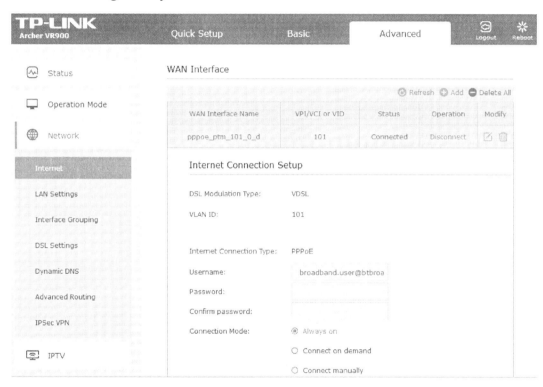

Configuring DSL modem settings. Note that this VDSL modem is connecting to a Fiber to the Curb (FTTC) service. The DSL segment only runs between the premises and the service provider's cabinet, located in a nearby street. From the cabinet, there is a fiber optic cable running back to the local exchange. (Screenshot courtesy of TP-Link.)

You can also use the management console to view line status and the system log. These might be required by the ISP to troubleshoot any issues with the connection.

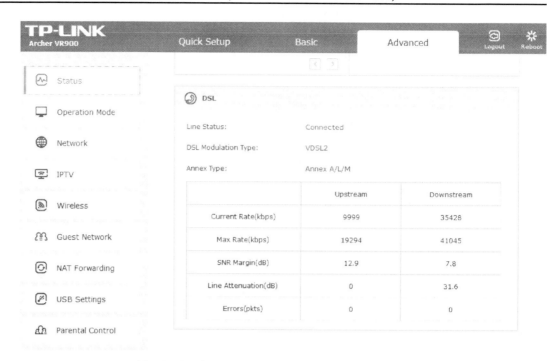

Viewing DSL line status. (Screenshot courtesy of TP-Link.)

WIRELESS SETTINGS

Having set up Internet access, the next step is to configure wireless settings. The majority of hosts will connect to the network wirelessly. Initial configuration is likely to be part of the device's setup wizard, but if you skipped that or need to reconfigure settings, the management software will have a separate page or section for wireless configuration.

Having checked the box to enable wireless communications, you can adjust the following settings from the default.

- Frequency band (2.4 GHz or 5 GHz)—on an 802.11ac access point, you can use the same network settings over both bands. Clients will connect to any supported frequency. Alternatively, you can configure different network names for each frequency. You might want to use one frequency but not the other, depending on the range of devices you have using the wireless network.

 Note: It is best practice not to enable services you do not need, especially on a multifunction device such as this. Most devices are now shipped in "security-enabled" configurations, meaning that you explicitly have to choose to enable services that you want to run.

- SSID (Service Set ID)—a name for the WLAN. This can be up to 32 characters and must be different to any other networks nearby.
- Security version and encryption type—always choose the highest mode supported by your wireless clients (WPA2 with AES). Note that WEP provides very weak security and should not be relied upon for confidentiality.
- Password (Pre-Shared Key)—on a SOHO network you will choose a password for use by all client devices to connect to the network. The password generates the encryption key. The same key must be configured on client adapters to enable them to connect.

 Note: Choose a strong passphrase and keep it secret. In order to generate a strong key, use a longer phrase than you would for a normal password.

- Mode—enable compatibility for different 802.11 devices. Performance may be improved if you disable support for unnecessary legacy standards. The typical configuration is to use the 2.4 GHz band for legacy b/g/n stations and the 5 GHz band for ac stations.
- Channel and channel width—the access point will try to auto-detect the best channel at boot time. You might adjust the settings manually if you subsequently experience a weak connection caused by interference from other devices. For 802.11n/ac access points, you may be able to configure the use of wide channels (bonding) for more bandwidth. This may only be practical in the 5 GHz band, depending on the wireless site design.

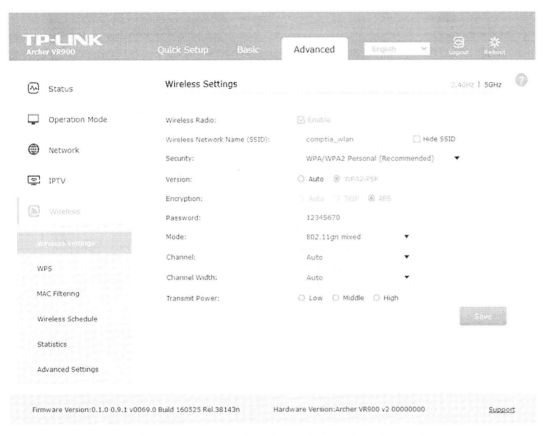

Configuring an access point. (Screenshot courtesy of TP-Link.)

DHCP AND IP ADDRESS CONFIGURATION

You may want to adjust the settings for the DHCP server. This assigns wired and wireless clients an appropriate IP addressing configuration. It is always enabled "out of the box" to allow users to connect to the configuration page easily. If you disable DHCP, IP settings have to be allocated and configured manually on client devices. This adds a lot of administrative overhead and introduces the possibility of configuration errors. Also, it is not difficult for a determined attacker to identify the IP scope in use.

Show Slide(s)

DHCP and IP Address Configuration

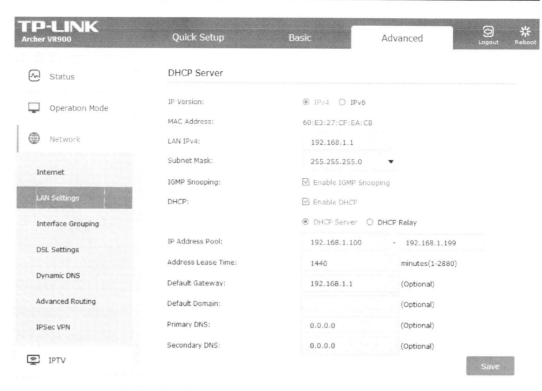

Configuring the DHCP server. (Screenshot courtesy of TP-Link.)

**Show
Slide(s)**

WPS

WPS

As setting up an access point securely is relatively complex, vendors have developed a system to automate the process called **Wi-Fi Protected Setup (WPS)**.

To use WPS, all the wireless devices (access point and wireless adapters) must be WPS-capable. Typically, the devices will have a pushbutton. Activating this on the access point and the adapter simultaneously will associate the device with the access point using WPA2. The system generates a random SSID and passphrase.

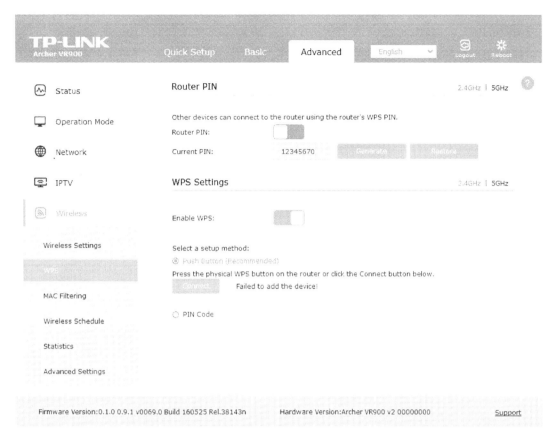

If you use WPS, disable the PIN configuration method if possible. (Screenshot courtesy of TP-Link.)

Note: *There is a WPS PIN method too but this is vulnerable to "brute force" attacks, where someone tries to guess the passphrase to get access to the networks. It is advisable to disable this method if possible.*

ACCESS POINT PLACEMENT

Antenna and access point placement is important for ensuring a robust network—one that clients can connect to wherever they are in the building. In a SOHO network, with an integrated router/modem/access point, placement of the access point is likely to be constrained by the location of the service provider's cabling. If this does not provide sufficient coverage, the typical solution is to use extenders to repeat and boost the wireless signal in locations where it is not strong enough.

A site survey can be performed with wireless signal measuring software (such as inSSIDer) to identify "dead zones."

CHANNEL SELECTION

The 2.4 GHz band for 802.11b/g/n is subdivided into 11 channels (in the US), spaced at 5 MHz intervals. However, the recommendation is to allow 25 MHz spacing between channels in active use. In practice, therefore, no more than three nearby 802.11b/g/n access points can have non-overlapping channels. This could be implemented, for example, by selecting channel 1 for AP1, channel 6 for AP2, and channel 11 for AP3. When using the 5 GHz band, more non-overlapping channels are available.

Show Slide(s)
Access Point Placement

Interaction Opportunity
Ask learners how they configure their home networks. Do they need to use extenders? Or power line adapters? Do any have structured cabling installed?

Show Slide(s)
Channel Selection

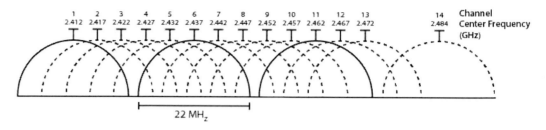

Frequencies and overlap of wireless channels.

Newer access points will auto-detect the channel that seems least congested at boot time. As the environment changes, you may find that this channel selection is not the optimum one. You can use a wireless spectrum analyzer to find which channels in your area are actually the least busy.

RADIO POWER LEVELS

Show Slide(s)

Radio Power Levels

You may want to turn the power output on an AP down to prevent "war driving." War driving is the practice of driving around with a wireless-enabled laptop scanning for unsecure WLANs. The main problem with this approach is that it requires careful configuration to ensure that there is acceptable coverage for legitimate users. You also expose yourself slightly to "**evil twin**" attacks, as users may expect to find the network at a given location and assume that a rogue AP is legitimate.

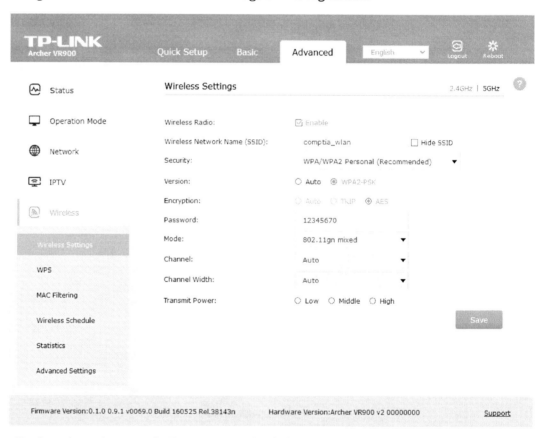

You have the option to set the Transmit Power level when configuring wireless settings on this access point. (Screenshot courtesy of TP-Link.)

Increasing power output to boost a signal is not always reliable. As you increase power, you also increase the chance of the signal bouncing, causing more interference, especially if there are multiple access points. Also, the client radio power levels should match those of the access point or they may be able to receive signals but not transmit back. Consequently, power levels are best set to autonegotiate. You should also be aware of legal restrictions on power output—these vary from country-to-country.

WI-FI SECURITY PROTOCOLS

Wireless LANs require careful configuration to make the connection and transmissions over the connection secure. The main problem with wireless is that because it is "unguided," there is no way to contain the signal. Anyone with a suitably equipped laptop or RF (Radio Frequency) scanner can intercept the signals. If the proper security has not been put in place, this could allow the interception of data or the unauthorized use of the network.

The crucial step in enforcing wireless security is to enable **encryption**. Encryption scrambles the messages being sent over the WLAN so that anyone intercepting them is not able to capture any valuable information. An encryption system consists of a cipher, which is the process used to scramble the message, and a key. The key is a unique value that allows the recipient to decrypt a message that has been encrypted using the same cipher and key. Obviously, the key must be known only to valid recipients or the encryption system will offer no protection.

WIRED EQUIVALENT PRIVACY (WEP)

The **Wired Equivalent Privacy (WEP)** encryption system is based on the RC4 cipher. RC stands for Ron's Cipher, after its inventor, Ron Rivest. Under WEP version 1, you can select from different key sizes (64-bit or 128-bit). A larger key makes it more difficult to attack the security system.

Although WEP might sound like a good solution at first, it is not as secure as it should be. The problem stems from the way WEP produces keys. Because of a flaw in the method, attackers can quite easily generate their own keys by using a wireless network capture tool to analyze network data and crack WEP in a short period of time.

Consequently, WEP is deprecated and should not be used to secure a wireless network.

WI-FI PROTECTED ACCESS (WPA)

Wi-Fi Protected Access (WPA) fixes most of the security problems with WEP. WPA still uses the RC4 cipher but adds a mechanism called **Temporal Key Integrity Protocol (TKIP)** to fix the issues with key generation.

The original version of WPA was introduced as an upgrade for equipment supporting WEP. The continued reliance on WEP meant that the protocol did not meet the requirements of the IEEE 802.11i security standard. An update, known as WPA2, was developed as a fully compliant 802.11i security protocol. The main difference to WPA is the use of the **Advanced Encryption Standard (AES)** cipher for encryption. AES is much stronger than RC4/TKIP.

The only reason not to use WPA2 is if it is not supported by adapters, APs, or operating systems on the network. WPA2 is very well-established now and most devices should support it. WPA is an acceptable fallback, especially on home networks, where the risk of intrusion is quite low.

 Note: WPA/WPA2 can still depend on the use of a passphrase to generate the key. If the passphrase is an easy-to-guess word or phrase, the key can be discovered and the encryption system cracked.

 Show Slide(s)

Wi-Fi Security Protocols (2 slides)

 Teaching Tip

Remind learners that WPA3 is being released at the time of writing. It is not on the exam objectives, but it is important for learners to know the main features. The key feature is better protection against offline passphrase-guessing attacks. There is also an Easy Connect mode for adding home automation devices to a network more easily. You can also use longer session keys (192-bit) and prevent use of legacy algorithms with possible weaknesses. Do stress that while it is included as an exam objective content example, no one should be using WEP.

 Teaching Tip

Some access points support option modes such as WPA-AES or WPA2-TKIP. These were designed to support legacy client chipsets when WPA2 was first released.

WI-FI AUTHENTICATION

It is possible to configure a WLAN as open, meaning that anyone can connect to it. In order to secure the WLAN, however, you need to be able to confirm that only valid users are connecting to it by authenticating them. WLAN authentication comes in two types.

PERSONAL

The personal authentication mode is based on a **Pre-shared Key (PSK)**. This is the key that is used to encrypt communications. A PSK is generated from a passphrase, which is like a long password. In WPA-PSK, the router administrator defines a passphrase of between 8 and 63 ASCII characters. This is converted into a 256-bit cryptographic hash, expressed as a 64-digit hex value where each hex digit represents 4 bits.

> **Note:** *It is critical that PSK passphrases be long (12 characters or more) and complex. This means that it should contain a mixture of upper- and lower-case letters and digits and no dictionary words or common names.*

The main problem is that distribution of the key or passphrase cannot be secured properly, and on a home network, the user acting as the administrator may choose an unsecure phrase. It also fails to provide accounting, as all users share the same key. The advantage is that it is simple to set up. Conversely, changing the key periodically (as would be good security practice) is difficult as the new key must be communicated to all users and updated on all their devices.

PSK is the only type of authentication available for WLANs that use WEP encryption technology. It is also suitable for SOHO networks and workgroups that use WPA or WPA2 encryption.

ENTERPRISE

WPA and WPA2 can implement enterprise mode authentication, where the access point passes authentication information to a **Remote Authentication Dial-in User Service (RADIUS)** server for validation. This type of authentication is suitable for server-/domain-based networks.

COMMON SOHO SECURITY ISSUES

Although encryption and setting a strong passphrase are the most important factors in configuring effective Wi-Fi security, there are other configuration changes you may want to make. Here are some additional security problems and solutions.

SERVICE SET ID (SSID)

The **Service Set ID (SSID)** is a simple name (case sensitive 32-bit alphanumeric string) for users to identify the WLAN by. Vendors use default SSIDs for their products based on the device brand or model. You should change it to something that your users will recognize and will not get confused between nearby networks. Given that, on a residential network, you should not use an SSID that reveals personal information, such as an address or surname. Similarly, on a business network, you may not want to use a meaningful name. For example, an SSID like "Accounts" could prove tempting to would-be attackers.

Disabling broadcast of the SSID prevents any adapters not manually configured to connect to the name you specify from finding the network. This provides a margin of privacy.

> **Note:** *Hiding the SSID does not secure the network; you must enable encryption. Even when broadcast is disabled, the SSID can still be detected using packet sniffing tools.*

PHYSICAL SECURITY

On a business network, physical access to important network infrastructure like switches and routers should be restricted to administrators and technicians. Most devices are stored in a locked equipment room and may also be protected by lockable cabinets. Many devices can be reset to the factory configuration with physical access. This could allow someone to disrupt the network or gain access to administrative settings (though probably not without being noticed).

UPDATING FIRMWARE

You should keep the firmware and driver for the Internet appliance up-to-date with the latest patches. This is important to fix security holes and to support the latest security standards, such as WPA2. To perform a firmware update, download the update from the vendor's website, taking care to select the correct patch for your device make and model. Select the **Firmware Upgrade** option and browse for the firmware file you downloaded.

Make sure that power to the device is not interrupted during the update process.

Upgrading device firmware. (Screenshot courtesy of TP-Link.)

ASSIGNING STATIC IP ADDRESSES

Assigning static IP addresses means that the DHCP server is disabled and clients must be configured manually to join the network properly. It would be trivial for an attacker to identify the appropriate subnet so this is not something that would deter a determined attack.

Note that devices such as the router/modem must be configured with a static address because it acts as a DHCP server, and client devices need to use it as the default gateway.

LATENCY AND JITTER

Quality of Service (QoS) means using a network protocol to prioritize certain types of traffic over others.

Show
Slide(s)

Latency and Jitter

Many networks are now being pressed into service to provide two-way communications, with applications such as Voice over IP (VoIP), video conferencing, and multiplayer gaming. Applications such as voice and video that carry real-time data have different network requirements to the sort of data represented by file transfer. With "ordinary" data, it might be beneficial to transfer a file as quickly as possible, but the sequence in which the packets are delivered and variable intervals between packets arriving do not materially affect the application. This type of data transfer is described as "bursty." Network protocols such as HTTP, FTP, or email are very sensitive to packet loss but are tolerant to delays in delivery. The reverse is applicable to real-time applications; they can compensate for some amount of packet loss, but are very sensitive toward delays in data delivery.

Problems with the timing and sequence of packet delivery are defined as latency and jitter:

- **Latency** (Delay)—the time it takes for a signal to reach the recipient. A video application can support a latency of about 80 ms, while typical latency on the Internet can reach 1000 ms at peak times. Latency is a particular problem for 2-way applications, such as VoIP (telephone), online conferencing, and multiplayer gaming.
- **Jitter**—variation in the delay; often caused by congestion at routers and other internetwork devices or by configuration errors.

Real-time applications are sensitive to the effects of latency and jitter because they manifest as echo, delay, and video slow down. End users are generally very intolerant of these kinds of errors.

It is difficult to guarantee Quality of Service (QoS) over a public network such as the Internet. Enterprise networks can deploy sophisticated QoS and traffic engineering protocols on managed switches and routers. On a SOHO network, you may be able to configure a QoS or bandwidth control feature on the router/modem to prioritize the port used by a VoIP application over any other type of protocol. This will help to mitigate issues if, for example, one computer is trying to download a Windows 10 feature update at the same time as another set of computers are trying to host a video conference.

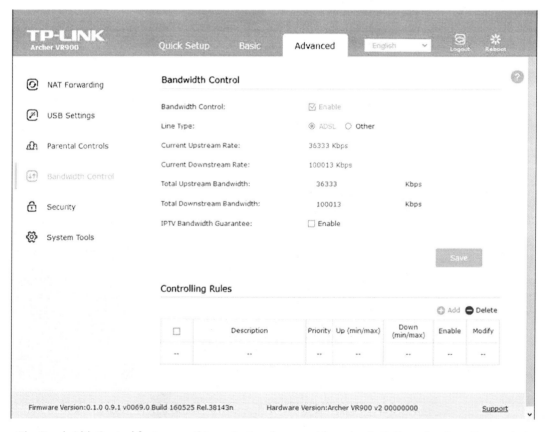

The Bandwidth Control feature on this router/modem provides a basic QoS mechanism. (Screenshot courtesy of TP-Link.)

Activity 9-3

Discussing SOHO Network Installation and Configuration

Show Slide(s)

Activity: Discussing SOHO Network Installation and Configuration

SCENARIO

Answer the following questions to check your understanding of the topic.

1. **What type of cable and connectors are used to connect a modem to a phone port?**

   Twisted pair with RJ-11 connectors. In the UK, the phone port might use a BT-style connector though.

2. **What is the function of a microfilter?**

   It screens noise from data signals on jacks for voice or fax devices if DSL equipment is connected.

3. **To configure a router/modem, what type of IP interface configuration should you apply to the computer you are using to access the device administration web app?**

   Set the adapter to obtain an IP address automatically. The router/modem will be running a Dynamic Host Configuration Protocol (DHCP) server that will allocate an appropriate IP address and DNS server.

4. **What is the effect of reducing transmit power when you are configuring an access point?**

   It reduces the supported range of the access point. You might do this to prevent interference between two access points in close proximity. You might also reduce power to prevent the network being accessible outside a particular area (such as making the network accessible to indoor users only).

5. **Which standard represents the best available wireless network security?**

   Wi-Fi Protected Access version 2 (WPA2). It is also worth noting that this can be configured in personal mode (using a passphrase shared between all users) or enterprise mode. Enterprise mode is more secure. Each user connects with his or her network credential, which is validated by an authentication server (typically RADIUS).

6. How can QoS improve performance for SOHO Internet access?

A Quality of Service (QoS) mechanism allows you to elevate certain types of traffic to a higher priority to be processed by the router/modem. For example, you could create a rule reserving 80% of bandwidth for a Voice over IP (VoIP) protocol. This means that whenever the VoIP application is active, other protocols can use only 20% of the router's link bandwidth, making it less likely that ordinary file downloads or web browsing will interfere with a call.

Activity 9-4

Installing and Configuring SOHO Networks

 Show Slide(s)

Activity: Installing and Configuring SOHO Networks

 Teaching Tip

The steps in this activity are written for Windows 10. Windows 7 users might need assistance, as the methods of managing networks are quite different.

BEFORE YOU BEGIN

Ideally, you would set up a mix of networks with different modes and frequencies. Experiment with using the same network name for 2.4 GHz and 5 GHz bands. Try setting up clashing network channels to see if there is any adverse effect.

If you do not have physical access points to use, consider asking learners to connect to an emulator, such as

- **https://www.cisco.com/assets/sol/sb/AP541N_GUI/AP541N_1_9_2/Getting_Started.htm**,
- **http://ui.linksys.com/**, **http://support.dlink.ca/emulators/wbr2310/index.htm**,
- **https://tools.netgear.com/landing/gui/wireless/wg102/simulators/wg102_v_1_0_31/start.htm**, or
- **https://www.tp-link.com/us/support/emulators**.

If the equipment is available, you will join a wireless network set up by your instructor, or you will configure your own wireless network as part of a group. Depending on the equipment available, you may receive either a dedicated access point or a multifunction router/modem/access point, or you might be asked to connect to a wireless access point emulator.

Use this table to record the wireless settings that your group will configure, or that your instructor will configure for you to connect to.

Option	2.4 GHz Band Settings	5 GHz Band Settings
SSID		
Mode/Compatibility		
Channel		
Security/Authentication Type		
Pre-shared Key/Password		

SCENARIO

In this activity, you will connect computers together in a wireless network, depending on the devices available in your learning environment.

---

1. If you have a physical wireless access point, reset it to the factory configuration, and then connect to the management interface.
   a) Connect the access point to a power source and switch it on.
   b) Unless you are advised otherwise by your instructor, press the access point's reset switch and hold for about 20 seconds (or as instructed) to apply the default configuration.

The reset switch will be a recessed button on the back of the access point. You might need to use a paper clip to press it.

c) Verify that the network adapter on your HOST computer is set to obtain an IP address automatically.

d) Disconnect the network cable from your HOST computer's network adapter. Connect an RJ-45 patch cable from the HOST computer's network adapter to one of the **LAN** or **Ethernet** ports on the access point.

e) If the network location banner appears prompting you to trust the network, select **Yes**.

f) Start a web browser, and open the device's management URL.

This may be printed on a sticker on the device.

g) If prompted, log in using the default user name and password.

Again, this may be printed on a sticker on the device.

h) If you are prompted to change the default user name and password, set the user name to *admin* and password to *Pa$$w0rd*

2. Configure the access point to use the settings suggested by your instructor (the ones you recorded in the table).

a) Locate the menu option for manual or advanced wireless settings.

In the environment shown in the following figure, you would select **Advanced→Wireless→Basic Settings**.

Teaching Tip

If the access point is dual band, learners can either use the same settings (SSID, encryption type, and passphrase) for each band or configure separate networks. Optionally, ask different groups to use different options.

Teaching Tip

The exact substeps shown in this step are for the TP-LINK AP300. If you are using a different wireless router, be prepared to guide learners on accessing the equivalent settings for their device.

Access point configuration. (Screenshot courtesy of TP-Link.)

 Note: *Your instructor will guide you through this activity if you are using a different wireless router than the one depicted in the previous screenshot.*

b) If there is an **Operation mode** option (as shown above), set it to **Access Point**.

The device may also support being configured as a repeater or bridge.

c) Enter the settings you recorded in the table, and then save the settings using the options appropriate for your configuration page. This might be a **Save** button, **Apply Changes** button, or something similar.

3. Install a wireless network adapter in your HOST computer.

Your instructor will provide you with a wireless network adapter. This may be a plug-in card or a USB device.

a) If your adapter has a setup-based install, run the **Setup** program to install the adapter driver software.

b) Physically connect the wireless adapter to the HOST computer.

- If you have a USB wireless adapter, connect it to a USB port.
- If you have a plug-in card, power off the PC, and remove all the cables. Follow instructions from your instructor to add the card to a spare slot, and then reassemble and restart the computer.

c) When the adapter is installed, restart Windows if necessary and wait for the adapter to be detected or for the **Device Setup** wizard to start.

d) If necessary, point to the location of the driver files, and follow any other prompts required to install the device and drivers.

4. When the adapter is physically installed, connect to the access point configured by the instructor or by your group.

a) In the notification area, select the network status icon.

b) If more than one network is detected, select the SSID associated with your access point, and select **Connect**.

c) Enter the network key and select **Next**.

d) If prompted, select **No** to set the network location as **Public**.

e) Open **File Explorer** and browse the **Network** object.

You should not see any computers listed, as the firewall settings for public networks prevent discovery.

f) Select the yellow **Network discovery is turned off** bar and select **Turn on network discovery and file sharing**.

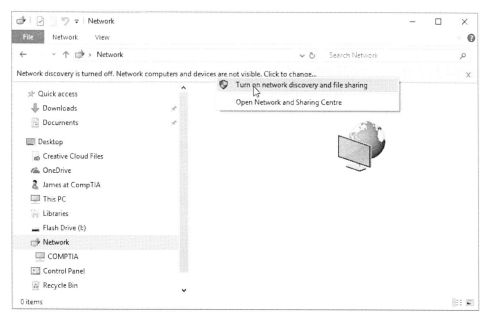

Click the bar to enable network discovery. (Screenshot used with permission from Microsoft.)

g) At the prompt, select **No, make the network that I am connected to a private network**.

    h)   Browse for other computers again.

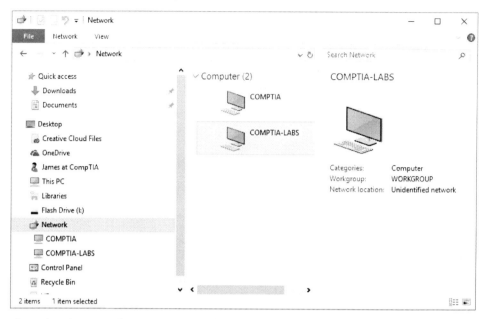

Browsing the network—two computers have joined this network (COMPTIA and COMPTIA-LABS). (Screenshot used with permission from Microsoft.)

5.   View the network properties using the **Settings** app.

    a)   Select the network status icon and select **Network & Internet Settings**.

    b)   In the **Settings** app, select **Wi-Fi**.

    c)   Select the network name.

        You can change the network location type here.

    d)   Scroll down the page to view the IP settings and connection properties, including the network band and channel.

    e)   Record the **Physical address (MAC)**.

    f)   Close the Settings app.

6.   View the Wi-Fi adapter's driver properties in Device Manager.

    a)   Right-click **Start** and select **Device Manager**.

    b)   Expand **Network adapters** and then right-click the wireless adapter and select **Properties**.

    c)   Select the **Advanced** tab.

    d)   Locate settings for preferred wireless mode and frequency. Are there options to set any of the following: **Transmit Power**, **QoS**, or **Wake-on-Wireless LAN**?

        Answers will vary depending on the wireless adapter.

    e)   Select **Cancel**.

7.   If you are managing an access point in your group, change the settings on the AP to use a different SSID, and ensure that it is not broadcast.

Option	2.4 GHz Band Settings	5 GHz Band Settings
SSID		
Mode/Compatibility		
Channel		
Security/Authentication Type		

Teaching Tip

Depending on features available on the wireless adapter, learners might not see these properties, or they might have different labels.

Teaching Tip

Assist learners in identifying the function of the different properties. Explain that the driver software may use different labels for these options. Note that some adapters come with more customizable properties than others.

Teaching Tip

If you are managing the access point, change the SSID and suppress broadcast. Change the passphrase as well.

Option	2.4 GHz Band Settings	5 GHz Band Settings
Pre-shared Key/ Password		

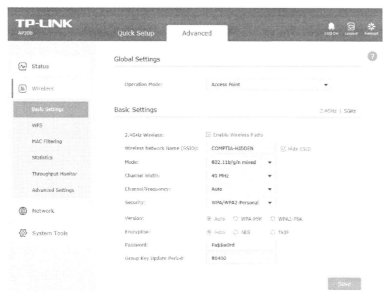

Setting the SSID to hidden. (Screenshot courtesy of TP-Link.)

8. When the AP has been reconfigured, manually connect to the wireless network.
- a) Select the network status icon and select **Network & Internet Settings**.
- b) In the **Settings** app, select **Wi-Fi**.
- c) Select the **Manage known networks** link.
- d) Select **Add a new network**.

e) Enter the network connection details. Make sure you check **Connect automatically** and **Connect even if this network is not broadcasting.**

Configuring a wireless network connection manually.

f) Select **Save**.

g) If you are prompted to enable discovery and file sharing, select **Yes**. If no prompt appears, enable network discovery via Explorer as you did before.

h) In Explorer, browse the network, and verify that other computers are visible.

9. Optionally, configure MAC filtering to prevent one of the stations in your group from connecting.

Configuring a MAC filter to blacklist stations. (Screenshot courtesy of TP-Link.)

10. At the end of the activity, if requested, uninstall the wireless adapter and return it to your instructor. Reconnect your computer to the classroom network.

Topic C
Configure SOHO Network Security

 EXAM OBJECTIVES COVERED
1001-2.2 Compare and contrast common networking hardware devices.
1001-2.3 Given a scenario, install and configure a basic wired/wireless SOHO network.
1002-1.5 Given a scenario, use Microsoft operating system features and tools.
1002-1.6 Given a scenario, use Microsoft Windows Control Panel utilities.
1002-1.8 Given a scenario, configure Microsoft Windows networking on a client/desktop.
1002-2.10 Given a scenario, configure security on SOHO wireless and wired networks.

 Teaching Tip

Both Core 1 and Core 2 exams require exam candidates to be familiar with firewall settings.

 Show Slide(s)

Firewalls (2 slides)

 Teaching Tip

The basic function of a firewall is traffic filtering. A firewall resembles a quality inspector on a production line; any bad units are knocked off the line and go no farther. The firewall processes traffic according to rules; traffic that does not conform to a rule that allows it access is blocked.

 Teaching Tip

More advanced firewalls (proxy and stateful inspection) can analyze data at a higher level (application, for instance).

Although security models stress the importance of defense in depth, the network edge must still be closely guarded. As a CompTIA A+ technician, you must be able to configure firewall settings and other types of access controls to ensure safe Internet use. In this topic, you will learn how to configure common security features of SOHO router/modems, use the Windows Firewall, and set browser options.

FIREWALLS

There are many types of **firewalls** and many ways of implementing them. One distinction can be made between network and host firewalls:

- **Network firewall**—placed inline in the network and inspects all traffic that passes through it.
- **Host firewall**—installed on the host and only inspects traffic addressed to that host.

Another distinction is what parts of a packet a firewall can inspect and operate on.

PACKET FILTERING FIREWALL

Packet filtering describes the earliest type of firewall. All firewalls can still perform this basic function. A **packet filtering** firewall can inspect the headers of IP packets. This means that rules can be based on the information found in those headers:

- IP filtering—accepting or blocking traffic on the basis of its source and/or destination IP address.
- Protocol ID/type—TCP, UDP, ICMP, and so on.
- Port filtering/security—accepting or blocking a packet on the basis of source and destination port numbers (TCP or UDP application type).

This configuration is referred to as an **Access Control List (ACL)**. The firewall may provide the option to accept all packets except for those on the reject list or, alternatively, it may provide the option to reject all packets except for those on the accept list. Generally, the latter is the best choice, since it is more secure and involves less configuration.

HOST FIREWALL

A host (or software or **personal firewall**) is one that is implemented as software on the individual host PC or server. This might be deployed instead of or in addition to the network firewall. As well as being able to filter traffic based on data in network packets (IP address and port number, for instance), a host-based firewall can be defined with rules for whether particular software programs and services (processes) or user accounts are allowed or denied access.

Having two firewalls is more secure; if one firewall is not working or is misconfigured, the other firewall might prevent an intrusion. The downside is complexity; you must configure rules in two places, and there are two things that could be blocking communications when you come to troubleshoot connections.

 Note: Using both a network firewall to secure the "perimeter" and a host firewall provides defense in depth. This is the concept that multiple, well-coordinated layers of defensive controls make a system harder to compromise than a single defensive barrier.

FIREWALL SETTINGS

Most Internet router/modems come with a basic firewall product; some come with quite sophisticated firewalls. On a SOHO network, it is more typical to filter incoming traffic than outgoing traffic. Some router/modems may not support outbound filtering at all.

 **Show Slide(s)**

Firewall Settings (2 slides)

DISABLING PORTS

One of the basic principles of secure configuration is only to enable services that must be enabled. If a service is unused, then it should not be accessible in any way. The most secure way of doing this is to remove the service on each host. There may be circumstances in which you want a service port to be available on the local network but not on the Internet. This is where a firewall is useful. If you configure an ACL to block the port, or if the port is blocked by the default rule, then Internet hosts will not be able to access it.

MAC FILTERING

The MAC is the hardware address of a network card, in the format aa:bb:cc:dd:ee:ff. Firewalls, switches, and access points can be configured either with whitelists of allowed MACs or blacklists of prohibited MACs. This can be time-consuming to set up and it is easy for malicious actors to spoof a MAC address. On a SOHO network, the security advantages are unlikely to outweigh configuration and troubleshooting issues.

CONTENT FILTERING/PARENTAL CONTROLS

Most Internet appliances also support the configuration of filters to block websites and services on the basis of keywords or site rating and classification services. Another option is to restrict the times at which the Internet is accessible. These are configured in conjunction with services offered by the ISP.

One issue for ISP-enforced parental controls is that the filters are not usually able to distinguish account types, so the filters apply to all Internet access unless the filtering is manually disabled, which requires the ISP account holder's password. Parental controls can also be enforced at the OS level in Windows 10, where different filters can be applied based on the account type.

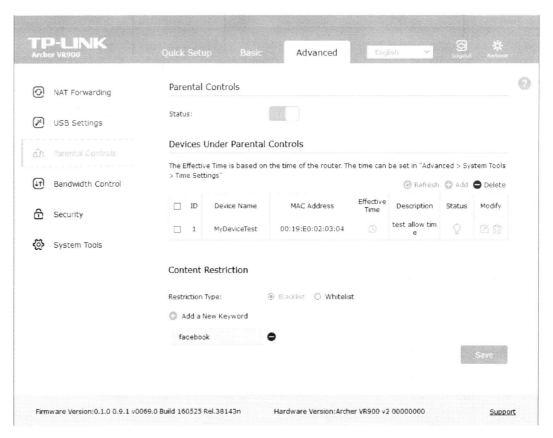

Configuring parental controls to restrict when certain devices can access the network. (Screenshot courtesy of TP-Link.)

WHITELISTS/BLACKLISTS

Content filtering works on the basis of **blacklists** of URLs that are known to harbor a particular type of content. There will be separate blacklists for different types of content that users might want to block. There are also blacklists of sites known to host malware. The firewall will block any IP address or domain name appearing on a blacklist for which a filter has been configured.

Conversely, **whitelisting** a site means that it will be accessible even if a filter is applied. If you want to lock down Internet usage very tightly, it should be possible to configure a filter so that only whitelisted sites are accessible.

NAT

Show Slide(s)

NAT

All router/modems implement **Network Address Translation (NAT)**. More specifically, they implement **Network Address Port Translation (NAPT)**, which is also referred to as NAT overloading or **Port Address Translation (PAT)**. The router/modem is issued with a single public IP address by the ISP. Some ISPs might allocate a static address, but it is more common for it to be dynamic (issued by the ISP's DHCP server).

Hosts connected to the router/modem's switch or access point are configured with local (private) addresses, typically in the range 192.168.0.0/24 or 192.168.1.0/24. When one of these devices tries to contact a host on the Internet, the router identifies the connection using an ephemeral port number, adds the original private IP address and port number to a NAT table, and sends the transmission to the Internet host, using its public IP address and the new port number. When (or if) an Internet host replies to that port, the router looks up the port number in the NAT table, locates the original IP address and port, and forwards the response to the local device.

NAT overloading on a SOHO router/modem generally works without any configuration. There might be an option to configure an Application Layer Gateway (ALG) for one or more protocols. NAT can pose problems for some types of protocol. ALG mitigates these problems by opening ports dynamically to allow connections.

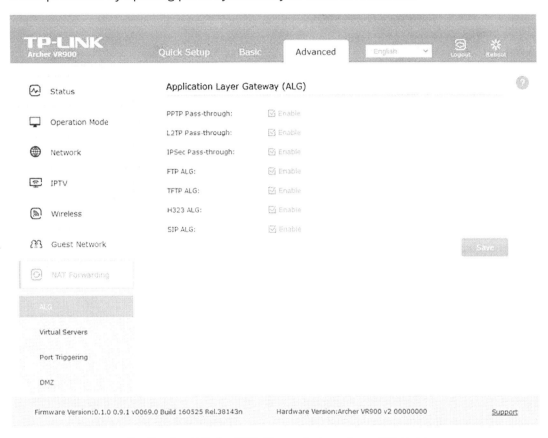

Configuring ALGs for NAT. (Screenshot courtesy of TP-Link.)

PORT FORWARDING AND PORT TRIGGERING

When NAT overloading is deployed, hosts on the Internet can only "see" the router and its public IP address. If you want to run some sort of server application from your network and make it accessible to the Internet, you need to set up port forwarding or Destination NAT (DNAT).

Port forwarding means that the router takes requests from the Internet for a particular protocol (say, HTTP/port 80) and sends them to a designated host on the LAN. The request could also be sent to a different port, so this feature is often also called port mapping. For example, the Internet host could request HTTP on port 80, but the LAN server might run its HTTP server on port 8080 instead.

Show Slide(s)

Port Forwarding and Port Triggering

Interaction Opportunity

Ask learners if they have ever configured port forwarding on their home networks. What did they use it for? Were there any problems?

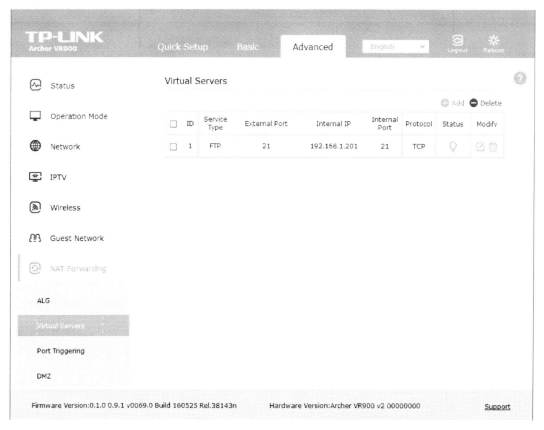

Configuring port forwarding for FTP. (Screenshot courtesy of TP-Link.)

Port triggering is used to set up applications that require more than one port. Basically, when the firewall detects activity on outbound port A destined for a given external IP address, it opens inbound access for the external IP address on port B for a set period.

DMZ

Show Slide(s)

DMZ

When making a server accessible on the Internet, careful thought needs to be given to the security of the local network. A simple firewall with port forwarding will only support servers on the local network. There can only be one set of access rules. If a server is compromised, because it is on the local network there is the possibility that other LAN hosts can be attacked from it or that the attacker could examine traffic passing over the LAN.

In an enterprise network, a **Demilitarized Zone (DMZ)** is a means of establishing a more secure configuration. The idea of a DMZ is that hosts placed within it are untrusted by the local network zone. Some traffic may be allowed to pass between the DMZ and the local network, but no traffic is allowed to pass from the Internet to the local network through the DMZ.

Most SOHO routers come with only basic firewall functionality. The firewall in a typical SOHO router screens the local network, rather than establishing a DMZ.

However, you should note that many SOHO router/modem vendors use the term "DMZ" or "DMZ host" to refer to a computer on the LAN that is configured to receive communications for any ports that have not been forwarded to other hosts. When DMZ is used in this sense, it means "not protected by the firewall" as the host is fully accessible to other Internet hosts (though it could be installed with a host firewall instead). This also means that the LAN is still exposed to the risks described previously.

Configuring a SOHO router version of a DMZ—the host 192.168.1.254 will not be protected by the firewall. (Screenshot courtesy of TP-Link.)

UNIVERSAL PLUG-AND-PLAY

ACLs and port forwarding/port triggering are challenging for end users to configure correctly. Many users would simply resort to turning the firewall off in order to get a particular application to work. As a means of mitigating this attitude, services that require complex firewall configuration can use the **Universal Plug-and-Play (UPnP)** framework to send instructions to the firewall with the correct configuration parameters.

On the firewall, check the box to enable UPnP. A client UPnP device, such as an Xbox, PlayStation, or Voice-over-IP handset, will be able to configure the firewall automatically to open the IP addresses and ports necessary to play an online game or place and receive VoIP calls.

Show Slide(s)

Universal Plug-and-Play

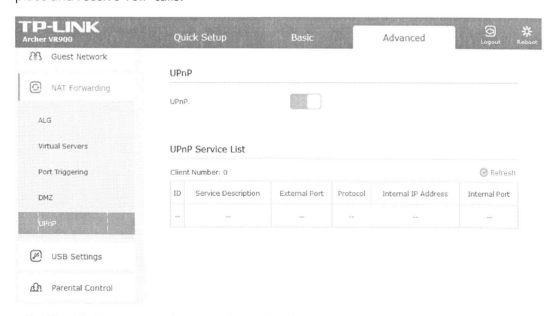

Enabling UPnP—there is nothing to configure, but when client devices use the service, the rules they have configured on the firewall are shown in the service list. (Screenshot courtesy of TP-Link.)

UPnP is associated with a number of security vulnerabilities and is best disabled if not required. You should ensure that the router does not accept UPnP configuration requests from the external (Internet) interface. If using UPnP, keep up-to-date with any security advisories or firmware updates from the router manufacturer.

> *Note: Also make sure that UPnP is disabled on client devices, unless you have confirmed that the implementation is secure. As well as game consoles, vulnerabilities have been found in UPnP running on devices such as printers and web cams.*

Windows Firewall (2 slides)

WINDOWS FIREWALL

As well as configuring the network firewall, you may want to configure a personal firewall on each host. Windows ships with bundled firewall software.

> *Note: There are also third-party firewalls. If you install another firewall product, it should disable Windows Firewall. Do not try to run two host firewalls at the same time. The products may interfere with one another and attempting to keep the ACLs synchronized between them will be extremely challenging.*

CONFIGURING WINDOWS FIREWALL

To configure the firewall in Windows 7, open **Windows Firewall** in Control Panel to view a status page, then click **Turn Windows Firewall on or off**. The Windows Firewall can be turned on or off depending on whether the network location is private (home/work) or public or domain. For example, you could have an Internet connection through an open access point set to public with a VPN to your corporate network running over the link, but set to domain.

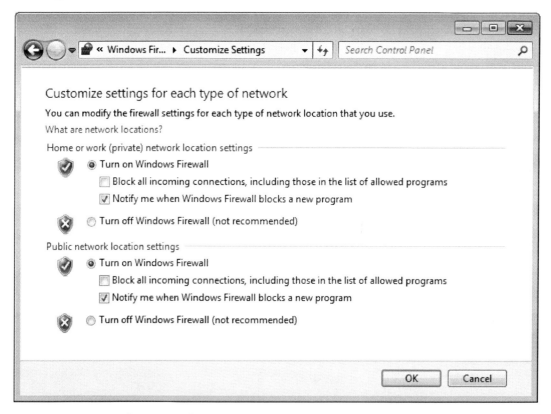

Customizing Windows Firewall settings in Windows 7. (Screenshot used with permission from Microsoft.)

CONFIGURING EXCEPTIONS

To allow or block programs (configure exceptions), from the **Windows Firewall** status page, click **Allow a program or feature through the Windows Firewall**. Check the box for either or both network type or use **Allow another program** to locate its executable file and add it to the list.

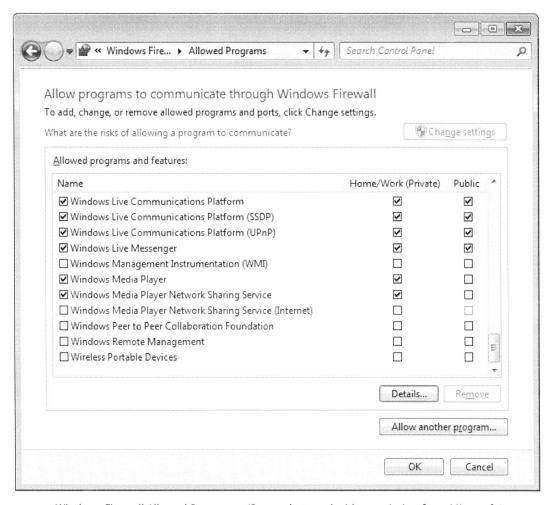

Windows Firewall Allowed Programs. (Screenshot used with permission from Microsoft.)

WINDOWS DEFENDER SECURITY CENTER

In Windows 10, you can turn the firewall on or off and access the configuration applets shown previously via the **Firewall & network protection** page in the Windows Defender Security Center.

WINDOWS FIREWALL WITH ADVANCED SECURITY

An add-in to the basic firewall (Windows Firewall with Advanced Security) allows configuration of outbound filtering, as well as IPsec connection security and additional monitoring tools.

The Advanced Firewall can be configured through group policy on a domain; on a standalone PC or workgroup, open the `wf.msc` management console (or enter "firewall" at the Search box or use the **Advanced settings** link in the Windows Firewall Control Panel applet). On the status page, you can click **Windows Firewall properties** to configure each profile. The firewall can be turned on or off and you can switch the default rule for inbound and outbound traffic between **Block** and **Allow**.

You can also set which network adapters are linked to a profile and configure logging.

Show Slide(s)
Windows Firewall with Advanced Security (2 slides)

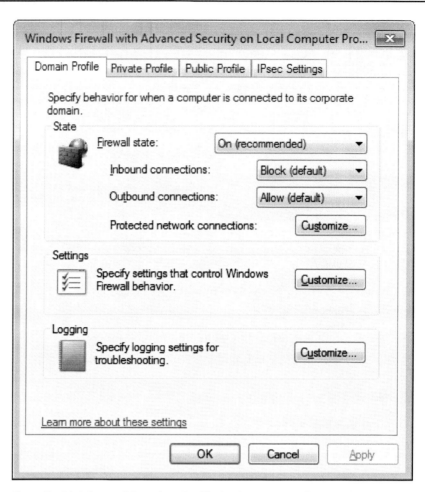

Windows Firewall with Advanced Security—Profile Settings. (Screenshot used with permission from Microsoft.)

 Note: Block stops traffic unless a specific rule allows it. Conversely, Allow accepts all traffic unless a specific rule blocks it. You can also use Block all connections to stop inbound connections regardless of the rules set up.

Back in the main Advanced Firewall console, you enable, disable, and configure rules by clicking in the **Inbound Rules** or **Outbound Rules** folder as appropriate. Rules can be based on a number of triggers, including program, Windows Feature, service, protocol type, network port, and IP address range.

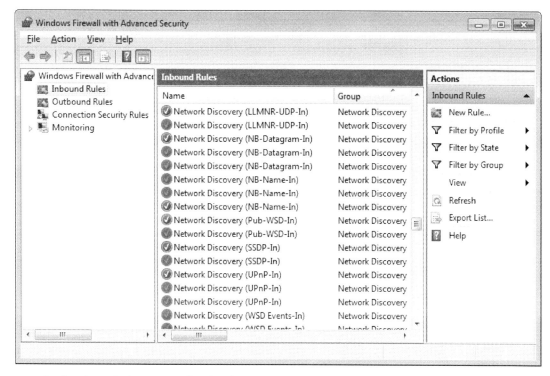

Configuring Windows Firewall with Advanced Security. (Screenshot used with permission from Microsoft.)

LOCATION AWARENESS

Different Windows Firewall settings can be applied depending on the network to which the PC is connected. When Windows 7 detects a new network (wired, wireless, dial-up, or VPN), the **Set Network Location** dialog box is displayed.

You can make the following choices:

- **Home**—enables network discovery (the ability to contact other computers on the network) and the use of homegroups.
- **Work**—enables network discovery.
- **Public**—disables network discovery and file sharing.
- **Domain**—you cannot choose this option, but if the computer is joined to a domain, then the firewall policy will be configured via Group Policy.

Show Slide(s)

Location Awareness (2 slides)

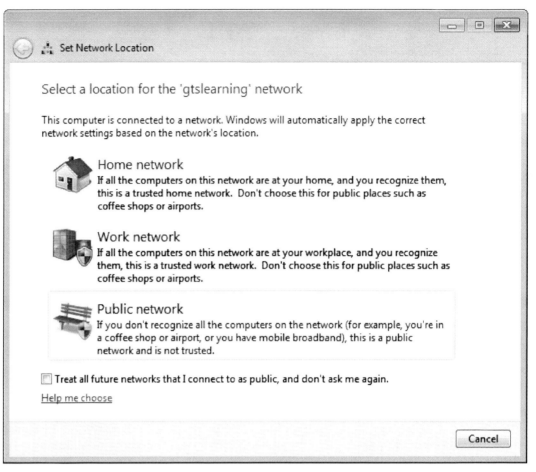

Set Network Location dialog box. (Screenshot used with permission from Microsoft.)

To change the location defined for a network, open the **Network and Sharing Center**. Click the network location label under the network name.

In Windows 8 and Windows 10, the concept of home and work networks has been discarded. Networks are either public or private depending on whether you choose to enable discovery and file sharing or not. If the computer is joined to a domain, then the network type will be set to domain.

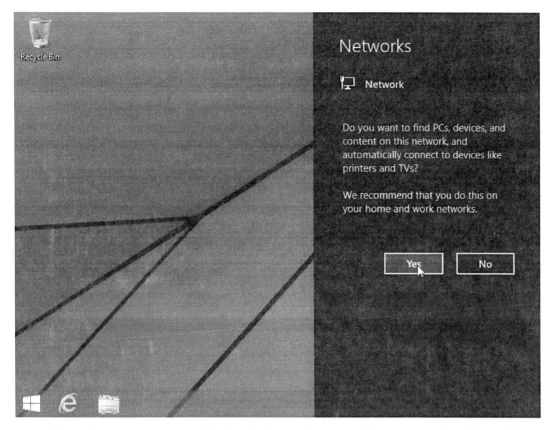

Setting network location type in Windows 8. (Screenshot used with permission from Microsoft.)

You can subsequently change the setting via the **Settings** app.

BROWSER CONFIGURATION

The browser has become one of the most important bits of software on a computer. As well as actual web browsing, it is frequently used as the interface for many types of web applications. The basic browser is also often extended by plug-ins that run other types of content. Internet Explorer (IE) used to be completely dominant in the browser market, but alternatives such as Google's Chrome™ and Mozilla's Firefox® now have substantial market share. This section describes the **Internet Options** applet for Internet Explorer®, but similar settings can be configured for other versions and browsers.

 Note: In fact, in Windows 10, the Internet Explorer browser is replaced by the Edge browser. IE is still available in Windows 10, but its use is deprecated.

GENERAL TAB

The main functions of the **General** tab are to configure home pages (pages that load when the browser is started) and manage browsing history. On a public computer, it is best practice to clear the browsing history at the end of a session. You can configure the browser to do this automatically.

 Show Slide(s)
Browser Configuration (7 slides)

 Teaching Tip
Make sure that learners know their way around these configuration screens.

This course focuses on IE because the exam objectives list the associated Control Panel applet as a content example. Consider asking learners to view the configuration settings for other browsers, such as **about:preferences** in Firefox or **chrome:// settings** in Chrome.

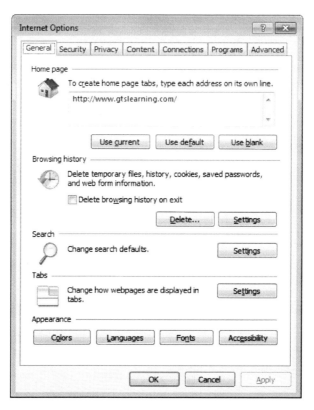

Internet Options—General tab. (Screenshot used with permission from Microsoft.)

 Note: *You can also start an "In Private" mode session by pressing **Ctrl+Shift+P**. This mode disables browsing history, cookies, and browser toolbars and extensions.*

CONNECTIONS TAB AND PROXY SETTINGS

The **Connections** tab sets the method Internet Explorer uses to connect to the Internet.

- To use a dial-up connection, select either **Dial whenever a network connection is not present** or **Always dial my default connection**. You would typically select the former option for a laptop computer that connects via the LAN in the office but a modem elsewhere. If the connection selected in the **Dial-up Settings** box is not the default, click **Set Default**.

- To use a router, you simply need to configure the Default gateway and DNS server parameters in TCP/IP properties for the local network adapter (though more typically, this would be configured automatically using DHCP). The browser will use this connection when you select **Never dial a connection** or **Dial whenever a network connection is not present**.

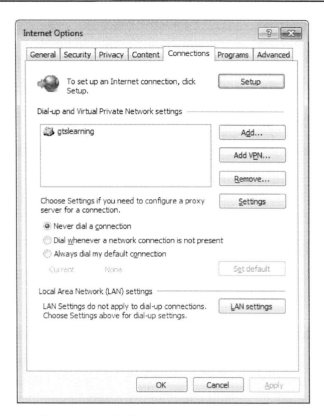

Internet Options—Connections tab. (Screenshot used with permission from Microsoft.)

On some networks, a proxy may be used to provide network connectivity. A proxy server can be used to improve both performance and security. User machines pass Internet requests to the proxy server, which forwards them to the Internet. The proxy may also cache pages and content that is requested by multiple clients, reducing bandwidth. The proxy may be able to autoconfigure the browser but if not, its address must be configured manually. Select the **LAN Settings** button to do this.

Local Area Network (LAN) Settings dialog box. (Screenshot used with permission from Microsoft.)

Note: *In Windows 10, use the* **Settings→Network & Internet→Proxy** *configuration page.*

SECURITY TAB

The **Security** tab is designed to prevent malicious content hosted on web pages from infecting the computer or stealing personal information.

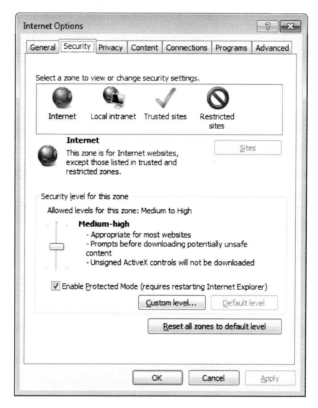

Internet Options—Security tab. (Screenshot used with permission from Microsoft.)

There are lots of security settings, configuring things such as whether scripts and plug-ins are allowed to run or install, files to download, and so on.

Internet Explorer operates a system of zones, each with different security settings. Everything off the local subnet is in the Internet zone by default; the user (or a domain's group policy) can add particular sites to the **Trusted** and **Restricted** zones as appropriate. The settings for a particular zone can also be changed using the **Custom Level** button.

PRIVACY TAB

The main function of the **Privacy** tab is to control sites' use of cookies. A cookie is a text file used to store session data. For example, if you log on to a site, the site might use a cookie to remember who you are. If the site is prevented from setting these cookies, it may not work correctly. On the other hand, a modern website might host components from many different domains. These components might try to set third-party cookies, most often to track pages you have been visiting and display relevant advertising at you.

You can use the slider to set the default policy for the Internet zone and use the **Sites** button to always block or allow cookies from particular domains.

The **Privacy** tab also allows you to configure the Pop-up Blocker, which prevents sites from spawning new windows through scripting.

Internet Options—Privacy tab. (Screenshot used with permission from Microsoft.)

PROGRAMS TAB

You can use the **Programs** tab to check whether IE is the default browser.

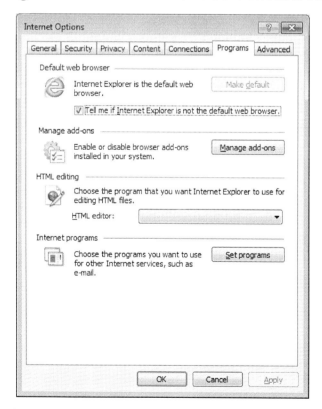

Internet Options—Programs tab. (Screenshot used with permission from Microsoft.)

Click **Set programs** to open the **Default Programs** applet to make another browser the default. You can also manage add-ons from here. Add-ons are code objects that extend the functionality of the browser. Examples include toolbars, malware scanners, content players (such as Adobe® Flash® player), and document readers (such as PDF viewers). **Manage add-ons** lets you disable or uninstall these objects.

ADVANCED TAB

The **Advanced** tab contains settings that do not fit under any of the other tabs.

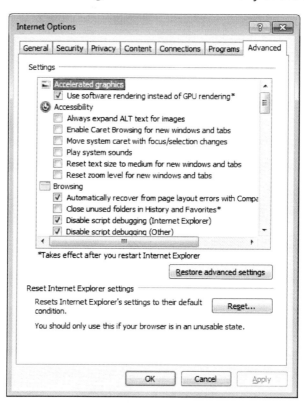

Internet Options—Advanced tab. (Screenshot used with permission from Microsoft.)

Some notable options include:

- Disable certain types of content (pictures,for instance).
- Enable a script debugger.
- Enable or disable passive FTP.
- Allow or prevent active content from running on local computer drives.

You can also use this tab to completely reset the browser.

Activity 9-5

Discussing SOHO Network Security

Show Slide(s)
Activity: Discussing SOHO Network Security

SCENARIO

Answer the following questions to check your understanding of the topic.

1. **True or false? A firewall can be configured to block hosts with selected IP address ranges from connecting to a particular TCP port on a server that is available to hosts in other IP address ranges.**

   True. A firewall's access control entry ruleset can combine any supported criteria.

2. **What sort of configuration options are available to apply parental controls, as opposed to packet filtering via a firewall?**

   You can set restrictions to block access at times of the day or night. You can blacklist web addresses (URLs), optionally on the basis of site rating schemes. You may also be able to block access on the basis of keyword filtering.

3. **What security method could you use to allow only specific hosts to connect to a SOHO router/modem?**

   You could configure a whitelist of permitted Media Access Control (MAC) addresses.

4. A user wants to be able to access an FTP server installed on a computer on their home network from the Internet. The home network is connected to the Internet by a DSL router.

   How would you enable access?

   Configure port forwarding on the router to send incoming connections on port 21 to the LAN computer.

5. You are setting up a games console on a home network.

   What feature on the router will simplify configuration of online multiplayer gaming?

   Universal Plug and Play (UPnP).

6. **True or false? To allow a PC game to accept incoming connections over a custom port you need to configure the Advanced Security Firewall.**

   False. You can allow a process to connect via the basic firewall interface.

7. **What option on the General tab of the Internet Options dialog box is most relevant to user privacy?**

   Delete browsing history.

8. **How would you configure a Windows 7 computer to use a proxy server for web browsing?**

   Open the **Internet Options** dialog box, and select the **Connections** tab. Select **LAN Settings** and enter the address of the proxy.

Topic D

Configure Remote Access

EXAM OBJECTIVES COVERED

1001-2.1 Compare and contrast TCP and UDP ports, protocols, and their purposes.
1002-1.5 Given a scenario, use Microsoft operating system features and tools.
1002-1.8 Given a scenario, configure Microsoft Windows networking on a client/desktop.
1002-4.9 Given a scenario, use remote access technologies.

A remote access utility allows you to establish a session on another computer on the network. There are command-line and GUI remote access tools. These are very useful for technical support and troubleshooting. The fact that remote access is so useful shows how important it is that such tools be used securely. In this topic, you will learn about the features of different remote access tools and security considerations of using each one.

WINDOWS REMOTE ACCESS TOOLS

Windows comes with several remote access features. Two of the GUI remote tools are Remote Desktop and Remote Assistance. These use some of the same underlying technologies but suit different purposes.

REMOTE DESKTOP

Remote Desktop allows a remote user to connect to their desktop machine. The desktop machine functions as a terminal server and the dial-in machine as a Windows terminal. This allows the user to work as if physically connected to their workstation.

This would ideally suit laptop users working from home with a slow link. Having gained access to the corporate network (via the Internet using a VPN, for example) they could then establish a remote desktop connection to their own office-based system. A technician can also use Remote Desktop to configure or troubleshoot a computer.

Remote Desktop runs on TCP port 3389.

 Note: Windows Home editions do not include the Remote Desktop server so you cannot connect to them, but they do include the client so you can connect to other computers from them.

REMOTE ASSISTANCE

Remote Assistance allows a user to ask for help from a technician or co-worker. The "helper" can then connect and join the session with the user. This session can include an interactive desktop, whereby the helper can control the system of the user.

Remote Assistance assigns a port dynamically from the ephemeral range (49152 to 65535). This makes it difficult to configure through firewalls, but remote assistance is designed more for local network support anyway.

REMOTE SETTINGS CONFIGURATION

By default, Remote Assistance connections are allowed but Remote Desktop ones are not. To change these settings, open **System Properties** then click **Remote settings**.

Teaching Tip

As with a lot of the networking objectives, SSH, Telnet, and RDP appear on both the Core 1 and Core 2 exams.

Show Slide(s)

Windows Remote Access Tools

Teaching Tip

There are many third-party remote access tools optimized for use over the web.

Show Slide(s)

Remote Settings Configuration

Teaching Tip

Describe the function of Network Level Authentication. This forces the client to authenticate before starting a session on the server (preventing a Denial of Service attack whereby multiple false sessions are created).

If NLA is enabled on the server, legacy RDP clients will not be able to connect.

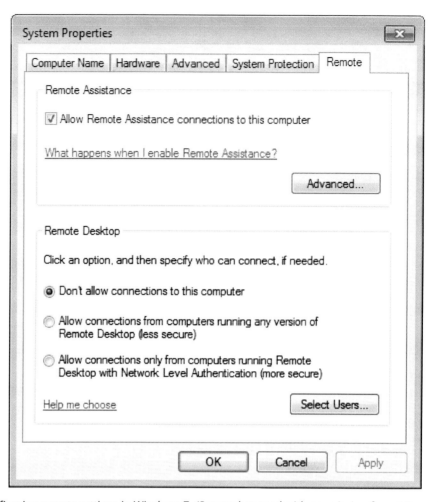

Configuring remote settings in Windows 7. (Screenshot used with permission from Microsoft.)

You can choose between allowing older RDP clients to connect and requiring RDP clients that support **Network Level Authentication (NLA)**. NLA protects the computer against Denial of Service attacks. Without NLA, the system configures a desktop before the user logs on. A malicious user can create multiple pending connections in an attempt to crash the system. NLA authenticates the user before committing any resources to the session.

RDP authentication and session data is always encrypted. This means that a malicious user with access to the same network cannot intercept credentials or interfere or capture anything transmitted during the session.

Click the **Select (Remote) Users** button to define which users can connect remotely. Users in the local administrators group already have this property. You can select from members of the local accounts database or from the domain of which your machine is a member.

Note: The biggest limitation of Remote Desktop on Windows is that only one person can be logged in to the machine at once, so once you log in using Remote Desktop, the monitor at the local computer will go to the login screen. If a local user logs in, the remote user will be disconnected. Remote Desktop is not really a remote diagnostic and troubleshooting tool as much as a management tool.

Show Slide(s)
Remote Credential Guard

REMOTE CREDENTIAL GUARD

If Remote Desktop is used to connect to a machine that has been compromised by malware, the credentials of the user account used to make the connection become highly vulnerable. **RDP Restricted Admin (RDPRA) Mode** and **Remote Credential Guard** are means of mitigating this risk. You can read more about these technologies at **docs.microsoft.com/en-us/windows/security/identity-protection/remote-credential-guard**.

THE REMOTE ASSISTANCE PROCESS

A request for remote assistance is made using the **Windows Remote Assistance** tool. You can send an invitation as a file, via email, or using Easy Connect. The tool will generate a password and a connection file for you to transmit to the helper.

To provide assistance, open the invitation file and enter the password and wait for the user to accept the offer of assistance. When the offer is accepted, a remote desktop window is opened with an additional chat tool that you can use to communicate with the user.

Remote Assistance sessions are encrypted using the same technologies as RDP.

Show Slide(s)
The Remote Assistance Process

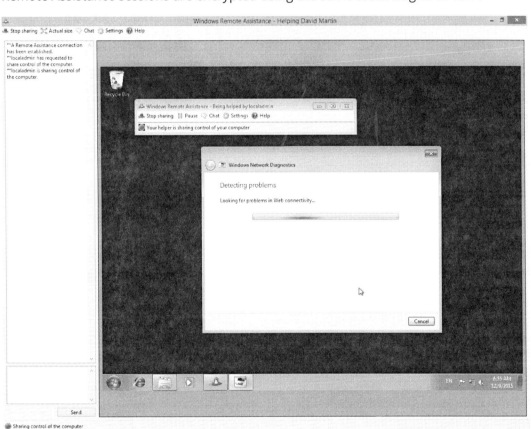

Using Remote Assistance. (Screenshot used with permission from Microsoft.)

REMOTE DESKTOP

To connect to a server via Remote Desktop, from the **Communications** menu in **Accessories**, open the **Remote Desktop Connection** shortcut, or run `mstsc` at a command prompt or the **Run** dialog box or **Instant Search** box. Enter the server's computer name or IP address to connect. The server can be installed with a certificate to identify it securely.

Show Slide(s)
Remote Desktop

Teaching Tip
Remind learners that a remote desktop server can be any type of Windows computer. "Server" here doesn't have to mean a server-class computer; it can include a desktop PC or laptop.

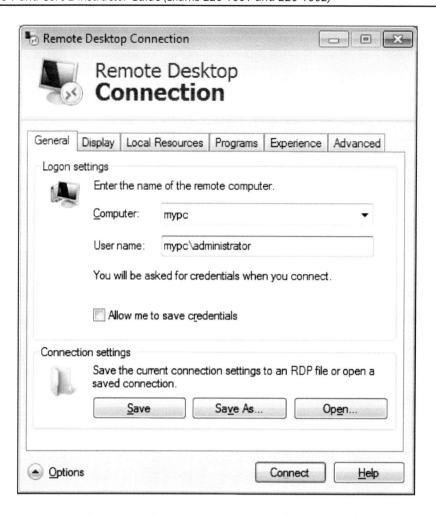

Remote Desktop Connection client. (Screenshot used with permission from Microsoft.)

You will need to define logon credentials. To specify a domain or computer account, use the format *ComputerOrDomainName\UserName*. In addition, you might need to define display properties. You can use either full screen or some windowed display. Also, you can configure the quality of the color scheme. The **Local Resources** tab allows you to define how key combinations (such as **Alt+Tab**) function—that is, will they affect the local computer, the remote computer, or the remote computer in full screen mode. Because the connection may be over a slow link, such as dial-up, you can configure optimization based on the line speeds (modem, LAN, and so on). This affects bitmap caching and video options.

Once you have your remote desktop connection established, you can work quite normally, as if physically adjacent to the target machine—but be aware that no one else can use the target system while in remote mode. The system becomes locked and can be unlocked by the administrator or the remotely connected user only.

REMOTE ACCESS TECHNOLOGIES

Show Slide(s)

Remote Access Technologies

Remote Desktop and Remote Assistance are technologies for Windows networks. There are versions of the `mstsc` client software for Linux®, macOS®, iOS®, and Android™ so you can use devices running those operating systems to connect to an RDP server running on a Windows machine.

Other protocols and software tools are available for accepting incoming connections to non-Windows devices.

TELNET

Telnet is a command-line terminal emulation protocol and program. The host server runs a Telnet daemon listening for connections on TCP port 23. The client system runs a Telnet program to send commands to the daemon. When you connect, your computer acts as if your keyboard is attached to the remote computer and you can use the same commands as a local user.

 Note: Telnet sends all messages in clear text. Anyone able to intercept ("sniff") network traffic would be able to see the passwords for accounts.

If you enter `telnet` at a command prompt, some of the basic commands you can use are listed in the following table.

Command	Use
`open HostPort`	Starts a session with the host on that port. Host can be a host name, FQDN, or IP address.
`?`	Displays help.
`status`	Check session status.
`close`	Ends the current session.
`quit`	Exits the telnet prompt.

Telnet is sometimes still used for troubleshooting services such as SMTP or HTTP. For example, to connect to an SMTP server at the IP address 192.168.1.2, you would enter `telnet 192.168.1.2 25`.

Telnet session with an SMTP server. (Screenshot used with permission from Microsoft.)

Another application of Telnet is router or switch configuration. The Telnet application is used to connect to the Telnet Daemon on the router and then command-line instructions can be issued to configure it.

 Note: Telnet is not installed by default in Windows. You can add it using Programs and Features. On a Windows network, you are more likely to use Windows Remote Shell (WinRS), which has better functionality and security features.

 Show Slide(s)
Telnet (2 slides)

 Teaching Tip
Point out that Telnet is unlikely to be used on a modern network. The security risks are too high.

Explain that "daemon" is a UNIX/Linux term for service or background process. The server process is usually appended with a "d" to indicate this.

For example `sshd` is the Secure Shell server while `ssh` is the client command.

SSH

Secure Shell (SSH) is designed to replace unsecure administration and file copy programs such as Telnet and FTP. SSH uses TCP port 22 (by default). SSH uses encryption to protect each session. There are numerous commercial and open source SSH products available for all the major OS platforms (UNIX, Linux, Windows, and macOS).

SSH servers are identified by a public/private key pair (the host key). A mapping of host names to public keys can be kept manually by each SSH client or there are various enterprise software products designed for SSH key management.

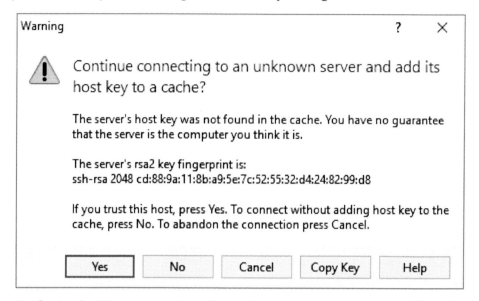

Confirming the SSH server's host key. (Screenshot used with permission from Microsoft.)

SSH CLIENT AUTHENTICATION

The server's host key is used to set up a secure channel to use for the client to submit authentication credentials. SSH allows various methods for the client to authenticate to the SSH server. Each of these methods can be enabled or disabled as required on the server:

- Username/password—the client submits credentials that are verified by the SSH server either against a local user database or using an authentication server.
- Kerberos—this allows Single Sign On (SSO) on a network that runs the Kerberos authentication protocol. Windows Active Directory domain networks use Kerberos.
- Host-based authentication—the server is configured with a list of authorized client public keys. The client requests authentication using one of these keys and the server generates a challenge with the public key. The client must use the matching private key it holds to decrypt the challenge and complete the authentication process. This provides non-interactive login but there is considerable risk from intrusion if a client host's private key is compromised.

 Note: With host-based authentication, managing valid client public keys is a critical security task. Many recent attacks on web servers have exploited poor key management.

- Public key authentication—host-based authentication cannot be used with fine-grained access controls as the access is granted to a single user account. The same sort of public key authentication method can be used for each user account. The user's private key can be configured with a passphrase that must be input to access the key, providing an additional measure of protection compared to host-based authentication.

SCREEN SHARING AND VNC

In macOS, you can use the Screen Sharing feature for remote desktop functionality. Screen Sharing is based on **Virtual Network Computing (VNC)**. You can use any VNC client to connect to a Screen Sharing server.

VNC itself is a freeware product with similar functionality to RDP. It works over TCP port 5900. Freeware versions of VNC provide no connection security and so should only be used over a secure connection, such as a VPN. However, there are commercial products packaged with encryption solutions. macOS Screen Sharing is encrypted.

Show Slide(s)

Screen Sharing and VNC

FILE SHARE

Setting up a network file share can be relatively complex. You need to select a file sharing protocol that all the connecting hosts can use, configure permissions on the share, and provision user accounts that both the server and client recognize. Consequently OS vendors have developed other mechanisms for simple file sharing between devices.

Show Slide(s)

File Share

- AirDrop®—supported by Apple iOS and macOS, this uses Bluetooth® to establish a Wi-Fi Direct connection between the devices for the duration of the file transfer. The connection is secured by the Bluetooth pairing mechanism and Wi-Fi encryption.
- Near Share—Microsoft's version of AirDrop. Near Share was introduced in Windows 10 (1803), partly replacing the previous Homegroup feature.

There are plenty of third-party and open source alternatives to AirDrop.

Although the products have security mechanisms, there is the potential for misuse of features such as this. Users accepting connections from any source could receive unsolicited transfer requests. It is best only to accept requests from known contacts. The products can be subject to security vulnerabilities that allow unsolicited transfers.

Activity 9-6

Discussing Remote Access Configuration

Show Slide(s)

Activity: Discussing Remote Access Configuration

SCENARIO

Answer the following questions to check your understanding of the topic.

1. **Which edition(s) of Windows support connecting to the local machine over Remote Desktop?**

   The Remote Desktop server functionality is available in Professional, Enterprise, and Ultimate editions.

2. **What is the goal of RDP Restricted Admin (RDPRA) Mode and Remote Credential Guard?**

   If the local machine is compromised, malware may be able to obtain the credentials of a user account connecting to the machine over Remote Desktop. RDPRA Mode and Remote Credential Guard are designed to mitigate this risk.

3. **True or false? SSH is not available for use with Windows.**

   False. Support for an SSH client and server is being included in feature updates to Windows 10, and there are numerous commercial and open source products.

4. **How can you confirm that you are connecting to a legitimate SSH server?**

   The server displays its host key on connection. You need to keep a record of valid host keys and compare the key presented by the server to the record you have.

Topic E

Troubleshoot Network Connections

EXAM OBJECTIVES COVERED

1001-2.8 Given a scenario, use appropriate networking tools.
1001-5.7 Given a scenario, troubleshoot common wired and wireless network problems.
1002-1.4 Given a scenario, use appropriate Microsoft command line tools.
1002-3.1 Given a scenario, troubleshoot Microsoft Windows OS problems.

As a CompTIA A+ technician, you will be expected to be able to troubleshoot basic network connectivity issues. At this support level, you will be focusing on client issues. As you have learned, networks are complex and involve many different hardware devices, protocols, and applications, meaning that there are lots of things that can go wrong! In this topic you will learn how to identify and diagnose the causes of some common wired and wireless network issues.

COMMON WIRED NETWORK CONNECTIVITY ISSUES

When troubleshooting a network issue, it is often a good idea to rule out any problem with connectivity at the hardware layer. If a single host is unable to connect to the network, the first thing you should check is whether the network cable is properly connected. If the problem is not that obvious, then there are a few other tools you can use to diagnose a problem with network hardware (adapters and cabling).

TROUBLESHOOTING WIRED CONNECTIVITY

To diagnose a cable problem, perform a basic local connectivity test using the `ping` utility (discussed later) with a known working system on the local subnet. If you can ping another local system, the problem is not in the cabling (at least, not this cable).

If you can't ping anything then, assuming you've physically checked the back of the machine for the cable's presence, verify that the patch cord is good. The easiest thing to do is swap the patch cord to the wall socket with another—known working—cable.

Can you ping anything now? If not, verify the patch cord between the patch panel and the switch. Swap with another known good cable and test again. If this still fails, try connecting a different host to the network port. If the other host connects, suspect a problem with network adapter in the original host. Use Device Manager to verify that the adapter's link properties are set correctly (typically to autonegotiate). If there is no configuration issue, swap the network adapter with a known good one and re-test.

Note: *The link LEDs on network adapter and switch ports will indicate whether the link is active and possibly at what speed the link is working. The LEDs typically flicker to show network activity.*

If you still haven't isolated the problem, try plugging the problem computer into a different network port. By testing from different ports, you should be able to establish the scope of the problem and the likely location of the fault. Eventually, through the process of substituting working components for suspect components, you should resolve the cable problem. Remember that if several users have the problem, you should check the switch in this way too.

Teaching Tip

Again, this topic covers a mix of objectives from the Core 1 and Core 2 exams. Most of the issues are content examples on Core 1, but the crucial command-line tools you use to diagnose them are on Core 2.

Show Slide(s)

Common Wired Network Connectivity Issues (2 slides)

Teaching Tip

As with the other troubleshooting topics, ask learners to recall the basic troubleshooting approach and CompTIA model.

Note: *If you have suitable tools, you can use them in place of substituting and transposing devices. For example, a loopback plug can be used to test whether a port is working (and therefore indicate that the problem is with the cable).*

Problems with patch cords are simple as you can just throw the broken one away and plug in a new one. If the problem is in the structured cabling, however, you will want to use cable testing tools to determine its cause, especially if the problem is intermittent (that is, if the problem comes and goes). The solution may involve installing a new permanent link, but there could also be a termination or external interference problem.

TROUBLESHOOTING SLOW TRANSFER SPEEDS

The transfer speed of a cabled link could be reduced if the network equipment is not all working to the highest available standard. Check the configuration of the network adapter driver (via Device Manager) and the setting for the switch port (via the switch's management software). Slow transfer speeds can be caused by a variety of other problems and can be very difficult to diagnose.

- There may be congestion at a switch or router or some other network-wide problem. This might be caused by a fault or by user behavior, such as transferring a very large amount of data over the network.
- There could be a problem with the network adapter driver.
- The computer could be infected with malware.
- The network cabling could be affected by interference. This could be from an external source but check the ends of cables for excessive untwisting of the wire pairs as poor termination is a common cause of problems.

COMMON WIRELESS NETWORK CONNECTIVITY ISSUES

Show Slide(s)

Common Wireless Network Connectivity Issues (2 slides)

Teaching Tip

Make sure learners are familiar with this terminology and the effect of allowing client devices supporting only legacy standards to join the WLAN.

When troubleshooting wireless networks, as with cabled links, you need to consider problems with the physical media, such as interference and configuration issues.

The **Radio Frequency (RF)** signal from radio-based devices weakens considerably as the distance between the devices increases. If you experience slow transfer speeds or you cannot establish a connection, try moving the devices closer together. If you still cannot obtain a connection, check that the security and authentication parameters are correctly configured on both devices.

TROUBLESHOOTING WIRELESS CONFIGURATION ISSUES

If a user is looking for a network name that is not shown in the list of available wireless networks (**SSID not found**), the user could be out of range or broadcast of the SSID name might be suppressed. In the latter scenario, the connection to the network name must be configured manually.

Another factor to consider is **standards mismatch**. Choosing a compatibility mode for an access point will reduce the features available (no WPA for 802.11b compatibility, for instance). If an access point is not operating in compatibility mode, it will not be able to communicate with devices that only support older standards. Also, when an older device joins the network, the performance of the whole network can be affected. To support 802.11b clients, an 802.11b/n access point must transmit legacy frame preamble and collision avoidance frames, adding overhead. If at all possible, upgrade 802.11b devices rather than letting them join the WLAN. 802.11g and 802.11n are more compatible in terms of negotiating collision avoidance. In a mixed 802.11g/n WLAN, performance of the 802.11n devices operating in the 2.4 GHz band is only likely to be severely impacted when 802.11g devices perform large file transfers. As these take longer to complete, there is less "airtime" available for the 802.11n clients.

Note: With 802.11n dual-band APs operating in mixed mode or with 802.11ac, it is typical to assign the 2.4 GHz band to support legacy clients. The 5 GHz band can be reserved for 802.11n or 802.11ac clients and bonded channels can be configured.

Also consider that not all clients supporting 802.11n have dual band radios. If a client cannot connect to a network operating on the 5 GHz band, check whether its radio is 2.4 GHz-capable only.

LOW RF SIGNAL/RSSI

A wireless adapter will be configured to drop the connection speed if the **Received Signal Strength Indicator (RSSI)** is not at a minimum required level. The RSSI is an index level calculated from the signal strength level. For example, an 802.11n adapter might be capable of a 144 Mbps data rate with an optimum signal, but if the signal is weak it might drop to a 54 Mbps or 11 Mbps rate to make the connection more reliable. If the RSSI is too low, the adapter will drop the connection entirely and try to use a different network. If there are two fairly weak networks, the adapter might "flap" between them. Try moving to a location with better reception.

TROUBLESHOOTING WIRELESS SIGNAL ISSUES

If a device is within the supported range but the signal is very weak or you can only get an **intermittent connection**, there is likely to be interference from another radio source broadcasting at the same frequency. If this is the case, try adjusting the channel that the devices use. Another possibility is interference from a powerful electromagnetic source, such as a motor or microwave oven. Finally, there might be something blocking the signal. Radio waves do not pass easily through metal or dense objects. Construction materials such as wire mesh, foil-backed plasterboard, concrete, and mirrors can block or degrade signals. Try angling or repositioning the device or antenna to try to get better reception.

Note: The ideal position for an access point is high up and in the center of the area it is supposed to serve.

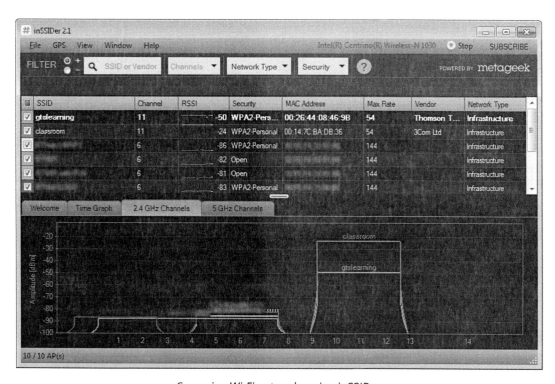

Surveying Wi-Fi networks using inSSIDer.

Wi-Fi Analyzer software, such as inSSIDer, is designed to support a site survey, to identify nearby networks that may be causing interference problems, and to measure signal strength. You can use a Wi-Fi Analyzer for troubleshooting, too. It shows the signal strength, measured in dBm. This can also be expressed as a percentage; for example, -35 dBm or better would represent the best possible signal at 100%, -90 dBm or worse would represent 1%, and -65 dBm would represent 50% signal strength.

The analyzer will also show how many networks are utilizing each channel. Setting the network to use a less congested channel can improve performance.

IP CONFIGURATION ISSUES

Show Slide(s)

IP Configuration Issues (2 slides)

Teaching Tip

Make sure that learners know the usage and typical output of each tool.

If a host does not have an appropriate IP configuration for the network that it is connected to, it will not be able to communicate with other hosts, even if the physical connection is sound. There are a number of command-line tools for testing and troubleshooting the IP configuration.

VIEWING IP CONFIGURATION (ipconfig)

In Windows, IP configuration information is displayed through the adapter's status dialog (Windows 7/8) or Windows Settings (Windows 10). You can also view this information at a command line using the `ipconfig` tool. Used without switches, `ipconfig` displays the IP address, subnet mask, and default gateway (router) for all network adapters to which TCP/IP is bound. Typical ipconfig switches and arguments are as follows.

Switch	Description
`ipconfig /all`	Displays detailed configuration, including DHCP and DNS servers, MAC address, and NetBIOS status.
`ipconfig /release AdapterName`	Releases the IP address obtained from a DHCP server so that the network adapter(s) will no longer have an IP address.
`ipconfig /renew AdapterName`	Forces a DHCP client to renew the lease it has for an IP address.
`ipconfig /displaydns`	Displays the DNS resolver cache. This contains host and domain names that have been queried recently. Caching the name-to-IP mappings reduces network traffic.
`ipconfig /flushdns`	Clears the DNS resolver cache.

Note that omitting the *AdapterName* argument releases or renews all adapters. If *AdapterName* contains spaces, use quotes around it (for example, `ipconfig / renew "Local Area Connection"`).

TROUBLESHOOTING WITH ipconfig

You would use `ipconfig` to determine whether the adapter has been correctly configured. `ipconfig` can resolve the following questions:

- Is the adapter configured with a static address? Are the parameters (IP address, subnet mask, default gateway, and DNS server correct)?
- Is the adapter configured by DHCP? If so:
  - An address in the range 169.254.x.y indicates that the client could not contact a DHCP server and is using Automatic Private IP Addressing (APIPA). If this is the

case, Windows will display a yellow alert icon and a notification that the adapter has only **Limited connectivity**.

- A DHCP lease can be static (always assigns the same IP address to the computer) or dynamic (assigns an IP address from a pool)—has the computer obtained a suitable address and subnet mask?
- Are other parameters assigned by DHCP correct (default gateway, DNS servers, and so on)?

```
C:\Users\Admin>ipconfig /all

Windows IP Configuration

   Host Name . . . . . . . . . . . . : ROGUE
   Primary Dns Suffix  . . . . . . . :
   Node Type . . . . . . . . . . . . : Hybrid
   IP Routing Enabled. . . . . . . . : No
   WINS Proxy Enabled. . . . . . . . : No
   DNS Suffix Search List. . . . . . : classroom.local

Ethernet adapter Ethernet:

   Connection-specific DNS Suffix  . : classroom.local
   Description . . . . . . . . . . . : Microsoft Hyper-V Network Adapter
   Physical Address. . . . . . . . . : 00-15-5D-01-CA-0E
   DHCP Enabled. . . . . . . . . . . : Yes
   Autoconfiguration Enabled . . . . : Yes
   IPv4 Address. . . . . . . . . . . : 10.1.0.131(Preferred)
   Subnet Mask . . . . . . . . . . . : 255.255.255.0
   Lease Obtained. . . . . . . . . . : Wednesday, January 4, 2017 2:40:05 AM
   Lease Expires . . . . . . . . . . : Thursday, January 12, 2017 2:40:03 AM
   Default Gateway . . . . . . . . . : 10.1.0.254
   DHCP Server . . . . . . . . . . . : 10.1.0.1
   DNS Servers . . . . . . . . . . . : 10.1.0.1
   NetBIOS over Tcpip. . . . . . . . : Enabled
```

Using ipconfig. (Screenshot used with permission from Microsoft.)

If any of these results are negative, you should investigate either communications between the client and the DHCP server, the configuration of the DHCP server, or whether multiple DHCP servers are running on the network (and the client has obtained the wrong configuration from one).

ifconfig

UNIX and Linux hosts provide a command called `ifconfig`, which provides similar output to Windows' ipconfig program. Note some differences between the Windows and Linux commands:

- `ifconfig` can also be used to bind an address to an adapter interface, set up communication parameters, and enable or disable the adapter.
- The Windows switches for configuring the adapter with DHCP and DNS are not supported by `ifconfig`.
- The `ifconfig` command output does not show the default gateway (use `route` instead). It does show traffic statistics, though.

> **Teaching Tip**
>
> `ifconfig` is starting to disappear from default software selections in many Linux distributions. Make sure learners are aware of it, but point out that the `ip` tool should be used going forward.

```
administrator@lamp:~$ ifconfig
eth0      Link encap:Ethernet  HWaddr 00:15:5d:01:c0:9f
          inet addr:192.168.1.1  Bcast:192.168.1.255  Mask:255.255.255.0
          inet6 addr: fe80::215:5dff:fe01:c09f/64 Scope:Link
          UP BROADCAST RUNNING MULTICAST  MTU:1500  Metric:1
          RX packets:0 errors:0 dropped:0 overruns:0 frame:0
          TX packets:36 errors:0 dropped:0 overruns:0 carrier:0
          collisions:0 txqueuelen:1000
          RX bytes:0 (0.0 B)  TX bytes:1728 (1.7 KB)

lo        Link encap:Local Loopback
          inet addr:127.0.0.1  Mask:255.0.0.0
          inet6 addr: ::1/128 Scope:Host
          UP LOOPBACK RUNNING  MTU:16436  Metric:1
          RX packets:57 errors:0 dropped:0 overruns:0 frame:0
          TX packets:57 errors:0 dropped:0 overruns:0 carrier:0
          collisions:0 txqueuelen:0
          RX bytes:4153 (4.1 KB)  TX bytes:4153 (4.1 KB)

administrator@lamp:~$ _
```

Using ifconfig. (Screenshot used with permission from Microsoft.)

 Note: *Additionally, a separate command (`iwconfig`) is used to manage wireless interfaces. Note that both these commands are deprecated in favor of the newer `ip` and `iw` utilities.*

Show
Slide(s)

IP Connectivity Issues
(3 slides)

IP CONNECTIVITY ISSUES

If the link and IP configuration both seem to be correct, the problem may not lie with the local machine but somewhere in the overall network topology. You can test connections to servers such as files shares, printers, or email by trying to use them. One drawback of this method is that there could be some sort of application fault rather than a network fault. Therefore, it is useful to have a low-level test of basic connectivity that does not have any dependencies other than a working link and IP configuration.

ping

The `ping` utility is a command-line diagnostic tool used to test whether a host can communicate with another host on the same network or on a remote network. It is the basic tool to use to establish that a link is working. `ping` uses the **Internet Control Message Protocol (ICMP)** to request status messages from hosts. The following steps outline the procedures for verifying a computer's configuration and for testing router connections:

1. Ping the loopback address to verify TCP/IP is installed and loaded correctly (`ping 127.0.0.1`)—the loopback address is a reserved IP address used for testing purposes.
2. Ping the IP address of your workstation to verify it was added correctly and to check for possible duplicate IP addresses.
3. Ping the IP address of the default gateway to verify it is up and running and that you can communicate with a host on the local network.
4. Ping the IP address of a remote host to verify you can communicate through the router. If no router is available, Windows will display a yellow alert icon and a notification that the adapter has **No Internet access**.

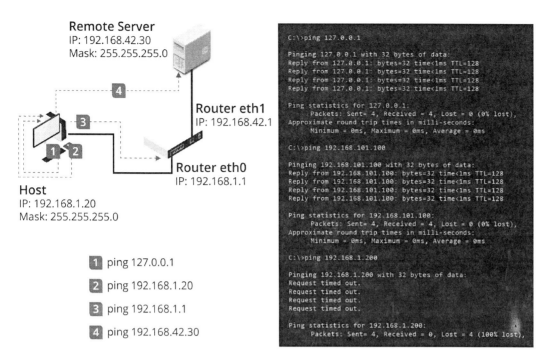

Remote Server
IP: 192.168.42.30
Mask: 255.255.255.0

Router eth1
IP: 192.168.42.1

Router eth0
IP: 192.168.1.1

Host
IP: 192.168.1.20
Mask: 255.255.255.0

```
C:\>ping 127.0.0.1

Pinging 127.0.0.1 with 32 bytes of data:
Reply from 127.0.0.1: bytes=32 time<1ms TTL=128
Reply from 127.0.0.1: bytes=32 time<1ms TTL=128
Reply from 127.0.0.1: bytes=32 time<1ms TTL=128
Reply from 127.0.0.1: bytes=32 time<1ms TTL=128

Ping statistics for 127.0.0.1:
    Packets: Sent= 4, Received = 4, Lost = 0 (0% lost),
Approximate round trip times in milli-seconds:
    Minimum = 0ms, Maximum = 0ms, Average = 0ms

C:\>ping 192.168.101.100

Pinging 192.168.101.100 with 32 bytes of data:
Reply from 192.168.101.100: bytes=32 time<1ms TTL=128
Reply from 192.168.101.100: bytes=32 time<1ms TTL=128
Reply from 192.168.101.100: bytes=32 time<1ms TTL=128
Reply from 192.168.101.100: bytes=32 time<1ms TTL=128

Ping statistics for 192.168.101.100:
    Packets: Sent= 4, Received = 4, Lost = 0 (0% lost),
Approximate round trip times in milli-seconds:
    Minimum = 0ms, Maximum = 0ms, Average = 0ms

C:\>ping 192.168.1.200

Pinging 192.168.1.200 with 32 bytes of data:
Request timed out.
Request timed out.
Request timed out.
Request timed out.

Ping statistics for 192.168.1.200:
    Packets: Sent= 4, Received = 0, Lost = 4 (100% lost),
```

1 ping 127.0.0.1

2 ping 192.168.1.20

3 ping 192.168.1.1

4 ping 192.168.42.30

Troubleshooting with ping.

If `ping` is successful, it responds with the message **Reply from IP Address** and the time it takes for the server's response to arrive. The millisecond measures of Round Trip Time (RTT) can be used to diagnose latency problems on a link.

If `ping` is unsuccessful, one of two messages are commonly received:

- **Destination unreachable**—there is no routing information (that is, the local computer or an intermediate router does not know how to get to that IP address). If the host is on the same network, check the local IP configuration—IP address, subnet mask, and so on. If you can discount any configuration error, then there may be a hardware or cabling problem. If the host is on another network, check the IP configuration and router.
- **No reply (Request timed out)**—the host is unavailable or cannot route a reply back to your computer. Check physical cabling and infrastructure devices such as the switch. If the host is on a remote network, try using `tracert` (described shortly).

Note: Be aware that ICMP traffic is often blocked by firewalls, making a response such as request timed out or destination unreachable inevitable. As well as network firewalls, consider that a host firewall, such as Windows Firewall, might be blocking ICMP.

TESTING DNS

You can also ping DNS names (`ping comptia.org`, for example) or FQDNs (`ping sales.comptia.org`, for instance). This will not work if a DNS server is unavailable. Use the `-a` switch to perform a reverse lookup on an IP address to try to get the host name. For example, `ping -a 192.168.1.1` should return the message "Pinging *HostName* [192.168.1.1]."

TROUBLESHOOTING AN IP CONFLICT

Two systems could end up with the same IP address because of a configuration error; perhaps both addresses were statically assigned or one was assigned an address that was part of a DHCP scope by mistake. If Windows detects a duplicate IP address, it will display a warning and disable IP. If there are two systems with duplicate IPs, a sort of "race condition" will determine which receives traffic. Obviously, this is not a good way for the network to be configured and you should identify the machines and set them to use unique addresses.

ROUTING ISSUES

Show Slide(s)
Routing Issues

Teaching Tip

If you have an Internet connection, show learners examples of `tracert`. Note the increase in hop time when you trace the route to a host on the other side of the Atlantic.

In the screenshot, note that not every router replies. This is likely to mean that the router is blocking ICMP.

The `tracert` command-line utility is used to trace the route a packet of information takes to get to its target. Like `ping`, it uses ICMP status messages. For example, a user might type the following: `tracert 10.0.0.1`. This command would return details of the route taken to find the machine or device with the IP address of 10.0.0.1. `tracert` can also be used with a domain name or FQDN, such as: `tracert comptia.org`.

```
C:\Users\localadmin>tracert 10.0.0.1

Tracing route to 10.0.0.1 over a maximum of 30 hops

  1   HOST [192.168.1.110]  reports: Destination host unreachable.

Trace complete.

C:\Users\localadmin>tracert gtslearning.com

Tracing route to gtslearning.com [185.41.10.123]
over a maximum of 30 hops:

  1    <1 ms    <1 ms    <1 ms   ARCHER_VR900 [192.168.1.1]
  2     *        *        *      Request timed out.
  3     *       11 ms    11 ms   31.55.187.181
  4    11 ms    11 ms    11 ms   31.55.187.188
  5    12 ms    11 ms    11 ms   core2-hu0-17-0-1.southbank.ukcore.bt.net [195.99
.127.188]
  6    12 ms    12 ms    12 ms   195.99.127.70
  7    13 ms    13 ms    13 ms   peer2-et-9-1-0.redbus.ukcore.bt.net [62.172.103.
43]
  8    13 ms    13 ms    18 ms   linx2.ixreach.com [195.66.236.217]
  9    20 ms    20 ms    20 ms   r1.tcw.man.ixreach.com [91.196.184.181]
 10    19 ms    23 ms    20 ms   rt1-tjh-ixr.as200083.net [46.18.174.222]
 11    20 ms    20 ms    20 ms   server1.gtslearning.com [185.41.10.123]

Trace complete.

C:\Users\localadmin>_
```

Using tracert—the first trace to a local private network has failed but the trace over the Internet to gtslearning.com's web server has succeeded, passing first through the SOHO router then through the routers belonging to the user's ISP, then the routers belonging to the web host. (Screenshot used with permission from Microsoft.)

If the host cannot be located, the command will eventually timeout but it will return every router that was attempted. The output shows the number of hops (when a packet is transferred from one router to another), the ingress interface of the router or host (that is, the interface from which the router receives the ICMP packet), and the time taken to respond to each probe in milliseconds (ms). If no acknowledgement is received within the timeout period, an asterisk is shown against the probe.

Note: `ping` and `tracert` use Internet Control Message Protocol (ICMP) traffic. A firewall may be configured to block this traffic to prevent network snooping.

UNAVAILABLE RESOURCES

Show Slide(s)
Unavailable Resources
(5 slides)

If you cannot identify a problem with the cabling, switches/routers, or the IP configuration, you should start to suspect a problem at a higher layer of processing. There are three main additional "layers" where network services fail:

- Security—a firewall or other security software or hardware might be blocking the connection.
- Name resolution—if a service such as DNS is not working, you will be able to connect to file/print/email services by IP address but not by name.
- Application/OS—the software underpinning the service might have failed. If the OS has failed, there might not be any sort of connectivity to the host server. If the server can be contacted, but not a specific service, the service process might have crashed.

When troubleshooting Internet access or unavailable local network resources, such as file shares, network printers, and email, try to establish the scope of the problem. If you can connect to these services using a different host, the problem should lie with the first client. If other hosts cannot connect, the problem lies with the application server or print device or with network infrastructure between the client and the server.

TROUBLESHOOTING INTERNET AVAILABILITY

When Windows reports that a network adapter has "No Internet access," it means that the IP configuration is valid but that Windows cannot identify a working Internet connection. Windows tests Internet access by attempting a connection to `www.msftncsi.com` and checking that DNS resolves the IP address correctly.

If the local PC settings are correct, locate your ISP's service status page or support helpline to verify that there are no wider network issues or DNS problems that might make your Internet connection unavailable. If there are no ISP-wide issues, try restarting the router/modem.

> **Note:** *Do not restart a router without considering the impact on other users!*

If these measures don't help, also consider that there might be some sort of security issue, such as a proxy configuration not working or a firewall blocking the host.

PERFORMING A NETWORK RESET

If there are persistent network problems with either a client or a server, one "stock" response is to try restarting the computer hardware. You can also try restarting just the application service.

> **Note:** *As before, do not restart a server without considering the impact on other users. A restart is probably only warranted if the problem is widespread.*

In Windows, you can try running the network troubleshooter app to automatically diagnose and fix problems. Another option is to reset the network stack on the device. In Windows, this will clear any custom adapter configurations and network connections, including VPN connections. These will have to be reconfigured after the reset.

In Windows 10, there is a **Network reset** command on the **Settings→Network & Internet→Status** page. In Windows 7/8, you can use the Network Adapter troubleshooter or run the following commands (as administrator):

```
ipconfig /flushdns
netsh int ip reset resetlog.txt
netsh winsock reset
```

Use Device Manager to remove any network adapters. Reboot the computer and allow Windows to detect and install the adapter(s) again. Update network settings on all adapters to the appropriate configuration.

netstat

netstat can be used to investigate open ports and connections on the local host. In a troubleshooting context, you can use this tool to verify whether file sharing or email ports are open on a server and whether other clients are connecting to them.

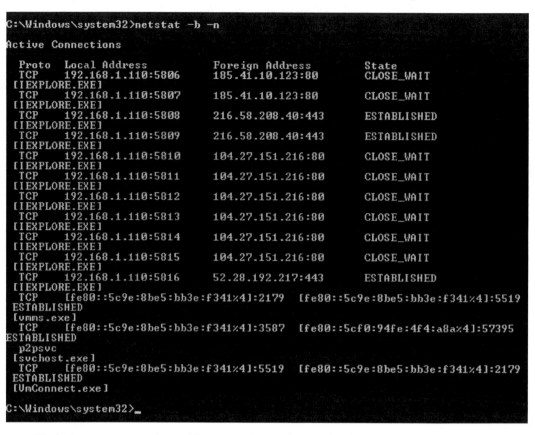

Displaying open connections with netstat. (Screenshot used with permission from Microsoft.)

The following represent some of the main switches that can be used:

- -a displays all the connections and listening ports.
- -b shows the process that has opened the port.
- -n displays ports and addresses in numerical format. Skipping name resolution speeds up each query.

Linux supports a similar utility with slightly different switches.

nslookup

If you identify or suspect a problem with name resolution, you can troubleshoot DNS with the nslookup command, either interactively or from the command prompt:

```
nslookup -Option Host Server
```

Host can be either a host name/FQDN or an IP address. Server is the DNS server to query; the default DNS server is used if this argument is omitted. -Option specifies an nslookup subcommand. Typically, a subcommand is used to query a particular DNS record type.

For example, the following command queries Google's public DNS servers (8.8.8.8) for information about comptia.org's mail records:

```
nslookup -type=mx comptia.org 8.8.8.8
```

```
C:\Users\James>nslookup -type=mx comptia.org 8.8.8.8
Server:  google-public-dns-a.google.com
Address:  8.8.8.8

Non-authoritative answer:
comptia.org     MX preference = 10, mail exchanger = comptia-org.mail.protection.outlook.c
om
```

Using nslookup to query the mail server configured for the comptia.org domain name using Google's public DNS servers (8.8.8.8). (Screenshot used with permission from Microsoft.)

If you query a different name server, you can compare the results to those returned by your own name server. This might highlight configuration problems.

Note: The *dig* utility is often used as a more up-to-date and flexible alternative to *nslookup*. *dig* allows you to query a name server directly and retrieve any of the information known about the domain name. It is helpful in determining if the server is running correctly and if the domain record is properly configured.

Activity 9-7

Discussing Network Connection Troubleshooting

Show Slide(s)

Activity: Discussing Network Connection Troubleshooting

SCENARIO

Answer the following questions to check your understanding of the topic.

1. You are trying to add a computer to a wireless network but cannot detect the access point.

   What would you suspect the problem to be?

   The computer's wireless adapter is not supported by the AP, the computer is not in range, or there is some sort of interference.

2. **What readings would you expect to gather with a Wi-Fi analyzer?**

   The signal strength of different Wi-Fi networks and their channels within range of the analyzer.

3. You have restarted the DHCP server following a network problem.

   What command would you use to refresh the IP configuration on Windows 7 client workstations?

   ```
   ipconfig /renew
   ```

4. **What command can you use on a Linux computer to report the IP configuration?**

   Historically, this could be reported using the `ifconfig` tool. The `ip` command is now preferred.

5. A single PC on a network cannot connect to the Internet.

   Where would you start troubleshooting?

   You could test the PC's IP configuration, specifically the default gateway or name resolution, or you could check that the cable is good.

6. A computer cannot connect to the network. The machine is configured to obtain a TCP/IP configuration automatically. You use ipconfig to determine the IP address and it returns 0.0.0.0.

What does this tell you?

If a DHCP server cannot be contacted, the machine should default to using an APIPA address (169.254.x.y). As it has not done this, something is wrong with the networking software installed on the machine (probably the DHCP client service, TCP/IP stack, or registry configuration, to be specific).

7. **If a host has a firewall configured to block outgoing ICMP traffic, what result would you expect from pinging the host (assuming that the path to the host is otherwise OK)?**

Destination unreachable.

8. **What Windows tool is used to test the end-to-end path between two IP hosts on different IP networks?**

`tracert`

Teaching Tip

Learners might find this question challenging; they will need to derive the answer from what they know about APIPA addressing.

9. **Which command produces the output shown in this graphic?**

This is output from `netstat`. Specifically, it is `netstat -ano`. The switches show all connections, with ports in numeric format, and the PID of the process that opened the port.

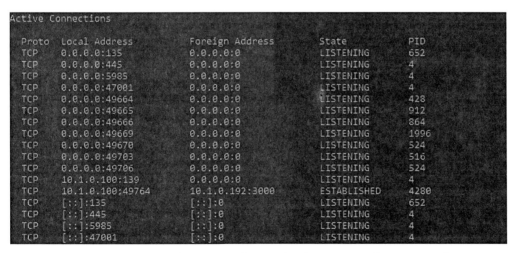

```
Active Connections

  Proto  Local Address          Foreign Address        State           PID
  TCP    0.0.0.0:135            0.0.0.0:0              LISTENING       652
  TCP    0.0.0.0:445            0.0.0.0:0              LISTENING       4
  TCP    0.0.0.0:5985           0.0.0.0:0              LISTENING       4
  TCP    0.0.0.0:47001          0.0.0.0:0              LISTENING       4
  TCP    0.0.0.0:49664          0.0.0.0:0              LISTENING       428
  TCP    0.0.0.0:49665          0.0.0.0:0              LISTENING       912
  TCP    0.0.0.0:49666          0.0.0.0:0              LISTENING       864
  TCP    0.0.0.0:49669          0.0.0.0:0              LISTENING       1996
  TCP    0.0.0.0:49670          0.0.0.0:0              LISTENING       524
  TCP    0.0.0.0:49703          0.0.0.0:0              LISTENING       516
  TCP    0.0.0.0:49706          0.0.0.0:0              LISTENING       524
  TCP    10.1.0.100:139         0.0.0.0:0              LISTENING       4
  TCP    10.1.0.100:49764       10.1.0.192:3000        ESTABLISHED     4280
  TCP    [::]:135               [::]:0                 LISTENING       652
  TCP    [::]:445               [::]:0                 LISTENING       4
  TCP    [::]:5985              [::]:0                 LISTENING       4
  TCP    [::]:47001             [::]:0                 LISTENING       4
```

Command output exhibit. (Screenshot used with permission from Microsoft.)

Activity 9-8
Troubleshooting Network Connections

BEFORE YOU BEGIN

Take a moment to review the VMs available on the virtual network.

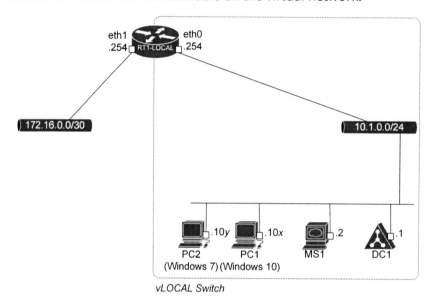

Network environment for troubleshooting network connections.

SCENARIO

In this activity, you will run scripts that simulate network connectivity problems. You will then use troubleshooting tools and techniques to detect and fix the problems.

---

1. Start the VMs to create the network.

   You do not need to open connection windows for the VMs unless you are specifically prompted to do so.

   a) If necessary, in Hyper-V Manager, right-click **RT1-LOCAL** and select **Start**.
   b) If necessary, right-click **DC1** and select **Start**.
   c) Wait until the **DC1** thumbnail shows the logon screen, and then start **MS1**.
   d) Wait until the **MS1** thumbnail shows the logon screen, and then start **PC1** and **PC2**.
   e) Open a connection window for **PC1**.
   f) Sign on, using the account *515support\Administrator* and password *Pa$$w0rd*

2. Test that the VMs on the local network can communicate with one another.

   a) On the Windows 10 VM, open a command prompt.
   b) Type `ipconfig /all` and press **Enter**.
   c) Examine the details of your IP configuration, and verify that the configuration of the Ethernet adapter matches the information shown in the figure at the start of the activity.

---

d) Run this command: `ping 127.0.0.1`

    This command verifies that IP is installed correctly by performing a connection test with the loopback adapter (essentially pinging the local host).

e) Run this command: `ping 10.1.0.`*x* where *x* is the value reported by `ipconfig` for the IPv4 address.

    This command checks the IP assigned by DHCP.

f) Run this command: `ping 10.1.0.254`

    This command checks the connection to the default gateway.

g) Run this command: `ping DC1 -4`

    This command tests name resolution and connectivity with the other hosts on the network. The -4 switch forces ping to use IPv4, rather than IPv6.

h) Run this command: `ping MS1 -4`

    This command tests name resolution and connectivity with the other hosts on the network. The -4 switch forces ping to use IPv4, rather than IPv6.

i) Run this command: `ping PC2 -4`

    This command tests name resolution and connectivity with the other hosts on the network. The -4 switch forces ping to use IPv4, rather than IPv6.

j) Leave the command prompt open.

k) Start a web browser, and open ***http://updates.corp.515support.com***

l) Open File Explorer, and browse **\\DC1\LABFILES**.

m) At the command prompt, run `netstat -no`

    This command checks the connections that you just established.

n) Run this command: `nslookup -type=SOA corp.515support.com`

    This command checks information about how the DNS service is administered.

o) Switch back to the web browser, select the **Settings and more** button at the top right, and then select **Settings**.

p) Select the **Choose what to clear** button.

q) Select **Always clear this when I close the browser** to toggle this setting to **On**.

r) Close the browser window.

3. Run a script to create a problem with the network configuration that you will diagnose and correct.

    a) On the **PC1 VM** computer, activate the **Instant Search** box, and type `powershell`

    b) Right-click the **Windows PowerShell** icon and select **Run as administrator**.

    c) In the UAC prompt box, select **Yes**.

    d) In the **Windows PowerShell** window, type `c:\labfiles\netprob1` and press **Enter**.

    e) Leave the PowerShell window open.

    f) Repeat the tests you performed in step 2 of this activity to try and identify the problem that was introduced.

    g) Think about the problem and how you would you fix it. Apply the appropriate fix for the problem you discovered.

    h) If you could not resolve the problem, at the PowerShell prompt, run `c:\labfiles\netprob1-fix` to reset the configuration to its original state.

4. Run another script to introduce another problem to troubleshoot.

    a) At the PowerShell prompt on the **PC1 VM**, type `c:\labfiles\netprob2` and press **Enter**.

    b) Leave the PowerShell window open.

Teaching Tip

The script sets a static configuration that will not work on this network.

Teaching Tip

The script sets the default outbound firewall rule to block, rather than allow. This prevents the PC1 VM from accessing the web server. Other connection types (ICMP plus file and printer sharing) are allowed by specific rules. Encourage learners to try to connect to the server from another VM to rule out a server-side issue.

    c)   Repeat the tests you performed in step 2 of this activity to try and identify the problem that was introduced, along with a proposed solution.

    d)   Apply the appropriate fix for the problem you discovered.

    e)   If you could not resolve the problem, at the PowerShell prompt, run `c:\labfiles\netprob2-fix` to reset the configuration to its original state.

5.   At the end of each activity, you need to close the VMs and discard any changes you made.

    a)   From the connection window, select **Action→Revert**.

    b)   If you are prompted to confirm, select the **Revert** button.

    c)   On the **HOST PC**, in the **Hyper-V Manager** console, right-click each VM that is still running and select **Revert**. At the end of the activity, the state of each VM should be listed as **Off**.

Topic F

Install and Configure IoT Devices

EXAM OBJECTIVES COVERED
1001-2.3 Given a scenario, install and configure a basic wired/wireless SOHO network.
1001-2.4 Compare and contrast wireless networking protocols.

As a CompTIA A+ technician, you should be alert to the need to stay up to date with new technologies. The market for home automation systems is expanding all the time, and these technologies are also starting to appear in office buildings. In this topic, you will learn about the main types of devices and networking standards plus basic procedures for setting up a smart hub and connecting devices to it.

INTERNET OF THINGS

Wi-Fi dominates wireless networking for devices like computers and laptops. It is also supported by smartphones and tablets. Wi-Fi requires quite powerful adapters with large antennas, however. Other wireless technologies support communications between smaller devices, where low weight, bulk, and power consumption are the primary requirements.

The term **Internet of Things (IoT)** is used to describe the global network of personal devices—such as phones, tablets, and fitness trackers, home appliances, home control systems, vehicles, and other items that have been equipped with sensors, software, and network connectivity. These features allow these types of objects to communicate and pass data between themselves and other traditional systems like computer servers. This is often referred to as **Machine to Machine (M2M)** communication.

Each "thing" is identified with some form of unique serial number or code embedded within its own operating or control system and is able to inter-operate within the existing Internet infrastructure either directly or via an intermediary.

IoT WIRELESS NETWORKING TECHNOLOGIES

When you work with IoT devices, you might encounter one or more of these network connection technologies.

BLUETOOTH AND BLUETOOTH LOW ENERGY

Bluetooth uses radio communications and supports speeds of up to 3 Mbps. Adapters supporting version 3 or 4 of the standard can achieve faster rates (up to 24 Mbps) through the ability to negotiate an 802.11 radio link for large file transfers (BT + HS [High Speed]).

Bluetooth does not require line-of-sight and supports a maximum range of 10 m (30 feet), though signal strength will be weak at this distance. Many portable devices, such as smartphones, tablets, wearable tech, audio speakers, and headphones now use Bluetooth connectivity. Bluetooth devices can use a pairing procedure to authenticate and exchange data securely.

Version 4 introduced a **Bluetooth Low Energy (BLE)** variant of the standard. BLE is designed for small battery-powered devices that transmit small amounts of data infrequently. A BLE device remains in a low power state until a monitor application

Teaching Tip

Sharing examples of home automation devices may help learners better understand. Otherwise, encourage them to browse vendor sites to learn about the features of individual systems.

Show Slide(s)

Internet of Things

Show Slide(s)

IoT Wireless Networking Technologies

initiates a connection. BLE is not backwards-compatible with "classic" Bluetooth, though a device can support both standards simultaneously.

Z-Wave

Z-Wave is a wireless communications protocol used primarily for home automation. It was developed in 2001 by Zensys, a Danish company, but with interest and investment from other technology and engineering companies such as Cisco, Intel, Panasonic, and Danfoss, the Z-Wave Alliance was formed. Z-Wave operates a certification program for devices and software.

Z-Wave creates a mesh network topology, using low-energy radio waves to communicate from one appliance to another. Devices can be configured to work as repeaters to extend the network but there is a limit of four "hops" between a controller device and an endpoint. This allows for wireless control of residential appliances and other devices, such as lighting control, security systems, thermostats, windows, locks, swimming pools, and garage door openers. Z-Wave has been registered in most countries worldwide and uses radio frequencies in the high 800 to low 900 MHz range. It is designed to run for long periods (years) on battery power.

Zigbee

Zigbee has similar uses to Z-Wave and is an open source competitor technology to it. The Zigbee Alliance operates a number of certification programs for its various technologies and standards.

Zigbee uses the 2.4 GHz frequency band. This higher frequency allows more data bandwidth at the expense of range compared to Z-Wave and the greater risk of interference from other 2.4 GHz radio communications. Zigbee supports more overall devices within a single network (65,000 compared to 232 for Z-wave) and there is no hop limit for communication between devices.

RFID AND NEAR FIELD COMMUNICATIONS (NFC)

Radio Frequency ID (RFID) is a means of tagging and tracking objects using specially encoded tags. When an RFID reader scans a tag, the tag responds with the information programmed into it. A tag can either be an unpowered, passive device that only responds when scanned at close range (up to about 25 m), or a powered, active device with a range of 100 m. Passive RFID tags can be embedded in stickers and labels to track parcels and equipment and are used in passive proximity smart cards.

Near Field Communications (NFC) is a peer-to-peer version of RFID; that is, an NFC device can work as both tag and reader to exchange information with other NFC devices. NFC normally works at up to 2 inches (6 cm) at data rates of 106, 212, and 424 Kbps. NFC sensors and functionality are starting to be incorporated into smartphones. NFC is mostly used for contactless payment readers, security ID tags, and shop shelf-edge labels for stock control. It can also be used to configure other types of connection (pairing Bluetooth devices, for instance).

IoT DEVICE CONFIGURATION

Show Slide(s)
IoT Device Configuration

One of the applications of Internet of Things (IoT) functionality is the use of home automation devices, also called a smart home. A smart home essentially means that ordinary controls, such as the thermostat or lighting, can be controlled using a simple computer interface. The interface could be an app on your smartphone or a voice-enabled home automation hub (or both).

For consistency and the use of a single point-of-control, you ideally need to pick devices that are all compatible. There are two main compatibility considerations:

- That devices all share the same networking protocol, such as Z-Wave or Zigbee.
- That devices are all compatible with the same virtual assistant or hub.

ENDPOINT DEVICES

In home automation, endpoint devices are the things that physically interface with or implement the system you are controlling.

- Thermostat—operate heating and hot water controls and measure the current temperature.
- Light switches/bulbs—turn lights on or off or set to a particular dimmer level or color (in the case of smart bulbs).
- Security cameras—the main function is to record images to cloud storage, but these come with a very wide range of features, including intruder alerting/motion detection, face recognition, night vision, two-way microphone, zoom, and tracking.
- Door locks—a smart lock can be operated using voice or a tap and can be set to lock automatically if your smartphone is more than a certain distance away. Locks can also log events.

Depending on type, an endpoint device might need to be fitted by a qualified installer, such as an electrician or heating engineer. The next step is to register the device with some sort of controller. This could either be a smartphone app or some sort of smart hub.

SMARTPHONE CONTROL

Smartphones can only be used to control a device directly over Wi-Fi, Bluetooth, or NFC. There are no smartphones with Z-Wave or Zigbee radios (at the time of writing).

SMART HUB AND SMART SPEAKER CONTROL

Devices using Z-Wave or Zigbee can be controlled using a smart hub. Most of the major hub vendors support both technologies (as well as Wi-Fi and Bluetooth). You can then use a smartphone to operate the devices via the hub.

Most Z-Wave or Zigbee smart devices will come with their own dedicated hub or bridge. A dedicated hub can only usually control devices made by a single vendor. Dedicated hubs tend to be fairly limited devices that you can configure via a management URL or mobile app.

It may be possible to replace or supplement use of a dedicated hub with a more generic smart speaker/digital assistant-type hub. Examples of smart speaker brands include Samsung SmartThings, Amazon Echo, and Google Home™. Note that most of the brands include different models with different capabilities.

To set up a smart speaker, you usually install the product's app on a smartphone or tablet then use it to connect to the speaker. Configure the speaker to connect to your home Wi-Fi network. You should now be able to start configuring specific settings and integration features.

Integration with a digital assistant depends on the hub model and smart device. As an example, Amazon's Alexa digital assistant can be configured with "skill" shortcuts. A smart device vendor could create skills to allow Alexa to respond to commands to "Alexa, dim the lights" or "Alexa, turn the heating up" by sending appropriate commands to the relevant device.

 *Note: In most cases, the dedicated hub will have to remain in place. When you issue a command to Alexa, Alexa sends a command to the dedicated hub, and the dedicated hub sends the command to the device. As smart device ecosystems evolve, the integration between devices and hubs is likely to become tighter. Another option is the Wink Hub (**wink.com/products/wink-hub**), which is specifically designed to act as a smart home systems integrator. The web platform If This Then That (**ifttt.com**) represents another means of integrating diverse technologies.*

When you connect a new smart device, you can use the hub to scan for it. The device will be allocated a node ID to register it on the network operated by the hub. If you

Teaching Tip

Note that the configuration of these devices tends to involve multiple components. You connect the hub to Wi-Fi then connect to the hub and then use the hub's Z-Wave or Zigbee radio to discover and configure the devices.

have to register a number of similar devices, it is best to do so one-by-one, so that you can give them meaningful names. If you connect multiple devices of the same type at the same time, it can be tricky to distinguish them in the hub management app. If you have to do things this way, look for a unique serial number or code printed on the device. That value might be reported to the hub as a device property.

> **Note:** *The node ID is assigned by the network controller rather than coded into the device. Zigbee devices have burned-in MAC addresses but Z-Wave devices do not.*

Show Slide(s)

Digital Assistants

DIGITAL ASSISTANTS

A **digital assistant** (or **virtual assistant**) is a voice interface designed to respond to natural language commands and queries. Most smartphones and computers now support a voice assistant and they are also implemented on smart speaker hubs. The voice interface transfers requests for processing by a backend server, reducing processing demands on the device but raising privacy and security concerns.

The market is dominated by the major smartphone OS and smart hub vendors. Each voice assistant can be configured to respond to a wake word.

- Google Assistant™—"OK Google."
- Amazon Alexa—"Alexa."
- Apple® Siri®—"Hey Siri."
- Microsoft Cortana®—"Hey Cortana" or just "Cortana" (Microsoft is dropping the "Hey" requirement at the time of writing).

There are obviously considerable difficulties in providing a natural language interface that can cope with the diversity of languages, accents, and speaking styles used by people around the world. As vendors gather more voice data, however, they can make the assistants more accurate and more capable of providing a useful, individualized service.

To use a voice-based virtual assistant, the feature may first need to be enabled and then trained by completing a setup wizard to configure the assistant to recognize the user's voice.

Activity 9-9

Discussing IoT Devices

Show Slide(s)

Activity: Discussing IoT Devices

SCENARIO

Answer the following questions to check your understanding of the topic.

1. **What type of network topology is used by protocols such as Zigbee and Z-Wave?**

    A wireless mesh network topology.

2. **What types of home automation device might require specialist installer training?**

    A device such as a thermostat has to be wired safely and correctly to the heating controls, door locks must be fitted securely by a joiner or carpenter, and even a security camera would be better fitted by someone with the skills to evaluate the best placement. While a homeowner might attempt these as DIY jobs, a service or support company should not allow untrained staff to attempt this type of installation.

3. **What are the two main options for operating smart devices?**

    Using a smartphone/tablet app, or using a voice-enabled smart speaker. Some devices might also support configuration via a web app.

4. **True or false? Voice processing by a smart speaker is performed internally so these devices can be used without an Internet connection.**

    False. The speaker passes the voice data to a backend server for processing.

Activity 9-10
Configuring IoT Devices

BEFORE YOU BEGIN

In addition to the actual IoT equipment, you will need a wireless network with an Internet connection and a computer with a wireless adapter to perform this activity.

SCENARIO

Depending on the equipment available, you might watch as your instructor sets up some home automation devices, or you might assist in setting them up yourself. This suggested activity requires an Echo Dot smart speaker, a Philips smart bulb kit, and one or more lamps.

You will configure the smart speaker so that it can respond to your voice queries. Then you will install the smart bulbs and configure the smart speaker to operate them.

1. Configure the smart speaker hub. The specific steps provided here are for configuring an Amazon Echo Dot smart speaker.
   a) Connect the smart speaker to the power supply.
   b) Unless you are instructed otherwise, reset it to factory settings. For example, with an Echo Dot, press and hold the **Microphone off** and **Volume down** buttons until the LED turns orange.
   c) Open **https://alexa.amazon.com**.
   d) If you do not already have an Amazon account, create one, and then sign in.
   e) If you are prompted to accept terms and conditions, select **Continue**.
   f) Select the model of smart speaker you are configuring.
   g) When you are prompted to connect your computer, use the network status icon (on the Windows taskbar) to connect to the **Amazon-XXX** wireless network, making sure to check the **Connect automatically** box.

Connect to the built-in Echo access point when prompted to continue with setup.

h)   Switch back to the browser setup app.

You should see a prompt to connect the smart hub to your own wireless network.

Echo Dot Setup

Select your Wi-Fi network

Previously Saved to Amazon.   Learn More

No Wi-Fi networks have been saved.

Other Networks

COMPTIA-WLAN

Cancel setup   Rescan

Your Echo Dot's MAC address is 5C:41:5A:56:E9:38

Join the smart hub to your own wireless network.

i)   Select the appropriate wireless network to join the smart hub to (it must have an Internet connection).

j)   Enter the PSK for the network.

k)   Uncheck the **Save password to Amazon** box.

l)   Select **Connect**.

m)   Select **Use built-in speaker**.

Alexa should now be available to respond to your queries, though possibly not able to answer complex ones such as:

```
Alexa, how do I configure smart bulbs?
```

2.   Use a Philips Hue account to set up the smart bulbs and bridge.

The detailed steps are for a Philips Hue smart bulb kit (with bridge). Philips smart bulbs use Zigbee wireless networking. This means that you must install a Zigbee-capable hub to facilitate a connection to the Echo Dot smart speaker or allow control via a smartphone or computer with Wi-Fi. The hub must be connected to the cabled network (it does not support Wi-Fi itself).

a)   Connect the smart bulbs to lamps and switch them on.

b)   Connect the Hue bridge to the power supply.

c)   Unless you are instructed otherwise, reset it to factory settings, by using the button on the bottom of the device.

d)   Connect the Hue Bridge to a LAN port on the router/modem, or if you are using a standalone access point, connect it to a switch port on the same network.

e)   In the Alexa web app, select **Skills**.

f)   Search for the **Hue** skill by Philips Hue.

Teaching Tip

Newer smart hubs are being released with support for Z-Wave and Zigbee.

g) Select the **Enable** button.

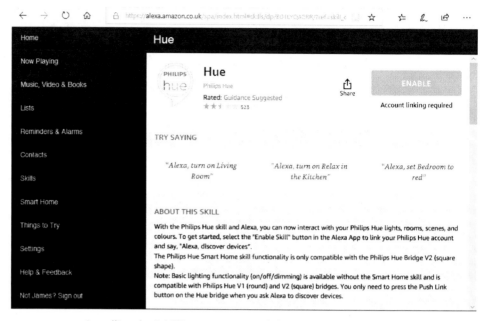

Installing the "skill" to use to control devices of a specific type.

h) When the separate browser window opens to **https://account.meethue.com/login**, either sign in or create an account and sign in.

i) When you are prompted, press the button on the Hue Bridge to allow the app to manage the bridge.

j) In the web app, select **Continue**.

k) When you are prompted, select **Yes** to trust Alexa.

l) Close the MeetHue browser tab.

m) In the Alexa app browser tab, select **Discover Devices**.

The device list should be populated with the smart bulbs (their names may vary). Note that "All lights" is treated as an independent device. This allows you to configure actions that operate on each light at the same time—"Alexa, turn off all lights" for example.

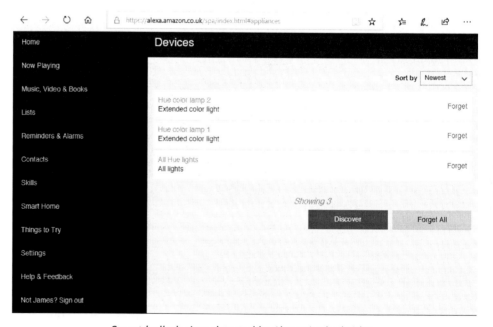

Smart bulb devices detected by Alexa via the bridge.

n) If necessary, refresh the view by selecting **Smart Home→Devices**.

o) When the bulbs are listed, you will be able to control the lamps with voice commands such as the following:

```
Alexa, turn off hue color lamp one.
Alexa, dim hue color lamp two.
Alexa, make hue color lamp two blue.
```

3. Optionally, if you have time, explore other options for configuring the smart bulbs.

Philips provides a management app only for Android and iOS. You can use a third-party app such as Huetro for Hue from Windows.

Summary

In this lesson, you configured and performed troubleshooting on SOHO and other networks. Ensuring consistent access to network resources is often an integral part of an A+ technician's day-to-day duties.

What experiences do you have in working with the networking technologies discussed in this lesson?

A: Answers will vary according to the backgrounds of different individuals. Possible experiences include: how do you access library card catalogs from the library, from home, or from the office? How do you troubleshoot your own Internet connectivity problems? Have you ever set up a home network using a router or switch?

Do you have any experience working with SOHO networks? What do you expect to support in future job functions?

A: Answers will vary, but will likely include connecting and setting up a small home wireless network. Most technicians will be installing and supporting SOHO wireless networks within their job role.

 Practice Question: Additional practice questions are available on the CompTIA CHOICE platform within the **Assessments** tile.

ISBN-13 978-1-6427-4173-5
ISBN-10 1-6427-4173-6